DANCE ON ITS OWN TERMS

Dance on Its Own Terms

HISTORIES AND METHODOLOGIES

Edited by

Melanie Bales and Karen Eliot

OXFORD UNIVERSITY PRESS

OXFORD
UNIVERSITY PRESS

Oxford University Press is a department of the
University of Oxford. It furthers the University's objective
of excellence in research, scholarship, and education
by publishing worldwide.

Oxford   New York
Auckland   Cape Town   Dar es Salaam   Hong Kong   Karachi
Kuala Lumpur   Madrid   Melbourne   Mexico City   Nairobi
New Delhi   Shanghai   Taipei   Toronto

With offices in
Argentina   Austria   Brazil   Chile   Czech Republic   France   Greece
Guatemala   Hungary   Italy   Japan   Poland   Portugal   Singapore
South Korea   Switzerland   Thailand   Turkey   Ukraine   Vietnam

Oxford is a registered trade mark of Oxford University
Press in the UK and certain other countries.

Published in the United States of America by
Oxford University Press
198 Madison Avenue, New York, NY 10016

Library of Congress Cataloging-in-Publication Data
Dance on its own terms : histories and methodologies / edited by Melanie Bales and Karen Eliot.
    p. cm.
Includes bibliographical references and index.
ISBN 978-0-19-993998-5 (hardback)—ISBN 978-0-19-994000-4 (pbk.)
1. Dance—History.   2. Dance—Research.   3. Dance—Methodology.
I. Bales, Melanie.   II. Eliot, Karen.
GV1601.D38 2013
793.309'012—dc23   2012029766

Contents

DANCE ON ITS OWN TERMS

Introduction

DANCE ON ITS Own Terms: Histories and Methodologies emerges from our concern that many dance scholars, newly launched into academia, lack the historical information and the requisite tools to analyze the art form in which they are expected to be well versed. Often they lack the core disciplinary knowledge that is widely expected of scholars in literature, music, theatre, and the history of art. This anthology is designed to address that gap through its inclusion of a range of subjects examined from a variety of dance-centered methodologies—modes of research that are emergent, are based in relevant systems of analysis, use primary sources, and rely on skills developed through critical, informed observation of movement. We present these essays as case studies organized into three categories of significant dance activity: performance and reconstruction, pedagogy and choreographic process, and notational and other written forms used to analyze and document dance. The field of dance is immense, and with the benefits of new media, few research topics are out-of-bounds for today's scholars. It is our intention to value the richness and vibrancy of the dance field, although we make no claims to address all of it. The essays included in this anthology are deeply informed examinations that serve as windows opening onto the larger world of dance; conceptually, though, the concerns and questions they raise point to broadly inclusive methodological applications.

Spurred by new technologies and a media-driven wave of popularity of dance in movies and on television, dance has moved to the forefront of public consciousness, and today, scholars face few restrictions in selecting their subjects for study. We live in an era that affords us access to information about almost any dance form at any time and in any geographical location; many of us have virtually unlimited access to digital media, and we have at our disposal, as well, an array of published materials that would have surprised (and probably delighted) dance scholars of earlier decades. We are encouraged by the breadth and generosity of the field and hope that subsequent generations of scholars will be trained in dance's history, and equipped with the critical skills and the analytical tools to further its study.

As dance historians, we recognize that we build on the work of our predecessors. In the second decade of the 21st century there are a number of battles we no longer have to fight: previous scholars championed dance as an academic discipline so that it has now claimed its status as "a culturally significant and intellectually viable field for study."[1] This was not always the case, of course. As Gay Morris points out in her 2009 "Dance Studies/Cultural Studies," since at least the 1990s dance scholars were prompted to follow their academic cohorts in bringing interdisciplinary perspectives to what might be perceived as an area too highly specialized, too internal, and too selective to have any relevance to the world outside the studio doors.[2] Writing in the mid-1990s, Amy Koritz argued that the pursuit of dance scholarship within larger interdisciplinary frameworks "helped to bring dance closer to the intellectual mainstream."[3] A long-marginalized practice, dance profitably adopted concepts from cultural and literary studies. These approaches led scholars to challenge received history, prompting them to recover the experiences and tease open the stories of disenfranchised populations omitted in more conventional accounts. The melding of historical and ethnographic methodologies encouraged a broader view of the field, challenging the practice that left non-Western dance out of mainstream dance history research and neglected the study of forms not typically considered high art.[4]

However, in their eagerness to adopt theoretical language from other disciplines, dance scholars have lost fluency in their own language. The body is theorized as a site for the study of race, class, and gender, but many dance students are inadequately equipped to observe and write about bodies in movement, and to analyze choreography in its context with a requisite and responsible level of scholarly rigor. Monolithic assumptions impose themselves on our attention where nuance and sophisticated criticism is needed instead. For better and for worse, interdisciplinarity has been the watchword for the last two decades. In their 2007 *Dance Discourses: Keywords in Dance Research*, editors Susanne Franco and Marina Nordera suggest that two camps emerged in response to the explosion of theoretical concepts and methodological tools drawn from disciplines outside of dance. One response was to embrace cross-disciplinarity in the interest of promoting dance and the body as subjects of academic study. The other response was cautious about employing methodologies drawn from literary and cultural studies. This second group, write Franco and Nordera, "emphasized the need to find methods and instruments of analysis within dance itself. The former perceived an interdisciplinary approach as a preliminary and unavoidable condition, while the latter saw it [the interdisciplinary approach] as a sort of colonization of a terrain, still considered marginal and thus constitutionally fragile, endowed with its own laws and 'original' identity that only a gaze from within could make known."[5]

We seek to employ methodologies we adapt from disciplines outside of dance, but we are not satisfied with a cursory and simplistic understanding of the art form within which we locate ourselves. At this juncture, we seek to re-focus the scholarly lens on a subject that is too easily scuttled and set aside: dancing. Dance, we can remind ourselves, is important because it is a rich human endeavor with a distinctive identity that emanates from who we are and have been throughout history. It is dance's distinctive identity that concerns us here.

A dance-centered methodology is one that is emergent and fluid; it can be flexibly applied to all forms, including for instance popular dance, classical ballet, early dance, and film dance. Dance-centered methodologies allow scholars to avoid formulaic investigation of their subjects, and provoke research questions that arise from the process of studying and writing about dance. Rather than employing theoretical lenses from disciplines outside dance to produce foregone conclusions, our effort in this book has been to analyze and tease apart the materials of the dances themselves, and to cross these boundaries with attention to disciplinary validity and rigor. Thus, each essay emanates from a specific topic and from this center moves outward to a broader examination of the world in which the dance or dance activity might find itself. Often, in the rush to build bridges out from dance's center, scholars ignore the profundity and complexity of dance in situ, thus threatening to erase from history the materiality and layers of meaning available through the examination of dance and its constitutive elements. In gathering these essays we have a number of specific aims: we strive to listen to the past and hear what its concerns are, allow theoretical inquiry to emerge from the subject matter itself, and be aware in its application of its ideological implications. Finally, and no less importantly, believing in the power of language, we value clarity of expression and writing that aims to communicate to readers in and outside the discipline.[6] Each of the following chapters seeks to illuminate some aspect of dance that is ripe for a more profound analysis or for examination from a dance-centered perspective.

Grounded in dance's history and practice, many of the authors represented here use modes of movement analysis or analyze music and dance relationships, and several attend to issues of the oral and physical transmission of dance. They raise questions about notation systems, pedagogical practices, spectatorship, and the potentially prickly topics surrounding reconstruction. Across the range of these diverse inquiries have emerged a number of interrelated questions. Some authors ask what people see when they watch dance, their examinations prompted by the realization that interpretations of dance vary across time and geography as well as among individuals and within diverse population groups. Also intriguing is the prominence of geometric forms and visual patterns, occurring both in the ways dance may be recorded and in the ways in which it is analyzed or taught. This recurrence of pattern and visual referencing derives from Western notions of classical perspective that have largely determined how, in the West, the dancing body is conceived in space and dancing bodies move through space. Thus, even though the chapters in this collection are discrete—each essay treating some aspect of dance in its unique historical moment—they are, at the same time, thematically linked.

Examining dance in its historical moment is significant as dance is both a living practice and an artifact of the past, one in which the political life of a specific time and culture reveals itself. In an essay titled "Dance and the Political," Mark Franko describes his frustrations in writing about the political nature of dance; as he puts it, the effort to determine politically "astute" dance studies inevitably gets the scholar knotted up in complexity. Franko writes, "I became tangled in the phenomenal presence of dance, the politics of the relation between dancer, choreographer, and institution, and so-called real-world politics; the political sphere itself."[7] And this, in fact, is where we wish to start. These essays emerge from the premise that it is critical to examine the phenomenal presence of dance and untangle its integral elements to better comprehend and more clearly write about the complexities of this rich art form and its often-fraught relationship to the world in which it exists.

The "gaze from within" is not a limitation and does not necessarily lead to intellectual stagnation, for an examination of dance's phenomenal presence does not preclude theorization or the forging of cross-disciplinary links. Nor does scholarship that starts from dance's materiality necessarily obviate its historical and political importance. We echo Franko's statement that dance may be regarded as political to the degree that its "forces and motives" "partake of the personal, the artistic, and the institutional. Politics are not located directly 'in' dance, but in the way dance manages to occupy (cultural) space."[8] The political nature of dance is, we think, inarguable. The question, though, is Whose politics? Whose history? We owe it to our predecessors to pursue their lives and experiences, and learn—as best we can—to wear their clothes and dance in their shoes. And, going still further, we aim to bring their political concerns into some kind of intersection with our own. Our ancestors were no more simplistic than we are. They were not necessarily ideologically straightforward; nor were they monolithic in their approaches to creating dance. In this collection, we hope to represent the wealth and ambiguity of dance's history along with the complicated and profound creative potential that resides in dance.

Our approach to history is aptly described by Martha Howell and Walter Prevenier in their book *From Reliable Sources*:

> The dominant mood today is considerably less celebratory, more self-reflective, and more revisionist than it was a century, two centuries, or ten centuries ago. It is also very often decidedly more progressive in tone. Such historiography typically seeks to include a wider variety of historical actors than historians of the past thought worthy of study. It often seeks, moreover, to expose the ways the political, social, and intellectual hierarchies that we have inherited from the past were fashioned, in this way working to demystify those hierarchies, making what once seemed natural and unchangeable appear artificial and malleable.[9]

That is, even though we approach history with skepticism, we emphasize the importance of knowing and critically examining sources, and of evaluating them with skills built up through a profound knowledge of dance and its history.[10]

Our questions can often be illuminating, but we realize that they *are* contemporary concerns, concerns that we do not necessarily share with our historical subjects. The authors in this book draw from an array of methodologies and contemporary theories; still their engagement with dance presumes an examination backward and forward in time, as well as an acknowledgement of the line where these two perspectives meet. As dance scholars, we are shaped by our global, technological preoccupations, and our musings and questions about the past emerge from these points of view. Nevertheless, the exercise of examining dances within their own contextual frames, and of extending our scholarly empathy toward our historical subjects, is a fruitful one; to slightly paraphrase Melanie Bales in her essay included in this volume, dance's "center is always moving, even as we think we have located it."

NOTES

1. Alexandra Carter, ed., "General Introduction," *The Routledge Dance Studies Reader.* London and New York: Routledge, 1998, 1.

2. Gay Morris, "Dance Studies/Cultural Studies," *Dance Research Journal.* 41/1 Summer 2009, 82–100.

3. Amy Koritz, "Re/Moving Boundaries: From Dance History to Cultural Studies," in Gay Morris, ed. *Moving Words: Re-Writing Dance.* London and New York: Routledge, 1996, 89.

4. For more on the melding of historical and ethnographic methodologies, see Theresa Jill Buckland, *Dancing from Past to Present: Nation, Culture, Identities.* Madison: University of Wisconsin Press, 2006.

5. Susanne Franco and Marina Nordera, eds., "Introduction," *Dance Discourses: Keywords in Dance Research.* London and New York: Routledge, 2007, 1–8.

6. In her review of the 1995 *Choreographing History*, Deborah Jowitt decried the tendency of writers to "drape even the most basic of concepts in torrents of language." We aim for clear communication and seek to avoid creating "thickets of thought." See Deborah Jowitt, untitled review, *Dance Research: The Journal of the Society for Dance Research.* 15/1. Summer 1997, 113. http://www.jstor.org/stable/1290962. Accessed Nov. 21, 2010.

7. Mark Franko, "Dance and the Political: States of Exception," in Franco and Nordera, *Dance Discourses*, 12.

8. Ibid., 13.

9. Martha Howell and Walter Prevenier, *From Reliable Sources: An Introduction to Historical Methods.* Ithaca, NY: Cornell University Press, 2001, 15–16.

10. Ibid., 16.

PART ONE

In the Moment of Re-Creation and Performance

A DANCE EXISTS uniquely and fleetingly in the moment of performance; yet in spite of, and perhaps because of, its resistance to re-creation, dance scholars in the last decades have been increasingly consumed with questions surrounding reconstruction and spectatorship. This section explores dance's rich relationship to its own past, provoking questions about what dance might mean in a specific time and place and how it might be translated to audiences for whom it was not first intended; it asks also what it is that viewers see in dance, and how their viewing might be mediated by social determinants. We find that spectatorship and reconstruction practices are in large part determined by local and unique conditions. That is, determinations of a dance's value (perhaps its aesthetic, moral, social, or commercial worth) dictate which works are most likely to be produced, and these determinations themselves generally hinge on the needs of a particular community of spectators at a specific moment in history.

Attitudes toward reconstruction are both deeply philosophical—asking what stories we tell about ourselves and about our past through dance—and pragmatic—identifying the structures that make it possible to re-create dance of the past. Karen Eliot's chapter, "Dancing the Canon in Wartime: Sergeyev, de Valois, and Inglesby and the Classics of British Ballet," examines the philosophies behind competing approaches to restaging the 19th-century classics in Great Britain, before, during and just after the Second World War. Her chapter also questions notions of "authenticity" in re-creating a dance from the past, and it looks at modes of transmitting dance. Directors Ninette de Valois and Mona Inglesby made individual choices in staging those canonical ballets, decisions that emerged from, and responded to, their specific moments in history and the needs of their unique communities of viewers.

Often, dance of the past can serve as a lens through which to more sharply focus on the present. A dance is always absent and present, says Ann Dils: it exists in its own historical moment, while in the present-day moment of its reconstruction it is inflected with new meanings and new associations. In "Reimagining *Le Boeuf sur le Toit*," Dils describes her project to restage the 1920 Jean Cocteau/Darius Milhaud farce for a contemporary college dance department in the United States, and her efforts to help her audiences experience the piece through a process of "double vision." In preparing her recent staging, she explored the racial and gender politics of early-20th-century Paris while reconsidering those same charged issues in modern-day Greensboro, North Carolina, a community that continues to confront its own racially divisive history.

In Deborah Friedes Galili's analysis of the Israeli dance scene, "Reframing the Recent Past: Issues of Reconstruction in Israeli Contemporary Dance," the key concept is not restaging but rather recycling dance. Galili treats the recent past in her survey of Israeli contemporary dance, framing her study within an examination of that country's own complex relationship to its dance identity and history. She finds that re-mixing and re-framing, rather than reconstruction in any strict sense of the term, may be the strategies most suited to contemporary Israeli dance at this point in its history as a nation. Galili suggests that in making choices about how and what to reconstruct, a dance community is challenged to confront its identity and to define its relationship to its past. Lacking any real infrastructure to support dance reconstruction, and ambivalent about their dance's history, contemporary Israeli choreographers conceive of themselves as continuously generative; re-mixing strategies allow them to plumb older work to reveal creative possibilities in the new.

In "The Body Censored: Dance, Morality, and the Production Code During the Golden Age of the Film Musical," Betsy Cooper asks both what viewers saw when they watched dance in the movies during the Golden Age of the Hollywood musicals and how dancers and choreographers accommodated social agendas imposed by the Production Code Agency (PCA). Cooper trains her focus on the PCA's strategies to fix criteria for rating dance as appropriate or indecent. Her examination traces these criteria to the distant past; the roots of these moral codes, she finds, lie in the classical and Renaissance values that for centuries shaped how audiences in the West have viewed dance and how they have learned to distinguish "high art" from "popular culture," and the "aesthetic" from the "indecent."

Harmony Bench explores the participatory culture of "viral choreographies," focusing her analysis on the explosion of male dancers' versions of Beyoncé's "Single Ladies" posted on YouTube. These viral choreographies, says Bench in "'Single Ladies' Is Gay: Queer Performances and Mediated Masculinities on YouTube," not only serve the needs of the performer for self-expression but also permit the multiplication of spectators' interpretations. Posting videos of themselves performing Beyoncé's song has allowed some men to open up expressions of masculinity that exist in dialogue—not in contrast—with the feminine.

Each of these chapters reminds us that reconstruction is a process that relies on the availability of modes of transmission, including possibly video documentation and notation systems, as well as the oral/kinesthetic learning that, although largely undocumented, transpires and has transpired for centuries and that exists in the intangible relationship between one dancer and another. Bodies, of course, are always central: training practices evolve, dancers' bodies are altered, body awareness changes and dance's relationship to its past becomes ever more fraught with challenges. These are the issues that emerge throughout this book, making the unraveling of dance's phenomenal presence all the richer and more thrillingly complex.

I

Dancing the Canon in Wartime

SERGEYEV, DE VALOIS, AND INGLESBY AND

THE CLASSICS OF BRITISH BALLET

Karen Eliot

DEBATING THE CANON

ALTHOUGH THE 21ST century has ushered in an emphasis on cross-pollination in the arts, the unique characteristics and histories of individual disciplines cannot be dismissed. In fact, the circumstances dictating the creation and re-creation of dance might press us to look closer at distinctions between various art forms, and to query the mechanics and politics of canon formation, which do not operate uniformly across the disciplines. As we celebrate the potential richness of cross-disciplinarity, the process of teasing apart the materials and history of the production of ballet reminds us that it is nevertheless still important to examine dance on its own terms. For those elements of a pre-20th century ballet that survive to be handed down are usually the textual and narrative components, such as the libretto and the musical score,[1] while the steps, the stuff of the dancing itself— even in the most canonical ballets—have typically been unceremoniously altered to suit the talents of new performers, or freely adapted to match the constraints of the performance venue. Similarly, sets and costumes are commonly re-imagined in light of changing economic and aesthetic concerns. Balletomanes and ballet scholars have been late in acknowledging that their form even had a history; thus, ballet's canonization process has taken on a distinctive character, one that demonstrates that classical ballets are, to adopt Mark Franko's phrase, (perhaps surprisingly) continuous with "all that circulates around and 'outside'" them.[2] Whereas across the disciplines the canon wars of the 1980s and 1990s resounded with allegations of "exclusion" and "monopoly," decisions about staging the ballet masterworks have always been framed through interactions within a community of spectators and presenters in an accretive process that has mostly been overlooked by dance scholars.

In her 1998 *Dancing Women: Female Bodies on Stage*, Sally Banes argued that studying the dance canon continued to be an important project: "The canon we have inherited— the dances that have survived for myriad reasons, including both the test of time and the fallibility of human memory as well as the distribution of cultural capital—cannot be wished away by fiat." Furthermore, she wrote, what is left out of the canon, including "various histories of popular, vernacular, and avant-garde dance performances," would fill many additional volumes. Without a doubt this is the case. I would suggest, however, that there are still other reasons to re-examine the masterworks of ballet: the canonical ballets warrant further examination for their potential both to be shaped by the needs of their respective viewers and to *include* elements of the "popular, vernacular, and avant-garde."[3]

THE CANON WARS ACROSS THE DISCIPLINES

When literary scholars talk about the canon, they typically generate lists of readings, preeminent texts that, it is argued, should (or should not) form the study of uninitiated undergraduates. Speaking for the pluralists in the 1990s, Henry Louis Gates, Jr., opposed the conservative list—one reflective of the view of the "West versus the Rest"—with a proposition that culture is "porous, dynamic, and interactive" and not "the fixed property of particular ethnic groups." For Gates, foundational readings emerge from a multicultural world where "mixing and hybridity are the rule, not the exception."[4] For his part, Harold Bloom argues that the list's (or the lists') inclusiveness is beside the point. What matters for Bloom is an individual text's perceived "supremacy" over all others of its kind. A canonical work, argues Bloom, determines its own fate; it "nudg[es]" its place into the tradition from within. Created in response to tradition, greatness in art is forged through "conflict between past genius and present aspiration."[5] For Bloom, a great book announces its place in our collective memory because it is quite simply better than all its contemporaries.

Anna Bryzski, summarizing the debate in art history circles, argues that, though tarnished, *a* canon perforce persists. Textbooks and museum exhibits implicitly identify *the* great works of art, although the collections themselves actually derive from practical considerations that include market forces and the economies of power. "All canons are created and revised under particular historic circumstances," writes Bryzski, "and they are shaped by conditions present on a local or a regional level. They are affected by external events and pressures, and are formulated in response to deeply held yet seldom articulated beliefs grounded in particular value systems."[6]

Touched to some degree by all of these issues, the conditions surrounding canonization in dance are still distinct, reflecting the unique history, politics, and materiality of the form. In the 21st century, the ballet canon remains small and mostly unchallenged, although questions of performance and authenticity loom large.[7] The "seldom articulated beliefs" Bryzski refers to hinge not so much on what is included in the canon but rather on all-too-often unexamined choices about how traditional ballets are to be performed. Western balletomanes have relatively recently acknowledged and established the history of their art form and the resultant canon—here meaning those 19th-century ballets accepted as the classics, including *The Sleeping Beauty, The Nutcracker, Swan Lake, Giselle* and *Coppélia*—was somewhat haphazardly constituted, as will be discussed.[8] Thus the chief concern for ballet company directors might be whether these ballets—in something approximating their authentic versions—continue to have emotional resonance for viewers. Because a performance is a live event, shaped by the unique bodies and interpretations of individual dancers and inflected by novel staging choices and design elements, it succeeds to the degree it can generate meaning in the moment. A 19th-century classical ballet is then valued for its capacity to project vitality through tradition, and the canon comprises works that endure for their properties of both historicism and immediacy. A canonical ballet satisfies box office demands through its responsiveness to the cultural needs of a unique historical moment, and endures because it can be continually re-made while retaining its hold on some version of an authentic text. On one level, spectators apprehend the classic ballets as fixed artifacts drawn from a great and enduring tradition; on another level, they experience them in the moment, as immediate, live events, capable of communicating in overlapping and multi-layered ways. Meanwhile, those who are in the business of reviving, recreating or restaging classic works do so with distinctly different attitudes toward the past, approaches that shape what the spectators see and how they experience the canon. These attitudes range from strict reverence for what is assumed to be an authentic historical text to a more heterodox approach to reviving the perceived masterworks of the past. Correspondingly, attitudes toward restaging the canon are rooted in the social and aesthetic impulses of the day and manifest a variety of responses to the *danse d'école* and the history and tradition of ballet.

In this chapter, I analyze divergent attitudes toward restaging the ballets of the past as demonstrated in Great Britain in the years leading up to the Second World War through the immediate post-war period of economic austerity. The classic ballets satisfied audiences in this context because they could mean different things to people across the social spectrum, who came to the ballet for a variety of reasons and with a range of expectations. The classics fed anxious audiences, hungry for relief, entertainment and recreation, many of whom, at the same time, craved tradition, stability and transcendence. Building on Beth Genné's research into the foundation of the ballet canon by Ninette de Valois during the 1930s, it is possible to examine the ballet canon at a unique historical moment through a focus on the ballets reconstructed by Nikolai Sergeyev for two wartime British ballet companies, de Valois' Vic-Wells/Sadler's Wells Ballet and Mona Inglesby's International

Ballet.[9] These two directors' distinct production decisions and their individual stances toward ballet's authenticity can be located within larger social and cultural debates of the early and mid-20th century.

CREATING AND DEFENDING THE CANON

> Today Great Britain is guardian of the culture of Europe. It is an inspiring thought, it is inspiring to be British at this moment. We who love and understand an art rich in tradition, an art that has developed and grown in Europe are in an admirable position to appreciate that to the full.... Yes, it is good to be British, to be the guardians of all the arts that make life worth living. One day we will restore them to the conquered nations and our own contributions to art will shine with a brighter light.[10]

So wrote the dance critic Arnold Haskell in August 1940 when it appeared that it might be Britain's destiny to act as a bulwark against Nazi depredations. In his impassioned column in *The Dancing Times*, Haskell anointed Great Britain the guardian of European culture, and more specifically of European-Russian ballet. The future of civilization was at stake and, it seemed, Britons were called to preserve a centuries-old ballet tradition for the day when sanity, reason, and peace would be re-established. Haskell's apparent chauvinism here—read against the heightened emotionality of war preparations—is both poignant and weighted with significance. After all, British ballet aficionados had worked assiduously, especially after the death of Serge Diaghilev in 1929, to ensure the stability of ballet in its uniquely British iteration and to assert its place in ballet's supranational tradition. Having established the foundations of a national ballet, would balletomanes watch this edifice crumble? In 1940 it was crucial to re-assert the stability of the form itself and declare its importance in British culture.

During the interwar period and throughout the 1930s, British dance critics had sought to define their national ballet's identity and declare its strong historical roots. A paper Haskell delivered to the Royal Society of Arts as war loomed in June 1939 was one statement of this project.[11] In this narrative—subscribed to by a number of British dance writers and patrons—various streams of ballet tradition converged, and for a brief but influential period in the 1930s, they coalesced in the co-operative venture known as the Camargo Society, an association Haskell labeled "the shop window of English Ballet" for the opportunities it afforded British dancers and choreographers to test their wings.[12] According to the narrative redacted by Haskell, the British ballet traced its lineage from the Danes and the French through Adeline Genée and her uncle, Alexander, and from the Russians and the Italians through Diaghilev's Ballets Russes and Anna Pavlova.[13] This generally accepted narrative of the development of British Ballet permitted the dance writer Janet Leeper, for instance, in her 1944 *English Ballet*, to identify a clear line of descent: English Ballet, wrote Leeper "traces its descent through Russian Imperial Ballet right back to the *Ballet de Cour* of Louis XIV."[14]

A noble tradition demanded great works, artifacts that dancers, scholars, patrons, and general audiences could point to as evidence of ballet's status as high art. In the early decades of the 20th century, British ballet supporters aptly analyzed and critiqued the new works of choreographers including Ninette de Valois, Frederick Ashton and Antony Tudor. But, as Genné explains, it became clear to some, and especially to de Valois, one of the most influential women in dance history, that the British ballet must also distinguish itself by striving to meet the challenges of dancing the great works of the past. The historical works were necessary to her drive to found a recognized national ballet both because these 19th-century ballets would challenge her young dancers to attain virtuosity and because her audiences needed to know the classical works in order to appreciate the tradition inherent in contemporary ballets. The ballet canon was thus laid down with measured deliberation at a unique moment in history by the far-sighted de Valois.

In spite of de Valois' energy and drive, when viewed in hindsight it is clear that the actual constitution of the canon was highly serendipitous, for it depended on a number of timely circumstances: the fortuitous presence in 1930s London of Alicia Markova, a classically trained ballerina, uprooted after Diaghilev's death and looking for opportunities to extend her performing range; the emigration to the west of former Imperial Ballet *régisseur* Nicolai Sergeyev, who staged the first productions of these ballets from the Stepanov notations stashed in his valise; and de Valois' own steady progress toward building a strong and dynamic ensemble prepared to take on the challenges of dancing the classics.[15] De Valois' goal, writes Genné, was "to create a repertory that stood outside of fashion and 'time', and as with the other 'high' arts, to present the range of its history to the public.... This was an entirely new goal in the history of dance.... It marks a new moment in the history of Western dance and can be linked with a growing perception of dance as a high art form in its own right and with its own history." Thus, by the 1940s, writes Genné, "critics and public alike were invoking ballet's noble past—*Sleeping Beauty*, *Swan Lake* and *Giselle*—as a gold standard by which to measure present dancers and choreographers."[16]

DIAGHILEV'S LEGACY: MODERNISM AND TRADITION

But what values did that gold standard represent, and what was the tradition from which these canonical works emerged? The large-scale Petipa ballets initially held out dubious rewards, for fervent British dance enthusiasts, many of them Diaghilev alumni/alumnae, were mostly intrigued by the capacity of the *danse d'école*—ballet's classical step vocabulary—to be made relevant to the modern era. During the interwar period, much of what drew the London intelligentsia to the Ballets Russes was the company's modernism, if not its outright weirdness. W. J. Turner, writing in *The New Statesman*, proposed that the "chief delight" of Diaghilev's enterprise was "that one never knows what one is going to see when the curtain rises." The audience in attendance was equally delightful: "The audience itself is less middle-class and respectable [than the opera audience], better looking and more amusing." Turner responded to what he described as the "weird, comic, puzzling" new ballet *Mercury* (*Mercure* premiered in Paris in 1927 with music by Erik Satie, choreography by Léonide Massine and sets and costumes by Pablo Picasso): "Let us admit that the whole thing is a joke, but what a superb joke!"[17] The Diaghilev Ballets Russes in London drew a distinctive audience compounded of the educated, the fashionable, and the intellectual avant-garde who mostly disdained convention and the middle-brow popularization of theatre, dance, music and literature. Post-Diaghilev, some in this audience—at least those most committed to the development of a national ballet—coalesced around the youthful Camargo Society, the Vic-Wells and Rambert's Ballet Club.

Diaghilev's experimentalism aroused in some members of his audience a desire for ballet as novelty, and these viewers were mostly intrigued by the form's potential to depict and engage fashionable modern life. The early decades of the 20th century were witness to the creation of new ballets and the small-scale *ballets intimes* that were, in any case, more suited to the young British companies' practical and physical constraints.[18] Like her contemporaries, de Valois sought to bring classical ballet into alignment with modern trends in the arts.

De Valois participated in these modernist trends herself. In the late 1920s and early 1930s, she collaborated with her cousin, Terence Gray, at the Festival Theatre in Cambridge, and with W. B. Yeats and Lennox Robinson at the Abbey Theatre in Dublin, contributing movement direction for their avant-garde theatre productions. As Kathrine Sorley Walker puts it, "Gray and [his partner] Ridge were reacting against the theatre of realism and toward the theatre of imagination and illusion, the theatre of Edward Gordon Craig and Adolphe Appia, of W. B. Yeats's poetry, of Central European expressionist techniques. Their concept of production included the use of dance and dance movement, mime and masks." On the basis of her experimental leanings, de Valois was "the perfect choice to bring these elements into action."[19] Among the influences on de Valois in her theatre work was her training under Léonide Massine and Bronislava Nijinska, as well as her familiarity with the activities of Isadora Duncan, Rudolf von Laban, and Mary Wigman.[20]

In a 1926 article entitled "The Future of Ballet," de Valois established her view that the *danse d'école* should be deployed in the service of contemporary ballet: "The true aim of modern ballet is a serious practical effort to extend the authentic methods of the classical ballet. It is to forward and expand the possibilities of the art of dancing in harmony with the other arts of the theatre."[21] De Valois' skepticism toward the 19th-century Petipa ballets stemmed from her apprenticeship with Diaghilev and her involvement in the cultural vortex of her times. In her memoir *Come Dance with Me*, de Valois confessed her initial bafflement at witnessing Diaghilev's production of *The Sleeping Princess* (Diaghilev's preferred title for *The Sleeping Beauty*) at the Alhambra in 1921.[22] "It took time," she wrote, "for me to understand the influence of the classical tradition on the

Company's work: enlightenment did not come until after I had left, and I had found time to reflect on the whole experience." Only in retrospect, she acknowledged, was she able to comprehend the continuity of the *danse d'école* underpinning Diaghilev's experimentalism.[23]

Still, if for no other reason, the vocabulary of the *danse d'école*—fully developed and on display in the lavish four- and five-act Petipa ballets—had its usefulness as a training tool. Genné points out that Marie Rambert, founder of the tiny but influential Ballet Club (later the Ballet Rambert) and herself an alumna of Diaghilev's Ballets Russes, asserted the important role the traditional ballets could play in training dancers and frequently taught variations from the classics in her school.[24] But it was de Valois who eked out the resources to produce these works and who made it possible to establish a repertoire balanced between the traditional and the new.

For his part, although he maintained a deep reverence for the past, Diaghilev had anything but a sacrosanct approach to staging the Petipa ballets. Meeting up with Sergeyev in Paris in 1920, the impresario engaged the former *régisseur* to help mount his new production of *The Sleeping Princess*. A perturbed Sergeyev resigned, though, before the work's London opening, provoked by Diaghilev's request that various "alterations" be made to the choreography.[25]

When he premiered his pivotal production of *The Sleeping Princess*, Diaghilev did so with a characteristically theatrical flair. His "gorgeous calamity" included choreographic interpolations by Nijinska, set designs by Leon Bakst and orchestral arrangements by Igor Stravinsky; for Diaghilev, as for many ballet presenters of the early 20th century, tradition was an open and flexible category.[26]

Following Diaghilev's retrospectivism, it was de Valois' self-assigned task to introduce the full-length classic ballets to a somewhat ambivalent British public. Her decisions to present canonical works as living entities—her reliance on a choreographic text represented with new dress and modern staging elements—was both forward-thinking and fully in line with the cultural ethos of her day. Her decisions were shaped by two contemporary cultural impulses: ongoing debates about the role of tradition in the arts of the 20th century; and the efforts by British artists and intellectuals to foster an educated and selective audience characterized by discrimination and good taste.

TRADITION, SENSIBILITY, AND THE INTELLECTUAL ELITE

"By losing tradition, we lose our hold on the present," wrote the modernist poet and critic T. S. Eliot in his 1920 "The Possibility of a Poetic Drama."[27] Acknowledging that in some instances traditions were not worth keeping (in this case, he referred to the impoverished dramatic writing of the Romantic poets), he proceeded to describe the greatest works of the past as those that achieved both a structural control and a de-emphasis of personality, and that, like the Shakespeare sonnets, emerged from "a precise way of thinking and feeling." Eliot championed a new modernist literature while he simultaneously insisted on the critical importance of tradition in the modern era: "It is part of the business of the critic to preserve tradition—where a good tradition exists."[28] For Eliot, discrimination, refinement, and the sensibility to distinguish the baggy, outworn conventions of the past from true greatness in art rested with the educated, dispassionate critic. The capacity to analyze art was not given to ordinary minds: "The moment an idea has been transferred from its pure state in order that it may become comprehensible to the inferior intelligence it has lost contact with art."[29] De Valois' own view of the long-term effects of Diaghilev's production resonated with this impulse, as in her memoir she emphasized that only a small portion of the ballet audience was initially prepared to appreciate the classical tradition: "I regard the failure of the Diaghilev *Sleeping Beauty* as of secondary importance when compared with the interest that it aroused in traditional classical ballet: it could be said that the seed of true appreciation had been sown in a minority of the slow-but-sure British public, but it was a minority that remained steadfast and faithful to this new aspect of the ballet."[30]

Also influential in the late 1920s and 1930s (and through the 1960s) was the literary scholar F. R. Leavis, whose writings on the value of tradition and civilization's reliance on an educated minority were widely read and taught. Standing in opposition to the dandy-aesthetes and to what he considered the dilettantism of the Bloomsbury Group, Leavis perceived the major threat to culture as coming from the pernicious effects of film, advertising, and technology. In *Culture and Environment*, published in 1933, Leavis warned that in an era of constant change and the steady deterioration of traditional ways of life, education must be viewed as a positive avenue for change.[31] Leavis' position that "in any period it is upon a very small minority that the discerning appreciation of art and literature depends," fit squarely with the initiatives launched by a number of influential British critics to train ballet audiences to appreciate ballet's lineage and view that classical tradition with discrimination.[32]

The art historian and ballet writer Adrian Stokes was just one of several who sought to inculcate discernment and who brought a new kind of studied rigor to the practice of writing about ballet. In his 1934 *To-night the Ballet*, for instance, he presumably wrote for a small but artistically informed audience, as yet unfamiliar with ballet. Stokes described ballet as one of the central enduring traditions of European art, with its contemporary vitality deriving from its basis in classical values:

> For ballet dancing is the European way of dancing. In the scheme of this technique whole eras of our civilization are embodied. In ballet alone do the eighteenth and nineteenth centuries support the twentieth. Ballet is our major reassurance, our sole grip upon continuity, the sole ancient art that lives, and more than that, lives at its height, *revitalized by the modern spirit*. And this we owe to Diaghilev who created the modern ballet, projected contemporary thought into terms of ballet[33] [emphasis added].

In his 1936 *Russian Ballets,* Stokes continued his efforts to educate audiences, proposing to resolve for his readers the seeming paradox in ballet performance: that "we go to the ballet for amusement and relaxation," but in doing so we "most frequently enjoy sublime and superlative art that is unmatched by our other arts." His analyses of selected ballets are addressed to "those who have, or propose to have some acquaintance with their performance."[34]

Haskell's extensive writings were also educative and treated ballet with an equivalent measure of intellectual seriousness.[35] He sought to instruct readers who might be new to ballet, emphasizing ballet's enduring tradition and ensuring that British audiences should be equipped with the requisite knowledge to appreciate its particular characteristics. In the 1938 Introduction to his *Ballet Panorama* Haskell declared his intention "to write a narrative of the continuity of tradition, to show how and in what way the companies and the dancers that we applaud to-day have arisen out of the past."[36] In the Introduction to his revised 1942–43 edition of the same work, however, Haskell added another note of concern. By the 1940s Haskell perceived a threat to ballet's traditional values: "Ballet has done more than retain its popularity, it has increased it. There has, however, been a sad falling off in critical standards and applause has often come through gratitude rather than merit.... Only a strict adherence to the principles of Noverre and Fokine will give permanent life to ballet."[37]

It was in this climate—threatened by war and a purported decline in critical standards due to the insidious effects of mass popular entertainment[38]—that de Valois and Inglesby staged the classical ballets for steadily growing, and increasingly more populist, British ballet audiences.

POPULARIZING THE CLASSICS DURING WAR

As Haskell put it in his 1940 *Dancing Times* column quoted earlier, Nazi incursions prompted many Britons to feel the need to serve as the "guardians of culture"; Hitler's annexation of Czechoslovakia, the invasion of Poland, and the recent fall of France made it all the more critical to preserve civilized values for the future of Europe and the world. Average Britons took it upon themselves to meet the challenges of the Nazi war machine in both grand and quotidian gestures as they resolved to fight back against Hitler. The day war broke out, for instance, many listened and responded to the King's radio message, broadcast twice that day for maximum dissemination: "For the sake of all that we ourselves hold dear and of the world's order and peace it is unthinkable that we should refuse to meet the challenge.... To this high purpose, I now call my people at home and my peoples across the seas. I ask them to stand firm and united in this time of trial."[39]

As the call-up began, average Britons volunteered to serve in a number of capacities. As Peter Clarke put it, "Saving for victory, digging for victory, sewing for victory—this was a war in which everyone could 'go to it' and do their bit on 'the home front.'"[40] Artists volunteered as well. Kenneth Clark, who became director of the National Gallery in 1933, wrote in his memoir of Myra Hess' proposal that she should offer free concerts at the gallery during the lunch hour:

> We decided that the concerts should take place between 1 and 2 o'clock, and that the admission fee should be 1s. Thanks to the ingenuity of our head attendant, Mr. Smith (who should have been a Field Marshall), we were able to rig up a make-shift platform under the dome. I suppose that we put a notice in the paper, but there was no other form of publicity. We had no idea whether or not people would come. On the day there were queues all along the north side of Trafalgar Square, and our concert area was packed with tired and anxious people, standing or sitting on the floor. Myra gave the first concert, and played Beethoven's *Appassionata* and her own arrangement of Bach's *Jesu joy of man's desiring*. I confess that, in common with half the audience, I was in tears. This was what we had all been waiting for—an assertion of eternal values.[41]

As Hess' playing evoked "eternal values" for audiences preoccupied with the survival of their civilization, so too did dance lovers flock to performances of the gold standard, the 19th-century classic ballets.[42] Miss Heather MacDonald, whose memories of her childhood experiences during the war are archived at London's Imperial War Museum, told of the almost giddy pleasures of attending the ballet throughout the nightly bombings:

> In 1943 we rediscovered Sadler's Wells Ballet. (We had paid occasional visits before the war.) Tickets and fares were cheap, and Mother's employer often sent her on errands near the theatre, paying her fare. I gave up my comic and we sold books, to help pay our way. Now we were often in London at night, hearing shrapnel fall as we walked home. Few left the theatre during raids.... The premiere of a new production of 'Swan Lake' caused a small group of us to queue all night for tickets, outside the theatre. When there was a raid, the air raid warden was not amused! He moved us, so we walked round the block and returned to our place![43]

When she established her company, Mona Inglesby, founder, director, sometime choreographer, and prima ballerina of the International Ballet, organized her troupe to fill a set of cultural needs dictated by war-time conditions that also had roots in a wide-spread populism, a set of conditions, that is, that were radically different from those underpinning de Valois' effort in the 1920s and 1930s. A former pupil of Marie Rambert who had also trained in Paris with Mathilde Kschessinskya, Lubov Egorova, and Olga Preobrajenskaya, and in London with Nicholas Legat, Inglesby began to present her choreography in London in 1938 and 1939. She established a company in 1940 but, when the war broke out, temporarily disbanded it, volunteering as an ambulance driver. By 1941, she had decided her true service lay in bringing ballet as entertainment to anxious and weary audiences; she thus reestablished the company and launched her ambitious plans to tour the provinces. The International Ballet made its official debut at the Alhambra Theatre in Glasgow in May 1941, and Inglesby set out to "save the classical ballets from complete disappearance." Whereas de Valois had worked to establish a select, critically astute London audience, Inglesby found her niche presenting ballet to audiences who were mostly unfamiliar with the art form: "it was considered our contribution to the war effort to help keep theatres open, allowing a population starved of relaxation and entertainment to have an opportunity to savour classical ballet of a high standard throughout blacked-out Britain."[44]

Critic Fernau Hall summarized Inglesby's achievements:

Ever since 1941 the International Ballet has played in the largest provincial theatres, big London cinemas, the Butlin camps, the London Casino, and so on; year by year it has built up an enormous audience for ballet among people who would normally never have dreamt of going to ballet. In fact, Mona Inglesby's achievement is in some respects comparable to that of Sir Henry Wood in the early years of the Proms—when his programmes consisted to a considerable extent of the musical equivalent of the 'classics' on which the repertoire of the International Ballet is based.[45]

By invoking the name of Henry Wood, Hall linked Inglesby to a wider view of the role of art in the entertainment life of average middle- and working-class Britons. Wood, who in 1895 became music director of the Promenade Concerts at Queens Hall, was lionized for introducing "serious" music to average audiences at modest ticket prices. According to J. A. Fuller-Maitland, the music critic and scholar, Wood could be credited with providing "nourishment" to music lovers as he steadily built audience attendance for the Proms Concerts.[46] Inglesby's initiative, shaped by the immediate impact of the Second World War, followed in the tradition of Wood's more Victorian approach to educating while entertaining the public.

To some extent, Inglesby's path may also have been paved—paradoxically—by de Valois' patron, Lilian Baylis, whose life work it was to bring high art to the masses at the Old Vic, and who hired de Valois in 1926 to teach, and arrange dances for Shakespeare and opera productions. Baylis was an inspiring and unconventional woman whose long-term influence was vast. Like Inglesby several decades later, Baylis was absolutely "committed to bringing what was considered the very best of high culture—Shakespeare, Wagner, Mozart, *Giselle*—to working people." Her biographer, Elizabeth Schafer, describes Baylis as a missionary who sought "to alleviate existing social conditions rather than trying for a radical, fundamental change in society," while her protégée, Ninette de Valois, moved generally in much more experimental artistic circles.[47]

Finally, Inglesby's mission must be seen in light of Anna Pavlova's ambitious goal to bring ballet to the wider public. Through her 20 years of touring the world, Pavlova, who died in 1931, is estimated to have covered about 500,000 miles. She was, said A. H. Franks, the "most hardworking dancer of all time," her fervor taking her to perform for audiences in "areas which nobody ever appeared to have heard of before." "Disdaining the beaten track," writes Franks, Pavlova was "quite happy to carry out her pioneering work anywhere it was possible for her to dance before an audience that had expressed a desire to see her."[48] These pioneering efforts made it possible for Inglesby to envision that her work lay outside the London theatrical circles, and to identify a popular need for ballet that mixed high art and entertainment. For this, she, like de Valois, turned to the classic ballets as staged by Sergeyev.

SERGEYEV AND THE PUZZLE OVER AUTHENTICITY

Nicolai Sergeyev is a puzzle. Although his role in bringing the classics to the West is undisputed, details of his professional life remain murky. Born in 1876, Sergeyev was trained at the Imperial ballet school in St. Petersburg and, upon his graduation in 1894, performed as a mostly undistinguished dancer in the company. Nevertheless, he was promoted through the ranks to first dancer, and after serving as assistant to Alexander Gorsky, the "Teacher of the Theory and Notation of Dances," he was appointed company *régisseur* in 1903.[49] Nevertheless, his fluency in Stepanov notation has been challenged, and in spite of his ire over Diaghilev's tinkering with *The Sleeping Princess*, his negotiation of the authentic choreographic text is open to question. His contemporaries were mostly unfriendly. For one, Fyodor Lopokov, his former student and the chief choreographer at the Kirov beginning in 1922, accused Sergeyev of making "uninspired changes" in his 1914 staging of Petipa's *The Sleeping Beauty*.[50]

Ultimately, it may be impossible, as Roland John Wiley notes, to get a balanced view of Sergeyev's tenure at the Maryinsky because "imperial period sources refer to him but rarely," and "Soviet writers, who are uniformly unflattering, make no attempt to treat him impartially."[51] Furthermore, the professional rivalries and personal ill feelings he experienced in Russia may have accompanied him to Europe, for the portrait that emerges of him in the memoirs of dancers in the West is equally jumbled and unclear.

In his 1939 article for *The Dancing Times* entitled "Memories of Marius Petipa," Sergeyev claimed for himself the role of Petipa's pupil, one who was presumably impartial and sufficiently knowledgeable to unmask the choreographer who by that time had garnered a near-mythic reputation in the West.[52] First, he declared, Petipa's major creations were made possible on the backs of the hard-won accomplishments of the "maestros of ballet" who preceded him.[53] His second allegation was that Petipa frequently absorbed the unacknowledged choreographic contributions of his more modest but equally gifted collaborators (including the classroom *enchaînements* of Sergeyev's own teacher,

Christian Johannsen, and the choreographic interpolations of his assistant, Lev Ivanov). Finally, Sergeyev reminded British readers that Petipa had at his disposal an exclusive cadre of the finest dancers and artists in Russia, and that the Imperial government spent lavish sums of money to support the production of his multi-act spectacles. Thus, even though Sergeyev positioned himself as the champion of Petipa's authentic ballets, his relationship to his mentor is not unambiguous. "I admit the great service rendered by Petipa to the Russian classical ballet," Sergeyev concluded. "I think he brought the foundation principles of our Imperial ballet to their logical full development, but we must also admit that Petipa, as a man ambitious in the highest degree, showed great skill in freeing himself from any dangerous competition and competitors."[54]

Sergeyev's expertise in using the Stepanov notation system is also a matter for speculation, and here again the picture is slightly out of focus. Sheila Marion, in her "Recording the Imperial Ballet: Anatomy and Ballet in Stepanov's Notation" (Chapter 12 in this volume), suggests that the eventual discontinuation of the notation system may have stemmed in part from the personal resentment that existed between Petipa and Sergeyev. For in spite of its limitations in capturing the newer style ballets of Michel Fokine, the system had characteristics that made it well suited to notate the classic 19th-century ballets. For instance, it was adequate for recording choreographic patterns in space and was useful for notating many aspects of Petipa's large-scale ballets. Although the system assumed a knowledge of classical ballet positions and step conventions, it may have served Sergeyev as a sort of *aide-mémoire*, useful for recording the symmetrical patterns, mirroring actions, and repetitions found in ensemble dances and in much of the choreography for the *corps de ballet*. The Stepanov notation was a conservative system, proposes Marion, and its chief usefulness was as a tool for the preservation of the repertory of the past.

Though not questioning the usefulness of the notation system, some of Sergeyev's contemporaries—including Lopokov—challenged Sergeyev's fluency in the system. "We soon noticed," Lopukov recalls, "that Sergejev was poorly versed in this [notation] system. I, for example, studying in the most advanced class, submitted the same assignment during the course of an entire year, which Sergejev would correct every week—re-correcting, as it were, his own correction."[55]

Ballerina Tamara Karsavina saw little of value in the notation itself. She was introduced to the system as a student in the Imperial ballet school and she, along with her classmates, strove to master its anatomical features. After having spent a great deal of time and energy learning "how to mark down the 'pliant' or the 'rotatory' work of every joint contributing to a step," she wrote, "our generation of dancers found no use for the system, preferring to rely on the visual memory." Furthermore, Karsavina did not think Sergeyev relied much on the Stepanov system either. Acknowledging that the Vic-Wells revival of *The Sleeping Princess*[56] owed much to Sergeyev's "notes," Karsavina nevertheless suggested the reconstruction depended much more on the elderly Russian's memory. "In his capacity as regisseur he must have rehearsed this ballet hundreds of times; one is therefore justified in surmising that his visual recollection must have remained vivid and true." Had he not already known the work thoroughly, she declared, the notation alone would have rendered only a "palimpsest" of the original ballet.[57]

What were Sergeyev's "authentic" versions of the classics, then? From whence did they derive, and what relationship did they have to Petipa's originary texts?

SERGEYEV, DE VALOIS, AND HER CANON

De Valois credited Lydia Lopokova (the sister of the above-mentioned Fyodor Lopokov and a former Diaghilev Ballets Russes ballerina, as well as the wife of the Bloomsbury Group member, economist and ballet patron John Maynard Keynes) with alerting her to Sergeyev's residence in Paris. It was Lopokova who mediated and translated during the initial business arrangements and rehearsals. De Valois engaged Sergeyev to produce for her company Acts I and II of *Coppélia* in 1933, and the complete ballet in 1940; *Giselle, Casse-Noisette* (*The Nutcracker*), and the four-act *Le Lac des Cygnes* (*Swan Lake*) in 1934; and *The Sleeping Princess* in 1939. He was, she wrote, "a strange little man" whose experience and tradition were useful to her long-term project to establish a repertoire balanced between new creations and the classics. But his eccentricities (and, she implied, his inability to re-imagine the choreography in any viable contemporary form) meant that she had a great deal of cleaning up to do after his rehearsals. "He meticulously reproduced the choreography on our small company, complaining from time to time of our small numbers and the stage's lack of mechanical devices. He found my indifference to his mechanical requests rather strange, for he could not grasp that it was the choreography that was my principal concern at that moment, and not dozens of cardboard mechanical swans." She was forced to quietly handle ordinary stage business behind his back, arranging dancers' entrances and exits and dictating where and when they should deploy themselves on stage. From her perspective, Sergeyev lacked stage sense and any understanding of music:

> He was unmusical to a degree bordering on eccentricity; he always carried a blue pencil, and would carefully pencil out a bar of music, which, for some reason, wearied him. The offending bar would receive a long, strong blue cross through it. This would mean that I must 'phone Constant Lambert, who would come down in lunch break and put the bars back. Sergueeff would return, and because, in his absence, I had extended some small choreographic movement to cover Mr. Lambert's tracks, he would be unaware that the composition was musically where it had been before the onslaught of the blue pencil.[58]

Margot Fonteyn recalled those rehearsals quite differently, though, describing in her autobiography how Sergeyev arrived for rehearsal sessions with his personal pianist Ippolit Motcholov, and his notations, in tow. According to Fonteyn, the major difficulties the dancers encountered in the rehearsal studio resulted from language barriers and the elderly man's inability to fully demonstrate the steps.

> Sergeyev pored over his manuscripts, consulted with Motcholov, then demonstrated the steps to the best of his limited dancing ability, trying to clarify them with some mixed Russian-French-English vocabulary. Often there would be confusion about fitting the steps to the music, accent up or accent down. De Valois had so little confidence in his ability to get everyone together in the same rhythm that she called "secret" rehearsals to "tidy it up"....As soon as he started work the next afternoon, his beady little eyes saw what had been done, and he got pretty ratty with us, banging the Malacca cane on the floor and shouting. "No, no, no. Not change! Not change!"[59]

Fonteyn remembered a sharp-eyed, exacting rehearsal master who was otherwise a rather sad little man. "Heaven knows what he must have thought of us! But he was oddly indulgent, and I was very fond of him; he brought so much atmosphere of the old-style ballet school to Sadler's Wells Theatre."[60]

Markova's recollections also differ from de Valois', for the ballerina described a working relationship almost entirely dictated by musical values. In her coaching sessions with Sergeyev, preparatory to her first performance of *Giselle*, music served as the primary means of communication: "Because Sergueyev only spoke Russian and a little French, we tended to work together musically rather than by speech." And musicality was vital to the ballet as he taught it: "The mad scene in *Giselle* was set strictly to the music. This Sergueyev was very insistent upon, because of the timing and the fact that it was rather like an 'orchestration' in that it involved not only Giselle, but also Albrecht, Bathilde, the Duke, Hilarion and Berthe."[61]

Meanwhile, given her economic and space limitations, de Valois declared that she was only interested in the choreography. If this was so, she was also prepared to view the classics as open vessels within which to re-imagine the ballet and to revivify the past in contemporary terms. For her the dance was located somewhere in the interstitial tissue between Sergeyev's "meticulously reproduced choreography," Tchaikovsky's enduring music, and the immediacy of Margot Fonteyn's compelling artistry. The dance critic P. W. Manchester understood the rationale behind de Valois' plucky 1939 production of the Petipa classic: the sole reason, said Manchester, for this first staging of *The Sleeping Princess* was to show Fonteyn in "a supreme *tour de force* of classicism."[62] Setting her sights on the post-war institution of a national ballet company, de Valois was prepared to give her dancers—and especially Fonteyn—the challenges of performing Petipa's ballets before she had secured the necessary resources to fully decorate the stage. She was equally prepared to educate a critically astute audience about ballet's canon of 19th-century classics.

For her part, the production's designer, Nadia Benois, preferred an up-to-date approach to dressing the stage for this *Sleeping Princess*. She declared Bakst's costumes and décor for Diaghilev's production—which she had studied in preparing her own version—drowned the dancing in their lavishness. She determined, she wrote, to keep a lighter touch, relegating the backdrops to the background while paying attention to historical authenticity in her costuming choices. Functioning within the constraints of the Vic-Wells budget, she aimed to work "economically while yet preserving" the characters' "individuality and the harmony of the whole." In accommodating the vast numbers of characters who peopled the ballet, she aimed for a highly untraditional simplicity: "This simplification gave the finished décor inevitably a touch of the twentieth century."[63]

In spite of what she considered the drabness of the 1939 production, Manchester had to admit the theatre was packed every night and that audiences were uniformly enthusiastic about the Vic-Wells performance of this classic work.[64] Was it escapism, the anxiousness of world politics, that drew audiences to experience ballet's enduring tradition? De Valois' musical advisor, Constant Lambert, declared that if so then it was a very particular form of escapism, one that appealed only to those spectators with the most discriminating tastes. Those whom he labeled "low-brow" audiences would be disappointed by Tchaikovsky's score for *The Sleeping Beauty*, for "being accustomed to flamboyant melodrama and a rather too-ready lump in the throat, ['low-brow audiences'] were not prepared to appreciate a score which not only shows the utmost refinement (using that word in its most complimentary sense), but is one of the most purely *musical* scores ever written."[65] The ballet itself appealed to the more intellectually astute. It would not provide spectators with the easy propagandistic messages to which they were becoming accustomed before and during war:

> Such a world of art is sternly denounced by some modern critics as being "escapist," and certainly those who expect ballets to have a "message" will not find much to please them in "The Sleeping Princess." Ballet, to my mind, is of all mediums the least suited to conveying a message, and that is why it provides so welcome an oasis in a world where writers, painters, and composers keep on sending one messages whether one wants them to or not. "Escapism" in art may not be so bad a thing after all. The realm of the imagination which has given us the landscapes of Claude and Poussin the poetry of Coleridge and Keats, the "Magic Flute" of Mozart and the finest pages of "The Sleeping Princess," may well prove more enduring than the platform from which are hurled to us the urgent polemics of the present day.[66]

Music critic Edwin Evans, writing about the Sadler's Wells 1940 presentation of *Le Lac des Cygnes*, affirmed that de Valois and Lambert had met their goals in championing art for art's sake alone. Not only was Margot Fonteyn steadily developing as a significant artist, he noted, but the production as a whole "was a triumphant success, certified not only by the enthusiasm which has become almost normal with the [undiscriminating] Sadler's Wells audience, but by the whole-hearted approval of more discriminating" spectators. Further, Lambert, "bursting with energy," got as much as was possible out of "the sumptuousness of Tchaikovsky's music" in spite of the reduced orchestra under his baton.[67]

After the war and with the company's move to the Covent Garden Royal Opera House, de Valois continued her strategy of updating the classics. Cyril W. Beaumont described the revival of *The Sleeping Beauty* staged for the reopening of Covent Garden on February 20, 1946, as an improvement over the 1939 version, which was, he said, insufficiently brilliant. No expenses were spared on Oliver Messel's colorful costumes and ornate settings. Ashton's Garland Dance in Act I, substituted for Petipa's Villagers Dance, was "pleasing and well-arranged"; his Act III "Three Ivans," replacing the version choreographed by Nijinska for the Ballets Russes, lacked the "robust humour of the original [sic] dance," but, wrote Beaumont, "it is an excellent arrangement of Russian character steps, adroitly used to develop a mounting excitement."[68] According to David Vaughan, additional changes that made their way into the 1946 version included Ashton's newly created *pas de trois*, "Florestan and His Two Sisters," replacing the Jewel *pas de quatre* in Act III. (That is, it was somewhat new, as the first female variation, danced by Moira Shearer, was based on the earlier divertissement from the *pas de quatre*, presumably choreographed by Petipa and later acknowledged in a program note that read "by Frederick Ashton after Marius Petipa").[69] In 1952, Ashton added a solo in the Vision Scene for Beryl Grey as Aurora, this amendment of the original Sergeyev staging also being credited to Petipa. Vaughan describes the complicated line of descent of this dance:

> In the 1939 production Sergeyev had given [Aurora] a solo danced to the waltz variation from the Jewel *pas de quatre*; now [in 1952] the proper music was restored, with choreography that seems to have been based by Ashton on Violette (Prokhorova) Elvin's memories of the Bolshoi version, which may or may not have been authentic Petipa.

Still later, in 1955, Ashton created a solo for the Prince as danced by Michael Somes, though no such variation existed in Sergeyev's notes, "probably because the role was created by Pavel Gerdt when he was too old to perform one." Making attribution all the murkier, this male variation was also described as being "after Petipa."[70]

Over the years, other changes to Sergeyev's stagings began to creep in, as noted by ballerina Nadia Nerina, who joined the Sadler's Wells Ballet at Covent Garden in 1947. Nerina loved the "real classical mime" as she had learned it upon first joining the company, but it was deemed "old-fashioned" and was gradually streamlined for modern tastes.[71] Most London critics responded positively to this streamlining. The superior performances of the classics by Sadler's Wells, noted Audrey Williamson, when contrasted with Sergeyev's productions for other companies (probably including the International Ballet), "shows how much the first owe to Ninette de Valois' efficiency in clarifying details through a 'sweeping up' process. The mime in Sadler's Wells performances is incomparable in its expressiveness, accuracy and restrained beauty, and their team of classical soloists is to-day unique."[72]

A different atmosphere greeted Sergeyev when he left the Sadler's Wells Ballet to be engaged by the International Ballet in 1942, for Inglesby contended that de Valois had always devalued Sergeyev's professionalism and the wealth of tradition he brought to staging the classics. During the International Ballet's lifetime (1941–1953), Sergeyev staged a number of canonical ballets, bringing to the stage *Coppélia* and *Giselle* in 1942, the one-act divertissement "Aurora's Wedding" in 1944, and *The Sleeping Princess* and *Le Lac des Cygnes* in 1947. Running consistently through Inglesby's interviews and writing is a deep vein of reverence for Sergeyev, the teacher and rehearsal director she affectionately referred to as Maestro, and to the ballets as he reconstructed them from his notes in her rehearsal studios.

For her, the classics represented a rampart against the tides of war and a shield against the depredations of unchecked experimentalism. Inglesby did not question Sergeyev's production of the classics; nor did she doubt his musicality. She regarded the Russian émigré as uncompromising in his high standards and dedicated to preserving the riches of his Imperial legacy. The Maestro she described was slight of build and erect in carriage; "he was not altogether prepossessing to look at until one looked at his eyes beneath their heavy lids, and realised that within him was a formidable will to overcome all obstacles which might stand in the way of the fulfilment of his purpose." When working to revive a ballet, he frequently half closed his eyes in concentration, as if bringing the various elements into his memory: "When he was ready, and rose to show what was required in every single role throughout the ballets, he became transformed into the character he was demonstrating—the fierce Chieftain in *Prince Igor*, the gentle mother in *Giselle*, or a delicate Princess Aurora in *The Sleeping Princess*."[73]

Indeed, she claimed, it was Sergeyev's confidence in her and her enterprise that allowed her to persevere through challenging circumstances and the frequently dismissive reviews of the London dance critics: "Without his decision to work with us, the company would never have come into being, but he placed his full weight behind us, constantly encouraging us, grooming and preparing us for the great roles to come. He never flagged." Still, Inglesby admitted that she had first to counter the misimpression, rife even among the dancers in her own company, that the classical ballets he staged were "museum pieces." "It was a struggle to reverse this opinion," wrote Inglesby, "to make members of our company understand just what a treasure house Maestro held in his hands in the form of his choreographic notations. These, with his dedicated teaching, ensured the presentation and preservation of the priceless heritage of Russian classical ballet."[74] Congruent with Inglesby's reverence for the past as restaged by Sergeyev, though, was her Pavlova-like zeal to make ballet responsive to the needs of the wider populace.

Sergeyev's 1942 production of *Coppélia* was important both to her audiences and to the future growth of her company. The tuneful, beloved ballet "filled a great need in the war years for escapism," affording "light-heartedness in a time of danger and darkness." For her audiences, the ballet offered an "escape" from the grimness of wartime existence, said Inglesby, using that word in its literal sense and not, as had Lambert, to suggest an escape into the artist's creative imagination. At the same time, staging the work gave the company a reason to expand its ranks "in preparation for Maestro's promised great four-act ballets in their entirety, with their original choreography"[75]

De Valois, like Diaghilev, reached into the ranks of modern British painters to design her productions,[76] as evidenced in this example of Leslie Hurry's 1944 Surrealist décor for Sadler's Wells *Swan Lake* (Figure 1.1). Inglesby, though, more often turned to theatre professionals like Hein Heckroth and Doris Zinkeisen for her stagings of the classics.[77] In a coy wink to her audiences, who no doubt were more familiar with the world of musical theatre, Inglesby often layered a subtle message of popular appeal atop the choreography's classicism. Heckroth's costumes and décor for *Coppélia* were "ravishing," said Inglesby, whose personal favorite was her second act costume for Swanhilda. "'Very delicate, very sexy,' said Hein, unheard by Maestro, who would not have approved of anything so suggestive." Nevertheless, Inglesby took obvious delight in dancing in the "delicious concoction."[78] The critic for *The Times* (London) sensed these doubly coded messages. In a review of the company's June 1943 performance of *Giselle* at the Lyric Theatre, he wrote, "Miss Doris Zinkeisen has designed some gay and colourful scenery and costumes for Act I and her forest scene is suitably macabre, but she is too amused at the period to take it quite seriously, and *Giselle* should not be gayed, even so deliciously."[79]

In 1946, on the occasion of the International Ballet's fifth anniversary season at London's Coliseum, a writer for the journal *Carnaval* asserted that the company was "no highly-coloured replica of the Wells."[80] What distinguished Inglesby's project was her goal to produce "a company dancing ballet as it should be danced, well presented, well dressed, technically perfect." "There was nothing arty-crafty about the International," wrote this critic, in a clearly aimed reference to de Valois' enterprise. "The 'Bloomsbury' approach to ballet may be all very well, but when a work can be adequately staged and finely dressed who can blame Miss Inglesby for rejecting the home-spun and two pianos for a full orchestra and a sparkling décor."[81] For Inglesby, the dance was located in the larger theatricality that emerged when all the elements of ballet—choreography, mime, music and décor—were brought together. Her classical works would be aimed, not at the Bloomsbury intellectuals or the artistic elite but at audiences outside London who attended ballet (often for the first time) in cinemas, amphitheatres, and other large venues. A publicity announcement issued by the company in August 1947 declared the mission of the company's forthcoming appearances in the Gaumont cinemas.[82] The company's four-month tour of the provinces was

FIGURE 1.1 Leslie Hurry, *Lac des Cygnes* drop Curtain, 1943. Jerome Robbins Dance Division, The New York Public Library for the Performing Arts, Astor, Lenox and Tilden Foundations. By kind permission of The Victor Batte-Lay Trust, VBLT Catalogue http://www.vbltcollection.org.uk/index. asp.

an event of considerable importance and encouragement in that it brings the art we foster to what must largely be a new public. Also, it has always been a source of keen regret to us that at every one of our London Seasons we have had to turn away large numbers of our Patrons, because they could not afford to pay the high West End prices and there were not enough of the lower-priced seats to go round.[83]

Critics registered that Inglesby often met her goals. One writer for *The Derby Evening Telegraph* noted the audience's rapturous applause for the company's 1943 *Giselle,* and particularly praised Inglesby as Giselle and Harold Turner as Loys as actors who exemplified the "depths of emotional expression which can be achieved in ballet."[84] Although James Redfern's May 1944 review of the International Ballet's new *Coppélia* was not unqualified (the orchestra was "slack in rhythm" and the *corps de ballet* lacked precision), the production served as a good introduction, he wrote, for those "who have even yet not acquired a taste for this delightful and for so long neglected art." And, he continued: " 'Coppélia' is given here a sufficiently adequate production to delight any audience susceptible to its extraordinary beauty and dramatic interest. Also, I would emphasise again to those who, though ardent theatre-goers, have not yet fallen under the spell of ballet that a visit to 'Coppélia' may immediately convert them and bring a new and most exquisite source of pleasure and entertainment into their lives"[85] (Figure 1.2).

From 1941 to 1953, the International Ballet toured lavishly produced and competently danced popular classics—the same works danced by the Sadler's Wells Ballet in London in different garb—to provincial audiences across Britain. In the company's later years, Inglesby and her troupe performed before enthusiastic crowds in the vast arenas of Swit-

FIGURE I.2 Lancelot Vining. Spinners and Reapers Pas de Quatre from Act III *Coppélia*, International Ballet Company. pf MS Thr 388 (234), Harvard Theatre Collection, Houghton Library, Harvard University.

zerland, Italy, and Spain, dancing the canon for audiences who, like their counterparts in Britain, were mainly unfamiliar with multi-act, full-length classical ballets. Arthur Franks described what many spectators witnessed in the company's initiative to perform canonical ballets to audiences in large cinemas:

> Before over four thousand souls in the Gaumont State Cinema the prologue of *The Sleeping Beauty* began to unfold. From near the back of an enormous auditorium bounded by gilt-encrusted walls the stage became a glowing miniature hung exasperatingly at too great a distance. An insufficiently raked floor and absence of staggered seats necessitated constant readjustment of neck and shoulders. Nevertheless, as the curtain fell on the pageantry of that opening scene the great audience burst into applause sufficiently vigorous to hearten everyone concerned with the project of presenting ballet in a super cinema.[86]

Reviewing the same Kilburn performances, Mary Clarke similarly weighed the pitfalls and benefits of the whole enterprise. Although the auditorium of the Gaumont cinema was grand, the stage itself was wide and shallow and afforded little wing space, and the inadequate lighting made the spectacle fatiguing to watch. Her seat, wrote Clarke, felt "at least half a mile from the stage," and from that distance, the sets appeared blurry and the colors of the costumes were distorted. As reconstructed by Sergeyev, the production was alleged to be closer to the Maryinsky original than any other. "This claim is probably justified," she wrote, "since International retain all the fairy-tale characters (nine couples) of the original and ignore all the emendations made by Diaghileff in his 1921 revival." To this the wearied Clarke snapped, "My admiration for Diaghileff grows continually. The fairy-tale divertissements may be original but are anything but interesting choreographically and their inclusion means that one is practically in a state of coma before the grand adagio." Nevertheless, all was not lost, for the audience was clearly appreciative. Sergeyev, she noted, had done a fine job drilling the *corps de ballet*, Claudie Algeranova made a feminine and appealing Princess Florine, and Michel de Lutry had some superb moments as the Blue Bird. Ernest Hewitt as Prince Désiré fell short of standard, as did Sandra Vane in her efforts as the Lilac Fairy. As Aurora, though, Inglesby revealed her finest qualities: "She has remarkable elevation and speed, and can be quite sensational in allegro passages. She has poise and assurance and is beautifully light."[87]

In producing the recently canonized 19th-century ballets, Inglesby and de Valois represented very different ideals and aims, and they responded to shifting cultural and artistic climates as well as to divergent audience expectations. De Valois worked to build the foundations for a strong national ballet composed of a repertoire of new and classical works that would appeal to a critically astute audience and would lead her company to eventual recognition as Britain's Royal Ballet. Meanwhile, Inglesby, holding fast to what she believed were original choreographic texts, managed to respond to the needs of her own more populist audiences, allowing her productions to be (again quoting Franko) continuous with "all that circulate[d]" around them. Ultimately, although the two women differed in their regard for the choreographic "text," each was responsive to the perceived demands of her audience, and each, to some degree allowed the inclusion of the popular, the vernacular, or the avant-garde.

Then too, both approaches proved important; in the 1950s some in the Sadler's Wells audience came to de Valois' enterprise after having been first introduced to ballet through the zealous efforts of Mona Inglesby, just as her International Ballet nurtured many young dancers who would later achieve recognition dancing with other companies.[88] For it was always clear where Inglesby's loyalties lay; included in the program for the International Ballet's production of *The Sleeping Princess* at the Kilburn Gaumont State cinema was a lengthy tribute to Sergeyev in which she expressed her reverence for the Maestro and her conviction that she was presenting classical ballets as they should be seen:

> The name of Nicolai Sergueeff needs no introduction or explanation, but on the occasion of his third revival of 'The Sleeping Princess' it seems only fitting that we, who have had the privilege of working with him since the Company's inception in 1941, should try and express our gratitude for this and all the other productions he has given to us.... M. Sergueeff informs us that this present rendering of 'The Sleeping Princess' is closer to the Marinsky production than any other now being performed, and we are deeply conscious of the honour he has paid us in allowing

International Ballet to present this famous work so closely in accord with the original conception.

We hope we may long continue to merit the confidence he places in us and we believe we can best express our appreciation and gratitude by trying to keep safe the traditions and spirit of the classical ballet to which he has devoted a lifetime of service.[89]

CONCLUSION: CANON FORMATION IN THE REALM OF BALLETOMANIA

In the closing decades of the 20th century, literary scholars and visual artists continued to debate the viability of the Western canon. Which works have transcended local origins to endure in the new millennium? How could (or should?) the canon be extended to include the creations of non-white, non-Western artists? Although Gates and those on the left of the political spectrum might argue for a broader and more inclusive list of canonical works, some on the right seized on these same lists in order to reassert their notions of the supremacy of the Western tradition, institutionalizing them as bulwarks of civilization.[90]

Meanwhile, discussions of the ballet canon must acknowledge dance's heterogeneous constitution, and its inherent capacity to be directly responsive to the needs of a community of spectators. Like the other art forms, ballet carries the potential to communicate timely, political messages; yet unlike these other forms, the authenticity of ballet's foundational text is always uncertain; even when producers and performers claim an authentic staging, they are really depending on some consensus about what that original text might be. Furthermore, the hybrid nature of any particular version of a well-known ballet allows multiple messages to be communicated to a wide range of audience members who carry with them their individual preconceptions, expectations, and previous experiences with ballet. To adapt the language of literary scholar Gates, each restaged version of a canonical ballet is inherently "porous, dynamic, and interactive," while, following Bloom, each also has some enduring essence that identifies it as a recognizable classic. And, in line with Anna Bryzski's discussion, each decision about how to restage a canonical ballet—made, in this example, by de Valois and Inglesby, and more widely by regional dance company directors and executives of major ballet companies today—is contingent on market forces and dictated by power structures. It is presumed that the canonical ballets, in some version of authenticity, will resonate with audiences, giving them the (widely varied) relationships to tradition they might desire at any particular moment in history. Moreover, the multi-layered performance of ballet, comprising performers' unique interpretations along with choices about staging, design, and production, may elicit intended and unintended meanings at many levels.

Precariously derived, the ballet canon was born at a unique historical moment and its construction bears only slight resemblance to the canonization process in the other arts.

Genné notes that the ballet canon was "the result of decisions taken by a group of individuals at one particular point in time for a variety of cultural and historical as well as aesthetic reasons."[91] The creation of a canon gave Western ballet both a ready repertory and a tradition. The classic ballets were deemed important to the training of young, non-Russian dancers, but they also gave Western dance lovers an adopted tradition, a link to a heritage that was, to some degree, a latter-day invention. Dance writer Marcia Siegel acknowledges that "we confer great power on the past, even though the past has no fixed meaning." Balletomanes may look backwards to reassure themselves of ballet's tradition, but the origin of canonical works is always uncertain. Hybridity, fluidity, and change are the natural conditions of dance; as Siegel puts it, "longtime critics return to the great works over the years, understanding that they are looking at objects in evolution."[92]

As we move into the 21st century it remains to be seen which ballets from the rich repertory of 20th-century ballets created by choreographers including George Balanchine, Frederick Ashton, Antony Tudor, and Kenneth Macmillan will make their way to the canon. Which of the ballets created in the 20th century will find homes in the repertories of today's ballet companies, given evolutions in audience taste, dancers' training regimes, and arts budget allocations? Furthermore, what are the aesthetic and other values that will dictate their re-creations? We can be aware that in the past the canon has been molded by serendipity, historical circumstances, and the forceful personalities of a handful of individuals who shape, and are shaped by, the local needs of a community of spectators. The intelligent use of technologies and documentation along with a deeper understanding of dance's history can help ensure that the future trajectory of balletomania is both more conscious and less tenuous.

ACKNOWLEDGMENTS

Research was made possible through an Ohio State University Arts and Humanities Research Enhancement Grant and a Howard D. Rothschild Fellowship in Dance from the Houghton Library Visiting Fellowship Program at Harvard University. My thanks to Sebastian Knowles, Associate Dean for Faculty and Research at The Ohio State University, for reading an early draft of this manuscript; and to my superb research assistant, Veronica Dittman-Stanich.

NOTES

1. On rare occasions, the scholar might find additional clues to reconstructing past works in the annotated rehearsal scores known as the *répétiteurs*. Marian Smith documents her discovery of a number of "spectacular treasures" in the archive of the Theater Museum in St. Petersburg. See Marian Smith, "The Earliest *Giselle*? A Preliminary Report on a St. Petersburg Manuscript," *Dance Chronicle* 23.1 (2000), 29–48.

2. Mark Franko, "Period Plots, Canonical Stages, and Post-Metanarrative in American Modern Dance" in *The Returns of Alwin Nikolais: Bodies, Boundaries and the Dance Canon*, eds. Claudia Gitelman and Randy Martin (Middletown, CT: Wesleyan University Press, 2007), 171.

3. Sally Banes, *Dancing Women: Female Bodies on Stage* (New York: Routledge, 1998), 11.

4. Henry Louis Gates, Jr. "Introduction," *Loose Canons: Notes on the Culture Wars* (New York: Oxford University Press, 1992), xvi.

5. Harold Bloom, *The Western Canon: The Books and School of the Ages* (New York: Harcourt Brace, 1994), 8–9.

6. Anna Bryzski, ed., *Partisan Canons* (Durham, NC: Duke University Press, 2007), 8.

7. Vida L. Midgelow has examined diverse choreographic responses to these classics. Newly created by contemporary choreographers, the works she examines have "contradicted, criticised, dislocated, fragmented, updated, celebrated, refocused and otherwise reimagined the [original] ballet." Although Midgelow's examination is timely, one might also tease apart the canonical works (as they have come down to us in some version of authenticity) for their potential to revise and refocus the originals and to invest them with new meaning for modern viewers. Vida L. Midgelow, *Reworking the Ballet, Counter-Narratives and Alternative Bodies* (London: Routledge, 2007), 1.

8. *Giselle, ou Les Wilis* premiered in Paris in 1841. The original choreography was by Jean Coralli and Jules Perrot. *Coppélia,* with choreography by Arthur St.-Léon, premiered in Paris in 1870. Both of these ballets come down to us mainly in versions staged by Petipa, who was also responsible for choreographing *Swan Lake* (with Lev Ivanov) at the Maryinsky Theatre in St. Petersburg in 1895; and *The Sleeping Beauty*, also in St. Petersburg, in 1890. Petipa's assistant, Lev Ivanov, was chiefly responsible for *The Nutcracker,* which premiered in St. Petersburg in 1892.

9. Beth Genné, "Creating a Canon, Creating the 'Classics' in Twentieth-Century British Ballet," *Dance Research* 18.2 (Winter, 2000), 132–62.

10. Arnold Haskell, "Balletomane's Log Book," *The Dancing Times*, August, 1940, 652.

11. Arnold Haskell, "The Birth of the English Ballet," *Journal of the Royal Society of Arts*, June 16, 1939, 784–802.

12. Haskell, "Birth," 791.

13. In an article entitled "The Camargo Society," which first appeared in *Dance Journal* in December 1930, Cyril W. Beaumont respectfully disagreed with Lydia Lopokova's opening remarks at the Camargo Society's first performance. Lopokova's claim that the audience assembled had witnessed the Birth of the British Ballet prompted Beaumont to include a list of other groundbreaking pioneers, including some whose efforts he thought had been overlooked: Miss Bedells, Miss Craske, Miss Ninette de Valois, Miss Fairbairn, Miss James, Mme. Rambert, Miss Marian Wilson, Mr. Ashton, Mr. Dolin, Mr. Doone, Mr. Espinosa, Mr. Haines, Mr. Michael Harvey, Mr. Leighton Lucas, Mr. Quentin Todd. In *Dancers Under My Lens. Essays in Ballet Criticism* (London: C. W. Beaumont, 1949), 20. For a more contemporary critique of this view, see Alexandra Carter, *Dance and Dancers in the Victorian and Edwardian Music Hall Ballet* (Burlington, VT: Ashgate, 2005).

14. Janet Leeper, *English Ballet* (London: King Penguin, 1944), 27.

15. Genné writes: "Thus, *Swan Lake, Sleeping Beauty* and *Giselle* come to us, in a sense, by default, for de Valois' choice of 'classics,' which Haskell subsequently 'canonised' in writing, was limited to the ballets in Sergueyev's collection and to those which she (and he) saw on the London stage. These came largely through the filter of the Russian companies, most prominently the

Ballets Russes, but also through Pavlova and other visiting Russian artists who...performed regularly in London variety theatres." "Canon," 150.

16. Ibid., 153, 136–37.

17. W. J. Turner, "Mercury and the Nightingale," *New Statesman*, July 23, 1927, 479.

18. For example, many of Frederick Ashton's early ballets were influenced by his study under late Diaghilev choreographers Bronislava Nijinska and Léonide Massine, who themselves created ballets depicting stylish, modern life. Like them, in his first work for Marie Rambert, "A Tragedy of Fashion" (1926), Ashton initially hoped to collaborate with the chic fashion designer Coco Chanel and the modern composers Georges Auric and Francis Poulenc. Although Rambert quickly dispensed with such outsized notions, reviewers commented on Ashton's stylistic links to late Diaghilev ballets. One of Ashton's wittiest depictions of "the bright young things" of the 1920s occurred in his 1931 ballet "Façade," to music by William Walton, based on poetry by society figure Edith Sitwell. In this regard, see Geraldine Morris' discussion of "A Wedding Bouquet," included in this volume. The reader is also referred to David Vaughan, *Frederick Ashton and his Ballets* (New York: Knopf, 1977).

19. Kathrine Sorley Walker, "The Festival and the Abbey: Ninette de Valois' Early Choreography, 1925–1934," Part One, *Dance Chronicle* 7, No. 4 (1984–1985), 380.

20. Ibid., 384.

21. Ninette de Valois, "The Future of the Ballet," *The Dancing Times*, February 1926, 589–91.

22. Lynn Garafola describes the gamble Diaghilev and Oswold Stoll took in staging the production in a London unaccustomed to the tradition of the full-length ballet: "Unlike Diaghilev's earlier season at the house, where *La Boutique Fantasque* had sent London 'off its head with delight,' the Petipa classic ended in failure. The ballet closed on February 4, 1922, as Diaghilev, a trail of debts in his wake, beat a retreat across the Channel." Lynn Garafola, *Diaghilev's Ballets Russes* (New York: Da Capo Press, 1998), 213.

23. Ninette De Valois, *Come Dance with Me* (1957; repr. London: Dance Books, 1973), 65.

24. Genné, "Canon," 140.

25. Roland John Wiley, "Dances from Russia: An Introduction to the Sergejev Collection," *Harvard Library Bulletin* 14 (January 1976), 99. The dancer Lydia Sokolova recorded in her memoirs Diaghilev's probable line of reasoning:

Looking back, one can see how Diaghilev's mind would have worked, and one can imagine him ticking off on his fingers the various problems he had to face, one by one. First of all there was Tchaikovsky's huge score, parts of which were unsatisfactory and parts inadequately orchestrated. Some of the weak numbers must be cut and replaced by others from *Swan Lake* or *Casse-noisette*; and Stravinsky must be interested in the music and persuaded to re-orchestrate one or two dances: thus might the nineteenth-century master appear to be given the blessing of a hero of the *avant garde*. Secondly...as it was not in his nature to leave well alone, one or two new dances by a young choreographer must be inserted. Thirdly, a suitable designer must be found for the gigantic production.... [fourth, a suitable classical ballerina, or ballerinas, needed to be found]. Lastly, public opinion must be swayed in favour of this five-act academic ballet, which might prove more novel and sensational than anything he had ever put on, simply through being so old-fashioned. (Lydia Sokolova, *Dancing for Diaghilev: The Memoirs of Lydia Sokolova*, San Francisco: Mercury House, 1989, 186.)

26. Garafola reports that "Ironically, both the idea of mounting *The Sleeping Princess* and the financing of this full-length ballet came from the popular stage." Although Petipa's 1890 *La Belle*

au Bois Dormant was an aesthetic cornerstone for many of the *Mir isskusstva* artists, Diaghilev's motive for producing his retrospective staging was a desire to finance his other modernist, experimental works. Garafola, *Diaghilev's Ballets, Russes*, 221–22. For "gorgeous calamity," see 223. The role of the popular stage and an openness toward staging the classics characterized the ballet of the first decades of the 20th century. In her memoir, Phyllis Bedells describes a similar effort to introduce a version of the classics in a program at the Royal Court Theatre in 1920: "Although classical ballet was not much in public favour, Novikoff and I opened the programme with an arrangement of the *adagio* from *Le Lac des Cygnes*, Act II. Novikoff and I both felt that English audiences ought to be given a taste of the serious, traditional ballet which we ourselves enjoyed so much." Phyllis Bedells, *My Dancing Days* (London: Phoenix House Ltd., 1954), 107. Cyril W. Beaumont documented the performances of abbreviated versions of standard ballets prior to the arrival of the Diaghilev Ballets Russes, including, in 1909, Tamara Karsavina at the Coliseum; and in 1910, Anna Pavlova and Mikhail Mordkin at the Palace Theatre, Lydia Kyasht and Adolph Bolm at the Empire, Olga Preobrajenskaya with a company of 20 dancers at the Hippodrome in a condensed version of *Le Lac des Cygnes*, and Karsavina with a company of 13 at the Coliseum in *Giselle or la Sylphide*, presumably *Giselle ou les Wilis*. Cyril W. Beaumont, *The Diaghilev Ballet in London* (London: Putnam, 1940).

27. T. S. Eliot, "The Possibility of a Poetic Drama," *The Dial*, November 1, 1920, 441–447.

28. T. S. Eliot, "Introduction," in *The Sacred Wood: Essays on Poetry and Criticism* (London: Methuen, 1928), xv.

29. Eliot, "Poetic Drama."

30. De Valois, *Come Dance,* 48.

31. F. R. Leavis and Denys Thompson, *Culture and Environment: The Training of Critical Awareness* (London: Chatto and Windus, 1933), 4.

32. F. R. Leavis, *Mass Civilisation and Minority Culture* (1930; repr. Folcroft Library Editions, 1974), 3. Leavis began his studies at Cambridge in 1919 and started teaching in 1927. He assumed the position of director of studies in English at Downing College in 1930. Arnold Haskell, born in 1903, entered Cambridge in 1922, where he studied for four years, and although he studied law and history he also wrote extensive criticism on film, drama, and literature. I hear strong echoes of Leavis' proposal for educating an intellectual elite in much of Haskell's critical writing.

33. Adrian Stokes, *To-Night the Ballet* (London: Faber and Faber, 1934), 45.

34. Stokes, *Russian Ballet* (New York: Dutton, 1936), 9–10.

35. There is much more to be said about the enormous influence of the British dance critics and historians of the period. Through their publications, many of them aimed to educate the ballet public, elevate the art form, and increase the size of dance audiences. In addition to those mentioned here, influential writers of the period include Lionel Bradley, Caryl Brahms, C. V. Coton, Peter Noble, and P. J. S. Richardson.

36. Arnold Haskell, *Ballet Panorama: An Illustrated Chronicle of Three Centuries*, 2nd ed. (1938; New York: Scribner, 1942–43), 1.

37. Ibid., 1, 2.

38. This pernicious popular entertainment was not confined to American movies. In *Music-Ho! A Study of Music in Decline*, originally published in 1934, Constant Lambert launched an astringent badinage against the mechanisms of popular entertainment, including the gramophone, the wireless, and the loudspeaker. In "The Appalling Popularity of Music," he took aim at

the indiscriminate appropriation of sound technology, and the "overproduction" of music, warning that "today the chances are that one's host is a gramophone bore, intent on exhibiting his fifty-seven varieties of soundbox, or a wireless fiend intent on obtaining the obscurest stations irrespective of programme. It is to be noticed that the more people use the wireless, the less they listen to it." Constant Lambert, *Music-Ho! A Study of Music in Decline* (London: Hogarth Press, 1985), 200.

39. Quoted in Norman Longmate, *How We Lived Then: A History of Everyday Life During the Second World War* (London: Hutchinson, 1971), 33.

40. Peter Clarke, *Hope and Glory: Britain 1900–1990* (London: Penguin Press, 1996), 207.

41. Kenneth Clark, *The Other Half: A Self-Portrait* (London: John Murray, 1977), 28.

42. Mary Clarke, *The Sadler's Wells Ballet: A History and an Appreciation* (New York: Macmillan, 1955), 152.

43. Heather MacDonald, Miscellaneous Documents, Accession number: 99/66/1, Imperial War Museum.

44. Mona Inglesby, *Ballet in the Blitz, The History of a Ballet Company*, with Kay Hunter (Debenham, Suffolk: Groundnut, 2008), 2–3.

45. Fernau Hall, *Modern English Ballet: An Interpretation* (New York: Andrew Melrose, 1951), 279.

46. Fuller-Maitland quoted in Reginald Pound, *Sir Henry Wood* (London: Cassell, 1969), 79. For the "social experiment" launched by Robert Newman and Henry Wood in opening the stalls to popular-priced tickets and to shifting musical tastes in London, see Jenny Doctor and David Wright, eds., *The Proms: A New History* (London: Thames and Hudson, 2007).

47. The musicologist Edward Dent described the paradoxical relationship between de Valois and Baylis at the Old Vic: "It is amusing to see how the proletarian theatre which Miss Cons and Miss Baylis thought they were creating has brought forth a type of ballet which is anything but proletarian in its appeal—not indeed a ballet for the aristocracy of imperial Moscow, but certainly for the intellectuals of Bloomsbury." Quoted in Elizabeth Schafer, *Lilian Baylis: A Biography* (Hertfordshire: University of Hertfordshire Press, 2006), 219. For "Committed to bringing," see 1; "alleviate existing social conditions," see 261.

48. A. H. Franks, "A Biographical Sketch" in *Pavlova: A Collection of Memoirs*, A. H. Franks, ed. (New York: Da Capo Press, 1956), 27.

49. Wiley, 94–95.

50. Lopokov charged that Sergeyev had removed, for instance, the key moment in the Prologue when Carabosse and her rat entourage sprawl across the King's throne, effectively disrespecting the aristocracy. "The action was very incisive, and I feel that here, Petipa, who was considered a courtier, revealed his true feelings about the social order of those years." Fyodor Lopukhov, "Annals of 'The Sleeping Beauty,' I. The Choreography," *Ballet Review*, 5. 4 (1975–76), 22–23.

51. Wiley, 95.

52. Nicolas Sergueeff, "Memories of Marius Petipa," *The Dancing Times*, July 1939, 396–97.

53. These included Charles Didelot, Antoine Titus, Jules Perrot, and Arthur St. Léon.

54. Sergueeff, 397.

55. Quoted in Wiley, 98.

56. Following Diaghilev's practice, the Vic-Wells Ballet and the International Ballet referred to the ballet as *The Sleeping Princess*. In later revivals, the Royal Ballet reverted to the title *The Sleeping Beauty*, a title that more closely translated Marius Petipa's original *La Belle au Bois Dormant*.

57. Tamara Karsavina, "Revival or Mutilation," *The Dancing Times*, June 1954, 539–40.

58. De Valois, *Come Dance*, 111–12.

59. Margot Fonteyn, *Autobiography* (New York: Knopf, 1976), 70. Former Sadler's Wells dancer Richard Ellis seemed to confirm Fonteyn's recollections that language was the major obstacle in Sergeyev's rehearsals. In a transcript of an interview from 1976, Ellis recalled that in spite of living in England for years, Sergeyev never mastered the English language: "Ninette [de Valois] used to get us all together on Sundays and we'd try and decipher what he'd taught us during the week to get *Sleeping Beauty* on." According to Ellis, everyone spoke up during those ad hoc rehearsals, each dancer offering suggestions about what the *régisseur* might have intended in his flawed demonstrations of the steps. Richard Ellis and Christine DuBoulay, interview by Nancy Reynolds, 1976, transcript. Oral History Archive, Jerome Robbins Dance Division, New York Public Library for the Performing Arts, 14a.

60. Fonteyn, 53.

61. Alicia Markova, *Markova Remembers* (Boston: Little, Brown, 1986), 45–46.

62. P. W. Manchester, *Vic-Wells: A Ballet Progress* (London: Victor Gollancz, 1946), 42.

63. Nadia Benois, "Décor and Costumes" in *The Sleeping Princess, Camera Studies*, ed. Gordon Anthony (London: George Routledge and Sons, 1940), 33.

64. Manchester, *Vic-Wells*, 136.

65. Constant Lambert, "Tchaikovsky and the Ballet" in *The Sleeping Princess*, 18.

66. Ibid., 25–26. Although Lambert does not further identify these "urgent polemics," Richard Overy has described the interwar years as "the first real age of mass communication," a period characterized by explosive growth in mass publishing. Overy notes the wide availability of foreign works in translations and the prevalence of radio broadcasts, reading groups, and social clubs that helped to fuel a sense of imminent crisis. The threat of the impending destruction of civilization sparked a pervasive and habitual sense of anxiety that found expression in the works of artists and intellectuals, and flourished, as well, in the ordinary discourse of citizens of all political persuasions. Richard Overy, *The Twilight Years: The Paradox of Britain Between the Wars* (New York: Viking, 2009). Philip M. Taylor notes the widespread efforts by political parties to sway voters through "mass persuasion" in popular media, including cinema and radio. In the 1920s, says Taylor, the primary threat to civilization appeared to be Bolshevism and the insidious invasion of American culture through Hollywood films; in the 1930s, the onslaught of Nazism presented the most immediate and the greater danger. Philip M. Taylor, "Propaganda in International Politics, 1919–1939," in *Film and Radio Propaganda in World War II*, ed. K. R. M. Short (London: Croom Helm, 1983), 27, 37.

67. Edwin Evans, untitled review, *The Dancing Times,* May 1940, 464.

68. Cyril W. Beaumont, " 'The Sleeping Beauty,' (Sadler's Wells Ballet)" in *Dancers Under My Lens*, (London: Beaumont, 1949), 50, 53.

69. David Vaughan, *Frederick Ashton and His Ballets*, 202–3.

70. Ibid., 203.

71. Barbara Newman, *Striking a Balance: Dancers Talk About Dancing* (London: Elm Tree Books, 1982), 140.

72. Audrey Williamson, "Classical Revival," *Ballet Renaissance* (London: Golden Galley Press, 1948), 132.

73. Inglesby, *Blitz*, 6.

74. Inglesby, *Blitz*, "Without his decision," 2; "It was a struggle," 6.

75. Ibid., 8.

76. From 1931–1939, de Valois employed Duncan Grant, Vanessa Bell, George Sheringham, Edward Burra, Rex Whistler, E. McKnight Kauffer, Sophie Federovich, Cecil Beaton, and André Derain. After the war, she also commissioned Graham Sutherland, John Piper, Leslie Hurry, and Michael Ayrton. See Clement Crisp, "Artists Design for Dance in the Twentieth Century" in *Artists Design for Dance, 1909–1984*, ed. Rupert Martin (Bristol: Arnolfini Gallery, 1984).

77. Doris Zinkeisen, whom Inglesby hired to design *Planetomania* (1941), *Giselle* (1942), "Aurora's Wedding" (1945) and *The Masque of Comus* (1946), was an artist who worked in the public sphere. For instance, she designed posters and graphics for the London Underground and frequently worked in musical comedy. Similarly, Hein Heckroth, whom Inglesby hired to design *Coppélia* (1944) and "Danses Espagnoles" (1944), came from the world of film design and designed for the Ballets Jooss.

78. Inglesby, *Blitz*, 9.

79. Unattributed review, "Lyric Theatre Season of Ballet Opened," *The Times*, June 29, 1943, 2.

80. "The Almost Legendary Miss Inglesby" in *Carnaval: The Magazine of Ballet and Ballet Personalities*, November–December 1946, 55.

81. Ibid, 54–55.

82. These cinemas with their low ticket prices were open to all social classes. The interiors were typically highly ornate and designed to provide a luxurious ambience. They sprang up in small towns across the country in the early 20th century when movies replaced the once-popular melodramas of an earlier age. See Simon Trussler, *The Cambridge Illustrated History of British Theatre* (Cambridge: Cambridge University Press, 2000).

83. International Ballet Announcement to Patrons, August, 1947, International Ballet Company file, Theatre Museum.

84. Untitled review, *Derby Evening Telegraph*, September 10, 1943, International Ballet Company file, Theatre Museum.

85. James Redfern, *The Spectator*, May 26, 1944, International Ballet Company file, Theatre Museum.

86. A. H. Franks, "The Inglesby Legend: A Short Factual Survey of the International Ballet," in *Ballet Decade*, ed. Arnold L. Haskell (New York: Macmillan, 1955), 182.

87. Mary Clarke, "International Ballet, 'The Sleeping Princess' at The Gaumont State Cinema, Kilburn," in *The Ballet Annual 1949: A Record and Year Book of the Ballet*, ed. Arnold Haskell (London: Adam and Charles Black, 1949), 23–24.

88. P. J. S Richardson, "Ten Years' Work, The Progress of 'International Ballet,'" *Dancing Times*, July 1951, 583–85.

89. Program in the International Ballet Company file in the Theatre Museum, "The Sleeping Princess Premier Presentation," Monday Evening 24th May, 1948, Gaumont State Kilburn, lists the following credits: The International Ballet with International Ballet Orchestra under conductor James Walker; Reproduction Nicolai Sergueeff; Choreography Marius Petipa; Décor and costumes Prince A. Chervachidze and Nandi Heckroth

90. David Denby, *Great Books: My Adventure with Homer, Rousseau, Woolf, and Other Indestructible Writers of the Western World* (New York: Simon and Schuster, 1996), 12.

91. Genné, 154.

92. Marcia B. Siegel, *Mirrors and Scrims: The Life and Afterlife of Ballet* (Middletown, CT: Wesleyan University Press, 2010), xi.

2

Reimagining *Le Boeuf sur le Toit*

Ann Dils

THE 1920 JEAN Cocteau/Darius Milhaud farce *Le Boeuf sur le Toit (Or the Nothing-Doing Bar)* was a performance event of its moment. In part a work of surrealist theatre in which clowns in giant papier-mâché heads moved in slow motion to peppy music, *Boeuf* was more convincingly an instance of "lifestyle" modernism.[1] The work celebrated jazz and popular culture from the United States, both in vogue in Paris at the time, while poking fun at character types and social concerns presented as American. Set in a bar during Prohibition, *Boeuf* depicted a group out for a night of drinking, dancing, and flirtation.[2] The characters suggest caricatures of well-known Americans such as boxer Jack Johnson and dancer Maude Allan and also represent a spectrum of American racial, ethnic, and gendered or sexual types.[3] Led by the three Fratellini Brothers, the cast were celebrity performers borrowed from the Circus Medrano. At its opening, a dress rehearsal to which Cocteau invited artists and well-off friends, he created a *succès de scandale* by overselling the house and delivering a pre-curtain speech about the seriousness of the performance. The evening also included an acrobatic dance act and modernist music that referenced jazz and social dance melodies.

Although *Boeuf* was ambivalently received after the first Paris performances, it has continued to intrigue performance historians and artists. In addition to research exploring the music and performance by scholars in the arts and popular culture, two collections of information about the work exist. *The Drama Review* included a "reconstruction" of *Boeuf* in their 1972 "puppet" issue, conjuring up the performance through the detailed scenario that Cocteau wrote for the work, as well as a collection of reviews, essays, and images from the 1920s. Daniella Thompson maintains a collection of materials and

43

opinion about *Boeuf* on a website, "The *Boeuf* Chronicles. How the Ox Got on the Roof: Darius Milhaud and the Brazilian Sources of *Le Boeuf sur le Toit.*"

Milhaud's energetic music remains popular, and is often performed and recorded. Available in orchestral and four-hand piano versions, the work weaves jazz and South American social dance music into motifs that conjure up the characters in the farce: a polka for the bookmaker and tangos for the women, for example. The music is a tribute to the two years that Milhaud spent in Brazil as part of a French diplomatic delegation. George Balanchine created a version of *Boeuf* as part of an evening of "Young Ballet" in Petrograd in 1923. Elizavets Anderson-Ivantzoff directed the work at the American Laboratory Theatre in New York in 1930 in conjunction with a production of Cocteau's *Antigone.*[4] More recent stagings of *Boeuf* include a 2004 production by the Chicago-based Mime Company, a version by the National Circus School in Montreal in February 2009, and my own setting of the work for female dancers at the University of North Carolina at Greensboro in 2009.[5]

My version generally followed Cocteau's 1920 scenario in which Prohibition-era Americans dupe a policeman into believing a bar is an ice cream parlor; it adhered to the entrances and dances designated on Milhaud's score. Beyond this, the work was largely re-imagined. Instead of over-sized heads, my dancers wore makeup, wigs, and muscle and fat suits. Instead of depicting specific characters and a variety of skin colors and ethnic backgrounds, this *Boeuf* delivered sexual and gender-based types, among them a woman-in-charge, a lecher, and a lout. Rather than slow-motion mime and acrobatics, my dancers moved through the scenario using silent-film-inspired mime and theatricalized social dances.

In my research and setting of the work, I continually asked a number of questions: What did the work look like in 1920, and how might audiences have understood what they saw? What will my audience, sitting in a theatre that is almost exclusively used for contemporary dance, make of *Boeuf*? How do college dance goers understand dance, and what do they know about modernist performance? How can I provide them with a rich experience that goes beyond the fun of seeing friends dressed up as a flapper, a pool-playing boy, and a gambler? Might I be able to "rehearse" the audience, however briefly, by imbedding information into the performance that prompts acts of historical imagination and critical reflection?

The research I report and reflect on in these paragraphs was shaped by these questions. In the section "*Boeuf* Reclaimed," I explore the work's performance history and reflect on how the work might have been seen by its first Parisian audiences. In "*Boeuf* Reconceived," I discuss my own work, and the contemporary concerns that influenced the 2009 version. The concluding section, "*Boeuf* Resituated," is an exploration of spectatorship for the work. These maneuvers—reclaim, reconceive, and resituate—suggest different attitudes toward performing the past: in order to better understand an historical event and its context, to provoke comparisons between past and present that inspire reflection about social change, and to provide an experience that transforms our sense of time and place.

BOEUF RECLAIMED

Boeuf provides a glimpse of the world in which Cocteau and his privileged circle lived. Born in 1889 into a conservative, wealthy family, Cocteau was a visual artist, poet, designer, scenarist, impresario, novelist, and filmmaker. Although seeking the respect and attention of modern artists, he also loved entertainments and the company of well-off friends. An evening out might consist of a silent film staring Mary Pickford or Charlie Chaplin, or a music hall performance that featured jazz music, a Chaplin short, and a skit involving rival California orange packers, along with chorus girls, singers, and comics. Attending a circus, Cocteau could see jugglers, animal acts, and clowns, as well as Barbette, the American female impersonator and aerialist. Another night, revelers might attend a Ballets Russes premiere or visit a cafe and Picasso's studio in Montparnasse. Parisian entertainment was informed by the speed and rhythms of America and by our new world cultural mix, and experienced alongside classical and modernist arts.

In *Boeuf*, Cocteau and designers Guy-Pierre Fauconnet and Raoul Dufy sample trends in high art without giving up popular culture. The use of false heads to make performers look like puppets had already been seen in Futurist and Cubist costume design. Giant forms such as a torpedo-like cigar and oversized bottles and glassware that dwarf the surrounding bodies were also reminiscent of Futurist and Cubist art and stage design. The nonsensical action—a gun is fired to cut the end off a boxer's cigar and the pool player falls down dead—has the sense of juxtaposition and non sequitur of dadism and surrealism. Admiring response to avant-garde ballets such as the Nijinsky/Stravinsky *Sacre du Printemps*, Cocteau engineered *Boeuf* performances to incite a clash of aesthetic opinion and inspire vocal audience response.

The unresolved eclecticism of *Boeuf* was typical of Cocteau's work in dance.[6] An admirer of Diaghilev and Nijinsky, Cocteau came to regard the Ballets Russes as a kind of family. He hoped to realize his own love of the everyday—variety shows, cinema, jazz music, and circus—in this vaunted context. Cocteau proposed a number of scenarios to Diaghilev that were never realized. *Parade* was the first of his works to be produced.[7] Created in 1917, when Cocteau was just twenty-eight years old, *Parade* had music by Erik Satie, costumes by Pablo Picasso, and movement by Léonide Massine. A theatricalized side show, *Parade* has turns for barkers or theatrical managers and performers including a Chinese juggler, a Little American Girl, and acrobats. The Little American Girl, with a blue blazer and an oversized bow in her hair, is reminiscent of silent screen heroines, especially Pauline of "Perils of Pauline." On stage she uses a typewriter, jumps aboard a train, and dances a kind of Charleston. Cocteau described her in later writing as "A girl more interested in her health than in her beauty."[8]

In the production stages, Cocteau remarked that *Parade* was "the greatest battle of the war," meaning the greatest artistic triumph of the war period. But he was disappointed with the performances: Picasso and Satie nixed the sound effects he'd written into the scenario, and he was snubbed in a program note. Cocteau severed his relationship with Diaghilev.[9]

Cocteau created *Boeuf* with an independent production team. He asked to use Milhaud's score, originally written with the idea that it would accompany a Chaplin film, and then wrote a long scenario detailing the characters and their actions.[10] Fauconnet designed the heads, costumes, and décor. Dufy finished these items after Fauconnet's sudden passing in 1920. Irritated that some members of the French press thought that *Parade* was a farce, Cocteau endeavored to create an actual farce for modern times. Unhappy with the importance placed on Picasso's Cubist costumes in *Parade*, he hoped to employ giant costumes and set pieces that worked expressively, overwhelming the performers rather than serving primarily as fantastic design (Figure 2.1).

Cocteau describes the movement as in slow motion and performed against the music by "the best mechanical puppets in the world."[11] Various dances are indicated on the musical score, and their sequence and length are clear: a triumphant dance for the jockey, a tango for the women, a waltz for the policeman, and a Salome dance for the red-haired woman. Samba, maxixe, and tango appear throughout. The scenario details the movements that surround these dances, including many non sequiturs. As the players flirt and fight, dance, drink, and gamble, the red-haired woman puts the tulle smoke rings that emanate from a giant cigar around her arm as bracelets. The bookmaker's oversized pearl

FIGURE 2.1 Raoul Dufy, *Le Boeuf sur Le Toit*. Lithograph. Used with the permission of Artists Rights Society.

stickpin is used to knock the boxer unconscious. The policeman is decapitated, but brought to life near the end of the evening by the barman.

As there is no mention of a choreographer, the original *Boeuf* performers may have made their own way through the scenario, moving in slow motion against the musical structure using their skills as mimes and acrobats. Milhaud described the movement as "like a slow motion film," while Cocteau saw the performers as "divers at the bottom of the sea."[12] Although Louis Laloy, writing in *Comoedia*, thought the movement "did not go beyond the ordinary buffoonery of the circus of music hall,"[13] the heads, combined with the slow movement, may have had an interesting element of stylization, elongating the bodies and movement into shapes against the fast, rhythmically complex music. The scenario calls for the red-haired woman to walk on her hands around the severed head, and then off stage. Seeing this in slow motion, with the added problem of balancing an enlarged head, must have been quite spectacular. When *Boeuf* was later performed in London, it did not survive the transition, perhaps because the newly auditioned British cast did not have the improvisational gifts of the Paris performers.[14] One reporter, reacting to its slow motion speed, reported that *Boeuf* looked as if it was "inspired by something considerably more potent than gin—probably Cannabis Indica."[15]

Boeuf was first shown in a small upstairs theatre at the Comédie des Champs Elysées, as the closing offering in an evening that included Tommy Footit and Jackly in an acrobatic dance to Georges Auric's foxtrot *Adieu, New York* and songs and orchestral music by Francois Poulenc and Erik Satie. A jazz band called American Cocktails played at intermission.[16] Cocteau situated his work as high art, but sophisticated audiences of the period could be boisterous and opinionated. Cocteau had been in the audience at the 1913 first performance of the *Rite of Spring*, presented in a larger theatre in the Comédie des Champs Elysées, and wrote extensively about the glorious brouhaha that accompanied the performance. Cocteau felt the audience had "played the part written for it" that night; through their differing reactions to Stravinsky's music and Nijinsky's ballet, the mix of conservative Parisian upper crust and liberal artists in attendance had goaded each other into a riot.[17] *Parade*, the 1917 Ballets Russes production with a script by Cocteau, also caused an impassioned audience reaction. With its appeals to popular culture and to modern art, *Boeuf* seems calculated to split audience reaction.

Three performances of *Boeuf* were scheduled, a closed dress rehearsal for an invited audience of artists and friends on February 21, 1920, followed by an open performance and a benefit for the war wounded on succeeding evenings. For dress rehearsal, Cocteau got a friend to send out three hundred "pneumatiques" (special delivery letters), each entitling the bearer to a private box. There was a crush at the door that had to be sorted out by Cocteau and the house manager. Michel Georges-Michel, writing in *Paris Midi*, reports that the audience included "Princess de Lucinge and the Marquise du Mun,... the clown Fleur de Jasmyn,... the younger Tolstoy, Picasso and Mme. Picasso... and Massine, the young choreographer, [who] turned toward Sergei Diaghilev from time to time to ask... questions."[18] Having settled the audience, Cocteau stood before them and gave a speech about the negative impact of scandal, directing the audience toward the serious-ness of his work: "a scandal is a lively thing, but it disturbs the artists, the orchestra, and prevents the few serious members of the audience from grasping the…nuances of a work."[19]

How was the challenge of reframing the popular as avant-garde taken up by the audi-ence? In a critique of the performance in *Matinee*, Jean Bastia reports that Cocteau con-vinced only his followers:

> There were three types of audience members:
> The Coctellists, fervent, transported, fanatic—the most numerous.
> The Rebellious—a minority.
> The Neutrals—a few.
> Some said: Astonishing! Full of genius!
> The others: Stupid!
> The Neutrals—…!
> What imagination! What sensibility!
> It seems to me that I have caught lethargic encephalitis and that I am awakening in another epoch.
> Mr. Conductor, is it soon that we will return to France?
> The Neutrals—…![20]

Bastia claims that *Boeuf* was disappointing: charming, but closer to circus or musical hall than the elevated art that Cocteau hoped to create. The audience laughed out loud at the clowns who were *Boeuf*'s first cast members, and may have whistled and catcalled the male performers portraying women, as they would have in circus or music hall settings. The remarks Bastia records may have been more than polite asides, and shouted aloud in response to the performance.

In his writing about *Boeuf*, Cocteau discusses creating archetypes based on American films, but he does not connect the work to any particular person. Surely an audience already familiar with Cocteau's drawn caricatures of Diaghilev and his circle, and with works such as *Parade*, would make obvious connections to well-known Americans. With these references in mind, *Boeuf* is a farce about an America that should embody modern progress but is too unsophisticated to get beyond its own racism and prudery.[21] Throughout the scenario and the staging are a series of reversals that leave the audience feeling nothing is certain and no progress has been made. The characters seem headed for heterosexual romance, but this becomes a tango for two women. The policeman, a period John the Baptist, is beheaded to please revelers in a bar; his sacrifice leaves him footing the drinkers' bar tab. This is the "nothing doing" of the title, the narrative that never really advances or amounts to much.

In the original program, the males are Le boxeur nègre, Nègre qui joue au billiard, Le barman, Le monsieur en habit, Le policeman, and Le jockey, elsewhere called a bookmaker. The women are named La dame décolletée and La dame rousse; the latter is described as a woman in male clothing. The African-American boxer must have been equated with Jack Johnson, one of the most photographed and written-about Americans of the Progressive era. Johnson was, from 1908 to 1915, the first African American heavyweight champion of the world and the first African American pop culture icon. Parisians would have seen the film of the 1910 Johnson–James Jeffries "Fight of the Century," and known about the race riots that occurred after Johnson's victory. In addition to his boxing victories, Johnson was a nightclub owner and womanizer, the perfect type to be found in an American bar.[22] In *Boeuf*, he is knocked unconscious by a stickpin and spends most of the performance passed out in a chair.

The Negre qui joue au billiard character has a number of referents. One possibility is Chocolat, of the clown team Footit and Chocolat. The Afro-Cuban performer was sometimes described as a dwarf.[23] Dressed as a dandy, but subject to the jokes of Footit, Chocolat was modeled on stereotypes based in minstrelsy, transplanted to France by the mid-1800s.[24] Parisians of the early 1920s would have seen the team as children and been familiar with Henri de Toulouse Lautrec's sketches of Chocolat, especially 1896 *Chocolat Dancing*, sometimes entitled *Chocolat Dancing in the Irish-American Bar* or the *Bar Darchille*.[25] The reference to a jockey also suggests five-foot-tall American jockey Jimmy Winkfield. Horseracing was dominated by African Americans through the early 1900s, and Winkfield was one of the most successful jockeys, winning the Kentucky Derby twice and then working as a jockey in Russia, Germany, and France. He spent the years between 1920 and 1930 in Paris.[26] The pool player is subject to a number of indignities in *Boeuf*, being hauled around by one of the women and shot in an attempt to cut the tip from a cigar.

Cocteau's "mannish woman," combined with the John the Baptist–like decapitation of the policeman, suggests Maud Allan, the most famous of the Salome dancers performing in variety theatres in the 1910s. A Canadian who grew up in California, Allan worked for years in Europe, creating her 1906 production, *Vision of Salome*, in the wake of Oscar Wilde's play. Allan was in the news in 1918 because she was embroiled in a court battle in the United Kingdom, accused of promoting (or in some accounts, having) "unnatural vices."[27] She is among the most active of the *Boeuf* characters, dancing with the boxer and the elegant woman, and walking around the severed head on her hands.

Although images of the barman don't look like Charlie Chaplin, his actions suggest the silent screen star. He instigates trouble—shooting a gun to cut the end off a cigar, for example—but shuffles through the action unscathed. The bookmaker, policeman, gentleman, and well-dressed woman may have read as caricatures to Cocteau's audience, but the references are less obvious. They may have been seen as period ethnic stereotypes. American bookmakers of the early twentieth century were often Italian or Eastern European Jews.[28] The policeman may have been a "dumb Irish cop." Though the gentleman and well-dressed woman rarely interact on stage, they suggest a French stereotype for upper-middle-class Americans: the man meek and ineffectual inside the home but ruthless in capitalist pursuits, the woman overbearing and manipulative. In working through the scenario with dancers, it became clear that the women initiate most of the interactions in *Boeuf*, through flirting, chastising male behavior, and goading one male into attacking another.[29]

For some audience members, Cocteau's representation of America may have been too benign. Louis Laloy, writing in the *Comoedia,* noted that he had expected "animal jaws." This might refer to the animal masks Fauconnet created for the play *Tales of Renard,* but it might also refer to giant-jawed caricatures of the American Yankee.[30] Among the images and descriptions of Americans written in the late 1800s and early 1900s is Jules Hurey's description of the Yankee in *Le Figaro*: a shrewd, uncouth capitalist with giant jaws that he exercises by chewing steak and chewing gum.[31] There was no Woodrow Wilson reference, an American president the French vilified for keeping the United States from entering World War I and discussed as puritanical and paranoid.[32] Wilson had just been in Paris in 1919, along with other Allied leaders, to negotiate the terms of the post–World War I peace.

Other audience members may have found the *Boeuf* characters quaint. In her work on Diaghilev, Lynn Garafola calls Cocteau's work "sanitized art," the "stuff of elite entertainment," and an "appropriat[ion]…of the avant-garde for essentially conservative ends."[33] She sees the *Boeuf* masks as appealing to elite culture. The Futurists used padding and false heads to emphasize form and color and make the body more machine-like,[34] but Cocteau's puppet-like figures had a nostalgic appeal. Garafola relates these huge-headed masks (and those in other Cocteau works) to "image d'Epinal," a tradition of French printmaking featuring idealized folkloric, political, or popular characters with enormous heads on tiny bodies. These would have had an innocent appeal for bourgeois French audiences.[35]

For some, circus conventions may have served as interpretive lenses. Clowns of the early twentieth century performed small plays, or *entrées*, that contained dialogue and physical comedy. The Fratellini brothers were especially known for these, performing such skits for up to forty-five minutes. *Boeuf* could have been seen as an entrée, and perhaps it was this tradition that Cocteau built from, and hoped to move the audience past, with Cubist/Futurist costume and stage design. The three best-known performers, François, Albert, and Paul Fratellini, were cast respectively as the elegant woman, the red-haired woman, and the barman, characters that continue to read as central to the performance. François, who usually performed as a whiteface clown, a character described as pompous and smart, may have lent the Elegant Woman these qualities through movement skill, but also by association. Albert was an *auguste* clown, a character type whose clumsiness, stupidity, and reactions to the abuse of whiteface clowns come from specialized physical skills. The red-haired woman reads as clever in Cocteau's scenario, but Albert's work as a clown may have set him in contrast to his elegant brother. With its handstands, the role of the red-haired woman is especially physical. The slow-motion Salomé dance may have picked up comic elements with Albert Fratellini's performance.

Paul served as a go-between for his brothers, and his clowning sat midway between their two styles. The barman serves this conciliatory function for all of the cast in *Boeuf*, as he wends his way through their encounters, serving drinks and engineering the change from bar to ice cream parlor.[36]

The heads for the boxer and the Negre qui joue au billiard seem very like minstrel show masks to the contemporary eye, and Cocteau's audience may have been reminded of that tradition, even as they understood the images as celebrity caricatures. In his article "Race as Spectacle in Late-Nineteenth-Century French Art and Popular Culture," James Smalls describes the changing ways in which images of people of African descent were used and understood. Looking at posters of Chocolat and Footit, Smalls describes the duo as playing on oppositions. Chocolat is a minstrel show dandy and bumbling fool, well dressed but slow and inarticulate, delivering his lines in a mixture of Cuban-accented English and French. Footit, his British partner, is quick and intelligent, abusing Chocolat verbally and physically, while dressed in the baggy polka dots and stripes of a clown. Chocolat's image, and those of others of African descent, were used to advertise bananas, chocolate, and shoe polish. Associations with this imagery were supported not only by minstrelsy but by France's own colonial history and by the "human zoos" that were popular at colonial and international exhibitions such as the 1889 Exposition Universelle in Paris.

Smalls believes that these images changed as the century wore on, and that artists such as Degas began to fashion representations that emphasized the activity or celebrity of people of African descent, rather than the tired stereotypes of minstrelsy. His example is Miss Lala, a late-nineteenth-century African American trapeze artist and human cannonball who was the subject of Degas's *Miss Lala at the Cirque Fernando, 1879*.[37] He sees the image as emphasizing Miss Lala's muscularity, skill, and speed, and as an erasure or transformation of her status as a woman of African descent. Like African Americans, people from French West Africa and the French Antilles, moved to Paris after World War I, drawn there by the myth of color-blind France. Smalls suggests that, for urban Parisians, images of people of African descent signaled modernity—progress, the nation, reason—but also anxieties about shifting post-war identities.

Some may have also seen shifts and ambiguities of gendered and sexual identities. The red-haired woman of Cocteau's cast, with her pearls and jacket, seems lady-like to contemporary eyes, but she is described as having a "mannish slouch." Though some scholars assume this character is a transvestite,[38] the existence of a severed head in the scenario points to Maude Allen and her Salome interpretations. The strength exhibited by this character might have been seen as an overturning of gender expectations, or seen as one more moment of humorous impossibility. The identity of the clown playing the character can't have been too far from any audience member's mind.

After *Boeuf*, Cocteau continued to seek a balance between popular culture and modern art in his dance works. Cocteau created *Les Mariées de la Tour Eiffel* for Ballets Suédois in 1921. In that work, a wedding party posed for photos on the platform of the Eiffel

Tower. The dancers were doll-like, highly made up and padded. Cocteau created "phono-graphic pavilions" through which commands could be issued throughout the performance. When a voice said "watch the birdie," an interloper popped out of a hunch-backed pho-tographer's giant camera. The uninvited guests included an ostrich, a lion, hunter, fat boy (the newlywed's future son), and bathing beauty, as well as human telegrams.[39]

By 1924, Cocteau worked again for Diaghilev, their relationship mended in part by young composers such as Georges Auric who were friends with both men. *Le Train Bleu*, a dance about the smart set cavorting at the Riviera, had a scenario by Cocteau, score by Milhaud, choreography by Bronislava Nijinska, costumes by Coco Chanel, sets by Roma-nian sculptor Henri Laurens, and a curtain by Picasso. The ballet is a tribute to fashion and pop culture in the 1920s. Set at the seaside, two couples, a golfer and tennis player, and the swimmers Beau Gosse and Perlouse flirt and fight. There is a series of jealous mis-understandings involving cabanas. The gigolos and flappers of the corps are in swimming attire. They don dark glasses to look up at an imaginary airplane, pose for snapshots, walk like Charlie Chaplin, and do stylized Charleston steps. Milhaud's score was inspired by music-hall tunes.

BOEUF RECONCEIVED

The 2009 *Boeuf* is a farce in which two women fascinate and manipulate a group of bumbling men. The characters are done up with makeup, wigs, and padding to suggest a spectrum of ages and classes; all appear to be Euro-American and all are performed by Euro-American women dancers. The boy (once called the pool player) is young, inno-cent, and impressionable. The ineffectual, drunken gentleman is elegantly dressed in a frock coat. The bookmaker schemes and picks fights with the preening boxer. The barman, dressed in a pink tuxedo and with a pink toupee, is stooped and shuffling. The women are flashily dressed and made up: the elegant woman is in a red flapper dress and heels, and the red-haired woman is in black velvet pencil pants, bra, and jacket. The policeman is the only character with a giant, papier-mâché head (Figure 2.2).

The performers move in time to the music, carrying out their actions in silent-movie-inspired mime and movement adapted from social dancing. The two women dance a tango similar to those taught at tango teas from about 1913. Other characters cakewalk and bunnyhug, Charleston, and apache.[40] When not the central focus of the action, the dancers organize their movement by moving only on a one or five count and then main-taining stillness. These are big gestures, the emotional gestures of silent films or everyday movement such as playing dice, slugging back a drink, or holding a cigarette, exaggerated in shape and timing. While this visually and rhythmically organizes the action, it is not the slow motion of Cocteau's version.

In rehearsals, we found Cocteau's scenario difficult to translate into action. In a typical passage, Cocteau describes: "The smart lady powders herself, notices the negro boy. He

FIGURE 2.2 Kelly Ozust as Elegant Woman, Amanda Diorio as the Policeman, Loren Groenendaal as the Gentleman, Sarah Wildes Arnett as the Bookmaker, and Melissa Pihos as the Red-haired Woman. Image by Justin Tornow. Used with permission.

climbs onto a stool, she takes him on her shoulders and carries him into the billiard room. The red-headed lady crosses the stage, collects the smoke-rings with her arm, empties them around the neck of the barman, and entices the boxer. The boxer gets up from his arm chair to follow her."[41]

In the small performance space indicated by the period images, crowded with a bar, stools, armchair, chaise lounge, and eight performers, this might have been accomplished in slow motion if the performers covered very little ground. In our space, even overlapping the action, we exceeded the time allotted by the music if we moved in slow motion. Too, some of the movement seems physically impossible, or at least to require sophisticated circus skills. Slinging another performer across your shoulders and marching off with her is easy enough. Doing it in slow motion is more difficult. While we decided not to use the puppet heads early on, we tried to imagine how this, and other actions, might have been engineered with a large, heavy head. Coming to terms with *Boeuf's* movement would provide a fascinating intersection of clowning, acrobatics, and social and theatrical movement. Intriguing as this was, I was not willing to close in the stage space or risk injuring dancers to accomplish this research.

What audiences saw in 2009 resulted from decisions made over a two-year period. The UNCG version of *Boeuf* was first produced by a cooperative group of theatre, music, visual art, and dance faculty for a 2007 conference in the School of Music. We had all read about *Boeuf* before making decisions about the work, but I had not done the research and thinking that led me to see *Boeuf* as a farce about a naïve, multicultural America. Looking at black-and-white images of Fauconnet/Dufy masks in journals, the renderings of the Negre qui joue au billiard player seemed to refer only to minstrel show stereotypes. We decided to do away with them.

Taking away references to African Americans in *Boeuf* was the best decision we could make at the time. The work was to be performed as the closer to a celebratory concert for an audience of scholars, musicians, and music educators from around the United States. Although I would give a lecture earlier in the day, there was no immediate way to contextualize those images. Surely most of the audience would have the same reaction that we did. As a group of white faculty members in an institution trying to increase diversity on campus, and a group of concerned citizens mindful of Greensboro history, we shied away from offending anyone in the audience.[42]

The women are the center of this world. The tallest members of the cast, except for the policeman with the giant head, the women are made taller with high heels. They are the instigators of much of the action. They spurn the boxer and the bookmaker in turn, and the men spend much of the piece competing for the women's attention. The boy manages to snag a drink at the bar and the elegant woman throws him over her shoulder, marches across stage, and sets him down for a lecture. The women dance a tango together while the rest of the cast ogles them. When the cast discovers they have no money, it is the women who organize the subterfuge that allows them to skip out on the bill (Figure 2.3).

As a farce, *Boeuf* works because of the humorous situations that Cocteau envisioned and because of the characterizations the performers build. The crafty, competitive bookmaker is at times quick and emphatic, pointing accusingly at the boxer or offering an insincere handshake, and at times evasive, quickly changing direction and level to sneak up on the boxer as he dances with the red-haired woman. When performed in a theatre usually reserved for serious dance, the work has a carnivalesque appeal, as accepted values are overturned. There is a great deal of fondling and ogling in *Boeuf*, some of it suggested by the scenario and some invented during the reconstruction process. The beheaded policeman, stumbling around with his arms outstretched, gropes the red-haired woman. To distract the barman, the elegant woman invites him to ogle her breasts and bottom, and provocatively runs a flower down his body until his legs shake. The boxer tries to kiss the red-haired woman and ends up on the receiving end of a violent apache.

Boeuf is performed by a group of women who are usually seen as technically virtuosic dancers, many of whom are technique teachers in our programs. To have these women give up release technique, sleek bodies, and unisex clothing for shuffling around in a pink toupee with a bulging stomach or dancing the tango in a flapper dress and too much makeup is also a source of laughter. Dance students probably laughed in response to their own anxieties about appearing foolish on stage. The performers, on the other hand, were happy to be released from perfection and enjoyed pushing their own outrageousness.[43] The 2009 *Boeuf* is a hedonistic debauch in the church of contemporary dance. Paired with ghostings of the 1920 version, it is also an opening to more serious reflection (Figure 2.4).

FIGURE 2.3 Kelly Ozust as Elegant Woman and Melissa Pihos as the Red-haired Woman. Image by Justin Tornow. Used with permission.

BOEUF RESITUATED

The Greensboro *Boeuf* was included in Paris Dancing in the 1920s, an evening that was part music hall performance and part history lesson.[44] I hoped to inspire active spectatorship in the audience that accomplished curricular and critical work, and set up the evening to encourage the audience to think about the historical *Boeuf* and its social setting, as well as the performance work before them. I opened the concert by describing how an audience might have behaved in the 1920s, and I worked with audience members on contemporary expressions of pleasure and displeasure: appreciative catcalls, cheers, laughter, whistles, and clapping and negative hissing and booing. Next was a series of projections that introduced Cocteau's *Boeuf*, including information about the production's history and the 1920s caricatures and their real-life sources. *Boeuf* led into a rhythmic play on popular music of the twenties featuring a singer, piano player, and several tap dancers. Both of these works drew a great deal of audience participation. The rest of the evening included excerpts from a Charlie Chaplin film, as well as a new version of the 1924 Cocteau/Milhaud/Nijinska *Le Train Bleu*, preceded by contextualizing projections. The audience also had programs that included historical information. By imbedding particular

FIGURE 2.4   Tricia Zweier as the Bartender. Image by Justin Tornow. Used with permission.

types of information and images into the evening, I hoped to influence what the audience thought about and did, providing a spectatorial rehearsal, however brief, that allowed the audience to catcall, cheer, and boo, but also encouraged them to speculate, imagine, and interconnect.

What would my audience bring with them to the theatre that would help them think about *Boeuf*? Greensboro has rich artistic offerings, but I do not think the theatrical counterpart to Milhaud's well-known score is general knowledge. All of my dance history students know something about Ballets Russes and Ballets Suédois, but only the current students have discussed *Boeuf*. Despite our dance history offerings, there is still a tendency to think of danced modernism as modern dance, as exemplified by the American moderns of the 1930s to 1950s. Audience members might know about early-twentieth-century modernist painting, literature, theatre, or film and recognize surrealism or dada, but the current costumes and set do not carry those associations. Some might know about early-twentieth-century popular culture and the vogue for American jazz in French music, dance, circus, and music hall. Stock characters performing overblown gestures to get laughs would be familiar, although not necessarily in a dance context. For contemporary audiences, farce is usually experienced in television sitcoms and romantic comedy feature-length films. Although Paris Dancing was well publicized and I did a number of pre-performance presentations in classrooms, most would expect contemporary dance, as that's the usual fare in our theatre.

In creating Paris Dancing, I hoped to take advantage of ways of seeing and creating meaning familiar to dance audiences. Understanding is shaped even before an audience member attends a performance, cued by advertising and reviews, and in the case of a university population, by direct and inferred relationships between the performance and the curriculum.[45] Here, audience members deliberate the various codes and conventions that cue their own response: Is the work contemporary or traditional? Should I expect a narrative, spectacle, or social critique? This process uncovers what Roland Barthes has referred to as *déjà lu*, the already read, the cultural understandings that cue the interpretation of any text, and that readers can use to understand and deconstruct their own habits of thought.[46] I hoped that audience members would quickly apply the information I supplied to begin asking questions about the dance they were seeing, as well as to question their own expectations.

My own dance history students, and I think contemporary dance goers in general, are adept at seeing performances that provoke questions about the nature of history and that ask audience members to use what they already know to understand the performance at hand. Dance works studied throughout our curriculum include 1990 *Last Supper at Uncle Tom's Cabin/The Promised Land*, in which Bill T. Jones incorporates references to Stowe's *Uncle Tom's Cabin* and to the theatrical traditions based on that work as well as to da Vinci's *Last Supper*. Matthew Bourne's 1995 restaging of *Swan Lake,* in which the swans are dangerous, seductive males, and the prince's royal parentage is a decadent and unhappy single mother, is also a favorite.[47]

As with these works, I wanted the audience to consider several things simultaneously. I hoped that they would conjure up an historical *Boeuf,* only partially present through images and text, as well as that work's context and meanings. I also hoped they would see the current performance and realize the choices that had been made, especially about the now-absent caricatures, and that much of the historical context that gave the work meaning had simply slipped away and was no longer common knowledge.

Further, I hoped to promote "double vision." In her essay "*Ghostcatching*: An Intersection of Technology, Labor, and Race," Danielle Goldman reminds readers that performance questioning occurs not just as "either-or" questions but as "both-and" considerations. She reports a public interview in which Bill T. Jones asks a student audience to be mindful of the formal aspects of choreography *and* the politics of gazing at another person: "When you look at my stage now, can you look with two sets of eyes? Do you see the sexual preference of the person, the race of the person, the gender of the person, and then, can you see what they're doing? And how the two come together to create a vision that is, that makes you want to look more carefully, want to dance, to want to touch one another?"[48]

Goldman underscores that "the most radical aspect of Jones's call, and perhaps the easiest to miss, is that he genuinely seeks a doubling, a vision whose sum is larger than its parts"...a "both/and type of vision."[49] Jones describes a double realization of identity and the performer's ability to thwart any easy association with a fixed identity.

Living bodies also move through texts and images from the past, reminding viewers of accepted historical narratives even as they shift the actors and outcomes of that history. He doesn't use the term directly, but performance theorist Baz Kershaw concludes his 2002 reception study, "Performance, Memory, Heritage, History, Spectacle—*The Iron Ship*" by discussing types of "double vision" that might occur as audiences consider performances with historical content. Kershaw notes that questions beginning in audience members' minds, often questions related to their own professional interests, provide "a rich stimulant for varied uses of memory work" in which they "construct a 'dialogue' between current identity and different *types* of history-making, and therefore [different] versions of 'history.'" Further, Kershaw speculates that "though this is more debatable,...somatic spectacle may be a powerful medium for setting this process of deconstructing the past-as-received in motion."[50] In other words, looking at a contemporary performance of history can help audience members enter into their own acts of history making, and to realize the contingent nature of any history. Like the moving body, meaning slips around and changes as performances enter new eras and contexts.

I did not systematically study how the audience understood *Boeuf*, but I noticed some recurring concerns that suggest audience members were speculating about the images in the historical and current *Boeuf*s. Many students asked about the African American boxer and pool player and what Parisians would have made of them. Were they minstrel show stereotypes? An equal number of students felt cheated by not seeing those figures, as my version erased historical figures and with them important social history. The Jack Johnson caricature is most obvious. With this figure gone, there is no reason to speculate about who the bookmaker or the policeman might represent.

Comments and questions about the woman characters tended to have generational differences. Older audience members saw the women as impossible amazons and laughed as the elegant woman slung the boy over her shoulder or the red-haired woman hauled the boxer around by his lapels. The women's costuming and makeup, their sexual manipulations, and the ogling troubled middle-aged people, who saw these as reinforcing sexist stereotypes. College-age students often remarked that they saw the interactions as typical bar behavior, or wondered if they could still see the cross-dressed clowns within the current portrayals of the elegant and red-haired women.

Although no one mentioned an experience of "double vision" in the performance, I know the possibility is there. The Euro-American boxer in my version of *Boeuf* is ineffectual, a braggart with a glass jaw. This is especially evident when the bookmaker knocks him out by hitting him over the head with a stickpin in a fit of jealousy over the boxer's dance with the red-haired woman. This is a moment of Dadist impossibility, but it can also be read as a reference to Jack Johnson's life, the champ running afoul of the law because of women, drink, and gambling. Like the policeman, he comes back to life at the end of the work, brushing himself off and moving on to the next thing, as Johnson did in his life and continues to do as a boxing and popular culture icon.

The 2009 *Boeuf* cast is female, and there are some steamy moments when the women dance together and flirtations that develop between women being women and women being men. I am tempted to see this as women celebrating and making fun of their own abilities to manipulate potential sexual partners. Thinking about this work as performed by an all-male cast in the 1920 reverses the message: women are funny when they're powerful, and men are funny when they allow themselves to be manipulated by women. It is still possible to see this in the 2009 production. Humor must have also been produced in *Boeuf* through associations that combined gender and race, or gender, race, and class. Although no longer a humorous image, the playing out of the French stereotype of the American capitalist who is brow-beaten at home is an example.

There is a moment in *Boeuf* when the various images of the red-haired woman, the more demure character of Cocteau's time, and the 2009 showgirl slide together in an especially powerful way. In my version, the dancer performs a number of handstands around the policeman's severed head. The performer always allows herself to linger in a vertical, inverted pose, allowing us to wonder how she will return her feet to the ground. This moment of suspension provokes consideration of the many identities she is suspended among: a skilled performer in an assertive female role; a current incarnation of a cross-dressed male clown; and a stand-in for Maude Allan, whose own daring was met with morals charges. Much that defines the historical red-haired woman seems tame today; her contemporary performance suggests that she can choose to maintain her historical identity or slip the past and forge new images and associations.

In the introduction, I mentioned three ways of working with the past that are all present in my *Boeuf* research: reclaim, reconceive, and resituate. Performative and academic research undertaken for the reconstruction led to rethinking audience reception for the original work, and to potential connections to clowning practices and to French understandings of American culture. Reconnecting the *Boeuf* characters with real-life Americans of the early twentieth century seems an important discovery. This doesn't do much to dignify Cocteau's artistry, but it does allow a reading of the work as a French commentary on American celebrity and social failings. I have reclaimed some of the *Boeuf* scenario as action, and through this realized the reversals and lack of narrative progress that gave the work its name. The modernist aspects of the work, especially the puppet figures and the slow motion movement that might relate the work to surrealist or futurist performance, remain a mystery, as do the techniques that made some of the action possible. The dance as the cast and I reconceived it, and the larger evening of performance and film that set it in relationship with the past, provided a fun evening that transformed performers, spectators, and our performance space. It was wonderful to rearrange the rules an audience adheres to and to hear laughter from usually silent spectators. I also find it inspiring, however hopeful on my part, to think about audience members' individual flights of historical imagination and the webs of memory they used to understand the performance, the 2009 *Boeuf* joined by visions of the historical *Boeuf* and by the questions this imagining generated.

NOTES

1. Lynn Garafola coined the term "lifestyle modernism" in her *Diaghilev's Ballets Russes* (New York: Oxford University Press, 1989), 98. It refers to work in which the artist examines the

conditions and materials of modern life: urban isolation, speed, consumerism, fashion, film, the Parisian revue, celebrity, and the like.

2. *Boeuf*'s Prohibition setting is curious. Although Americans had been moving toward Prohibition with state and interstate commerce restrictions during the 1910s, the Volstead Act had been in force for only a month when *Boeuf* was first staged. It's also interesting that Prohibition was seen as American. Religious groups worked to ban alcohol in Australia, New Zealand, and Canada in the 1910s and several countries banned alcohol, prohibited access to strong spirits, or controlled where alcohol could be consumed, including Russia and Norway. Perhaps Cocteau was thinking about the high-living American ex-pats he knew in Paris in making this joke.

3. There is no direct evidence that Cocteau intended the characters to be read as caricatures or that the audience saw them in that way. Parallels to famous Americans of the early 1920s seem obvious, however. Cocteau's drawn caricatures and references to real people in *Parade* and *Le Train Bleu* also suggest this possibility.

4. See Frank W. D. Ries, *The Dance Theatre of Jean Cocteau* (Ann Arbor: UMI Research Press, 1986), 69. On her website, Danielle Thompson discusses several projects taking the name *Le Boeuf sur le Toit*, including a Paris bar and restaurant that opened in 1923 as well as a novel, *Au Temps de Boeuf sur le Toit*, by Maurice Sachs in 1939. The 1960s-era literary/arts review *Nothing Doing* in London took its name from the subtitle.

5. An early reader of this paper suggested that other choreographers have used Milhaud's *Boeuf*. I can find no evidence of this. For other productions, see "T. Daniel Productions," accessed October 1, 2011, http://www.tdanielcreations.com/leboeuf.html, and "On Stage with Orchestre de Chambre i Musici," accessed October 1, 2011, http://www.nationalcircusschool.ca/en/actualite/stage-with-orchestre-de-chambre-i-musici.

6. Sources that establish Cocteau's history in relationship to ballet include Garafola, *Diaghilev's Ballets Russes*, 98–143; Ries, *The Dance Theatre of Jean Cocteau*, 31–104; and Francis Steegmuller, *Cocteau: A Biography* (Boston: Little, Brown, 1970), 160–97; 238–45; 265–68; and 330–31. I have relied on repeated information from these sources throughout this paper.

7. In 1914, excited by the Ballets Russes production of *Petrushka* with its fairgrounds scene, Cocteau thought of doing a production entitled *David*. He envisioned it as featuring a clown enticing people to enter a show (a show that bore the title "David") through a megaphone, while an acrobat attracted attention. He consulted his friend Paul Thévenaz, a Swiss painter and the founder of the Paris School of Dalcroze Eurythmics, about the movement for this production, and he asked Stravinsky to create a score. This production, never realized, contains the seeds for *Parade* (1917).

8. Steegmuller, *Cocteau: A Biography*, 166. Steegmuller adds this footnote, quoting Paul Morand: "Perhaps Cocteau was with Paul Morand and Misia Sert the evening of December 27, 1916 when they saw, at the Alhambra music hall in Paris, a number consisting of a 'contest between the champion California lady orange-packer and the champion orange-crate maker, staged by an impresario with a megaphone.' 'It's the beginning of the invasion of the American style,' said Misia. 'Think of what's to come!' "

9. *Parade* was performed again in December 1920 with more satisfactory results. Cocteau's sound effects were added and public response was more positive. See Steegmuller, *Cocteau: A Biography*, 261–62.

10. In Daniella Thompson, "The *Boeuf* Chronicles: Scenario of Jean Cocteau's *The Nothing-Doing Bar*," accessed October 1, 2011, http://daniellathompson.com/Texts/Le_Boeuf/Nothing-Doing1.htm.

11. In Ries, *The Dance Theatre of Jean Cocteau*, 62.

12. Darius Milhaud and Jean Cocteau in *The Drama Review: TDR*. The "Puppet" Issue 16, (3) September: 29 and 31.

13. Louis Laloy, *Drama Review*, 40.

14. *Boeuf* ran in London for two weeks at the Coliseum as part of a vaudeville bill, along with acts such as Japanese acrobats, a Persian pianist, American monologist Ruth Draper, and a Swiss clown. Cocteau found *Boeuf* perfectly placed; the English press found it hard to grasp. Also, *Boeuf* was extracted from its reinforcing context from other references to America and to popular culture. With these changes, *Boeuf* must have edged closer to bad slapstick and further from charming farce.

15. *Sackbut*, August 1920, 58 in Ries, *The Dance Theatre of Jean Cocteau*, 68.

16. In Thompson, http://daniellathompson.com/Texts/Le_Boeuf/Au_Temps_du_Boeuf2.htm.

17. Jean Cocteau, *Oeuvres Complètes*, 11 vols., Geneva, IX: 43–49, in Modris Eksteins, "*Rites of Spring": The Great War and the Birth of the Modern Age* (New York: Houghton Mifflin, 1989), 11.

18. Michel Georges-Michel in *The Drama Review*, 1972, 37.

19. Jean Cocteau, *A Call to Order*, translated by Rollo Meyers (London: Faber and Gwyer, 1926), 226. Quoted in Ries, *The Dance Theatre of Jean Cocteau*, 66.

20. Jean Bastia in *The Drama Review*, 1972, 41–42.

21. Philippe Roger, *The American Enemy: A History of French Anti-Americanism*, translated by Sharon Bowman (Chicago: University of Chicago Press, 2006), 211–12.

22. Gerald Early, "Rebel of the Progressive Era," website for Ken Burns' PBS documentary *Unforgiveable Blackness*, http://www.pbs.org/unforgivableblackness/rebel/June 1, 2008. In the mid-1930s, Cocteau briefly managed a boxer named Panama Al Brown and considered creating a kind of *Le Boeuf* spectacle that included him. (Steegmuller, *Cocteau: A Biography*, 433).

23. I don't know if Cocteau thought of the United States when he thought of America or of the Americas in general. The use of music with Brazilian folk rhythms to create a farce about an American bar suggests a general notion of America as the Americas. It's possible that after the period of the Spanish-American War (1898–1901), when the United States was involved with Cuba militarily and commercially, Cuba was generally thought of as part of the United States.

24. Smalls, 363–69.

25. Steegmuller, 8.

26. Jimmy Winkfield's history was found in Schmidt. Steegmuller (7) says Cocteau was born and spent summers in Maison-Lafitte, a center for French horseracing, and he must have encountered jockeys there. Although Le jockey is listed in the original program, Dufy presents this character as a bookmaker, perhaps to include yet another ethnic stereotype.

27. Lacy McDearmon, "Maud Allan: The Public Record." *Dance Chronicle*. 2(2): 98; Felix Cherniavsky, "Maud Allan, Part V: The Years of Decline, 1915–1956." *Dance Chronicle*. 9(2): 177–236, 215–16.

28. In the *Boeuf* score, the bookmaker dances to a polka.

29. 1920 is also the date when, with the passage of the Nineteenth Amendment to the Constitution, women's suffrage was finally secure in the United States. French women waited until 1944 to vote.

30. In *The Drama Review*, 1972, 43, and in Ries, 65.

31. Roger, *The American Enemy*, 194–95.

32. Ibid., 266.

33. Garafola, 100.

34. Garafola, 77–82. Also see Gunter Berghaus, ed. *International Futurism in Arts and Literature* (New York: Walter de Gruyter, 2000).

35. Garafola, 105–06.

36. Schechter's review of Tristan Rémy's *Clown Scenes* was especially helpful in making these connections.

37. James Smalls, "'Race' As Spectacle in Late-Nineteenth-Century French Art and Popular Culture." *French Historical Studies.* 26 (2), Spring: 351–82, 369–81.

38. Daniel Albright, *Untwisting the Serpent: Modernism in Music, Literature, and the Other Arts* (Chicago: University of Chicago Press, 2000), 277.

39. Ballets Suédois was begun in 1920 by Rolf de Maré, a Swedish art collector. Other Ballets Suédois works include *Skating Rink* (1922), in which a group of factory workers, prostitutes, and dandies skate together in a work reminiscent of Charlie Chaplin's *Rink* (1916); and *Within the Quota* (1923), a work about a Swedish immigrant in New York with music by Cole Porter. A costly enterprise reliant on de Maré's resources and those of his friends, the group lasted through 1925.

40. In creating movement for our version of *Boeuf*, I was influenced by reconstructions of two works with Cocteau scenarios, *Parade* and *Le Train Bleu*, and by Chaplin films. DVDs and videotapes consulted include *Picasso and Dance.* 2005. DVD. Paris Opera Ballet. Kultur; Carol Teten. 2001. *How to Dance Through Time* vol. II. Dances of the Ragtime Era 1910–1920. Dancetime Productions; *Modern Times* [videorecording], written and directed by Charlie Chaplin; *A King in New York*; *A Woman of Paris* [videorecording], written and directed by Charles Chaplin. The cast and I also looked at clips available on YouTube, especially cakewalk, Salome, and Apache dancing.

41. Thompson, http://daniellathompson.com/Texts/Le_Boeuf/Nothing-Doing1.htm.

42. This change may have been especially important at the University of North Carolina at Greensboro. UNCG was, traditionally, the all-white Women's College of North Carolina. Across town are two historically black schools, Bennett College for Women, and North Carolina Agricultural and Technical State University (NCA&T). Greensboro was the site of two major events related to the Civil Rights Movement. During the 1960 Greensboro sit-ins, NCA&T students, joined later by Women's College and Bennett students, occupied the local, segregated Woolworth lunch counter. In 1979, five labor leaders were killed at an anti-Klan rally, gunned down by Ku Klux Klan and American Nazi Party members in an event that has come to be known as the Greensboro Massacre. No one was ever convicted of these crimes. The Greensboro Truth and Reconciliation Commission, a body assigned to clarify the events of 1979 as well as facilitate community healing, had just concluded its work in 2006. The UNCG campus participated in the Truth and Reconciliation process by staging plays and dances based on the events. The International Civil Rights Center and Museum opened at the site of the old Woolworth Building in downtown Greensboro in 2010. In this environment, gender play and sexual ambiguity are less charged possibilities.

43. People who came to dress rehearsal and saw the performance without a program told me that they did not recognize the dancers at all. One mother remarked that seeing her daughter shuffling across the stage in the hunched posture of old age brought her mother in law to mind.

44. I am grateful to Linda Caldwell and others who attended my World Dance Alliance delivery of a short version of paper, who conceptualized *Boeuf*, with its "prepared" audience, as a kind of site-specific performance.

45. I visited dance appreciation and history classes to introduce the evening.

46. Michael Moriarty, *Roland Barthes* (Stanford: Stanford University Press, 1991), 132.

47. Other examples include Mark Morris's *The Hard Nut* (1991), a reworking of *The Nutcracker* with references to 1960s popular culture; Mark Dendy's *Dream Analysis* (1998), in which he evokes both Vaslav Nijinsky and Martha Graham; and Doug Elkins's *Frauline Maria* (2007), in which he refers to characters and employs parts of the score for the *Sound of Music*, and also makes use of Graham technique, breakdancing, and release technique.

48. Bill T. Jones, interview by Michelle Dent and M. J. Thompson, New York University, March 20, 2002. Quoted in Danielle Goldman, "*Ghostcatching*: An Intersection of Technology, Labor, and Race," *Dance Research Journal* 35/2, 36/1: 71.

49. Goldman, "*Ghostcatching*," 71.

50. Baz Kershaw, "Performance, Memory, Heritage, History, Spectacle—The Iron Ship." *Studies in Theatre and Performance* 21(3): 141–42.

3

Reframing the Recent Past

ISSUES OF RECONSTRUCTION IN ISRAELI

CONTEMPORARY DANCE

Deborah Friedes Galili

ON MARCH 18, 2009, an excited audience packed the main theater in the Suzanne Dellal Centre, Tel Aviv's premiere dance venue, for the opening night of the Shades of Dance festival. First held in 1984 and subsequently instituted as a biennial event, Shades of Dance has offered a vital platform for young, novice choreographers presenting new works; operating on a competition format, it often crowned the rising stars of Israel's contemporary dance scene.[1] Yet the works about to be performed this evening were not premieres by unknown artists. Instead, to pay tribute to the America-Israel Cultural Foundation's seventy-year history and its continued support of Shades of Dance, four previous recipients of the competition's first prize were returning to the stage in a program called "Then and Now." The playbill announced that Liat Dror and Nir Ben Gal, Noa Wertheim and Adi Sha'al, Ronit Ziv, and Barak Marshall would offer excerpts of their original award-winning works alongside sections of their latest creations.[2] This rare line-up of leading choreographers and popular, groundbreaking works on a single bill—and the promise of appearances by Dror, Ben Gal, Wertheim, and Sha'al, none of whom had performed in recent seasons—were ample reasons for the audience to greet "Then and Now" first with great anticipation and then with wildly enthusiastic applause. But within the framework of Israeli concert dance, this celebratory program was even more excep-tional for its presentation of older works that had not been performed in many years.

Although the roots of Israeli contemporary dance can be traced back to the 1980s, with a growing push to develop new choreographic voices through initiatives such as

Shades of Dance, the works premiered during the 1980s and 1990s have not, by and large, appeared on stage in the 2000s. Nor have dances by choreographers who worked in earlier periods, like artists who pioneered concert dance forms in the 1920s and 1930s, German expressionist-influenced choreographers who shaped the field in the 1930s to 1950s, or those who worked with Batsheva Dance Company, Bat-Dor Dance Company, and their own groups in the 1960s to 1980s. And even though the sphere of Israeli modern dance during the latter half of the twentieth century encompassed works by foreign choreographers ranging from Martha Graham and Kurt Jooss to Paul Taylor and Mark Morris, stagings of dances by these and other non-Israeli artists are now noticeably absent within the repertory of Israeli companies.

In contrast, American stages have recently been dotted with full-scale reconstructions of historically significant dances by choreographers who worked centuries ago and by ones who are still active.[3] Why is the landscape of reconstructions in Israel so different from that in the United States? This article posits that the nature of reconstructive practices—a term encompassing a wide range of approaches to staging earlier works—is dependent upon the particular unfolding of concert dance's development and the current terrain of concert dance in a given country.[4] After contextualizing the state of reconstruction in Israeli modern and contemporary dance by surveying the art form's history and its institutional infrastructure, this study examines how Israeli choreographers in the still-young field of contemporary dance are starting to creatively re-present their earlier works using innovative approaches that add a different dimension to the reconstructive methods practiced, observed, and outlined by Americans, and in many cases their European counterparts. Because the existing literature on reconstruction of modern and contemporary dance focuses overwhelmingly on the American and European arenas, this article opens a new dialogue about activity outside these realms while simultaneously elucidating an alternative model for how works from more recent artistic movements, regardless of their origin, might be revisited onstage in this postmodern age.

CULTURE OF RECONSTRUCTION

In an article published in a 1994 issue of *Dance Theatre Journal*, Roger Copeland opens by listing what he calls "Words imbued with the spirit of the Zeitgeist: 'reconstructing', 'reviving', 'reworking', 'remounting', 'restaging', 'restoring', 'recreating'." Arguing that revivals have been among the most noteworthy dance events in the United States over the previous seasons, he then wonders, "what accounts for the high level of interest in [revival and reconstruction] (as well as in documentation and preservation) at this particular moment of our cultural history?" With this question—and with his attempts to answer it—Copeland draws a direct relationship between the presence of reconstructions and the specific conditions of a country's dance scene. The possible causes he suggests for the prevalence of revivals are, indeed, very tightly bound to the particular cultural history of concert dance in America: the aging and passing of the pioneering generation of choreographers, the devastating effect of AIDS on a younger generation of creators, and the view that the dance boom of the 1960s and 1970s was followed by a "bust" with poorer-quality dance.[5]

Historical factors such as those delineated by Copeland are part of a larger set of variables—including institutional structures and artistic and scholarly discourses—which, taken together, foster a *culture of reconstruction* comprising attitudes and approaches towards reconstructive practices. Each culture of reconstruction encompasses a set of stances regarding the value and purpose of reconstruction, the volume and frequency of reconstructions, the context in which reconstructions are staged, the means through which reconstructions are conducted, and the preferred form(s) of reconstructions. Because of its reliance on specific historical background and present conditions, a culture of reconstruction may vary greatly from country to country. In order to identify a variety of factors that may shape a culture of reconstruction and to offer a point of comparison for the discussion of reconstructive practices in Israeli contemporary dance, this article will first examine the culture of reconstruction in the familiar American modern dance scene.[6]

Both at the time of Copeland's writing in the 1990s and during the early 2000s, the culture of reconstruction in American modern dance could be described as a relatively lively one that supported and even promoted the return of older works to the stage. If the purpose of reconstruction is to establish what both Copeland and Helen Thomas call a "usable past" for the most ephemeral of art forms, then a key prerequisite for reconstruction is a mineable past—a past that, first and foremost, contains natural resources (choreographic works).[7] By the end of the twentieth century, the simple passage of time and accrual of decades worth of rich modern dance activity in the United States had certainly provided a mineable past ripe for reconstruction. The country boasted an unparalleled unbroken lineage of development stretching back to Isadora Duncan and Ruth St. Denis's first experimentations in the early 1900s. Even if the only works deemed eligible for reconstruction were to be those widely considered as masterworks—an approach to reconstruction favored by some practitioners, notably Millicent Hodson and Kenneth Archer[8]—the American modern dance repertory contained ample acclaimed material by choreographers ranging from Martha Graham and Doris Humphrey through to José Limón, Merce Cunningham, Paul Taylor, and Alvin Ailey and then onward to Trisha Brown, Yvonne Rainer, Twyla Tharp, and others. Indeed, although new trends and movements emerged over the course of the twentieth century, there were enough works in the American repertory that stood the test of time and continued to be hailed as groundbreaking, entering the developing canon of modern dance.

The passage of time, coupled with the longevity of many leading American choreographers, has allowed revivals of well-known works by the original creators themselves or with the artists' involvement.[9] Some dances essentially remained in active repertory or were revived after only short periods of dormancy. Other works remained absent from the stage for decades before their revivals, like "Steps in the Street" from Martha Graham's *Chronicle* (1936), which was reconstructed by Yuriko Kikuchi and Graham in 1987 after having long been "lost." As the decades progressed, the American dance scene reached milestones—anniversaries of establishment of companies, centennials of choreographer birthdates—that occasioned revivals. And the passing of time also brought the passing of prominent choreographers, which tends to spur interest in and reconstructions of these artists' work. Witness the flurry of activity following the death of Merce Cunningham in 2009, both with his own company's last tour before its dissolution and with other companies mounting the master's repertory. Although some choreographers' groups ultimately disbanded after their founders died, other well-established companies have survived. Significantly, the Alvin Ailey American Dance Theater, the Limón Dance Company, and others have not only preserved the legacy of their founding choreographers but also transformed into repertory companies that stage reconstructions of works by a variety of artists.

The progression of time and the concomitant accumulation of significant repertory certainly fostered an environment in which reconstruction was possible and even desirable, but the comparably strong culture of reconstruction in the United States is also attributable to an array of supportive institutions. Besides groups that began as single-choreographer organizations before transitioning into broader entities after the founder's death, other professional companies, such as Repertory Dance Theater in Utah, Paul Gordon Emerson's CityDance Ensemble and subsequently his Company E in Washington, D.C., and the now-defunct American Repertory Dance Company in Los Angeles, assumed the mantle of performing a range of dance including revivals of older works. University dance departments have also provided fertile ground for reconstructions. Repertory classes as well as student concerts featuring existing repertory offer opportunities for choreographers, dancers, and stagers to revive works from memory, video, or notation. Moreover, many American universities offer courses in Labanotation, and these facilitate partial or full reconstructions in either a class or performance setting. The prevalence of Labanotation in universities and usage of Labanotation scores in professional contexts is thanks to the activity of the Dance Notation Bureau (DNB), the central body for Labanotation in the United States. Since its founding in 1940, the DNB has offered classes in Labanotation; trained notators, stagers, and teachers of notation; commissioned new scores; and maintained an extensive library that now contains scores of dances by more than 155 choreographers. The DNB estimates that every year it aids in the staging of approximately forty works from Labanotation score.[10]

Although Labanotation has proved a valuable tool for reconstructing dances, stagers have also used other visual records as the basis for remounting works. The film record of dance from the early half of the twentieth century is admittedly patchy, but both informal and professional films of choreographic works are housed in the archives of some companies and universities as well as in such dance collections as the Jerome Robbins Dance Division of the New York Public Library. Such records have enabled dancers and scholars to reconstruct early works, among them Doris Humphrey's 1929 solo *Quasi Waltz*.[11] The advent of video in the latter half of the twentieth century, combined with subsequent technological improvements, the growing availability of video cameras, and the decreasing costs of recording on video, have established this medium as a widespread form of documentation and subsequently a frequently used tool for restaging.[12]

The comparatively high volume of reconstruction in the United States—whether conducted with the help of Labanotation scores, film or video, or memory—is possible thanks to a relative wealth of capital for such projects. Both the National Endowment for the Arts (NEA) and the National Endowment for the Humanities as well as private organizations such as the Ford Foundation have supported reconstructive practices, and in more recent years some monies have been specifically earmarked for preservation, which in turn involves the act of reconstruction. In 1999, one year after the Save America's Treasures program was established through Executive Order, the DNB received a substantial grant to notate works by major choreographers; although the allotted $250,000 was intended for the documentation of dances, the resulting scores enabled future stagings.[13] Meanwhile, in the mid-2000s, the NEA began a new initiative, American Masterpieces: Three Centuries of Artistic Genius, further reflecting a broad cultural interest in honoring and preserving the past. These NEA funds were spread out across multiple artistic disciplines and at first focused on other art forms, but in 2009 and 2010 dance received the largest sums of any category, with forty-three grants totaling $1.5 million in 2009 and sixty-three grants totaling $2,331,500 the following year. Although a few grants were designated for residencies, conferences, festivals, and documentaries, the vast majority were awarded to universities and companies for projects described as restagings, revivals, and reconstructions of works by more than fifty choreographers.[14]

The vibrant culture of reconstruction in the United States, which is first and foremost made possible by the country's long and rich history of dance and is then supported by a variety of institutions and funding structures, is made even more dynamic by a substantial ongoing dialogue about reconstructive practices. American critics, scholars, and stagers alike have written about the theory and implementation of reconstructive practices in both American and European journals ranging from the highly specific *Dance Notation Journal* to broader publications, among which *Dance Research Journal*, *Dance Theatre Journal*, *Choreography and Dance*, *Ballet Review*, and *Ballett International*. Chapters on reconstruction have been included in dance studies anthologies such as *Rethinking Dance History: A Reader* and *Moving History/Dancing Cultures: A Dance History Reader*. And in 1992, a critical mass of artists and scholars gathered at Rutgers University in New Jersey for a Society of Dance History Scholars conference entitled Dance Reconstructed: Modern Dance Art, Past, Present, Future. The discourse generated at this conference, in writing, and in other contexts builds the rationale for reconstruction; outlines and defines the spectrum of reconstructive practices conducted through various means and in an array of settings; provides a platform to address theoretical and logistical challenges; and suggests best practices.

Thus the noticeable presence of and heightened interest in reconstructions in the United States that was observed by Copeland and others in the 1990s and has continued in the twenty-first century can be attributed to several interlinked factors. A mineable past with decades worth of significant choreographic works provided ample raw material, and a perception that the 1930s to 1970s were the glory days of American dance fueled a desire to revisit the works of this era. A network of professional companies and educational institutions offered a stage for revivals. The reconstructions themselves could be realized through the use of widely accepted reconstructive tools, particularly Labanotation and video, and with the help of funding structures that facilitated revivals. Lastly, a lively discourse served both to clarify theory and practice and to further spur interest in reconstructions. With these factors, the culture of reconstruction that developed in the United States is one in which the full-scale reconstruction of critically acclaimed choreographic works is not only possible but also popular; indeed, a tradition of fully restoring older dances and re-presenting them in their entirety has emerged as a characteristic of the American modern dance scene in the late twentieth and early twenty-first centuries.

ISRAEL'S CULTURE OF RECONSTRUCTION

Because the dance field in the United States is significantly larger than that in Israel—a country roughly the size of New Jersey and with a total population of seven and one-half million people, albeit with a thriving dance community that has achieved international prominence—it follows that the sheer number of reconstructions in America should exceed those in this small country. But were the rate and nature of reconstructions not so culturally dependent, one would expect that Israeli stages would also have hosted a noticeable number of older works mounted in recent decades. This phenomenon, however, has not transpired, for the culture of reconstruction in Israel is by definition fundamentally different from that in the United States. Each factor that contributed to the U.S. culture of reconstruction is directly linked to that country's particular historical and institutional landscape. These factors necessarily have a different shape in Israel, on the basis of that nation's own past and present context, and consequently they informed a set of approaches distinct from that in America. To bring this unfamiliar terrain of reconstructive practices into focus, it is necessary to examine how these factors have unfolded and functioned within the Israeli scene; the following discussion attempts to provide a survey of this subject while raising points that may deserve further exploration in the future.

First, concert dance in Israel developed on a different time frame and underwent a dramatically different progression of stages. The 1920s saw the beginnings of modern dance in what was then called Palestine, with Baruch Agadati's attempts to fashion a uniquely Hebrew style and Margalit Ornstein's synthesis of the prevailing approaches from her native Vienna. Whereas Agadati's lack of a school hindered the promulgation and preservation of his work, Ornstein did teach, and her synthesis of methods ranging from Mensendieck and Dalcroze to Duncan and Laban was the preferred model both for the dancers who emerged from her school and a wave of dancers from Central Europe who fled the rise of Nazism, bringing their own direct experience in this source material.[15] Among these immigrants was Gertrud Kraus, who had worked with Gertrud Bodenwieser and Rudolf von Laban and achieved widespread renown throughout Central Europe in the German expressionist style. Upon her arrival in 1935, Kraus became a leading teacher and choreographer in Israeli modern dance. Some other pioneers of this era such as Yardena Cohen, who studied in Dresden and Vienna, took larger strides away from expressionism, but ultimately the influence of Ausdruckstanz prevailed on Israeli modern dance during the 1930s and 1940s.[16]

The popularity of this genre and the artists working in it quickly faded once foreign companies, including those of the Americans Martha Graham, Pearl Primus, and Talley Beatty, toured to Israel in the 1950s. These artists were at the forefront of what then was considered the most progressive and popular modern dance scene in the world, and after seeing their work Israeli dancers and audiences alike perceived the Israeli modern dance as out-of-date and subpar.[17] As immigrants from the United States such as Rina Shaham and Rena Gluck brought their expertise in American modern dance techniques and began teaching and choreographing, a virtual full eclipse occurred. Dancers flocked to these new teachers and to Anna Sokolow, who first visited from the United States to provide professional training for Sara Levi-Tanai's Yemenite-influenced Inbal Dance Theater and then returned yearly to teach modern dance and run her own Lyric Theater, founded in 1962 and composed of Israeli dancers. Faced with competition, the early schools modeled on the German style emptied out.[18] At the same time, those who had led the field until the 1950s left the stage. Even in earlier years, Margalit Ornstein had rarely appeared as a dancer, instead choreographing for her students and her twin daughters Shoshana and Yehudit; Shoshana was diagnosed with a heart condition and stopped dancing in 1949, while her sister turned to literature. Kraus's more notable performing career ended in the early 1950s. After presenting her last solo concert in 1954, she turned her attention to teaching in her studio and at the Jerusalem Academy of Music and Dance. Meanwhile, Agadati had long since left the profession. Thus a chapter of Israeli concert dance was effectively closed.[19]

Thanks to the American immigrants' teaching in the 1950s and the Batsheva Dance Company's establishment in 1964 with Graham as artistic adviser, Graham's technique and aesthetic reigned supreme during the next period in Israeli dance. The rise of Batsheva marked the demise of a few small companies run by independent choreographers as well as the end of Sokolow's Lyric Theater, and for the next few decades the vast majority of dance activity in Tel Aviv was effectively concentrated in Batsheva and the Bat-Dor Dance Company. Both of these troupes drew most of their repertory from foreign choreographers, among them the Americans Beatty, Sokolow, Donald McKayle, Robert Cohan, Pearl Lang, Glen Tetley, Jerome Robbins, Alvin Ailey, Paul Taylor, and later, in the 1980s, Mark Morris, Daniel Ezralow, and David Parsons. Some Israelis did choreograph for Batsheva and Bat-Dor in the 1960s and 1970s, including Moshe Efrati, Oshra Elkayam, Mirali Sharon, Rina Schenfeld, and Yair Vardi, but critics often noted that their styles stemmed either from that of Graham or a more generic modern technique also born from the American context.[20] Slowly, however, a few of these Israeli choreographers broke off from the main company system to found their own groups, and in the 1970s a handful of young independent artists, among them Ruth Eshel, Rachel Cafri, Hedda Oren, Ronit Land, and Ruth Ziv-Eyal, struck out on their own, creating a fringe scene.

Just as American modern dance had overthrown the German expressionist influence in Israel, new developments during the late 1980s and 1990s radically changed the landscape of Israeli dance, ending the dominance of Graham and other foreign styles while also altering the small but growing fringe. New Israeli voices brought a different flavor to the country's major troupes. Ohad Naharin assumed the helm at Batsheva in 1990 and quickly revitalized the troupe with his own repertory while also nurturing young Israeli artists and importing some adventurous choreographers from abroad. In the north of the country, the Kibbutz Contemporary Dance Company became a more significant force and showcased more and more of Rami Be'er's work through the 1980s and 1990s, ultimately elevating him to artistic director in 1996. A young generation of artists emerged outside the companies as well, supported by the Shades of Dance platform as well as by the Suzanne Dellal Centre, a multi-theater venue with a strong dance agenda that opened in 1989, and by Curtain Up, a festival of premieres by local choreographers that began the same year. While drawing on existing trends from abroad such as minimalism, contact improvisation, and dance theatre, these young artists more successfully shaped distinctive and innovative voices than their predecessors who had adopted the Graham aesthetic. In theory, these choreographers joined an existing fringe, but in practice they were replacing the other independent artists who had started this alternative scene. Whether because of personal decisions or increased competition from fresher artistic voices, most of the Israeli choreographers who populated the dance scene from the 1960s through the early 1980s were no longer active in the 2000s.

The progression of these three major periods in Israeli dance and the response of existing Israeli choreographers to each of these shifts provide a vastly different backdrop for reconstruction in contemporary times.[21] Whereas American choreographers such as Graham, supported by well-established schools and companies, kept producing new dances and sometimes revisited older works even as new trends arose, Israeli choreographers did not have the same institutional buffers to weather the still more radical sea changes in their country's modern dance. The result was essentially a turnover of choreographers instead of a prolonged overlap of generations, and as the older artists left the stage they took their works and the chance for their self-directed revivals with them.[22] Further jeopardizing the possibility of reconstructions of works by these earlier choreographers has been the perception that, with the rise of substantially different styles in later years, these older dances were outmoded. Ruth Eshel, who not only spearheaded the fringe dance scene in the late 1970s but also has written extensively about Israeli dance as a critic and scholar, accounts for the lack of reconstruction by citing the rejection of the expressionist aesthetic in the 1960s and 1970s and describes the prevailing attitude toward revival in Israel as "why reconstruct something old-fashioned?"[23] The particular character of the expressionist dance adds to the complication of successfully reconstructing Israeli works from the 1920s to 1950s. Eshel notes that in Ausdruckstanz the interest lay in "spirit of the dance" rather than "the movement lexicon"; indeed, she emphasizes, "when you are talking about Ausdruckstanz, it's all soul and fire." Thus without the passionate feeling of the original performers trained in the expressionist style, and without a sufficiently compelling movement vocabulary to catch the eye of contemporary viewers, a few historical reconstructions shown in the late 1980s and early 1990s were disappointing.[24] It is perhaps telling that in one of the few historical reconstructions that took place, Naomi Aleskovsky's revival of three dances by Gertrud Kraus for a tribute evening to the choreographer in 1988, the works did not enter the regular repertory of some of the companies that performed them.[25] The fate of Kraus's dances may have caused other artists to pause when considering reviving older works.[26]

Even if an outside stager wishes to restore a work made in Israel between the 1920s and 1970s, the logistical challenges are substantial. The types of institutions that support reconstructions in the United States—decades-old single-choreographer companies, repertory companies, and university dance programs—largely do not exist in the current landscape of Israeli concert dance. Single-choreographer modern dance companies have not survived after the death (or more likely, the retirement) of their founders and thus have not continued their choreographic legacy. Moreover, the repertory companies that were the mainstay of the Israeli modern dance scene in the 1960s and 1970s have shifted their mode of operation or folded entirely. Batsheva's earliest seasons in the mid-1960s included productions of Graham's *Herodiade* (1944), *Errand into the Maze* (1947), and *Diversion of Angels* (1948); in the late 1960s, the company mounted José Limón's *The Exiles* (1950) and *La Malinche* (1949) as well as Sophie Maslow's *The Village I Knew* (1950), while in the mid-1970s it acquired productions of such masterworks as Donald McKayle's *Rainbow 'Round My Shoulder* (1959), Anna Sokolow's *Rooms* (1955), and Kurt Jooss's *The Green Table* (1932), staged by Anna Markard. Yet these and other older works receded from view in the 1980s as Batsheva's repertory focused on newer works created by both Israeli and foreign artists, and for a period during the first decade of the twenty-first century the company presented only works by Naharin and house choreographer Sharon Eyal. Like Batsheva, Bat-Dor Dance Company also drew from the American modern dance canon during its early decades of operation, staging works such as Sophie Maslow's *Prologue* (1959), Paul Taylor's *Three Epitaphs* (1956), and Doris Humphrey's *Shakers* (1931). In fact, Bat-Dor's repertory was so tied to restaging that, for a time, the company employed choreologists including Ilana Sofrun, who was sent to study at the Benesh Institute by Bat-Dor's artistic director Jeannette Ordman.[27] Yet the practice of reviving significant dances was the exception rather than the norm in the late 1990s. Writing about Bat-Dor's financial and artistic struggles, Eshel lamented in 1998, "The country is lacking a modern company that focuses on the mounting of masterpieces of modern dance," and she suggested that the company could redeem itself by turning to this task.[28] Instead, the company continued on its shaky path and finally disbanded in 2006. The country's third major repertory company, Kibbutz Contemporary Dance Company, always tended to present newer works rather than revivals, and ultimately it turned its attention to the dances of artistic director Rami Be'er. There are some more recently founded groups that have adopted a repertory model, but their scope is limited. Located on the periphery in Be'ersheva since 2002, Kamea Dance Company centers its programming on new works, especially those of its co-director, Tamir Ginz. Meanwhile, The Project—a joint initiative of the Israeli Opera and Suzanne Dellal Centre that started in 2010—has brought in European and Israeli choreographers to build what is a decidedly contemporary, up-to-date repertory. All the other companies in Israel are one- or two-choreographer companies, established to present the new work of their founders. Consequently, the varied repertory that was performed in Israel during the 1960s through the 1990s has virtually no avenue to appear on the professional stage, and likewise there is no logical outlet for reconstructions of earlier work.

Nor is there an academic platform in Israel for these revivals. Dance has not attained the same position in Israeli higher education as it has in American universities; indeed, there are no major universities that have dance programs. The two primary institutions that grant degrees in dance, the Jerusalem Academy of Music and Dance and the Kibbutzim College of Education, are both ostensibly aimed toward training dance teachers, and the curriculum and performance opportunities are designed accordingly. Older works might figure into repertory classes on a limited basis, but performances by these schools' students feature either brand-new or relatively new works rather than reconstructions.[29]

Compounding the absence of institutions that might support revivals is a relative lack of tools to bring them to fruition. Israel does boast its own form of movement notation, developed by Noa Eshkol and Abraham Wachman in the 1950s, but Eshkol-Wachman Movement Notation (EWMN) has not been used to document and subsequently reconstruct choreographic works to the same extent as Labanotation or Benesh Movement Notation. Indeed, Eshkol acknowledged that her motivation for developing a system of notation "was primarily for a way of composing in movement, and not for a method of writing down movements."[30] Thus the published scores in EWMN focus on choreographic works developed using the system by Eshkol and her associates, including Tirza Sapir and Einya Cohen, as well as readers for students and some documentation of movement forms outside the realm of concert dance, such as T'ai Chi, Feldenkrais, athletic activities, sign language, and Arab, Yemenite, and Israeli folk dances. Apart from one EWMN score of an eighteenth-century gavotte, published in a joint edition with Labanotation and Benesh notation of the same dance, there are no EWMN scores of dances by Israeli or foreign choreographers who worked outside of the EWMN community.[31] Only a few dance professionals in Israel are fluent in other notation forms, and consequently they have had a limited impact on the scope of reconstruction in the country. Amira Mayroz trained at the Benesh Institute in London, and during the 1980s and 1990s she reconstructed Renaissance and Baroque dances using Beauchamp-Feuillet notation. Naomi Perlov also studied at the Benesh Institute after her exposure to choreology as an apprentice in Bat-Dor. Yet asked if she has worked with Benesh here in Israel, she notes that there is no place for it within the current scene; her extensive career as a choreologist and stager has been conducted abroad.[32]

A comparative lack of film and video further impedes the reconstruction of older works in Israel. As is the case in the United States and elsewhere, film of the earliest dance trailblazers in Israel is virtually nonexistent. Although Baruch Agadati later turned his creative attention to film, the only visible evidence of his groundbreaking dance solos are photographs and newspaper articles. The same is true of Margalit Ornstein's choreography for her twin daughters, Shoshana and Yehudit.[33] Due to the expense of filming during Gertrud Kraus's career from the 1920s in Vienna through the early 1950s in Israel, traces of her repertory also lie solely in photographs, drawings, and written accounts. Writing about the problems of addressing Kraus's work in the latter part of the twentieth century, Giora Manor notes that during the span of her career there were very few recordings of dance.[34] The dearth of original filmic records from the 1920s through the 1950s is far more extreme in Israel than in the United States, and the loss of this documentation is magnified by the subsequent lack of reconstructions conducted during the choreographers' active careers—reconstructions that could have been more easily recorded with updated technology. Choreographers working in Israel during the 1960s and 1970s fared somewhat better with regard to the preservation of their work on film, but the visual record is still far from complete. In her memoir-history of her career with the Batsheva Dance Company, Rena Gluck recalls that certain pieces such as guest artist Pearl Lang's *Voices of Fire* were never filmed and consequently never revived. She also notes that Bethsabee de Rothschild, the company's founder and backer, did not believe in filming works if a film already existed and as long as there were no choreographic changes for the company, as was the case with some dances imported from abroad.[35] Moreover, de Rothschild did not fund any documentation of works by Israeli choreographers within the company since those artists were available to rehearse their own creations.[36] Amira Mayroz, who became Batsheva's rehearsal director in 1974, adds that filming a dance became a matter of the lowest priority in the budget once de Rothschild stopped supporting the company in 1975; this attitude toward documentation continued during the rest of Mayroz's tenure with the company, which ended in 1977.[37]

Further complicating the possibility for reconstruction—and perhaps reflecting the prevailing attitude toward revivals—is the funding structure for dance in Israel. Particularly since the mid-to-late 1980s, when the Shades of Dance and Curtain Up festivals were established, government funding for dance has effectively promoted the development of young local choreographers and the creation of premieres. This emphasis on the new also characterizes more recently founded festivals that have shaped the fringe scene, notably Machol Acher (Other Dance), Tmuna Theatre's Intimadance, and the Jerusalem-based Machol Shalem and Zirat Machol. Meanwhile, large-scale international festivals that include local choreographers, such as the Israel Festival in Jerusalem and Tel Aviv Dance, tend to program recently premiered offerings and commission works by some of the country's leading artists. There are no specific platforms, either in the form of festivals or grants, explicitly geared toward revivals or historically informed reconstructions, and securing general funding for reconstructive activities is challenging. Gaby Aldor, a grand-daughter of Margalit Ornstein and a dance scholar, reconstructed Ornstein's *The Rivals* (1934) in 1991 from photographs and from her mother Shoshana's memory in honor of the Ornstein sisters' eightieth birthdays. Aldor undertook this challenge with negligible support and recalls that there was no obvious source to appeal to for funding such a project.[38] When Amira Mayroz reconstructed Renaissance and Baroque dances in Israel in the 1980s and 1990s, she too received only minimal support and resorted to funding the productions herself; she notes that this is in direct contrast to the large sums of money available for the historically informed reconstruction of early dance in England, France, and other countries.[39]

With regard to the last factor outlined in the discussion of America's culture of reconstruction—a scholarly and artistic discourse that both clarifies and stimulates reconstructive practices—it is perhaps not surprising that such a dialogue is all but non-existent in Israel. There have been neither conferences nor major publications about reconstruction, as there have been in both the United States and Europe.[40] Musings about the purpose and nature of reconstruction have been printed primarily in programs of the rare revival or in newspaper articles about these infrequent restagings; for the discourse to expand, it seems, more reconstructive activity would need to occur. But the few writings that do exist, primarily by dance critic Giora Manor, underscore the tenuous place of reconstruction in Israeli dance by highlighting tensions between the problems of reconstruction and the perceived value of revisiting works. On the one hand, Manor cites the logistical "difficulties" stagers face in mounting early works.[41] In other sources, he further problematizes the reconstruction of earlier dances on a philosophical level by invoking the choreographers' unwavering focus on the new. "I am quite sure she would have preferred to make new ones instead, lest they become museum pieces," writes Manor of the late Gertrud Kraus just prior to the 1988 reconstruction of three of her works.[42] About Sara Levi-Tanai, whose dances were revisited by the Inbal Dance Theater in the early 2000s, he opines, "As any creative artist who always is in love with a new baby that has yet to be born, in this case a new creation, Sarah [sic] Levi-Tanai never wanted to hear about preserving her creations. It never crossed her mind to have former dancers stage her works with young dancers performing."[43] Previewing Gaby Aldor's 1991 reconstruction of Margalit Ornstein's *The Rivals*, Manor simultaneously questions the purpose of reconstruction and reveals the need to justify or at least explain revivals to an Israeli public largely unfamiliar with reconstructive practices by opening with the provocative query, "Why, actually?" Yet ultimately Manor defends this and other reconstructions. Concerned that the dancers' lack of curiosity about the past will lead to superficiality and the repeated reinvention of the wheel, Manor argues, "Therefore, it seems to me that the effort to reconstruct dance works, and almost with no real connection to the contemporary artistic value of the reconstructed pieces, is a wise and right act."[44]

Despite Manor's eventually enthusiastic endorsement of reconstruction, there have been few other restagings of Israeli modern dance from the early and mid-twentieth century other than those already mentioned. In 1994, the Karmiel Dance Festival included "Expressionist Dance in Israel 1920–1940," a program dedicated to the first generation of Israeli choreographers. The tribute featured only a couple of live performances, including the previously reconstructed versions of Ornstein's *The Rivals* and Kraus's *Carousel*. Meanwhile, four of Kraus's solos were revived for a 1998 program commemorating twenty years since the choreographer's death. Fringe dance of the 1970s and early 1980s has also remained absent from the stage since its heyday. One exception is Ruth Eshel's solo *The Gown of Stones* (1981), danced in a robe designed by the artist Avraham Ofek; notably, however, Eshel's performance at the opening of an exhibition of Ofek's work in 2010 was an expanded and altered version rather than a strict reconstruction of the original.[45] Somewhat outside the realm of modern dance, a few other works have been revisited. As noted earlier, the Inbal Dance Theater has reconstructed some of the repertory of its founder, Sara Levi-Tanai, who drew inspiration from traditional Yemenite dance and culture. And in the mid-1980s, Deborah Bertonoff—then in her seventies—performed snippets of the "Beggars' Dance" from the Habima Theater's 1928 production of S. Ansky's play *The Dybbuk*.[46]

The reconstructions mentioned in this chapter are not highlights but instead compose the bulk (and perhaps even the sum total) of Israeli reconstructions of dances from earlier eras. Ultimately, the disjunctions between phases of Israeli concert dance history, the absence of reconstruction-friendly institutions such as repertory companies or university dance departments, the lack of reconstructive tools including notated scores and archival footage, and the scarcity of funding for revisiting older works erected daunting and some-times insurmountable challenges to reconstruction. Compounding these impediments are other factors specific to the Israeli context, such as the comparatively limited audience available to see a given work in a tiny country. Choreographer Barak Marshall, who is based part-time in Tel Aviv and part-time in Los Angeles, points out that in Israel "there's only a certain number of times you can perform a piece before everyone has seen it."[47] Marshall and others also suggest that a broader cultural attitude may be another barrier to reconstruction, affecting and perhaps underlying some of the other factors. Discussing both the absence of notation in particular and reconstruction in general, Naomi Perlov emphasizes, "We're a young country; we don't yet rely on the past as we should…the problem is not only time but is the mentality of considering the past as something impor-tant."[48] Marshall reflects, "I think in general in Israel, there is an issue of throwing away history. We dealt with that in 1948 when we threw away everything we considered old in order to build a new Israeli identity. As a result we lost too much of our cultural heritages." He adds that in Israel "there is a real hunger for the new, with a real neglect of the old."[49] Thus until now Israel's culture of reconstruction has been one with a small volume and low frequency of reconstructions, one in which revivals are undertaken occasionally to commemorate a landmark or enliven a special event rather than performed as an integral part of regular programming.

RECONSTRUCTING THE RECENT PAST: RESTAGINGS
OF ISRAELI CONTEMPORARY DANCE

Notably, as the first decade of the twenty-first century drew to a close, the Israeli concert dance scene celebrated several milestones related not to earlier generations of artists but instead to the current crop of choreographers, some of whom started their careers in the late 1980s and early 1990s. The most recent chapter of Israeli dance has now accumulated enough years and enough significant works to warrant restagings, and as the Suzanne Dellal Centre reached its twentieth anniversary and the Shades of Dance festival continued twenty-five years after its first incarnation, revivals from the repertory of Israeli contemporary dance began to appear onstage. Besides the "Then and Now" program which gathered together partial reconstructions for the 2009 Shades of Dance, a couple full-length revivals have recently graced the country's concert stages. Ido Tadmor staged an all-female rendition of his *Cell* (1996) for the Ashdod-based Ginolia Dance Company in 2010. And the Inbal Dance Theater mounted a full-length reconstruction of Marshall's *Aunt Leah* (1995) a half-year prior to the "Then and Now" program that included an excerpt from this breakout work. However, this revival was initiated not by the choreographer himself but by the company's artistic director, Razi Amitai, who according to Marshall was searching for continuity from Inbal's past to its present and thus "wanted a piece that reflected an investigation of this Yemenite heritage and yet also contained a contemporary pulse"[50] (Figure 3.1).

Perhaps not surprisingly, reconstruction of earlier works is not foremost in the mind of Marshall and other active contemporary choreographers. This is in part due to the nature of art making and the progression of individual artists' careers. Extending from Angela Kane's study of the restaging of Paul Taylor's *Airs* (1978), a living choreographer's approach to revivals must be contextualized within his or her current creative activity.[51] Still at the height of his productivity, Paul Taylor explained that although he revived older works every year, "I'm not wild about seeing any of them, really, because I'm always more interested in whatever the new baby is. It's just more alive."[52] Working choreographers in Israel articulate similar desires to focus on the present and the future rather than the past. Although Marshall's choreographic career included an extended hiatus due to injury, fifteen years after his choreographic debut with *Aunt Leah* he feels he has moved far beyond

FIGURE 3.1 From *Aunt Leah* by Barak Marshall. Photography by Gadi Dagon.

his first work. Marshall admits that it might be interesting to revisit an earlier dance such as *Emma Goldman's Wedding* (1997), but he asserts that he is "more hungry to develop something new."[53] Nir Ben Gal echoes this sentiment, elucidating, "It's much more interesting to create a new world and new language and to continue with this"; accordingly, it was with some reluctance that he returned to perform an excerpt from *Two Room Apartment* (1987) with his partner Liat Dror in the 2009 Shades of Dance retrospective.[54] Inbal Pinto, who started choreographing in the early 1990s and with her partner Avshalom Pollak is currently in great demand internationally, recognizes that there is limited time to work and consequently chooses to channel her energy toward new dances. She articulates, "If I have the dilemma between going back and going forward, I would prefer now to go forward."[55] Meanwhile, for Noa Dar, who also has focused on the presentation of new works since she founded her company in 1993, her investment in the creative process often precludes the possibility of revival not only because of time constraints but also because of concerns about the vitality of a restaging performed by dancers who did not experience the original work's development.[56]

Whereas revivals of dances by living choreographers account for just a portion of reconstructions in the United States, they are effectively the only restagings that populate the Israeli arena as the second decade of the twenty-first century dawns. And as Ohad Naharin contends, "There is a difference between [reviving the work of] dead choreographers and living choreographers." Naharin notes that stagers attempt to respect what they perceive as the intentions of deceased choreographers and consequently aim for reconstructions that hew as closely to the original as possible.[57] Yet when the person reviving the dance is the choreographer himself or herself, there is a greater opportunity for artistic license to be exercised and for changes to be implemented. In Israel, where the scenario of the choreographer revisiting earlier work is the rule rather than the exception in the pantheon of reconstructive practices, this license has been wielded liberally and creatively—and concomitantly, an innovative approach involving the remixing and reframing of older material in a new format has emerged.

REMIXING AND REFRAMING IN THE REPERTORY OF OHAD NAHARIN

Choreographing since 1980 and directing Batsheva since 1990, Ohad Naharin has amassed arguably the largest and deepest repertory of any contemporary Israeli choreographer. The magnitude of Naharin's creative output—with regard to size and artistic merit—makes his body of work the ripest for revisiting. And especially during the first decade of his tenure at Batsheva, Naharin did restage some of his earlier works, among them *Pas de Pepsi* (1980), *Innostress* (1983), *Black Milk* (1985), *60 a Minute* (1985), *Tabula Rasa* (1986), and *Passomezzo* (1988). The younger Batsheva Ensemble, which also operates under Naharin's direction, has in particular performed these shorter, older dances; indeed, even as the main company gravitated toward presenting new full-length works by Naharin, the ensemble mounted *Arbos* (1989) in 2004, ending the work's seven-year absence from the Israeli stage.

Though there is little visual record that would support a thorough comparison of the original works to their remounted versions, programs and newspapers reveal that Naharin did make at least some significant alterations when he returned to his early dances. *Black Milk*, for instance, was first composed for five female dancers of the Kibbutz Dance Company. Five of Batsheva's female dancers performed the work in 1990, but soon after Naharin cast a quintet of men; reflecting on this shift more than a decade and a half later, critic Ora Brafman still recalled that *Black Milk* was "drastically changed in 1991 when Naharin introduced it to his company as an all-male dance"[58] (Figure 3.2).

Naharin's general conception of reconstruction also suggests that the revivals of his repertory from the 1980s were not necessarily exact replicas of the originals. Recognizing the variation inherent in different performers, Naharin explains, "even if a choreographer restaged a piece exactly the way it was, two people will do it in two different ways." Talking broadly about the idea and practice of reconstruction, he also notes that even a choreographer who seeks to present faithful reproductions may mistakenly remember his or her work while in the process of restaging. Consequently, he stresses, "it's really impossible to reconstruct [a work] the same as it was."[59] Beyond this understanding of the limitations of reconstruction, Naharin's wider perspective on the creative process may also have affected the shape of these revivals. Naharin has noted more than once that a premiere is not an end point but rather a beginning. At a 2010 press conference prior to a round of performances of *Three*, which has remained in

FIGURE 3.2 From *Black Milk* by Ohad Naharin. Performed by Batsheva Dance Company. Photography by Gadi Dagon.

active repertory since its creation in 2005, he likened a premiere to a birth after which many changes occur.[60]

Thus for Naharin, a return to previously choreographed material is an extension of the choreographic process rather than a separate exercise in mounting existing works as they were originally made. "I don't have an interest to show the works as they were," he remarks. "I have an interest in constantly looking at it with a fresh eye and continuing a process with everything that is still onstage, whether it is six months old or a twenty-year-old piece."[61] He elaborates that even though he engages in a form of revisiting older work, he is also "changing the place as [he] revisits" and adds, "The changing of the place that I revisit is even more fun than the visit itself." Indeed, for Naharin, producing an exact replica of an earlier work is not simply a process that holds little interest; instead, he views this endeavor as "a missed opportunity." It is this opportunity to actively reengage with his choreography, reassess it, and actually rework it that serves as his rationale for revisiting older works. When Naharin finds weak spots in the original dance, he says the process of returning to it "gives me the chance to find those solutions.... This is one of the main reasons I come back to it, because I do feel fulfilled by constantly finding better solutions."[62] With this mindset, the passage of time is not a disadvantage, a barrier to recapturing an original, but an advantage, allowing Naharin to improve his earlier choreography with an accumulated wealth of information and insight. "We constantly learn, we're constantly gaining new tools, we're gaining an ability to see things, to solve things in a new way," he acknowledges, "and by acquiring those new tools, I like to use them on my older works too."[63]

The mode of revivals that has predominated during Naharin's second decade at Batsheva clearly reflects this perspective. Full revivals of the choreographer's earlier works—

revivals in which changes may well be present but not evident to the audience—have faded from the company's repertory in the 2000s. Instead, Naharin has frequently remixed material from his evening-length and shorter works and reframed them as new entities, a practice in which alterations are an inherent and visible part of the product.[64] This process of remixing is part and parcel of Naharin's larger perception of choreography. Speaking about the field as a whole rather than about his specific repertory, he attests that the creative process relies fundamentally on the act of rearranging and avers that good choreographic moments can be "shuffled" without hindering the work.[65] This principle has perhaps been most thoroughly illustrated by Merce Cunningham. Not only was the sequence of many of Cunningham's individual works determined through chance methods, but in the more than eight hundred performances of what he termed Events, a series of excerpts from across Cunningham's repertory were similarly ordered using chance operations. Yet in contrast, Naharin states that within his approach to remixing earlier dances, "It's not chance; it's not Merce Cunningham shuffling." His compositional process in creating remixed and reframed works is positively infused with intention; indeed, he notes that his rearranging is "not something that's done carelessly. You still place it very carefully," and adds that with shuffling he is able to find possibilities which are "more dramatic, more funny, more surprisingly satisfying."[66] The popular and critical success of several of Naharin's remixed and reframed works—*Deca Dance* (shown in various permutations since 2000), *Project 5* (2008), and *Kyr/Zina 2010* (2010)—testifies that this approach does in fact yield highly satisfying dances. An examination of these three pieces reveals further dimensions of Naharin's philosophy and approach.

Initially intended as a retrospective to commemorate Naharin's ten-year anniversary with Batsheva, *Deca Dance* soon expanded beyond its four planned performances. But in a move that highlights his interest in an ongoing process, Naharin has repeatedly altered the composition of *Deca Dance* to reflect the continuing development of his repertory. Describing the work before a 2009 tour to the United States, he explained, "*Deca Dance* is something I have been playing with for some time. It's a modular piece that keeps changing. I can reconstruct my work and create something coherent from the broken pieces, that gives me, the dancers, and the audience pleasure."[67] The Batsheva Dance Company and the Batsheva Ensemble have performed numerous versions containing roughly seven to nine excerpts each from an ever-growing roster of dances including *Black Milk* (1985), *Passomezzo* (1988), *Queens of Golub* (1989), *Kyr* (1990), *Mabul* (1992), *Anaphase* (1993), *Z/na* (1995), *Sabotage Baby* (1997), *Zachacha* (1998), *Moshe* (1999), *Naharin's Virus* (2001), *Three* (2005), *Telophaza* (2006), *George & Zalman* (2006), *MAX* (2007), *Seder* (2007), and *B/olero* (2008).[68] Certain segments—most notably a whimsical section in which the performers pull audience members up onstage to dance and a building, powerful movement accumulation to the Passover song "Echad Mi Yodea" ("Who Knows One")—are present in almost every rendition.[69] Yet at its core, *Deca Dance* is a fluid work in a perpetual state of evolution (Figure 3.3).

FIGURE 3.3 From *Deca Dance* by Ohad Naharin. Performed by Batsheva Ensemble. Photography by Gadi Dagon.

The inclusion of so many shorter excerpts from a range of sources has prompted reviewers to liken *Deca Dance* to a "tasting menu," a "puzzle," and a "collage."[70] Such metaphors illuminate two intriguing aspects of this work and shed light on the larger practice at play. First, as the phrase "tasting menu" suggests, *Deca Dance* supports an overarching familiarity with the breadth of Naharin's repertory that is not typically possible with the viewing of a single dance. Interestingly, if one goal of reconstructive practices is assumed to be the fostering of firsthand knowledge of previously choreographed works, *Deca Dance* fulfills this aim—albeit in packaging that explicitly underscores the inevitable distance between what is currently onstage and the original. At the same time, although *Deca Dance* comprises several shorter components drawn from disparate sources, the product is perceived as a "puzzle" or a "collage," a whole entity that presents a united picture rather than a loose series of unrelated pieces. Describing a version called *Super-Deca-Dance* performed outdoors in Israel's Timna Park as part of the 2003 Phaza Morgana festival, Naharin reflects on the fusion of unconnected elements into a new dance with its own logic, explaining, "it was like telling just the beginning, the middle, and the end of different stories. The way in which I connect the different excerpts creates the coherence and the dynamics of the show, and sometimes the result is even more moving than the original works."[71] Viewers already well acquainted with Naharin's repertory may recognize each excerpt in *Deca Dance* from its source, but ultimately the audience member sees a freshly composed full-length dance that contains significance of its own. As critic Lily Abudi wrote in 2010, "The combinations created new contexts and gave added value and meanings to familiar creations."[72] Allowing the old to be viewed from a novel angle and generating wholly new meanings, Naharin's approach can be understood as a relative of the postmodern reworkings of story ballets described by scholar Vera Midgelow and is thus situated within the postmodern wing of reconstructive practices.[73]

Like *Deca Dance*, *Project 5* (2008) also culls its component parts from several works spanning a few decades, but these chamber selections remain fixed: the quintet *George & Zalman* (2006), the duet *B/olero* (2008), a trio called "Park" from *Moshe* (1999), and the revised 1991 version of the 1985 quintet *Black Milk*. The impetus for *Project 5* stemmed from the graduation of five women from the Batsheva Ensemble. Naharin wished to keep working with these talented dancers, and so he undertook the challenge of designing what he calls "the right frame" for showcasing them.[74] Originally created for members of *Project 5*'s first cast, *George & Zalman* and *B/olero* were obvious choices. Naharin then chose "Park" because the trio fit logically after the duet *B/olero*, and *Black Milk* offered an ideal platform to once more bring all five of the dancers together at the dance's conclusion.[75] Only a short film of the dancers was made specifically for *Project 5*, but nonetheless the sum total emerged as, in the words of critic Ora Brafman, "a solid new piece."[76] Indeed, Naharin masterfully formulated an equation that delicately balanced segments with the differing dynamics, moods, and numbers of dancers. The choreographer's choices of the parts themselves and his subsequent decisions about order, transitions, and costuming contribute to the sense that *Project 5* is a complex but coherent work; when the two dancers from *B/olero* matter-of-factly carry on three microphones for the performers of "Park," it is possible to imagine that the trio always followed the duet, and the fact that the dancers are clothed in simple black outfits for the first three sections further links these together visually into a single framework. Again, as in *Deca Dance*, there is an intricate relationship between older components and a novel construction that simultaneously offers a glimpse at the past and a wealth of new meanings. This unique tension was evident to Brafman, who was familiar with *Moshe* and *George & Zalman* but not *B/olero* and observed, "The first three segments attached in this new context offer a fresh outlook on the two sections we've seen before."[77]

Whereas both *Deca Dance* and *Project 5* remix excerpts from numerous dances, *Kyr/Zina 2010*, premiered by the Batsheva Ensemble as Naharin celebrated twenty years with Batsheva, focuses exclusively on material from two dances that loom large in Naharin's body of work. *Kyr*, the first evening-length work that Naharin created for Batsheva, closed the prestigious Israel Festival in 1990 and boasted live onstage performances by the popular band The Tractor's Revenge; it was performed for many years by the main company before moving to the Ensemble's repertory in 1997, and it also introduced audiences to the now-famous "Echad Mi Yodea" accumulation, which later was absorbed with different costuming into *Anaphase* (1993) and *Deca Dance* and has become the choreography most associated with Naharin. *Zina* also appeared in the Israel Festival, opening the 1995 season, and it electrified audiences with memorable scenes and surprising props, including an oversized stuffed cow. Although Naharin has revived all of the dances several times in full and considered doing so in 2010, he explained, "I decided to concentrate on the parts that I liked…and invest in the process, and it was a very meaningful process in those sections."[78] The concentrated investment in this process yielded a number of changes in the parts that Naharin chose to revisit, particularly in those that have not been restaged in other contexts such as *Deca Dance* or the Batsheva Ensemble's *Kaamos + Love*.[79] In some sections, such as the opening of *Kyr* and a later segment from that dance for a line of seated women and a female soloist, Naharin retained the concept and structure but re-choreographed the movement itself. An additional excerpt from *Kyr* remained mostly the same but received a new ending, with the dancers sharply, quickly, and repeatedly twisting, building into a near frenzy before collapsing. This process of re-working segments also "opened up room" for a brand-new section placed in between two excerpts originally drawn from *Z/na*.[80]

The tension between old and new is perhaps more palpable in *Kyr/Zina 2010* than in a more varied remix such as *Deca Dance*. The title of the framework directly references the two sources, raising their specters from the outset, and as certain sections unfold one from the next as they did twenty or fifteen years ago some semblance of these full-length originals is resurrected. Yet Naharin's changes, as well as the complete absence of substantial parts of each dance, serve as a constant reminder that although *Kyr/Zina 2010* grants audiences a valuable opportunity to approach these landmark works, it is neither *Kyr* nor *Z/na*. Instead, aided in part by the transitions built to connect sections that were not previously contiguous and by casting choices, it emerges as its own coherent entity replete with new meanings as well as old significance. The same man who wields a grating noise-maker in an excerpt from *Kyr* later lassos a rope during the portion of the evening culled from *Z/na*; the same woman who suddenly stops the noisemaker's incessant rotations positions herself provocatively in the path of the man's circling rope and then ties it around him. For viewers who seek it, a throughline is available, and the audience can choose to interpret the work as a whole by considering the entire frame instead of just the component parts from separate sources (Figure 3.4).

Naharin does not use the term *reconstruction* to describe his work in *Deca Dance*, *Project 5*, and *Kyr/Zina 2010*, and these projects are clearly not reconstructions in the traditional sense of the word. Yet as he returns to older choreography in the process of creating these works, Naharin engages with many of the same issues as do choreographers and stagers who revive and reconstruct dance. For one, although he freely makes changes in his material, he is concerned with its essence, noting, "The only rule I have is that I keep connected to what I call the soul of the original piece. This I don't change." Even as this connection to the original "soul" is sought, Naharin, like other stagers dealing with older works, seeks to establish the dance's relevance in its present setting. He asserts, "When we work on something that I've done in the past—it doesn't matter how long ago—it always has to feel to me that it's current, that it's not a museum piece." Ensuring that older choreography—whether it is fully restaged or remixed and reframed in the case of Naharin's work—does not become fossilized but instead truly lives requires a

FIGURE 3.4 From *Kyr/Zina* by Ohad Naharin. Performed by Batsheva Ensemble. Photography by Gadi Dagon.

significant amount of attention to the new dancers' understanding and performance of the material. Naharin emphasizes that he does not simply teach his dancers the steps but instead "[invests] in giving the keys to the dancers to interpret the work."[81]

Notably, although Naharin is engaging with his own repertory, he encounters something that many outside stagers face when they reconstruct earlier dances by other choreographers: differences in the training of the new dancers as compared to the original ones. Naharin's movement language, Gaga, is constantly evolving and has come into its own as a training method since the early 2000s. Whereas the dancers who first performed some of the older works featured as excerpts in Naharin's reframed dances trained daily in ballet, Batsheva now holds a morning Gaga class instead. In accordance with the nature of Naharin's philosophy and process, he does not coach his dancers to achieve what might be considered a strictly "authentic" performance of the excerpted material and instead welcomes the information that Gaga brings to the current interpretation. Reflecting on *Kyr/Zina 2010*, Naharin notes that Gaga has increased the dancers' stamina and enhanced their connection to their explosive power, therefore improving their performance of the demanding, highly athletic movement. Simultaneously, Gaga fosters attention to smaller details and a fine-tuning of subtleties, and as a result the current dancers can offer a modulated, nuanced rendering of what was, initially, more incessantly high-voltage choreography.[82]

Finally, Naharin's remixing and reframing results in the mounting of a work that offers some audience members the chance to re-view earlier choreography, albeit with a twist that more traditional reconstructive processes do not produce. He recounts that his way of working gives him a chance "to communicate to [his] audience, to make people come and see again something they've seen before and see from a different angle and also from a fresh point and another point in their life."[83] Thus in a country where full-scale reconstruction is nearly nonexistent, this novel method provides an alternate path for approximating the "usable past" so elusive in dance, even as the contemporary choreographer's creative process continues into the future.

REMIXING AND REFRAMING IN OTHER ISRAELI CHOREOGRAPHERS' WORKS

Naharin is not the only Israeli choreographer who has favored remixing and reframing. At the beginning of 2001, shortly after the premiere of *Deca Dance*, one newspaper wondered if a "trend" was sweeping across Israeli companies, noting that the Kibbutz Contemporary Dance Company (KCDC) was also staging an evening composed of excerpts from existing choreography. *Ratel Saka* (2000), by KCDC's artistic director Rami Be'er, was described by the journalist as "a new work that is built from a collage of previous creations by Be'er, that were sewn anew into a complete creation."[84]

Be'er, who like Naharin has been choreographing since the early 1980s, has similarly developed an extensive repertory and won acclaim for his vivid artistic vision; his body of work also contains multiple candidates for revival. And perhaps thanks to the support of the well-established company he leads, Be'er has kept certain dances such as his renowned *Aide Memoire* (1994) in active repertory long after its premiere. But throughout the 2000s he has more frequently opted to revisit his repertory not through large-scale revivals but by remixing excerpts into new frameworks like *Ratel Saka*. Another such framework, *Multifidus* (2004), was created for the Karmiel Dance Festival and drew from the spectrum of Be'er's output, prominently *Real Time* (1991), *Naked City* (1993), *Aide Memoire*, *Makomshehu* (1995), *When Most I Wink* (1996), *On the Edge* (1999), *Screen Saver* (2002), and *Foramen Magnum* (2004). The costuming, set pieces, and distinctive props as well as the internal composition of each section enabled critics and viewers familiar with Be'er's body of work to identify its source, but again the overarching product was novel. One writer marveled that "in an almost mystical fashion [Be'er] creates a new work in front of our eyes."[85] Other reviewers used the metaphor of sewing to describe the choreographer's process. After noting that Be'er created a "new fabric," Tikva Heter Yeshi opined, "What is interesting in this kind of show is the choice of excerpts and the connection that is formed between them."[86] The "new and surprising transitions and connections" caught the attention of fellow writer Lily Abudi, who elaborated, "Sometimes they easily slide from piece to piece, connecting to a previous one as though it sprung out of it; sometimes the scene is cut at once, and immediately a scene from another creation bursts onto the stage."[87] The transitions in Be'er's *Kef Kafim* (2007) are similarly fashioned. Short excerpts from dances including *Real Time*, *Naked City*, *Aide Memoire*, *Makomshehu*, *On the Edge*, *When Most I Wink*, *Screen Saver*, and *Upon Reaching the Sun* (2005) are spliced together, but even though it draws from many of the same works as *Multifidus* this collage takes on quite a different feel as it scraps much of the original costuming and props to focus on the design of the movement itself. Indeed, Be'er describes *Kef Kafim* as "a young, fresh, colorful dance, which emphasizes the joy in dance, movement, energy, rhythm, virtuosity, and poetry acting together in a mix."[88]

Whereas Be'er has remixed and reframed his repertory numerous times in the last decade, other Israeli choreographers are just starting to venture into this territory. As the Suzanne Dellal Centre marked its twentieth anniversary in 2009, its director, Yair Vardi, approached the planning of the celebratory Big Stage festival with a retrospective eye. Besides Be'er's *Aide Memoire* and Batsheva's performance of a *Deca Dance*-type bill, Vardi programmed an evening by Ido Tadmor, who rose to prominence as a choreographer at the center in the mid-1990s.[89] But rather than simply revive one of his popular dances, Tadmor revisited sections from two of his large-scale works, *Sima's Pot* (1995) and *Cell* (1996). The excerpts from *Cell* transitioned directly into those from *Sima's Pot* with no break, and with a special appearance by guest artist Rina Schenfeld at both the start and finish of the evening, the evening was viewed within a single frame.

Noa Dar's first experiment with remixing and reframing, a work called *Arnica* (2007), is more blended in nature. After returning to the stage herself with a short series of solos to Tom Waits's songs in the 2007 Israel Festival, she decided to examine the aspects of a female dancing solo by mining her previous creations. Dar extracted dancer Michal Mualem's solos from *Achilles Tendon* (1999) and *Strange* (2000) and reset material from *Water Music* (2006) on a third dancer, Shira Rinot. Then she arranged them with her new Waits solos, alternating among the three characters, constructing transitions between each dancer's sections, and placing them on an intimate stage with a male guitarist as an interloper. On the one hand, *Arnica* provided an opportunity for what Dar calls "a retrospective look, researching my language and its development over these years." Simultaneously, though, Dar noted that these solos "became something completely different because of the context" of *Arnica*. Placed in a new framework with altered surroundings, the moods and mental states of each character shifted.[90]

Inbal Pinto and Avshalom Pollak launched their remixed work from another starting point. The pair absorbed *Rushes* (2007), a work they created for Pilobolus, into their company's repertory in late 2009, but since it was a shorter dance they needed a companion piece to fill out a full evening of programming. Strapped for time, the creative couple decided to collect excerpts of previously choreographed dances that could, in Pinto's words, "create a dialogue with this piece," and they gathered "all kinds of things that we wanted to retouch or recreate or see how they work together."[91] Through trial and error Pinto and Pollak assembled several selections from *What Good Would the Moon Be* (2004) as well as a quirky duet that had premiered in 1997 and subsequently became part of the Bessie Award-winning *Wrapped* (1998). Although the material itself is older, again, something fresh was created. Pinto recalls, "we took [these excerpts] from their context, and we created something new. It has its own logic and its own world, and it feels like it is one unit and not just parts that are glued to each other." She adds that the final work, which is shown in the evening-length program under the umbrella title *Rushes Plus*, is "something I can relate and connect to today."[92]

CONCLUSIONS AND FURTHER RESEARCH

When the increasingly common approach of remixing and reframing is recognized as a legitimate method of revisiting older works, the landscape of reconstructions in Israel—which at first glance appears to be relatively bare—reveals itself to simply have an alternative shape to that observed in the United States. In Israel's culture of reconstruction, which is contingent on the country's distinctive history of modern and contemporary dance and its particular institutional infrastructure, a unique set of attitudes and approaches to the revival of older works has developed, in turn giving rise to a new palette of possibilities and opportunities for revival. Full-scale reconstructions of dances from earlier eras have been challenging and consequently rare, whether mounted from a single, complete source or pieced together in an approximation from scraps; brought to life through the use of memory, notation, or video; or staged by the choreographer or another person. Yet in the hands of the choreographers themselves, the nation's more recently accumulated contemporary repertory is returning in some format to the concert stage. Establishing a "usable past" may not be the driving force behind these artists' creatively remixed stagings of earlier material. But by using the past to fill new theatrical frames, these choreographers offer audiences a panorama of previous works that, thanks to the ephemeral nature of dance, would be otherwise absent.

As the contemporary dance scene in Israel continues to mature and grow, moving further away from its historical roots and amassing decades of repertory from younger generations of choreographers, questions arise about the evolving place and shape of reconstruction. Will works from the earlier decades of Israeli dance be revisited at all, or will they become irretrievable as the original choreographers, dancers, and audience members pass away? Will full reconstructions of works from the recent past become a more present part of future programming, or will they remain primarily relegated to special events? Will remixing and reframing continue to be the preferred method of revisiting work, and will other choreographers adopt it once they reach a point of reflection on their repertory? The unfolding of revivals in the future, as in the past, is linked to the already existing culture of reconstruction, and the currently held attitudes may well become self-perpetuating as time progresses. Choreographers who enter a dance scene with a vibrant, active culture of reconstruction may perceive revivals as a more natural extension of their creative activities; dance artists in the United States, for instance, may follow the lead of Paul Taylor, who while professing a greater interest in current projects acknowledges the importance of revivals and therefore stages some every season.[93] But in a culture of reconstruction where traditional full-length restaging has not been practiced or encouraged, younger choreographers may not have the wherewithal to give such revivals much consideration. Instead, scanning their dance scene for role models, Israeli artists will find choreographers such as Ohad Naharin and Rami Be'er, who have engaged in remixing and reframing.

There are also issues to examine further about the deeper connection of a culture of reconstruction to the wider culture of a given country. How much of Israel's culture of reconstruction is purely reflective of the inner workings of the dance field there, and how much of it is affected by the larger society's approach toward history and culture? Could the popular practice of remixing and reframing be a product, in part, of a broader Israeli emphasis on the new and an attraction to innovation? And finally, there is likely more to be explored about the postmodernist theoretical underpinnings of remixing and reframing as well as the ramifications of these intertwined practices not only within Israel but also on a global scale. The variations created through the updating of excerpts in reframings may complicate future attempts to revive the original full-length sources of these remixed parts. When reconstructing a work like Naharin's *Kyr*, for example, should the revival include the changes made within the framework of *Kyr/Zina 2010* or remain loyal to the first production? And what might it mean to reconstruct a reframed work like *Deca Dance* that is fashioned from constantly changing components and thus has existed in numerous forms?

Despite the potential challenges, the field of reconstruction has much to gain through the approach of remixing and reframing. The creation of a usable past for dance must begin in the present, ideally with the involvement of contemporary choreographers along with those stagers whose interests lie in works of a more distant era. Not all choreographers can or will engage in traditional start-to-finish revivals of their older works. For those active choreographers who prefer to invest their energies in an ongoing creative process, remixing and reframing may offer a more palatable option for revisiting old dances anew. By reframing the recent past, choreographers can simultaneously embrace the ephemeral character of dance and enact their own changes while keeping their repertory alive in a refreshed, relevant form for rising generations of dancers and audiences alike.

NOTES

1. Shades of Dance operated on a competition format from its second edition in 1987 through 2005 and again in 2011. But in 2007 and 2009, the platform for young choreographers was held without a contest.

2. The restaged works were Liat Dror and Nir Ben Gal's duet *Two Room Apartment* (1987); Noa Wertheim and Adi Sha'al's duet *Vertigo* (1992); Ronit Ziv's duet *Rose Can't Wait* (1999); and Barak Marshall's *Aunt Leah* (1995), a group work. Although the playbill itself listed these four works as the winning compositions from their respective years—and the few newspaper articles about this program also highlighted these as prize-winning dances—an examination of archival records held at the Dance Library of Israel reveals that only Barak Marshall's *Aunt Leah* and Ronit Ziv's *Rose Can't Wait* won awards at Shades of Dance. Nir Ben Gal was indeed noted as the best choreographer at the 1987 festival, but he was given this distinction for *Wrong Catch*, created without his partner Liat Dror and performed by Batsheva Dance Company. Ultimately, though, it was Dror and Ben Gal's *Two Room Apartment* that won most of the critical acclaim, and only a few years after its premiere at Shades of Dance it was mentioned in newspapers and subsequent playbills as the winner of the 1987 festival. Similarly, Noa Wertheim and Adi Sha'al won first place at the 1993 Shades of Dance (after the 1992 Shades of Dance festival was postponed), but they received this honor for *Contact Lenses* and not for *Vertigo*, which instead garnered them the On the Way to London Award at a previous competition.

3. Writing in 1994, Roger Copeland commented on the prevalence of reconstructions on the American stage. Introducing the proceedings of the 1997 conference on reconstruction held at the University of Surrey Roehampton—which encompassed both America and Europe—Stephanie Jordan notes that "the reconstruction of lost work has burgeoned into a major enterprise." Although some European countries may also have a significant amount of reconstructive activity, this chapter will focus on the United States as a counterpoint to Israel. See Roger Copeland, "Reflections on Revival and Reconstruction," *Dance Theatre Journal* 11, no. 3 (1994): 18; Jordan's preface to *Preservation Politics: Dance Revived, Reconstructed, Remade*, ed. Stephanie Jordan (London: Dance Books, 2000).

4. The existing literature on reconstruction includes an array of contested terminology. Authors such as Ann Hutchinson Guest, Selma Jeanne Cohen, and Susan Manning have proposed definitions for terms, including reconstructions, revivals, reproductions, re-creations, reinventions, and restagings, relating each term to particular methodologies and circumstances, but the exact meanings of the terms have not been agreed on. Consequently, this article draws from the terminology without connecting each word to a specific approach. The term *reconstructive practices* is used as a broad umbrella phrase that reflects a spectrum of methodologies for reconstruction and also implies a range of outcomes that stretch beyond a full-length, strictly faithful remounting of original choreography. For various definitions, see Ann Hutchinson Guest, "Is Authenticity to Be Had?" in *Preservation Politics: Dance Revived, Reconstructed, Remade*, ed. Stephanie Jordan (London: Dance Books, 2000), 65–66; Helen Thomas, "Reconstruction and Dance as Embodied Textual Practice" in *Rethinking Dance History: A Reader*, ed. Alexandra Carter (London: Routledge, 2004), 36–37; Susan Manning, "Perspectives in Reconstruction: Keynote Panel" in *Dance Reconstructed: Modern Dance Art Past, Present, and Future* (New Brunswick, NJ: 1992), 15–16.

5. Copeland, "Reflections on Revival," 18. The article was adapted from a presentation given at the 1992 Dance ReConstructed conference.

6. Although the culture of reconstruction surrounding American ballet may well influence and interact with the culture of reconstruction within American modern dance, this chapter hones in on American modern dance to provide a more direct counterpoint for the Israeli modern and contemporary dance scene.

7. For more on a "usable past," see Copeland, "Reflections on Revival," 18; and Thomas, "Reconstruction and Dance," 33.

8. Kenneth Archer and Millicent Hodson, "Confronting Oblivion: Keynote Address and Lecture Demonstration on Reconstructing Ballets" in *Preservation Politics: Dance Revived, Reconstructed, Remade*, ed. Stephanie Jordan (London: Dance Books, 2000), 1.

9. Sarah Rubidge cites both Doris Humphrey and Martha Graham as either orchestrating or overseeing revivals of their earlier works, in "Reconstruction and its Problems," *Dance Theatre Journal* 12, no. 1 (1995): 32.

10. Dance Notation Bureau, "About the DNB," http://www.dancenotation.org/ (accessed June 3, 2010).

11. Early Humphrey-Weidman dancer Ernestine (Henoch) Stodelle reconstructed *Quasi Waltz* in the 1980s from a silent black-and-white film of Doris Humphrey dancing the solo outdoors, and that work is held in the NYPL collection. The work was subsequently notated in Labanotation by Muriel Topaz, facilitating additional stagings, such as one in 2006 by the author of this chapter, and the dance has been further documented on video.

12. The practical and philosophical concerns of restaging from video frequently surfaced at Dance Reconstructed: Modern Dance Art Past, Present, and Future, a conference held at Rutgers University in New Jersey in 1992. The proceedings reveal that speakers, including Sali Ann Kriegsman and Stuart Hodes, referred to or more deeply examined video in their talks, while video was a recurring subject in the panel Strategies for Documentation and Retrieval.

13. See Heritage Preservation: The National Institute for Conservation, "First Lady Announces $30 Million in Save America's Treasures Grants," http://www.heritagepreservation.org/news/grants1.htm (accessed May 30, 2010).

14. National Endowment for the Arts, "Recent Grants," http://www.arts.gov/grants/recent/index.html (accessed June 3, 2010).

15. Ruth Eshel, *Lirkod im hahalom: Rashit hamachol ha'omanuti b'eretz Yisrael 1920–1964* [Dancing with the Dream: The Development of Artistic Dance in Israel 1920–1964] (Tel Aviv: Sifriat Poalim and the Dance Library of Israel, 1991); from the English synopsis, n.p.

16. Ibid.

17. Ibid.

18. Ibid., 48.

19. Ibid., from the English synopsis, n.p.

20. Reviews from Batsheva's 1970 and 1972 tours indicate that the Israeli-made repertory did not always distinguish itself either in quality or style from the company's American-made repertory. Frances Herridge of the *New York Post* wrote on December 16, 1970, that Rina Schenfeld "[expressed] herself in the Graham manner" upon seeing her *Curtains*. On February 8, 1972, Anna Kisselgoff of the *New York Times* noted in "Dance: Two by Batsheva" that both the Canadian Linda Rabin and the Israeli Mirali Sharon were using an "all-purpose modern-dance

technique." In "Graham is Good—But Then What?" on December 24, 1972, Clive Barnes of the *New York Times* called the few Israeli works "apprentice efforts."

21. Ruth Eshel notes two distinct periods in the development of Israeli concert dance and proposes that a third era may be beginning in the 1990s, in her article "1992—A Year of Transition," *Israel Dance*, no. 2 (April 1993): 63.

22. Of all the Israeli choreographers who created dances for Batsheva in its first decade and a half, only Rina Schenfeld is still active in the concert dance scene in 2010. Rather than return to pieces that she made in the 1960s to 1990s, she continues to produce a new dance almost every year.

23. Ruth Eshel, telephone interview with the author, July 7, 2010.

24. Ibid.

25. Aleskowsky and dancers from Kraus's company revived three works: *Schubert's Dream* (1944) was performed by Moshe Efrati's Kol Demama Dance Company; *Allegro Barbaro* (1938) was performed by Batsheva Dance Company; and *Carousel* (1942) was performed by the Kibbutz Dance Company (now Kibbutz Contemporary Dance Company). The program Tribute to Gertrud Kraus was performed twice within the framework of the Israel Festival. Despite Batsheva's public performance of *Allegro Barbaro*, a comprehensive listing of the company's repertory published in *Israel Dance* in October 1994 does not include any reference to Kraus's work. The Kibbutz Dance Company did perform *Carousel* again as well as *Schubert's Dream* in Vienna at the Tanz '90 festival on a program called "Expressionismus"; however, it is unclear whether this group or Kol Demama performed the works within the framework of their regular repertory performances.

26. Eshel, interview. Eshel recounts that Yardena Cohen had wanted to reconstruct some dances on her but then repeatedly postponed rehearsals. She suggests that Cohen heard what had happened with Aleskovsky's reconstructions of Kraus's work and subsequently became afraid about returning to her own work.

27. Naomi Perlov, interview with the author, Tel Aviv, July 18, 2010.

28. Ruth Eshel, "And What Shall Become of Bat-Dor," *Israel Dance*, no. 12 (Winter 1998): 19. Eshel notes that funding from Bat-Dor's patron, Bethsabee de Rothschild, was dwindling by this point, and the company's style seemed dated in contrast to that of Batsheva, the Kibbutz Contemporary Dance Company, and fringe artists.

29. Most professional dancers in Israel do not receive their modern training in university but instead in performing arts high schools and independent studios. Again, some of these dance programs, such as Naomi Perlov's Maslool at Bikurei Haitim, expose their students to snippets of older works in a repertory class. Yet the dancers' performance experience emphasizes more contemporary choreography by currently working artists.

30. Noa Eshkol, foreword to *Language of Shape and Movement* by John G. Harries (Holon, Israel: Movement Society, 1983), vii.

31. Noa Eshkol, *Tomlinson's Gavot* (Israel: Tel Aviv University, 1985).

32. Perlov, interview.

33. Gaby Aldor, telephone interview with the author, July 2, 2010. In her article "Sand, sand everywhere…" for the *Jerusalem Post* on August 2, 1990, Sraya Shapiro also laments, "What a pity that the video camera was invented too late to capture the Ornsteins' charm!"

34. Giora Manor, ed., *Gertrud Kraus* (Tel Aviv: Sifriat Poalim and the Dance Library of Israel, 1988), 60.

35. Rena Gluck, "Batsheva Dance Company 1964–1980: My Story" (computer files of unpublished English manuscript, 2006), Chapter 5, 123, and Chapter 8, 220. In e-mail correspondence from September 30, 2010, Gluck notes several dances that fell into this category, notably Martha Graham's *Cave of the Heart, Sarabande, The Learning Process,* and *Embattled Garden*; Sophie Maslow's *The Village I Knew* and *Neither Rest Nor Harbor*; John Cranko's *Ebony Concerto*; and Herbert Ross's *Caprichos.*

36. Rena Gluck, e-mail message to the author, September 30, 2010.

37. Amira Mayroz, interview with the author, Tel Aviv, June 24, 2010.

38. Aldor, telephone interview.

39. Mayroz, interview.

40. The conference closest to the topic in Israel was an international congress of movement notation in 1984.

41. Giora Manor, "Gertrud Kraus," in Program: Israel Festival, Jerusalem 1988, Tribute to Gertrud Kraus, file no. 121.18, Gertrud Kraus, Dance Library of Israel–Archive, Tel Aviv.

42. Ibid., 51.

43. Giora Manor, "The Future Leads to the Past," in undated booklet for Ethnic Arts Center, Inbal, featuring *The Story of Ruth* and *The Song of Songs,* file no. 111.4C, Inbal Mercaz Etni Rav-Tchumi [Inbal Ethnic Arts Center], Dance Library of Israel–Archive, Tel Aviv.

44. Giora Manor, "Shoshelet Ornstein" [Ornstein dynasty], *Davar,* November 15, 1991. This and all translations are by the author with the assistance of Tal Galili unless otherwise noted.

45. Eshel, telephone interview. Eshel intended to relearn this avant-garde solo directly from video. Yet as she watched the footage, she realized that she could not simply reenact what she had done nearly three decades ago; instead, she remarks, she felt that she "could enrich it much more" and decided that the revival "has to reflect what I am today."

46. The daughter of famed Habima actor Yehoshua Bertonoff, Deborah Bertonoff studied ballet in Moscow before immigrating to Palestine with her family and performed the "Beggars' Dance" with the theater company's *The Dybbuk* while in her young teens. She went on to study modern dance in Berlin and London and had a successful career as a solo dancer performing character sketches, particularly during the 1930s and 1940s. In the 1980s, Bertonoff returned to "Beggars' Dance" at a congress in New York and subsequently at the Ninth Conference of Jewish Studies in Jerusalem and for festivities celebrating Habima's seventieth anniversary.

47. Barak Marshall, telephone interview with the author, June 23, 2010.

48. Perlov, interview.

49. Marshall.

50. Ibid. As Marshall notes, *Aunt Leah* offered this continuity not just stylistically but also historically, since it was originally built on dancers from Inbal in 1995.

51. Angela Kane, "Issues of Authenticity and Identity in the Restaging of Paul Taylor's *Airs,*" in *Preservation Politics: Dance Revived, Reconstructed, Remade,* ed. Stephanie Jordan (London: Dance Books, 2000), 73–74.

52. Taylor quoted in Kane, 74.

53. Marshall, interview.

54. Nir Ben Gal, telephone interview with the author, June 30, 2010. Ben Gal and his partner Liat Dror have made a definitive break from their earlier repertory, leaving the contemporary dance establishment in Tel Aviv behind for the quiet of the desert, founding a dance center called Adama, and developing a gentler approach for moving and creating dances. Now perceiving an

element of cruelty in *Two Room Apartment*, Ben Gal was initially resistant to the prospect of reconstructing ten minutes from the dance for the Shades of Dance retrospective; he chooses not to teach *Two Room Apartment* or his other early works to others.

55. Inbal Pinto, interview with the author, Tel Aviv, June 15, 2010.

56. Noa Dar, telephone interview with the author, July 21, 2010.

57. Ohad Naharin, interview with the author, Tel Aviv, July 20, 2010.

58. Ora Brafman, "Dance Review," *Jerusalem Post*, November 6, 2008.

59. Naharin, interview, July 20, 2010.

60. Ohad Naharin, press conference for *Three*, Tel Aviv, January 27, 2010. Naharin also discussed the idea of a premiere as a beginning of an ongoing process during an interview with the author in Tel Aviv on June 2, 2010.

61. Ohad Naharin, interview with the author, Tel Aviv, June 2, 2010.

62. Naharin, interview, July 20, 2010.

63. Naharin, interview, June 2, 2010.

64. This twin endeavor of remixing and reframing has especially characterized Naharin's work for the Batsheva Ensemble. To build a repertory that is suitable for the ensemble's target young audiences but remains artistically challenging for dancers and viewers alike, Naharin has frequently retooled material from his recent creations for the Batsheva Dance Company. *Zachacha* (1998) combines excerpts from *Perpetuum* (1993), *Anaphase* (1993), and *Sabotage Baby* (1997). The ensemble's popular *Kamuyot* (2003) takes much of its inspiration from *Mamootot* (2003), which is similarly performed in the intimacy of the studio, as well as from *Moshe* (1999). And *Seder* (2007) draws much of its choreography from *Telophaza* (2006), *Three* (2005), *Furo* (2006), *MAX* (2007), and *George & Zalman* (2006). Also in the Batsheva Ensemble's repertory—though not intended for school or family audiences—is *Kaamos + Love* (2009), which features not only Naharin's *Kaamos* (1994) and excerpts from *Seder* (2007) and *Passmezzo* (1988) but also a significantly reworked rendition of *Love* (2003) by Sharon Eyal, Batsheva's house choreographer.

65. Naharin, interview, July 20, 2010.

66. Ibid.

67. Ohad Naharin, quoted in "Israel's Batsheva Dance Company Makes Its Philadelphia Debut with Deca Dance," *Dance Journal*, January 17, 2009, http://philadelphiadance.org/blog/2009/01/17/israels-batsheva-dance-company-makes-its-philadelphia-debut-with-deca-dance/print/ (accessed July 30, 2010).

68. Although Batsheva Dance Company and the Batsheva Ensemble have presented several permutations of *Deca Dance*, the New York-based Cedar Lake Contemporary Ballet took one variation of the dance into its repertory and continues to perform it under the title *Decadance 2007*. Several other groups, among them Nederlands Dans Theater, Les Grands Ballets Canadiens, Hubbard Street Dance Chicago, and students at Juilliard, have performed *Minus One*, *Minus 16*, and *Minus 7*, a series of related works ranging from twenty to ninety minutes that draw from a similar pool of excerpts as *Deca Dance*.

69. "Echad Mi Yodea" was originally from *Kyr* (1990) before becoming a part of *Anaphase* (1993), in which the dancers wear black suits rather than more work-like outfits of shorts and shirts. It is this later version that is performed in *Deca Dance*.

70. Alice Kaderlan, "'Deca Dance' is an extraordinary feast of movement," *Seattle Post-Intelligencer*, March 19, 2004, http://www.seattlepi.com/classical/165376_bathsheva19q.html (accessed July 29, 2010); "M'hamidbar l'New York u'behazara" [From the desert to New York and back],

Col-Bi (Be'ersheva), September 11, 2003; Lily Abudi, "Rokdim collage" [Dancing collage], *Malabs* (Petach Tikva), January 15, 2010.

71. "Ohad Naharin al 'Super-Deca-Dance'" [Ohad Naharin on 'Super-Deca-Dance'], *Fun Time*, November 2003.

72. Abudi, "Rokdim collage."

73. Vera Midgelow, "Revisiting History in Postmodernism: Resurrecting *Giselle*…again…and again!" in *Preservation Politics: Dance Revived, Reconstructed, Remade*, ed. Stephanie Jordan (London: Dance Books, 2000), 220.

74. Naharin, interview, June 2, 2010. *Project 5* was initially created for Iyar Elezra, Shani Garfinkel, Bosmat Nossan, Michal Sayfan, and Bobbi Smith; due to injury, Ariel Freedman replaced Garfinkel in the premiere. The five dancers were ultimately accepted into the main company. *Project 5* was subsequently performed by different female casts, and in 2010, all-male casts also began dancing the work.

75. Ibid.

76. Ora Brafman, "Dance Review," *Jerusalem Post*, November 6, 2008.

77. Ibid.

78. Naharin, interview, July 20, 2010.

79. Outside of full or partial revivals of the original works, some sections used in *Kyr/Zina 2010* have been performed more recently, such as "Echad Mi Yodea" in *Deca Dance* and a part of *Z/na* called "Kaamos," which entered the Batsheva Ensemble's repertory in 2009 as part of the framework *Kaamos + Love* (itself another example of remixing).

80. Naharin, interview, July 20, 2010.

81. Ibid.

82. Naharin, interview, July 20, 2010; Ohad Naharin, press conference for *Kyr/Zina 2010*, Tel Aviv, February 22, 2010.

83. Naharin, interview, July 20, 2010.

84. "Gam lekibbutzit collage mishelah" [The Kibbutzit has its own collage], *Tzomet Hasharon*, January 12, 2001.

85. Eliakim Yaron, "Yofi mehamem" [Stunning beauty], *Maariv*, November 23, 2004.

86. Tikva Heter Yeshi, "Mayim mitoch habe'er" [Water from the well], *Yediot Ahronot*, December 15, 2004.

87. Lily Abudi, "Kesem shel olam" [Magic of a world], *Achbar Ha'ir*, December 1, 2005.

88. Rami Be'er quoted in Eyal Ochana, "Mix Me" (Hebrew article with English title), *Achbar Col Ha'ir* (Jerusalem), February 7, 2008.

89. Nati Ornen, "Rikuday shnot ha-20" [Dances of the '20s], *Achbar Ha'ir*, March 2009.

90. Dar, telephone interview.

91. Pinto, interview.

92. Ibid.

93. Kane, 74.

There are certain things in Hollywood, however, which are not hampered by restrictions. One is the censors.[1]

4

The Body Censored

DANCE, MORALITY, AND THE PRODUCTION CODE DURING THE GOLDEN AGE OF THE FILM MUSICAL

Betsy Cooper

VIOLATING THE CODE

WHEN VETERAN DANCER, choreographer, and theater director Jack Cole entered the Hollywood studio system as a dance director, one of his first assignments was to recreate a Seminole Indian ritual number with Betty Grable for the musical comedy *Moon over Miami* (1941), in which he also performed. After shooting was complete, Cole learned that he had violated four provisions of the Motion Picture Production Code, and that his choreography was deemed too erotic by the Production Code Administration (PCA)— the industry's internal censorship bureau—to be viewed by movie goers. One of these transgressions involved exposing his navel. The code prohibited "dancing costumes intended to permit undue exposure," and a strict taboo against showing any "scenes of child birth in fact or in silhouette," resulting in a common practice of having to cover the navel with tape and then apply body makeup to hide the tape. Cole also learned that a man and woman could not lie prone on the floor together; at least one partner had to stand. Cole's highly stylized Seminole ritual also included "some kind of betrothal Indian thing where the girl got a crack on the face"[2]; that didn't go over too well with the censors either. The editors went to work cutting the Seminole number to shreds in order to get a seal of approval from the PCA. Yet even after extensive cuts, Cole's choreography was screened in only four of forty-eight states.[3]

97

THE PRODUCTION CODE: HOLLYWOOD'S TEN COMMANDMENTS

From 1934 to 1968 the PCA, instituted as a means to keep the federal government out of the movie business, operated as an internal censorship bureau for the motion picture industry.[4] Expected to ensure that the content of films would not threaten or diminish the moral fiber of movie audiences, PCA censors were entrusted to keep all morally, socially and politically suspect content out of motion pictures. "The sympathy of the audience should never be thrown to the side of crime, wrong-doing, evil or sin," such as "when evil is made to appear attractive and alluring and good is made to appear unattractive."[5] Thus scenes of passion were treated with the greatest delicacy so as not to excite the baser emotions. The code eliminated from the screen overt displays of intimacy, and shunned as immoral any sexual union outside of marriage. Without the PCA's seal of approval, motion picture studios faced serious impediments to mass distribution and were thus more susceptible to significant financial losses.

The campaign to "improve" the content of films was fueled largely by morality groups and Catholic organizations such as the National Legion of Decency.[6] The Motion Picture Production Code was co-authored in 1930 by the Jesuit priest Daniel A. Lord[7] and the lay Catholic Martin Quigley. Its tenets, stewarded initially by the Studio Relations Committee, and subsequently under the staunch leadership of Joseph Breen, a devout and politically active Catholic, were scripted to ensure that films would become 20th-century morality plays for the masses.[8] The crusade to clean up the motion picture industry was a fairly straightforward and systematic affair with regard to the spoken and sung word. It proved to be far more ambiguous when it came to controlling the dancing body in the Hollywood musical.

THE BODY CENSORED (OR NOT): IMPLEMENTATION
OF THE CODE UNDER JOSEPH BREEN'S PCA

This chapter looks at how censors appraised dance performance and choreography in film musicals made between 1934 and 1955,[9] in particular how a perception of "decent" or "correct" dance stemming from classical and Renaissance notions of moral virtue influenced the manner in which Hollywood's Production Code Administration implemented the tenets of the production code. A central query in this chapter is to understand to what degree the authors of the code, and those who enforced it, perceived and responded to the dancing body as a locus of meaning within the film's narrative. Were the PCA's requests for censorship informed by the meaning(s) embodied within choreography, or factors completely ancillary to choreographic intent and performance, and by what mechanisms were some dances able to transgress the code's guiding principles without being excised from a film?

Section VII of the motion picture production code states:

1. Dances suggesting or representing sexual actions or indecent passion are forbidden.
2. Dances, which emphasize indecent movement, are to be regarded as obscene.

The reasoning given is as follows:

Dancing in general is recognized as an art and as a beautiful form of expressing human emotions. But dances which suggest or represent sexual actions, whether performed solo or with two or more, dances intended to excite the emotional reaction of an audience, dances with movement of the breasts, excessive body movements while the feet are stationary, violate decency and are wrong.[10]

A close reading of film musicals ranging from 1938 to 1955 indicates that PCA censors focused their attentions on the most blatant and superficial transgressions of the production code when assessing dance numbers. The skimpiest costumes, the fullest shimmies, and the raunchiest bumps and grinds were excised, while censors passed over choreography that violated the letter and moral intent of the code when it exhibited an aesthetic stemming from Western concert dance, typically a blend of classical ballet and modern dance forms. The PCA's seeming failure to subject choreography to a consistent and comparable level of scrutiny, as that applied to dialogue and dramatic action, is an indication that Joseph Breen and his staff tended to view dance as a decorative element of film, underestimating its power to stimulate an audience on some level: emotional, intellectual, kinesthetic, or moral. But this is only part of the reason some film choreography evaded the censors' hatchets. Ultimately, the operation of a culturally (and implicitly racially) biased aesthetic criteria had an impact on how choreography was perceived and appraised on a moral basis by censors. Under Breen's watch, the scenic setting of a dance as well as the demeanor of the characters became important means by which censors gauged moral acceptability.

SELF-REGULATION: THE LESSER OF TWO (OR MORE) EVILS

In order to appreciate more fully the complex relationship between the PCA and the Hollywood studio system, it is important to understand that industry self-regulation was the result of financial concerns exacerbated by the onset of the Great Depression. Motion picture executives balked at the notion that they bore any responsibility for public morality, but competing social, political, and economic pressures forced their hand. They endorsed the motion picture production code because it was the most expedient means for the studios to anticipate and circumvent more stringent and potentially costly interference by the federal government, state censorship boards, and morality groups.[11]

The Catholic Church had been at war with the motion picture industry since the early days of silent film; relations worsened with the introduction of talking pictures.[12] Fed up with the ineffectual performance of the Studio Relations Committee, precursor to the PCA, the Church and its Legion of Decency appealed to millions of Americans across all denominations, threatening a massive boycott of all morally indecent films; seven to nine million parishioners joined the campaign, many in large urban centers. With the advent of the New Deal and the creation of the National Recovery Act (NRA), the motion picture industry, like other American businesses, also faced the prospect of federal regulation.[13] By 1933, studio moguls were growing increasingly concerned that federal bureaucrats might instigate both economic and moral oversight of the motion picture industry, interference they actively sought to avoid.[14] Financiers also had an influence in the adoption of the code. Studios had turned to investment bankers for the purchase and expansion of sound technology in the late 1920s. Bankers also financed productions and purchased new theaters. Seeking a guarantee on their investments, they viewed the production code as a means to promote more financial stability in the motion picture industry because it forestalled government intervention, which could considerably delay the release and distribution of a film.[15]

With the creation of the Production Code Administration under Breen's firm leadership, no film could begin production prior to script approval by his office. Furthermore, the PCA had the authority to prevent any film not awarded their seal of approval from being distributed to any theater owned by, or affiliated with, the Motion Picture Producers and Distributors of America (MPPDA), which constituted the majority of movie theaters in the country.[16] Yet despite the administration's internal mechanisms for controlling content and distribution, the PCA was first and foremost an industry sponsored institution committed to promoting the profitability of Hollywood films. According to Jeffrey Shurlock, Breen's assistant, the PCA's task was to ensure that the elements within a picture were managed (through rewrites and reshooting) so that the film would receive a seal of approval, not ban it from distribution, destroying any money-making potential.[17]

"I CAN'T QUITE VISUALIZE IT": SELF-REGULATION
AND THE PROBLEM OF DANCE

Though self-regulation was built into the movie making process, the PCA was involved primarily in the pre-production stages of the film, at the level of text, which included plot synopsis, treatments, all drafts of a screenplay, and song lyrics. PCA staff met daily to review material submitted by the studios. Within a day or two of these meetings, the studios would receive memos outlining those parts of the script, lyrics, and designs considered unacceptable under the provisions of the code. The process involved a system of give and take among producers, writers, and directors, leading to revisions, alterations, and cuts.[18] The PCA's focus on textual analysis is likely a contributing factor to why the content of choreographic sequences received less scrutiny than other aspects of film content; it is difficult to put down in words the elements of a dance such that a layman can envision and comprehend them.

In a 1994 interview, Gene Kelly referred to his own frustration of communicating his "dance as narrative" concepts to studio heads:

> The executives didn't know how to read a musical script—they still don't! There would be a line like "I love you" which was followed by three minutes of song and dance and they never quite understood that. One time, somebody upstairs insisted that we write out the dances, so I got together with other choreographers and wrote out – glissade, arabesque, boy takes girl in his arms, lifts her down into a fish. It's a classic dance language, but of course it was Latin to them and we soon went back to the old way.[19]

In a scene from *Singin' in the Rain,* Kelly pointedly pokes fun at the studio executives' inability to understand the language of dance. It comes at the conclusion of the "Broadway Ballet," the film's culminating dance sequence. The scene cuts from the end of the mass choreographic spectacle back to the studio screening room at which point Kelly, portraying Don Lamont, says to the studio executive, "Well, that's the idea of the number, RF. What do you think of it?" To which RF responds quizzically, "I can't quite visualize it. I'll have to see it in film first."[20]

LOCATION IS EVERYTHING: THE IMPORTANCE OF ATMOSPHERE AND DEMEANOR

In addition to script development and song lyrics, PCA censors appraised certain non-verbal aspects of a film during pre-production. In 1935, Breen reported to his boss, Will Hays, that an increase to his staff enabled the PCA to undertake a more extensive review of costumes and set construction.[21] In Breen's report to Hays the following year, he stressed the importance of atmosphere in the evaluation of films, stating, "Low tone alone may render a whole production unacceptable. The location of scenes, and the conduct, the demeanor, the attitude of the players enter very much into the question of the flavor of the appeal of the right or the wrong presented."[22] The "flavor" of these elements became crucially important to how PCA censors assessed the moral acceptability of the dancing body, such that choreographic intent was secondary to the relative measure of vice or virtue of the locale and its denizens.

DANCE AS DECORATION: JACK COLE'S FRUSTRATIONS
WITH THE STUDIO SYSTEM

Though Breen does not mention choreography explicitly in either of these reports, we
know that dance was frequently used to provide atmosphere or "local color" to a scene, as
attested by dance critic Arthur Knight in a 1959 *Dance Magazine* article on the inclusion
of dance in the non-musical film:

> One of the chief functions of dance, at least so far as the film makers are concerned,
> would seem to be the quick establishment of a locale or an atmosphere.... Rarely
> are they functional or built integrally into the plot.... Even when these atmospheric
> dances are inserted somewhere along the way... one is often genuinely surprised to
> note that the credits include a choreographer (frequently well known). What hap-
> pens, all too often, is that in the preparation of the picture the producer decides that
> a nice, lively dance number could be used at this point in the story for color, visual
> variety and production values. The choreographer is hired, handed an outline of the
> plot, told to come up with something extraordinary... a memorable highpoint of
> the film. Enchanted with the prospect, he creates an eight-minute sequence;
> complete in its self... the producer is delighted. They assemble a hundred or so of
> the best dancers in Hollywood and rehearse the sequence for six weeks, another
> two weeks is spent on the shooting. And what ultimately comes out on the screen
> is perhaps ninety seconds of assorted leaps and turns, broken by lines of dialogue
> between the hero and his sweetheart. "The picture ran too long," is the usual expla-
> nation and the first thing that gets cut is the dance sequence.[23]

Knight's commentary supports the notion that choreography was an undervalued feature
of many films, given minimal thought until filming had begun. Jack Cole, dance director
for 20th Century-Fox, Columbia, MGM, and United Artists, corroborates this view. Initially a dancer with the Denishawn and Humphrey-Weidman companies before turning
to commercial theater, Cole created his own unique brand of theatrical jazz dance by
blending elements of Latin American, Caribbean, Asian, East Indian and African
American vernacular dance forms with modern dance, introducing the use of complex
and precise movement isolations into his work. Cole's "melting pot of 'ethnic impressions' "[24] defied easy classification. In a 1948 *New York Times* review, John Martin noted:

> Cole fits into no easy category. He is not of the ballet, yet the technique he has
> established is probably the strictest and the most spectacular anywhere to be found.
> He is not an orthodox "modern" dancer, for though his movement is extremely
> individual, it employs a great deal of objective material—from the Orient, from the
> Caribbean, from Harlem.... His art is strictly high-tension; nervous, gaunt, flagel-
> lant, yet with an opulent sensuous beauty that sets up a violent cross current of

conflict at its very source.... When he has finished he leaves you limp with vicarious kinesthetic experience.[25]

According to dancer/actress Ann Miller, Cole absolutely rejuvenated dancing through a renewed sense of heightened and sexually charged physicality. He taught the audience how a dance should feel—that a dancer worked with the whole body and whole being, not just steps.[26] He "asked dancers to use their hips, groins and their libidos."[27] The animalistic quality and "cool" sensuality of his choreography caused havoc with the PCA and state censorship boards.

Cole was exacting and meticulous in his approach to training dancers and staging choreography. He advocated for more collaboration between film director and dance director, and for greater input in the overall artistic vision of musical films, including camera setups and the connection of dance sequences to narrative structure. He was outspoken in his criticism of the motion picture studios' general disregard for dance: "Everybody considers dancing as merely decorative—and that's how it's staged in a theatre or shot in a studio...We move just enough so as not to disturb the composition of the set. This convention can be traced back to Busby Berkeley and his passion for making wallpaper with real people...the trouble is that outside of ballet, nothing intelligent is ever expected of dancers or dance."[28]

Cole's comments stem from years of experience working within the Hollywood studio system. His insights, however, point to a broadly institutionalized bias toward "high art," specifically concert dance, that appears to have been widespread and insidious, as evinced by Martin's comments in the *New York Times*: "In the type of dance he [Cole] has created thus far for musical shows, night clubs and movies, he has had no opportunity to concern himself with content and substance, but if he were really to turn his hand to the creation of an independent ballet or to the serious repertory of the concert field, his almost fanatical concentration and creative power would probably result in some pretty staggering things."[29]

Martin's critique of Cole is glowing throughout: he sees an "undeniable genius" in his compositions, yet summarily dismisses the substantive nature of Cole's choreographic work because it is not for the concert stage.[30] The serious repertory to which Martin refers was almost exclusively the domain of the white dancer, whereas dancers of color, in particular African American performers, were "confined almost exclusively to the inertias of the entertainment field," leading one to infer that commercial dance work was perceived as a "lesser" and un-intellectual activity based on a "racialized" and racist concept of the genre and its history.

BALLET'S RISING STAR IN HOLLYWOOD

Though it is debatable whether studio heads deemed ballet an intellectual activity, there is ample evidence to suggest that the glamour and mystique of the female ballet dancer and aesthetic provenance of the *danse d'école* brought a desired cachet to the popular medium of film.[31] The popularization of ballet in Hollywood films began in the 1930s following a wave of Russian dance émigrés led by Pavlova and other members of Diaghilev's Ballets Russes, most notably George Balanchine, whose impact on the standard of training and the establishment of ballet as an American rather than European art form was profound and unparalleled. With the availability of more polished classical dancers, ballet was seen as an untapped source of commercial entertainment, attracting the attention of entrepreneurs from both stage and screen.[32]

When Balanchine arrived in the United States in 1933 to establish a school and company, he found Broadway and Hollywood more hospitable terrain for his choreographic inventions than the concert stage or opera house. More broadly, the perception of classical ballet in America was paradoxical; John Martin, dance critic and chief apologist for the modern dance, referred to Balanchine's repertory as "evidences of the decadence of the classic tradition as it is found in certain European environments, examples of what someone has aptly called 'Riviera esthetics'."[33] Ballet was revered and alluring, yet deemed incongruous with the pace and substance of the American experience and viewed by many with suspicion as an effete and elitist practice because of its European heritage and aristocratic trappings.

With its high-art status and exotic mystique, the inclusion of ballet could lend both variety and prestige to a musical theater production. The classical form, however, was often satirized in the films, a device that accentuated the divide between ballet's aristocratic traditions and elitist patrons and the populist roots and mass appeal of American musical theater dance. Numerous musicals from the 1930s, 1940s, and 1950s exploited this high-art, popular-entertainment binary by juxtaposing ballet choreography with an array of vernacular dance forms.[34] One of the earliest uses of this device in a film is seen in Balanchine's *Romeo and Juliet* ballet from the 1938 backstage musical *The Goldwyn Follies*.[35] In this musical sub-genre, dance and song are presented using the conventions of the vaudeville stage revue or within the context of "putting on a show"; neither element is intrinsically connected to character or plot development, and rather than move the story toward resolution the insertion of a song and dance number more often "disrupts" the narrative structure of the film. The backstage musical, as typified by Busby Berkeley's popular films from the 1930s,[36] features the aspiring chorus girl as heroine, performing tap routines along with lavishly orchestrated dance spectacles composed of highly synchronized drill-like pageantry. The dances are intended to tantalize and delight the eye.

Goldwyn Follies diverges somewhat from this formula: the film depicts a Hollywood producer who selects a forthright young woman, "Miss Humanity," to critique his film from the perspective on the "common (wo)man." Symbolic of the ordinary American moviegoer, Miss Humanity shares her refreshing insights as she and the producer watch an eclectic array of songs, dances, and comedy skits. The movie audience is meant to assume Miss Humanity's perspective; thus Balanchine's dances for the *Goldwyn Follies* are not filmed from a backstage or performer perspective. They are self-contained performances in which the audience is made aware of the dance's site, and their location in relationship to it. In his *Romeo and Juliet* ballet, the viewer is shown the theater's interior, the curtain and the proscenium frame delineating the dance space. The dance unfolds between two competing hotels operated by the balletic Capulets and the jazz-inspired, tap dancing Montagues. The feuding families employ their respective dance forms to battle one another. The idiomatic sparring culminates in a mock sword fight, at which point, the *corps de ballet* and platoon of tappers are shooed off stage by the family patriarchs: the lyre-playing[37] Capulet and sax-toting Montague.

Ballet and its aesthetic framework became increasingly prominent in Hollywood musicals in the 1940s, a trend that continued into the 1950s with the introduction of the integrated musical and its requisite dream ballet and "dance as narrative" elements.[38] In this musical sub-genre, dance is an essential (integral) component of the film's narrative and dramatic structure.[39] Staging and camera work were devised to heighten the meaning and impact of choreographic sequences, which were conceived to drive plot and character development, and often to explore the internal conflicts and desires of the main characters.

EVALUATING DANCE THROUGH THE LENS OF THE HIGH-ART, POPULAR-ENTERTAINMENT BINARY

The rise of the integrated musical in the 1950s is concurrent with both a rise in ballet's popularity and the beginning of a trend in musical theater scholarship that promoted an evolutionary model of its history in which the steady progression toward "seamless integration of plot and music" came to signify the form's aesthetic pinnacle.[40] This perspective resulted in a propensity to evaluate backstage and integrated musicals using a popular-entertainment, high-art binary, whereby popular entertainment denoted a mass produced commodity designed to please the eye, and high art possessed the potential to elevate, transform, and imbue meaning to its audience through its medium. The question remains as to whether this aesthetic hierarchy was at play in the minds of PCA censors. The evidence suggests that (whether consciously or not) censors evaluated dances using a double standard that privileged ballet-based choreography over movement informed by vernacular dance forms, such as jazz dance. Significantly, the backstage musicals and "dance as atmosphere numbers" were more heavily censored and more frequently cut from films than was choreography in the integrated musicals, in part because of this conceptual distinction between dance as entertainment and dance as art.

At the Columbia studio, Jack Cole worked with a group of handpicked and exceptionally skilled and versatile dancers. Cole worked most often in the sub-genre of the backstage musical, however, with leading ladies—Rita Hayworth[41], Betty Grable, Marilyn Monroe, and Jane Russell—who could move well and were adept in popular dance forms, rather than classically trained and proportioned ballet dancers who could act—such as Vera Zorina, Cyd Charisse, and Leslie Caron. Though Cole's artistic contributions to musical theater dance are tremendous, studio executives did not perceive Cole as an artist. Instead they regarded his choreography as a decorative element, important to atmosphere, not dramatic structure. Cole experienced frustration at the haphazard manner in which his dance numbers were inserted into a film after the script had already been completed: "If they had confidence in you…you might be called in when the script is only two-thirds done. Then you still have some chance of influencing the character development, or creating integration between your dance sequences and the story line. My own feeling is that the dance director should work with the film director on the three or four minutes that immediately precede and follow the dances to create a smooth transition."[42]

Cole was intent on creating meaning through dance. His interest in spurring a synergistic relationship between choreography and the film's narrative superseded the outward form of the dance or musical sub-genre. In 1947, he wrote:

A subject can only be rendered in any medium by approaching it with an informed mind, sympathy, and understanding. Therefore, let us hope that the minds of those who plan motion-pictures become aware of the large possibilities of the dance, other than the spectacular and the decorative, that the choreographer learns to use the camera as the remarkably fluid instrument it can be, and also that he becomes aware of its severe limitations, and that the cameraman learns to look at the dance as an expressive and communicative form.[43]

In this sense, Cole was ahead of his time, though other factors certainly contributed to thwarting his ambitions. Cole was relegated to "films built around Broadway, vaudeville and Hollywood studio situations."[44] He worked primarily at Columbia and 20th Century-Fox with the industry's leading sex goddesses: Hayworth, Grable, and Monroe, rather than MGM, the major producer of integrated musicals. Add to this his unparalleled ability to infuse musical theater dance with jazz and panoply of "ethnic" dance forms, which may have made him the obvious choice for the "dance as atmosphere" assignments, despite his distaste for the practice.

Cole considered the PCA's attitude toward the body and human sexuality arbitrary and idiotic, but his *Moon over Miami* experience made him attuned to what he could and could not get away with in his choreography. Cole's biographer notes that the choreographer spent many hours of spectator time in burlesque houses and, over time, became adept at integrating bumps and grinds into his cinematic work. One had to be careful though: a forward bump was considered erotic, while a backward bump was permissible. Likewise, a side grind could be incorporated but never a full rotating one.[45] It is evident when watching Cole's dance numbers that he was a master at pushing the boundaries of the code to the extreme, especially in the deliciously tantalizing numbers he staged for

Marilyn Monroe in such films as *There's No Business Like Show Business* (1954). In her rendition of "Tropical Heat Wave" Monroe simply oozes female sexuality. The choreography is sultry, pelvic-oriented, and full of innuendo cleverly tailored to the number's lyrics.[46]

TRANSGRESSING THE CODE IN THE INTEGRATED MUSICAL

The working environment appears to have been markedly different for Gene Kelly, Michael Kidd, Eugene Loring, and Agnes de Mille, all of whom worked in the sub-genre of the integrated musical and had backgrounds in ballet. A principal component of the integrated musical is the self-contained "dance as narrative," often realized in the form of the dream ballet. Typically choreographed in a style that blends classical ballet with modern dance; the dream ballet is highly symbolic and intended by the choreographer to be interpreted on a number of levels. In the dream ballet, the central characters expose and explore internal conflicts and desires and work toward a resolution of those feelings, and sexual longings, whether sanctioned or taboo.[47] In the musicals *On the Town, American in Paris, Singin' in the Rain, Band Wagon*, and *Oklahoma!*, emotional ambiguity, libidinous desires, seduction, and even murder are portrayed through dance. In all these films, the intent is to create meaning through movement. But the meanings encoded in these dances can be fully realized only when the viewer engages actively with the choreography, imbuing the dance and dancers with the power to unleash a range of individual responses. The archival record brings into serious question whether PCA censors engaged significantly with the content and meaning of the choreography they reviewed. If one examines the manner in which PCA censors evaluated the dance as narrative or dream ballet sequences, we see that the true import of the choreography either went unrecognized or was consciously overlooked. Censors' comments and their subsequent request for cuts demonstrate that PCA staff responded only to the most obvious violations of the code, most pertaining to costume and setting rather than choreographic content and performance. Were PCA censors simply unable to recognize the potential of these dances to create meaning capable of eliciting strong emotional and visceral reactions from viewers, or is there some other explanation for their failure to act?

DOS AND DON'TS IN *SINGIN' IN THE RAIN* AND *GOLDWYN FOLLIES*

In a 1973 interview, Gene Kelly recalled PCA censors requesting cuts to a duet from *Singin' in the Rain* (1952) that he performed with the classically trained Cyd Charisse. Censors told Kelly, "Don't allow her to wrap her legs around your middle," to which Kelly responded, "they do in ballet on the stage all the time."[48] In the end, Kelly seems to have toned down this element of the choreography, rather than omit it. The duet, part of the "Broadway Melody" ballet, takes place in a speakeasy, with Charisse as the gangster's moll dancing a classic *femme fatale* role. It is a dance of pure seduction in which Charisse exploits her long legs, slow shimmies, and pelvic isolations to taunt Kelly until his sexual appetite is aroused and he becomes the aggressor in the dance. The turning point of the duet is signified when Kelly grabs Charisse's arm and pulls her toward him into a chest-to-chest lift with her legs thrown behind her. Now in a position of dominance, Kelly releases Charisse slowly, allowing her to slither down his thigh onto her back. He pulls her up from the floor, into a whip turn and a side fall. Then, standing directly in front of him, Charisse and Kelly perform a deep, hinged *plié*—a sensual zenith in the dance—followed by a series of rhythmically accented pelvic isolations. Toward the end of the *pas* Charisse entwines her leg around Kelly's waist in a serpentine fashion. This *posé* is fleeting, however, and far less suggestive than the preceding sequences in the duet.[49]

Kelly's comment about this partnered step (in which Charisse faces Kelly and encircles his waist with a leg in *attitude devant*) resonated strongly when I sat down to view Balanchine's choreography for Vera Zorina in *The Goldwyn Follies* (1938). One need only look at Zorina's first *pas de deux* in the film to see an example of the double standard referred to earlier in this essay. In this abridged *Romeo and Juliet* duet, Zorina, dressed in a 1930s white satin dress and heels, descends the ladder placed beneath her window by Romeo. As they stand *tête-à-tête*, they are transformed into Shakespearean lovers. Zorina, now clad in blue tricot and chiffon and *en pointe*, displays a strong technique and beautiful classical line as her partner supports her. On two occasions she wraps her leg in an *attitude devant* around her partner's waist followed by a *grand ronds de jambe en l'air* into a *promenade en arabesque*. Toward the end of this very brief *pas de deux*, Zorina performs a *penchée en arabesque* toward the kneeling Romeo literally directing her bosom toward his face so that he has to arch his head backwards to avoid being nestled in her cleavage. It is a sustained *penchée* involving a series of interlacing *port de bras* followed by a mimed enactment of their suicides. The same *attitude devant* is performed *en pointe* in a classical *pas de deux* based on Shakespeare's tragedy and in a jazzy duet set in a 1920s speakeasy. Why did Breen's staff find this enveloping *attitude devant* acceptable in the first context but taboo in the second? (Figure 4.1)

MISE EN SCÈNE AND CENSORSHIP

I would argue that the bias at work in the PCA's evaluation and censorship of dance was heavily informed by the setting in which a dance was performed, an assertion supported by the fact that PCA censors also reviewed the opening *mise en scène* of the *Romeo and Juliet* ballet with great latitude. The shot reveals a small plaza situated between the hotels containing a fountain and stairs that ascend to a forced vanishing point. Clothes lines draped with women's intimate apparel connect the Capulet and Montague hotels. After establishing the scene, the camera traverses back and forth between a series of close ups of

FIGURE 4.1 Side-by-side views of the *attitude devant* position with Gene Kelly and Cyd Charisse (*Singin' in the Rain*) and Vera Zorina and William Dollar (*The Goldwyn Follies*)

beautiful young women in varying degrees of undress who take turns removing items of lingerie from the clothes line. The most striking of these close-up images, and what should have caught the attention of the censors, involves a young woman dressed in a slip who removes a pair of silk shorts from the line and conspicuously pulls them up over her stocking clad legs and under her slip. Balanchine's second dance number for the film, the *Undine* fantasy ballet for Zorina and *corps de ballet*, is even more tantalizing. Staged on an elegant set with Greek colonnades and de Chiricoesque horse, Zorina, as the water nymph, emerges from a placid lily pond dressed in "the flimsiest costume imaginable, made out of sheer gold lame," which when wet was "not only flimsy but transparent"[50] (Figure 4.2). The costume caused Zorina a good deal of embarrassment, but its sexual allure was "exactly what George [Balanchine] had planned."[51] Later in the scene Zorina, astride the colossal steed, appears stunningly dressed in a shimmering ball gown. A storm ensues and, with the assistance of huge airplane propellers set offstage, her dress is torn off by a fierce gust of wind.

When reviewing *Dance, Girl, Dance* (1940), a backstage musical telling the stories of an opportunistic burlesque dancer and an aspiring ballet dancer, the PCA repeatedly warned the studio not to portray any women's undergarments or any hint of a striptease in a burlesque[52] scene where gusts of wind carry off Lucille Ball's garments one by one, forcing her to take cover behind a tree. Interestingly, the studio complied with the PCA's demands, resulting in a very tame striptease act. Though hardly *risqué* by today's standards, the series of close-ups in the clothesline sequence and Zorina's *Undine* ballet from *The Goldwyn Follies* are sexually tantalizing. It is puzzling that PCA censors did not call for alterations to either of these scenes. One is left to speculate that the footage remained

FIGURE 4.2 Close-up of Vera Zorina emerging from her watery realm in gold lamé (*The Goldwyn Follies*)

intact because it was within self-contained ballets by Balanchine—one based on a Shakespearean tragedy, the other inspired by Romantic literature—and therefore deemed to be high art rather than mere entertainment.

State and foreign censorship boards were not part of the industry's self-regulation process. They acted with impunity, scrutinizing films for morally questionable material and exercising free reign in banning films or expunging material regardless of how it affected the film's legibility or artistic integrity. The PCA archives indicate that state and foreign censorship boards tended to scrutinize choreographic sequences more vigorously than PCA censors. Gene Kelly stated that when *Singin' in the Rain* was released in Spain, foreign censors excised the part of the dream ballet in which Kelly "kissed her in the white thing."[53] Here, Kelly refers to the immense swath of white fabric in which the couple becomes enveloped. The *pas de deux*, performed by Charisse in bare legs and feet, is highly balletic in form and execution. Filmed on a vast sound stage, the set is bathed in soft light that elicits an almost celestial quality. In this surreal setting, Charisse, clad in flowing white fabric, assumes a virginal quality *apropos* for this apollonian portrayal of "pure" love. Kelly and his collaborators thought the piece was "very lovely and charming." He was incensed that Spanish censors cut it from the film, "because they thought it was very symbolic of lovemaking. A Catholic country…I remember writing them a letter saying, 'I'm a Catholic; I don't understand your attitude.' But it didn't do any good. That's what you'd be up against."[54] Although the PCA staffers did not find any aspect of the dream ballet objectionable, the Spanish censors were correct in their appraisal of the *pas de deux*. Kelly's choreographic intent is very clear. The dream ballet is an abstracted interpretation of a couple's lovemaking in which heterosexual male desire is actualized, and, as such, the dance violates the code stipulating that dances suggesting or representing sexual actions or indecent passion are forbidden.

As the dance unfolds, Kelly's sexual urges seem to dictate Charisse's actions. A series of expansive runs and *bourées* symbolize the lovers' mutual desire and creates a heightened sense of sexual tension before the lovers unite. Charisse has an immensely long and flowing white scarf as part of her costume that is wind-blown with the aid of huge off-screen fans. As Kelly falls to his knees enraptured, Charisse encircles him, letting the fabric caress him. She runs up a short flight of steps, takes a striking pose on *demi-pointe* and looks at him beneath her. This is a visual and musical climax; the white scarf shoots straight up, clearly representative of male sexual climax. Kelly remains in a full hinge on his knees, his head thrown to one side in a state of post-coital ecstasy. It is a beautiful lyrical moment, but there is nothing subtle in its symbolism. The tone of the music and dance shift into a denouement as Charisse tenderly descends the stairs to Kelly and allows him to cradle her in his arms. He releases her gently. She circles him again, this time letting the scarf entwine them. Kelly takes her once again into his arms, their lips nearly touching. Slowly, he lets her glide down onto his knee, until she is stretched out, her back gently arched over his knee. They share a passionate kiss as the orchestra strikes another climatic note. As Charisse departs, the white fabric caresses Kelly's torso once again. They face each other from a distance with arms stretched out. The fantasy concludes.

The Spanish film censors' ability to look past the apollonian qualities of the *pas de deux* and grasp the erotic nature of the choreography demonstrates the power of dance to elicit an empathic response from viewers. The disparity between the responses of PCA staff and the Spanish censors is a further indication that PCA censors did not engage with choreographic intent or meaning, and were predisposed to evaluating balletic movement with greater latitude due to its high-art status.

AN AMERICAN, IN LOVE, IN PARIS

A year earlier, MGM released *An American in Paris* (1951), containing an extended seventeen-minute ballet choreographed by Kelly and featuring French ballerina Leslie Caron. The *American in Paris Ballet* commences after Kelly, portraying the American painter Gerry, must say goodbye to his beloved Lise at the Beaux-Arts Ball so that she can honor her engagement to a prominent French entertainer. In the ballet, Gerry pursues Lise through the city of Paris. The journey serves a dual function: it pays homage to Paris and its great artists, and recapitulates their relationship—replaying the stages of discovery, courtship, love, and loss.[55] Gerry first glimpses Lise at the fountain at the Place de la Concorde but loses her instantly. Later in the ballet, they are reunited at the fountain and perform a sensual *pas de deux* beneath the fountain's spray and amongst its statuary. Though the setting, lighting, and costuming are patently different from the dream ballet in *Singin' in the Rain*, this *pas de deux* is also symbolic of a couple's lovemaking and is imbued with an eroticism that unquestionably violates the moral intent of the production code. Here, Kelly and Caron are shrouded in mist and bathed in an array of deep, saturated colors, creating the impression of an intimate interior space. At one point in the dance, Caron reclines back on a statue as if she were arching over the edge of a bed, her lover on the floor beneath her. Though Caron is not dancing *en pointe* (as she does throughout much of the ballet) the choreography is balletic, featuring Caron's classical line, vertical comportment, and superbly arched feet. The absence of *pointe* shoes only contributes to the intimacy of the duet. There are a number of lifts in the dance, but the one that most appears to violate the code occurs toward the end of the *pas de deux* at the musical climax of the piece. Kelly supports Caron in a lift in which she straddles his waist with bent knees, swoons back into a full arch, and is swayed side to side. She slides down his thigh into a supported hinge and is pulled up by Kelly so that their lips almost meet. They pull away briefly, turn to face one another, and are drawn into a kiss. There is no mention of this sultry *pas de deux* in the PCA files (Figure 4.3).

The only dance number in *American in Paris* that raised any concern was in the Toulouse Lautrec scene, where Caron and a small ensemble perform a Cancan in a Moulin Rouge setting. The files do not specify what censors found objectionable in this, though one can presume it is the dance's setting in a cabaret and the association of the Cancan with titillating costumes, and disreputable behavior. Although censorship boards in Indonesia, Spain, and several states removed the Cancan scene, the PCA approved the film after only minor edits to the script and cautions regarding the costuming of women.[56]

FIGURE 4.3 Leslie Caron and Gene Kelly in the sultry *pas de deux* from "The American in Paris Ballet" (*An American in Paris*)

OKLAHOMA!: DEMILLE'S DREAM/NIGHTMARE BALLET

Agnes De Mille is credited with developing the concept of the integrated musical on Broadway with the 1943 landmark production of *Oklahoma!*.[57] De Mille's choreography for *Oklahoma!* contains perhaps the most famous dream ballet captured on film, one rooted in classical vocabulary and performed by professional ballet dancers. In the dream sequence, the heroine, Laurie, is confronted with her own decision to have Jud, a rough farm-hand and the film's dark-natured antagonist, take her to the box social rather than Curly, her true love and future mate. It is a decision calculated only to make Curly jealous, with no regard for Jud or for the repercussions of her action. De Mille's choreography demonstrates a binary structure. We begin with dream Laurie and dream Curly. Their dance is light, soaring, and ebullient, unfolding beneath clear blue skies. A church bell signals their wedding day, and the procession begins; yet just as Laurie is about to kiss her betrothed, she is confronted by Jud. He rips the veil from her face, catapulting her dream into a torrid nightmare. The *corps de ballet* becomes immobilized and recedes off stage. Curly symbolizes wholesome love—marriage, procreation, and security—but Jud embodies the baser animal instincts. Jud is unkempt, savage, sexually promiscuous, and destructive.[58] The Dionysian dance that ensues takes place in a gambling house set against a searing red-orange background. A Cancan, performed by stony-faced women in fancy dress to the reprise of "I'm just a girl who can't say no," gives both the song and dance a whole new meaning and leaves little doubt that these are women of ill repute. Laurie, desperate for help, is thrown into Jud's embrace. He begins to drag her around the dance floor but is easily distracted and enticed away by a saloon dancer who seductively lifts her skirt to reveal her thighs. A group dance follows. The camera angle offers numerous "crotch shots" of the dancers as they fan-kick their legs and are swept into lifts with their legs straddled and feet flexed. At one point the lifted women appear stiff, with eyes shut, as if they are corpses. Interestingly, when Laurie begins to dance, the camera angle does not alter, but she is shot only from the waist up. Only her emotional/intellectual zone is in view, in direct contrast to the focus on the libidinous zones of the saloon dancers. Laurie escapes this macabre scene by fleeing up a narrow flight of stairs. But this is not the end of the nightmare. The dream ballet concludes with Jud murdering Curly and carrying Laurie off while the crowd stands by, immobile as before.

De Mille's dream/nightmare ballet violates a number of the code's provisions: it includes lustful embraces, sexually suggestive postures, and gestures that could stimulate baser instincts as well as non-sexual poses that could be regarded as indecent or obscene. But of course, this was the choreographer's objective; the dance is intended to be crude and disturbing, and it succeeds brilliantly. The ballet is also crucial to the development of plot and character, especially in how we understand Laurie's motivation and internal conflict. When Jud awakens Laurie in her rocking chair on the porch, she shudders and her nightmare continues in earnest as they depart for the box social.

De Mille's dream ballet was subjected to censorship by the PCA. It was, however, the scene's setting rather than the choreography that was found to be offensive. "When the Legion declared that it was implicit that a dancer who runs up a staircase pursued by the villain in *Oklahoma!* was heading for a brothel, the scene was re-shot to establish that it was, in fact, a gambling hall."[59] The code stipulates, "Certain places are so closely and thoroughly associated with sexual life or with sexual sin that their use must be carefully limited."[60] The re-shoot portrays Laurie peering down a dimly lit corridor with closed doors. The setting does not convincingly announce it as a gambling house but is instead left ambiguous. In fact, the choreography so firmly establishes the locale as a saloon/brothel that the re-shooting of the scene seems inconsequential and ineffectual. Again, the PCA left the brilliant choreography intact despite the potency of its subject matter and impact of its performance. The earlier success of *Oklahoma!* on Broadway may have protected De Mille's choreography from censorship once it reached the film stage, though it is more likely that it was the dream ballet's role in plot and character development, and the decreasing power of the PCA to enforce the Legion of Decency's moral agenda, that helped save it from further tampering. By 1955, the year *Oklahoma!* was released, Joseph Breen had relinquished directorship of the PCA to his assistant, Jeffrey Shurlock.

CULTURAL LEGACIES AND BIASES IN THE PRODUCTION CODE

To an extent, the wording of the production code laid the foundation for censors to employ a culturally biased (high-art, low-art) lens in determining the approbation or censure of dance numbers based on a set of guiding moral principles. To begin, the code classifies motions pictures as both entertainment *and* art. It states:

Motion pictures are to be regarded *primarily as entertainment*—entertainment has long been recognized for its value in rebuilding bodies and souls of human beings. But it has always recognized that entertainment can be of a character either helpful or harmful to the human race....Correct entertainment raises the whole standard of a nation. Wrong entertainment lowers the whole living conditions and moral ideals of a race...e.g. note for example the effect on ancient nations of gladiator combats, the obscene plays of Roman times.

Motion pictures are very important as art. Though a new art...it has the same object as the other arts, the presentation of human thought, emotion, and experience, in terms of an appeal to the soul through the senses....Art can be morally good, lifting men to higher levels. This has been done through good music, great painting, authentic fiction, drama....[61]

In describing art—and by extension, dance—as a means of appealing to man's soul through the senses, the authors of the code confer dance with great moral responsibility: the power to affect an audience (for good or for bad) through an emotional, kinesthetic, and visual connection to the form. In arguing the potential for art to elevate or degrade moral standards, the authors of the code turned to ideals they considered central to the teachings of the church, but which are actually part of the broader legacy of Western civilization.

PLATO, DANCE, AND THE BODY POLITIC

The notion of dance as an instrument of socialization and moral education has its foundation in ancient Greek philosophy. In *Laws,* Plato stresses the participation of the entire citizenry in choral activity, either as participants or spectators, as a means to transmit and reaffirm the shared beliefs of the entire body politic, and to reverse the natural human tendency toward moral degeneration.[62] He proclaims that an educated man is one trained to participate in a chorus, performing those songs and dances associated with spiritual or bodily excellence. Conversely, songs and movements associated with vice are deemed to be bad. He distinguishes between two types of dancing: decent dances portray fine physiques and noble characters and are exemplified by the movements of graceful people with the purpose of creating an effect of grandeur. A composed temperament and rigorous training generate movement that is deliberate and measured: correct posture is erect, in a state of vigorous tension, with the limbs extended nearly straight. Whereas disreputable dances present the movements of unsightly people in an unattractive light, such as the coward who dances in a wild manner altering his postures violently.[63] Plato also addresses regulations for correct female and male performances such that "an elevated manner and courageous instincts must be regarded as characteristic of the male, while a tendency to modesty and restraint must be presented—in theory and law alike—as a peculiarly feminine trait."[64] One cannot help see a correlation between Plato's description of decent dance and the comportment, movement characteristics, and gender specificity of European court dance, classical ballet, and the categories of *danseur noble* and *ballerina.*[65] Correspondingly, dances with the opposite postural, physical, and stylistic characteristics—a stooped, relaxed stance, movement initiated from the core and mid-range areas rather than distally, and the inclusion of ("seemingly uncontrolled") improvisatory elements—can be understood as incorrect and morally indecent.

RENAISSANCE NOTIONS OF DANCE: MORAL VIRTUE OR CARNAL PLEASURE

The concept of a decent versus disreputable type of dance is one that humanist scholars and theologians—both apologists for and detractors of dance—appropriated for their own purposes when discussing the proper moral conduct and education of well-bred gentry. Writing in 1531, Sir Thomas Elyot devoted seven chapters of *The Book Named the Governor* to the subject of social dance instruction, which he believed necessary for acquiring grace of carriage and imparting moral virtues.[66] The abundance of Renaissance tracts offering firm defenses of dance based on classical authorities are testament to the fact that the activity of dancing was not embraced universally.[67] Puritan clergyman John Northbrooke asserted: "[Dances] are…snares and offenses, not only to the dancers, but also to the beholders; for they stir up and inflame the hearts of men, which are otherwise evil enough…O deceitful dance! IT is the mother of all evil, the sister of all carnal pleasures, the father of all pride."[68] The influence of humanism led the Jesuits to adopt a radically different stance toward dance than the Puritans. Seeing it as a useful tool in the moral instruction and socialization of youths,[69] Jesuit educators incorporated ballet interludes into Biblical plays to expand on the Christian-humanist moral elements within the drama.[70]

THE CODE: AN AMALGAM OF CATHOLIC ETHOS AND CLASSICAL IDEALS

Whether dancing provides a path to moral instruction, socialization and control of the body politic, or moral degeneration has been a matter of public debate since the time of Plato. It is of great interest that these same concerns appear with such prominence in the argument proffered by Daniel A. Lord and Martin Quigley in the 1930 motion picture production code. Officially, Breen, Quigley, and Lord sought to appease Protestant reformers and the predominantly Jewish movie executives by claiming that the code was based on the Ten Commandments—a Judeo-Christian amalgam that all decent men could agree on. Breen, however, referred to the code in 1934 as "an overall authority, which would function on a platform of Catholic understanding and interpretation of moral values."[71] Though Breen, Quigley, and Lord associated the code's moral values with Catholic theology (strongly influenced by Thomistic philosophy), the ideals expressed within the code are nonetheless rooted in Platonic philosophy, synthesized with Catholic theology through the treatises of the Neo-Platonist Plotinus and Christian Neo-Platonist St. Augustine, who was instrumental in merging "Greek philosophical tradition with the Judeo-Christian religious and scriptural tradition."[72]

As a Jesuit priest, educator, and dramatist, Lord would have been well versed in classical philosophy, literature, and art. An essential principle of Jesuit educational philosophy expressed in the *Ratio Studiorum* (Plan of Studies, 1599) is the conviction that the Greek and Latin classics and scholastic philosophy are constants in any educational schema because they offer "abiding and universal values" for the formation of virtue and character. The *Ratio Studiorum* prescribed a method of instruction designed to bring students into "close and inspiring contact with classical culture" in order to develop "high human standards by which to appraise not only works of art and literature but also social and political theories and movements."[73] The production code drafted by Lord reads much like a scholarly treatise.[74] It contains a logically constructed philosophical justification for the code's specific tenets, leading into a list of permissible and prohibited content areas for motion pictures. Through the inclusion of ideals expressed by Plato and Renaissance humanists, Lord aimed to confer gravitas and moral authority on the production code.

OUT OF STEP: THE CODE'S WANING RELEVANCE IN 1950S AMERICA

As the head of the PCA, Breen believed that he and his staff had a moral obligation to uphold the code's tenets.

> Motion pictures, I need not remind you, constitute a peculiar and a powerful influence, for good or evil, upon all those who see it. Because of their widespread popularity, the vividness of their presentation and the facility with which they never fail to impress and to stimulate, too much emphasis cannot be placed upon the need for the exercise of the greatest possible care in the construction of the pictures, and at the same time, the likely effect the picture may have upon the minds of those who set it.... This Code is a *moral* Code. No other industry, so far as I know, has undertaken to pattern its products in conformity with the basic tenets of *decency* and *morality*.[75]

Those having to comply with the code, including producers, directors, writers, lyricists, designers, and choreographers, may have agreed with the necessity for industry self-regulation as a means to avoid government intrusion and even greater scrutiny by morality groups, but not necessarily with the narrowly conceived classifications of what comprised decent and moral content as laid out by Lord and Quigley, and enforced by Breen. The tensions inherent in self-regulation increased as the decades wore on and the film industry struggled to keep up with a rapidly changing social and moral milieu, especially with regard to attitudes about sex, marriage, and divorce.[76] In his 1950 study of the popular arts, the media critic Gilbert Seldes wrote, "Although I do not exaggerate the influence of the movies (or any other art) I think the Code, its frivolous applications, and the evasions it encourages have become a dangerous and destructive element in American life."[77] By the mid-1950s it became evident that the PCA and the National Legion of Decency were losing the battle to control motion picture content, and that the code was viewed as anachronistic by those closely involved in the film industry, as well as the movie-going masses. The tenets of the original production code were revised in 1956, coinciding with a discernable waning in the number of musicals being produced by Hollywood studios that speaks to a radical shift in the post-war cultural milieu and the film industry's response to this change.

CONCLUSION

Dance in the Hollywood musical was assessed in an inconsistent and biased manner by PCA censors, with the result that certain types of dance transgressed the tenets of the code, while others were more heavily scrutinized for signs of moral indecency. The reasons for the inconsistency in valuation are multifaceted and intricately connected to cultural and implicitly racist biases rooted in classical and Renaissance ideals regarding proper decorum and decent versus indecent modes of dance. These ingrained and ethnocentric notions affected how censors judged an array of components pertaining to choreography and performance in film musicals, including comportment, demeanor, gender specific behavior, movement initiation, and musical accompaniment. Instead of recognizing and placing value on how meaning is created and transmitted through movement alone, PCA censors concentrated on dance genre, scenic location, and costuming. Dance was largely treated as a decorative feature of a film—another scenic effect—as attested to by veteran film choreographer Jack Cole. This means of assessment can be traced to Breen's 1936 memo to Hays in which he emphasizes the importance of atmosphere, location, and demeanor of performers in the evaluation of films and what is deemed permissible. Breen's directive became the basis for a crude method of appraising the moral acceptability of dance based on setting, character, and conduct. Put simply, dances set in locations associated with illicit behavior or performed by disreputable characters were more likely to be viewed as indecent and thus were more prone to censorship. Dance scenes filmed in more abstract settings, locations associated with high art and culture, or with the daily activities of the average law-abiding citizen were overwhelmingly approved by the PCA, even when the choreography was in obvious violation of the code's tenets pertaining to costume, sex, and indecent passion.

Censors had neither the capacity nor the inclination to engage critically with choreographic intent, interpretation, and reception.[78] PCA censors reviewed several hundred film scripts and treatments annually, in addition to lyrics, scenic and costume designs, ads, and multiple re-writes. Working at this pace called for standardization and expediency, with the end goal of approving a film for mass distribution. Breen's understanding of the Code as the basis for inculcating and sustaining a strong Catholic ethos in motion pictures led him to enforce its tenets with an unwavering moral certitude, and a blind eye to the nuances of interpretation.

Using setting, character, and conduct as a litmus test for gauging the moral acceptability of dance created a sort of chain reaction with regard to censorship because locale was so closely associated with dance genre, and genre in turn was connected to specific movement characteristics judged according to culturally determined notions of decency and virtue. The dream ballets and dance as narrative pieces were set in proscenium theaters, glamorous art deco sets, vast sound stages, or amidst elaborately constructed urban or rural backdrops; the (oft thin) plots of the backstage musical unfolded in nightclubs, second-rate theaters, dressing rooms, and burlesque houses. The heroine is often a virtuous young woman from humble means who finds a job in a theatrical revue hoping to tap her way to fame and fortune. In contrast to the apparent glamour of the stage spectacles she performs, her "offstage" life is neither charmed nor secure. Her dream of a "better" life spurs her to work hard and keep on dancing. These films typically feature dancers performing burlesque, jazz, or tap routines; rarely did they conform to classical or Christian concepts of decent and virtuous dance, or appropriate female behavior. Thus a narrowly conceived characterization of "good" or decent dance had the result of privileging balletic-based choreography, in particular the dream ballet and dance as narrative forms, over theatrical and vernacular dance forms stemming from non-Western dance traditions, relegating the latter to a lesser aesthetic and moral standing.

The film *Dance, Girl, Dance* epitomizes the high-art, popular-entertainment binary and the association of dance genre with locale, conduct, and moral stature. Lucille Ball, as the sensationally successful burlesque artist Bubbles, is portrayed as a loose woman—unhappy, scheming, and opportunistic—while her female co-star Judy O'Brien (Maureen O'Hara), an aspiring ballet dancer from humble means, embodies the four cardinal virtues: prudence, temperance, justice, and moral fortitude. In the film, Judy serves as the warm-up act, or stooge, to Bubbles's featured burlesque number. Each night she performs a lyrical ballet variation of her own creation to the jeers and mockery of the low-class, thrill-seeking audience—a prime example of casting pearls before swine. In the film, we watch Judy go through this demeaning ordeal a number of times. She continues to endure the humiliation and denigration because times are tough and the rent must be paid. She convinces herself that she will not be tainted by her surroundings as long as she maintains her devotion to the ballet and the integrity of her performance. Judy's nightly sacrifice in the burlesque house has the effect of accentuating the virtue of her character and her artistic practice. She assumes a martyr-like persona—the beautiful young Christian thrown to the lions—who meets her fate with bravery and dignity. In the end, Judy confronts the hostile crowd, reproaches them for their lustful behavior, and quits the burlesque house. At the film's conclusion, she is rewarded for her valor and her relentless devotion to classical ballet. Unbeknownst to her, a famous impresario had been sitting in the audience. Enthralled with her artistic potential, sterling character and spunk, he hires her as the newest talent for his world-class ballet company.

FILMOGRAPHY

An American in Paris (MGM, 1951)
Band Wagon (MGM, 1953)
Cabin in the Sky (MGM, 1943)
Cover Girl (Columbia, 1944)
Dance, Girl, Dance (RKO, 1940)
Doll Face (Fox, 1945)
Down to Earth (Columbia, 1947)
The Gay Divorcee (RKO, 1934)
The Goldwyn Follies (United Artists, 1938)
Guys and Dolls (Samuel Goldwyn, 1955)
Moon over Miami (Fox, 1941)
My Sister Eileen (Columbia, 1955)
Oklahoma! (United Artists, 1955)
On the Town (MGM, 1949)
The Pirate (MGM, 1948)

Shall We Dance (RKO, 1937)
Singin' in the Rain (MGM, 1952)
Stormy Weather (Fox, 1943)
There's No Business Like Show Business (Fox, 1954)
Words and Music (MGM, 1948)
Yolanda and the Thief (MGM, 1945)

NOTES

1. Joris Ivens, "Notes on Hollywood" in *New Theatre and Film 1934 to 1937: An Anthology*, ed. Herbert Kline (San Diego: Harcourt Brace Jovanovich, 1985), 296.

2. Jerome Delamater, *Dance in the Hollywood Musical* (Ann Arbor: UMI Research Press, 1981), 113.

3. Glenn Merideth Loney, *Unsung Genius: The Passion of Dancer-Choreographer Jack Cole* (New York: F. Watts, 1984), 128. Viewing *Moon Over Miami*, I found that PCA censors completely excised any hint of erotic content from the Seminole dance. After PCA approval, state censorship boards had license to cut any portion of a film they deemed objectionable before a film was distributed to theaters in their states.

4. The Studio Relations Committee was tasked with enforcing the production code, but only as an advisory committee to motion picture producers. It had neither a mechanism nor strong incentive for securing all scripts or enforcing compliance with their recommendations, and it was replaced by the far more powerful Production Code Administration in 1934.

5. "Working Draft of the Lord-Quigley Draft Proposal," printed in Gregory D. Black, *The Catholic Crusade Against the Movies, 1940–1975* (New York: Cambridge University Press, 1997), 248.

6. The faith-based morality organization was originally called the Catholic Legion of Decency but changed its name in April 1934 as part of an active campaign to include all denominations in their activities. Stephen Tropiano, *Obscene, Indecent, Immoral and Offensive: 100 + Years of Censored, Banned and Controversial Films.* (Milwaukee: Limelight Editions, 2009), 78.

7. Lord was also a prolific playwright, author, and musician. He was initially invited to Hollywood to serve as technical advisor on Catholicism during Cecil B. DeMille's filming of *King of Kings*. When Quigley invited him to consider writing a new moral code for the motion picture industry, Lord leapt at the opportunity. See Gregory D. Black, "Hollywood Censored: The Production Code Administration and the Hollywood Film Industry, 1930–1940," *Film History*, vol. 3, no. 3 (1989): 170. Quigley stated that Lord prepared the original draft of the code. See Thomas Doherty, *Hollywood's Censor: Joseph I. Breen & the Production Code Agency* (New York: Columbia University Press, 2007), 42, 46.

8. Black, *Film History*, 171.

9. Though the PCA was operational until 1968, 1955 was chosen as the logical cutoff date for this research because it marked the conclusion of Joseph Breen's influential tenure as PCA director. The production code underwent revisions in 1956. Although I do not include close readings of films made prior to 1938, I did view and analyze musicals produced between 1934 and 1937 for this research.

10. Martin Quigley, *Decency in Motion Pictures* (New York: Macmillan, 1937), 56.

11. Lea Jacobs, "Industry Self-Regulation and the Problem of Textual Determination," in *Controlling Hollywood: Censorship and Regulation in the Studio Era*, ed. Matthew Bernstein, (New Brunswick, NJ: Rutgers University Press, 1999), 88; and Stephen Vaughn, "Morality and Entertainment: The Origins of the Motion Picture Production Code," *Journal of American History*, vol. 77, no. 1 (June 1990): 53, 56–57.

12. Black, *Film History*, 167; and Vaughn, 39.

13. Demands for government supervision of motion pictures took two forms: legislation to regulate film content and calls to abolish the monopolistic practices of the MPPDA. See Vaughn, 45.

14. Doherty, 61.

15. Ibid., 57.

16. Frank Walsh, *Sin and Censorship: The Catholic Church and the Motion Picture Industry* (New Haven: Yale University Press, 1996), 104.

17. Jacobs, *Controlling Hollywood*, 90–91.

18. Lea Jacobs, *The Wages of Sin: Censorship and the Fallen Woman Film* 1928–1942 (Madison: University of Wisconsin Press, 1991), 21.

19. Excerpted from a 1994 interview with Gene Kelly and Hilary de Vries in the *Los Angeles Times*. Larry Billman, *Film Choreographers and Dance Directors: An Illustrated Biographical Encyclopedia, with a History and Filmographies 1893 Through 1995* (Jefferson: McFarland, 1997), 96.

20. Dialogue from *Singin' in the Rain* (Stanley Donen, Gene Kelly), MGM, 1952.

21. *Annual Report* February 15, 1935, from the MPPA files in Jacobs, *Controlling Hollywood*, 98. Studios were required to submit all costume designs to the PCA to ensure they were not too revealing. Tropiano, 55.

22. Ibid., *Annual Report*, March 15, 1936, MPPA files.

23. Billman, 86. See page 102 for the story of the young (and not yet famous) Agnes DeMille's distressing experience choreographing the court dances for MGM's *Romeo and Juliet* (1936), directed by George Cukor.

24. Constance Valis Hill, "From Bharata Natyam to Bop: Jack Cole's 'Modern' Jazz Dance," *Dance Research Journal*, Vol. 33, no. 2 (2001): 32.

25. John Martin, "The Dance: Jack Cole," *New York Times* (November 7, 1948): X6.

26. Billman, 79–80.

27. Ibid., 78.

28. Ibid., 80, excerpted from an interview in *Dance Magazine*, May 1946.

29. Martin, 1948, X6.

30. From John Martin, *The Dance*, as quoted in Joe Nash, "Pioneers of Negro Concert Dance: 1931 to 1937," http://www.pbs.org/wnet/freetodance/behind/behind_pioneers_d.html. Recent scholarship has brought to light the major contributions of African and African American dancers to the concert field, as well as the racist policies and attitudes they encountered. See, for example, John O. Perpener, *African-American Concert Dance: The Harlem Renaissance and Beyond* (Urbana: University of Illinois Press, 2001); and Thomas F. DeFrantz, *Dancing Many Drums: Excavations in African American Dance* (Madison: University of Wisconsin Press, 2002).

31. For an extensive look at ballet and ballet dancers in narrative film, see Adrienne L. McLean, *Dying Swans and Madmen: Ballet, the Body and Narrative Cinema* (New Brunswick, NJ: Rutgers University Press, 2008). When Balanchine brought his American Ballet Company to Hollywood—complete with musicians, wardrobe assistants, make-up artists, and other experts—he

made demands that were previously unheard of from a choreographer, including the construction of a dance studio on the lot. "Goldwyn cheerfully ordered a new building…. The more unreasonable Balanchine's request, the more he respected it. He sensed that he now owned a genuine group of first-rate artists, that he was somehow entertaining royalty." Susan Roper, "Balanchine in Hollywood," *Ballet Review* 23:4 (Winter 1995): 53.

32. Delamater, 85. Viennese-born ballerina Albertina Rasch had tremendous success on Broadway and in Hollywood in the 1920s and 1930s. The Albertina Rasch Girls "became a staple of most of MGM's 1930s musicals and historical dramas, adding beauty and the 'class' of their ballet work, plus greater demands on the dancers themselves." Billman, 39.

33. John Martin, "The Dance: The Ballet," *New York Times*, March 10, 1935, X9. The exception to Martin's classification was the Americana ballet *Alma Mater*, though he dismisses "the college ballet" as unoriginal and of no consequence.

34. For example, the films *Shall We Dance, Goldwyn Follies, Dance, Girl, Dance, Down to Earth, American in Paris, Band Wagon,* and *Silk Stockings* exploit the ballet versus vernacular dance binary to highlight differences of class, culture, age, and political persuasion.

35. Balanchine first employed this device in 1936 on Broadway for the ensemble piece "On Your Toes" in the hit musical of the same name, where he paired twenty tappers with twenty ballet dancers. In 1938, he returned to the juxtaposition of classical and popular forms in *The Boys from Syracuse*. According to historian Camille Hardy, "Balanchine combined tap and ballet to shape an image that expanded the plot"—a man pursuing two relationships simultaneously and the resultant conflict he experiences. In the dance, Heidi Voessler's "classical dancing expressed the delicacy of conjugal love. [Betty] Bruce's tapping showed a steamier side, appealing to more carnal interests." Camille Hardy, "Bringing *Bourrées* to Broadway: George Balanchine's Career in the Commercial Theatre," *World Literature Today* (March/April 2006): 16.

36. For example, Berkeley's *Gold Diggers of 1933, 42nd Street,* and *Footlight Parade* for Warner Brothers. According to Martin Rubin, this sub-genre was more important and more popular in film than on the stage. It continued to flourish in the 1940s, often "overlapping with the musical-biography and let's-put-on-a-show-for-the-USO modes." Martin Rubin, *Busby Berkeley and the Tradition of Spectacle* (New York: Columbia University Press, 1993), 35.

37. The lyre appears in many forms in a number of Balanchine's ballets. It is a reference to the god Apollo and the ballet *Apollon Musagete* from 1928 (now called *Apollo)* and of great symbolic importance to Balanchine and the New York City Ballet. The lyre is the official symbol of the NYCB, representing the apollonian qualities of lightness, harmony, measure, clarity of form, and reason.

38. Larry Billman states that the critical and popular success of *The Red Shoes* (1948) removed ballet from the realm of the cultural elite and delivered it to the masses, and it also encouraged Gene Kelly and Eugene Loring to include ballet in extended dance sequences in film. Billman, 83.

39. Beth Eliot Genné, *The Film Musicals of Vicente Minnelli and the Team of Gene Kelly and Stanley Donen: 1944–1958 Volume I* (Ann Arbor, MI: UMI, 1984), 132.

40. Rubin, 12. Rubin points to the work of Cecil Smith, Richard Kislan, Stanley Green, David Ewen, and Gerald Bordman as "traditional chroniclers of the stage musical," typifying "the pro-integration position." He argues that non-integration, or disruption of narrative, represents a "formulized resistance to the hierarchy of discourse" and is "essential to the musical genre," which he describes as a "shifting and volatile dialectic between integrative and non-integrative elements."

41. Rita Hayworth came from a family of dancers. Her father was a Spanish dancer and her mother was a Ziegfeld girl. Hayworth received a broad variety of dance training at an early age—ballet, tap, ballroom, and Spanish dance. Her film roles, however, called on her acting ability and talent in popular dance forms.

42. Loney, 116.

43. Ibid., 152.

44. Ibid., 126.

45. Ibid., 211.

46. It is important to note that this film was released in 1954, the year of Breen's retirement. By this time, Breen and the Legion of Decency were less able to control the moral content of films in the face of a changing populace, the success of foreign films, television, and a series of films that had been successful at the box office without receiving the PCA's seal of approval.

47. Rick Altman, *The American Film Musical* (Bloomington: Indiana University Press, 1987), 188. Beth Eliot Genné draws a parallel between the development and popularity of the dream ballet form from 1936–44 to the influx of Freudian analysts into the United States. Genné, 174–75.

48. Delamater, 225.

49. The relationship with Joseph Breen and the Legion of Decency reached a nadir in 1953 when an official, Father Thomas Little, reprimanded Breen's handling of dance sequences in several films, including Charisse's performance in *Singin' in the Rain*, which he found highly "suggestive." Here Father Little is most likely referring to Charisse's performance as the gangster's moll, a performance of fairly unbridled sexuality in which Charisse's taunting behavior unleashes Kelly's carnal desire. The fact that this scene passed the watchful eye of the PCA seemingly intact indicates Breen's waning authority. Walsh, 262.

50. The Production Code stipulates, "Transparent or translucent materials and silhouette are frequently more suggestive than actual exposure." Quigley, 69.

51. Vera Zorina, *Zorina* (New York: Farrar, Straus, Giroux, 1986), 189.

52. The PCA was consistent in rejecting dance forms associated with burlesque. Censors completely rejected the idea of Fanny Brice spoofing a fan dance in *Ziegfeld Follies* and as well as a scene from *Gilda*, which suggests that Rita Hayworth is about to perform a striptease. Censors' comments include this statement: "Any suggestion of the actual dance could not be approved." Margaret Herrick Library, Academy of Motion Picture Arts and Sciences, and Primary Source Microfilm (Firm). 2006. *History of Cinema: Selected Files from the Motion Picture Association of America Production Code Administration Collection. Series 1, Hollywood and the Production Code.* Woodbridge, CT: Primary Source Microfilm, Reel 22.

53. Delamater, 225.

54. Ibid.

55. Genné, 340.

56. Margaret Herrick Library, *History of Cinema*, Reel 26.

57. A number of dance scholars have asserted that Balanchine should receive credit for the introduction of the integrated musical based on his choreography for *On Your Toes*, in particular the ballet "Slaughter on Tenth Avenue," which drives the narrative and resolves the conflict within it. John Mueller argues that Fred Astaire's choreography for stage and film contributed significantly to the development of the integrated musical, anticipating both Balanchine's and DeMille's contributions to the form. See John Mueller, "Fred Astaire and the Integrated Musical," *Cinema Journal*, (Autumn 1984), vol. 24, no. 1: 28–40.

58. Altman, 313.

59. The studio refused to make all the changes requested by the Legion of Decency in order to move the film from a B to an A-II rating by the Legion, an indication of the waning power of morality groups after Breen's departure. Walsh, 267.

60. Quigley, 69.

61. Ibid., 57–58.

62. Choral activity was understood as a means to conduce order in the soul and in the body politic. Plato states that an uneducated man (*achoreutos*) is one who has not been trained to take part in a chorus. Trevor J. Saunders, translated Plato, *The Laws* (Baltimore: Penguin Books, 1970), Book II, 87–89.

63. Ibid., Book VII, 307–9. Both types of dance have two subdivisions. Decent dance is divided into the *Pyrrhic* (war dance) and *Emmelei* (dance of peace). Plato places *Bacchic* dances in a separate category, apart from the *Pyrrhic* and *Emmelei*. He defines the *Bacchic* as presentations of drunken persons they call Nymphs, Pans, Sileni, and Satyrs performed during purifications and initiations.

64. Ibid., 291.

65. These physical characteristics also apply to types of Renaissance and Baroque dance and certain ballroom dance forms. The connection of classical ballet to Platonic philosophy can be traced to ballet's roots in European court dance and to the Neo-Platonist ideals of l'Académie de Musique et de Poésie, which sought to recreate in a unified presentation the components of ancient Greek drama: measured dance, measured music, and measured verse.

66. Within these chapters, Elyot combats the accusations of stricter moralists by establishing the respectability of dance, supporting his argument with the citations of classical poets and philosophers. Elyot's ideas are drawn primarily from Plato, Aristotle, and Lucian, but it is evident that Plato's *Laws* and the *Republic* exerted the greatest influence on his beliefs. Sir Thomas Elyot, *The Book Named The Governor*, ed. John Major (New York: Teachers College Press, 1969), 164–65.

67. Fifteenth-century educator P. P. Vergerius forbade youths to practice dancing on the grounds that it bred "lasciviousness and vain conceit." John Major, "The Moralization of the Dance in Elyot's Governor," *Studies in the Renaissance* vol. V: 27–28.

68. John Northbrooke, *A treatise wherin dicing, dancing, vaine playes or enterludes…are reproved* (Shakespeare Society reprint from the earliest edition, 1577), 155–56. Northbrooke is primarily opposed to any dance forms where men and women dance together.

69. Writing under the pseudonym Thoinet Arbeau, the Jesuit cleric Jehan Tabourot published one of the most important dance manuals of the Renaissance period, *Orchesographie*. Written in the form of a Socratic dialogue between teacher and student, the work chronicled French social dance forms, style, and etiquette from the 1550s to 1580s.

70. In the late Renaissance and Baroque, Biblical dramas were performed in Latin and based on subject matter from the Old Testament, but the *ballet d'attache* used a combination of the baroque *danse d'école*, classical mythology and complex allegory, serving as a didactic tool within the play. Judith Rock, "Baroque Ballet, the Bible and the Jesuit Stage," *Choreography and Dance* (1992), vol. 2, part 3: 39–40.

71. Doherty, 174.

72. Michael Mendelson, "Saint Augustine," *The Stanford Encyclopedia of Philosophy (Fall 2009 Edition)*, ed. Edward N. Zalta, http://plato.stanford.edu/archives/fall2009/entries/augustine/.

73. Allan P. Farrell, *The Jesuit Code of Liberal Education: Development and Scope of the Ratio Studiorum* (Milwaukee: Bruce, 1938), 403.

74. Doherty, 44.

75. Tropiano, 58.

76. Ibid., 84.

77. Doherty, 295–96.

78. This may explain why the Spanish film censors, acting according to a different set of principles and independent of the PCA, called for cuts to Kelly's dream ballet with Charisse in *Singin' in the Rain*, while PCA censors make no mention of the overtly sexual nature of the choreography.

Masculinity has become a relentless test by which we prove to other men, to women, and ultimately to ourselves, that we have mastered the part.[1]

The conventions of [theatrical dance] generally ensure that the male dancer does not embarrass any male spectator: the male dancer should not appear sexually desirable and should direct the audience's gaze towards his female partner; if noticed at all he should be tested and must prove himself through bravura display.[2]

5

"Single Ladies" Is Gay

QUEER PERFORMANCES AND MEDIATED MASCULINITIES ON YOUTUBE

Harmony Bench

MASCULINITY THEORIST Michael S. Kimmel suggests that in U.S. culture masculinity is a test. Men must prove their masculinity; it cannot be taken for granted but must be performed over and over—not for women so much as other men. Furthermore, Kimmel argues that "masculine identity is born in the renunciation of the feminine, not in the direct affirmation of the masculine, which leaves masculine gender identity tenuous and fragile."[3] Defined through negation, the pool of masculine possibility shrinks for men as it expands for women, both because the contours of American femininity have proven more flexible than those of masculinity, and because female masculinity (e.g., being a tomboy) is not as socially scrutinized and abhorred as male femininity (e.g., being a sissy). Given the precariousness of masculinity, I am fascinated by the number of male dancers who, in 2008 and 2009, posted online videos of themselves dancing the choreography from the music video for Beyoncé Knowles's hit song "Single Ladies (Put a Ring on It)," directed by Jake Nava. The phenomenon of male dancers performing "Single Ladies" runs counter to long-standing attempts to "butch up" male dancing in concert dance as well as dance on television.[4] How, then, do men and boys stage themselves as males when dancing like a woman (i.e., like Beyoncé) to a song about female (dis)empowerment? We could follow Kanye West's proclamation of the "Single Ladies" music video as "one of the best videos of all time"[5] and suggest that the dance transcends the gender of its performers. However, as demonstrated in online comments that respond to young men's performances of "Single Ladies," many online viewers believe that "Single Ladies" is such a gender-specific dance that it should be performed exclusively by women.[6] Even toddlers and young boys are cautioned against performing the dance, for fear they will grow up gay.[7] For these spectators, submitting to this particular test of dancing skill—a challenge first extended in the abstract and later concretized with the announcement of dance contests sponsored by Beyoncé and any number of daytime talk shows—is to already fail as a man, this ultimate test that "is never over or in some reliable sense passable."[8]

If, as Kimmel suggests, masculinity is built on a renunciation of femininity, access to attitudes and attributes characterized as "feminine" is constantly mediated by the figure of the homosexual as a failed man. Even male dancers who do not embody queer kinesthetic stereotypes are taunted with gay slurs for their audacity to perform "Single Ladies." Policing the boundaries of masculinity while at the same time making possible an ambiguity of masculine expression, the figure of the homosexual fills the gap between masculinity as a receding horizon and the femininity against which it is defined. As an "internally excluded difference,"[9] this figure stands as both interdiction and as possibility, creating the space in which young men can perform "Single Ladies" but also restricting their means of access by subsuming all performances under the sign "gay."

In his essay "The Performance of Unmarked Masculinity," dance theorist Ramsay Burt reflects on the importance of dancers as mediators between choreographers or choreographic material and audience members: "The spectator responds to the performance itself, while the performer frames the material in ways that limit and direct the kinds of interpretive manipulations a spectator can make."[10] Though Burt locates this specific intermediate relation in "live performance" where dancers can "sense the audience's response,"[11] this same relation exists, perhaps to an even greater extent, in social media environments. Indeed, approaching the many re-performances of "Single Ladies" is, in some ways, more revealing than looking exclusively at the choreographic content of Beyoncé's video. As the number of imitations and reproductions of a given choreography increase thanks to social media's participatory culture, each performance provides new framing and delimitations, which means that as performers bring their own interpretive and performative lenses to bear on a choreography, the possible interpretations multiply. Taken together, the performances do not limit a spectator's "interpretive manipulations" but instead expand a choreography's possibilities with every restaging. Burt goes on to suggest, following art theorist Mieke Bal, that performance should not be considered a transparent expression of a "choreographer's intentions" and that one must shift the site of analysis from choreography to performance in order to discern the "affective, political, and intellectual relationship [that] is created between dancer and spectator [which is] crucial to the ideas about gender that are brought into play during a performance."[12] Though Burt suggests that in analyzing gender individual performances surpass choreography in importance, I hold choreography as centrally important in considering the diversity of male performances of "Single Ladies" and try to sustain equal attention to both.

Pointing to tensions between the choreographic precedents on which Beyoncé's "Single Ladies" relies and individual performances by Beyoncé and male dancers online, and to the (sometimes) antagonistic relationship between online performers and online commentators, I aim to show in this essay how male performances of "Single Ladies" on YouTube illuminate the perceived possibilities and limitations of queer masculinities. I argue that online responses to these performances show the conceptual labor of the homosexual figure, which both holds the place for and mediates the performances of non-normative masculinities. In putting their masculinity on the line *en masse*, these dancers collectively open a space for masculine expression not predicated on the renunciation of the feminine but existing in productive physical dialogue with it.

I have organized this essay as a series of encounters between dancers on YouTube. Each dance-off or dance challenge is a response to or reiteration of "Single Ladies" that presents a new framework for analyzing the music video and choreography. My emphasis is on how the dancers approach and perform the dance, how YouTube viewers respond to those performances, and my own reading of the videos and comments.[13] I have chosen this method of organization because the dance challenge—a dance that demands a response from a larger community of dancers—works well as a metaphor for how dance circulates through social media sites, with performers trying to out-dance one another or parody/clown others' performances. The dance challenge also mirrors the structure of negotiations around masculinity online, with physical declarations and renunciations of masculinity in the videos and verbal jousting in the comments. Although I focus in this essay on male performances of "Single Ladies" on YouTube from 2008 to 2009, I begin with a much earlier incarnation of the "Single Ladies" choreography: the short dance "Mexican Breakfast," choreographed by Bob Fosse and performed on television in 1969. The background relationship between these two pieces circulating online as Internet memes—units of cultural information that spread through the Internet in shifting configurations[14]—informs a historicization of later "Single Ladies" performances. I then turn to effeminate performances of "Single Ladies," comedic and failed performances of gender, and finally, the difficulty of using "Single Ladies" as a platform for performing more conventional versions of masculinity.

SINGLE LADIES AS A SHARED OBJECT: ON DANCE IN SOCIAL MEDIA

Elsewhere I have delineated some prominent aspects that characterize the contemporary trend of dance in social media sites, highlighting their articulation of social media's ideologies of participation in choreography, performance, and spectatorship.[15] Because they travel from body to body in a way that recalls the operations of viral media, I call choreographies such as "Single Ladies" *viral choreographies.* "Single Ladies" and similarly circulating dances accumulate performances into a complex network of movement citations. Because it was created in response to remix and mash-up culture, re-performances of "Single Ladies" are integral to the music video's online identity. As such, "Single Ladies" is a special instance of dance in social media. Beyoncé's "Single Ladies" is a privileged performance, a version that sits within a constellation of "Single Ladies" performances that mimic it, reify it, or rework it.

By now it is well known that in their choreography for the "Single Ladies" music video Frank Gatson and Jaquel Knight quoted lengthy sequences of Fosse's "Mexican Breakfast." When critics and online commentators discovered that Beyoncé's choreographers did not so much compose as arrange the "Single Ladies" dance, they accused Beyoncé of stealing the choreography. In spite of such condemnations, "Single Ladies" sits well within the norms of contemporary cultural production, which art curator and theorist Nicolas Bourriaud has described as an era of "postproduction"—the reuse of existing works and blurring of "distinction[s] between production and consumption, creation and copy, readymade and original work."[16] Just as contemporary artists working in a fine arts setting recycle and recontextualize materials to allow new signification, Beyoncé has repurposed existing choreographic material for her music videos.[17]

Dance off: Gwen Verdon vs. Beyoncé Knowles
    "Most of the same steps, done at twice the speed."[18]
        Sporting a yellow dress shirt under a white vest with white bellbottom slacks, Gwen Verdon is flanked by two dancers in bright pink. Sunglasses perched in their poofy hair, they bob their heads to the beat, slinking forward by circling their hips and dragging their feet, maintaining a triangular formation with Verdon at its apex. They rock their hips forward and back as they gently press the space around them outward with their hands, circle the stage perimeter in a prance, and collapse their upper bodies into high kicks. Arms overhead, backs curved slightly, left feet in a forced arch and knees bent, they rapidly jackhammer their weight-bearing right heels—a vibration that travels upward to subtly shake their buttocks. The dancers return to their slinking, bobbing, and rocking. Although they sometimes strut and take up the stage space, their gestures are mostly small and contained, creating an overall rhythmic pulsation rather than a bravura display of technical virtuosity. Verdon and her dancers remain "cool" throughout, not appearing to overexert themselves in their execution of the choreography.
        Dancing in the guise of her alter ego Sasha Fierce, Beyoncé Knowles and her backup dancers Ebony Williams and Ashley Everett[19] bring more attitude, higher high-heeled shoes, and barer legs to the choreography than Verdon's trio. The dancers' long hair falls over their shoulders and whips through direction changes, and the cut of their black leotards frames their sideways-popping hips. The dancers bring viewer awareness to their collective marital status, pointing out the absence of rings on their ring fingers to the refrain "If you liked it, then you shoulda put a ring on it." Beyoncé sings of her former beau's infidelity and his jealousy that she has moved on. Beyoncé and her dancers bounce in their upper bodies while allowing their hips to smoothly rotate or

strike with the beat. They wave their arms around their heads with vogue style and drill team precision, float above the music with small turns and syncopated chassés, and they smack their rumps and shake their hips.

The sharp attack of Beyoncé's striking hips figures as prominently in the "Single Ladies" music video as Gwen Verdon's constantly rocking pelvis in "Mexican Breakfast." Whereas Verdon's movement is continuous with occasional punctuation, Beyoncé's is mostly punctuated with occasional continuity in its flow. Everything about "Single Ladies" is bigger than "Mexican Breakfast." If Verdon's trio of white women is cool, then Beyoncé's trio of African American dancers is hot, hot, hot. Although Beyoncé and her dancers remain choreographically faithful to the sequences pulled from "Mexican Breakfast," Beyoncé pops her gestures to her song of (dis)empowerment, infusing her motions with an "in your face" attitude that Verdon's playful and inviting performance does not share.

The day after the "Single Ladies" music video was released, Beyoncé remarked in an interview on the BET television show *106 & Park*:

I saw this…on YouTube and it's these three ladies and one of them is Bob Fosse's wife, who's this choreographer, and they're doing 'Walk It Out'—they put 'Walk It Out' to the music, it's from like the 60s—and it's one take [...] and I thought, 'wow, how amazing would that be now,' because videos have so many different cuts and different takes, just to see a non-stop dance video, one take all the way through, very simple.[20]

What Beyoncé saw was not a recording of the original 1969 "Mexican Breakfast" performed by Gwen Verdon and two other dancers on *The Ed Sullivan Show*, but a video mash-up called "Walk It Out, Fosse." Posted online in 2007 by team members of the design company Diamond Creative, "Walk It Out, Fosse" was part of a wave of mash-ups that followed the 2006 release of D. J. Unk's song "Walk It Out."[21]

Whereas the Diamond Creative team responsible for "Walk It Out, Fosse" engaged in a form of digitally enabled appropriation, combining Unk's music with the "Mexican Breakfast" video via electronic means, Beyoncé and her dancers engaged in a bodily appropriation of Fosse's movement. In her essay "'Stealing Steps' and Signature Moves: Embodied Theories of Dance as Intellectual Property," dance historian Anthea Kraut argues that in so-called vernacular dance forms—particularly those promulgated by early-twentieth-century African American performers and entertainers—copying, lifting, or stealing other dancers' steps has been integral to the learning process and the creation of movement communities around certain dance styles. This is precisely the activity in which Beyoncé herself engages, supported by choreographers Gatson and Knight. As Kraut explains, "social dances depend on the give-and-take that makes the idea of granting a dancer a performance monopoly on a particular step or set of steps both problematic and impractical."[22] One could argue that "Mexican Breakfast" is neither a social dance nor a "set of steps" and should consequently be subject to the performance monopoly Kraut describes as impractical for vernacular and social dance forms. However, in the contemporary domain of social media, once-copyrighted materials circulate following the same logic of appropriation and intertextual reference as the performers Kraut analyzes.[23] Indeed, as Bourriaud describes in his analysis of the aesthetics of postproduction, "Single Ladies" repurposes "objects that [were] already circulating on the cultural market"[24] and gives them new meaning through their recontextualization.

Combining imitation with innovation, Gatson and Knight intersperse Fosse's sampled choreography with J-settes or eight-counts, which are precision movements that punctuate each count of an eight-count musical phrase. The style was popularized in the 1990s in gay clubs throughout the U.S. South[25] and was picked up by the Atlanta-born Knight for inclusion in the "Single Ladies" video. Though rarely mentioned, the music video also borrows sequences from "There's Gotta Be Something Better Than This" in Fosse's *Sweet Charity*—most notably the rump smacking, and a stylized version of the hip hop dance move Whoop Rico can also be spotted.[26] Like creators of video or audio mash-ups, Gatson and Knight remix distinct movement practices in order to create something new from their conjuncture, offering a challenge to dancers and viewers alike with the "mimicry with a difference"[27] of their choreographic arrangement. Additionally, by including Fosse's choreography in her music video, Beyoncé sets it in circulation among a generation of dancers and viewers who are likely unfamiliar with Fosse and Verdon. She recuperates and disseminates Fosse's movement as a shared object that those who imitate her likewise embody. The filming and editing techniques used for the music video, also borrowed from the television incarnation of "Mexican Breakfast," facilitate this task of bodily transference and/or reproduction. Beyoncé and her two dancers are in full view for most of the piece and few edits disrupt their dance sequence, making the transition from a digital media platform to bodily platform reasonably easy.

On February 23, 2009, after many "Single Ladies" fans (and critics) had posted videos of their own dancing to YouTube, Beyoncé announced a dance contest in which participants were to "adhere precisely to the iconic 'Single Ladies' dance routine performed by Beyoncé and her two dancers in the original clip." Although performances and parodies were already proliferating online, Beyoncé refused contestants the liberty of what Tricia Rose calls versioning, that is, of adapting or putting a new spin on an existing piece of music or series of steps. The contest rules specifically stipulated that "no new choreography should be added."[28] Beyoncé could not police the spoofs and other remakes of her video, but she did step in to oversee the reproduction of her version as a way to assert artistic ownership over the material while at the same time inviting its imitation. In this instance, imitation does not diminish Beyoncé's status as author, because the copies, accompanied by Beyoncé's music, continuously pointed back to her (rather than Fosse or Verdon, for example). Yet the migration of dance steps from one body to another across identifiers of race, gender, and sexual orientation does cause this choreography to multiply in its significations.

Tying "Single Ladies" to Internet culture by first incorporating choreography from a viral video and then promoting the dance in an online contest, Beyoncé integrated social media source material and reflected its modes of participation in the creation and dissemination of "Single Ladies." Although the dance contest did not serve as the catalyst for the emergence of "Single Ladies" as a viral choreography, it helped to ensure a future for the routine in electronic and bodily memories by occasioning the multiplication of performances. Beyoncé established ideal conditions for a viral choreography, which requires ongoing performance in order to sustain itself as a shared cultural object and what I call, adapting cultural theorist Sara Ahmed's terminology, a shared object of embodiment.

In *The Cultural Politics of Emotion*, Ahmed analyzes what she calls the sociality of emotion—the ways emotions circulate between bodies. Feelings do not transfer in a contagious manner, Ahmed argues, as though they were some property that could pass from hand to hand unchanged. Objects of emotion, rather than emotions as such, circulate and accumulate affective responses with continued circulation. Like commodities for Marx, emotions convert "the movement between signs or objects" into affect. For Ahmed, these movements form a shifting and growing set of associations—objects of hate that are linked together out of fear, for example, and that derive their meaning from their relation. Affect is thus the cumulative effect of circulation: "Affect does not reside in an object or sign, but is an effect of the circulation between objects and signs."[29] Beyoncé's "Single Ladies" is just such a circulating cluster of intertextual objects accruing affect—as a song, video, and choreography. Indeed, as a shared object the song outpaces the choreography; listeners sing along with the song playing on the radio more frequently than dancers embody its moves. With "Single Ladies" and other viral choreographies, the set of associations that grow out of movement among its surrounding signs generate affect, but it is movement of a corporeal nature, such as dancing a choreography, that links the affect back to embodiment. Although Beyoncé's status as pop icon and the success of the music video secured "Single Ladies" as a shared object of feeling, it is the choreographic component that renders "Single Ladies" a shared object of embodiment—that is, an object subject to physical restaging and not just digital reproduction, an object embedded in muscle memory rather than a surface of projected affects.

Just like viral videos such as "David After Dentist"[30] or "Charlie bit my finger—again!"[31]—videos that create a common ground of Internet cultural literacy without requiring their restaging but that nevertheless seem to compel users to post their own versions—"Single Ladies" invites YouTube users to perform, record, and post their performances of the music video's choreography online. Dancers thereby extend the reach of this shared choreographic object, participating in its circulation by incorporating its motions and disseminating the videated result. As a shared object of embodiment, Beyoncé's "Single Ladies" circulates online alongside other versions that imitate, approximate, and parody the music video. Each version accrues affective value in relation to the others, and online commentators often compare a video to other versions in their posts. As Ahmed argues, "Signs increase in affective value as an effect of the movement between signs: the more signs circulate, the more affective they become."[32] "Single Ladies" migrates from body to body and its ever-multiplying iterations travel the Web. But, like emotions, which are attached to circulating objects rather than being transmitted themselves, the choreography of "Single Ladies" does not copy exactly; it looks different on every body.[33] Furthermore, in the bodies of dancers, the "Single Ladies" choreography has undergone a process of resignification, morphing from a site of female (dis)empowerment to a site that supports the performance of a spectrum of masculinities and male femininities.

MAKING A SPECTACLE OF THEMSELVES: MALE DANCERS
AND THE FEAR OF QUEER

In the networked world of social media, male dancers have discovered a space in which to perform for a public audience—often at their peril. As the authors in *When Men Dance: Choreographing Masculinities Across Borders* make clear, to be a male dancer in the United States is already to render one's manhood suspect. Taking the additional step of posting recordings of one's dances to social media sites is to submit one's performance of non-normative masculinity to the judgment of a national and sometimes global Internet audience. If, as John Berger famously suggested in the 1970s, men act and women appear, to be on display as a dancer is to be visually consumed, which is already to occupy a feminized position in relation to a viewer. A man who dances makes a spectacle of himself by offering himself up to be seen. As Peggy Phelan argues in her critique of the visibility politics pursued by the political Left, "Visibility is a trap ...; it summons surveillance and the law; it provokes voyeurism, fetishism, the colonialist/imperial appetite for possession."[34] Male dancers, particularly those who present themselves within an eroticized queer frame, not only fall prey to the trap of visibility and come under the scrutiny of those who would police, fetishize, and challenge expressions of minority masculinities. They thereby violate the cardinal rules of male performance as observed by Ramsay Burt: do not appear sexually desirable, and do not embarrass male spectators.[35] Dancers must negotiate this politics of address differently in the space of social media than they would in theatrical venues, as Burt discusses, or even social dance clubs, as Jonathan Bollen describes in his essay "Queer Kinesthesia: Performativity on the Dance Floor." For Bollen, there are queer kinesthetic sensibilities, "queer styles of moving as a sexualized body" that viewers read,[36] whether in the context of a dance club or YouTube. Through their fashion choices and movement styles, queer dancers orient their performances of desirability toward specific audiences keyed into a similar register of desire. Viewers who fall outside that register but who nevertheless read the sexual overtones in their dancing may very well feel embarrassed or even scandalized at such a display.

Dance off: Shane Mercado vs. Chris McMillon (Angel Pariz)
"As gay as that was. . . . He did the choreography perfectly."[37]

On October 18, just five days after Beyoncé's music video for *"Single Ladies (Put a Ring on It)"* premiered on *MTV*, dancer Shane Mercado posted his video *"Single Man dances to SINGLE LADIES"* to *YouTube*. Mercado dances in his orange and grey bedroom surrounded by everyday objects: dressers against the walls, an umbrella propped in the corner, towels hanging on his door, a plastic sack peeking out from its spot on the doorknob. For this version, which has been flagged as inappropriate for viewers under 18, Mercado wears a costume as revealing as Beyoncé's: accentuating his slender physique, the top does not reach his nipples and the bottoms are Speedo-like in their simplicity. Mostly bare, Mercado ecstatically wriggles, hyperextends, and flexes his way through the *"Single Ladies"* dance. Even though his movements are clearly confined by the space in which he is dancing, his skill with hip/pelvic isolations comes across the screen unhindered. Mercado begins the dance with a cool, almost cold attitude and a hesitation born, perhaps, of concentration. He sings along, a smile curling at his lips, and by the time he reaches the second chorus of *"If you liked it, then you shoulda put a ring on it/Don't be mad when you see that he want it,"* the attitude has melted into a boyish grin. He plays to the camera with irrepressible energy—except for when he worries about running into the furniture. Mercado neither introduces his dance, nor does he say anything at its conclusion; he just walks over and turns the camera off as though his performance speaks for itself.

A day after Mercado's *"Single Man"* appeared online, Chris McMillon (aka Angel Pariz) posted his own version, *"Angel Pariz 'Single Ladies' By Beyonce Dance Cover."* McMillon (Angel), who maintains an online presence and personality on *YouTube* (Angel has a video channel that contains his performances of many music video dances, including those of Britney Spears, Lady Gaga, and Beyoncé), dances in a sparsely furnished room. He wears a black and green fitted top, black booty shorts, boots, and a do-rag. Unlike Mercado, McMillon's whole body remains in the frame but the image is low quality. The pixilation of the image, combined with his skill at performing a dance associated with women, renders McMillon's sex unreadable, or so he seems to himself believe, declaring to viewers through his captioned video *"O!. . . and by the way. . . I'M A BOY I'M A BOY I'M A BOY I'M A BOY!!!!!"* In fact, McMillon calls attention to many aspects of his dancing, filling the frame with text bubbles encouraging viewers to go to his Facebook page and to help send him to the Ellen DeGeneres Show, or to visit his Twitter feed or MySpace page. This video of McMillon dancing, in other words, is an advertisement for McMillon and is connected to other videos all referring to McMillon's attempts at fame (part of his Facebook address is *"makemefamous"*).[38]

Both performers over-exaggerate their movements, filling their confined rooms with exuberant torso articulations (Mercado) or head and arm motions (McMillon), bringing the percussiveness of clubbing and the largess of drag queen performances to bear on their dancing. They both overplay the Fosse-derived movements, the rocking *pelvis becomes, dare I say, penetrating, and the "butt jiggle" that results from rapidly raising and lowering the heel of an outstretched leg becomes a different kind of ass-shaking all together. Mercado, for example, sets his buttocks swaying from his tailbone while McMillon seems to stomp at the floor with bug-squashing insistence. The absence of high heels may be the genesis of these dancers' errant backsides, but more likely their mis-performances are linked to their reading of Fosse via Beyoncé rather than via his unparalleled interpreter Gwen Verdon. This is not to say that following Verdon's style would have altered the reactions of online viewers, many of whom criticize Mercado and McMillon for their spectacularly gay performances, but in following Beyoncé, they magnify (and queer) some of her movement tendencies not visible in Verdon's rendition.*

What seems to be at issue for many viewers is a combination of Mercado's and McMillon's queer movement styles, their revealing outfits, as well as the fact of latching onto "Single Ladies" as a shared object of embodiment. According to some viewers, the choreography should be the exclusive domain of women; its embodiment should not be shared across gender lines. Yet, as choreographer of a large portion of the sampled steps, Bob Fosse made more of a distinction between male and female sartorial styles than movement vocabulary.[39] Given that "Mexican Breakfast" was a "family-friendly" performance for television audiences, the sequences that Gatson and Knight borrowed are not particularly gender-coded or even highly sexualized. It would be incorrect, then, to assert that the choreography itself excludes male performers. It seems, rather, that it is the inevitable residue of Beyoncé's singing and dancing image that founds such assertions, despite the choreographers, lyricists, music composers, and music video director all being men. If Beyoncé as a commercialized fantasy haunts and informs male dancers performing "Single Ladies" on YouTube, the latter are also circumscribed by a circular logic that suggests all males (including children) who dance ("Single Ladies") are gay because only gays would be caught dancing (to "Single Ladies").

In his analysis of choreographer Joe Goode's stage-based work "29 Effeminate Gestures," David Gere argues that fear of effeminacy, or perceived effeminacy, is at the root of this gay-induced anxiety. "What exactly, then, are the physical codes that signify effeminacy?" he asks.[40] Reading Goode's performance, Gere observes that "Enthusiasm comes unbridled. The gestures are effulgent, ... *excessive.* .... Excess is enabled when the [societal] chains constraining one's corporeality break and shatter to the floor."[41] Similarly, Mercado and McMillon dance big, luxuriating in their "gestural freedom,"[42] even in the small rooms in which they dance. But following in the footsteps of the sexually assertive, body-confident Sasha Fierce rather than the softer, more vulnerable, "feminine" Beyoncé persona, Mercado and McMillon invest their performances with the maximum energy possible. Their dancing is truly over the top, uncontainable, effulgent and excessive—effeminate but not exactly feminine, a point to which I will return later on.

Regardless of their approach, Mercado and McMillon unapologetically frame their queer bodies for online viewers. Neither dancer has disabled comments on his YouTube videos, which offer readers a repository of viewers' sentiments. Many of the comments praise the dancers for their skill, but some viewers respond with slurs such as "faggot," "bicha," or extended statements such as "Damn this is just disturbing…straight up awful. yeah maybe he is imitating Beyonce pretty good but the dance is suppose to be done by WOMEN! Is feminine so yeah that makes this dude pretty much a fag" [sic][43]; and "errrr ugly lady boy, u got a dick mate act like you fucking got 1!" [sic].[44] Other comments are a little subtler ("wtf?"; "that was weird") or offer qualified praise ("I think yur the gayest person in the world but yu got talent man" [sic]).[45] Even some commentators who identify themselves as gay are reticent to advocate for Mercado and McMillon's performances of "Single Ladies," arguing implicitly or explicitly that such performances fulfill shameful and toxic gay male stereotypes. Queer theorist Judith Halberstam suggests that contemporary politics around gay pride offer gay men a way to "work through gay shame by producing normative masculinities and presenting themselves as uncastrated, muscular, whole."[46] Halberstam notes that the shame experienced by gay men as children "has to do with exposing their femininity and dramatizing their failure to access the privilege that has been symbolically reserved for them"—their failure to perform phallic masculinity.[47] Performances such as those by Mercado and McMillon undermine attempts by gays and lesbians pursuing a politics of assimilation, who, in hopes of garnering recognition and validation by the dominant straight culture, promote the collective embodiment of gender norms.[48] The fear of queerness and of effeminacy in particular, in other words, is a shared fear.

The threat Mercado and McMillon pose to some viewers seems tied to what the latter perceive as the dancers' shamelessness. Halberstam contends that "the sissy boy is the incarnation of shame,"[49] but by appearing online in all their sissy glory Mercado and McMillon refuse to be ashamed of their dancing. Viewers' caustic comments on their videos thus supply shaming mechanisms to offset the performers' lack of shame—a lack that appears as threatening to these viewers as the symbolic castration the dancers seem to represent. Though the performers are no longer children, viewers continue to exert social pressures toward gender conformity, engaging in what Bollen calls "the forcible production of abject homosexuality,"[50] exposing femininity and diagnosing homosexuality wherever alternative masculinities appear. What plays out in the comments, however, is not a uni-directional shaming of queer subjects by hetero/homonormative subjects. In addition to shaming the dancers, the viewers who post negative comments are also shamed: first by the videos themselves in which queer shamelessness shames viewers and prompts them to post their homophobic or effemino-phobic indictments, and a second time when commentators voicing support for the performers shame those viewers for their offensive and socially unacceptable posts. Shame is volleyed back and forth with each successive retort, the parties involved incensed by their inability to adequately shame those who are affectively alien to them.

Sara Ahmed uses the term *affect alien* in her essay "Happiness and Queer Politics" to describe the killjoy, specifically a (black) feminist killjoy who ruins the enjoyment of others by pointing out the sexist and racist implications of what those in an affective community enjoy. She explains, "When we feel pleasure from happy objects, we are aligned [with others]. We become alienated—out of line with an affective community— when we are not happy in proximity to objects that are attributed as being good."[51] If a majority of Mercado's and McMillon's viewers value the videos and, through their enjoyment, constitute an affective community around the videos as happy objects, those who find displeasure disrupt that affective community with their derisive remarks and contribute to "the loss of a shared atmosphere."[52] But if one community of viewers can be discerned through their displeasure at what they read as the dancers' queerness, on what grounds are positively inflected affective communities established in relation to the dancers or their videos? A survey of the comments seems to suggest that it is not the performers' queerness that turns the videos into "happy objects," since even viewers who do not chastise the dancers for being gay deflect into accepting the dancers "just the way God made them," or make it known to other commentators that even though they are complimentary toward the performers, they themselves are not gay. It would seem, then, that the competence of the dancers affords spectatorial enjoyment on which to construct an affective community among viewers. In these videos, skill and sexuality are tethered. Mercado and McMillon are clearly skilled dancers, but for a male dancing in this style, to dance in a competent way is to dance in a "gay way."

As I mentioned earlier, the male performers I have observed on YouTube perform not so much in a feminine way as in an effeminate or queer way, as though performing-woman remains beyond reach and the only access to femininity available to men (regardless of their sexual orientation) is through the stereotypical figure of the homosexual. There are many viable reasons for the figure of the homosexual mediating and transfiguring male femininity into queer effeminacy in online performances of "Single Ladies": dancers are gay and are not afraid to show it; dancing "like a woman" is subtler than the showier style of dancing "like a homosexual" (which is why women continuously lost "Single Ladies" dance contests on daytime television shows); Beyoncé's alter ego Sasha Fierce is a drag queen, that is, a fantastical version of femininity at home in the exaggerated aesthetics of camp; male femininity as such does not exist in the cultural imaginary except as gay, and for various reasons people (regardless of orientation or gender identity) feel compelled to continuously diagnose queerness wherever attributes coded as effeminate appear without female bodies. As masculinity theorist R. W. Connell suggests, the category or "social identity of being gay [...] is now so well formed and readily available that it can be imposed on people whether they like it or not."[53] The label *gay* erases all nuance and subsumes all slantwise performances of masculinity under its singular rubric. Alternate tactics of performance such as comedy, parody, and clowning offer a partial way out of this bind, but accusations of gayness/queerness have become so habitual that any escape is tenuous and provisional.

GENDER FAIL

Although colloquial usage has adapted the meme *fail* to express any kind of displeasure independent of competence assessment, the term was once framed by the tragedy of a sincere but inadequate performance. In a curious development of gender norms, young men have built on the success of television shows such as *Jackass*, which showed guys engaged in dangerous pranks and stunts, and the amateurism of Internet culture to articulate failure as a technique of (white) masculinity. The success of failure, it seems, has given young men leave to perform acts of superlative stupidity, as well as feats for which they do not possess the requisite skills, in front of a camera. Epic failure, that is a failure that is so complete and so miserable as to have been previously unimaginable, is a type of failure that is so satisfying to viewers that it becomes a "win" in its own right. Spectacular failures of the "epic" variety rival skillful execution. Whereas for the most part this results in so-called fail blogs being populated by extreme sports accidents and misadventures with power tools, this same ethos seems to have also opened up a space for "gender fails," or failed performances of gendered identities. The term *gay* has adapted many of the same features as "fail," though it is more derisive. As an insult directed at a person,[54] it has largely taken the place of "retard," which was used with excessive frequency in the 1980s and which has since largely fallen out of favor as a socially unacceptable derogatory term. However, where "retard," as crass as it is, pointed to a failure of competence based in mental acuity, "gay," usually directed at men or boys, links that same failure to manhood and sexual orientation. Whereas "fail" connotes a misfire or mistake, when used derisively toward a person, "gay" implies that the failure is one of gender. In other words, "fail" points to the action undertaken (You failed at …), while "gay" points to the person undertaking that action (You are gay).[55]

Dance off: Joe Jonas and Cubby
"hilarious!!!! and at the same time totally wrong!!!!"[56]
"It's for the fans," his brothers coax, and after much persuasion, singer Joe Jonas emerges from behind his brother, revealing himself to be dressed in a long-sleeved black unitard and high heels. As part of the countdown to the fourth Jonas Brothers album release, Joe Jonas dances to "Single Ladies." "Dances" is perhaps too generous. Rather, Jonas wobbles, wags his finger, grimaces, and lip synchs while the "Single Ladies" song plays. Perched atop high heels, Jonas is unable to maintain his balance and he sways from the torso up. True, he does manage to shake his butt, presumably for the pleasure of his female audience, but otherwise Jonas's performance is nearly unwatchable. He is alternately geriatric in his attempt to remain upright and electric in his body's flailing about as though prodded by shocks. Jonas is clearly watching the video while performing, and he doesn't know the words to the song. He does not dance with the intent of showing his skill. Instead, he stages a form of self-mockery that strategically foregrounds the absence of skill.

It is unclear what has motivated the Charlotte, North Carolina, radio personality Cubby (Jase Edwards Squires) to remake music videos by Beyoncé, Lady Gaga, Rihanna, and others. His version of "Single Ladies," performed in his living room, seems to have initiated his series of music video remakes. His black leotard and bare legs have now become something of a trademark in his home-based performances, but what really makes Cubby stand out from the crowd of imitators is his bulging belly. Unapologetically overweight, Cubby dances to songs by some of the leading contemporary female vocal artists and posts his videos online. For his video, "Cubby dances to Beyonce Single Ladies," Cubby has edited together several takes. He doesn't indicate if the cuts are a result of displeasure with his performance or lack of stamina, though the introduction of a handkerchief after the third cut suggests the latter. After editing, his video is under two minutes long, while the "Single Ladies" video is over three minutes.

While Joe Jonas's mockery is both self- and other-directed, which is to say, Jonas pokes fun at Beyoncé's "Single Ladies" and his performance of it, Cubby's seems mostly self-directed, as his dances seem to be sincere acts of fandom. Jonas stages his embarrassment at appearing in a unitard (one cannot be too eager to don a unitard and still be considered a "real" man) and his failure at "Single Ladies" in order to secure a masculine position, though some online commentators find proof of Jonas's rumored homosexuality in his having performed this dance at all. Cubby, in contrast, is not embarrassed and in fact seems rather empowered in his performances. What viewers mostly respond to in watching Cubby's videos is his obesity.

There are, to be sure, innumerable instances of young men and women failing at prescribed performances of gendered identities online. In fact, a search for "Single Ladies fail" on YouTube results in mostly female performers, who have identified their own performances as fail(ure)s through titles and tags, who do not posses the skill to perform either the "Single Ladies" choreography or Beyoncé's/Sasha Fierce's diva-like femininity. In her essay " 'Throwing Like a Girl'?: Gender in a Transnational World," dance theorist Susan Leigh Foster analyzes similar misperformances that lead to gender's choreographic undoing in contemporary postmodern dance choreography. Of interest for Foster is the way gendered movement citations function such that performers "underscore the pretence of their performance."[57] She suggests that citing and parodying gender's codes by putting on and taking off gendered identities destabilizes gender as a cultural construct. Foster points to British choreographer Lea Anderson's full-length work *Yippee!!* and the Japanese performance collective KATHY as examples of artists mining a "globally circulating set of [gender] codes" as gestural fodder for performing feminist critique.[58] This "repository of codes," Foster suggests, "can be tapped to accessorize any body."[59] Although Foster's analysis centers on femininity as accessory and the spaces of failure that performers carve out for themselves within femininity as a representational terrain, her provocative suggestion that gender, now globally uploaded, can be corporeally downloaded to suit various purposes is evidenced by the sheer number and variety of male performances of "Single Ladies" that can be found online.

However, the effects of what Foster might consider gender-destabilizing performances can also be put to the service of gender restabilization in the comments viewers leave in response to a video. As Judith Butler notes in *Gender Trouble*, "we regularly punish those who fail to do their gender right."[60] According to Foster, Anderson's performers offer viewers "a slightly different flavor of the feminine" with each glamour-infused scene,[61] but male dancers performing parodies of "Single Ladies" on YouTube miss the mark in their portrayals of feminine movement codes. They do not seem to have privileged access to the feminine gender codes-as-accessories that Foster describes,[62] even as they clearly leave (a dominant version of) masculinity behind in their performances of slightly different flavors of queer.

Take, for example, Joe Jonas, who fails remarkably in his parodic portrayal of femininity. Despite framing his performance as one demanded by fans, Jonas's sexuality comes under intense scrutiny. With more than 25.5 million views on YouTube and around 275,000 comments, it is not surprising to find a range of responses to Jonas's performance. What is surprising is that the term *gay* is the statistically most common word used in the video's comments.[63] Some viewers suggest that the "horrible…unwatchable" quality of Jonas's dancing of the video proves he is straight, implying that a "proper" gay man would/should dance well,[64] while others think his spastic dance is a cover and that "a straight man would have worked [the choreography] out."[65] Most viewers are simply shocked to see Jonas wearing a unitard and heels.

As a point of comparison, it is useful to examine how the television shows *Glee* and *Saturday Night Live* parodied "Single Ladies." I will not discuss these in detail since they were made for television, which has its own history of repackaging cultural material for popular televisual consumption. However, along with Cubby's performance, they offer representational strategies of which Jonas does not avail himself.

In the first season of *Glee*, the show's gay character, Kurt, who has joined the McKinley High School football team (it's a long story…), dances to "Single Ladies" to help him make a field goal.[66] Though it requires much convincing, the entire team eventually learns a sequence of "Single Ladies," which they dance on the field as a diversionary tactic. "Single Ladies" is deployed in the hypermasculine space of a football game where it lends the element of surprise to an underdog team. Dressed in football uniforms, it is impossible to tell the sex of the dancers, though the context suggests that television audiences read them as all male. The dancers move somewhat gruffly, as they would not want to be seen as effeminate by the other team. They are already taking a risk by performing this dance. It is crucial for both the narrative and the framing of the dance that McKinley scores—otherwise the football players' embarrassment at losing a game would be compounded by the humiliation of their out-of-place, cross-gender dancing. In performing "Single Ladies," they are risking public humiliation; they put their masculinity on the line as their last best hope for winning the game.

In the *Saturday Night Live* parody starring Beyoncé and Justin Timberlake, a trio of male "dancers" also put their masculinity on the line, but their uniform is quite different from that adopted by the cast of *Glee*: black unitards and high heels, but more important, affected hand gestures, body postures that emphasize their hips, and lisps when they speak. In other words, the men perform gay in order to deflect accusations of being gay. Instead of female impersonation, theirs is a form of gay impersonation. The skit suggests that Beyoncé and the three men are in a studio to record the "Single Ladies" music video, but the male dancers are hopeless—even Timberlake, a former member of dancing boy band 'N Sync. They do not know the choreography and appear not to have much experience wearing high-heeled shoes, so with each take they shake their butts, bump and grind, and devolve into a hot mess until Beyoncé refuses to put up with their dancing any longer. Though the men physicalize queer codes, they are neither fierce nor competent in their dancing; they are bumbling, hapless, and humorous.

In contrast to the performers on *Glee* and *SNL*, Cubby appears in his living room rather than on a television comedy. It would seem that he should have been subjected to the same biting criticisms as Mercado and McMillon, but this proves not to be the case. There are some gay slurs in his videos' comments, but the humor users find in watching him dance almost cancels out negative responses regarding Cubby's weight or perceived sexual orientation. Like Mercado, McMillon, Jonas, and Timberlake, Cubby shows a lot of leg in his leotard. His dancing is more restrained than Mercado and McMillon, however, and it is clearly difficult for him to perform the choreography. Cubby is no "twink"; he does not have the youth, slender build, stamina, or practice that many other dancers have. Cubby does have amateurism on his side, which has been valued in social media, but it is really Cubby's corpulence that sets him apart from the sea of both amateur and practiced dancers performing Beyoncé's "Single Ladies" online. Cubby's skin-tight costuming challenge to the cultural desexualization of obese people even turned him into something of a folk hero for a time. Some users post things like "omg," "my eyes, my eyes!" or "I can't unsee that," but comments also tip over into a strange form of admiration: SexyGal127 says, "mad props to you man, you got some guts for dancing like that" and magicalpoop declares, "You have balls of steel, sir."[67] Humor as the demonstrated absence of dancing skill does not rescue Jonas from gay slurs, but it almost works for Cubby. This discrepancy can be traced to their performances: Jonas has tried too hard to fail, revealing his insecurity and rendering his performance just a regular "fail," while Cubby's self-sure performance is so unexpected and such a breach of decorum that it earns him an "epic fail" and thus boosts his status according to the logic of social media.

In contrast to the performances of "Single Ladies" by Cubby and those shown on *SNL* and *Glee*, all of which demonstrate preemptive maneuvers or gimmicks that help stabilize the masculinity of the performers (football gear, playing gay, being overweight), Joe Jonas has no cover, no defensive tactic to deflate criticisms. Whereas the other situations enable their performers to accrue cultural capital for their performances that make up for a lapse in gendered behavioral protocols—McKinley High wins the game, Justin Timberlake gets to be popular again, Cubby gets millions of views online and appeared onstage with Beyoncé in an Atlanta concert—Jonas does not set himself up to gain anything from his performance. His is a defensive rather than offensive or anticipatory performance. Whereas Timberlake embraces his parodic gay character, Joe Jonas cowers behind his brother, reluctant to expose himself. Already suspected of being gay, hounded by paparazzi to come out, and catering to an audience of teen and pre-teen girls (with their crushes and school girl fantasies), Jonas is right to be anxious about his scrutinized masculinity. Without a narrative in which to couch his performance or an ingenious scenario in which to recuperate his gender fail, he opts instead for a spastic performance in which he actively repels the feminine codes placed on his body through Beyoncé's fashion and the "Single Ladies" choreography. In an attempt to not be emasculated by his unitard, high heels, and broken wrists, Jonas fails at performing both masculinity as well as femininity. Because he is suspected of being gay and because his young fans (or their parents) might take offense at any allusion to queerness—his own or that of imagined others— Jonas also has no recourse to the figure of the homosexual as a way to defend his challenged heterosexuality through a mockery of minority masculinities. But even though he does not embody or parody queer kinesthetic codes, his performance is nevertheless criticized as evidence of homosexuality.

To be sure, there are plenty of online viewers who have no fondness for the Jonas Brothers or their music and who take cheap shots at them and other boy bands. But explaining away some of the comments on the YouTube video does nothing to alleviate the ridiculousness of Jonas's grimacing performance. For comedians and others who perform parodies of gender for the sake of humor, the gender fail is necessarily double: one must initially fail at one's own gender and then fail at the gender one portrays in order to resecure the first. The second failure must be greater than the first, outwitting it. In the realm of social media, only a male's spectacular failure at femininity offers to compensate for performing feminine codes in the first place. Even then, the outcome is not guaranteed as the online reception of Jonas's performance demonstrates. Nor are there assurances for those men who abandon unitards and high heels in favor of conservative but stylish men's clothing. They do not martyr themselves to their clothes[68] in the way that Mercado, Mc-Millon, Cubby, and Jonas do, yet they too find their masculinity questioned.

DANCE LIKE A MAN

Given the widespread failure of gender in male performances of "Single Ladies"—a failure welcomed by some and abhorred by others—is it even possible to dance "Single Ladies" "like a man"? Although I admit I am not sure what that phrase means as a physical practice, since masculinity is an impossible test, I will nevertheless venture to suggest that it is possible to dance the "Single Ladies" choreography in a masculine manner, but to do so requires that performers bypass Beyoncé's Sasha Fierce personality and sexualized performance quality. In a sense, such performances return to the classic style and comparative gender neutrality of "Mexican Breakfast"—whether or not the performers acknowledge any intention to dig down into this sedimentary layer of Beyoncé's performance.

Dance off: Purple Haze (Darius Crenshaw, Grasan Kingsberry, Brian Brooks) vs. ts19180 (anonymous)

"no homo but you guys can dance"[69]

Purple Haze performs their rendition of "Single Ladies" with, they note, some choreographic adaptations. The dancers are from the touring Broadway musical The Color Purple, *and as such they wear early twentieth-century slacks, vests, and caps, and they are framed by the golden hues of the musical's set and lighting. They are very dapper indeed. The leader struts backward to take his place downstage, and as music begins the other men join him in a triangle of shifting weight—side to side, hand on hip or rib cage, with an occasional flourish of the hand and wrist. "Now put your hands up": they kick at full height, outdoing Beyoncé's 45 degrees. Taking up the stage space, the dancers do not mince their steps but take their time, filling the music by sitting gently into their hips. They maintain a low center of gravity—the movement of their upper bodies rests atop rooted lower halves. They initiate their movements cleanly, remaining very close to Beyoncé and her dancers in performance quality. Reinforcing their gentlemanly qualities, they occasionally remove and gesture with their caps, and, crucially, they omit the choreographic keystone: instead of gliding their heads back and forth atop their shoulders, continuously rotating their left hands from one side to the other to display the absence of a ring, they insert entirely different choreography. The choice to exclude such a strong symbol of female (dis)empowerment is striking.*

Visually establishing their maleness at the outset, the two unnamed male dancers in ts19180's "Single Man Single ladies Beyonce" perform bare-chested, exposing the shapeliness of their well-developed muscles. They have mastered the choreography's sequencing and phrasing but dance somewhat conservatively, keeping close to Beyoncé's energy and effort. These young men neither underplay nor overplay Beyoncé's gestures and the femininity with which she executes her movement, and they are nuanced enough in their imitation that they even copy Beyoncé's facial expressions, smiling when she smiles. Though they miss a few changes of head direction, their performance remains one of the most accurate imitations on YouTube in terms of duplicating Beyoncé's movement quality and intention.

Both Purple Haze and the two anonymous dancers approach "Single Ladies" as a sexy but gender-neutral dance that anyone can perform. In their period-style costumes, the dancers in Purple Haze move through the choreography in a genteel manner that fosters a refined masculine expression, while the bare-chested anonymous young men in baggy jeans suggest participation in street dance aesthetics that embrace fluid movements alongside the more familiar percussive and discontinuous moves. Neither group attempts to undermine homoerotic registers; nor do they amplify them. They perform without overtly embracing queer (kin)aesthetic sensibilities and without fearing femininity or queer possibility.

Fashion choices, as it should by now be apparent, are crucial to how men frame their dancing bodies on YouTube. In dance clubs, Bollen argues, the bodily orientation of dancers indicates to whom they address their dancing. This facing, along with proximity to other dancing bodies, becomes the foundation upon which "social relations are ventured, negotiated, and sustained on the dance floor."[70] In contrast, YouTube dancers perform in the absence of other dancing bodies and thus do not manifest their affiliations through their spatial proximity to others. Dancers in videos nevertheless create their own kind of facing or what, following Rosalyn Diprose, Bollen calls "opening onto others."[71] Fashion is the key to this mode of address.[72] For example, whereas Mercado and McMillon dance in outfits that sartorially signify the performers' queer identities, the unitards that Jonas and Cubby (and Timberlake) sport are intended as a farcical doubling back to position the wearer as one who would never or should never wear such an item of clothing, while the attire of the anonymous brothers and Purple Haze does not itself suggest the sexual orientation of the performers. Nor is it clear from the dancers' performance style toward what target audience(s) they orient their dancing.

The dancers in Purple Haze and ts19180 permit homoerotic readings without dampening the enthusiasm of (purportedly) straight female audience members. Indeed, both groups perform a conventional fantasy of the smooth, sexy, sensitive guy who can sweep a woman off her feet. Responding to this portrayal of masculinity, women offer mock proposals of marriage, and both men and women comment on how sexy the performers are. This is also true for other performers who adopt a similar approach to the piece in terms of fashion and movement styles. For example, online commentators compliment Joner Hall, who won a "Single Ladies" dance contest on the *Rachel Ray Show*, for his dancing skills as well as his physique (his butt is particularly admired),[73] and Jeremy Cox and Alex Wong of the Miami City Ballet (the latter also of the 2010 season of *So You Think You Can Dance*) are adored for their fun and boyishly innocent version performed in dress shirts and ties.[74] Comparing comments across all the videos mentioned in this chapter, it is clear that viewers tend to be more comfortable with the masculinities that Purple Haze and ts19180 perform, and the tone of their language shifts accordingly. It helps that they perform in groups, distributing masculinity across bodies in such a way as to render masculinity a cumulative effect rather than the singular property of any one body. Still, masculinity reads primarily through the dancers' physical appearance, including developed muscles, choice of attire, and movement styles. The dancers masculinize the space around them in socially familiar ways, and as a result they are criticized far less frequently than other "Single Ladies" dancers. Despite performing "Single Ladies," the dancers seem to embrace gender norms at the level of self-presentation, troubling viewers' ability to visually apprehend their sexual orientations.

Removing fashion choices and bulging biceps from the equation, Purple Haze and ts19180 make a strategic aesthetic choice that further differentiates them from other online performers. Simply put, they do not attempt to embody Beyoncé. They neither demonstrate the likeness of their approximation to Beyoncé's own performance as do Mercado and McMillon, nor do they show how their imitation falls short like Jonas and Cubby. Instead, they bypass Beyoncé's performance, dancing the choreography rather than performing Beyoncé. With this maneuver, they set themselves alongside Beyoncé as interpreters of this choreography rather than as derivative performers—Beyoncé wanna-bes. This frees them to move through the choreography in a manner different from Beyoncé, but because of this difference their renditions are closer to Beyoncé's than are the videos in which dancers try to copy her. Performing on Broadway, where, no doubt, all the performers have encountered Fosse-style movement, surely assists Purple Haze in reaching the choreography behind Beyoncé's performance. Because ts19180 gives viewers no personal information, I cannot say what has facilitated the performers' interpretation of the choreography, in which, ironically, they copy minute details of Beyoncé's performance.

Though obviously skilled performers, neither group allows their own personalities to overshadow the choreography, thus allowing the subtlety—and gender ambiguity—of Fosse's movement to show through. Whether the dancers are aware of it or not, the choices Purple Haze and ts19180 make return "Single Ladies" to a movement style one can imagine Fosse performing himself. They recuperate the possibility of Fosse's own masculine presence, first sidestepped by Verdon in "Mexican Breakfast" and later erased by Beyoncé in "Single Ladies"—an absence compounded by the song's lyrics. Indeed, though Fosse does not himself perform in "Mexican Breakfast," he and other male dancers perform many of the same movements as Verdon and her female dancers, examples of which can be found in *Liza with a Z* ("Bye Bye Blackbird"), *Sweet Charity* ("Rich Man's Frug"), and *Pippin* ("Glory"), among many others. Where Beyoncé's rendition choreographically references Fosse, viewers and dancers who are unfamiliar with dance's gestural histories and repertories are likely to miss its presence in "Single Ladies" as a critical residue. In her book *Queer Phenomenology*, Ahmed suggests that heterosexuality constitutes a field in, around, and against which we orient ourselves. "Heterosexual bodies 'extend' into spaces," she says, "as those spaces *have taken form by taking on their [heterosexual] form*."[75] Although "Single Ladies" strongly implies heterosexuality, (theatricalized) femininity is foregrounded as constitutive of this particular field. Performers thus orient themselves around femininity as they extend into the space carved out by Beyoncé, a space that has relegated Fosse to the background in order to take on Beyoncé's form.

I began this chapter with Michael Kimmel's assertion that masculinity is a test, of which the renunciation of femininity is a crucial component. Yet over the course of this essay, I've surveyed a diverse group of men willing to submit to a test of dancing skill that requires proximity to "the feminine" in its alignment with the pop icon Beyoncé. Some of the men I've described performing "Single Ladies" complicate their performances of masculinity with effeminacy, and others don the trappings of femininity (unitard/leotard, high heels) while rejecting feminine (kin)aesthetic codes. Still others assert their masculinity through performances of gentility. Dancing "Single Ladies" and posting their recordings online, these dancers submit their performances to the scrutiny of viewers outside their affective communities. Many are berated for failing to appropriately perform the gendered behaviors assigned to their sex, for embodying a dance many viewers perceive as gender-specific, and for dancing in a way that online commentators designate as gay or queer regardless of whether or not the performers use such terms to describe themselves. Though viewers continue to approach their dancing through the mediating figure of the homosexual, reducing deviations from conventional masculinity to the adjective "gay," these performers shift the ground of contemporary expressions of masculinity within a broader U.S. cultural milieu. They collectively refuse the renunciation of femininity as the essential qualification for masculinity, and they do so not tucked away in dance clubs and theaters or even in the character "types" represented on television sitcoms; they do so circulating online in front of an anonymous audience of millions. For that, as one viewer put it, they have "balls of steel."

NOTES

1. Michael S. Kimmel, "Masculinity as Homophobia: Fear, Shame, and Silence in the Construction of Gender Identity," in *Privilege: A Reader*, ed. Michael S. Kimmel and Abby L. Ferber (Cambridge, MA: Westview, 2003), 71.

2. Ramsay Burt, *The Male Dancer: Bodies, Spectacle, Sexualities* (London: Routledge, 2007), 172.

3. Kimmel, "Masculinity as Homophobia," 60.

4. Jennifer Fisher, "Maverick Men in Ballet: Rethinking the 'Making it Macho' Strategy," in *When Men Dance: Choreographing Masculinities Across Borders*, ed. Jennifer Fisher and Anthony Shay (Oxford: Oxford University Press, 2009), 37.

5. West infamously interrupted Taylor Swift's acceptance speech for Best Female Video in order to announce this public assessment of Knowles's work. *MTV Video Music Awards*, MTV, September 13, 2009.

6. Other commentators compliment male performers by suggesting that they dance to "Single Ladies" better than Beyoncé did or better than a woman could.

7. See, for example, "Single Ladies Devastation," posted March 29, 2010, http://www.youtube.com/watch?v=sb9eL3ejXmE, and "Little White Boy Does Beyonce's Single Ladies," posted April 18, 2009, http://www.youtube.com/watch?v=hnFxOsIy1Ew. In contrast, a girl of about four years old in the viral video "Arianna dancing to Beyonce's 'Single Ladies' (Picture-In-Picture)" is accused of being too sexy for her age or a target for online sexual predation. Posted December 17, 2008, http://www.youtube.com/watch?v=5CU2JhYM8tY.

8. Avital Ronell, *The Test Drive* (Urbana-Champaign: University of Illinois Press, 2007), 139.

9. Leo Bersani, *Homos* (Cambridge, MA: Harvard University Press, 1995), 36.

10. Ramsay Burt, "The Performance of Unmarked Masculinity," in *When Men Dance: Choreographing Masculinities Across Borders*, ed. Jennifer Fisher and Anthony Shay (Oxford: Oxford University Press, 2009), 152–53.

11. Ibid., 152.

12. Ibid., 153.

13. YouTube comments are not an unproblematic "archive of feelings" (see Ann Cvetkovich, *An Archive of Feelings: Trauma, Sexuality, and Lesbian Public Cultures*, Durham, NC: Duke University Press, 2003), but because they contain viewers' responses in their own words and offer a range of responses, from the inflammatory and reactionary to the complimentary and appreciative, I find them valuable as a gauge of audience attitudes and reception.

14. The idea of Internet memes has been adapted from Richard Dawkins's *The Selfish Gene*. The author postulates the presence of gene-like entities, which he calls memes, that spread ideas and cultural phenomena such as catch-phrases, fashion trends, and beliefs. Memes are units of information that repackage themselves through variation and mutation to survive new cultural scenarios. This concept has been applied to viral media and can refer to any object, image, or idea that spreads through the Internet, whether forwarded and uploaded in unchanged form or recontextualized with each iteration. Examples of Internet memes include "Om nom nom nom," "Evil Bert," "Hitler Finds Out," and "LOL Cats." Users reinvigorate Internet memes by applying familiar phrases or images to new contexts, and they create branching memes from content joined in mash-ups. See Richard Dawkins, *The Selfish Gene* (Oxford: Oxford University Press, 1989).

15. See Harmony Bench, "Screendance 2.0: Social Dance-Media," *Participations: Journal of Audience and Reception Studies* 7.2 (November 2010).

16. Nicolas Bourriaud, *Postproduction: Culture as Screenplay: How Art Reprograms the World*, translated by Jeanine Herman (New York: Lukas & Sternberg, 2002), 7.

17. Beyoncé has used Fosse-inspired choreography before. For example, Beyoncé's "Get Me Bodied" music video borrows movement and scenery from "Rich Man's Frug" in Fosse's *Sweet Charity*. Her apocalyptic Afro-futurist music video for "Run the World (Girls)" similarly incorporates movement created by the Mozambican dance group Tofo Tofo, though in that instance the Tofo Tofo dancers also appear in the video.

18. Bienbiensuper, comment on "Beyonce confirmed that 'Single Ladies' video was indeed inspired by Broadway choreographer Bob Fosse," posted November 18, 2008, http://www.YouTube.com/watch?v=e-SlfHHd3qI&feature=related.

19. See Duncan, "Beyonce 'Single Ladies' Put a Ring on It," posted August 18, 2009, *The Inspiration Room*, accessed March 1, 2011, http://theinspirationroom.com/daily/2009/beyonce-single-ladies-put-a-ring-on-it/; and Margaret Fuhrer, "The Many Sides of Ebony Williams," posted June 1, 2009, *Dancespirit*, accessed March 1, 2011, http://www.dancespirit.com/blogs/2130.

20. "Beyonce confirmed."

21. "Walk It Out, Fosse" went viral after being mentioned by blogger and gossip columnist Perez Hilton.

22. Anthea Kraut, "'Stealing Steps' and Signature Moves: Embodied Theories of Dance as Intellectual Property," *Theatre Journal* 62 (2010): 178.

23. It is noteworthy that choreographic works were not even covered by copyright law in the United States until 1976—seven years after "Mexican Breakfast" appeared on *The Ed Sullivan Show*.

24. Bourriaud, *Postproduction*, 7.

25. J-setting was developed by the dance line at Jackson State University, known as the Prancing J-Settes. See "Fosse and JSettes," *Effervescent Collective*, no post date, http://effervescentcollective.org/projects-and-performances/fosse-and-jsettes/.This page is no longer available.; and Lewis Liddle, ed., no post date, "The Prancing J-settes: Origin and Development of the Prancing J-Settes," *Sonic Boom of the South*, http://sonicboomofthesouth.com/history/the-prancing-j-settes/.

26. Many thanks to D. Sabela Grimes for this observation.

27. Kraut, " 'Stealing Steps,' " 181.

28. "Beyoncé Announces Official 'Single Ladies' Dance Video Contest," last modified February 23, 2009, *Beyonceonline*, http://www.beyonceonline.com/us/news/beyonc%C3%A9-announces-official-single-ladies-dance-video-contest.

29. Sara Ahmed, *The Cultural Politics of Emotion* (New York: Routledge, 2004), 45.

30. "David After Dentist," posted January 30, 2009, http://www.YouTube.com/watch?v=txqiwrbYGrs.

31. "Charlie bit my finger—again!" posted May 22, 2007, http://www.YouTube.com/watch?v=_OBlgSz8sSM.

32. Ahmed, *Cultural Politics*, 45.

33. See performance scholars Ann Cooper Albright on dancers' "movement signatures" in *Traces of Light: Absence and Presence in the Work of Loïe Fuller* (Middletown, CT: Wesleyan University Press, 2007) and Erin Brannigan on screen performers' "idiogest" in *Dancefilm: Choreography and the Moving Image* (Oxford: Oxford University Press, 2011).

34. Peggy Phelan, *Unmarked: The Politics of Performance* (London: Routledge, 1993), 6.

35. Burt, *Male Dancer*, 172.

36. Jonathan Bollen, "Queer Kinesthesia: Performativity on the Dance Floor," in *Dancing Desires: Choreographing Sexualities on and off the Stage*, ed. Jane Desmond (Madison: University of Wisconsin Press, 2001), 303.

37. PrinceTraumatizine, comment on Shane Mercado, "Single Man dances to 'SINGLE LADIES,' " posted October 18, 2008, http://www.youtube.com/watch?v=SGemjUvafBw.

38. In McMillon's second "Single Ladies" video, "Beyonce 'Single Ladies' Part 2," he notes the shops from which he has purchased each item of his clothing, again turning his body and his video into an advertisement.

39. Male and female fashion choices also converged at times in Fosse's work, for example, with women appearing alongside men in top hats and coat tails.

40. David Gere, "29 Effeminate Gestures: Choreographer Joe Goode and the Heroism of Effeminacy," in *Dancing Desires: Choreographing Sexualities on and off the Stage*, ed. Jane Desmond (Madison: University of Wisconsin Press, 2001), 350.

41. Ibid., 356–57, original emphasis.

42. Ibid., 357.

43. Ariask617, comment on Chris McMillon [Angel Pariz] "Angel Pariz 'Single Ladies' By Beyonce Dance Cover," posted October 19, 2008, http://www.youtube.com/watch?v=7rknRJVdpOo. This video is no longer available.

44. Tangledup86, comment on Shane Mercado, "Single Man dances to 'SINGLE LADIES.' "

45. AaronAcodisin13, comment on Shane Mercado, "Single Man dances to 'SINGLE LADIES.' "

46. Judith Halberstam, "Shame and White Gay Masculinity," *Social Text* (Fall/Winter 2005): 228.

47. Halberstam, "Shame," 226. Halberstam is specifically referring to white gay men and to gay shame as a movement in the service of white gay men, but her comments on male privilege and normative masculinity are more broadly applicable.

48. Jonathan Bollen notes that "there are gay men for whom 'girly' is a style against which to define their dancing" (305). He goes on to state that gay men tend not to dance "girly" while cruising, and that one adopts a style of dancing according to what one hopes to accomplish through dancing, namely, having fun or cruising/getting cruised (305).

49. Halberstam, "Shame," 226.

50. Bollen, "Queer Kinesthesia," 302.

51. Sara Ahmed, "Happiness and Queer Politics," *World Picture* 3 (2009), 4.

52. Ahmed, "Happiness," 5.

53. R. W. Connel, *Masculinities* (Berkeley: University of California Press, 2005), 151.

54. "Gay" can also be directed at any object or situation a speaker dislikes or by which he or she is inconvenienced. Because I am concerned in this essay with videos of dancing that people have posted online, I attend to the human-directed uses of this term and do not consider its wider range of meanings as intended primarily by U.S. teenagers.

55. It is possible that some YouTube users who simply write "gay" as their comment intend their truncated insults to mean "that performance is gay" rather than "the performer is gay." However, when directed toward a person, I find the distinction untenable.

56. 01MZBIEBER, comment on Joe Jonas, "Joe Jonas Dances to 'Single Ladies,'" posted June 3, 2009, http://www.youtube.com/watch?v=rP-KFnYg6Hw.

57. Susan Leigh Foster, "'Throwing Like a Girl'?: Gender in a Transnational World," in *Contemporary Choreography: A Critical Reader*, ed. Jo Butterworth and Liesbeth Wildschut (London: Routledge, 2009), 61.

58. Ibid., 61.

59. Ibid., 60.

60. Judith Butler, *Gender Trouble* (New York: Routledge, 1990), 178.

61. Foster, "'Throwing Like a Girl'?," 60.

62. Ibid., 60.

63. I used the Google Chrome ad-on OpinionCloud, which analyzed the 999 most recent comments (as of 22 March 2011) on Jonas's YouTube video.

64. 3GPalmSprings, comment on Joe Jonas, "Joe Jonas Dances to 'Single Ladies.'"

65. sflachuck, comment on Joe Jonas, "Joe Jonas Dances to 'Single Ladies.'"

66. "Preggers," *Glee*, season 1, episode 4, FOX, September 23, 2009.

67. Comments on Cubby [Jase Edwards Squires], "Cubby dances to Beyonce 'Single Ladies,'" posted December 26, 2008, http://www.youtube.com/watch?v=o_lrKhmx2WU.

68. Kathryn Bond Stockton, "Cloth Wounds, or When Queers Are Martyred to Clothes: Debasements of a Fabricated Skin," in *Beautiful Bottom, Beautiful Shame: Where "Black" Meets "Queer"* (Durham, NC: Duke University Press, 2006), 39–66.

69. Vorido, comment on Purple Haze, "Beyonce's 'Single Ladies' by Purple Haze," posted December, 27, 2008, http://www.youtube.com/watch?v=3UPGWvAzRJA.

70. Bollen, "Queer Kinesthesia," 293.

71. Ibid., 293.

72. Tags, descriptions, and other metadata are another key way to designate "facing."

73. Joner Hall, "SINGLE LADIES' CHOREOGRAPHY by Joner Hall aka 'The Answer,'" posted January 14, 2009, http://www.youtube.com/watch?v=eTL6bLfbVR0.

74. Jeremy Cox and Alex Wong, "Beyonce—'Single Ladies'—Alex & Jeremy," posted March 26, 2009, http://www.youtube.com/watch?v=uxjolKcx6e8.

75. Sara Ahmed, *Queer Phenomenology: Orientations, Objects, Others* (Durham, NC: Duke University Press, 2006), 92, original emphasis.

PART TWO
Within the Body and Mind of the Dancer
and Choreographer

THE CHAPTERS WITHIN Part Two provide deep analyses or examinations of particular works or creative artists. The authors in this part avoid monolithic treatments of genre or style and allow the points of inquiry to emerge from the works themselves. Counterparts to oral histories exist in dance as physical histories, many of which have been built up over countless hours shared in the studio. Teacher-pupil and choreographer-dancer relationships are frequently deeply intertwined and are complicated to unravel, so these interactions in the studio are difficult to document. Most often reconstructors, choreographers and teachers communicate by physically embodying the essential attributes of dance, literally handing down their traditions through the demonstration and corresponding imitation of steps, gestures and movement phrases. Several chapters in Part Two explore the processes of transferring kinesthetic phenomena from one body—even one historical context––to another, critiquing, and paying homage to, individual dancers as they communicate across time and through their bodies, using the various physical languages of dance.

Some authors examine the role of collaboration and the variety of ways choreographic meaning can be established through the layering of constitutive elements. The relative independence of movement creation and exploration from other elements of a dance, such as the music or the design aspect, surfaces in more than one chapter here. Considering the role of collaboration provides another way into analyzing dance, prompting a number of questions: Where is the dance? Is it distributed across the various parts— music, text, scenic elements—the way an image is reflected in each piece of broken glass, or does the movement itself carry the greatest significance? Where do we see elements that clearly identify the choreographer's style? Where can we see contributions of dancers and collaborators? How is a work affected by the inevitable changes that happen over time and place to any work that endures? The fact that a dance is embedded not only in the choreographer's imagination and the dancers' enactment but also in the times and places of those enactments creates unlimited possibilities for cross-referencing influences from within and without the arenas of dance creation. In the following chapters, subjects range from online choreographic communities to the ultra-classical Petipa *pas de deux*, from mid-20th-century modern dance figures to considerations of teaching from contexts within the Baroque period and up to today.

In *"La Cosmografia del minor mondo*: Recovering Dance Theory to Create Today's Baroque Practice,"* Catherine Turocy demonstrates how Baroque dance of the 18th century occupied its own cultural space, informed by a set of values and aesthetic notions that prefigure, but are still distinct from, those assumed in most of the West today. That Baroque cultural space must be approached first on its own terms before contemporary dancers can accurately and respectfully enter into it. The dance of the past, insists Turocy, can be reclaimed by today's dancers, but only if they make the imaginative journey from the Renaissance forward in time, through the 16th and 17th centuries, learning and embodying the prevailing physical, spatial and aesthetic concepts articulated by prominent thinkers and artists including Leonardo da Vinci, Girard Thibault, Jeronimo de Caranza, and Don Luis Pacheco de Narvaez.

In "Pavlova and Her Daughters: Genealogies of Contingent Autonomy," Carrie Gaiser Casey is drawn to rethink the mother-daughter and master-apprentice relationships at the heart of Anna Pavlova's touring company. Drawing on feminist history, she asks how an examination of these conflated relationships might extend scholars' notions of ballet's pedagogical lineage. She proposes that the transmission of codified ballet technique is more open and adaptable than scholars generally acknowledge. Casey examines, in particular, the deep, rich and complicated phenomenal aspects of the relationship of dancer Muriel Stuart to her mentor. A photographic analysis of Stuart's bodily gestures reveals the dancer's indebtedness to, as well as her autonomy from, the powerful presence of her teacher and surrogate mother, Anna Pavlova.

Melanie Bales closely juxtaposes three duets from different centuries and styles, though each is located within the ballet idiom, in "Touchstones of Tradition and Innovation: *Pas de Deux* by Petipa, Balanchine and Forsythe." The comparative analysis forces inquiries into the codes and values of the balletic form itself, and a consideration of those values as they emerge through the steps and structure of the dances, the identities of the choreographers and the social and political climates surrounding the creation of each work. Her three examples are signposts by which to see the effects of time on a tradition, and to consider how both individual artists and collective choices have shaped that tradition. Various forms of analysis, including LMA, serve to anchor each piece in its own particular place and to show the gaps and overlaps among the dances.

Geraldine Morris' essay, "Joined-up Fragments in A *Wedding Bouquet*: Ashton, Berners and Stein," shares some similarity to other chapters in the book that locate a work inside a collaborative frame and are written from the perspective of an informed practitioner. In her analysis of Frederick Ashton's 1937 *A Wedding Bouquet*, she pulls apart the constitutive elements—music, movement vocabulary and text—asking how each was regarded in its own time and what the work as a whole might offer to audiences and dancers of today. Through her multi-layered examination, she uncovers the profundity at the heart of what might otherwise appear a relatively lightweight work in Ashton's *oeuvre*. Additionally, she proposes a complex view of Ashton's choreographic process; the choreographer simultaneously engages with a centuries-long tradition, working out his own creative fascinations and responding in a more immediate way to his own unique time and place.

The choreographer's identity, as woman, Jew, activist and dance artist, comes into focus in "*Kaddish* at the Wall: The Long Life of Anna Sokolow's 'Prayer for the Dead'." As seen in this work, the various strands of Sokolow's identity generated both friction and resolution; *Kaddish* is a deeply personal dance that also speaks to its audiences and has been a vehicle for performing artists other than the choreographer who, through their performances, come into dialogue with its creator. Hannah Kosstrin considers *Kaddish* a collection of iterations by analyzing documentation as well as performances of the dance, and the work emerges as one where different-but-equal interpretations point to the multifarious possibilities of art to communicate to its audiences and express the profound feelings of its performers.

As Jessica Zeller points out, ballet pedagogy has been mainly treated as a homogeneous entity, with teachers' individual contributions to the larger tradition of classical dance training often overlooked or dismissed as charming, but insignificant idiosyncrasies. In "Developing the American Ballet Dancer: The Pedagogical Lineage of Rochelle Zide-Booth," Zeller identifies Zide-Booth as a representative teacher whose role in helping develop the so-called eclectic approach to American ballet training stemmed, in part, from her desire to resolve her own physical questions and contradictions. In identifying the unique contributions of this ballet teacher—herself the product of a varied and eclectic array of teaching styles—Zeller further complicates the notion that classical ballet exists as an unbroken and monolithic teaching practice; she prompts us to think, instead, of the fluidity, heterogeneity and capaciousness of that centuries-old tradition.

6

La Cosmografia del Minor Mondo

RECOVERING DANCE THEORY TO CREATE TODAY'S
BAROQUE PRACTICE

Catherine Turocy

DIAGRAMS OF THE body in the Renaissance, such as Leonardo da Vinci's Vitruvian man (Figure 6.1), have influenced Western art for centuries, and they are thus useful to dance scholars and those interested in the reconstruction of Baroque dance. These diagrams, though, are not typically discussed in the dance manuals of Raoul Auger Feuillet (c. 1650–c. 1709) or Pierre Rameau (1674–1748), dancing masters who, in their day, were more concerned with recording step patterns in choreography than with theorizing about the body.[1] Nevertheless, period body image and movement theory can be recovered by today's dancers from diagrams of the still and moving body as seen in disciplines outside dance, and from descriptions of "good dancing" in period sources. Valuable sources include those of the artist and scientist Leonardo da Vinci, the fencing master Girard Thibault and the orator and minister Gilbert Austin.

As one who is active in Baroque reconstruction and choreography, I am interested in making historical dance come to life in today's performances of period works, and I have developed ways to enable dancers to experience the pre-performance state from which Baroque dance emerges.[2] Encouraging dancers to achieve this state requires their engagement in a historical style and aesthetic, informed by a particular set of body images and movement theories. In this research, preparing historically attuned performance, I set out to discover the scientific principles shaping the art of dance that emerged from a culture that believed there was a science to every art and an art to every science. Instead of looking from the 21st century back to the Baroque, I propose an alternative for contemporary

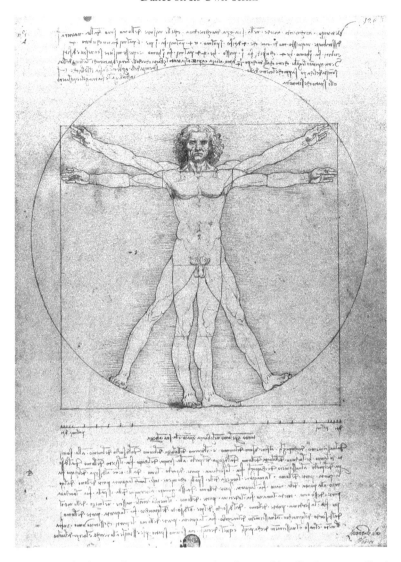

FIGURE 6.1 Leonardo da Vinci's Vitruvian Man, taken from Wikimedia Commons. The image is in the public domain because its copyright has expired. http://en.wikipedia.org/wiki/File:Da Vinci Vitruve Luc Viatour.jpg.

dancers: experiencing these body images and movement theories from the Renaissance forward. This perspective, reflecting as it does the natural growth and evolution of the form, encourages today's dancers to engage their kinesthetic knowledge in understanding the moving body in Baroque dance. Three fundamental principles are to be examined:

1. The historical body within a circle/sphere (a concept carried forward from the Renaissance to the Baroque and beyond)
2. Early concepts of *terre à terre* (17th and 18th centuries)
3. Original meaning of *le mouvement* (17th and 18th centuries)

THE HISTORICAL BODY WITHIN A CIRCLE/SPHERE

The Ancients, having taken into consideration the rigorous construction of the human body, elaborated all their works, as especially their holy temples, according to these proportions; for they found here the two principal figures without which no project is possible: the perfection of the circle, the principle of all regular bodies, and the equilateral square.

—from *De divina proportione* by Luca Pacioli, illustrations by Leonardo da Vinci

It is useful to begin by envisioning the active body within a circle or sphere, particularly using Leonardo da Vinci's Vitruvian man as a point of departure. Although this work is from the late 1400s, da Vinci's writings were published and disseminated in the 17th century and were much discussed in intellectual gatherings. Notably, in 1516 da Vinci entered the service of King Francis I, being given the use of the manor house in Clos Luce near the king's residence at the royal Chateau d'Amboise. The young King of France, who is generally credited with bringing the Renaissance to France, was tutored by da Vinci during the last three years of his life. Da Vinci's impact on French culture was enormous, and the artist was even to die in France in 1519. Because of his prominent role in French art and aesthetics, it makes sense to include da Vinci's concepts on the body when studying the origins of French ballet.[3]

Da Vinci used both image and text to express the ideas and theories of Vitruvius, a first century Roman architect and author of *De Architectura libri X*. The Vitruvian ideas as presented by da Vinci formed the basis of Renaissance proportion theories in art and architecture. Today's standard reference on da Vinci's anatomical notebooks is K. D. Keele's *Corpus of the Anatomical Works in the Collection of Her Majesty the Queen*. Keele discusses the drawing of the Vitruvian man, with his body first standing inscribed in a square and then, with feet and arms outspread, inscribed in a circle. Leonardo describes the drawing thus: "If you open your legs so much as to decrease your height 1/14 and spread and raise your arms till your middle fingers touch the level of the top of your head you must know that the centre of the outspread limbs will be in the navel and the space between the legs will be an equilateral triangle. The length of a man's outspread arms is equal to his height."[4] The center of the square is the pelvis. According to Pythagorean tradition, the circle represents the spiritual realm, and the square represents material existence. Thus, according to da Vinci's formulation, the human body represented the perfect marriage of matter and spirit.

Da Vinci related man to nature and considered the Vitruvian man a *cosmografia del minor mondo* (cosmography of the microcosm). He believed the workings of the human body were an analogy for the workings of the universe:

By the ancients man has been called the world in miniature; and certainly this name is well bestowed, because, inasmuch as man is composed of earth, water, air and fire,

his body resembles that of the earth; and as man has in him bones the supports and ·
framework of his flesh, the world has its rocks the supports of the earth; as man has
in him a pool of blood in which the lungs rise and fall in breathing, so the body of
the earth has its ocean tide which likewise rises and falls every six hours, as if the
world breathed; as in that pool of blood veins have their origin, which ramify all
over the human body, so likewise the ocean sea fills the body of the earth with infinite springs of water.[5]

For today's dancer, working with the theory of *cosmografia del minor mondo* may suggest
an image of the body as earth and the veins as rivers connected to the ebb and flow of the
sea. The uneven flow of water in the cycle of the wave with its cresting and falling suggests
an uneven rhythm of energy flow; before the body even begins to move in space it is associated with the sea's movement. Using images of nature can remind today's dancer that, in
the Baroque period, art was seen as nature perfected. Truth and beauty existed in a work
of art precisely because it was rooted in nature. Da Vinci's drawing and text for the Vitruvian man gives dancers a visceral sense of their own bodies standing still. I often liken this
state to a "premovement or pre-performing state" from which the first breath of movement
emerges.[6]

THE SPANISH CIRCLE

The next circle to be considered is known in fencing as the Spanish Circle, or the Myste-
rious (also Magic) Circle, and is drawn from a discipline outside, but directly related to,
dance.[7] The fencing master and the dancing master in the 17th through the early 20th
centuries often taught in the same school, sharing spaces. Indeed, it was not uncommon
for the dancing master to also serve as the fencing master. Such a circle as this would have
no practical use in a dance manual; however, anyone who fenced and danced would have
this spatial concept in his well-practiced body.

The diagram, by Girard Thibault of Antwerp, is originally found in his *Académie de
l'Espée*, published in 1628.[8] On the basis of earlier theories of fencing masters, Thibault
"anatomized" the art of sword fighting and used this diagram to explain attacks and
retreats. As in da Vinci's drawing, the center of the body in Thibault's image is the
navel. But in place of da Vinci's square, Thibault envisions the body inside a diamond,
with the space conceived of as a web of intersecting points, describing attacks and
retreats from a strong center. The stance, attack and defense are all conceptualized
within a circle with the fencer remaining inside his sphere as he moves around his
opponent. This circle continued to be used as a spatial image in fencing instruction
well into the 1800s.

Although da Vinci's drawing is a flat circle, the body within the circle suggests life, with
its flowing hair and sculpted muscles. Da Vinci emphasizes the proportional balance of

the body with the navel as the center of the spiritual world represented by the circle, and the genitals as the center of the physical world represented by the square. In contrast, the Spanish Circle with its diagonal web of lines suggests paths in three-dimensional space, even though at first glance the drawing appears flat. The size of the Spanish Circle is in proportion to the man. However, one must read the foot symbols in the drawing, imagining that the man is standing in a perpendicular relationship to the paths in the drawing. This physical relationship of the real body to the diagram is the same relationship one experiences when reading a map while searching for an address, or when deciphering Feuillet dance notation from the page. In other words, a 17th century man would see the body in the Spanish Circle as a reference to the circumference of the circle in proportion to his own body and would read the shifts of movement described by the foot symbols as choices for foot movement while fighting.

The Preamble in the official papers for the establishment of L'Académie Royale de Danse in Paris in 1670, housed in the archives of the Bibliothèque de l'Opéra, reads in part: "The King equates the importance of dance with that of the military. In wartime, nobles are in the service of the King's army, but in times of peace, they are in the service of his ballet."[9] The French fencing salute of the period defines a sphere with the foil being raised over the head and lowered to engage the opponent's foil. In fencing, as in dancing, the elbows, and often the knees, are maintained in a supple, bent position. However, such pliability in the joints does not make the movement weak; on the contrary, the joints are spring-loaded and ready for attack. The line of attack often takes the fencer beyond his own sphere as he attempts to penetrate that of his opponent. Hence, the fencer is very aware of his kinesphere (the space his body occupies when the limbs are extended) and his opponent's, and he understands too what it means to penetrate the kinesphere with the attack of the foil. The nonfoil arm acts to balance the attacks and the retreats of the body. This sensation of the movement reaching beyond the physical limit of one's limb is common in ballet, where the gesture is meant to project outward in space, according to the dimensions of the theater.

One begins to see commonalities between early ballet technique and the body in combat. The *plié* position (knees bent) is grounded; quick, shifting movements allow one to retreat or to attack; the foot feels the ground, testing for stability and changes in slant as one adjusts one's balance. The back foot helps to push the body forward in an advance, much the same way as the supporting foot eventually pushes the body forward in the danced *demi coupé*. The upper part of the body elongates or contracts and weaves from side to side as the combat or dance ensues. Normally, the upper body is held with a slight vertical spiral (possibly akin to *épaulement*) with the intention of minimizing the available target area. The motion of the upper body must be supported by a strong lower body. Oppositional forces in attacks and retreats are held together through a strong center in the body. In addition, both the opponent in combat and the partner in dancing share a back-and-forth play, a keen kinesthetic awareness of the physical space; each senses the movement and emotional impulses of his partner.

THE SPHERE

The long-lasting influence of the sphere on the practices of Baroque dancing masters is emphasized by its continuation into the post-Baroque era, here seen in the book *Chirono-mia*, by Reverend Gilbert Austin (1753–1837), published in 1806.[10] Intended for the public speaker and the actor, Austin's sphere reflects the body's space in shifting postures and gesture (Figure 6.2). Austin does not use a sphere to demonstrate proportion, but rather to organize expressive directions in space, using the body as the center of the sphere from which these gestures expand and retract. His system pinpoints the end of a gesture in space. Spatial directions are coded with letters of the alphabet. The system is a memory aid to an actor or orator. To employ the system, one merely writes the letter of the alphabet above the word corresponding to the placement of the gesture. Austin used pictograms with his notation, printed above the spoken words, to illustrate his employment of the system when reciting a poem. This example clearly reveals the concept of the body moving within a sphere, where spatial directions and shifts of the body from a stationary position possess dramatic implications. Hence, Austin suggests, the body lives within this expressive sphere.

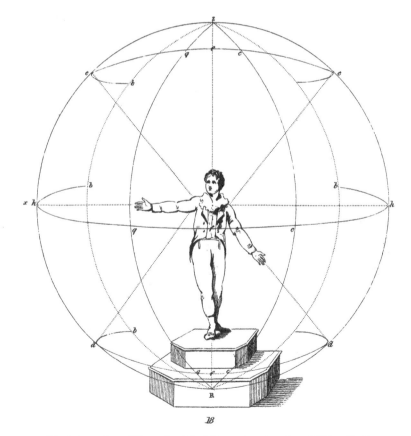

FIGURE 6.2 The Sphere, from Gilbert Austin's *Chironomia*, taken from Wikimedia Commons. The image is in the public domain because its copyright has expired. http://en.wikipedia.org/wiki/File:Chironomia%20Sphere.jpg.

My application of the idea of the sphere for dance is that the dancers remain inside their individual spheres when they move in space. Whether traveling in space or resting in one spot, dancers have an awareness that the declamatory gestures are made within their individual spheres and are executed in proportion to their own body size. In my teaching I have christened this sphere "the Baroque Bubble." Just as a bubble bursts if it is touched, so the dancer's Baroque Bubble will disappear if the limbs are fully extended in a locked position. In the Baroque period, straight arms and gestures, locked knees and any rigidity in the joints was considered ugly. Furthermore, in the fencing or fighting body, this locking of the joints could result in death as such stiffness of movement made it more difficult to sense and overtake the opponent. Meanwhile, the attacker's thrust must be rigid, piercing the opponent's bubble, so as to cause physical injury or death.

It is a long stretch to go from da Vinci to Austin, but I would like to propose that the image of viewing the body in its own spherical universe is part of European culture and intrinsic to the dancer's concept of the moving body in space. In translating to dance practice these concepts of the body encased in a sphere with the ebb and flow of the blood (energy) within the body—itself the microcosm of nature—I have devised a series of exercises to bring today's dancer to a mental and physical understanding of the Baroque dancing body.

Exercise 1: Reaching Diagonally in Space

Imagine you are in a sphere. Define the sphere by touching its outline in space. Be aware of the height, depth and width.

Stand in a wide fourth position, left foot forward. Reach diagonally high back, to the right with the right arm, and let the fingers carve an oblique line to a point low, forward and to the left across the body.

Return the arm to place diagonally high, back and right, this time initiating the movement from the center of the back so the motion comes from the center of the body and unfurls sequentially through the back, the length of the arm and finally the finger tips. Do this three times.

Now, reach the right arm diagonally across the body to a point high, forward and to the left, and then let it fall to the lower right diagonal behind the body, initiating the movement from the muscles in the center of the body near the navel and allowing the fall to drop through the lengthening of the arm and through the fingertips. Repeat three times.

Repeat this series to the left with the left arm, etc.

Exercise 2: Exploring the Standing Position

1. Stoop to the ground in a standing fetal position, letting the head drop forward, hands on the floor. Feel the feet spread and root into the floor with the weight

equally balanced over the two feet. Allow the weight of the head to stretch the spine. Be aware of the top and tail of the spine. Breathe and exhale.

2. Next, imagine the feet are roots of a tree, going into the ground. Feel the strength of the lower limbs as if they were the trunk of a tree. Rest here and feel the strength of the body related to the earth and gravity. Now gradually unfurl the body, straightening in succession through the limbs and then stacking one vertebra upon another, while you breathe, moving on the exhalation. Arrive in a standing position. Feel as if you are joining the earth to the heavens, much as the tree sends its roots into the ground and reaches for the sunlight with its branches. Thinking of da Vinci's Vitruvian man, envision the navel as the center and send a vertical flow of energy downward from this point through the lower body; send a vertical flow of energy upward through the upper body. Working with da Vinci's concept of the navel as the center of the body seems logical as it divides the body into upper and lower halves. In the structure of Baroque choreography, the lower part of the body is concerned with the steps and following the track of the choreography in space, while the upper part of the body is used for decoration and expression. In fact, it is not uncommon in rehearsal to practice the steps, or the upper body coordination, in isolation.

3. To further demonstrate the effect of this imagery, stand with attention only to the vertical flow of energy from the navel going downward or descending. Walk maintaining this sensation.

4. Now, stand with attention to only the vertical flow of energy from the navel going upward or ascending. Walk maintaining this sensation.

5. Now join the two concepts to achieve the noble stance of the body joining the earth to the heavens as the flow of energy goes downward from the navel through the feet and upward from the navel through the head. Walk maintaining this sensation.

Exercise 3: Exploring the Horizontal Plane

Continuing to experience the navel as the center of the body, gently twist your torso side to side around your vertical axis. Let the arms swing out from the body and describe the horizontal plane. Begin small, add the vertical dimension by using a plié simultaneously with the twist and gradually let the arms swing around the body, higher and higher as they create a horizontal plane that extends out from the body.

Now let the action diminish and the arms lower.

These exercises help the dancer imagine the diagonal paths of the body, experience the vertical dimension of the body within the horizontal plane and place all these movements within the concept of the sphere or Baroque Bubble. After exploring the idea of the body in the sphere, I take the dancers into motion adding rhythm, balance and moving into space. They must first understand the Baroque dance convention of arriving on the down-beat with an upward motion of the body springing forth from the *plié*. I see the *plié* not as position but rather as an action. The resulting balance on the downbeat is a caught moment sustained between two opposing forces. The idea of the caught moment corre-sponds with the other arts such as painting and sculpture, where the figure or figures are caught in a moment. The Baroque aesthetic celebrates the moment of motion, not stasis.

I begin by taking the dancers' whole body into a swing, reminding them of the ebb and flow of the blood in the veins, connected to the ebb and flow of the ocean as described by da Vinci. I also use this quote, dated 1715 from the Italian Martello, to inspire their motions:

The Frenchman dances in a way that gives you the impression that he is swimming. His arms, always raised and supple, break the waves graciously, and he frisks in a thousand turns with his waist as though he were following the motion of the current with these gentle bendings. From time to time he skips, as a swimmer who lets the crest of the wave push him high in order to be carried forward. You can see him turn again and again, with no set pattern which can be recognized as square, oval or circle. Then there are unexpected releases and retractions, which nevertheless follow the orchestra with such grace that one is enchanted.[11]

Exercise 4: Swinging

Place your body in the middle of your sphere with the feet planted on the floor and the upper body reaching toward the heavens.

Feel the energy drain first through the bottoms of the feet, then the ankles (let them bend), the knees (let them bend) and the hip joints. Let the body begin to fold over from the waist, the spine and finally the head, until you have reached the stooped fetal position we experienced in the earlier demonstration. Be sure to articulate each vertebra of the spine as you reach the vertical placement of the head.

Now feel the energy reenter the body through the feet and flow back up the body in sequence. Do this three times.

Feel the energy drain from the feet, but this time, when you are fully bent over, take the hips up to the ceiling and lengthen the back of the legs. Pause here and feel the feet spread and root to the floor. Release any tension found in the back and neck. Then start from the feet with a bend in the ankle, then the knees, and unfurl the body, letting the pelvis drop as the head rises; finish standing straight and joining the earth to the heavens. Do this three times.

Add the uneven timing of the water's ebb and flow, and change this into a swing. Stand evenly on two feet rooted into the ground. The arms are up and reaching toward the heavens. This exercise is in two parts: the first stroke of the swing is a release of the energy through the bottom of the feet, with the end of the swing being the half-folded-over position of the body (hips up) and the backs of the legs extended. The second part of the swing also begins in the feet; first the ankles and then the knees bend, and then you fling your upper body in a sagittal plane, moving upward to recover a standing position with the arms touching the "north pole" of the sphere—the topmost region as you raise them upward to the beginning pose. Concentrate on the principles of the action, beginning with the feet and the ebb and flow of the energy through the entire body. Do this three times.

Exercise 5: Moving the Body in Space to a Duple Meter

Dance during the Baroque period is married to music, and the dance steps have a different feeling in duple meter and triple meter. These exercises address the simplest version of these meters, not the complicated compound meters that are based on the same principles but are far too complex to be covered in this essay.

With the weight of the body supported on the left leg, *plié* on the upbeat, slide forward to the right leg with a pushing action from the left leg at the initiation of the forward progress, arriving on the right leg as it straightens on the downbeat. Allow the left leg to linger behind you. Pause on the second beat before executing the *plié* once more on the "and" of the second beat. Do this four times.

And—plié L
ONE—step R
(Rest two)
And—plié R
ONE—step L
(Rest two)

And so on, alternating legs as you move forward. During the rests, the leg without weight lingers back behind the body, in preparation for the next step.

Next, complete the movement in one beat and do not hold the second beat, but rather move forward again on the alternate leg. This time do not let the former supporting leg linger behind, but bring the foot to the detached first position (first position of the feet, with the heel of one foot detached from the ground; the free foot is not at the ankle of the standing leg but is near the standing leg with the heel off the ground and the ball of the foot on the ground). Do this four times. Repeat this exercise forward, back and side to side.

And—plié L
ONE—step R
And—plié R
TWO—step L
And—plié L
ONE—step R

And so on, alternating legs as you move forward.

To inspire the dancers' execution of this exercise in a triple meter, I often refer to a description of a sarabande (a dance in ¾ time) by the Jesuit priest, Francois Pomey. In his *Dictionnaire royale augmenté*, published in Lyon in 1671, Pomey says:

> At first [the dancer] danced with a totally charming grace, with a serious and circumspect air, with an equal and slow rhythm, and with such a noble, beautiful, free and easy carriage that he had all the majesty of a king, and inspired as much respect as he gave pleasure. Then, standing taller and more assertively, and raising his arms to half-height, and keeping them partly extended, he performed the most beautiful steps ever invented for the dance.
>
> Sometimes he would glide imperceptibly, with no apparent movement of his feet or legs, and seemed to slide rather than step. Sometimes, with the most beautiful timing in the world, he would remain suspended, immobile, and half leaning to the side with one foot in the air; and then, compensating for the rhythmic unit that had gone by, with another more precipitous unit he would almost fly, so rapid was his motion.[12]

The images of sliding and gliding; remaining in a suspended action; keeping a regular pulse so that when a rhythmic unit goes by the dancer can pick up the music on the next unit: these are the images we are attempting to portray in adapting the last exercise to a triple meter. These are also movement qualities related to the idea of a swing that can happen at regular intervals but within each interval uses an unequal force.

Exercise 6: Moving to a Triple Meter

Take the demonstration of moving the body in a duple meter, arriving on the downbeat with the completion of the step, but this time hold the second beat and begin the *plié* on the third beat rather than the "and" of the second beat. Allow the weight of the body to have a *falling* effort on the upbeat and a *recovery* effort on the downbeat, and then suspend the motion over the second beat until the fall of the body is repeated on the third beat. Allow the forward motion of the body to become a swinging transition of weight shifts through supple use of the *plié*.

3	1	2	3	1	2 and so on
Plié L	Step R	Suspend	Plié R	Step L	Suspend

Take this traveling forward.

One might add the movement of the arms with this action in either the duple or triple meter. The circular motion of the arms moving from hip level through the midline of the body and then opening to the raised arm position helps to define the sensation of the sphere mentioned earlier. One never leaves the sphere but rather takes the sphere with the moving body. (Picture the rudimentary image of a hamster traversing the space inside his toy ball.) The circular motion of the arms, like a policeman gesturing for the cars to move forward, has an uneven timing to the motion where the accent is in the upward position and is the end point of the swinging gesture. The timing of the arm's arrival corresponds with the "swing" of the *plié* and the arrival of the body on the downbeat (Figure 6.3). Moving both the arms and the body in this swinging action creates a sense of ebb and flow corresponding to the image of the body as a microcosm of the universe, with the water ebbing and flowing from the river to the sea.

Pomey further describes the execution of the sarabande:

Sometimes [the dancer] would advance with little skips, sometimes he would drop back with long steps that, although carefully planned, seemed to be done spontaneously....Now and then he would let a whole rhythmic unit go by, moving no more than a statue and then, setting off like an arrow, he would be at the other end of the room before anyone had time to realize he had departed.

This description suggests a sense of the dancer's spontaneity and control: while he dances within the pulse of the music, he takes occasional risks in executing the rhythm and dynamics of the choreography. The ongoing pulse keeps the heartbeat of the dance, but what happens between those beats can be unevenly timed, or it can be sailed through in a long sustained arc with the dancer once again landing on the grounded pulse. The pulse is self-renewing, just as the motion of the dance must be. This concept will be discussed further as we explore the notions *terre à terre* and *le mouvement*.

EARLY CONCEPTS OF TERRE À TERRE

An important concept in the noble dance style is that of *terre à terre*, which is discussed in every dance manual, including contemporary sources. Suppleness and easy bendings and risings are common descriptions of *terre à terre* dancing. The sliding and gliding described by Pomey above is a quality of *terre à terre*. Literally, dancing earth to earth means that one is very linked to the earth. Jumps in Baroque dance are not intended to show escape from the earth; rather, they emphasize its return, and at times the dancer

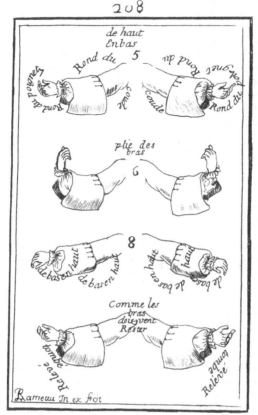

Representation des mouvements des poignets Coudes et de l'épaule

FIGURE 6.3 "Les ronds du poignet et du coude" from Pierre Rameau's *Le Maître à Danser*. Reproduced with the kind permission of Broude Brothers Limited. http://mediatheque.cnd.fr/spip.php?page=texte&id_article=130.

barely leaves the floor at all. In the 1807 edition of his *Lettres sur la danse et les ballets*, Jean Georges Noverre describes Marie Sallé's dancing as "simple touching graces…it was not with jumps and gambols that she touched the heart."

A related concept, *la belle danse*, also known as the serious style of dance, was considered to be the basic style from which all other genres sprang. One could not be a good dancer in the other styles unless one was accomplished in *la belle danse*, a form that barely left the floor and was known for displaying a noble body carriage, gentle balances and graceful arms.[13] Giovanni-Andrea Gallini in his 1765, *A Treatise on the Art of Dancing*, describes it best:

I have before observed that the grave or serious style of dancing, is the great groundwork of the art. It is also the most difficult. Firmness of step, a graceful and regular motion of all the parts, suppleness, easy bendings and risings, the whole accompanied with a good air, and managed with the greatest ease of dexterity, constitute the merit of this dancing. The soul itself should be seen in every motion of the body, and express something naturally noble, and even heroic. Every step should have its beauty.[14]

Exercise: Terre à terre

In a triple meter, begin with the weight of the body supported on the left leg; *plié* on the upbeat and on the downbeat slide forward to the right leg, arriving on the ball of the foot as the leg straightens on the downbeat. Then, without changing levels, step forward on the ball of the left foot and repeat with the right, stepping on beats 2 and 3 respectively. *Plié* quickly, and repeat this measure on the other side. For the third measure, instead of stepping on the third beat leap forward onto the new supporting leg (which means you will need to bend or *plié* before the leap, and you will land in a bend or *plié* on the third beat). However, when you leap do not leave the floor but merely skim over the floor as if leaping. Repeat this action for measure 4. Repeat the whole phrase four times.

Plié preparation L, then step on the ball of the foot R L R, *plié* preparation R, then step L R L, and so on.

The *plié* preparation is on the "and" before one, and the steps are on one, two, three.

When performing the small leaps, a *plié* preparation happens as well on the "and" of three before the leap.

The *plié* is a bending action, and the dancer must consider the quickness and weight of the *plié*. Most often in the Baroque style, the *plié* is very buoyant and limited to a bend in the ankle. The musical timing of the plié is not an exact time measurement, but rather a "feeling." This will be further explained in the next section of this essay, *Le Mouvement*.

This simple exercise should give you the feeling of *terre à terre* in its most basic description. The sensation of jumping from earth to earth and staying within the pulse of the music rather than escaping the earth and warping the timing of the music is very characteristic of the early ballet style and ties it to traditional or "folk" dance styles where emphasis is on returning to the earth. Both styles respect the ongoing pulse of the music and do not disturb the pulse with athleticism.

For those readers schooled in ballet, another exercise would be executing three *glissades* to the right direction without leaving the earth. In folk dance a simple grapevine to the right would give a feeling for the rise and fall of the body in the *terre à terre* style.

LE MOUVEMENT

Le mouvement, crucial to the training of the Baroque dancer, is currently translated by most of today's dance historians as *plié*.[15] However, French treatises do not use the word *plié* and *le mouvement* interchangeably. In Compan's dictionary of dance terminology published in Paris as late as 1787, one sees a listing for *le mouvement*, whereas the term *plié* has no listing at all. Compan points out that the bending of the ankle is very much connected to the bending of the knee and hip, and that these basic connections support a sense of motion throughout the body. Unlike the dance manuals, which teach the details of the action of the step, Compan underscores the importance of the whole body moving with a sense of *le mouvement*.

In her book *Terpsichore at Louis-le-Grand*, Judith Rock offers translations for *le mouvement* derived from Antoine Furetière's *Dictionnaire universal* (1691), and François Pomey's *Grand Dictionnaire royal* (1740). According to Rock, Pomey said of *le mouvement*:

The word is used figuratively of moral and spiritual matters, and means thought, feeling, and will…in rhetoric and poetry, one is said to excite *mouvements* when the passions of the hearer are affected by the force of eloquence. One says also that a theater piece is full of great *mouvements* when it has many vehement and pathetic figures and expressions…in music: It is the *mouvement* that makes sarabandes, gavottes, bourrees, chaconnes, and so forth different from each other. One uses the word also in dance to mean the various agitations of the body that one makes in order to move pleasingly in time to the music.

Rock quotes Antoine Furetière further in this description of a dancer who failed to achieve *le mouvement*: "This girl dances badly, because, however she makes the steps, they are never accompanied by the suitable *mouvement* of the body."[16]

When the same movement phrase is danced to different meters and tempos, *le mouvement* is revealed in the dancer's use of the *plié* and other bendings of the body as the dancer adjusts to the meters. It is the quality of the *plié*, as in soft, springy, taut, etc., that colors the effect of the motion and gives character to the dance form. The idea of *le mouvement* can also be extended to dramatic expression. As the dancer inhales and then steps on the ground, the ankle, knee and hip bend in response to the intention of the step, reflecting the quality or emotion to be portrayed by the performer. *Le mouvement* is the flow of the bendings incorporating the expression from which those bendings originate.

Giovanni-Andrea Gallini says:

Many who pretend to understand the art of dancing, confound motions with strength, with those of agility, mistaking strength for flight, or flight for strength; though so different in their nature. It is the spring of the body, in harmony with sense, that gives the great power to please and surprise. The same it is with the management of the arms; but all this requires both the theory of the art, and the practice of it. One will hardly suffice without the other; which makes excellence in it so rare.[17]

In referring to the "spring of the body," Gallini specifically means the quality of the plié from which the action originates. It is the first movement of the body that sets off the color, quality and emotion of the dancing body. Hence, the plié is a part of *le mouvement*, and it involves other bendings of the body in harmony with the intent of the motion. For example, when one is creeping onto the stage the bending of the ankle is cautious, careful, contained but soft and fluid so any motion is absorbed into the joints. ("It is the spring of the body, in harmony with sense, that gives the great power to please and surprise.") Consequently, when one is doing a *plié* as a preparation for a step sequence, it must be timed not only with the music but must be calculated as part of the quality and emotion of the step sequence. As an experiment, try these actions: stand very still, then slip by…now creep…then pounce. With each action one prepares the body and the bending of the joints in a very particular way before moving. This sensation is the *"mouvement"* in the joints and is the quality of the *plié*. Because of my view of the use of the *plié*, I do not recommend dancing to a metronome when practicing dance sequences as the metronome tends to even out or flatten the timing of the steps, forcing the *plié* into a metric unit. The regularity of a metric unit limits its expression and also runs counter to the sensation of water's ebb and flow, so crucial to the notion of *la cosmografia del minor mondo*.

CONCLUSION

Training today's dancers in period dance calls for an exploration of body image and period movement theory, gleaned from concepts of the moving body in disciplines outside dance, and from contemporaneous descriptions of "good dancing." The exercises delineated here are designed to begin enabling the dancer to experience these elements from dance as they emerge from an ongoing tradition, moving forward in time from the Renaissance toward the Baroque. The exercises are designed to further the dancer's ability to conceive of the historical body within a circle/sphere; to physically comprehend early concepts of *terre à terre*; and to reclaim original conceptions of the term *le mouvement*. These are areas where dance reconstructors need to explore beyond the notations printed on the page, and ask questions about how body-mind constructs in use in the historical period might inform today's performance. The physical knowledge gained through experiencing these body images and movement theories gives the scholar keener insights to the rich history of the period, allowing the dancer to attain a more vital understanding of the performance of dance from the Baroque world.

NOTES

1. Raoul Auger Feuillet, *Chorégraphie* (Paris, 1700; repr., New York: Broude Brothers, 1968); Pierre Rameau, *Le Maître à Danser* (Paris: Villette, 1725). However, the dancing master/choreographer John Weaver, working in 18th-century London, did address dance and anatomy, and he

encouraged his students to study the actions of the body. See, for example, John Weaver, *Anatomical and Mechanical Lectures upon Dancing* (London: J. Brotherton, W. Meadows, J. Graves, and W. Cherwood, 1721).

2. These ideas continue to evolve as I work on Baroque reconstructions and choreography, many times being challenged by my dancers, who are integral to the process.

3. In *The Eloquent Body*, Jennifer Nevile describes the prominence of *De divina proportione* in Renaissance dance manuals as dancing masters commonly aligned dance with music and Pythagorean theory. She also finds instances of Renaissance dancing masters referring to the *Cosmografia del minor mundo* and talking about the *"movements of the soul."* I have found references to *"the movement of the soul"* by Giovanni-Andrea Gallini in his 1762 *A Treatise on The Art of Dancing*. I believe this is shorthand for the concept of *cosmografia del minor mondo*. The Enlightenment certainly challenged beliefs of man in relation to the divine, but were humanist concepts so integrated into the structure of dance that they remained covertly present in European society into the 18th century? Jennifer Nevile, *The Eloquent Body: Dance and Humanist Culture in Fifteenth-Century Italy*. (Bloomington: Indiana University Press, 2004)

4. This is Leonardo's translation of Vitruvius' text; his drawing was originally an illustration for a book on the works of Vitruvius. Leonardo da Vinci, *The Notebooks of Leonardo Da Vinci*, vol. 1 (New York: Dover Press, 1970), 182–83.

5. Leonardo da Vinci, "Codex Leicester," in *The Notebooks of Leonardo Da Vinci*, vol. 2 (1883; repr. New York: Dover, 1970), 179.

6. I have found no references in period treatises directly related to concepts in the Vitruvian man. However, according to Richard Ralph, John Weaver was familiar with Leonardo Da Vinci's writings in "A Treatise of Painting," which were translated by an anonymous author and published in London in 1721. Richard Ralph, *The Life and Works of John Weaver: An Account of His Life, Writings and Theatrical Productions, with an Annotated Reprint of His Complete Publications* (New York: Dance Horizons, 1985), 856.

7. A good starting point in seeking a reproduction of the image is to search online for http://wikipedia.sfstate.us/File:Gerard_Thibault_Mysterious_Circle.jpg.

8. Girard Thibault, *Académie de l'Espée* (1628; repr. Paris: Kubik Editions, 2005).

9. Preamble. Official papers establishing L'Académie Royale de Danse, 1670. *Donné à Paris au mois de Mars, l'an de grace 1661 & de nostre regne le 19ᵉ. Signé LOUYS, & sur le reply par le Roy, DEGUENEGAUD.*

10. Reverend Gilbert Austin, *Chironomia; or a Treatise on Rhetorical Delivery; comprehending many precepts, both ancient and modern, for the proper regulation of the voice, the countenance, and gesture. (Together with an investigation of the elements of gesture, and a new method for the notation thereof; illustration by many figures.)* (1806; repr. Carbondale: Southern Illinois University Press, 1966).

11. Quoted in Marian Hannah Winter, *The Pre-Romantic Ballet* (London: Pitman Publishing, 1974), 65.

12. Father François Pomey. *Dictionnaire royal augmenté* (Lyon, 1671), 22.

13. For a more in-depth description of the kinds of dance in France during the 17th and 18th centuries that goes beyond the scope of this essay, see the entry "danse" in Marcelle Benoit, *Dictionnaire de la musique en France aux XVII et XVIII siècles* (Paris: Fayard, 1992), 201–4.

14. Giovanni-Andrea Gallini, *A Treatise on the Art of Dancing* (London, 1765), 75.

15. See Wendy Hilton, *Dance of Court and Theater: The French Noble Style, 1690–1725* (Stuyvesant, NY: Pendragon Press, 1997).

16. Judith Rock, *Terpsichore at Louis-le-Grand: Baroque Dance on the Jesuit Stage in Paris* (Saint Louis: Institute of Jesuit Sources, 1996), 190–91.

17. Gallini, 59.

7

Touchstones of Tradition and Innovation

PAS DE DEUX BY PETIPA, BALANCHINE AND FORSYTHE

Melanie Bales

THREE TOUCHSTONES

ALTHOUGH THE BALLET tradition may be referred to comprehensively as a style and form of presentation derived from Baroque court dances, that same tradition has, over time, gathered a vast collection of influences and contributions into its fold. Further, as each individual ballet simultaneously issues from and transforms the lexicon of the *danse d'école*, each also exists as a distinct choreographic statement of "oddities and inventions"[1] as well as a fixture within the frame of Western classical dance. If we recognize the concomitant conservative and generative forces that have carried the ballet tradition into the present time, we are prompted to ask: How does a dance work its way *through* time and also be *of* its time, and how does this fit into the notion of ballet as a cohesive genre? Any piece lucky enough to be performed often will change as it passes through different countries, decades and bodies, making the idea of a "timeless classic" largely fictional. Although any ballet might be seen as a microcosm of the whole of the genre and be examined as such, particular works can act as touchstones for surveying the scope of the balletic *oeuvre* and for appreciating the distinct individual profiles that have arisen. The purpose of this chapter is to allow three touchstone works to generate inquiry into both the complexity and cohesiveness of the ballet tradition, and to demonstrate the richness that emerges through comparative analysis.

This small collection of *pas de deux* is drawn from the bodies of work of choreographers who have achieved undisputed significance on the international ballet front: one was created at the end of the 19th century, Marius Petipa's *pas de deux* from Act 3 The

Sleeping Beauty; one in mid-20th century, George Balanchine's Aria II from *Stravinsky Violin Concerto*; and the third at the beginning of the 21st, an excerpt from William Forsythe's *One Flat Thing, reproduced*. The duet form, or *pas de deux*, has been the centerpiece of ballets over the centuries and is thus significant as such. Also, *pas de deux* are smaller nuggets within larger works and thereby provide a more focused aperture for examination. Each *pas de deux* in this study is situated within a ballet in current repertory; in fact, works by Petipa, Balanchine and Forsythe make up a substantial part of company repertories across the world. Many pieces by Petipa and Balanchine have achieved canonical status; it may be premature to call any of Forsythe's works canonical, but his international profile as a ballet choreographer is currently the highest of any living artist. And instead of choosing works that have been ignored or under-represented in the literature, I have deliberately focused on—if not the most well-known ballets—ones representative of what is actually being danced today, for one reason or another. Temporal and geographical space lies between the creations; no two choreographers share country of origin; the style of movement varies considerably, despite the fact that all are designated as ballets. These and other differences are among the obvious and not-so-obvious comparisons that present themselves.

The Petipa and Balanchine *pas de deux* are representative of sub-genres within their vast repertories—an evening-length story ballet and so-called leotard ballet, respectively. The Forsythe exemplar is a transitional piece between his neo-classic or contemporary ballets and later site-specific works that broke significantly from convention (such as *You Made Me a Monster*). Although I might have chosen the white swan *pas de deux* from Petipa/Ivanov or Balanchine's Sanguinic Variation *pas de deux* from *The Four Temperaments* from those same sub-genres, I selected Forsythe's *One Flat Thing, reproduced*, in part for the availability of the website resource on that piece. In addition to various forms of documentation and written resources at my disposal in researching the works, I have seen all them performed live. For this study, I refer specifically to *The Sleeping Beauty* Act 3 *pas de deux* across several versions as noted, to a video recording of the original cast of Aria II in *Stravinsky Violin Concerto*, and to the version of *One Flat Thing, reproduced* as represented on the website http://synchronousobjects.osu.edu/.

Before looking more closely at each *pas de deux*, a recent comment by the guardian of Balanchine's repertory offers a brief prelude to our inquiry. Barbara Horgan, who was interviewed as chairman of the Balanchine Foundation, said words to the effect that even when *Serenade*—the first work Balanchine made in America and one of the most durable—is performed badly, "it is still *Serenade*."[2] The statement contains several underlying assumptions: Balanchine's work is worth doing as great choreography to be commissioned and licensed relatively freely; his work furthers a tradition that is worth furthering; and that the dance comprises more than its momentary iteration (a bad performance). As if to answer "where is the dance?" Horgan seems to indicate that it safely resides within some kind of structural integrity, and that it can go on being itself by maintaining whatever conditions have brought it this far. This raises the idea that a dance exists as an artifact in some form beyond each of its performances, and one whose longevity depends not only on its ability to charm but, as we know, on funding and politics and the vagaries of individuals. Of greater concern than its durability here, however, is the fact that *Serenade* also exhibits the flexibility of a work that has remained within the balletic tradition by containing aspects that both uphold and challenge that tradition. First, we can examine which elements seem to reflect the adherence that formed the tradition, and secondly we can identify elements that expand or challenge that tradition. It may not be of primary concern to answer the questions "Is it ballet?" or even "How ballet is it?" But starting from those questions and suggesting the possibility that the balletic tradition is a moving target takes us deeper into considerations about style, choreographic intent and dance history. Three articles by critic/writer Alastair Macaulay provide jumping off points for the teasing apart of several critical and intertwined issues.

CLASSICISM AND ITS TRADITION

If there is something that goes through time, could it be classicism? Macaulay wrote two articles on the subject, the first "Notes on Dance Classicism" in 1987"[3] and the second 10 years later. In the first piece, he states: "As dance classicism has *evolved*, its great masterpieces have marked a steady *progression* away from literalism and representation"[4] (italics mine). We see from his remarks that he considers there to be a forward movement involved, and that it goes in the direction of more dance per square inch, and less need for other elements, including story. In the later piece, he identifies Marius Petipa and George Balanchine as the representatives of "the true orthodoxy of classical ballet" because their work celebrates the *danse d'école*, and for "the emphasis they give to the differences between masculine and feminine, and to the (deeply ambiguous) device which brings these polar forces together: namely, supported adagio."[5]

In another article from summer 2010,[6] Macaulay revisited the "deeply ambiguous" part, further interrogating the gender relations issue. In this piece, he also reconsiders the role of story and narrative drama in ballet. In fact, these two points are interrelated: much of the storytelling in ballets emerges through the *pas de deux*. This later article came in response to the opening by Gelsey Kirkland of a school devoted to "a renaissance of dramatic storytelling in ballet" in recognition that "the 20th century experiment with abstraction is coming to its logical end."[7] Clearly, for her the optimal definition of the classical balletic tradition includes a heavy dose of story and drama. Macaulay wonders in response if the stories told need to be more relevant or at least more interesting, and secondly, whether those "expressive possibilities of ballet are increasingly constricted today by the way it hinges on dichotomy of gender."[8] He also identifies the mid-20th century—including Balanchine, Frederick Ashton, Antony Tudor, Kenneth MacMillan and Jerome Robbins, noting that Kirkland danced for them all—as "the greatest era for choreography in ballet's history."[9] However, despite the fact that those choreographers furthered ballet classicism through the male-female supported adagio, he wonders about the future: "But a 21st-century art that knows no alternative to bringing men and women together in situations of love, chivalry or arrant manhandling will retain obvious limitations."[10]

Macaulay's three articles taken together with the introductory comments above provide a platform of assumptions and contentions for this analysis: (1) the balletic tradition[11] is not a fixed center, but rather a moveable collection of attributes and practices; (2) an essential attribute to consider is the interplay or balance between so-called pure dance and story, the *danse d'école* and narrative drama, technique and meaning; (3) each dance can be analyzed in terms of the balance between elements drawn from within the *danse d'école,* and those elements or practices that challenge, ignore or eventually expand it; and (4) the gender politics of the *pas de deux* are reflective of their times and thus should be analyzed within the context of those times. And further, the ideology[12] of a tradition or an individual dance can be revealed through an examination of its constituent parts.

THE *PAS DE DEUX* AND THE HISTORICAL CONTEXTS OF THEIR CREATIONS

In considering the choreographic voice inside the balletic tradition, it is important to have a sketch of each *pas de deux* over several contexts: historical, socio-political, aesthetic, individual. All three *pas de deux* are situated within ballets that are in current repertory, and all three choreographers were trained through the tradition of the ballet *danse d'école.* The Act 3 wedding *pas de deux* from *The Sleeping Beauty* was created in 1890 by Petipa; Balanchine's Aria II, the second *pas de deux* and third section from *Stravinsky Violin Concerto,* was first performed in 1972; and *One Flat Thing, reproduced (OFTR)* is a group work by Forsythe begun in 2000, from which a three-minute excerpt is the center of focus here.

For Petipa, *The Sleeping Beauty* was significant in many ways. As his first collaboration with the already renowned composer Pyotr I. Tchaikovsky, a new world of music opened up, but it also challenged the convention of the balletmaster's sovereignty.[13] He worked tirelessly with the director of the Imperial theatre I. Vsevoloszhsky on the libretto, and with the dancers of all ranks and temperaments. Despite the elaborate nature of the work, hours in length with hundreds of performers and gigantic sets, the choreographer took the opportunity to create some of his most inventive arrangements of the *danse d'école*[14] regardless of mixed reviews, including the Tzar's tepid "very nice." The ballet inspired the flow of re-creations still issuing from that first performance, which eventually linked "the period of Russian ballet's relative obscurity outside a small circle of Petersburg elite to a second period, when Russian ballet gained an international, popular audience."[15]

As noted earlier, Balanchine's *Concerto* comes under the heading of his spare and terse abstract or leotard ballets as distinguished from other pieces in his enormous opus that were more romantic in nature, or still others that reflected his own heritage as former student and dancer with the Maryinsky. The 1972 Stravinsky Festival, where the ballet premiered, came after an uncharacteristically fallow period where some wondered if his genius had run its course, and his muse, Suzanne Farrell, had not yet returned to the company after her departure in 1969. The ballet marked a triumph, and was offered as a tribute to his most revered collaborator, who had recently died. He considered it well made and only changed small things when it was later filmed.[16]

Forsythe's dance, a collaborative venture that has been expanded through the interactive website, is typical of other works that are created over a long period of time with many iterations, some in which one ballet is inserted into a later one (as *Enemy in the Figure* into *Limb's Theorem*). After his earliest pieces, which in retrospect are somewhat anomalous,[17] Forsythe's work could be roughly divided into the highly theatrical works (*Eidos:Telos, Impressing the Czar*) that feature substantial text or speaking, unconventional lighting effects, sound collages and overt contributions by the dancers; and his "ballet ballets"[18] such as *In the Middle Somewhat Elevated*, created for Paris Opera with ballet superstar Sylvie Guillem. *OFTR* is neither a "ballet ballet" (no pointe shoes or discernable classroom steps) nor a Bauschian/Dada extravaganza. Instead, 14–17 dancers interact with or negotiate 20 metal tables arranged in neat rows of five across and four down. The original score was composed by frequent collaborator Thom Willems.

The Sleeping Beauty is a ballet created by a Frenchman in Russia within a state institution under the auspices of an imperial family. Created "in reactionary times, the ballet expresses deeply conservative royalist politics."[19] Also, in the latter half of the 19th century, an "attitude of condescension existed toward the ballet"[20] and its audience expected pomp, not substance.[21] The ballet's subject, a warning that ignoring a royal (fairy), even a nasty one, can have dire consequences underscores these points. Petipa was constrained by intrigues and politics in casting. And yet, the ballet that issued from those circumstances is considered the pinnacle of classical ballet tradition, a "watershed in the history of the art."[22]

Balanchine, a Russian in America, may have emerged from a low point with *Stravinsky Violin Concerto*, but the 1970s found U.S. ballet in its "high tide"[23] and part of a dance boom. In her book *A Game for Dancers: Performing Modernism in the Postwar Years*, Gay Morris concludes her chapter on the success of the "Kirstein-Balanchine enterprise" in noting that by the 1950s "Balanchine's choreography embodied America's new position of world leadership; his choreography built on an imperial past that had been democratized and given youthful energy."[24]

Forsythe, the American transplanted to Germany, also created his work in the midst of some professional upheaval, as the city of Frankfurt, which housed and funded his operation, was in grave financial trouble. This eventually resulted in the choreographer leaving his artistic home of 20 years to create the Forsythe Company in 2003–04, an entity whose name closely reflects the nature of the new enterprise. Earlier in his career in Europe, things were more flush, and the growth of contemporary dance, including the influential work of Pina Bausch and *Tanztheater*, has prompted many to say that Europe

has now eclipsed the United States on several fronts. In the current global recession, Forsythe's Euro-ballet enterprise is still a hot ticket.

Petipa's Tchaikovsky ballets are often referred to as "the classics," with a meaning that
binds the (ancient) classic period of high art to classic revivals (such as *Beauty's* setting in
a court modeled after Louis Quatorze) to the idea of a classic work inside a lasting tradition, as discussed earlier. Indeed, those ballets have been disseminated across the world,
beginning with Petersburg régisseur N. Sergeyev fleeing to England during the revolution
with the Stepanov notation of Petipa's work.[25] Those same Petipa works can be found in
some version in every major ballet company. Even the neo-balletist Diaghilev tried to get
in on the act with his unsuccessful *Sleeping Princess* of 1921.

Balanchine's choreography has probably had every major art movement label of the
20th century attached to it, and his experimental spirit meant that he ranged over a large
territory of styles. His early work in 1920s Russia showed elements of constructivism, surrealism, symphonism, even expressionism.[26] He created a collection of romantic ballets
(such as *La Valse* and *Liebeslieder Waltzes*), and also many so-called neo-classics (*Diverti-
mento no. 15, Ballo della Regina*), so-called abstract works (*Agon, The Four Temperaments*)
and is a "formalist."[27] Others see him aligned with several tenets of modernism, such as
defying conventionality and medium-specificity.[28]

Forsythe's stickiest labels are postmodernist and deconstructivist,[29] but he considers
himself working within the same idiom and frame as Balanchine and Petipa. In a monograph, Senta Driver calls him "Nijinsky's heir" because, in her view, the two artists share
a commitment "to a personal vision rather than to the primacy of the classical materials."[30] The "isms" and other descriptive terms do help to situate choreography within
other art movements and create useful distinctions between choreographers, and across
the works of one artist. Unfortunately, labels can also generate dangerous over-simplifica-
tions in discourse and therefore should be used carefully. From this basic sketch of each
choreographer in his milieu, the pieces themselves will serve to reveal further commonalities and distinctions.

A HISTORY OF TENSION BETWEEN NARRATIVE AND MOVEMENT

The tension between story and dance, or the proper role of narrativity in ballet, has a
history as long as the form itself. Whether ballet needs to have meaningful content, or
whether the movement is enough, is still hotly debated by critics. Choreographers find
themselves framed in terms of this tension; audiences often wonder if they are supposed to look for plots and characters when those elements are not explicitly drawn
either through gesture or theatrical devices. Just following Petipa's time, the great critic-
writer André Levinson wrote rapturous prose extolling the great master's ability to
resolve the "antimony" between realism, literalism and pantomime and the metaphoric
truth and formalism of the classical dance.[31] For Levinson (and Akim Volynsky, as

found in *Book of Exaltations*), the beauty and refinement of the *danse d'école* as arranged and developed by Petipa especially, was the heart of the ballet and its ultimate expression. Character dances were acceptable inclusions, but they needed to be transformed by style and elevated.[32] Mid-twentieth-century critic John Martin grappled with the tenets of modernism and non-representational art along with art critic Clement Greenberg, whose idea of each art form's autonomy (in dance's case movement) was complicated by the fact that the medium is the human body.[33] Balanchine himself called his ballets such as *Stravinsky Violin Concerto* "story-less" but countered with his famous aphorism, "How much story you want?"[34] suggesting that the mere presence of a man and woman dancing together on stage created story. The Judson Dance Theatre era of the 1960s in America prompted writer Jill Johnston to distinguish between two styles, "dramatic-realist" and "depersonalization"—terms she later replaced with gesture and abstraction.[35] Although Johnston was writing specifically about (post)modern dance, those ideas were part of Forsythe's dance milieu as a young American before his departure to Germany, where he came under the influences of that country's tradition of *Ausdruckstanz* and *Tanztheater*, genres fully invested in dramatic contexts for purposes of psychological and social engagement, and where he danced for John Cranko, renowned for his story ballets.

Going back to the era of the mid-19th century, we find that an article entitled "National Dance in the Romantic Ballet" about character dances proposes that in this era "the ebb and flow between the dancing and miming may have been akin to that between the aria and *scena* (the dramatic scene consisting largely of recitative) in opera."[36] Furthermore, "Ballet was considered first and foremost a dramatic genre, like opera and the spoken play.[37] As ballet continued during the Romantic era, the character dances—which authors Lisa Arkin and Marian Smith contend were of much greater importance than previously thought—echoed the alternating structure inherited from opera in their placement within the ballets, as the "white" classical *pas* were offset by colorful (in both senses) Spanish or Polish or Middle Eastern dances. Also, these "national *pas*, which were often characterized by driving rhythms, speedy footwork, and partnering that privileged rapid turns over stately arabesques, sustained poses, and adagio movements,"[38] provided an alternation in terms of qualities of movement, ensuring a balance between the two modes.

In *Giselle*, this antiphonal structure is reflected in a broader way over the two-act ballet, where the first act includes, if not true character dance, a peasant *pas de deux* and a rustic setting, with the second act a poetic realm of death and sacrifice in the formalism of the Willis groupings, and a series of *pas* using the *danse d'école*. This structure of alternation—of story and non-story, formal arrangements and expressive solos, fiery, emphatic steps and languid, airy Sylphides—inherited from earlier Western theatre forms, may be identified as one of the main structural characteristics of the balletic tradition. Yet, at the same time, old forms give way to newer versions of story and non-story, and become less literal.

In her chapter entitled "Ballet's Challenge," Gay Morris refers to theater director William Ball's idea of "connotative movement" by which gestures and images may be suggestive of human or dramatic situations many steps removed from pantomime, but still having the power of association. She states: "At a less mimetic level dance imagery may draw on other encoded systems to suggest associations, such as baroque sculpture or military drill. Or dance imagery may derive from movements and gestures that have no specific meaning in themselves but that suggest meaning through formal processes, including such devices as repetition, symmetry and recontextualization."[39]

If visual imagery and even formalized gestures allow the audience to attach shreds of plot lines or characterizations within the context of a dance that might otherwise be described as formalist, we should admit that what or what isn't "story" may sometimes be difficult to determine because of the suggestive and variable nature of association. Even if the story–not-story division may not always be easy to discern, is still possible to examine a dance for its structure, and see how other elements in addition to the story–not-story dualism might be related to the alternating system described above. How this dualistic or antiphonal interplay of content and form operates across the three *pas de deux* at hand necessitates further analyses of each work.

ANALYSIS OF CHOREOGRAPHY

The following structural outlines are sketched from my dancer's eye—the way a performer or choreographer might perceive of them—unless a specific musical or textual source is mentioned otherwise. Despite the staggering number of re-stagings, revivals[40] and national variations of Petipa's *The Sleeping Beauty*, the Act 3 *pas de deux* is remarkably stable in its basic structure and steps (see the Visual Sources list at the end of this chapter for versions consulted). Its overall structure of six sections matches up quite directly with the musical themes and follows the spatial pattern of: dance together, part from one another, set up for the next section. In most versions, Princess Aurora and Prince Désiré enter together (or are revealed standing together depending on the staging) and acknowledge their on- and offstage audiences with a grand welcoming gesture; there is an immediate sense of place and social order, and both the music and the movement unfold with the grandeur and unhurried confidence of an imagined nobility. The following summary of the *pas* is offered with full recognition that such a sketch squeezes out the juice of musical phrasing, nuanced individual interpretation and other essential charms that constitute the sum total of the dancing and the ballet itself. Rather, the focus is on the structural shape of the choreography.

After facing each other for a *révérence*, they begin to dance. Although there are many others on stage, none of them move beyond small mime gestures; focus is on the Prince and Princess front and center in the *tableau*. Part 1 establishes the main themes or codes of behavior that remain consistent throughout the *pas de deux*: she is more mobile (performing supported and unsupported classical steps), he is stable (providing physical support and giving his full attention to her); he presents her outwardly, with a few moments of address to each other. The classical shapes, both in movement and in repose, alternate between matching, where he usually completes her line, and mirroring each other. Part 2 follows a new melodic statement and is a series of lifts across one side of the stage to the other, finishing in a supported *pirouette*. Part 3 is a series of *en dedans* supported *pirouettes*, a figure repeated three times. Part 4 returns to a slower tempo with the recapitulation of the first musical figure, but part 5 picks up again with a repeated pattern of *pirouettes* coming downstage. Part 6 contains the moment I call the "sitting bird" because the ballerina sits on a folded leg with the other extended on the floor, but instead of folding her body over the extended leg (as in *Swan Lake* or Fokine's dying swan), she presents her hand to the Prince and climbs back up to an *arabesque* balance, after which he lets her hand go, recalling the earlier Rose Adagio with its series of daring balances. The *pas* ends with a risky final pose—a "fish" catch or shoulder lift, depending on the version—showing the characters' shared commitment to each other, her confidence and his trusty support. They exit and the ballet proceeds to the variations and coda, an order of events that has marked the partner dance in the development of Western theatrical dance since the 16th century.[41]

The ballet, according to Fyodor Lopukhov, was "built on a proportion of ninety-five percent dance to five percent pantomime,"[42] making it distinct from earlier works, and giving the audience and the dancers a lot of dancing. In his second essay on classicism, Macaulay notes that Petipa had solved the problem of how to "make academic dancing the centre of a story ballet" by making the protagonist(s) dance like crazy.[43] Although the rest of the ballet featured mime or stylized gesture, national dances (polonaise, czardas, mazurka), and formational movement or pageantry, the *pas de deux* is virtually all *danse d'école* as we define it today. And yet it is performed within the frame of a story derived from a 17th century French fairytale, reflecting both the court of the Russian Tzar and other royal courts of yore. There is no doubt that there is story here, as the fairy tale provides a narrative line on which to layer other narrative meanings, such as the demonstration of the "story" of Russian supremacy in ballet. The Act 3 *pas de deux* is the fourth supported adagio for the principals of the ballet and, as the Wedding *pas,* unites the royal couple and ensures the royal line. Sally Banes notes that "the four adagios of *The Sleeping Beauty's* four sections form not only 'the musical points of support for the whole course of action' in the ballet, but also the key moments of Aurora's biography."[44]

Both the *pas de deux* and the ballet as a whole reflect the alternating structure of story and dancing, up-tempo passages and drawn-out ones, following from the balletic tradition established earlier as noted by Arkin and Smith above.[45] The *pas de deux* may be seen as a miniature version of the whole ballet, in which narrative passages with character dances or stage action (such as Calabutte having his hair pulled out, or the Lilac Fairy miming how she will soften the blow) alternate with formational group dances such as the Garland Dance or classical *pas d'actions* such as the Jewel *pas de quatre* and variations.

The Wedding *pas* is placed within the whole ballet as an exposition of the *danse d'école* as opposed to a narrative passage, but inside it are smaller alternations of story and dancing through the gestures coming at the beginning of each change of section, such as Aurora giving the Prince her hand as she ascends from the "sitting bird." So the *pas de deux* functions both as a foil against the narrative sections and slows down the action so that the audience focuses on the hero and especially the heroine, while reflecting the overall structure of alternation in the way it progresses.

In Balanchine's *Concerto*, Aria II follows the lively opening group dance Toccata and the sinewy and strident Aria I *pas de deux*, in somewhat of an "upstairs-downstairs" relationship, the earthy-profane Aria I followed by the elegant-sacred Aria II. The ballet concludes with another group section, the up-tempo Capriccio. The ballet overall reveals an ABBA structure. The beginning and opening movements are large groups (albeit with many smaller duets, trios and quartets entering and exiting) and are formational to a large degree but also have elements of folk dance—Russian? Georgian?—with folded arms and turn-in, turn-out, heel-toe steps. The inside movements of the two Aria *pas de deux* lead us inside the intimate worlds of two very different couples: one combative or at least competitive, the other intertwined in a series of protective and enabling supports. Rather than following a back and forth or ABAB structure as with the four acts of *Swan Lake* or the two acts of *Giselle*, this arrangement maintains a structural symmetry in two ways: first, the outside movements are faster and more emphatic in tempo (following Stravinsky's score) and the inside movements have more melodic and legato lines; and second, the outside movements emphasize the steps, floor patterns and kaleidoscopic designs, while the two inside duets show us personalities.

Who are the dancers in Balanchine's tender and slow-moving *pas de deux*, nestled inside the somewhat boisterous group movements of *Stravinsky Violin Concerto*? The dancers here are referred to by their real names, as the version analyzed is taken from the Nonesuch DVD (see Visual Sources) danced by the original cast couple, Kay Mazzo and Peter Martins. The couple enters together and stays in close proximity with a few moments of separation. Unlike the formal and predictable distance between Aurora and her prince, they are enmeshed and entwined with long legato lines of slow twisting and turning. The overall choreographic structure falls into four parts, and uses Stravinsky's alerting "passport chord,"[46] a strident bowing of the violin, as a landmark through the dance.

Charles Joseph, in his music-dance analysis, agrees for the most part with my dancer-eye structuring of four main sections, saying that "Aria II... is set in a loosely cast tripartite structure: A (mm. 1–16, *but with a clearly defined A[1] in mm. 8–16*), B (mm. 17–24), and a varied reprise of A (mm. 25–33)"[47] (italics mine). Part 1 is the entrance as they travel across stage with Mazzo in front. The steps are balletic in tone and extension, but they are stretched beyond the usual range and shapes of the *danse d'école*, with Martins often literally extending her beyond her own balance and into large and sinewy shapes, yet keeping her close. Part 2 begins with the sudden and somewhat jarring passport chord and Mazzo quickly assumes a wide second position on pointe facing him, after which he slowly brings her knees together in a rather awkward but strangely supportive gesture. A long supported promenade follows, going again beyond the classical shapes as she dives and falls around him. There are also small flexings of the feet and hands that add delicacy and detail, referring back to the other sections of the dance in the folk element. As with the Petipa couple, he is the stabler one, she is mobile. He anticipates her pathways and moves in to support; she moves out searchingly, then draws in and back to herself or to him. With part 3 the tempo picks up and the mood changes. They are less entwined, moving side by side, and she leaves him momentarily to walk upstage. At the repeat of the chord with accompanying wide second position figure (signaling part 4), they return to the slow adagio movements until after a lift he sets her down in a sitting position with her legs tucked under her. Although she is facing offstage and away from him, and both legs are tucked under, this moment is reminiscent of *Beauty*'s "sitting bird" posture. Also, she then plants her foot and rises, in a similar way to Aurora's ascent, into a slow *développé allongé* while holding his hands. Interestingly, it comes at about the same point in each *pas de deux*, toward the end.

The last moments are dominated by gesture. Although the entire *pas de deux* has unfolded with the camera zooming in from the opening Toccata, it now zooms in further, literally and figuratively. Much has been made of the last gestures because they are both hieratic and provocative. Balanchine made this dance to music of his great, lost friend and celebrated colleague, and the tone of mourning and reverence increases over the last moments. Martins wraps his arm around Mazzo just below her throat as they both face downstage right, and makes an outward sweeping gesture with her still close, after which they both bow forward to a point in the distance, rather than to each other. He then wraps his arm around her forehead, covering her eyes, and pulls her into a deep back bend as he kneels. Is Balanchine (as Martins) paying homage to Stravinsky and taking his dancers (represented by Mazzo) with him?[48] The action overall is somewhat in reverse of *Beauty*: beginning with dance and ending with gesture, getting smaller and quieter versus the big finish, and ending rather than beginning with a *reverence* in homage to Stravinsky.

As a reflection of the ABBA structure of the whole piece, the Aria II can be said to have more dance at the beginning and more story at the end, through the concluding gestural passage (AB). The four-part progression of the movement action, punctuated somewhat regularly by the passport chord in the music and its attached action of Mazzo's sudden wide second position, further supports the sense of balance and wholeness through repetition—a statement finished with little left unsaid. So, as in *Beauty*, the *pas de deux* has its place carved out within the whole dance, and although we sense that a story, or at least a dramatic situation, is there in the dance, its specific meaning is not as explicit as in Petipa's duet.

A performance of *One Flat Thing, reproduced* opens with the roar of metal tables being dragged onstage by the entire cast. After the tables are meticulously and efficiently put into a neat grid pattern, the dancers retreat to the space behind them. Two male dancers begin to move through sequences that require them to interact or partner with the tables, while simultaneously reacting to and cueing each other from time to time. This cueing is a significant element of the dance, as it serves to initiate and coordinate what Forsythe calls "alignments," or patterns in space and time, among the dancers. After about a minute and a half, Yoko Ando and Fabrice Mazliah, who dance the duet I am choosing to call a *pas de deux* here, enter the dancing space by walking with fierce intent directly downstage center. The following summary draws from footage of a filmed rehearsal, my memory of a live performance, and multiple viewings of the Synchronous Objects website (see Visual Sources). Ando and Mazliah negotiate their way through an aisle between the 20 tables, both arriving at the same table where they sit facing outward, immediately beginning to move with each other mirroring each other's movement, then a few moments later moving screen right into unoccupied space. All four dancers on stage are now moving with a kind of purposeful and efficient hysteria. The tempo is exceedingly quick, considering the level changes in and around the tables, and the full-out and full-bodied nature of the material. Like an intricate traffic pattern, they seem to avoid collision by maintaining an intense alertness to one another amid the relatively breakneck speed and rapid changes of direction.

Unlike the Balanchine and Petipa *pas de deux*, the couple in this duet is summarily interrupted by another two dancers after about 30 seconds, just as they have overlapped with and supplanted focus from the two dancers before them. Therefore, my eye and attention wander off Ando and Mazliah momentarily, and then return to them. As a viewer, I am barely able to string the moments of their dancing together into one connected necklace of phrases. The movement has no discernable linkage to Thom Willems' score but relates to it rather more like a Cage-Cunningham piece, and it therefore produces no memory aid or reinforcement of the images in that conjunction.

As far as distinct sections within the period of time Ando and Mazliah dance together, seven moments emerge as discernable landmarks. These moments occur when the dancers are either looking away to see a cue—and thus stopping the action if very briefly—just stopping, or separating from each other spatially. Owing to the intriguing complexity of the partnering and the kaleidoscopic shape changes of the action, such stillish moments are resonant by contrast. There is a moment midway where they seem to be in stop action—he is holding her arm aloft with his arm—and suddenly they begin to move again. At one point, she is standing still on top of a table before he comes to move her. Later, they briefly exchange roles in terms of who moves whom—he moves her more often than she moves him—when she grabs his mid-section and rolls him over on top of a table at about the three-minute mark. Then he is under the table, as she seems to match another dancer's arm gesture. They separate to opposite ends of adjacent tables, and as she is still, he tips the downstage edge of the table up and then hangs over it. She then exits going upstage screen right (or stage left) at about the 3.5-minute mark. This interaction/*pas de deux* could perhaps end at the point at which they separate, but she watches him tip the table and is still involved if not physically, then attentively, so the end comes with her exit.

The material for the Ando-Mazliah duet is the fourth movement Theme with variations, as explicated on the website. Theme 3 is only a short sashay downstage, and the first two Themes have been performed by the opening duo. On the website, Ando and Mazliah perform Theme 4 under a heading entitled Movement Material Index, and this is the material that forms the basis for their interaction in the passage I have designated as the *pas de deux*. Other dancers perform parts of it, but Ando and Mazliah introduce it and explore it more thoroughly during their two-minute duet. In this sense, it is *their* material, just as the dancers in *Beauty* or *Concerto* have special material created for them. In all three cases, some of the steps or motifs of the *pas de deux* are danced by others, but in *OFTR* the repetitions of material are more obvious. The piece continues on to around 20 minutes, so this excerpt comes quite near the beginning. The sequence of events does not establish a developmental or linear pattern, yet eventually actions accumulate into a skeletal narrative, such as "they are alone there, but then others come and join them," or "everyone stops and faces upstage and then moves very slowly together."

Like the Petipa and Balanchine examples, the Forsythe *pas* is a part reflective of the whole. The piece as a whole has no soloists in terms of rank or time dancing, and this *pas de deux* is not "centered" in its placement chronologically or spatially. Mazliah and Ando emerge from the group, walking side by side, but do not really dance together until they begin the Theme. They do not end their duet together either, although by the end of the piece everyone has pushed the tables back again. Very roughly, *OFTR* has an ABA structure, but within the action between tables on and tables off, events are asymmetric and unpredictable in their unfolding. The symmetry of design of the inanimate props, recalling rows of Swan maidens or dancers in the final movement of Balanchine's *Symphony in C*, contrasts the chaotic and explosive character of the human action. The cool and sharp metal offsets the heated and highly toned character of the dancing. In such ways a loose binary structure or dual nature of contrast does emerge. Unlike the Petipa and Balanchine couples, this couple does not dance within a designated spaciousness, but rather must literally fit among other dancers, sometimes vying for a place, and at other times, oddly separated as if lost, as when Mazliah drapes over the table. Likewise, it is difficult in the Forsythe piece to separate the story–not-story through either an alternating structure or a separation of gesture and dance, unless one counts the cueing as brief, but knowing, glances. We have come a rather long way from princesses and *révérences*.

EXPANDING AND ALTERING THE TRADITION: THE *DANSE D'ÉCOLE* AND MOVEMENT VOCABULARY

If the balletic tradition can be located in terms of choreographic structuring, conventions of presentation and the steps and figures of the *danse d'école*, choreographers such as the three in this study also import material and ideas as resources for commenting on and expanding that tradition in the creative process. Such decisions range from how far they "stray" from the *danse d'école* itself to what influences of all kinds take shape during the creation of the piece, including the contributions of dancers in the studio, and other collaborative elements such as scene design, costumes, lighting and dramaturgy. The choice of subject matter is naturally another significant determination, but not specifically included in this study. The scope of this consideration will focus on three particular aspects of the ballet–not-ballet question: the movement vocabulary across the dances, and two collaborative areas (the role of the dancer in the creative process, and the significance of the music-dance relationship). Other aspects that would yield further insights are there to be mined by other writers.

Just as the debates continue over too much story or not enough, too much dancing or not enough, writers on ballet continue to argue about whether or not the dancing is "ballet enough." Levinson, Volynsky and Arnold Haskell, among others, have championed the notion that the authenticity and expressive power of classical ballet rests solidly on the *danse d'école*. Critics like these were leery of too much digression, as seen in Levinson's strong distaste for the "new" ballet of his time, namely Fokine's ballets with their Isadora-infused freedoms.[49] Had Levinson lived longer than 1933, we might have seen his views change. It is interesting to speculate what he would have thought of *Stravinsky Violin Concerto*; he thought Balanchine's *Apollon Musagète* showed promise, but *Concerto* came forty-plus years later and shows evidence of further movement experimentation. As viewers, we see out from our own times and experiences, so although we can watch dances from other eras, the *way* we see them is time-bound to some degree. Today, *Beauty* is in part beloved *because* of the elaborate staging, period costuming, Tchaikovsky score, and the colorful characters and national dances; these elements speak to us from and about the past. But in its day, it was distinguished by the central role of the *danse d'école* and the expanded boundaries of the technique. Petipa was interested in showing off the riches of Italian virtuosity brought to the Imperial theatre via dancers such as Carlotta Brianza, the first *Beauty*, and by ballet master and first Bluebird Enrico Cecchetti. Petipa is now identified as the center of the classical ballet tradition, but in truth he holds a place on a continuum. Such a continuum does not necessarily flow in one direction but has circularities and repetitions, tributaries and main streams. In my selected three dances, the examples from Balanchine and Forsythe can be put in relation to Petipa's example as other, later signposts along that continuum.

As the lexicon grows and shifts, there is simply more in the physical arsenal for ballet dancers and choreographers to use. It is true that some steps are lost and styles die out, but many more are born to take their places for better or worse. As choreographers draw from sources outside the *danse d'école* to enrich and expand it, dancers learn to move in new ways; and dancers' abilities push choreographers into new territory. Second, training methods have benefited from a collected storehouse of knowledge, which has accumulated over the years. The resulting competition pushes dancers and teachers to continue to up the ante—sometimes crossing the line into vulgar displays or irrelevant vocabularies. Deborah Jowitt wondered recently if virtuosity was "the new porn."[50] Also, not only are the dancers today probably stronger and faster and (excepting Nijinsky?) jump higher, but the range of their extensions is far larger, the latter being perhaps the most marked.

Another aspect reflected within this trio of works is a change in the bearing or carriage of the dancers themselves, their Body Attitudes in Laban Movement Analysis terms.[51] To some degree, this mirrors Western society as our social interactions have become less formal and proscribed. In Petipa's time, his more physically substantial dancers were relatively upright; torsos were held, calling back to Baroque corseting, and the gestures were smaller and closer. In the era of *Beauty*, those costumes were heavy, and it was crowded onstage. Subsequent performances have retained some of those characteristics through mimetic gesture and noble bearing, but the dance movements have increased in size, both spatially and bodily. The 1999 Kirov revival of the ballet prompted at least one critic to comment on an obvious anachronism. Clive Barnes noted that "Zakharova's 'twelve o'clock high' extensions looked stylistically out of place."[52] Here is an example of a nearly 21st-century body in a 19th-century ballet, an interesting dilemma for dancers and directors. It seems that when Aurora woke up this time, she could get her leg up a lot higher! These things are quantitative to a large degree, not qualitative. Can we say that any dancer of today is "better" than any dancer of yesteryear? No, certainly not. And when dancers note that Margot Fonteyn, for example, would not have had a chance as a professional dancer today with her less-than-spectacular technique, we could argue: if she had lived today, she would have danced differently. There has certainly been a progression toward speed and flexibility from Petipa to Balanchine to Forsythe. Where it will go, who knows; but it could be that audiences are ready for a turn in another direction, as Kirkland seems to indicate on her website blurb.

As for the Balanchine *pas de deux*, the classically trained dancers are wearing, if not tutu and royal jacket, enhanced practice wear of leotards, tights and pointe shoes (for her). Unlike Petipa, the vocabulary is far too off-center and off-balance to be primarily *danse d'école* as it is still practiced in class settings. Clearly evident is the influx of Balanchine's other dance interests such as American Broadway and African American vernacular dance, acrobatics, all kinds of vestiges from his long, rich background of early Russian influences, including the ballets of the iconoclast Goleizovsky.[53] In the stretched and sinewy phrasing, along with the chiseled shapes and overall high tone, there is something of mid-century modern dance too, in the Graham-like tension and countertension of the partnering. Although Mazzo and Martins assume positions that are far more intimate, sensually explicit and full of struggle than those of Petipa's dancers, their conduct is still within a theatrical formality that is presented outwardly to an acknowledged audience.

Critics frequently put Forsythe's works into relief against Balanchine's for various reasons. John Percival describes Forsythe's 1984 *Artifact* thus: "Think of the difference between Balanchine's early classical duets and the more contorted choreography of say his Webern *Episodes* or *Stravinsky Violin Concerto*; then develop those changes for

another two or three decades, and you're about there."⁵⁴ Despite the fact that Balanchine's early duets weren't all that classical in the sense Percival means, the influence
of Balanchine upon Forsythe is as undeniable as the influence of Petipa upon Balanchine. Speaking directly of *OFTR*, Jowitt, in a piece from 2003, says that the Forsythe work "knocks the classically trained body off its Apollonian verticality."⁵⁵ She
goes even further in the 2010 article, in naming Forsythe, who "has ventured way
beyond George Balanchine in pushing ballet moves off-center and disorienting the
classical line," as the "brainy forefather" of a trend in a new kind of technical prowess
that, instead of "implying superhuman perfection and accomplishment," is "used to
convey imperfection, disconnectedness, and alienation"⁵⁶ though a celebration of the
grotesque. The material and phrasing of the movement also owe something to Trisha
Brown's continuous layers of initiation and follow-through, and to contact improvisation, which digested the push and retraction of martial arts such as Judo or Aikido.
Forsythe's closest dancer-collaborator, Dana Casperson, says: "He looks for [a dancer's] …
ability to coordinate the highly complex ways, creating folding relational chains of
impetus and residual response,"⁵⁷ not unlike a description of so-called release technique of post-modern dance. In the Forsythe duet I have excerpted, and in the piece as
a whole, the *danse d'école* per se is nowhere in sight, except for its significant traces on
the physiques and knowledge banks of the dancers.

The idea that the Body Attitude or postural model varies across the dancing bodies of
the three pieces has been mentioned above in connection with Laban Movement Analysis (LMA), a framework that can be used to elucidate several other distinctions among
the three dances. The so-called kinesphere,⁵⁸ a virtual spatial form that the dancer
describes with his or her movement, takes its shape and size from the parameters of that
movement. Laban distinguished the kinespheric space—in common parlance akin to
personal space—from general space. So, between your kinesphere and my kinesphere is
general space. Petipa's dancers describe smaller kinespheres than those of their expansive
counterparts in the Balanchine and Forsythe choreography, but the space between
Aurora's and Desire's kinespheres is roomier. He never moves beyond a certain distance
to her, unless in direct physical support, and even then maintaining a polite distance. This
enactment separates the royal couple from the masses onstage who are relatively closer
together, therefore reinforcing their superiority in their greater realm. The separation creates for the audience a more generously delineated view of their bodily designs. In the
Balanchine piece, the dancers have moved much closer to one another, often dancing
within a shared kinesphere of intimacy and support. The Forsythe piece illustrates a case
of colliding and inter-penetrating kinespheres, where no zone of space is left unexplored,
including jabbing and kicking into the personal space or kinesphere of other dancers,
such as when Ando and Mazliah unceremoniously supplant the space/kinespheres of the
duet preceding them.

Laban identified the ballet genre with a particular spatial form—the octahedron
(Figure 7.1)⁵⁹—because both the geometric solid and the dance style exemplify stability

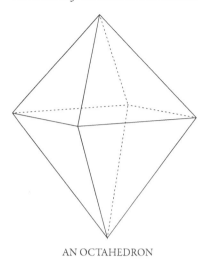

AN OCTAHEDRON

FIGURE 7.1 An Octahedron

through the interplay of three-dimensional counter-tensions: up and down (vertical), side and side (horizontal) and forward and back (sagittal). Maintaining Jowitt's "Apollonian verticality" above requires that the classical dancer master the art of balancing out all the opposing forces that might take her off her pointes, and toward the floor. Also, the positions in ballet, despite the gentle curves of the *port de bras* and the twisting of *épaulement,* generally describe the lines of the three dimensional axes: vertical as in the extended and upright spine, and the straight standing leg; horizontal as in the *à la second* positions of the legs and arms; and sagittal as in the leg in back of the body in first arabesque while the opposing arm reaches forward. In broad terms, Petipa's dancers move within the octahedral model, rarely showing diagonal pulls or lines, whether in terms of body design or pathways. Balanchine delighted in taking his dancers off their pointes, and he valued risk-taking movers, especially Suzanne Farrell for her capacity to pull off balance. In *Concerto,* Martins pulls Mazzo off her balance and into space, he extends her beyond the confines of an octahedral stability. This contrasts with the Petipa couple, where the male's role is mostly that of a steadying influence or *porteur.* Balanchine was said to be particularly fond of *éffacé* positions,[60] which often allow the dancer to give in to a twisted and open diagonal line. Forsythe's couple, in their interactions with the tables and each other, is clearly describing geometries outside of the octahedron, and these dancers exhibit little body zone congruency. As they move through each other and around obstacles, heads may be down and feet up, and the tables provide a horizontal surface that subverts a vertical relationship to gravity. In summary, if Petipa's choreography in *Beauty* exemplifies ballet mostly inside the octahedron, Balanchine's and Forsythe's pieces have both stretched the form out of shape and toppled it, albeit in individual ways.[61]

All three choreographers work(ed) with dancers thoroughly trained in ballet academies. In a 1998 program, Forsythe said, perhaps somewhat defensively to people wondering, "I use ballet, because I use ballet dancers, and I use the knowledge in their bodies. I think ballet is very, very good idea."[62] The role of the dancers' contributions is a subject that deserves much more attention. Autobiographies, such as Suzanne Farrell's, often contain nuggets of real insight into the working process.[63] The subject of how each choreographer worked with his dancers would fill another essay, but I have touched on the fact that Forsythe elicited phrase material from his company, with some dancers giving more than others. It is well known that Balanchine claimed to need the dancers in the studio to give him direction; but he certainly worked on his own analyzing the scores or visualizing the phrases (while ironing!). Many principal dancers note the degree to which they could get him to customize solo material on most occasions. Petipa also worked methodically outside the theatre, creating models of the stage, complete with little figurines of the dancers he could move into position; but he certainly had the qualities of specific dancers in mind once he began to design the actual steps. High-ranking dancers also contributed; the traces of Carlotta Brianza's *jetés en manège* are still there for future Auroras, alongside some of *their* pet steps. In his direction to Tchaikovsky on the ballerina's variation after the Act 3 *pas de deux*, the note reads: "Don't compose it, I must speak with the *danseuse*."[64]

In Petipa's time, it was the tradition for several choreographers to contribute to one ballet, although the ballet master maintained his status as director. Balanchine followed the Diaghilev period of the old ballet, new ballet wars, where concern with authorship and competition among choreographers created a heated atmosphere. Balanchine may have described himself as a craftsman and placed himself within a continuum, but his work had his individual stamp on it, a stamp that defined the New York City Ballet as an institution. Forsythe has moved from inside an existing institution that he made highly visible to create a group that bears his name and operates more like a European modern dance company. He considers his present company to be composed exclusively of soloists; dancers who contribute significantly to the choreography are credited in the program and paid accordingly. This acknowledgment of compositional contribution is not wholly unlike the system of rank—the *premiere danseuse* of Petipa's time or the principal dancer in the New York City Ballet—where a dancer inspired as well as contributed to the individualized solos and *pas* within a group work. Suffice it to say for our purposes that all three *pas de deux* emerged from a complex interaction among choreographer, dancers and other collaborators.

In his 1997 piece on classicism, Macaulay muses: "In dance, the classical sense of harmony probably has its origin in the age-old marriage of dance to music."[65] He wonders if "dance has its centre in its union with music. Is that centre holding?"[66] Writing at the end of the 20th century about more than the balletic tradition, he notes that the music-dance relationship has had many iterations and "estrangements" over time. Leaving aside the question of whether or not a certain *kind* of music-dance relationship is more or less related to the balletic tradition, instead I will note some differences among the pieces, especially with regard to Forsythe. For Petipa and Balanchine, the music-dance relationship was central—inarguably so for Balanchine—and an intrinsic part of the balletic tradition, as such nearly inseparable. The idea of music's supremacy over the other collaborative elements is expressed in Balanchine's comment about what he learned from Lopukhov via Petipa: "The dancer's body is his or her main *instrument*, and it must be visible...Lopukhov used to say, 'Forward toward Petipa!' That is, dance expresses everything with the help *only of music*"[67] (italics mine). Balanchine, as an accomplished musician in his own right, always had music at the center of his works, even in his wide range of subject matter and style. He compared dancers to fish swimming in the sea of music, with music as the environment for dance, and not merely one of many components coming together. The particular synergy between Stravinsky and Balanchine has been a topic in several books by musicologists, among them Stephanie Jordan, Charles Joseph, Paul Hodgins and Richard Taruskin. This is not surprising given the stature of the composer, but it also attests to the central place each artist's work occupied in the other's.

Forsythe himself said that one of his interests in making *OFTR* was to find an "organizational counterpoint that did not depend on music."[68] Although that particular goal may have been newly articulated, it is not a new direction in relationship to previous endeavors. In Driver's book of 2000, Forsythe says: "I used to be in service of the music, providing an interpretation of the music, but at the moment I'm more interested in *working with dance ideas*"[69] (italics mine). The music-dance relationship is an aspect of his work that often disappoints critics. Jordan found little to like of Forsythe's work on a musical level in a 1991 article: "Forsythe does respond to the musical pulse, but the effect is still of unphrased choreography, at full pressure."[70] Many critics simply don't like Thom Willems' music, with or without dance. One writer seemed confused by the mood contributed by the score: "It is possible to see the frantic movement as release and play, but with Willems' loud, pounding music I found the overall affect [sic] made me think of apocalypse."[71]

The way the piece was constructed probably influenced the formation of the score. The movement material came from improvised sequences contributed by dancers and was shaped over time by the system of complex cues among dancers, generating a concurrent sound score of slapping tables, moving tables and intermittent vocalizing. The phrasing of solo and partnering sequences were necessarily modified because of the dancers having to negotiate the tables in amazingly creative ways. Also, as noted earlier, the process of collaboration between Willems and Forsythe more closely resembled a Cage-Cunningham relationship, where each acted independently until the performance. I viewed the piece online both with the sound score and without, and although the low knocks and tones of the Willems score, suggestive of the inside of a submarine, created an atmosphere of mystery and sometimes foreboding, I could not really directly connect the score with the action. The table slaps and cue calling are as much a score as the music. Imagine Petipa or Balanchine inviting, as Forsythe does, the audience/user to watch a dance without the score, as occurs on the Synchronous Objects website. In *Beauty* and *Concerto* the dance phrasing is, if not completely inseparable from the musical phrasing, far closer to the heart of the intention. Tchaikovsky's score was commissioned, often with Petipa giving him measure-by-measure instructions as to the instrumentations and rhythms, with assurance that, in style and tone, music and dance were a matched set. Although the music and movement are not matched as closely as the Petipa, the counterpoint in Balanchine's piece is palpable, and the mood set by the strings especially, infiltrates with both sadness/longing and a quiet joy/acceptance.

In summary, what we know about Petipa's interaction with his dancers is that it was like Balanchine's in that both choreographers worked in close collaboration with their principal and soloist dancers to create their new roles. This is also true of Forsythe, who more overtly acknowledges the collaborative efforts of his dancers whether they add movement phrases, text or structural ideas, and he often makes his creative resources transparent in part through explanatory program notes. However, in terms of the music-dance relationship, Petipa and Balanchine are closer to one another in a more integrated use of the two arts, with Forsythe representing a different (and possibly more indifferent) interface with music. Tchaikovsky's music supplied the underpinnings or rhythm and phrasing for Petipa's choreography and boosted the status of the work; Balanchine's *Concerto* was created for a festival in honor of the composer. The piece paid homage to Stravinsky, whose death is arguably the subject matter of the *pas de deux* examined here. Willems' score for *One Flat Thing, reproduced* was created in the spirit of a separate but equal Cage-Cunningham venture; it goes along with the movement and other elements, but not in a parallel or structurally important manner.

THE CHOREOGRAPHIC WORLDVIEW

If the balletic tradition has produced certain conventions of form or style, does it uphold or express some kind of ideology or worldview? A return to Macaulay's essays allows an entry for wrestling with, if not answering, the question, apropos the three examples in this study. In the earlier essay, he suggests that classical dance represents a worldview that, although not "repressed," does respond to a "code of manners."[72] He proposes that these manners of outward behavior often "give an ideal or idealist view," and that the "use of dance techniques, ballet or other, that demand clarity, precision, rigour, propose some kind of perfection."[73] He does not equate ballet with classicism in this context; for example, he argues strenuously that Cunningham's work is classicist, while ballet choreographer Gerald Arpino's is not. Forsythe also separates the two notions when he calls *OFTR* "not balletic, but classical."[74] Local definitions of classical are messy and often contradictory, not to mention large in scope; therefore for our purposes, the focus will shift to assessments of how the three examples reflect or deflect some of the attributes Macaulay lists above.

All three *pas de deux* represent ordering processes of different kinds: Petipa shows us theatrical conventions and social hierarchies; Balanchine follows musical structuring; and Forsythe's busy and complex piece, appearing to be more of a game between the players than a presentation to the audience, has a code of sorts, a system beyond the arrangements of steps and gestures. Sulcas notes that in creating the piece he was interested in the "same organizing principles he has always used in his choreography, notably counterpoint, alignment and *épaulement*."[75] The development and exposition of the Themes certainly demand clarity, precision and rigor on the part of the dancers. In fact, systems and processes are front and center here, and Forsythe wants to share them, just as Petipa displayed his elaborate *entrées* and Balanchine his intricate musical responses. His practice of providing program notes has gone further with the mounting of a website that invites visitors to see visual connections through technological means, and to construe new meaning by asking how choreographic systems are congruent to fields of knowledge far outside dance. This statement by the co-creators of the website indicates a post-human aspect: "can choreographic ideas be expressed other than through the body…became one of the central questions underpinning the development of Synchronous Objects."[76] Or perhaps this kind of interactivity and transparency of method and meaning represents another kind of metaphoric functioning. Although Petipa's piece is ostensibly about its central character, it suggests hope, renewal and the stability of love. Balanchine's piece, although intimate and emotionally toned, has already been said to stand for other relationships, either between the choreographer and his dancers, or between himself and Stravinsky. In any case, all three pieces' structural components serve to support the meaning, however interpreted.

What of Macaulay's notion above about the classicist code of behavior often expressing an ideal or idealist view? Oleg Petrov, in an article on Russian ballet during the latter half of the 19th century, finds that "it was the classical dance that was capable of conveying to a person the form of a complete, harmonically organized, and thus ideal world."[77] Petipa certainly presents a world where order prevails and love (and the aristocracy) reigns supreme. The stage *tableaux* presented at the end of the wedding *pas de deux* and at the conclusion of the whole ballet create meticulously arranged frames with a place for everyone and everyone in their place. Balanchine's couple is not floating in a realm of easeful bliss, but he carefully wraps and encloses them within a package of formally structured, extroverted dance invention—the first and fourth sections—that ends felicitously and with the music. The *pas de deux* itself has both a cool restraint and an emotional charge, but the ending furnishes us with a sense of closure and acceptance. If Mazzo, as a ballerina or a metaphor for grief, is vulnerable, she has been taken care of, so to speak, and is literally in good hands at the end. The eye-covering motif appears several times in Balanchine's *oeuvre*, often a dancer is led forward by a protective figure behind him or her, indicating blind trust and imbued with religiosity. Here the motif is stationary as Martins kneels behind Mazzo while she arches back, but it suggests a similar theme.

In contrast, the dancers in *OFTR* occupy, if not a full-out dystopia, certainly not an idealized world. In a reaction from critic Holly Messitt, the breathlessness and jarring intensity of the phrasing is connected to the view of the piece as a crisis situation: "Most of the time it was impossible to watch all the dancers at once. They moved as one would in an emergency, partnering and connecting for a moment before moving off to something else."[78] Ando and Mazliah, as other pairings or small groups in *OFTR,* dance together, part and return to each other later in the dance, even repeating their Theme briefly, but they have no space or time "of their own" in a theatrical sense. In a way, they have to keep checking in with the group through the cues given and received, in order to direct their action. Their abrupt separations and somewhat frenzied reunions are more like a real, slightly dysfunctional couple than a romantic ideal. In that way, they are related to the combative, competitive dancers in Aria I of *Concerto,* who perhaps exemplify the struggle of creativity. Forsythe's duet folds back into the group and takes its place in the community, as do all the other small group interactions, and the piece ends in reverse of the beginning, everyone running upstage dragging the tables. Dana Casperson's program note expresses the tone of the piece in terms of a storm: "The piece begins with a roar. Twenty tables, like jagged rafts of ice, fly forward and become the surface, the underground, and the sky inhabited by a ferocious flight of dancers. A pack of bodies raging with alacrity, whipping razor-like in perilous weaves, in a hurtling intelligence. The music begins quietly and then blows up into a gale, hurling the dancers toward the end, their bodies howling in a voracious, detailed storm."[79]

What happens to the dancers: Do they survive the storm? Or as they rush away at the end, are they carried into oblivion, all of their signals to each other in vain?

A further consideration recalls Macaulay's question of whether or not the *pas de deux,* as an essential part of the balletic tradition, can go beyond "love, chivalry or arrant manhandling." A partial answer would be that it already has. But perhaps there is more implied within those terms themselves. To translate the three alternatives into choreographic terms: love could be dancing equally, side-by-side, either in unison, mirroring or united in some other way; chivalry arises when one person supports or presents the other, or takes support graciously or with obvious pleasure; arrant manhandling implies bullying, when one partner is too forceful and the other is too passive, but it might also imply equal-opportunity aggression or just plain conflict. Although I am keeping these descriptions gender neutral, the word *man*handling speaks for itself. Robbins' *The Cage* may be one of very few ballets where the woman is the aggressor, and in that case she isn't human. There is no question of there being elements of the first two modes of love and chivalry in all three of the *pas de deux,* if played out in very different ways, so let us get to the juicy one: the arrant manhandling.

Both Petipa's couple and Balanchine's are decidedly heterosexual, and male and female roles are clearly delineated in both ballets overall, through costume and actual movement material. Although the couple in *OFTR* is a man and a woman, I could have chosen man-man or woman-woman pairings, since there is no central or featured *pas de deux*, as in the other two examples. Some consistent contrasts between the two do exist in the choreography, however. He lifts and moves her far more often that she does him; he is more often at a lower level spatially, she higher, above the table or above him. So, there are patterned distinctions, but they are not as evident in qualitative ways as can be seen in the other two couples. Ando does not have special steps or step sequences as does Aurora in her variations, or specially featured movement qualities as in Mazzo's pliability and delicacy. In terms of movement material, costumes, and character or attitude, Ando and Mazliah are almost, but not wholly, unisex. The post-Balanchine era, undoubtedly a reflection of all forms of contemporary and vernacular dance, has seen more same-sex *pas de deux*, along with other groupings not seen in earlier ballets, so this is not surprising given the times and Forsythe's catholic dance interests.

Although to our modern eyes Petipa's royal couple dances within a strictly formal realm of proscribed distances and formalized gestures, in its day the ballet pushed limits in terms of the physicality of the partnering. Descriptions of the opening night performance include accounts of Brianza grazing herself on her partner's costume and tearing some hair out.[80] As for manhandling, the male dancer played a decidedly subordinate role in Petipa's ballets for the most part, and took the role of *porteur* to the celebrated ballerinas. In later versions of the ballet, as technical virtuosity has ramped up, with increases in speed and flexibility, the partnering has become more forceful and "hands on," but it still does not approach what could be called manhandling.[81] The male is there to facilitate and amplify her movements, whatever the challenges she faces.

Balanchine's experimental work in the 1920s began a project he continued until his death, although some maintain that it lessened in intensity after he created *Apollo*; that is, he explored the art of partnering, pushing the envelope of the idiom of the time. These innovations were considered distortions by many critics, including Levinson[82], and were criticized for being destructive of ballet's ideals. Just as some of the classical lines were extended in flexibility and pulled off-balance, the partnering itself developed in response, with the male dancer catching the ballerina from falling, pulling her beyond the point of balance, and following her line further in space. Referring to a part from *Le Fils Prodigue* of 1929 where the Siren wraps herself around the torso of the Prodigal, who then holds her at the groin and waist to bring her to the floor, writer Juliet Bellow agrees with many other contemporary critics[83] in saying that "such sequences emphasized the male dancer's control of the ballerina's movements."[84] But what is the line between helping, presenting or clearly directing the movement (chivalry) and manipulating an objectified body (manhandling); between a man carrying a woman on his back as he trudges forward, or dragging her like a caveman? If the woman is the lighter and more flexible, it follows that a choreographer will work with that difference until two like-sized bodies become the focus. Every partnering sequence offers a chance to look for evidence of compliance or resistance on the part of the woman being handled and other clues as to the intention behind the choreography in interpreting it. At the end of *Concerto*, Martins pulls Mazzo's head back, covering her eyes with his arm and then bending her back quite far. Is it uncomfortable? For the dancer, and for some viewers, it may be. During the *pas de deux*, he has been following her body for nearly the entire time, although there are moments when they separate and dance apart. Mostly, however, it is a dance of interdependency, as he has no other purpose within the dance apart from moving and being moved by her. It is against that context that the final gestures rest.

Forsythe's couple is also not openly combative; nor do they keep a formalized distance or display a troubling intimacy. They seem to be working to get something done. Citing no piece in particular, Jowitt says in her virtuosity article: "Taking the human body apart onstage in extreme ways, as Forsythe has done, can express some of our most disturbing fears,"[85] a statement somewhat similar to complaints that Balanchine's works can be dehumanizing. However, in *OFTR* the intensity and scale of gesture are markedly extreme, while the dancers also move in a perfunctory way, if at times somewhat more playful and at others more anxiously. Their movement recalls a term from the Judson era: "task-oriented." Ando and Mazliah are dancing together but also continue to check in with the group, suggesting the group has supremacy over the individual. Their specialized bodies, trained through the *danse d'école* but shedding its actual vocabulary, dance within an ethos closer to Sally Banes' "Democracy's Body"[86] of the post-modern period. Their interaction with each other puts them on basically equal footing, but it doesn't tell us much about who they are as individuals or in their relationship. Their relationship to the group is of greater importance; they are one of many smaller groupings that emerge out of the group and fold back into it. Finally, the endings of the three works encapsulate some interesting contrasts in terms of artistic statement: *Beauty* and *Concerto* end with reassembled full casts presenting themselves to the audience, although Petipa's opulence and pomp contrasts Balanchine's black-and-white geometric arrangement of bodies in space. Forsythe's dancers appear to have finished the tasks or solved the issues at hand when they run in unison back upstage and out of our view; they, too, reunite as a group, but they do not present themselves to us, the audience, hurrying off to somewhere else instead.

CONCLUSION

Each shift in the baseline vocabulary that underlies all three dances distinguishes one choreographer's style from others. However, some basic features of the balletic tradition expressed through movement qualities of the overall style, if not the steps of the *danse d'école* themselves, leave traces on choreography as evidence of those balletic roots. Among those things evident across our three examples are precision and articulation, muscularity and resiliency, extension into space and clarity of line and spatial intent. These features, among others, are all reinforced by the physical practice that underpins at least a major portion of the bodily training of dancers and choreographers working in the ballet idiom, including the examples here, no matter how far the choreographic invention falls from that center. Therefore, on some level, despite the differences in choreographic movement resources and preferences that we have seen across the three excerpts, there is a uniting thread of practice tradition. *Pliés* and *tendues* look different now than they did then, but something of the basic step and intention persists for each dancer to embody, as well as the qualitative traces that come along with those steps.

This particular trio of works is connected and represents a progression of relations that includes the very real legacy each inherited from the other. Balanchine's "Forward to Petipa!" comment shows that the old master was present for him as he created; the first work he performed as a boy at the Imperial Theatre was the Garland Dance of *The Sleeping Beauty*. Forsythe said early in his career, he "moved through Balanchine,"[87] studying and appreciating the work of the 20th-century giant. The movement profile from Petipa to Forsythe traces a continued increase in flexibility and lability, in speed and rate of change that obviously mirrors an uptick in the rapidity of the pace of life from the 19th century to the 21st. A progression toward democratization or the ideal of a classless society finds a parallel in the settings of the ballets: from the imperial court to the elite (inter)national ballet company to an interactive collective of problem solvers.

In terms of the relative balance of abstraction and literalism, our three *pas* demonstrate interplay, although differently constructed, between pure-dance and non-dance elements, form and content. Macaulay identified Petipa as the beginning of a route through Balanchine that exemplified a shift in favor of abstraction and non-representation. Forsythe is still actively making work, but his trajectory seems to be in a direction away from earlier neo-classical pieces, though not necessarily toward abstraction in the sense to which Macaulay refers. Part of this trajectory involves questioning the mode of presentation (audience participation, site specificity, developing an online presence), any direct use of the *danse d'école* and the supremacy of one choreographic voice. Another indicator of a possible pendulum swing away from abstraction can be found in the evident interest in story ballets of high-profile choreographers Christopher Wheeldon and Alexei Ratmansky. Although Macaulay and other writers regard the progression toward abstraction as a marker of excellence and purity of the classical impulse, the idea that quality—or Western or Anglo-American canonical status of a particular dance or choreographer—should be aligned with such a progression, is contested by at least two scholars recently.[88]

A dance work is the confluence of contributions and practices coming from many sources. Despite the fears of choreographers and dance lovers, dances do survive in the imperfect and time-battered (or time-enhanced) versions that follow the initial creations. Writer Sara Rubidge discusses the particular difficulties of preserving "open work" or pieces that are intended to have radically different solutions to a choreographic problem, including structured improvisation. Although the three pieces discussed here are not that sort of enterprise,[89] these particular passages in her article are eye-catching: "The open work is necessarily in flux. It has a 'career'...a history, rather than an essential nature." And, "However, under the rubric of an ontology of flux, these changes do not damage the identity of the work, for they are part of what that work is. This contrasts directly with an ontology of substance."[90] Forsythe's piece comes closest to the definition of flux, at least in its creation through multiple authorship (dancers' contributions) and the cueing aspect (increased possibilities for timing changes). Paradoxically, *Beauty* is close to the idea of the changes becoming "part of what the work is" simply by virtue of its many iterations and versions through time. It is to some degree left to chance which parts of a dance—structure, style or themes—retain their identity as they are danced again and again.

Petipa's ballets currently sit squarely within the ballet tradition; in fact, his surviving ballets have come to *mean* the confluence of both the classical and the balletic. *The Sleeping Beauty pas de deux* as quintessential Petipa has become a template for choreographers since his time, but it also represents the distillation of qualities over time. Those ballets have formed the basis of repertories, which is to some degree happenstance.[91] The question is: could this happen to other ballets or figures? Balanchine has already spread his repertory worldwide, and has influenced another generation of choreographers. His name has taken its place next to Petipa's, as Petipa took his place next to Perrot and St. Léon. Forsythe's *pas de deux*, although not necessarily representative of his entire opus, may be a tributary flowing away from the main stream of the balletic tradition as it has been constructed. Further, balletic tradition is always changing as its creators—choreographers with their inventions and their collaborators—keep inventing new versions of it. Paradoxically, its center is always moving, even as we think we have located it.

VISUAL RESOURCES CONSULTED

The Sleeping Beauty. Long Branch, NJ: Kultur DVD, c. 1994.

The Sleeping Beauty. New York: HBO/Cannon Video, c. 1983.

Tchaikovsky: The Sleeping Beauty. BBC/Opus Arte, 2006.

Tchaikovsky—The Sleeping Beauty. VAI DVD, 2004.

Choreography by Balanchine: Program One and Program Two. Nonesuch Records, DVD, 2004.

Balanchine, Long Branch, NJ: Kultur DVD, 2004.

William Forsythe: From a Classical Position and *Just Dancing Around?* Long Branch, NJ: Kultur DVD, 2007.

Synchronous Objects site: *One Flat Thing, reproduced* http://synchronousobjects.osu.edu/.

One Flat Thing Reproduced: A Film by Thierry de Mey. France: MD2, DVD, 2006.

NOTES

1. This phrase came from the following statement on how ballet and modern dance differ, which I feel is overstated by author Ismene Brown: "Unlike ballet, which has various mechanisms as well as a unified academic tradition to preserve it, modern dance is built on individualism, oddities and inventions that have no universal method of noting them for transmission without their creator being there." "After a Dancemaker Dies, BBC Radio 3," August 9, 2010. As examples to the contrary, Cunningham developed a codified vocabulary taught by his dancers and others who studied with him, and Bausch left a legacy of working methods that can be furthered by those with whom she worked. Systems of notation have been used for all kinds of dance, and there is no "universal method" available anywhere. Also, as can seen by other chapters within this book, those "various mechanisms" supposedly available within the ballet tradition are dependent on many factors, such as social and political forces, not to mention funding structures and the sheer force and gumption of certain personalities.

2. Horgan was interviewed by Frances Byrnes as part of the BBC broadcast Brown writes about (see note 1 above) and may have said something closer to "*Serenade* still survives." Shortly after I listened to the broadcast, it was taken offline, and as yet there is no available transcript, so I am relying on my notes. See Frances Byrnes, "After a Dancemaker Dies," *BBC Radio* 3, August 8, 2010.

3. Alastair Macaulay, "Notes on Dance Classicism," *Dance Theatre Journal* 5.2 (1987), and "Further Notes on Dance Classicism," *Dance Theatre Journal* 13.3 (1997).

4. Macaulay, "Notes," 36.

5. Macaulay, "Further Notes," 28–29.

6. Alastair Macaulay, "For Ballet, Plots Thicken, or Just Stick?" *New York Times*, August 4, 2010.

7. "Gelsey Kirkland Academy of Classical Ballet," accessed June 15, 2010, http://www.gelseykirklandballet.org/categories/mission. From a letter by Kirkland posted on the site: "My mission as a ballerina and as a teacher has always been to strive for theatrical depth of character and technical virtuosity in the classroom and onstage. I have come to believe over the years that the future of ballet lies in the art of dramatic story telling, drawing on the wellsprings of classical tradition."

8. Macaulay, "For Ballet."

9. Ibid.

10. Ibid.

11. I am choosing the term *balletic tradition* rather than forms of the words *classical* or *classicism*. Although useful terms, if loaded, and ones that deserve further discussion and consideration, spending time developing working definitions is outside the scope of my purposes here.

12. Ideology refers here to the working assumptions, *Weltanschauung,* and choreographic vision of the choreographer, as well as to possible other meanings beyond those intentionally embedded by the artist; in other words, viewpoint, content, and interpretation.

13. See Roland John Wiley, *Tchaikovsky's Ballets* (Oxford: Clarendon Press, 1985), 1–4.

14. See Natalia Roslavleva, *Era of the Russian Ballet* (London: Victor Gollancz, 1966), 119.

15. Tim Scholl, *From Petipa to Balanchine* (London and New York: Routledge, 1994), 119.

16. See Merrill Brockway's notes from the booklet to the Nonesuch edition of *Choreography by Balanchine*, Program Two.

17. See the titles as listed in Senta Driver, ed., *Choreography and Dance, an International Journal: William Forsythe* (Malaysia: Harwood Academic, 2000), 115. The titles of his early

works are revealing in that they describe a more traditional or neo-classical approach, unlike later titles that show the influence of his reading in philosophy, poetry, and other textual resources.

18. See Roslyn Sulcas, "DANCE: Using Forms Ingrained in Ballet to Help the Body Move Beyond It," *New York Times*, December 9, 2001.

19. Sally Banes, *Dancing Women: Female Bodies on Stage* (London and New York: Routledge, 1998), 42.

20. Oleg Petrov, "Russian Ballet and Its Place in Russian Artistic Culture of the Second Half of the Nineteenth Century: The Age of Petipa," translated by Tim Scholl, *Dance Chronicle*, 15.1 (1992), 41.

21. Deborah Jowitt, *Time and the Dancing Image* (New York: William Morrow, 1988), 242.

22. Arlene Croce, *Sightlines* (New York: Knopf, 1987), 201.

23. The title of the chapter on ballet mid-20th century in Nancy Reynolds' comprehensive history *No Fixed Points* is "Ballet's High Tide."

24. Gay Morris, *A Game for Dancers: Performing Modernism in the Postwar Years* (Middletown, CT: Wesleyan University Press, 2006), 62.

25. See Chapters 1 and 12 in this book for further consideration of Sergeyev and his role in this era of ballet history.

26. See Yuri Slonimsky's account of Balanchine's early years as a choreographer in Francis Mason's *I Remember Balanchine* (New York: Doubleday, 1991), 19–78. Also see Morris, *Game*, 53.

27. Jennifer Jackson, "Dancing Latin: William Forsythe's Challenge to the Balletic Text," in *Dancing Texts: Intertextuality in Interpretation* Janet Adshead-Lansdale (Hampshire: Dance Books, 1999), 107.

28. See Peter Gay, *Modernism: The Lure of Heresy* (New York: Norton, 2008).

29. See the transcripted BBC Radio 3 interview with John Tusa, *William Forsythe, Director, Ballet Frankfurt,* on ballet.co.uk for Forsythe's comments on various labels.

30. Driver, 1.

31. See Lynn Garafola, *Legacies of Twentieth-Century Dance* (Middletown, CT: Wesleyan University Press, 2005), 125–34.

32. Lisa C. Arkin and Marian Smith, "National Dance in the Romantic Ballet" in *Rethinking the Sylph,* Lynn Garafola (Middletown, CT: Wesleyan University Press, 1997), 52.

33. See Morris's chapter "Modernist theory: John Martin, Edwin Denby, John Cage."

34. A clip of Balanchine uttering that phrase can be seen on the DVD *Balanchine*, Kultur, 2004.

35. Morris, *Game*, 167.

36. Arkin and Smith, "National Dance," 29.

37. Ibid., 21.

38. Ibid., 29.

39. Morris, *Game*, 47.

40. In 1999, the Kirov staged a version that purported to be a faithful reproduction of the original 1890 version. See David Vaughan, "Further Annals of *The Sleeping Beauty*," in *Ballet Review*, (Winter 1999); and Tim Scholl, *The Sleeping Beauty, a Legend in Progress* (New Haven: Yale University Press), 2004.

41. "The structure for such sixteenth-century *balletti* for a *cavaliere* and his lady is not unlike that of the ballet *pas de deux* for a *danseur* and ballerina. Beginning as it does with an entrée and

adagio for the couple, the *pas de deux* proceeds to exciting variations performed first by the male dancer and then by his partner...." Sandra Noll Hammond, *Ballet Basics* (Palo Alto, CA: Mayfield, 1984), 9.

42. Fyodor Lopukhov, "Annals of The Sleeping Beauty," *Ballet Review* 5.4 (1975–1976), 25.

43. Macaulay, "Further Notes," 7.

44. Sally Banes, *Dancing Women*, 51.

45. It may be noted that dances such as the Fairy solos and the Blue Bird *pas de deux* are examples of a more "homogenized" blend of character and *danse d'école* in that Petipa infused them with movement qualities particular to each character.

46. See Stephanie Jordan, *Stravinsky Dances: Re-visions Across a Century* (Hampshire: Dance Books, 2007), 559.

47. Charles Joseph, *Stravinsky & Balanchine: A Journey of Invention* (New Haven: Yale University Press, 2002), 343.

48. Nancy Goldner says: "The dance [Aria II] strikes me as being 'about' a choreographer and a ballerina" and "to be a perfect instrument of someone else's imagination is a great achievement." Nancy Goldner, *Stravinsky Festival of the New York City Ballet* (New York: Eakins Press, 1973), 80.

49. See Joan Acocella and Lynn Garafola eds., *André Levinson on Dance: Writings from Paris in the Twenties* (Hanover and London: Wesleyan University Press, 1991); and Arnold Haskell, *Balletomania: Then and Now* (New York: Knopf, 1977).

50. Deborah Jowitt, "The Beauty and Limits of the Dance World's Ongoing Love of Virtuosity," *Village Voice*, August 11, 2010, http://www.villagevoice.com/2010-08-11/dance/the-beauty-and-limits-of-the-dance-world-s-ongoing-love-of-virtuosity/.

51. "Posture and body attitude are most often used interchangeably.... However, in common metaphorical usage, posture also indicates expressive content as, for example, in the reference to 'the posture' one assumes with regard to an issue." Irmgard Bartenieff, *Body Movement: Coping with the Environment*, with Dori Lewis (Langhorne, PA: Gordon & Breach, 1980), 109.

52. Clive Barnes, "Beauty Sleep," *Dance Magazine*, September 1999, 122.

53. See Mason, *I Remember*, 50.

54. John Percival, "Ballet Frankfurt, Sadler's Wells, London," *The Independent*, November 6, 2001.

55. Deborah Jowitt, "How Many Ways to Twist It?" *Village Voice*, October 7, 2003, http://www.villagevoice.com/2003-10-07/dance/how-many-ways-to-twist-it/.

56. Jowitt, "The Beauty."

57. Dana Casperson, "It Starts from Any Point," in Driver, *Forsythe*, 26.

58. "The kinesphere is the sphere around the body whose periphery can be reached by easily extended limbs without stepping away from that place." Rudolf Laban, *The Language of Movement: A Guidebook to Choreutics*, annotated and ed. Lisa Ullmann (Boston: Plays, 1974), 10.

59. "Ballet practice is a selection of [spatial elements], highly sophisticated—octahedral, central or peripherally placed. Laban's esoteric choreutic forms were, by contrast, icosahedral." Valerie Preston-Dunlop, "Choreutic Concepts and Practice," *Dance Research: The Journal of the Society for Dance Research* 1.1 (1983), 79.

60. *Éffacé* poses, whether held or momentary, "show off the dancer's figure more plainly and expansively than *croisé* poses" and "Balanchine had a preference for *éffacé* positions, Ashton for

croisé. Robert Greskovic, *Ballet* 101: *A Complete Guide to Learning and Loving the Ballet* (New York: Hyperion, 1998), 512–13.

61. Laban was writing about the ballet of his era, decades before Balanchine's 1972 piece. Since a big part of Laban's project was to distinguish himself and his dance (called alternately German, modern, *Ausdruckstanz,* or *Tanztheater,* depending on the circumstances) from the balletic tradition, he was eager to find cogent ways to describe and distinguish the two. Now that the genres of ballet and modern dance have cross-fertilized to the degree that they have, it should be more difficult to make clear distinctions across the board, and we must look for finer differences. In this regard, Balanchine's piece here must be taken as exemplifying itself, and not his entire opus, which includes pieces closer to the Petipa style.

62. Driver, *Forsythe,* 5.

63. See Suzanne Farrell, *Holding on to the Air* (Gainesville: University Press of Florida, 1990), 99. Farrell describes how Balanchine worked with her to tweak a passage from Symphony in C, the "weird, unorthodox" split *penché.* Also see Barbara Milberg Fisher, *In Balanchine's Company* (Middletown, CT: Wesleyan University Press, 2006) for more descriptions of how he worked with dancers.

64. Wiley, *Tchaikovsky,* 358.

65. Macaulay, "Further," 25.

66. Ibid., 30.

67. Solomon Volkov, *Balanchine's Tchaikovsky: Interviews with George Balanchine* (New York: Simon and Schuster, 1985), 162.

68. Roslyn Sulcas, "Drawing Movement's Connections," *New York Times,* March 29, 2009.

69. Driver, *Forsythe,* 84–85. The rest of the quote is: "There's something outdated about it: get a piece of music and interpret it."

70. Stephanie Jordan, "William Forsythe," *Dance Theatre Journal* 9.2 (1991), 38.

71. Holly Messitt, "Ballett Frankfurt, *The Room as It Was, Duo, (N.N.N.N.),* One Flat Thing, *reproduced,* October 2, 2003, http://www.ballet-dance.com/reviews/2003/BallettFrankfurt-20031002.html.

72. Macaulay, "Notes," 39.

73. Ibid., 37.

74. Sulcas, "DANCE," 2009.

75. Ibid.

76. Scott Delahunta and Norah Zuniga Shaw, "Choreographic Resources: Agents, Archives, Scores and Installations," *Performance Research* 13.1 (2008), 131.

77. Petrov, "Russian," 43.

78. Messitt, "Ballett."

79. Program notes by Dana Casperson and Ballett Frankfurt at Zellerbach Hall, 2004.

80. See Wiley, *Tchaikovsky,* 186–87.

81. See Yuri Slonimsky, "Marius Petipa," *Dance Index* 6.5, 6, (May–June 1947), 124. Slonimsky lamented the fact that Petipa did not do more with the male dancers of his time.

82. "Balanchine's work of the 1920s featured many of these choreographers' [Nijinska, Massine] most famous distortions of the *danse d'école.* His ballets broke with the classical ideal of bodily symmetry and balance, employing diagonal lines and uneven groupings, high leg extensions, extreme backbends and overhead lifts. He invented unconventional forms of partnering and support." Juliet Bellow, "Balanchine and the Deconstruction of Classicism," in *The Cambridge*

Companion to Ballet, ed. Marian Kant (Cambridge, UK: Cambridge University Press, 2007), 239.

83. See Ann Daly, "The Balanchine Woman," *Drama Review* 31.1 (Spring 1987), 8–21, and the author's reconsideration of that stance in "Feminist Theory Across the Millennial Divide," *Dance Research Journal* 32.1 (2000), 39.

84. Bellow, "Balanchine," 241.

85. Jowitt, "The Beauty."

86. From the title of Sally Banes' book *Democracy's Body: Judson Dance Theater, 1962–1964* (Ann Arbor: UMI Research Press, 1983).

87. Tusa, *William Forsythe*, 2.

88. See "The Specter of Interdisciplinarity," by Ramsay Burt, in *Dance Research Journal* 41.2 (2009), 3–22; and Mark Franko, "Period Plots, Canonical Stages, and Post-Metanarrative in American Modern Dance," in *The Returns of Alwin Nikolais: Bodies, Boundaries and the Dance Canon*, eds. Claudia Gitelman and Randy Martin (Middletown, CT: Wesleyan University Press, 2007), 170–90.

89. Sara Rubidge, "Identity and the Open Work" in *Preservation Politics*, ed. Stephanie Jordan (London: Dance Books, 2000), 204. Rubidge admits all performance works might be considered open texts to some extent but delimits her discussion to a specific range of work.

90. Rubidge, "Identity," 210.

91. See Karen Eliot's Chapter 1 in this book, "Dancing the Canon in Wartime."

The artist's consecration to his art must be absolute. Even in the absorption of work there are moments, terrible stretches of loneliness, long, tragic, relentless. One is in agony for a protecting home, the sympathetic companionship of the fireside.[1]
—ANNA PAVLOVA

8

Pavlova and Her Daughters

GENEALOGIES OF CONTINGENT AUTONOMY

Carrie Gaiser Casey

THE MEMORY OF ballerina Anna Pavlova is so associated with the glamorous, downy, and frail "Dying Swan" (1907) that few remember the historical details of her contributions to ballet history. Pavlova toured to almost every world continent continually from 1908 until her death in 1931, bringing ballet to new audiences to such far-flung destinations as Australia, South America, Asia, and Africa. Her peregrinations led her and her dancers through less-than-glamorous conditions. The company performed in school auditoriums, churches, and vaudeville theaters, where the wooden boards of the stage might be rotten, or the dressing rooms flooded with raw sewage, or the local town suffering from an outbreak of malaria. The company slept in train compartments and cattle rafts and practiced their ballet barres on the decks of schooners. Many of the female dancers in Pavlova's company were young teenagers when they joined these tours. In remembering their goodbyes to their own mothers, they recall how Pavlova became their maternal substitute. Hilda Butsova, who joined the company when she was 13, wrote, "When I was a little girl with braids over my shoulders my mother let me go away with her—and I was an only child. Pavlova tried to advise me and help me as Mother would; I always looked upon her as my second mother."[2]

This essay focuses on the mother-daughter framing that Pavlova and her dancers adopted to describe their relationships and to regulate their interpersonal conduct—and how these social regulations affected the form of the dance Pavlova sought to transmit to her metaphorical daughters. In particular, the essay attends to how Pavlova's relationships with her dancers might contribute to and complicate our understanding of feminist ballet history: What might it look like? What might it purport to accomplish? In personal ballet histories, links between teachers and students are often articulated in terms of a familial genealogy—a kind of artistic family tree. In the case of Pavlova's company, and in particular for its female members, entering into Pavlova's "genealogy" meant giving other "mothers"—Pavlova—a claim to their bodies. What did this mean for the women in terms of their self-development, their independence, and their autonomy? Moreover, if the transmission of dance centers in a conversation of mimicry and improvisation between two bodies in the dance studio, how do the particularities of the relationship between the two literally shape dance history?

When the "where" of the dance is located in the socially and inter-personally conditioned transfer of kinesthetic information, the question of bodily autonomy—often presumed as a marker of feminist achievement—arises automatically. Thus, attending to relationships alongside of the question of what kind of ballet Pavlova promoted affords the opportunity not only for recouping a neglected part of ballet history, the behind-the-scenes nitty-gritty that was a part of Pavlova's company life, but also for characterizing and analyzing the kind of "feminism" she promoted in her dealings with her dancers and indeed in her vision of what ballet itself should do for women. This is an important task, for one, because ballet has received the (partially deserved) label of anti-feminist art form that until recently has obscured alternate viewpoints and as such needs to continue to be coaxed back into three dimensionality. In addition, looking at the ambivalence of these relationships—how ballet both enabled and conscripted the movements of women—offers a productive example for understanding how qualifiers for selfhood such as "autonomy" and "independence" often function in a highly contingent fashion.

Why use Pavlova as an example here for both the pitfalls and potentials of ballet discipline? Pavlova was a potent symbolic figure for aspiring ballet dancers of an older generation and today remains as an icon. (Few ballerinas are brave enough to attempt her famous solo, "The Dying Swan," in the face of the inevitable comparisons.) Though she stands apart from her leggy, super-stretchy contemporaries, Pavlova still exerts a claim on the popular image of the subject matter of ballet: that ballet is a hyper-feminine province of swans, fairies, flowers, and princesses. Today, this subject matter may seem quaint, irrelevant, or even sexist, but Pavlova herself idealized ballet as part of a missionary effort to uplift audiences around the world. As such, Pavlova as symbol illuminates the paradoxical lure of ballet because she embodies how hyper-femininity might counterintuitively be harnessed for at-times feminist ends such as public visibility or professional independence.

THE WOMAN MOVEMENT, DISCIPLINE, AND KINSHIP

There are people who refuse to believe that a dancer's life can be otherwise than frivolous. But, in fact, the dancer's profession is altogether incompatible with a frivolous mode of living. If a dancer, yielding to temptation, ceases to exercise over herself the strictest control, she will find it impossible to continue dancing. She must sacrifice herself to her art. Her reward will be the power to help those who come to see her to forget awhile the sadnesses and monotony of life.

—ANNA PAVLOVA[3]

In defining what kind of "feminism" we might assign to Pavlova's work, we see how Pavlova's relations with her company demonstrate strong connections with one historical feminist formation in particular. Her attitudes toward the professional woman align within what historian Nancy Cott terms the "woman movement" of the early 20th century. Cott characterizes the woman movement as a precursor to the feminist movement (the word *feminism* was not in wide circulation until the 1920s). The woman movement in her analysis differs from the feminist movement primarily because it emphasized the self-sacrifice of public service rather than the attainment of equal rights.[4] Women of this era, Pavlova included, justified entering public life by framing their activities as good works in the public interest; they argued that as women they were more suited to this purpose because of woman's innately superior moral sense. What does it mean to align a ballerina—who has often functioned more as legend than as historical figure—with a moment in history belonging to a women's studies class? Doing so grants a historical legitimacy to Pavlova's mission, for one. It also highlights the doubled logic of the woman movement, which relied on the language of traditional feminine values, such as self-sacrifice, in service of non-traditional ends.

As historian Martha Vicinus argues, greater autonomy for those of the "woman movement" era was permitted as long as they imposed on themselves a strict discipline.[5] This discipline often took the form of celibacy, the rejection of marriage, and the consecration of the self to all-female communities. As we will see, all of these factors came into play for Pavlova's company. In return, the dancers enjoyed membership in an artistic community dedicated to a higher, almost sacred calling. Dancing was Pavlova's version of a missionary effort. Ballet would uplift the soul and change the world: "Really, some government should subsidize me as an artistic ambassadress. For that's what I am, isn't it? This my work of being ambassadress is very hard, difficult, sometimes even dangerous, and yet it is the work which the world most needs today."[6] The higher purpose she claimed for dance provided Pavlova and her dancers with a fulfilling identity, even as this purpose circumscribed their freedom.

For Pavlova, an artist's duty was to bring joy to her audience and relieve suffering, but in order to do this she had to sacrifice the usual familial arrangement of marriage and children. Pavlova was in fact married to the company's manager, Baron Viktor Dandré (although some contend that the marriage never took place—a certificate was never found), but she never spoke of him to the press. For her, forsaking family life meant not only refraining from speaking of herself as a wife, but also refraining from having children: "In my opinion a true artist must devote herself to her art. She has no right to lead the life that most women long for."[7] One company member, Rita Glynde, recalls how intensely Pavlova desired a child: "[T]owards the end of her life [she] often asked, 'Would it have been better if I had had a child? This unfulfilled wish explains many of Pavlova's actions."[8] It also explains how Pavlova's company members became Pavlova's "children," as Joan van Wort remembers: "You are all my children"—these were the words with which Pavlova concluded a conversation as to whether she should give up all dancing and bring up a family, which was her great ambition, or continue with her work. For her it was impossible to do both, for she maintained that no true artist of the dance could combine two such personal roles at one and the same time."[9]

The artistic demands of Pavlova's career, combined with her wish for a family, prompted her to create an alternate kinship structure. This was perfectly in keeping with the woman movement, where the non-normative social units of the women's college or the settlement house could be ordered through the metaphor of familial relations. In addition to refer-ring to her company members as her metaphorical children, Pavlova also drew from familial rituals to define her relationships with her dancers. Company members recall that the Christmas holiday, for example, held special significance for Pavlova. She went to great lengths to secure a tree for the company while on tour: this meant hiding a tree on a boat to South Africa, placing one on the stage in Holland for the divertissements, and even having a tree brought from the Himalayas on tour in Burma.[10] These trees Pavlova festooned with presents chosen individually for each company member—some with an educational purpose. Van Wort remarks of their Montreal Christmas: "Arriving at the hotel, we found a feast awaiting us, and the most beautiful Christmas tree one could wish to see, superbly decorated and hung with parcels, with a magnificent gift for everyone in the company: leather traveling clocks, handbags, photographs frames, cameras, and workbaskets for those who sat idle for hours on end in the trains! Madame did indeed know how to bring up her 'children'."[11]

As you might suspect, the workbasket (a sewing kit, apparently) was designated for one of the female company members. Pavlova's maternal concern extended much more extensively to the women in her group. As a result, the women belonged to a closer familial circle where the metaphor of a specifically mother-to-daughter relationship structured company life. And it is notable that these women used this particular meta-phor of mother and daughter in characterizing their interactions, when any number of other titles might have applied: a governess and her charges, mentor and mentees, aunt and nieces. As we will see, "mother" acknowledged a particular kind of reproductive rela-tionship between Pavlova and her dancers, one where her legacy was physically passed on to the next generation. The word signaled this specifically corporeal link between dancer generations. Certainly the reproduction of Pavlova's lineage through her "daughters" was not a strictly heterosexual operation that "mother" might seem to imply (although, as I analyze later, neither was it a simple copying or imitation of Pavlova). The use of this particular familial metaphor underscored the need to maintain the purity of a body-based legacy. When Pavlova disciplined her "daughters," the structure of this discipline asserted the values she held for her ballet family tree and for her legacy to the next generation. By shaping her family, she was also attempting to shape the kinds of associations her form of ballet would carry forward.

Pavlova took the responsibility for the welfare of her teenage charges very seriously: "It was naturally a worry to be in charge of more than a score of young girls traveling in trains and ships, staying in hotels and strange towns—many of the girls away from home for the first time. Pavlova had to impress very strongly on the girls the necessity for absolute propriety and moral sanity."[12] "Moral sanity" was especially important since ballet dancers still did not enjoy the best reputations: the 19th-century "ballet girl" was often equated with a prostitute in the popular imagination. Many of the countries the company toured to did not know what to make of the women—as in Ecuador, where the women went clothed head to foot in black and averted their eyes from the Pavlovitas (as they were called) in the streets; or in one town in America, where the authorities threatened to cancel the performances unless the company wore longer ballet skirts.[13] But the "good name" of the company prevailed. Dandré's depiction of two side-by-side pictures in a South American newspaper (in spite of his possible tendency toward hyperbole here) encapsulates the sea change of attitudes toward the "ballet girl": "The first, representing the arrival of the company, depicted the menfolk highly elated at the prospect, and smiling, while their wives were weeping and sad; the second, showing the situation a month after the arrival of the company, told a different tale—all the men were dejected and the wives beaming and laughing."[14]

Pavlova insisted on good behavior not just to maintain the reputation of the company, however; she also viewed discipline as a means of self-development. A newspaper article from a *Boston Sunday Post* dated November 1920 offers a sense of Pavlova's philosophy when it came to her "girls." The title summarizes her views succinctly: "Pavlowa Tells Girls how to Avoid 'Pitfalls' of Stage Life: Work Hard, Practice Often, Care for Own Room, and Keep Busy—These Equip the Character and Make Girls the Shapers of their own Destiny, According to Famous Dancer." In a section of the article titled "Hard Work Saves Girls"—an axiom that could very well have come straight from the "woman movement"—the interviewer asks, "What do you think is one of the greatest causes of girls who leave home 'going wrong' as they say, or at least, only learning to order their lives through terrible and tragic mistakes?" Pavlova answered:

Very largely, in my opinion, this: That at home everyone shelters them, thinks for them, looks out for them. They don't have to size up the world, or conduct their personal affairs for themselves. Well, when they join my company they have to do that. They have to take care of their own trunks, see to their own rooms in the hotels of which a list, in every city, is given them, and from which they can make their own choice. They have a maximum of personal responsibility for themselves, very strict rules, of course, as regards rehearsal hours and everything likely to affect the system and quality of their work. What is the result? I think I can say with safety that you will not find a company in which there are beautiful girls, talented, before the public in a way likely to attract attention and honors of different kinds, where there is so little nonsense, so much system, so much devotion to the most exacting work. To go out in the world, and have responsibility, does not hurt a girl. On the contrary, it equips her in character and as an artist to do great things and be mistress of her own destiny.[15]

The price of becoming "mistress of her own destiny" meant that the dancer had to follow strict rules about where she stayed, how she comported herself, and what kind of "nonsense"—code for romantic and sexual intrigues—she avoided. By learning the right way to be in the world through a sort of domestic discipline—looking after their trunks, cleaning their rooms, maintaining punctuality—the dancers earned a form of independence. What Vicinus wrote of the women in turn-of-the-century boarding schools applies here: "Self-discipline meant maturity, autonomy, and privilege."[16] The girls' cultivation of "so much system, so much devotion to the most exacting work," rather than enslaving them to a system of subjection, here functioned more as a condition of self-fashioning.

The discipline required to maintain such values extended to the women's free time. Pavlova also attempted to foster a kind of genteel cultural education by insisting that her younger female dancers go to the museums in the towns to which they toured.[17] Company member and Pavlova pupil Muriel Stuart remembers that Pavlova asked them to write essays about the artworks they had seen as exercises in self-cultivation:

> She felt a keen responsibility for having taken us out of school. When touring abroad she insisted that we see everything—go to all the museums, see the great churches, hear the music, see the dancing and the theatre of each country. She would ask us to write out our reactions. (At the time it seemed like torture.) Dates or historical facts were not important; what she wanted to know, what she wanted us to consider, was what each new experience meant to us inside.[18]

Although Pavlova ensured that her dancers received this privileged education—it certainly would have been easier to leave the women to their own devices, much less require written papers from each of them—their "reward" for good behavior in her company was also tightly circumscribed by her. In the face of such unusual homework assignments, not all of the young women welcomed the direction of their free time. Not surprisingly, how Pavlova's female company members relate stories about her off-stage discipline of conduct read very much like stories of mother and rebellious teenager. Butsova recalls conspiring with other company members to get out of these homework duties:

BUTSOVA: [S]he insisted and we couldn't get out of it, that we went to every museum.

KENDALL: Why?

BUTSOVA: Part of our education. Right? We were dying to do other things, but oh boy! I've seen every museum. I've seen every place of interest there is to see.

KENDALL: She was really a mother.

BUTSOVA: You couldn't say, "Oh yes." Unless maybe someone said, "Did you go to...?." "Yes." "Tell me what, in case I'm asked." You know. She'd ask you what you thought of this and what you thought of that. And you had to give a good explanation of why you liked this and why you didn't like that. Then any other dancer who was appearing, different performances, we had to go and see. We visited all the nightclubs so we could see the authentic dancing—Spanish, mostly South America and those places. Mexico. Everything. We didn't need a college education. What good are mathematics and psychology and all this? This all had to do with our work. And she herself—it wasn't as if she herself didn't go to these things, you know. She was the first one to give you money to go. She'd pay the expenses, whatever it was.[19]

Molly Lake also remembers Pavlova roaming the trains making sure the girls were reading the proper books in their off hours.[20] Stuart states that Pavlova gave the girls books such as *The Life of Napoleon* to shape their reading habits.[21] Once again, this discipline inspired adolescent acts of rebellion. Rita Glynde recalls the ruse used by the girls to deceive her:

Abhorring idleness of any kind, Pavlova believed in exercising the mind as well as the feet, and during the long train journeys necessitated by the great distances between 'one night stands" in the United States, she enjoyed nothing more than to walk up and down the full length of the corridor trains glancing right and left to see what the members of her ballet were reading—and woe betide any girl if Pavlova found her absorbed in one of the more lurid magazines popular at this time. To circumvent this "overseeing" of their literary tastes the girls devised a plan that worked like a charm.

For reasons known only to herself, *The Saturday Evening Post* was on Pavlova's "approved" list. Fortunately, it was large in format so that it was easy to conceal between its capricious covers any one of the smaller romantic novels in which, at this time of their adolescence, her girls took such delight. Poor Madame! She never discovered the subterfuge, and smiled charmingly when she saw her ewe lambs reading *The Saturday Evening Post* with such deep concentration.[22]

Pavlova's dedication in educating her "ewe lambs" is admirable. By fostering the personal responsibility and artistic sensitivity of her dancers, she did more than merely speak of her ideals; she attempted to instill them in her metaphorical daughters. This more holistic training focused on the development of the artist as a person and the sense of higher purpose she infused into her company were (and are) unique modes of ballet training at odds with the strict, strictly physical discipline associated with it today. A Pavlova dancer received the opportunity to prove herself capable in the world: the training meant "to equip her in character and as an artist to do great things and be mistress of her own destiny." At the same time, the image of Pavlova roaming the trains and surveying the reading material immediately calls to mind a kind of roving panopticon, Foucault's disciplinary architectural model made flesh. The girls called her "X" behind her back—"the unknown quantity," as Butsova put it. Her discipline was internalized and continued to function long after her dancers left her company. The sense of Pavlova always watching never left Butsova, who writes that for the rest of her life she would ask herself, "What would X say if she saw me doing this, or I wonder if X would like this number or, and so on."[23] Pavlova's ideals kept self-development channeled in particular directions; the women were free to develop, but only in the direction sanctioned by Pavlova herself—to long-lasting effect.

Thus Pavlova's dancers experienced a kind of contingent autonomy in keeping with the tenets of the "woman movement." For their time, these experiences constituted a kind of feminism. It may not have been the kind of feminism that we associate with the feminist movement today, but the opportunities Pavlova's dancers received would not have been possible without the rhetoric of self-sacrifice and the regulations on behavior she put in place. The resulting ambivalence might be said to be characteristic of this phase of the woman movement as a whole: from one angle the discipline involved could look like a foreclosure of individuality, but from another it appeared as the basis for self-cultivation.

THE REPRODUCTIVE LOGIC OF TRANSMISSION: PAVLOVA'S BODY DOUBLES

Bringing a ballet history moment together with a women's history moment is one way to rethink the question of feminism in ballet (in addition to offering an example of how cultural history contributes to the social history of feminism). Another way to think about feminism in ballet is to understand how contingent autonomy might be worked out through acts of cultural transmission, defined in this case as the passage and incorporation of a body of knowledge. This section considers more fully the notion of family that Pavlova articulated and analyze how, in the absence of an actual biological family, she created these relationships with daughter-heirs. By defining her legacy through the metaphor of kinship, Pavlova conjoined dance history in the sense of technique (what kind of ballet was Pavlova passing down?) with interpersonal relationships (whom did she choose as a successor, and why?). The word *genealogy* is especially useful here not only as a metaphor for the combination of artistic and familial relationships analyzed below with Pavlova but also as a performance studies term for a model of cultural transmission that might also be usefully applied to ballet. Joseph Roach defined genealogies of performance as the discontinuous transmission of cultural knowledge taking place through a "kinesthetic imagination"—a repertoire of received gestures, poses, and physical affects that may be literally re-membered in the space of performance as bodies reflect, converse, imitate, and reinvent these gestures to fit the needs of the moment.[24] In this case we have the question of how a familial genealogy affected a performance genealogy, or how the attempt to create a line of descent from Pavlova also directed the shape of the "kinesthetic imagination" that she strove to pass down and that her "daughters" received and altered. Transmission thus offers a different model of a feminist dance history, one pursued by understanding how bodies "converse" with one another in the context of a relationship. Moments such as when Pavlova "got down on her hands and knees" as her student Muriel Stuart stated, to fix the girls' feet, enacted a literal shaping of the lineage. These moments are only fleetingly referenced in the available historical materials, but they emerge in photographs of Pavlova and her students in the studio: in the way her dancers' bodies echo her own relaxed elegance, in how they reproduce the aesthetic values of grace, repose, and ethereality.

As in the photograph of Pavlova and students in what appears to be an impromptu moment in between exercises (Figure 8.1), the corporeal conversation between them is not recorded—but we can imagine its progression. The dancers strike poses, fiddling around and practicing, while their teacher watches; perhaps she stands and demonstrates a refinement of one, while the student adjusts her body more fully to embody the pose. The other girls watch, also incorporating the effects of these alterations. Pavlova approaches one, standing behind her, and with both of them looking into the mirror, she guides her body into position; a kind of pas de deux between her guiding hands and the body she holds ensues. Perhaps she encounters resistance, or tension, from that body; perhaps, in contrast, it is too easily molded. Gazing into the eyes of her student in the mirror, teacher and student attempt to move together; they respond to the energetic approach of the other, and their bodies calibrate one to the other. With each new

FIGURE 8.1 Anna Pavlova teaching. Courtesy of New York Public Library Dance Division.

corporeal conversation, with each new day in the studio, teacher and student improvise a relationship that is constantly changing. For ballet training specifically, which is often viewed as the passive reproducing of an inherited kinesthetic reservoir of steps, looking at transmission within the context of such a specific relationship, as we do later in this essay, demonstrates that on the contrary there is considerable negotiation going on between generations, even in one of the most codified of dance forms.

As we have seen, Pavlova regarded all of the female dancers in her company as potential daughters, but she also singled out specific successor candidates as possible "body doubles" for herself. Often, for one reason or another, these dancers would fail to live up to her expectations and would find themselves passed over (or, in extreme cases, out of the company). Genealogy here, in the absence of overt biological ties, was constructed by subtler cues attached to the body: whose body Pavlova dressed in her clothes, whose body Pavlova taught specific variations to, etc. The inter-corporeality of these genealogical overtures, or the invitation to be Pavlova's "body double," implied constrictions on where a successor candidate's body could go, how it moved in space, with what other bodies it mingled, and how it came into contact with other bodies. Within these restrictions we can begin to see what kind of legacy Pavlova hoped to transmit.

Some of the women Pavlova pressed into museum duty while on tour had been with her since childhood. In 1910, Pavlova held auditions to select eight pupils, all eight years old, to be trained by her in London in a house she rented on Golder's Green (Pavlova moved into her permanent London home, Ivy House, in 1912).[25] Muriel Stuart, who danced with Pavlova until the age of 27, was among the children selected. Pavlova's stated wish was that the children selected had no previous ballet training—a fact that demonstrates her desire to instill in her students her own form of ballet training. In these children's bodies we can glimpse the distillation of Pavlova's ideals concerning women in dance—the funneling of her legacy, or what she most wished her legacy to be. By all accounts, Pavlova was more interested in artistic expression than in technical brilliance. Certainly the girls performed all of the usual barre exercises (very simply, as Stuart recalls—eight tendus front, side, back, side; ronde de jambs, slow developpés; the girls didn't even do grand plié until Pavlova deemed them ready.) Pavlova started them at a 90 degree turnout rather than the standard full 180 degrees, and nothing on pointe (which made some of the mothers unhappy).[26] She placed great emphasis on port de bras and on the position of the head.[27]

A photograph of Stuart and her fellow students in the garden at Ivy House imparts a sense of the movement quality Pavlova sought to teach (Figure 8.2).[28] The students, clothed in white silk tunics draped in an Isadora Duncan style "Greek" fashion, hold instruments of various kinds: flutes, horns, lutes, violins, castanets. Stuart lies on the ground in front of them, fingering a tambourine with one hand and reclining sideways with a graceful curve as she looks coyly at the camera. One girl holds a wreath; others squint in the sunshine of the garden. Each girl is posed differently in S-shaped curves, her body sculpted with a sense of elongation and languid elegance. The photograph imparts an idealized vision of organic forms, yet, in spite of the affectations of tunic, garden, and

FIGURE 8.2 Pavlova students at Ivy House, 1913. Courtesy of New York Public Library Dance Division.

musical instrument, Pavlova's students appear totally without artifice. Though no doubt representing a conscious stylization of the body, the corporeal postures of this photograph certainly evoke a different kind of training from little soldiers at the ballet barre. (By Stuart's own admission, the girls learned more technique from Phyllis Bedells, an English ballerina who taught the girls at Ivy House when Pavlova toured.)[29] In an unpublished interview, Stuart characterized the kind of ballet she was taught as "organic":

We didn't do the difficult adagios that Cecchetti gave later on—I went to him for a short time—nothing like that. But her standard, she seemed to want beauty. She seemed to want a sense of movement which a child doesn't really possess. You don't possess this until you have some modicum of technique—until that comes. She was looking for something beyond this. I mean we did this every morning. We did the same exercises every morning, same simple porte [sic] de bras. But she wanted the porte de bras to sing; she didn't want it just to do this…(apparently demonstrates). In other words she was trying to make us move with some kind of—what shall I say—organic sense, not just…which, of course, you have to start in a very simple way.[30]

In post-class lectures, she told her students to observe strangers on the train ride home, to try to understand what made each one "tick," and to try to imagine what their lives might be like.[31] This fostering of a kind of artistic empathy assumed more importance for Pavlova, ultimately, than the development of complicated balletic tricks.

Two of Pavlova's Ivy House pupils removed themselves from successorship consideration by departing from Pavlova's more expressive, "organic" version of ballet. Pavlova once ran into one of her favorite students from her Ivy House days, June Tripp, at a casino in Monte Carlo. Upon learning that her "Juneshka" had become a musical comedy star, Pavlova offered to rescue her into her company, mistakenly believing that June was forced into this profession by reduced circumstances.[32] Dandré in his biography of Pavlova also disparaged a student of hers who had left her and "fell to the temptation of a music hall career in America."[33] Ballet dancers on tour outside of the major opera houses still shared venues with variety acts and vaudeville dancers. Because it wasn't always so easy in practice to distinguish ballet performed on opera house stages from ballet performed in music halls, Pavlova insisted on distinguishing her kind of ballet and her ballet dancers from other troupes and venues.

It wasn't enough just to identify one's self as a ballet dancer, however; one needed to be a certain kind of ballet dancer, interested just as much in artistry as in technical excellence. This became the problem with another Ivy House pupil, Beatrice Collenette. For a time Pavlova chose Collenette as her protégée and treated her almost as her adopted daughter, "dress[ing] her in her own cast-off clothes and show[ing] her all sorts of motherly attentions."[34] However, Collenette loved nothing more than turning multiple pirouettes and spent most of her time spinning away rather than working on her expressiveness. This irritated Pavlova: "She despised mere brilliance—the impertinent brilliance which, unimbued with imagination, presumes itself to be of importance."[35] Pavlova soon dropped her from consideration, although she kept Collenette in her company.

Keeping rein on genre was one rule Pavlova used to shape her lineage, but it was just one facet of a larger issue concerning the purity of her legacy. Unquestionably, the most important way Pavlova delineated her genealogy centered on the sexuality, and sexual purity, of her female dancers. On the surface, her concern had much to do with the negative moral reputation of the ballet girl and her desire to legitimize ballet as an artistic career. While Pavlova wanted her "girls" to have love affairs so that they could be better expressive dancers and actors, having presumably experienced deep emotions through these episodes, she contradicted this wish by her own actions.[36] Pavlova consistently responded to flirtatious behavior, or any situation where a love affair might occur, with protective hostility. According to one company member (Sylvia Kirkwhite), she showed up at nightclubs or restaurants where she thought her female dancers might be, just to keep an eye on them.[37] One morning "X" delivered a harsh lecture to a group of women who had stayed out all night in Buenos Aires, drinking champagne, dancing, and returning just in time to be ready for class the next morning:

BUTSOVA: Well, we thought we were being terribly smart, and putting something over Pavlova. We thought.

KENDALL: Did she know?

BUTSOVA: Well, the girls, not the men, were called to be on the stage at a certain time. And she appears, and in very few words—it didn't take too long, what she had to say. She had something to say to us. She just wanted to know if we intended to dance in her company or whether we wanted to be prostitutes. That's all![38]

In an extreme case, Pavlova fired a six-year veteran of the company, Elsa D'Arcy, for allegedly kissing a fellow dancer late at night on a steamer to Penang. (Pavlova happened to be walking by.) The firing grew into a lawsuit for slander; D'Arcy claimed that Pavlova and Dandré had unjustly ruined her reputation by calling her conduct "immoral and indecent."[39] (They settled the suit out of court, with Pavlova paying her expenses.) Company member Andre Oliveroff also recounts an episode with one "Tatiana" (a dancer whom Pavlova hoped to groom as her successor), whom Pavlova forced to repeat a difficult step on pointe from Fokine's *Seven Daughters of the Ghost King* (1912) in rehearsal until the girl fled the stage crying. Pavlova was angry with Tatiana for forsaking ballet for "the expensive clothes and jewels which an ageing and infatuated banker gladly squandered on her in return for what was, actually, her art itself."[40] These strict rules regarding sexuality reflected not only the fragile artistic status of ballet but also Pavlova's desire to preserve the status of her dancers as professional artists.

The rules regarding sexuality also reflected the logic of embodied transmission in that the passage of corporeal knowledge depended on the purity of the bodies involved in the exchange. In each of these examples, Pavlova perceived the physical transfer of her dancer's body and the psychological transfer of her dancer's desire over to another as a breach of lineage. To be an heir to Pavlova implied a kind of corporeal fidelity to her ideals that manifested itself not only in how one danced but for whom and for what purpose one shared one's body. Because transmission of a kinesthetic imagination from Pavlova to designated heir occurred via a conversing of their two bodies—the heir imitating Pavlova's dancing, Pavlova shaping the heir's body in rehearsal—its logic was already sexual, or at the very least, reproductive. This was the logic that demanded that most women leave the company on marriage (even on marriage to a fellow company member) so as not to confuse loyalties by simultaneously belonging to two family trees. In this way, the reproductive logic of transmission conflated both the dancing movements and sexual activities of Pavlova's dancers and placed boundaries around both. Although such rules may appear overly intrusive from today's standards, for Pavlova and her dancers they formed a structure within which alternate modes of relating and alternate modes of dancing had to be evolved in order to make the lineage habitable.

IMPERFECT INCORPORATION: MURIEL STUART AND EMBODYING PAVLOVA

What was it like to "live" in this genealogy from the dancer's perspective? What was it like to leave it? How did these claims to ownership affect dancers? Pavlova may have had her rules, but very few dancers actually lived up to her standards of behavior. What "genealogy" looked like in practice was very different from what Pavlova idealized (since ultimately Pavlova never really claimed a successor, but neither did she—or others—fully dismiss the familial metaphor they used to describe their connection, as we will see). Because the attempt to claim a clear heir failed and yet the need to produce or affiliate with a Pavlovian lineage endured, Pavlova and her dancers in particular cases improvised in and around the rules in order to maintain the genealogy. The failure of genealogy in its idealized form actually demanded a back-and-forth negotiation far different from a model of ballet transmission involving a simple copying or cloning of the original.

Here we examine one specific case in which Pavlova identified a successor (and identified with her), but now shifting perspective to the dancer, Muriel Stuart, herself. Stuart enjoyed a long career with Pavlova, beginning from her Ivy House days as an eight-year-old girl up through to the time she left to get married at the age of 27. With this longer association with Pavlova dating from her childhood came a stronger genealogical connection. What was it like to find a habitable place within Pavlova's legacy? As Pavlova's "body double," Stuart had to work out her place in Pavlova's genealogy throughout her life, sometimes welcoming and identifying with this connection, at other times distancing and differentiating herself from it. She worked out her place in two ways: through the kind of dancing she chose to practice and teach, and through the familial ties she chose to uphold. In both of these arenas, Stuart could move in and out of belonging to Pavlova, thereby exerting a kind of paradoxical autonomy.

Stuart landed the unenviable role of functioning as Pavlova's body double—sometimes quite literally. Contemporaries who saw her perform remarked on how closely she resembled her mentor, particularly in her use of her arms and hands. Oliveroff wrote that audiences routinely mistook her for Pavlova, most especially when she performed in the neo-Greek tunic dances: "Muriel unconsciously mimicked Madame and her work suggested Madame's more than anyone else's ever did. She was the only ballerina whom the public repeatedly mistook for Madame—her entrance time and again was greeted with riotous applause which we all (Muriel included) knew was intended only for Pavlova. This happened almost always in *Autumn Leaves* (1919) [a free-form, Duncan-esque dance choreographed by Pavlova]."[41] Later on in life, during her 50-year teaching career at the School of American Ballet (SAB), she continued to identify with and be identified with Pavlova. Stuart continued to perform her connection to Pavlova by recounting her memories in articles for *Dance Magazine*, in interviews, and in talks with students and parents at SAB. Such performances of genealogy legitimized Stuart's teaching ability and reminded parents of their own children's privileged, one-step removed connection to the legendary ballerina.

At other times, however, Stuart appeared to be deliberately defusing the aura of Pavlova she was supposed to embody and transmit. Pavlova wanted her to improve her technique, but Stuart liked being a "character" dancer more. At one point, Pavlova choreographed a "classical" ballet for Stuart, *Schubertiana* (1917), as a vehicle for improving Stuart's ballet technique. Instead of feeling flattered, Stuart in an unpublished interview with Tobi Tobias recalled a sense of horror.

> You see, I wanted very much to be a character dancer, a dramatic dancer. She wouldn't let me. She said, "No, Mugie [Pavlova's nickname for her, from *muguet*, or lily of the valley], this is easy for you. This is what you like doing. What I want you to do is work very hard and be technically able to do," which I lacked. I lacked the incentive. I'm being very honest with you. Nobody can make a person work.[42]

At the Maryinsky, Pavlova's home theater, dancers were divided into two groups: classical dancers and character dancers. The classical dancers attained higher prestige, while the character dancers filled secondary pantomime roles or performed stylized folk dances off pointe. A character dancer could not be a ballerina; her expertise (and thus her claims to a lineage) resided in a separate sphere with different mentors, standards, and movements. By refusing to aspire to "ballerina," Stuart effectively refused to assume the place Pavlova held for her in the genealogy: "[I]t was almost frightening all that she wanted me to become and do, which I was never able to accomplish (laughs). She really made me dance the Swan Dance once. She felt that I could have done so much more. She was angry because she felt that I lacked ambition."[43]

Stuart did not lack ambition per se, but she *did* lack the desire to step into Pavlova's swan costume.

When Stuart left the company and moved to San Francisco, her flirtation with non-classical styles of dance continued. Her teaching photos from her San Francisco days are dominated by women in Grecian tunics arrayed in languorous Dalcrozian poses. However, this apparent departure from classical ballet was not as paradoxical, coming from a member of Pavlova's company, as it might seem. Pavlova always encouraged Stuart to improve her classical technique, but Stuart emphasized in interviews that Pavlova fostered interest in other movement forms in her company members and encouraged them to experiment. She invited Dalcroze specialists to Ivy House to teach her young pupils rhythm;[44] she praised Isadora Duncan often to her students and brought them to see her in performance (Stuart was not impressed—she couldn't get past the hair, which she said Duncan had dyed "a rather ghastly carrot color");[45] she told the girls after they visited Mary Wigman's studio, "This is a wonderful new world that has been discovered."[46] Judging from the photographs and program books from company tours, moreover, a non-trivial number of dances performed by the company were done *à la grècque* in tunics and sandals. A photo from the South American tour, circa 1918, depicts the corps de ballet outside under a set of trees, taking "aesthetic posing" postures—slight backbends with the upper chest, sidebends with a leisurely dragged foot, Venus de Milo s-curved torsos with upraised arms (Figure 8.3).

Thus, although Pavlova was and is associated with "pure" classical ballet in the Russian tradition, and although she pushed Stuart to embrace this technique, the seeds of Stuart's

FIGURE 8.3 Pavlova Company in *Printemps*, Caracas, Venezuela, 1918. Courtesy of New York Public
Library Dance Division.

own departure from classical ballet were already in place through the exposures she
received while dancing in Pavlova's company.

Stuart took her departure from classical ballet one step further when she left Pavlova's
touring group. Some of the most animated moments in interviews with Stuart occur
when she discusses taking Martha Graham's modern dance class in New York in the
1930s: "I just peeked through the curtains and there was Martha sitting, just as Pavlova
sat. She had on a white sort of taffeta dress, and her black hair. And this (makes knocking
sounds) accompaniment. People sitting on the floor, contracting. Do you remember this
technique? Marvelous, really, to me. I just went insane about this."[47]

Graham also functioned as a kind of mentor to Stuart, although in a much more
limited way than Pavlova: she placed her in her first teaching job in New York, at the
Neighborhood Playhouse, before Stuart moved on to SAB in 1934. By the time Stuart
started teaching at SAB, therefore, she had considerable exposure to other dance styles.
Again, though, while attempting to break out of a classical ballet mold Stuart was also
replicating aspects of her touring with Pavlova—from the dabbling in other techniques
to the search for a mentor ("there was Martha sitting, just as Pavlova sat...").

The fact that Stuart could be declared the representative of Pavlova at SAB—John
Gruen wrote, "When she demonstrates, everything reflects the Pavlovian tradition"—
and asked by Vladimir Dimitriew, the director of SAB until 1940, to teach modern dance
at the school, illustrates the considerable ambiguities involved in placing Stuart in Pavlova's lineage.[48] (It also begs the question of why Pavlova is so strongly associated with
"classical" ballet.) When, if ever, did Stuart make her true departure from Pavlova?

Depending on the context, Stuart could be a ballet black sheep or a Pavlova look-alike. She stubbornly limited herself to character roles in Pavlova's company, refusing to work on her technique in order to develop her expression, and yet she was also the woman who co-authored a major ballet textbook with Lincoln Kirstein entitled *The Classic Ballet: Basic Technique and Terminology*. By choosing to work with other genres, Stuart demonstrated both her independence from and her indebtedness to Pavlova.

A curious series of photographs of Stuart in her scrapbooks at the New York Public Library supports the thesis of her hybridized genre identity (Figure 8.4).[49] In the pictures, Stuart is dressed in her teaching clothes (a long black skirt, a white wrap sweater, black soft shoes with pink ribbons, and a black cardigan that she wears on one arm only); she stands in ostensibly canonical ballet poses (tendu croisé front, tendu croisé back, and tendu back en face) but adds an idiosyncratic port de bras "twist" that throws off its academic squareness. The poses remain harmonized and balanced, but she upturns a wrist that is normally curled under, or extends an elbow that should be rounded; she also twists her torso a bit outside of the geometric frontalism cultivated by the eight-point center system used in ballet. Finally, her face is intensely expressive: wistful, earnest, uplifted, exposed, and yearning. She radiates an overflowing kinesthetic feeling, as though she had gathered too much of it with her arms. Her poses are simple, but totally unique to *her* even as they remain necessarily informed by her background. As it is a studio photo of her

FIGURE 8.4 Muriel Stuart. Courtesy of New York Public Library Dance Division.

as a teacher, dressed in teaching clothes, rather than as a dancer, the photo reads almost as a statement of her teaching philosophy: Stuart teaches and remains committed to certain basic inherited forms as her foundation, but these forms may be given an independent and idiosyncratic existence. The photographs suggest that Stuart worked out a personal style of dancing that was both separate from and yet beholden to Pavlova's influence: she negotiated a contingent and paradoxical form of autonomy in her relation to Pavlova's genealogical claim to her body, neither totally breaking with the past nor totally subsuming herself within it. If we take signs like Stuart's upturned wrist or twisted torso to be visual markers of the negotiation of a personal history through dance, moreover, it should also be noted that "transmission" here in no way resembles a simple copying of an ideal model. This point is often lost in comparisons of ballet to other genres, such as modern dance, where much more emphasis gets placed on radical breaks with the past.

The same paradoxical negotiation of personal autonomy that Stuart worked out through her dancing style also occurred in her family life. Stuart left Pavlova's company when she married the company violinist, in 1927, effectively ending her career as Pavlova's soloist. Perhaps she tired of never living up to the expectations of Pavlova and found in the marriage a convenient escape route. However, even though Stuart forced a geographical separation, her connection to Pavlova inspired a plan for an improvised kinship connection that could go beyond the proximity of the ballet studio. Pavlova, who had often told Stuart that not having had children was her "one great sorrow," asked Stuart to have a child when Stuart left. If she could not keep Stuart as her dancer, she could ask her to produce a surrogate—both for Stuart herself, and for the child Pavlova always wanted. On the day of Stuart's departure, Pavlova gave her a good-bye party:

> I left her in Australia. Instead of going back, I left her in Australia and came to San Francisco to be married. That's when I started teaching.... She gave me a certain sum of money which was in an envelope and said that I could join her at any time that I wished to leave him, in any part of the world, and to come right back to her. She thought that I wouldn't really stay very long. She knew that I was going to take a boat and go to San Francisco. My cabin was full of flowers. She gave me the most beautiful amber necklace, which was stolen, which I hate to even think about. She took it off her neck and she put it on mine, and this sum of money. She kissed me very fondly and she said, "Muriel, I want you to promise me one thing, have a child. I never did. But, if you're not happy, you must return to me, any time." I don't think they thought it would last.[50]

Even after Stuart left the company, Pavlova and Dandré continued to express their interest in Stuart having a child—and in particular, a female child, so that she could become a dancer. (Dandré apparently lost interest in Stuart's child years later when she had a son instead of a daughter.)[51] Stuart for her part took this request quite seriously. She often repeated in interviews Pavlova's request:

I don't really think she was a happy woman in the sense of a happy one. I know, she told me, she said, "Muriel, you're leaving me. You're going to be married. Have a child. I never did. This is my really great sorrow." (pauses) "But don't forget," she said, "you can come back to me at any time. It's not going to be so wonderful, maybe, as you think. But don't forget, darling, have a child." I never forgot this because I had my son. Bless his darling heart. He's not with his mother now; he doesn't need it. But in this respect I had to have my son. This woman has influenced me tremendously, unconsciously.[52]

Stuart also stated that she divorced her first husband in part because he didn't want children.[53] Pavlova's request, and the fact that Stuart consciously fulfilled it, suggests that Stuart shared Pavlova's desire for a continued link between them in the form of a successor/surrogate. This not only required stretching the definition of their family tree beyond more obvious ties, but it also underscored how conflated the relationships of mother-daughter and master-apprentice had become. The conflation centered on what Stuart produced with her body: dancing movements or children. In a sense, Pavlova was also partially responsible for both. She served as a kind of co-producer to whom Stuart granted a claim, as though once Stuart's bodily products—whether movement or babies— belonged to the lineage, they would always belong to the lineage. Thus, even while Stuart separated herself from her mentor by moving away and ostensibly joining a new family tree by marriage, she found ways to further her bond with Pavlova (and, in a sense, to enact a form of reproduction separated from the male reproductive partner). The marriage arrangement was simply an alternate form of proximity through which Stuart could continue on as Pavlova's "body double."

For Stuart, finding a space she could comfortably inhabit in Pavlova's genealogy took a lifetime of fine-tuning. The lineage did not fully own her, but neither could she completely stand outside of it. Choices such as the cultivation of a professional teaching identity that embraced other dance genres, or the decision to have children, functioned simultaneously as reflections of her connection to Pavlova and expressions of an independent personal will. The discipline involved in being a pupil of Anna Pavlova marked her for life, but she found a way to translate the discipline imposed into a discipline of choice—and it seems that the character of that discipline changed when she chose it, even as the choice itself remained conditioned by the discipline. The transmission of Pavlova's legacy to Stuart functioned less as a relentless machine of incorporation and discipline than it did as a mode of improvisation that necessarily redefined the contents of that legacy.

CONCLUSION

The dance history Pavlova and Stuart together created cannot be understood apart from their personal relationship. This fact points to another mode for defining the purpose of a feminist ballet history: to analyze how dance evolves in the context of the give-and-take of interpersonal relations. Focus in this mode of analysis shifts from the visual surface of performance and choreography to the more tactile experience of two bodies conversing in a studio. Such scenes illustrate how what dance looks like—what gets passed down—is strongly influenced by who is in the room and how they relate. These scenes also demonstrate how much personal choice may be involved in the incorporation of a ballet legacy, contrary to the more common notion of the unreflective ballet dancer who simply reproduces what is given to her. If the "where" of the dance centers in moments of kinesthetic transfer, thus, this centering simultaneously shapes and is shaped by "the who" of the individuals participating. Subjectivity cannot be abstracted from the process; indeed, it is uniquely formed through it.

However, as the relationships between Pavlova and her dancers demonstrate, the formation of a ballet lineage nevertheless depends on a discipline that sometimes appears to circumscribe tightly the development of the individual. How then ought we to judge what potentialities these practices offered? We have seen how Pavlova's discipline of her female dancers could function both as a platform for self-fashioning and as channeling behavior into controlled directions. If independence for Pavlova's dancers relied also upon their restraint, it would seem that characterizing this ballet genealogy means leaving intact considerable ambivalence. Ambivalence was also a part of Muriel Stuart's relationship with Pavlova, where leaving the lineage often looked like staying and vice versa, and where establishing independence often looked like reiterating the lineage. Rather than trying to explain away the complexities of such improbable pairings, writing a feminist ballet history also means articulating this ambivalence as an integral part of dancer experience. It seems the best way to respect the interpretive richness and historical nuance due to both the professional performer and the metaphorical daughter.

NOTES

1. Letter to Constance Paget-Fredericks, January, 1931. Quoted in J. Paget-Fredericks, "Pavlova Dances." Paget-Fredericks Collection, Bancroft Library, University of California, Berkeley.

2. Hilda Butsova, "Pavlova as Friends Recall Her," *Dance Magazine*, August 1931, 20.

3. "Pages of My Life" in Paul Magriel, ed., *Pavlova: An Illustrated Monograph* (New York: Henry Holt, 1947), 10.

4. *The Grounding of Modern Feminism* (New Haven: Yale University Press, 1987), 36.

5. *Independent Women: Work and Community for Single Women, 1850–1920* (Chicago: University of Chicago Press, 1985), 16.

6. Quoted in Margot Fonteyn, Roberta Lazzarini, and John Lazzarini, *Pavlova: Portrait of a Dancer* (New York: Viking, 1984), 116.

7. Magriel, 15.

8. Quoted in A. H. Franks, *Pavlova: A Biography* (London: Burke, 1956), 77.

9. Ibid., 88.

10. Franks, 89; Oleg Kerensky, *Anna Pavlova* (New York: Dutton, 1973), 71; Alexander Volinine, "In Memory of Anna Pavlova," *Dancing Times* (January 1937), 146.

11. Franks, 89.

12. Walford Hyden, *Pavlova: The Genius of Dance* (London: Constable, 1931), 86.

13. Fonteyn, 120.

14. Victor Dandré, *Anna Pavlova* (London: Cassell, 1932), 78.

15. Clippings File, Anna Pavlova Collection, Harvard Theatre Collection, Harvard University.

16. 178.

17. Muriel Stuart, interview by Jac Venza and Virginia Kassel, *The Legend of Anna Pavlova*. Sound recording at New York Public Library for the Performing Arts, Jerome Robbins Dance Division.

18. Muriel Stuart, "Pavlova Was Real," *Dance Magazine* (January 1956), 18.

19. Hilda Butsova, interview by Elizabeth Kendall, January and April 1975 in New York City. Typescript, Oral History Archive, New York Library for the Performing Arts, Jerome Robbins Dance Division, 50.

20. Naomi Benari, *Vagabonds and Strolling Dancers: The Lives and Times of Molly Lake and Travis Kemp* (London: Imperial Society of Teachers of Dancing, 1990), 27.

21. "Pavlova Was Real," 18.

22. Franks, 77–78.

23. "Pavlova as Friends Recall Her," 20.

24. *Cities of the Dead: Circum-Atlantic Performance* (New York: Columbia University Press, 1996), 26.

25. Keith Money lists the pupils as follows: Mabel Warren, Grace Curnock, Aileen Bowerman, Beatrice Beauchamp [later Collenette], Muriel Popper Stuart, Beatrice Griffiths, and June Tripp. Muriel Stuart also mentions one "Helen May" in her interview with Tobi Tobias. According to Stuart, Pavlova's original idea was to have each girl of a different nationality—an English girl, French girl, German girl, Russian girl, etc. She had to "settle" for a mostly English roster.

26. Muriel Stuart, interview by John Gruen, November 5, 1972, typescript, Oral History Archive, New York Public Library for the Performing Arts, Jerome Robbins Dance Division.

27. Muriel Stuart, interview by Tobi Tobias, September 5, 14, 19, October 10, 1978, typescript, Oral History Archive, New York Public Library for the Performing Arts, Jerome Robbins Dance Division.

28. Photo labeled #5 in Muriel Stuart, Photographs, New York Public Library for the Performing Arts, Jerome Robbins Dance Division.

29. Bedells, one of the first "openly English" ballerinas (to borrow a phrase from Beth Genné) began performing at the Empire theater in London at the age of 13. She received her training there in the Italian school from Malvina Cavallazzi, but also absorbed influences from the Danish and Russian schools through her association with the Empire's leading ballerinas, Adeline Genée and Lydia Kyasht. Pavlova actually invited her to be a leading dancer in her company, but Bedells declined in order to be the first English ballerina to receive the title of premiere danseuse at the Empire. See Beth Genné, "Openly English: Phyllis Bedells and the Birth of British Ballet," *Dance Chronicle* 18:3 (1995), 437–51, and Jennifer Borgnis, "The Forgotten Ballerina: A Portrait of Phyllis Bedells," *Dance and Dancers* (May 1982), 24–27.

30. Stuart, interview by Tobias.

31. Muriel Stuart, "With Pavlova at Ivy House by Muriel Stuart," *Ballet Review* 19:2 (Summer 1991), 54.

32. June [Tripp], "Pavlova: A Memory of Ivy House," *Dancing Times* (December 1934), 246.

33. 66.

34. Andre Oliveroff, *Flight of the Swan: A Memory of Anna Pavlova* (New York: Dutton, 1932), 137.

35. Ibid., 137.

36. Kerensky, 66; and Oliveroff, 195.

37. "The Genius of Anna Pavlova, Part One," *Dance and Dancers* (January 1956), 18.

38. Butsova, interview by Kendall.

39. Keith Money, *Anna Pavlova: Her Life and Art* (New York: Knopf, 1982), 200.

40. 123.

41. Oliveroff, 139.

42. Stuart, interview by Tobias.

43. Ibid.

44. Marian Horosko, "Pavlova and Muriel Stuart," *Dance Magazine* (January 1976), 64.

45. "Pavlova Was Real," 19.

46. Muriel Stuart, interview by Jac Venza and Virginia Kassel.

47. Stuart, interview by Tobias.

48. Jennifer Dunning, *But First a School: The First Fifty Years of the School of American Ballet* (New York: Viking, 1985), 80.

49. Muriel Stuart, Photographs, #9–11, New York Public Library for the Performing Arts, Jerome Robbins Dance Division.

50. Stuart, interview by Tobias.

51. Ibid.

52. Ibid.

53. Ibid.

9

Joined-up Fragments in *A Wedding Bouquet*

ASHTON, BERNERS AND STEIN

Geraldine Morris

IT IS APRIL 27, 1937, and in an elegant country house in Belley, France, the wedding of a bride and groom is taking place. They are Ashton's/Stein's/Berner's couple in the première of *A Wedding Bouquet*, Mary Honer and Robert Helpmann to be precise. Seventy years ago, these dancers had few problems performing Ashton's style. But can today's dancers, with the changes in both training and cultural context, access the work and the style of the period? Beyond notation, what do they need to know in order to interpret the choreography? To really get inside the work, learning the steps will not be enough. Interpretation without sufficient knowledge leads to dancers' misunderstanding the ballet, which, as a result, becomes inaccessible to audiences. In this article, a section of *A Wedding Bouquet* is analysed, and the diverse strands that contribute to the work are explored.[1] Rediscovering what might seem to be an old-fashioned work is a way of increasing our understanding and appreciation; the knowledge gained through analysis helps dancers and audiences alike to make sense of a past dance. Additionally, knowledge of all the elements contributing to a theatre dance—choreography, music, painting and writing—is crucial in contextualising the dance for performers, and in nourishing their interpretation of the dance movement.

From its first performance in 1937, Frederick Ashton's ballet, with music by Lord Berners and sung works by Gertrude Stein, was regarded as a "fine example of team work."[2] During the 1930s, collaboration was considered to be the essential ingredient of a ballet, a notion generated by the Ballets Russes and Serge Diaghilev. Central to Diaghilev's thinking was the belief that the arts of music, design and dance should be linked to form a single unit, and the Vic-Wells Ballet, the company with which Ashton worked, followed this assiduously.[3] Because choreographer, designer, composer and writer worked so closely together in *A Wedding Bouquet*, it is important to look at the work of all creators to acquire an in-depth knowledge of the dance.

But should a dance analyst confine the enquiry to the main components, be they movement, music or décor? An examination that focuses solely on these elements, although helpful for understanding the construction of the dance, could give a limited idea of the meanings that are embedded in the work. And because the work was made more than seventy years ago, such a limited study does not recognize the historical aspects of the dance movement; choreography, movement and training are not ahistorical. Hence, to consider a work's significance, we need deal with not only the cultural and historical features of the era but also the artistic intentions of the contributors.

THE COLLABORATORS

In London's fashionable, artistic circles Gertrude Stein (1874–1946) and Gerald (Lord) Berners (1883–1950), though not exactly household names, were well known, and by then Frederick Ashton (1904–1988) too had achieved a degree of fame, spreading beyond ballet and theatre fans. Both Stein and Berners were, to some extent, almost as celebrated for their eccentricities as for their work, yet Berners had already composed the music for a ballet for Diaghilev's Ballets Russes, *The Triumph of Neptune* (1926).[4] Stein's *Autobiography of Alice B. Toklas* (1933) and her opera *Four Saints in Three Acts* (1934)[5] had both been widely acclaimed, at least in the USA,[6] although even today, as Mary Clarke points out, "there are people who detest the whole affair 'don't understand it' and think it an absurd waste of time and talent."[7] And some still find Stein's work "unreadable."[8]

Stein was an American writer living in Paris, who also became an illustrious collector of paintings and from 1907 lived in a fairly open lesbian relationship with her companion Alice B. Toklas. As part of an avant-garde artistic circle, she was one of the earliest collectors of the work of Pablo Picasso. Recognising the value of cubism, she tried, in a sense, to adapt its principles to her writing. Her output was formidable and included novels, plays and poetry, though, as the scholar Ulla Dydo points out, Stein confronts our conception of reading, and sentences, and what words should do.[9] Yet her material was taken from everyday life. In *A Wedding Bouquet*, adapted from one of her plays, she dealt with the goings-on of the local French people in a village, near Aix-Les-Bains, where she had a country house. Her collaboration with Ashton and Berners produced a dance that was both avant-garde and proved to be long-lasting.[10]

Several people still regard Stein's work as impenetrable and in the 1930s it was considered to be "absolute rubbish" by some, including Berners, so it is to the Vic-Wells' credit that they were prepared to include her words in their repertory.[11] Ashton, however, liked the rhythms of Stein's works and, had war not intervened, he would have collaborated again with Her. Stein was a very serious writer who constructed her work under artistic concepts, using and rejecting material from past writers. This is evident both from examining her other works and knowing that she spent a lifetime writing books, plays, articles and autobiographies. She is considered by Sarah Bey-Cheng to be "the first genuine avant-garde dramatist, without whom experimental drama in the USA would never have happened."[12] And Bey-Cheng makes the point that her work needs to be understood in relation to three artistic trends of the twentieth century: the avant-garde, the development of cinema and "the emergence of homosexuality as an identity."[13]

Berners was a quixotic English lord who featured in Nancy Mitford's novel *The Pursuit of Love* (1945) and was notable for engaging in a number of frivolous activities, including dying his white pigeons various pastel shades. But he was a multi-talented man who not only composed music but also wrote novels and two volumes of autobiography, and produced a significant number of oil paintings. These were mainly landscapes, modelled on the work of Jean-Baptiste Corot, the French nineteenth-century artist. Like his backcloth for *A Wedding* Bouquet, these were gentle, possibly even conservative, paintings of the countryside.[14] In spite of his reputation for eccentricity, one of his most ardent admirers and friends was Igor Stravinsky, who, it is thought, recommended his work for publication to J. and W. Chester.[15] Berners' earliest music was considered avant-garde and described as having "originality in the writing [and] a true sense of irony in the music itself, not just in the humorous titles and amusing commentaries."[16] He was, and still is, frequently compared with Eric Satie, and his music is quite unlike that of English composers such as Edward Elgar and Ralph Vaughan Williams.[17] His score for *The Triumph of Neptune* had been acclaimed, and he was also praised for *Luna Park* (1930). This was a ballet, choreographed by George Balanchine, in a revue of Charles B. Cochran. It was set in a fairground and according to Philip Lane had musical links with *Petrushka* (1911), *La boutique fantasque* (1918), *Coppelia* (1870) and Ravel's opera *L'enfant et les sortilèges* (1925).[18] Ashton used some of the music from *Luna Park* in 1932 for his ballet *Foyer de danse* and so, by 1937, was already familiar with Berner's music.

Although Berners liked to present himself as an eccentric, he was a serious musician whose earliest music was considered to be avant-garde. After falling into obscurity for some time, his work gained fuller recognition during the celebrations of his centenary in 1983.[19] As the following account will demonstrate, his approach to both Stein and the writing of *A Wedding Bouquet* was highly professional; he spent over a year working on the score. Berners had met Stein during the 1930s, and Peter Dickinson, in his illuminating collection of interviews, claims that he "liked her because she was fashionable modern...and she did disconcert people";[20] yet this was to be the only time he ever worked with her. Although plans were made for an opera, the 1939–1945 war intervened and Stein died in 1946.

Berners wrote the music for two other Ashton ballets: *Cupid and Psyche* (1939) and *Les Sirènes* (1946), but neither outlived its initial run of performances. The former had a complicated narrative that was declaimed from the stage at the start of every scene, and this may have affected its success. David Vaughan argues that it was not without merit and had some excellent choreography, but the war intervened and because the Sadler's Wells Ballet (earlier known as Vic-Wells and now the Royal Ballet) moved to Covent Garden, with its huge stage and auditorium in 1946, it was probably too chamber-like to revive.[21] *Les Sirènes* flopped, perhaps because Ashton jumbled too many ideas together and lost sight of his initial thoughts, or because it was out-of-step with the prevailing post-war aesthetic.[22] It is unlikely, though, that the music was at fault.

Ashton is regarded as the Royal Ballet's founder choreographer.[23] His earliest training came from Marie Rambert, who nurtured his choreographic talents, but he was also helped by Bronislava Nijinska with whom he worked during his time as a dancer with Ida Rubinstein's company in 1928. Inspired to dance by a performance of Anna Pavlova, he tried to recreate her theatricality in his dances but he considered Nijinska to be his main choreographic mentor.[24] Joining the Vic-Wells Ballet in 1935, he made mainly short one-act ballets. He also choreographed for revues and film, but it was not until 1948 that he made his first three-act dance, *Cinderella*. Ashton's ballets consisted of narrative, non-narrative and hybrid works that used words; *A Wedding Bouquet* is a key example of the latter. Such composite works feature throughout Ashton's career.[25] They began in 1928 with Purcell's *The Fairy Queen* (re-choreographed for a new production in 1946) and ended in 1981 with Stravinsky's opera *Le Rossignol*, for which he provided the dance line.[26] Hybrid dances had figured in the repertory of the Ballets Russes; *Les noces* (1923) and *Les biches* (1924) both had words. Yet Ashton's word ballets were different; in both *A Wedding Bouquet* and *Persephone* (1961) words are central, and in the latter the dancer speaks throughout.

Ashton's subject matter is dance itself, but his works are often peopled with very human, fallible individuals. Vaughan believes he was not interested in what is sometimes described as "serious" subject matter, yet he offers a view of humanity that is profound and often moving, even when the plots are seemingly trivial.[27] Writing to Vaughan in 1956 he observed that "the older I get, the less interested I am in ballets of the pests, persecutions and cynicism of contemporary life, and frankly I only like ballets which give an opportunity for real dancing, and after all that is what the whole thing is about. A restatement of one's own personal idiom of the classical ballet is all I ask to be able to achieve."[28]

Commenting on Ashton's choreography Alastair Macaulay points out there is an "unusual relationship between the simplicity of Ashton's theme and the complexity of his treatment."[29] That this has not always been understood is evident in the performances of some of his works. Dancers try to add more character and humour to dances in which both are amply present, and because they lack the necessary background for dancing the Ashton style (and, often, the style of other choreographers), they fail to focus on the dance movement style; as a result, the ballet loses its significance.[30] The more ephemeral the theme, the more important the performance, and this is very true of *A Wedding Bouquet*.

THEORETICAL FRAMEWORK

In analysing a ballet, it is of particular importance to examine the genesis and stylistic attributes of the choreographer's movement. Over time, different training methods form different bodies and, consequently the aesthetic values differ between methods. Paradoxically this is not always considered to be important, but the training methods of an era affect both the dance movement chosen by a choreographer and the abilities of the dancers. Knowledge of a choreographer's larger body of work is equally essential in order not to misinterpret it. For instance, when watching the duet between Pigling Bland and Black Berkshire Pig in Ashton's *The Tales of Beatrix Potter* (1971), we might think that Ashton was interested only in portraying furry animals. But from examining others of his works, we know that his main concern was with dance itself, and, from his own comments and the references he makes to past established choreographers, that he regarded himself as part of ballet's traditions. The Piglet duet alludes to *Giselle* (1841), to Aurora's wedding duet in *Sleeping Beauty* (1890) Act III and to several of his own works, including *Cinderella* (1948) and *The Dream* (1963). These are ironic comments made about those lovers and on some of ballet's most revered works. We might find the duet sentimental, but we can applaud the subtleties of the choreography and recognise its place in Ashton's corpus.[31]

As Bonnie Rowell observes, analysing a work is thus not a straightforward process of describing the components. She argues that analysis of choreographic style involves both the seeing and hearing as well as revealing "why and how what you see and hear are as they are."[32] This requires understanding what Rowell describes as the choreographer's conceptual framework. She uses the work of several philosophers to explore the point, including that of Stanley Cavell (1969), but here I draw only on Cavell. I also discuss Graham McFee's notion of style (1992), which provides a framework for dealing specifically with the stylistic aspects.[33] The importance of Cavell is that he writes of art works as embodied ideas, which means that context can be regarded as part of the work and not as something outside it. In other words, artistic intention can be accessed by examining the artist's other works.

Cavell enters the intentional debate, controversially suggesting that art works are intentional objects. He argues that they embody the makers' ideas, though not their private thoughts, which are neither relevant nor accessible.[34] Cavell contests the opinions put forward by Wimsatt and Beardsley in "The Intentional Fallacy" (1946/1954). They claimed that because intentions are outside the work, they are not relevant to an understanding of that work; criticism should focus only on the work itself.[35] Cavell argues that, on the contrary, intention is part of the work because "everything that is there is something a man [sic] has done" and as a result is intrinsic to the art work and thus part of its significance.[36] Accordingly, knowing the era and the artist and her other works is a way of understanding artistic intention, and in dance this is important, even vital, knowledge for a dancer trying to interpret a past dance.

But, usefully for dance, Cavell observes that intention also includes the physicality of the art work; works are made in a particular medium, which only becomes a medium because of its use in the artwork. For instance, wood or stone would not be a medium *"in the absence of the art of sculpture."* Cavell's point is that it is important in the visual arts to know in which medium the artist worked—oil, tempera, etc.—because each has characteristic possibilities and, of course, limitations. It is not simply the physical material per se that is significant but, as he puts it, "materials-in-certain-characteristic-applications."[37] By the same token, in ballet, classroom movement remains a collection of training exercises and would remain so *in the absence of the art of choreography.*[38] Moreover, ballet's classroom movement is altered by different training systems, so the characteristic possibilities change accordingly. Further, dancers' bodies become useful choreographic materials only when the dancers are used for their technical and expressive possibilities. But because dancers' bodies are historically created, we need to have access to both the context and the physicality of the dance. Cavell's arguments can usefully be applied to dance because they lead us to consider such contextual elements as the artist's other works and the practices of the time. Doing so does complicate our interpretation, and should too affect dancers' interpretations, but it also gives us a framework for considering the work's significance. As I suggested earlier, it is easy to misunderstand and underestimate an Ashton work, and although *A Wedding Bouquet* may not appear to be a very serious work, the rich dance tradition it draws on and the carefully crafted choreography are evidence of its profundity.

McFee is one of the few writers in philosophy to address dance, and in particular the problem of style. He argues, like Cavell, that works are intentional objects. Consequently, in order to understand a dance it needs to be decipherable; otherwise it would not be possible to distinguish the work of an artist from that of, for example, a child.[39] Style, he points out, is dependent on decipherability. The work of children cannot be said to have a style because it is neither intentional nor consciously made against a background of tradition. He argues that an examination of the codes and conventions of the art, which the artist either employs or rejects, helps us discern style.

I have suggested that Ashton drew on past traditions and contemporary dance movement style, and an examination of these leads us to consider the specific aspects of the era that affected him as well as the training of the dancers with whom he collaborated. But to understand the work as a whole, we need to address not only Ashton's theoretical framework and that of his collaborators but also the circumstance of the collaboration, how, why and what was put into the work. This is at the heart of my inquiry, since I believe that only by looking at the work in context can we really engage with its significance. But because the main thrust of my discussion is with dance, I cannot deal as fully with Stein and Berners as I do with Ashton.[40]

FIGURE 9.1 David Drew and Kenneth Mason as Paul and John, with Deanne Bergsma as Josephine in *A Wedding Bouquet*. (Photograph by Roy Round by kind permission of Tobias Round).

GENESIS OF *A WEDDING BOUQUET* (FIGURE 9.1)

Gertrude Stein's Play and Its Metamorphosis into a Ballet

The structure and form of the play *They Must. Be Wedded. To Their Wife* shaped both the musical composition and the choreography, or at least, in its truncated version, for the ballet. Written in 1931, it was not published till 1949.[41] Although spread over thirty-four pages, it is probably a one act play; the pages are A5 size (or equivalent) and the lines short. Stein divides the play into four acts and numerous scenes, even if they are not scenes or acts in any conventional sense. She places Act III after Act IV and then puts in a second Act IV. According to Marc Robinson these "Acts" and "Scenes" "function like frames around paintings directing and focusing our attention on discrete sections of the perceived world."[42] Seemingly arbitrary, similar framing is found in several other Stein plays. In the ballet, the narrator or chorus names the scenes, so they are incorporated into the music and narrated text. There they seem to frame the text, dividing it between discussion of character and description of place. Time and place are mentioned before Act I and in Scene I: "Scene one is a place where they are." In Scene IV the wedding occurs and there is no Scene III, but in the play, Stein's divisions are a little different. This habit of disturbing and fragmenting the narrative has analogies with film technique. As Bey-Cheng argues, Stein was hugely influenced by film. Writing in 1935 Stein observed that "anyone is of one's period and this our period was undoubtedly the period of cinema and series production. And each of us in our own way are bound to express what the world in which we are living is doing."[43]

Adopting the fragmented sentences of the text and the play's brief scenes and acts, Ashton's ballet too is cinematic in form. The ballet's sections are short, and often fragmented, and include none of classical ballet's conventional variations or standard set-piece group dances. Significantly too, the words were first performed by a chorus and not, as is generally the case today, by a solo narrator.

For more than fifty years, scholars have been studying Stein's work with illuminating results.[44] Dydo, one of the leading scholars, argues that Stein never used words as signs, in the semiotic sense, and once embedded in the text they are no longer a reference to the existing world. Despite this, Dydo points out that the "vocabulary is generated by the daily life," by what she observed around her, uttered in Stein's distinctive manner.[45] Dydo claims that Stein's work is, in one sense, about the act of writing and, like the cubists, was concerned with structure. She sought to make the works self-contained. The words "point inwards to the piece," rather than "pointing outward to the world"; Stein has manipulated them for their sonic qualities, and their purpose is mainly rhythmic or textural.[46] Freed from their conventional meaning, words can have new forms, as can steps. So, nouns, for example, can be broken up, into verbs and nouns, thereby altering their function; for example, as Dydo points out, selfish can be separated into two new words sel fish. But Stein used no made-up or nonsense words, as some critics suggested when *A Wedding Bouquet* was first performed.[47] By the same token, steps can change their function, and Ashton did just this in *A Wedding Bouquet*, making linking steps important and frequently the main focus of the dance.

Stein deconstructed the word and changed its grammatical function just as Ashton did with the ballet step. Yet, she insisted that she did not invent but used what she observed.[48] And Dydo claims that because of this, reading Stein involves both an examination of the text's internal composition and the external references to Stein's own world: "The two are in constant creative opposition. The references make us attend to the world while the composition asks us to attend to the design."[49] The same could be said of Ashton's choreography, and it is the design and sound of the words that are also reflected in Berner's music.

Stein's acquisition of the lease of Bilingin, a country house in Belley, in the Department de L'ain in south-eastern France in 1929, had a substantive impact on her writing. Dydo argues that some of the writing of the late 1920s and early 1930s not only incorporates the landscape and the daily life of the countryside but is also a reflection of her own and Toklas' life there. In an interview with me, Dydo pointed out that marriage was central to country life of the time.[50] Making a good match was crucial to that society, involving property, the provision of indoor and outdoor help, extending the family and providing care for elderly relatives. Stein hints at the necessity for marriage throughout the play and mentions the duties and the worries inflicted by this need. So phrases like "Thérèse will always hear that she is not a disappointment Nor whether there will be her share"; and "John an elder brother who regrets the illness of his father because it deprives him of travelling as a vacation" are not just platitudinous comments but seem to reflect the anxieties of the characters, possibly caused by the French system of inheritance.

Ashton used the words to depict his characters and to give the ballet a hint of anxiety. Paul "has charm"; Josephine is "tall and true" and "married," though evidently not very happily as she ends up tipsy and is ousted from the party. "Josephine will leave"; Violet is slightly spinsterish and desperate to marry and "Violet oh will you ask him to marry you." Ernest, whom Violet approaches, is well-mannered, finicky and dapper. "Ernest Politeness" and he "may be a victim of himself"; Julia is "forlorn." Neither the Bride nor the Bridegroom is mentioned by Stein, but Ashton conceives of the one as dotty and the other as a rake. Sometimes he uses the text literally, as when Pépé, Julia's dog, attacks Arthur: "Julia could be called Julia Arthur Julia Arthur only this would make a dog uneasy"; or when Violet mimes that she is "older than a boat." The text, the choreography and the music are closely linked throughout, but because the ballet was first set to a chorus, there are times when the repetitions of the chorus are manifest in the dancing: as lines repeat over and over, so do dance phrases. These links are lost when the text is narrated.

Berners' Conception, Musical Contribution and Use of Stein's Text

Peter Dickinson comments that the ballet is "a satire on weddings by way of *Les noces*."[51] And when heard with the chorus, as opposed to the single speaker most commonly featured in contemporary performances, it resonates with that work. Yet the references in Ashton's choreography are to Nijinska's other masterwork, *Les biches*, though he hints that the Bride's future happiness is likely to be as bleak as that of the Bride in *noces*. The choral version was performed until 1940, when, because of the war (1939–1945), the company had to tour England as part of their war-effort contribution. Consequently, they were deprived of an orchestra and all dances were performed to two pianos. A chorus too was out of the question, so Constant Lambert suggested using a narrator. After the war, at Covent Garden, the narrator remained, and I have not been able to discover whether the chorus was ever reinstated.[52]

Berners' decision to write the music for an opera using Stein's text was made in March 1936. It appears to have been his intention to set the whole play, so when it was cut and changed into a ballet is not clear. But by July 18, 1936, Ashton had agreed to choreograph the piece.[53] In a letter to Stein, just after Ashton had visited her, Berners mentions that the music is nearly finished and includes "a fugue, a waltz, a tango and a very moving adagio on the theme 'Josephine will leave'."[54] The fugue is not in the final score, though

Bryony Jones, the music scholar, mentions that there are fugal entries, such as when the chorus' overlapping entries for "Josephine will leave," create the impression that everyone is talking at once.[55] Berners later informed Stein that he would do the décor himself, describing it thus:

> The backdrop is an oval landscape of a house a little like Bilingin only simplified and I have put it on the banks of a river and reflected in the water. The costumes are of no particular period—if anything slightly 1900 and the principal characters, Josephine Therese etc I have given a rather "endimanche" air. The curtain (shown during the overture) is an immense bouquet with a wedding couple standing on either side of it.[56]

The ballet is, presumably, set in the Ain region of France and looks back to the Edwardian era. Its backcloth depicts a well-ordered house, harmoniously set in the landscape. It could be either England or France, though the characters behave in ways that are assumed to be French; yet the overlay is English. Despite Josephine's drunkenness and Julia's erratic behaviour, the reaction to these by the other characters has a kind of English stiff-upper-lip quality, generated by the dance movement. The main focus of the movement is on the lower body and the expressive gestures are stiff and comical, not generous and extravagant. Neither are there exaggerated leg extensions or fabulous displays of turns; everything is understated, if at times somewhat eccentric.

After his visit to Bilingin in August, Berners wrote about it, observing that Stein drove him out in her car to show him things of interest. Tellingly he records that the "neighbours are interesting and curious. [that] Gertrude had a knack of dramatising them—and perhaps it [was] she who [made] them interesting and strange."[57] Some of these characters probably found their way into both the play and ballet.

From one reference to a dog in the text: "Julia could be called Julia Arthur only this. Would make a dog Uneasy,"[58] Berners added the dog Pépé. It was based on Stein's Mexican chihuahua, and Stein helped Berners construct the mask by sending a photograph of her dog. Later, not long before the opening, in a letter dated March 17, 1937, Berners discusses the dog: "Pépé's part is getting larger and larger. He now appears for a moment in a white gauze tutu and a wreath and does a short classical dance with pointes and entrechats and all that. As the English are a race of dog lovers it ought to have a great success."[59]

The dog's series of *entrechats* are taken from a phrase performed by Giselle in Act II of the ballet of the same name, another of Ashton's covert, even satirical, references. Giselle's tragic plight is burlesqued here by Pépé. By focussing on this moment from *Giselle*, Ashton could be cautioning the Bride. Like Albrecht, the Bridegroom is a man with a past, or at least with secrets. He has a back-to-front duet with Julia, who is "forlorn" and has clearly been rejected by him. Julia was played by Margot Fonteyn, who had recently taken on the role of Giselle. The allusion to *Giselle* may also be a comment on the ballet world's obsession with the ethereal, and ethereal *A Wedding Bouquet* is not.

It is likely that Berners had cut Stein's play before he invited Ashton to choreograph. The 1949 printed version of the play runs from page 204 to 238. The ballet uses virtually all of the text from pages 204 to 210 but also includes lines from page 227: "Let no one deceive. By. Smiling." in the ballet this reads as: "Let no-one be deceived by smiling." From page 232 Berners takes: "Thérèse Crowned with lace. With grace … In place of lace," which, in the ballet is inserted near the end after the lines "And once again they will sing and once again" and the lines are changed to "Thérèse is crowned with lace and crowned with grace in place of lace." From page 213 is taken:

Josephine May she be tall. And true.
[and] Julia may she also. Be new.
May she. Also. Be. One of few.

There are other places where Stein's text has been moved a couple of lines up or down, but apart from one or two word changes, the text of the play and that of the ballet are very close, if not quite identical. A major feature of the ballet's text is the use of repetition, which is not in Stein's play, but is in some of her other works.

Berners constantly repeats phrases and frequently stresses each syllable of each word, fragmenting the word. He threads these repetitions throughout the text, and they are sometimes picked up by Ashton, who parallels the musical repetition by repeating the dance phrases. The scholar Bryony Jones argues that repetitions came naturally to Berners because his musical style favoured repetition in preference to variation and development. But in the ballet, she assumes that the repetitions are Stein's, though in fact they were seemingly added by Berners. More importantly, she notes that Berners must have written the music before meeting Ashton and Lambert and had probably already constructed the libretto.[60] This is because "small sections of the text are set to short melodic fragments…which are reiterated as the words are repeated by the chorus" and the rhythm of the music is frequently dictated by the sound of the words.[61] Earlier suggestions that Lambert put the words to the music now seem less likely.

Ashton picks up on Berners' waltzes and tangos. He uses the waltz to celebrate the marriage, though the movement burlesques the traditional waltz and he adds movements from those performed by "chorus girls" in the stage dancing of the era. Later the waltz is used for a display of *grandes jetés* by several of the Guests, and in particular to show off those of Julia and the Bride, who make a circle of *grandes jetés* around a group of guests. Is he pitting one character against the other? At the ballet's conclusion, the cast exits to the waltz, which gradually tails off to leave Julia alone, "forlorn," with her dog Pépé. Although it has been clear right from his first entrance that the Bridegroom is not to be trusted, his participation in the tango quells any doubts we may have had. His persona reminds us of that of the seedy Dago in the tango from Ashton's *Façade*; here Ashton is using the music as a way of depicting character. Because Stephanie Jordan has amply dealt with Ashton's use of music, I do not deal with it extensively here.[62]

ANALYTICAL FRAMEWORK FOR THE DANCE MOVEMENT

Ashton considered himself to be part of a heritage and in an England dominated by the values of the Ballets Russes, Marius Petipa and Pavlova; it is hardly surprising that he refers to both Pavlova and Nijinska in most of his works. By the same token, as a choreographer working during the 1920s and 1930s, he also made dances for the commercial theatre. Consequently, *A Wedding Bouquet*, and many of his other works, includes aspects of the stage dancing of the era. Though because the work was made before the Vic-Wells Ballet incorporated *The Sleeping Beauty* into its repertoire, there are few allusions to Marius Petipa. And yet there is a grand *pas de deux*, and some trios, and the Bride has a solo. But it would be stretching the point to suggest that the spatial grouping owed much to Petipa. The references to Pavlova too are tenuous, and there is little that was typical of her performances: there are no attempts to highlight gorgeous feet and no moments of the kind of theatricality for which Pavlova was renowned.[63] Aspects of Nijinska's dance movement style and the popular culture of the era both figure in this work. There are numerous references to Nijinska's *Les biches* in both the dance movement and the use of a duo, which recalls the Grey Girls. And Ashton frequently re-uses dance movement material, both his own and that of others. Sometimes the quotations from others are used ironically as in the Piglet duet in *The Tales of Beatrix Potter* (1971), and sometimes to create associations between two works as with *Les biches*. These consciously made references to Nijinska and to the popular culture of the era are part of Ashton's style.

For the movement, Ashton draws on the *danse d'école* but breaks the rules, altering and adapting the steps.[64] Since it is not possible to deal with every altered step, when exploring Ashton's dance movement style, I identified several that could be described as "signature steps"; these are found in almost every one of his ballets.[65] The term is also used by Michael Somes[66] to describe the group of steps that make up the "Fred Step" (*posé en arabesque, coupe dessous*, small *développé à la seconde, pas de bourrée dessous, pas de chat*) and these, together with the *pas de bourrée, pas de chat, rond de jambe à terre* and the *ballonné simple*, I consider to be signature steps.[67] They are used in different ways, sometimes to create texture and arrest the flow of a phrase or as major steps in a phrase. In the latter case, the function of the step is altered, since those mentioned above are usually regarded as minor, linking steps. Ashton was not interested in presenting the "correct" version of the classroom code. For instance, he was more concerned with the qualitative elements of the movement than with the linear shape; for him, it was more important to retain the speed and emphasis than the correct shape or position.[68] These are the most frequently repeated signature steps. For this reason, I chose them to highlight stylistic characteristics of his movement. Altered codified steps are thus characteristic of his style, and as a result different criteria are required for their performance. They are no longer entirely dependent on the rules governing the performance of the *danse d'école*, and dancers need to take account of this aspect of Ashton's style.

The steps have significant stylistic traits, and the way Ashton groups them into short phrases, or clusters of phrases, is important and different from their typical deployment in the classroom *enchaînement*. The types of phrase fall into several categories. Here I explore two: phrases that depend on elaborate rhythmic patterning, and phrases in which there are no pauses between steps, the ending of one becoming the preparation for the next.

INVESTIGATION INTO ASHTON'S DANCE MOVEMENT
AND CHOREOGRAPHY

The ballet is peopled with friends and relations of the Bride and Groom: spinsters, re-jected women, drunks and "respectable" men. And, like Stein, and Berners through the costumes, Ashton attempted to capture the distinctive characteristics of a French country wedding. All the locals are there, the peasants, the two Gendarmes and the men "according to their social status, [wearing] dress-coats, frock-coats, jackets or waistcoats" and the ladies supporting "town-style dresses."[69] Each character enters and leaves before gathering with the others for the ceremony. The ballet glimpses at a disparate collection of very ordinary people made eloquent by Stein's words and Ashton's choreography. But, just like any wedding, we hear only half-finished phrases and see scraps of dance. Nothing is complete, and at the end we are aware that this is not the whole story, nor the happy-ever-after affair that story-book weddings usually assume.

Webster, the Edwardian housekeeper, manages the country house where the wedding happens. It is she who opens the ballet, performing one of the longest dances in the piece, lasting almost two minutes. She then beckons on the four peasants and eventually joins in with them. As Josephine enters, and the music changes to a more legato phrase, the peasants carry Webster off in a mock funeral lift, holding her horizontally and high above their heads. Various characters are then gradually introduced in ones, twos and fours. And for the first ten minutes of the ballet, apart from that of Webster, no dance lasts more than twenty to thirty seconds. Each character enters with a brief dance only to be interrupted by the arrival of the next. Ashton hurries the dancers on and off the stage, treating us to all the furore and general confusion that precedes a wedding. The Bride and Groom enter through a guard-of-honour-like grouping of the guests. There is a picture-taking event, followed by a group dance for all. As in Aurora's wedding in the last act of Petipa's *The Sleeping Beauty*, there are *divertissements,* but the typical order of classical ballet is reversed: the Bride's solo starts things off and the main *pas de deux* follows a little later. Two trios ensue before the tango brings the Bridegroom back on, marking the beginning of the end.

Each individual has a distinctive motif, a key to his or her character, but none more so than Webster. Dressed in the uniform of an Edwardian servant, she scurries from side to side, hands joined, held high to show sharply pointed elbows. Evidently, she is something of a tyrant, and the jabbing, spiky nature of her runs on pointe and picked-up *pas de bourrées* make this clear. With elbows akimbo, she scolds and gestures to no one in particular. At times, streaks of mischief and affection shine through, though; she is after all human. It is Webster who rushes to take the photograph of the wedding, and in the later trio, with John and Paul, she is frisky, even perhaps seductive, collapsing every now and then in order to be revived by the two men. This trio recalls a similar one involving the Hostess in *Les biches*. Webster was made for Ninette de Valois, on whom the Hostess dance was also choreographed. Ashton would have known this, and contemporary audiences might well have recalled the other trio in *Les rendezvous*, which Ashton did for her in 1933.

Ashton uses the *danse d'école* in Webster's opening phrases to convey her personality, but without abandoning his familiar stylistic characteristics. He elevates linking steps, like the *pas de bourrée* (step containing three quick weight changes) and makes them the major motif in the dance. Picking up on de Valois'/Webster's resourcefulness, Ashton provides her with a multitude of ingenious *pas de bourrées*[70]:

Phrase (a) moving in a circle and remaining on point, she performs three *pas de bourrées*, as if running, each ending/beginning with a low kick/attitude

Phrase (b) has two and a half repeats of the same *pas de bourrée*, travelling from side to side with larger steps

Phrase (c) comprises a high kick and shouting gesture into a jumped turn, repeated

Phrase (d) has a parallel *bourrée couru* with two *relevés* into the low kick/attitude

Phrase (e) is a flat-footed *pas de bourrée* from side to side

This cluster of triplets is eventually completed by the "Fred Step": he uses only the first four steps of the phrase, replacing the *pas de chat* with eight *ronds de jambs en l'air*. These are performed hopping on pointe, to *effacé*, preserving the aggressive industriousness of the character.[71] Ashton transforms the balletic *pas de bourrée* into a running series of triplets. The feet are almost parallel, and Webster remains on pointe virtually throughout the cluster of phrases (de Valois was known for her precise footwork). To convey character, the phrases initially depend on gestural movement, though for the rest the arms are kept close to the body, encouraging activity in the upper torso; this too is a feature of Nijinska's movement style.

The movement creates an image of a very driven, frenetic persona, amplified by the way in which the arms, bent, at shoulder height, are occasionally flung from side to side; the movement is emphatic, focused and purposeful. Throughout the ballet the *pas de bourrée* and *bourrée couru* recur, tailored to suit each female character. *Les biches* has a similar dominating motif. There, walks on pointe, off point and performed with long strides are used for each of the personae.

Josephine, the next guest, enters backwards, with a lazy, languid version of the *bourrée couru*. Her indolence is emphasised by the elliptical pathway and eye-shading gesture. The phrase that follows has a sliding movement into *arabesque* and a *pas de bourrée*. The contrast between these *pas de bourrées* and those of Webster is palpable; where Josephine's are languid and lazy, Webster's are strong and purposeful. Described by Stein as a "ca va bien" type, she is, almost, too sophisticated to attend a country wedding.[72] And when she engages with the smartly attired Paul and John, who interrupt her dance, she leans seductively from one to the other, anticipating her subsequent drunken behaviour. Violet and Ernest enter next in a flurry of runs/*bourrée couru* and fast, *saut de basque*, type of steps, two more recurring signature movements. Thérèse is the last to enter in this opening section. In a fast backwards *bourrée couru*, she crosses the stage, diagonally entering from upstage left, and ends by bumping suddenly into Violet. Almost immediately, the characters re-enter and this first introductory section is completed by a short ensemble dance. They exit, one behind the other, performing a staccato dance phrase of *chassé, coupé, pas de bourrée* with upper body comically twisting from side to side.

Ashton is not showing off the technical talents of his dancers, at least not their virtuoso talents. This opening section is almost shockingly limited, with its brisk *terre à terre* steps and fragmented phrases. If the ballet is not a showcase for technical exploits, it is undoubtedly an assessment of articulate footwork. These intricate steps and the complicated *épaulement*, or use of the torso, of the opening section set the tone and stylistic pattern for the rest of the ballet. Key movements are introduced: the *bourrée couru, pas de bourrée*, low *arabesque* and *pas de chat*, just the kind of steps that de Valois was interested in developing as characteristic of an English ballet style.[73]

It is now worth looking in more detail at this short ensemble dance, which ends the opening section. Not only does it give further clues to Ashton's movement style, but it also serves to highlight Ashton's use of music and text. The movement is clipped, echoing the sounds of the words "There can be no hesitation," and responding to the short musical notes. The vocal repetitions differ between the choral and spoken versions: the phrase is repeated (up to fifteen times) by the chorus but only four times by the Speaker in the narrative version.[74] The singers are heard throughout, fading as the group exits, but because of the Speaker's silence a long orchestral passage is heard instead and the waning effect of the exit is lost. Ashton of course choreographed to the chorus, and the Speaker affects how we see the dance; the spoken voice is declamatory, more nuanced, changing the tone. Ashton follows the words of the chorus, though in the final exit he draws attention to the mechanical beat of the base line ostinato with the rapidly changing *épaulement*. The continuous nature of the cluster of phrases responds too to the sense of the words "there can be no hesitation"; there is no hesitation between phrases. This, of course, is or would be much more evident in the choral version.

All the characters who have already been introduced perform the sequence, comprising six phrases of repetitions and no breaks:

Phrase group (a) eight hip-thrusting, jerky walks that accentuate the "there" and "no" of the text.

Phrase group (b) ten small *entrechat* performed in a circle with arms rising to fifth.

Phrase group (c) an *épaulement* rich combination of *glissades* ending in a hop to one leg with an extra *glissade* in the last phrase.

Phrase group (d) a *pas de bourrée* with two *entrechats*, repeated four times, though in the final phrase of the quartet an extra two *entrechats* are slipped in. During both the *entrechats* and *pas de bourrées*, the shoulders change, moving in the direction of the front foot, making the phrase highly active.

Phrase group (e) combines a turning jump and *jeté* followed by a turn on two feet, ending with four little *jetés*; these end heavily, each with a jolt.

Phrase group (f) is a recurring *pas de bourrée* with changing *épaulement*, travelling in a curve and taking the group off stage.

The steps, although standard to the ballet class, are not used in their classroom versions.[75] They are too fast, follow each other without preparation and are performed as a single long sequence. They are made lively, even effervescent, by the constantly changing *épaulement*. Although taken from the *danse d'école*, the steps break the rules in other ways. The arms are not correct, and the speed at which they have to be performed prevents them from being text-book copies. Instead, they are clipped, sharp versions of the original, not bothered by the need to close in an exact fifth position. The *épaulement* too is hugely exaggerated, and arms, apart from one incidence, are kept low or even held behind the back. The comedy depends on the speed of performance and the non-stop activity of the group of phrases. The humour is reinforced by the reference to stage dancing; the exaggerated entrance walk comes from the chorus line, the steps in Phrase group C also appear in the Popular Song in *Façade* (1931), itself a reflection of the dead-pan, soft-shoe, Music Hall, duet.[76]

Other aspects of Ashton's dance movement style are evident in this long sequence. Confining the arms is something he learnt from Nijinska. In both *Les noces* and *Les biches*, Nijinska also keeps the arms fixed, though in different ways: held to the face in *noces* and to the shoulders in *biches*. As a result, the movement has to be initiated from the torso. Similarly with *A Wedding Bouquet*, the impetus for the movement comes from the torso, forcing it to work harder; this creates a look of frenzy and underpins the comedy. There is no need to add funny faces, or a raised eyebrow; the sequence itself is humorous and reflects the gossipy excitement of those arriving for a wedding.

I have discussed some of Ashton's signature steps above, but particularly in this work, they are interspersed with quotidian gesture. Just before the group sequence, for example, Violet performs quick, travelling *sauts de basque*, which interrupt the flow of the running/*bourrée couru*. The phrase is accompanied by the gesturing, pleading arms of Violet, while Ernest occasionally covers his ears with clenched fists, a characteristic

Ashton gesture.[77] Throughout Violet's dance phrase, the narrator, or chorus, insistently chants "oh will you ask him to marry you." And we learn that she is not young any longer.

> Thérèse I am older than a Boat
> And there can be no folly in owning it.

Violet is dressed in a lavender gown with a high neck decorated with lace, accoutrements of the older Edwardian woman. Ashton does not present her as elderly, only as rather sad. According to Dydo, Stein was conscious of the position of women in France, and in particular the unmarried woman, who, at the turn of the twentieth century, had little power and little status.[78] Although Violet's plight may appear amusing to audiences, the reality is more chilling. These Chaplinesque elements are created by Ashton, for he makes the characters seems silly but forces us to sympathise with them because they are so human, mundane even. The references to *Giselle* and to *Les noces*, both disturbing works, help to reinforce these comic overtones.[79] Is Ashton, and is perhaps Berners too, suggesting that the Bride and Groom in *A Wedding Bouquet* are in an arranged marriage, like the couple in *noces*?

Ashton drew extensively from Nijinska, but one of his more significant quotes demonstrates his ability to tease his audience through movement. The phrase, stolen from *Les biches*, occurs in the dance of the two Bridesmaids, who, like the Grey Girls in *Les biches*, are joined but beneath a veil. A repeated phrase in the *Chanson Dancée* (Grey Girls) comprising *glissade, jeté en avant, demi contretemps, glissade pas de chat, pas de chat, glissade assemblé*[80] is picked up by the Bridesmaids and becomes *assemblé, sissonne* step across and two *pas de chat*. The *glissades, jeté en avant* and *demi contretemps* are missing from the Bridesmaids' dance, and there is no *sissonne* in that of the Grey Girls, but the rhythm and uninterrupted flow of the two phrases are similar; in neither do the dancers have time to think ahead. The reference is also clear because in both the women are physically attached to each other and the series of phrases follow a semi-circular path. Nijinska hints that the women in the *Chanson Dancée* are lesbians; the dance ends in a sudden embrace. It is quite likely that Ashton was referring both to this and possibly even to the relationship between Stein and Toklas. There are other quotes from *biches*, such as the moment when the four Guests duck down and hide behind the table. In *biches*, five women hide behind the sofa and after a short male duet jump up, startling the men.

In *A Wedding Bouquet*, there is an abundance of signature steps. There are references too to stage dancing and, most prominently, to both the dance movement style and choreography of Nijinska. Phrases are repeated and refreshed and picked up and used by other characters, and despite its fragmentary nature it has a vague structural similarity with *Les biches*: characters entering in small groups or solo, followed by a group dance and a series of short divertissements.

DANCERS' CONTRIBUTION

Ashton's dancers also play a part in his dance movement style. In this work, he used a range of dancers coming from different dance backgrounds, trained by such early twentieth-century pedagogues as Phyllis Bedells, Edouard Espinosa, Margaret Craske and Serafina Astafieva. The training at the Sadler's Wells School was, at this time, equally eclectic, drawing on Nicholas Sergueyev, Stanislas Idizikowsky and occasionally other Russian immigrants such as Anna Pruzina. There was nothing uniform about these teachers, since their dance experience was drawn from vaudeville, revues, musical theatre and the Ballets Russes, reflecting the dance world in Britain during the 1930s. The book *Who's Who in Dancing 1932* makes this clear.[81] It was edited by Arnold Haskell (dance critic and writer) and Philip Richardson (editor of *The Dancing Times*) and comprised a list of "the leading men and women in the world of dancing." This invaluable book summarises precisely the contemporary state of dance and ballet in Britain, the latter still referred to as operatic dancing. No distinction is made among ballroom, revived Greek dance, folk dancing, stage dancing and ballet, and it is frequently the case that many of the teachers taught several of these genres. In more than 120 pages of dense print, the teachers and dancers of the era are listed; nearly all the ballet teachers, from Astafieva to Espinosa and beyond, had performed in multiple genres. In effect this meant that the easy, relaxed style of stage dancing of the first thirty years of the twentieth century coloured the way in which ballet was performed and even perhaps perceived.

Typified by such popular dance artists as Fred Astaire, Jesse Matthews and Buddy Bradley, the appearance was of an effortless nonchalance and in ballet this translated into less emphasis on turnout and more on having a relaxed, flexible, natural looking upper body, though an ability to perform intricate footwork was also important. Although the Vic-Wells dancers looked nothing like the sleek, athletic dancers of today, they were exciting dancers of widely varied abilities. Despite the fact that many of the teachers listed above had studied with Cecchetti, whose classes encouraged a strong core, facilitating speed and a flexible upper body, their professional demands required that they expand beyond balletic technique. Indeed their training generally lasted only a few years before they became professional dancers. Many performed in revues before joining the Vic-Wells and did so again during an enforced three-to-four-month break in the summer. Tap dancing and the intricate footwork of the social dances figured prominently on most teachers' CVs, and it is likely too that the skills encouraged by these dance forms found their way into the ballet training. Certainly it is fair to say that the emphasis on beaten jumps and intricate, rhythmic *pas de bourrées* was an aspect of the early Cecchetti syllabuses and these features were emphasised in the classes of de Valois during the 1930s and later.

Ashton's passion for fast, intricate footwork was clearly echoed in this training and may also have been influenced by it—and the dancers were well equipped for these demands.[82] By the same token, Berners' long costumes, covering most of the body, dictate that footwork and gestural movement should dominate.[83] There is no account of the making of the choreography, though it is unlikely Ashton drew on the individual talents of the dancers because the ballet is more dependent on group dancing, but their specific personalities are indeed evident. Katherine Sorley Walker believes that Ashton cast his dancers carefully so that the characteristics of each dancer suited the role he or she was given.[84] Margot Fonteyn, at the time a rather legato dancer, played the "forlorn" Julia, while Helpmann, as the Bridegroom, was described by P. W. Manchester as having "captured exactly the spirit of burlesque...[he] never attempts to win any sympathy for this frustrated would-be-rake."[85] And of course, de Valois was wickedly typecast as the formidable Webster. Mary Honer, the Bride, was a virtuoso dancer who had performed in musical theatre until 1935. Her technical ease surely encouraged Ashton to include not only a series of fast turns but also *fouettés* in the choreography for the Bride. The choreography for the Bride demands technical skill, as she ends most of her *pas de deux* upside down and back to front and needs to accomplish these humorous reversals without looking ruffled by the experience. And the teenage Michael Somes, whose high jumps were described by Sarah Woodcock as extraordinary, has several displays of big jumping movements as Guy.[86] It is the only obviously virtuoso dancing in the ballet, and probably because Somes wanted to show off his abilities Ashton made use of them. Of the other dancers, June Brae's languid movement may well have inspired the character of Josephine, whose movement becomes slurred and unsteady as she grows more intoxicated. Brae's celebrated elegance probably came from the time she spent studying with Mathilde Kschessinskaya in Paris, a teacher renowned for her attention to the upper body.[87] For Ashton the dancer was the catalyst whose presence stimulates the dance movement. And despite the ensemble nature of *A Wedding Bouquet*, Ashton drew on and enhanced not only the technical abilities of the dancers but also their approach to movement. As with his other works, their dance movement and that of the era are inextricably linked with the choreographic style of this ballet. In spite of the eclecticism of the training, the dance movement has unity, probably because the choreography embraces the *zeitgeist* of the 1930s.

CRITICAL RECEPTION

A Wedding Bouquet has had well over a hundred performances by the Royal Ballet and is also in the repertory of several American companies. The last time it was performed in London was in 2004. After the first performance, Lionel Bradley found it amusing but unlikely to last beyond ten years.[88] The anonymous critic of *The Bystander* regarded it as a Berners ballet and wondered if he should "call Lord Berners a fifth Marx Brother or a Lewis Carroll of ballet? His 'Wedding Bouquet' is glorious nonsense, more witty than farce. His period is Edwardian, his theme is a French provincial wedding, set to his own music and words by Gertrude Stein, decorated by his own setting and dresses."[89]

Arnold Haskell, writing in the *Dancing Times*, made the point that the artists had been true to their intentions, which, he observes, was to show us something about the Edwardian period. He regards the piece as a burlesque of the Edwardian music hall but does not believe it to be an enduring masterpiece.[90] H. S. Sibthorpe, whose unpublished manuscript on the Vic-Wells recounts the early years of the company, was less enthusiastic. He argues that Ashton has given the cast very little dancing and that the addition of the Stein words provides a sort of differentness-at-all-costs effect.[91] James Monahan in *The Manchester Guardian* commented that "unquestionably the most observable nonsense came from Miss Stein," although he did regard it as funny.[92] Haskell again, writing in *The Daily Telegraph*, was more praising of Stein's words and suggested that they were not "unintelligible or deep in their hidden meaning [but that] they are just excellent theatre and [that] their rhythm forms an admirable accompaniment to the dancing."[93] In general, Stein's words were not highly regarded and none appeared to understand that the material came from her play *They Must. Be Wedded. To Their Wife.*

In later years, the ballet still had a following, though critics generally focus on the dancers' performances rather than the work itself. Most still admire it though find the performances poor, and James Monahan never really felt comfortable with it. He found the Stein words dated and "a bit of a private joke," with "the choreographic action … imprisoned in those words."[94] This may well have been because different Speakers imposed meaningless intonations on the words, and that might not have been the case had the words been sung. But more recently, when the ballet was revived for the centenary of Ashton's birth, the critics were very positive, about both the ballet and the performances. Judith Mackrell regarded it as an "*amuse-bouche*," something to "whet … appetites for the rest of the season,"[95] while Mary Clarke found the performance "lighthearted, witty, funny, sometimes a little sad."[96] But it was Jennings who recognised the sophistication and seriousness of the choreography, despite his attitude to Stein's words. He argued that although the choreography appears straightforward, with "nursery steps … match(ing) the libretto's simplistically prepared phrases," it comprises "pared-down *enchaînements* [which are] an essential stroke of the portraitist's pen."[97]

Regardless of the descriptions of a witty, frothy work, *A Wedding Bouquet* is a ballet in which the whimsical subject matter has been handled seriously by Ashton. His choreography treats dance very seriously, and the movement is tightly knit, drawn from a small pool of steps. Like Stein's sentences and Berners music, the structure is fragmentary. The solos have short scraps of dance, and even the pas de deux and trios are brief, lasting at best a couple of minutes. And Ashton was very fond of the work. In conversation with Clement Crisp in 1963, he observed that "although it is a humorous ballet, it's rather Chaplinesque in the sense that it has an underlying sadness. And … I think all the characters are very well rounded, and what humour there is is almost a tragic humour in a way."[98]

TO CONCLUDE

Throughout this chapter I have tried to show the integrated nature of this work and how important it is to deal with more than the dance components. What has transpired is that Stein's sparse, fragmented, internal-looking prose influenced the musical, dance movement and choreographic styles but without destroying the individuality of choreographer and composer. Believing that one element is as important as another, she never valued one word more than another, and this is reflected in Ashton's dance movement. He does not emphasise the virtuoso steps or give them prominence over linking steps; all are treated equally. Each of the three artists made compromises for the sake of the work as a whole: Stein allowed her text to be cut, Berners agreed to cuts in the music and Ashton responded to both text and music, adjusting his style accordingly. It emerges less as a light and frothy confection and more as a work that focuses self-reflectively on dance, music and literature. The analysis also shows that dancers interpreting the piece need to be conscious of the movement; that the comedy comes from understanding it and not from facial contortions; and, equally, that the steps cannot be treated like classroom movement. Speed and mobility are valued above turnout and limb flexibility. If Ashton was not a radical, this ballet with its mix of high art and popular culture shows him to be hugely inventive, and no one can watch the work and fail to be touched by the humanity of the characters and the ingenious use of the *danse d'école*.

NOTES

1. A different version of this chapter may be found in Geraldine Morris's *Frederick Ashton's Ballets: Style, Performance, Choreography*, published autumn 2012.

2. Arnold Haskell, *Bystander*, (June 2, 1937), no page numbers available.

3. This company became the Sadler's Wells Ballet in 1940 and the Royal Ballet in 1956.

4. The libretto for *The Triumph of Neptune* was by Sacheverell Sitwell with choreography by George Balanchine.

5. Stein collaborated with Virgil Thomson on this, and the production, which opened in New York, had choreography by Frederick Ashton.

6. Virgil Thomson, *Virgil Thomson* (London: Weidenfeld and Nicholson, 1967), 231–47.

7. Mary Clarke, "The First Wedding Bouquet," *Dancing Times* (November 1969): 69.

8. See Elaine Showalter, *A Jury of her Peers: Celebrating American Women Writers from Anne Bradstreet to Annie Proulx* (New York: Knopf, 2009).

9. Ulla Dydo, *The Language That Rises* (Illinois: Northwestern University Press, 2003), 12.

10. She did not, strictly speaking, collaborate with Ashton and Berners, since the play was written before the ballet, but she accepted the cuts and changes made by Berners and, probably, Constant Lambert.

11. Quoted in Kavanagh, Julie (1996), 215, but see also Showalter, Elaine, *A Jury of Her Peers*.

12. Sarah Bay-Cheng, *Mama Dada: Gertrude Stein's Avant-Garde Theatre* (New York and London: Routledge, 2004), 2–3.

13. Bey-Cheng, *Mama Dada*, 4.

14. Mark Amory, *Lord Berners: The Last Eccentric* (London: Chatto & Windus, 1998), 104–7.

15. Mary Gifford, *Lord Berners: Aspects of a Biography* (Ph.D. thesis, Kings College, University of London, 2007), 152.

16. Georges Jean-Aubry, "British Music Through French Eyes," *Musical Quarterly*, 5, no. 2 (April 1919): 210–11, quoted in Gifford.

17. See Gifford, *Lord Berners*, 157–158.

18. Quoted in Gifford, *Lord Berners*, 123.

19. See Peter Dickinson, *Lord Berners: Composer Writer Painter* (Woodbridge: Boydell Press, 2008).

20. Ibid., 18.

21. David Vaughan, *Frederick Ashton and His Ballets* (London: Adam and Charles Black, 1977), 169–70.

22. Vaughan, *Frederick Ashton*, 214–15.

23. Amongst others, see Mary Clarke, *The Sadler's Wells Ballet: A History and Appreciation* (London: Adam and Charles Black, 1955).

24. Theodor Wohlfahrt, "Ashton's Last Interview," *Dance Now*, 5, no.1 (1996): 25–30.

25. *The Fairy Queen* in 1928 and again in 1946, and the ballets *Façade* (1931), which was not performed to the words until 1972; *A Day in a Southern Port (Rio Grande)* (1931); *A Wedding Bouquet* (1937); *Illuminations* (1950); and *Persephone* (1961). He also directed and choreographed six operas. The following had strong dance elements: *Four Saints in Three Acts* (Virgil Thomson, 1934); *Orpheus* (Christoph Willibald Gluck, 1762/1953); *Death in Venice* (Benjamin Britten, 1973); and *Le Rossignol* (Igor Stravinsky, 1914/1981). The two remaining operas, *Manon* (Jules Massenet, 1884/1947) and *Albert Herring* (Britten, 1947), which were directed by Ashton, were also highly choreographed.

26. This is in John Dexter's production for the Metropolitan Opera House in New York in 1981. The solo for the Fisherman can be seen on the video/DVD Stephanie Jordan and Geraldine Morris *Ashton to Stravinsky: A Study of Four Ballets with Choreography by Frederick Ashton* (Alton: Dance Books, 2005).

27. Vaughan, *Frederick Ashton*, 404.

28. Quoted in ibid., 404.

29. Alastair Macaulay, *Some Views and Reviews of Ashton's Choreography* (Surrey: National Resource Centre for Dance, University of Surrey, 1987), 19.

30. See Katherine Sorley Walker, "Ashton Ballets: Post-Mortem Performance," *Dance Now* 3, no. 3 (1994): 45–52.

31. Bonnie Rowell makes a similar point about the choreography of Mark Morris in *Dancing Off the Page: Integrating Performance, Choreography, Analysis and Notation Documentation* (Alton: Dance Books, 2007), 110–11, and I am indebted to her for formulating this approach.

32. Ibid., 113.

33. The arguments in my 2000 doctoral thesis *A Network of Styles: Discovering the Choreographed Dance Movement of Frederick Ashton* (University of Surrey at Roehampton, 2000) were based on McFee's conception of style, taken from Graham McFee, *Understanding Dance* (London and New York: Routledge, 1992).

34. His arguments are fully dealt with in Cavell (1969), and a discussion is beyond the scope of this article.

35. Monroe Beardsley and William Kurtz Wimsatt, "The Intentional Fallacy" (1954), in *Philosophy Looks at the Arts,* ed. Joseph Margolis (New York: Scribner, 1978), 293–306.

36. Stanley Cavell, *Must We Mean What We Say?* (Cambridge: Cambridge University Press, 1969/1976), 236.

37. Ibid., quoted in Rowell.

38. For further discussion on this point, see Geraldine Morris, "Artistry or Mere Technique? The Value of the Ballet Competition," *Research in Dance Education*, 9, no. 1 (2008): 39–54.

39. Richard Wollheim, *Painting as an Art* (London: Thames and Hudson, 1987) and in "Pictorial Style: Two Views" in *The Concept of Style*, ed. Lang Berel (Philadelphia: University of Pennsylvania Press, 1979), 128–45.

40. I develop this more fully in my book on Ashton's style (*Frederick Ashton's Ballets: Style, Performance, Choreography* (Hampshire, U.K.: Dance Books, 2012)).

41. Gertrude Stein, *Last Operas and Plays* (New York: Rinehart, 1949).

42. Quoted in Bay-Cheng, *Mama Dada*, 49.

43. Gertrude Stein, "Portraits and Repetition" in *Lectures in America* (New York: Random House, 1935), 165–208.

44. Dydo, *The Language That Rises*.

45. Ibid., 7.

46. Ibid., 23.

47. Ibid., 16.

48. Ibid., 19.

49. Ibid., 19.

50. Interview, June 2008.

51. Dickinson, *Lord Berners*, 17.

52. The chorus was used in the early1980s.

53. Letters in Berners Archive, at present in the care of Dr. Mary Gifford.

54. Letter, July 18, 1936, from Berners to Stein. Berners Archive.

55. Bryony Jones, *The Music of Lord Berners (1883–1950) "The Versatile Peer"* (Aldershot, Hampshire: Ashgate, 2003), 95.

56. Undated letter from Berners to Stein, but probably written before March 17, 1936. Berners Archive.

57. Berners in Amory, *Lord Berners*, 164.

58. Stein, *Last Plays*, 206.

59. Letter written to Stein from Berners on March 17, 1937, Berners Archive.

60. Jones, *The Music of Lord Berners*, 93.

61. Jones, *The Music of Lord Berners*, 93.

62. See Stephanie Jordan, *Moving Music: Dialogues with Twentieth-Century Ballet* (London: Dance Books, 2000), 187–266; and *Stravinsky Dances: Re-Visions Across a Century* (Alton: Dance Books, 2007), 257–326.

63. Ashton describes Pavlova's very theatrical entrances and exits in an interview with the dancer Natalia Makrova. It is shown on YouTube from Golden Idol videos, 2008.

64. Muriel Topaz, "Specifics of Style in the Works of Balanchine and Tudor," *Choreography and Dance*, 1 (1988): 1–36.

65. The term was coined by Henrietta Bannerman to describe frequently recurring motifs in Martha Graham's choreography. See Henrietta Bannerman, *The Work (1935–1948) of Martha*

Graham (1894–1991) with Particular Reference to an Analysis of her Movement System: Vocabulary and Syntax (Ph.D. thesis, Roehampton, University of Surrey, 1998), 51.

66. Michael Somes, "Working with Frederick Ashton" in *The Ballet Annual*, ed. Arnold Haskell (London: Adam and Charles Black, 1961), 50–54.

67. In Vaughan, *Frederick Ashton*, 9n.

68. See Colin Nears and Bob Lockyer, *Dance Masterclass: The Dream* (BBC Production, 1988).

69. This and the previous quote are taken from Gustave Flaubert, *Madame Bovary*, translated by Alan Russell (London: Penguin Books, 1856–1857/1981), 39.

70. In July 1988, in an interview with some members of the Royal Ballet, de Valois makes a long plea for the teaching of all twenty-three *pas de bourrée* because knowledge of them gives rise to incredible floor patterns of the feet. Interview in the archives of the Royal Ballet.

71. There are two versions of this. In the 1965 version, she performs a quick *bourrée* movement before the eight *ronds de jambs*, whereas later this is omitted.

72. I have been unable to find an exact translation of this phrase, but it seems to mean someone who is sophisticated, unaffected by the rest of the world. Letter from Berners to Stein, March 17, 1936, in the collection of the Berners Trust.

73. Interview with Ninette de Valois, July 1988, in the collection of the archives of the Royal Ballet.

74. It is difficult to hear how many times the words are repeated in the choral version as the sound trails off at the end.

75. Luke Jennings, "They Must Be Wedded," *Dance Now*, 13, no. 4 (Winter 2004/2005): 20–23.

76. Vaughan, *Frederick Ashton*, 55.

77. Ibid., 13.

78. Interview with the author, June 10, 2008.

79. I am indebted to my colleague Victor Durà Vilà, who was at the time in the philosophy department at Roehampton, for making this point.

80. *Les Biches* (1924).

81. Arnold Haskell and Philip John Sampey Richardson, *Who's Who in Dancing 1932*, (London: Noverre Press, 1932, facsimile reprint, 2010).

82. An examination of the syllabuses of Enrico Cecchetti and the Royal Academy of Dancing testifies to this.

83. It seems from Berners' letters to Stein that the costumes were conceived before Berners met with Ashton, but presumably Ashton agreed to the long skirts as well and used them to his advantage.

84. Katherine Sorley Walker, "A Wedding Bouquet," *Dance Now*, 6, no.1, (1996/97): 76–81.

85. Quoted in ibid., 78.

86. Sarah Woodcock, "Michael Somes" in *International Dictionary of Ballet*, ed. Martha Bremser (Detroit, London, Washington: St James Press, 1993), 1322–24.

87. Interview with Pamela May, 1999.

88. Lionel Bradley, *Ballet Bulletin*, in the archives of the Theatre Museum, Victoria and Albert Museum, (London, 1937).

89. Anonymous, *The Bystander* (May 12, 1937), 263.

90. Arnold Haskell, "Balletomane's Log Book," *Dancing Times*, no. 321, June, 280 (1937): 281, 287.

91. H. S. Sibthorpe, *The Vic-Wells Ballet (1931–1940)*, unpublished manuscript in the Theatre Museum Victoria and Albert Museum, South Kensington (London, circa 1941).

92. James Monahan, "Ballet at Sadler's Wells," *Manchester Guardian*, (April 29, 1937): 12.

93. Arnold Haskell, "A New Choral Ballet," *Daily Telegraph*, (April 28, 1937): 12.

94. James Monahan, "Dividends of Nostalgia," *Dancing Times*, LV, no. 652, (January): 177–79.

95. Mackrell, Judith (2004) "Royal Ballet Triple Bill," *The Guardian* (October 25, 1965): no page numbers available.

96. Mary Clarke, "Royal Ballet," *Dancing Times*, 95, no. 1132, (December 2004): 51, 53.

97. Jennings, "They Must Be Wedded."

98. Ashton in Clement Crisp, "Frederick Ashton: A Conversation" in *Dance as a Theatre Art*, ed. Selma Jeanne Cohen (London: Dance Books, 1974), 169–73.

10

Kaddish at the Wall

THE LONG LIFE OF ANNA SOKOLOW'S "PRAYER
FOR THE DEAD"

Hannah Kosstrin

EVERY JEW RESPONDED differently to the Holocaust, so every dancer has her own version of *Kaddish*. This is the gist of what dancer and choreographer Ze'eva Cohen said in conversation after a performance celebrating Anna Sokolow's centennial on February 14, 2010, at the Jewish cultural institution of the 92nd Street Young Men's/Young Women's Hebrew Association ("92nd Street Y") on Manhattan's Upper East Side.[1] Sokolow (1910–2000), who grew up on New York's Lower East Side of Russian Jewish immigrant parents, is most widely known for her mid-century works of alienation and isolation, for her anti-war statements, and for her expressions of countercultural youth. In her work prior to her mainstream breakout *Lyric Suite* (1953) and masterwork *Rooms* (1954), however, her choreographic statements featuring women in positions of power reflected values from the Jewish community and from her own Communist worldview. *Kaddish* (1945), a memorial for Holocaust victims, was the last of a small group of Jewish-themed dances that Sokolow made in response to the Holocaust. The title references the Mourner's Kaddish, a Jewish prayer of comfort for those living who commemorate those lost.[2] *Kaddish*'s movement embodies Jewishness through its elements of opposition and stability, its ritualistic gestures, and Sokolow's act of saying Kaddish for the victims of the Holocaust.

In the five-minute solo, Sokolow wore a dress and *tefillin* (phylacteries), vestments made up of a leather strap and small prayer box, worn exclusively by Orthodox and

Conservative Jewish men around their left arm and head during prayer. Men must wear *tefillin* during weekday morning prayers, but not during Shabbat or the High Holidays; they have the option of wearing *tefillin* through the part of the morning service that includes the Mourner's Kaddish, but they are not required to do so.[3] In the 1940s, women were forbidden to wear *tefillin*; thus, Sokolow's defiant—even deviant—choice to lay *tefillin* opened a space for women's power in secular American Judaism, and in its representation in modern dance.[4] Although Jewish law prohibits women from wearing *tefillin*,[5] and it seems, as Naomi Jackson comments, that "nothing could be farther from Jewish tradition" than a woman dancing around a stage in bare feet wearing *tefillin*,"[6] *Kaddish* re-orients Jewish tradition with Sokolow's appropriation of men's vestments and prayer space. The *tefillin* are instruments of transgressive power instead of theatrical genderplay. They do not suggest that Sokolow's performance represents a man; instead, the *tefillin* register that she is a woman doing a man's job, praying in a way from which women were excluded, and literally embodying a privilege from which women were barred. Sokolow's performance challenges a gendered reality, but it does not mimic Jewish women's drag performance of the early 20th century, wherein some dancers, including Pauline Koner and Belle Didjah, performed as Jewish men or as androgens.[7] Instead, Sokolow mobilized the historical strength of Jewish women within the context of revolutionary women's actions to make a dance that was at once a pointed political statement and an intimate yet public prayer that became a thing of pride for a healing Jewish community.

After Sokolow premiered *Kaddish* at Mexico City's Palacio de Bellas Artes in August 1945, and then at Boston's Jordan Hall and New York's 92nd Street Y in May 1946, she infrequently presented the dance through the 1940s. Sokolow did not teach this work to any of her company members until she revived it in the 1970s for individual soloists, and in so doing she reportedly re-choreographed it. The *Kaddish* of the late 20th century became a solo tailored for the women who perform it, and each version shares ideas but uses different movements to express them. Recent scholarship has not specifically addressed the layered issue of Jewish women's power in the dance, and there has largely been a dearth of detailed attention to the dance's movement. This examination demonstrates the centrality of gendered and Jewish movements and signifiers to the decades-long, fluid, ongoing power of the solo.

Many women continue to perform and teach versions of *Kaddish* that Sokolow crafted specifically for them. Cohen, who first encountered Sokolow as a young dancer in Tel Aviv and then worked with her for many years in New York, learned a *Kaddish* that is swoopy and full to reflect her own movement style.[8] This differs from, for example, Deborah Zall's *Kaddish*, which contains the angularity and initiations through abdominal contractions that reflect her years of training in Martha Graham's technique. The essence of embodying the Kaddish prayer remains consistent from dancer to dancer.

Cohen's comment about individualized *Kaddish* solos came in the aftermath of a concert on which dancers performed two distinct versions of the dance. During the post-performance discussion Jim May, artistic director of the Sokolow Theatre/Dance

Ensemble, proposed a hypothetical vision of an imagined event in which a handful of soloists perform their versions of the dance side by side, as if lined up against the Wailing Wall.[9] (The Wailing, or Western, Wall is a contemporary standing remnant of the biblical destroyed Second Temple in the Old City of Jerusalem. Following Jewish law, men and women must pray on separate sides of a divider.) On the women's side of the Western Wall, wails mix with spoken and chanted prayers as women touch the stone with their hands, press their full bodies against it as they cry, and sit, trembling or in silence, as they await their turn. *Kaddish* carries this emotional weight. May's comment conjured a powerful image in which a mighty line of women would perform a kind of physicalized *yahrtzeit* (a ritualized commemoration of a loved one on the anniversary of his or her death) against the Wall, one of the most significant architectural and spiritual sites of modern Judaism. Both Cohen's comments, and May's vision of seeing many *Kaddish*es against the Western Wall, situate Sokolow's dance near the heart of contemporary Jewish Diasporic identity: an emotional dual relationship with the Holocaust and with Israel that unites Jews through a sense of common loss and connects them through communal strength. *Kaddish* continues to endure, through many versions and for Jews and non-Jews alike, in a performative space of reflection, haunting imagery, and women's power.

Kaddish is set to Maurice Ravel's *Deux Mélodies Hébraiques*, a breathy violin solo of minor notes in conversation with stark piano chords, with expectant pauses between phrases. Many versions include, as did Sokolow's, a chanted (sung) version of the Kaddish paired with the Ravel score.[10] Sokolow believed that one does not have to be Jewish in order to understand the Kaddish prayer.[11] She explained in 1990, "Kaddish is the Hebrew prayer for the dead, so that the theme of the dance is a prayer. How Ravel uses it, the first section is almost like someone singing it. For me, the second section is the inner feeling about it."[12] The dance, which critic Doris Hering called a "quavering lament,"[13] includes spiraling turns, oppositional pulls and twists through the torso, a floor section rising onto knees and hips, impatient thrusts from the gut, and contemplative moments, wherein pain meets anger and emerges with quiet hope and defiance. The movement pairs strength with vulnerability; there is internal turmoil from the quick, weighted body rotations, the labored steps, and the inner changes in direction.[14] According to Cohen, movement similarities in various *Kaddish* versions include beating the breast and tearing out one's hair, traditional Jewish gestures related to grief. When a dancer performs these movements in *Kaddish*, she notes, the actions are expressive of a whole community.[15] Although other gestures, including tearing one's collar (in reconstructions) or shielding eyes from the heavens (in a photograph of Sokolow), relate to Jewish ritual, the larger shape of the full-bodied movements, from torso contractions to throwing the body over a folding waistline to recruiting limbs in the service of the back, are characteristic of the abstract shapes of mid-century modern dance.

Contrary to popular legends—either that there is one definitive version of *Kaddish* to which few have access, or that Sokolow did not remember the dance and therefore re-created it years later—Cohen's explanation liberates *Kaddish* from a secretive, lost, or even stagnant existence and allows the dance to live and breathe across generations of dancers, and across generations of Jews. Unlike Sokolow's dances from the latter half of the 20th century, which are documented through photographs and film, early versions of *Kaddish* were photographed and widely reviewed, but they were not filmed. Since there is no extant recording of Sokolow performing *Kaddish*, and Sokolow notoriously recombined and re-titled dances according to the concert situation or the dancers performing the work,[16] it is instructive to bring the many versions of *Kaddish* into dialogue through considering it an "open work." Sarah Rubidge defines an open work as "a work the form and/or movement content of which alters from performance to performance. The author of the work provides the raw elements and/or instructions from which any performance of the work is constructed."[17] In *Kaddish*, the raw material includes bodily countertension, a nuanced attention to the weighted surfaces of the hands, and repeating patterns of three. The consideration of *Kaddish* as an open work, furthermore, reinforces the dance as a living, breathing form and affords it plasticity in relation to the Jewish community's changing connection to Jewish tradition and to the Holocaust, and with non-Jewish audiences as a canonical, though malleable, concert dance work.[18] Sokolow's *Kaddish* of 1945–46 responded to her specific time, place, and life experience; as she created more versions of the dance, it changed as did her interaction with the dancers, the social situation, and her own relationship to Israel, the Holocaust, and her Jewish identity. The movement embodied Jewishness, and it also aligned with a concert dance aesthetic. In *Kaddish*, Sokolow shaped her movement vocabulary to express the issues of Jewishness and gender that were central to her lived experience. She transgressed the assumptions associated with her position as a Jewish woman, necessarily taking on a man's agency in the face of larger tragedy, and she crafted an aesthetic statement through a secular art medium. Although *Kaddish* changed over many years and in many bodies, its throughline relies on the Jewish elements at its core.

JEWISHNESS AND GENDER

In *Kaddish*, Jewishness and gender inform each other. Many aspects of Jewish ritual and culture are prescribed specifically for men or women. Prior to the middle to late 20th century practice of progressive denominations of Judaism in the United States ordaining women clergy and allowing women to lead rituals that were previously exclusively men's domain, Jewish rituals and identity were tied closely to gender and to gendered power within Jewish culture.[19] As a member of the secular "second generation" of American Jews,[20] Sokolow was exposed to non-normative gender roles.[21] Her 1930s Workers/New Dance League leadership aligned her with many aspects of Jewish women's activism.[22] In *Kaddish*, Sokolow not only acted in ways forbidden for women but also blurred the lines between what could be considered "feminine" and "masculine" physical representation. She used tumultuous, edgy movement that at times contained brute strength, paired with tenderer, quieter moments. *Kaddish* comes from a cultural moment where, for Sokolow, social action, Jewishness, and women's power converged.

In all of her 1940s Jewish-themed dances, Sokolow shifted the traditional representation of Jewish women. In *Songs of a Semite* (1943), she presented portraits of biblical women as well as a stoic procession of Jewish women leading the community, and in *The Bride* (1945) she portrayed a young bride in an imagined Eastern European village questioning the Jewish tradition of arranged marriage and her role therein. In *Kaddish* in particular, Sokolow's shift in her presentation of gender by wearing men's vestments harkens back to her portrayal of male characters in her 1930s proletarian dances, such as her portrayal of criminal, neglected lower-class youths in *Case History No.—*(1937). If, according to Judith Butler, performativity is a discourse of power,[23] then Sokolow's performance of *Kaddish*— in which she acted as Jewish law forbade women to do—became a site for Jewish women's agency: the agency to publicly stage grief and mourning.

Although the costume's *tefillin* are part of the gendered power in this dance for audience members who recognize them, *tefillin* also visually mark the dance as Jewish. Yet the dance does not need the *tefillin* in order to be Jewish; in fact, when Sokolow performed *Kaddish* again in 1948, she removed the *tefillin*.[24] Jewishness resides both in the movement through gestures associated with Jewish rituals and traditions and through movement characteristics relating to opposing tensions. A defining characteristic of U.S. Jewishness is a tension between opposing forces, and navigation of the space between them. There is strain between religious observance and secularism, between retaining traditions and assimilating, and between blending into the "American" mainstream while retaining elements of difference from it. For the women of Sokolow's generation in particular, acculturation into U.S. society dictated, as Riv-Ellen Prell demonstrates, an embrace of sameness to "displace their fear of being different and their tensions around joining and staying in the middle class" amid pressures associated with white womanhood.[25] Thematic and physical tension make all of Sokolow's work Jewish, in terms of movement and thematic material, an identification acknowledged by the critical establishment.

Jewishness in concert dance encompasses dance that uses Jewish cultural history as a narrative, references based on Jewish spirituality, or biblical stories as themes in a dance; dance that teaches through questioning; dances that have an unresolved ending with lingering questions or accusatory statements open for discussion; dances that use irony, satire, or other nuance as part of a work's meaning; and dances with the goal of social action through *tikkun olam* (healing the world).[26] Rebecca Rossen has introduced the generative term "dancing Jewish," a "process that embraces the fluid and multifaceted nature of Jewish identity, and accounts for the ways in which meanings for Jewishness evolve historically and in concert with particular contexts."[27] As Jewish custom relies on teaching through questioning and on understanding a co-existence of opposing tensions, dancer Felix Fibich identifies Jewishness in dance as a matter of opposition in mood and in the body, where the body "[pulls] in two different directions."[28] In *Kaddish*, this manifests in the tension created by the movement's oppositional pulls and twists. Many dancers and critics discuss Sokolow's choreography as coming from the "gut"; beyond the emotion that this phrase references, Sokolow's movement originated from her abdominal core, with prominent spirals growing through the back. These movement elements likely stem from Sokolow's 1930s training with Martha Graham, but they are also Jewish, as Fibich identifies movement that grows "from the guts" as Jewish.[29]

The many versions of *Kaddish*—photographs of Sokolow performing in the 1940s, a Labanotation score based on one dancer's solo that Sokolow taught in the 1970s, and filmed examples of many soloists performing the dance in the 1990s and 2000s— contribute to my discussion of how the movement embodies Jewishness. Laban Movement Analysis (LMA), a tool for interpretation, establishes a framework with which to connect the movement in the dance to larger cultural themes, to discuss the movement essences of the different versions of the dance, and to bring them into dialogue with one another.[30] LMA focuses on movement's general shape and intent, instead of what specific moments looked like. It examines movement dynamics and connects positions of the body in space to values including stability, intention, and expression.[31] In LMA, the body is envisioned to exist within crystalline forms, such as an octahedron and an icosahedron, which group together movement ideas on the basis of where the body moves in space. Although using this system can sometimes be problematic, it is useful when talking about mid-century modern dance, as many movement ideas were shared between German and American modern dancers in the early and mid-20th century. LMA patterns allow an examination of the essence of *Kaddish* across versions, and movement description opens a discussion of the specific movements in these versions of the dance.[32] Program notes, scholarly and critical reviews, notes in the Labanotation score, and movement from a number of versions of the dance help construct an understanding of what *Kaddish* meant at the time of its early performances, and how the dance has been perceived and received in the years since.

KADDISH: HISTORICAL CONTEXT AND ANALYSIS OF A "LOST" DANCE

Sokolow's experience working in Mexico City between 1939 and 1945 reinforced her use of dance as a mobilizing, revolutionary force, as the visual and performing arts were central to postrevolutionary Mexican nationalism. The Mexican government did not fully grant women suffrage until 1953, following a failed vote in 1939 during which time the once-leftist government under President Lázaro Cárdenas swiftly turned conservative. As such, women were not full citizens under the law; instead, they performed their citizenship through their embodied actions more actively than did many women in the United States at the same time. These actions included organizing, exerting political power, and being present in the occupation of public space.[33] Sokolow's actions of appropriating men's privilege of laying *tefillin*, and publicly saying Kaddish without a *minyan* (a quorum of ten men necessary to hold a public prayer service), embody this power. Indeed, critic José Herrera Petere exclaimed in a review reprinted in *Tribuna Israelita*, a secular Mexican Jewish periodical, that Sokolow's 1945 concert opened his eyes to how modern dance could be an empowering vehicle of social statement, especially for Jewish voices in the wake of the Holocaust.[34]

Sokolow's first performances of *Kaddish* came at a crucial time for the international Jewish community. The Allied victory in Europe and the liberation of Holocaust concentration camps occurred in May 1945. Although many European Jews remained in Displaced Persons camps at the time of *Kaddish*'s August premiere, the war was over; still, mourning continued as details of the death camps surfaced. The Holocaust and its aftermath remained at the forefront of Jewish discourse in New York City during the U.S. premieres of *Kaddish* a year later.[35]

Photographs of Sokolow in *Kaddish* between 1945 and 1948 display how the dance transformed in the years that she performed it. Even though the most striking change is perhaps the removal of the *tefillin* in the later images, what is instead foregrounded is the development in emotional gravitas and choreographic complexity over a period of three years. In the photographs included here, it is unclear in what order these images might occur in the dance's sequential unfolding. Nor is it clear if the camera captured moments from Sokolow's *Kaddish* or staged shots for publicity.[36] These photographs do clearly demonstrate, however, the dynamic and emotional range of the work on which critics commented in their reviews. It is also notable that the same photographer, Marthe Krueger, produced the defining images of *Kaddish* that documented the dance's change. Perhaps as Sokolow's choreography evolved, Krueger's understanding of how to represent Sokolow's movement on film changed as well.

The *tefillin* in early versions of *Kaddish* identify the dance as "Jewish," despite the movement's more mainstream resonances. One pair of images from an early version of the dance not pictured here features stable shapes that remain in balance, despite the forceful movement that created them. Sokolow wears a long tunic with a "V" neck, without a discernible belt. She has a suggestion of a *tefillin* band wound around her left arm, and she wears ballet shoes. It is possible that these photographs were taken in Mexico, as many of the photographs of Sokolow working in Mexico in the early 1940s feature her in ballet shoes, while in the majority of photographs from the United States she is barefoot. In one of these images, Sokolow looks out toward the camera after whipping around in a turn as her hair and skirt flair in respective orbits.[37] With elbows wide, Sokolow presses her fists together in front of her chin and matches this force with a contraction in her abdominals. Her right foot reaches for the ground, as if she is landing from a jump, or as if the turn has taken her to the balls of her feet. The other image shows a quieter moment of the solo.[38] Sokolow, turned toward the left side of the frame, bends her torso gently to the right. Her head seems to hang off her neck behind her right shoulder, as her right arm dangles toward her knee. Her left arm is a gently weighted bow extended from her left shoulder, and her palm curves up; it looks as if there is a resultant reverberation through her body, and that this image, like the other one, is one of arrested motion. The movement, with the exception of the countertension between the upper and lower halves of the body to stop the turn, appears to present shapes from mid-century concert dance that do not necessarily register as "Jewish."

Two of Krueger's 1946 images display a similar scenario. In these photographs, Sokolow wears a dark sleeveless tunic belted by a thick rope.[39] She looks strongly grounded, with lyricism in her torso. *Tefillin* wrap tightly around her left arm, yet despite this Jewish signifier the abstract movement elements, such as curved limbs and an actively bent torso, relate more closely to concert dance vocabularies than to the opposition of Jewish dance (Figures 10.1 and 10.2).

Sokolow's use of *tefillin* is significant not only in a contemporary analysis of the dance and consideration of Sokolow's presentation of Jewish identity in a secular medium, but also in consideration of how Jewish audiences received the dance at the time of the premiere. Reviews of the piece in both mainstream and Jewish periodicals in Mexico City, Boston, and New York did not mention the *tefillin*.[40] In the weeks that followed Sokolow's concert at the 92nd Street Y, the *Y Bulletin* carried no reference to *Kaddish* or of any fallout from Sokolow's performance.[41] Mention of Sokolow's dance did not appear in the *Jewish Daily Forward* in the weeks following her concert. Perhaps Sokolow's use of *tefillin* was not as controversial as it may seem.[42] Perhaps no clergy came to Sokolow's performances, and the secular nature of the Y's general audience created an atmosphere

FIGURE 10.1 Anna Sokolow in *Kaddish*, 1946. Photographer: Marthe Krueger. Courtesy of the Sokolow Dance Foundation.

FIGURE 10.2 Anna Sokolow in *Kaddish*, 1946. Photographer: Marthe Krueger. Courtesy of the Sokolow Dance Foundation.

in which this was not a problem.[43] Most likely, Orthodox Jews did not attend a secular modern dance performance on the Upper East Side, and the Jews who were there did not find it significant enough to be bothered.

The *tefillin*, though a marker of Otherness, were also a tool of agency and empowerment. During this time many Jews questioned or turned away from religion because of their disillusionment with the Holocaust. In a period when many Jews, especially Holocaust survivors, questioned their faith, it is significant that Sokolow, in light of her reconnection to her Jewish heritage in Mexico[44] and her 1943 realization that the Holocaust affected her as part of the international Jewish community,[45] chose to specifically reference religious (men's) Judaism in this dance. Jews were not allowed to have *tefillin* in concentration camps, and the Nazis stripped Jews of all visual symbols of Jewish significance and replaced them with the yellow Star of David.[46] In *Kaddish* Sokolow reclaims *tefillin* for those who were denied them, while also making them a marker of religious freedom. So many Jews were killed in the Holocaust that there were not enough people to say Kaddish for the dead. In *Kaddish*, Sokolow becomes a universal everyperson, reclaims Jewish ritual, and says *Kaddish* for those who had no one to say it for them.[47] Through her embodiment of male space, the use of her body as both a political site and one of ritual, and her decision to craft *Kaddish* within the aesthetic conventions of concert dance, Sokolow twisted patriarchal traditions to suit contemporary needs. Through this action Sokolow not only defined herself as a Jew but also brought female identity into Jewishness, where it was previously unacknowledged, while creating a wide-reaching appeal for peace.[48]

Kaddish's secularism represents a larger current in American Jewry that at once addresses the Holocaust and foreshadows the postwar assimilation of the "second generation." Dancers such as Sokolow faced an increasingly progressive Jewish audience who expected superb modernist craft, even—or especially—in dances with Jewish thematic material.[49] In a 1948 article in the socialist periodical *Jewish Life*, critic Nathaniel Buchwald boasts of the talent of Sokolow, Sophie Maslow, and others, not because they were successful choreographers but because they were strong artists trained by Martha Graham who were also Jewish and who used modernist techniques to create dances with Jewish themes. He names Sokolow a "characteristic example" of this, as she "in her Jewish dances combines the technique and choreography of Graham with [Benjamin] Zemach's exaltation and intensity of emotional expression."[50] Most likely, Sokolow's progressive Jewish audiences saw the *tefillin* as a marker of Jewishness, and nothing more. Since Sokolow was a prominent choreographer, the *tefillin* likely gave her Jewish audiences a sense of pride for her visibility as a Jew in an otherwise mainstream modernist context. In a mixed audience of Jews and non-Jews, the *tefillin* were a silent triumph for the Jewish community instead of an ignition of religious scandal.[51]

Although Sokolow removed *tefillin* from later versions of *Kaddish*, the Jewish elements in the movement became more pronounced than they were in versions with *tefillin*, as is exemplified in Krueger's 1948 photographs of Sokolow. These images display Jewish elements of countertension, opposition, and questioning, as well as a simultaneous reverence for and accusation toward a volatile or wrathful god, especially in wake of the Holocaust. They show the relationship of Sokolow's movement to Jewish women's power through her body. This power also harkens back to Sokolow's 1943–1945 solo portraits of powerful Jewish women. In one photograph, Sokolow perches on her thigh, bracing one arm against the ground in opposition to her floating leg, pleading through her raised eyebrows. While this image could be from any moment of supplication, the oppositional tension reveals its Jewishness. The two halves of her body work in tandem, yet there is opposition between her low-level shape and the lightness of her weight in it. Sokolow stands in the other image, looking up. Her fingers dab her eyelids and her palms gently rest above her eyes, shielding them from what is above. Her face's quiet, internal expression contrasts the sharp angles of her elbows. Jewishness resonates in this private movement even in the absence of the "Jewish" *tefillin* signifier (Figures 10.3 and 10.4).

Sokolow's shielded upward focus makes this final image the most spiritual of the images in this collection. It is the only photograph in which her focus is internal, and the only one in which she does not acknowledge the camera's gaze. Many aspects of Jewish ritual include shielding one's eyes. One, both for men and women, is during the recitation of the *Sh'ma*, a daily prayer proclaiming singular dedication to God: the shielding comes

FIGURE 10.3 Anna Sokolow in *Kaddish*, 1948. Photographer: Marthe Krueger. Courtesy of the Sokolow Dance Foundation.

FIGURE 10.4 Anna Sokolow in *Kaddish*, 1948. Photographer: Marthe Krueger. Courtesy of the Sokolow Dance Foundation.

from respect for God's power. Another ritual, reserved for women, is to shield one's eyes while reciting the blessing over Shabbat candles. Even without the *tefillin*, Jewishness resonates here, in both the ritual of eye shielding and in the weight with which Sokolow dabs her eyelids. This nuanced weight of the hands' surfaces appears in Eastern European Jewish folk dance.[52] It is also familiar in relation to the way many second- and third-generation Jewish women gesture in conversation, as if they resiliently hold the weight of the world in the retreating palm of their hand. Although here the word *dab* offers an effective image, I specifically reference LMA's "dab": movement that is at once light, direct, and quick. This is not a hurried moment, but the specificity of Sokolow's gesture references that weight quality.[53]

Kaddish was empowering for the Jewish community, though its content did not read as clearly for non-Jewish audiences. Movement description of *Kaddish* is scarce in reviews. Although the solo concerts in which Sokolow performed *Kaddish* received wide coverage and generally high praise, mainstream critics largely glossed over *Kaddish* in their reviews, or instead discussed the dance as "ethnic," commenting on its relationship to Sokolow's heritage without any critical or content analysis of the work.[54] As such, critics Martha Coleman and Doris Hering both noted in 1948 that in *Kaddish* Sokolow used a "unique" movement vocabulary and style.[55] *Kaddish* presented these critics with a narrative difficulty. Unlike Sokolow's other Jewish dances of the time, which were based on biblical heroines, with explicit program notes, *Kaddish* was clearly "Jewish" but used a Jewish element not widely understood to make a larger social statement through abstracted movement. Gay Morris addresses how this content-driven tension became a "game for dancers" in the postwar era, wherein modern dancers had to stay within the rules of the "game" of modernism by creating movement that appeared to be only about itself instead of communicating emotional essences or societal criticism. Specifically for Sokolow, Morris notes the friction between *Kaddish*'s Jewishness and its abstraction: "*Kaddish* therefore points up the problem of encompassing difference within the rules of modernism.... In [expanding inflexible modernist boundaries, Jewish dancers] challenged notions of consensus culture where difference was muted."[56] In both the Labanotation score and the dance, the complications of Jewish themes within an abstracted, universal, white form point to Jewishness's Otherness within secular society.

ANALYSIS OF CONTEMPORARY VERSIONS OF *KADDISH*

Contemporary presentations of *Kaddish* reinforce its physical and emotional intensity and Jewish elements, while presenting possibilities for what may have been aspects of Sokolow's 1940s solo. *Kaddish* performances are emblematic of many of Sokolow's reconstructions of her own work. As Deborah Jowitt noted in a 1986 review, "Second thoughts inform every [Sokolow] revival.... Many of her changes simplify old material, slow down its reflexes a little."[57] The stark, unembellished movement that characterizes contemporary

Kaddish staging possibly reflects this kind of departure from earlier performances. Even though many elements, such as the costuming, movement choices, and accompaniment, differ from version to version, the lines of continuity that connect incarnations of *Kaddish* lead to understanding the essence of Sokolow's solo. Choreographic elements such as repetitions of three, spiraling and wrapping gestures, kneeling, and dialogue with a spiritual power—accusatory or beseeching—tie the versions together across time; yet the dancers' own performances reinforce the individuality that is also central to *Kaddish*'s life. The twisted, contorted shapes in *Kaddish* may represent the tumult of the Holocaust, or the situation of an American Jew living in its shadow. The unresolved endings, which Sokolow considered part of her expression as a Jew,[58] are stoic yet not somberly triumphant as postwar Holocaust work became.

Contemporary *Kaddish*es portray Jewish elements both through movement and through the reflection of the Kaddish prayer's gentle support. A dance of mourning may conjure images of erratic movement, but in LMA terms this dance is about stability and balance. With words that introduce peace instead of death, the Kaddish prayer, which Jews recite in its original Aramaic instead of in Hebrew, also reflects this stability. The chanted prayer creates a deep, guttural, almost wailing backdrop for some versions of the dance; the spoken prayer retains a soothing, refraining, comforting patter for others. Countertension abounds in the dance and, according to LMA definition, lends stability. The movements of the *Kaddish* stagings reside mainly in Laban's octahedron. By Laban's definition, movement through the octahedron's dimensional scale—which moves up and down, side to side, and front to back—affords the most stability.[59] Stability is also reinforced in the movement by recurring patterns of three; in Jewish faith, threes symbolize permanence.[60] Many Jewish rituals, such as dipping in a *mikveh* (ritual purifying bath) and rising onto the balls of the feet during a specific portion of the prayer service, include repeating motions three times. Whereas the placement of the movement in space relates to stability, the emotion of the dance is not always a calm reflection of it. Morris identifies Jewishness in such intensity. In a comparison of *Kaddish* with Graham's *Lamentation* (1930), an abstracted solo of grief and mourning, Morris notes that the tension between *Kaddish*'s jagged, broken emotional outbursts as compared to *Lamentation*'s mostly vertical, consistently contained energy are what make it Jewish.[61]

My analysis of *Kaddish* includes examination from video documentation and from Labanotation score. It focuses on two performances of *Kaddish* on video: Lorry May, who started dancing with Sokolow in 1968, and is now one of the trustees of her work, performs and teaches one version; and Deborah Zall, a Graham-trained solo dancer who was close friends with Sokolow from the 1980s until the end of Sokolow's life, performs the other one. Examples of May's version include her 1990 performance; Hadassah Segal's 2000 performance at The Ohio State University and Eryn Trudell's 1990 performance at the Juilliard School.[62] Zall's version is mainly based on a 2007 recording, and includes a 1990 film and a 2010 live performance.[63] The intention here is not to propose a definitive image of what *Kaddish* "looks like," but to offer a layered view of the dance, and to introduce multiple points of entry for a textual analysis of it.

Lynne Weber's Labanotation score of *Kaddish* records Sokolow coaching Hadassah Badock Kruger in the solo in 1974.[64] The score reveals the dancer's intention and initiation of the movement, which is important to a Sokolow work because of her use of inner motivation.[65] The notated symbols show the intention (as Sokolow coached Kruger, as Weber recorded it) of the direction, level, and placement of body parts in relation to each other and where they go in space. This is not always evident on film, especially if a movement is subtly initiated from within. The Labanotation score also supplies extensive glossary notes that specify descriptions of the Jewish cultural moments from which some movements originate. Weber's score includes LMA symbols denoting the intended Effort in addition to Labanotation symbols.[66] Labanotation symbols give a quantitative description of the movement and indicate where the body goes in space, time and duration. LMA symbols detail the dynamics and movement qualities of the dance. Language from both systems indicates what the movement looks like, and how it is performed. Weber used both Labanotation and LMA symbols in the score to denote a focus on weight. The focus on moving from the center of weight reflects the intention of initiating the movement from the pelvis, or from the body's core; it takes the direction of the movement from inner initiation instead of from outward manifestation of the whole body. Weber similarly represented the play with predominantly Strong Weight through LMA symbols. The score, furthermore, shows many quick changes in Effort, especially for changes in Time between Sudden and Sustained. The emphasis on Weight reflects how the metaphorical weight of the Holocaust bears down on the *Kaddish* performer, and the quick Effort changes bring intensity and urgency to the performance.

In addition to the performative insights of the intention, motivation, and Effort phrasing, Weber's *Kaddish* score reveals layers of Jewish intertext. The transliterated words of the Kaddish prayer run up the left side of the page alongside the staff, so that the dance moves to the rhythm of the prayer, and a glossary note connects the phrasing of the prayer with the music phrases. Although many contemporary versions use Ravel's score as the only accompaniment, some include a cantor or rabbi singing the prayer with the instrumentation. (A cantor is a member of the clergy who chants or sings certain prayers.) Other threads of Jewishness in the Labanotation score appear as extra directions in the glossary to contextualize Jewish ritual movements. These elements of Jewishness in the score create a tension counter to the universality triumphed not only in mid-century modern dance but also in a notation score.[67]

The following description interlaces these filmed and written versions of *Kaddish* to generate a layered image of the solo. It moves sequentially through the dance and matches movements in the versions either for similarity or for progression. For organizational purposes, I refer to each dancer by name to distinguish between the versions in discussion. In Lorry May's versions, the costume is a long black dress with a long right sleeve and no left sleeve, but with a black band around the left arm to suggest *tefillin*. Deborah Zall wears a long black dress with sheer black long sleeves, with a thick oxblood-colored band wound around her left arm. Zall did not originally have *tefillin* as part of her costume but later added it.[68] Hadassah Badock Kruger's costume has no *tefillin* and consists of a belted brown dress and a headscarf, a tradition expected of religious Jewish women in synagogue, with no explanation in the score for the costume alteration.[69] All versions use the Ravel score, and Zall's includes a cantor chanting the Kaddish.

The opening moments of all three versions contain ritual or gesture connected to Jewish spirituality and tradition. Zall's begins with a pose invoking mourning traditions of beating the breast and tearing the collar, and Kruger's begins with reading from a prayer book. May's version, performed by Hadassah Segal and Eryn Trudell, begins at the Western Wall.[70] The dancers in this (May's) version raise their hands as if they are pressed against the Wall's vertical surface. Sokolow worked in Israel from 1953 through the 1980s, and she found there a deep connection to Judaism. It may be due to this that she later included this imagery in *Kaddish*.

After turning from the Wall, Segal forcefully beats her chest thrice in one of the first repetitions of three. The third impact pulls her around to face the front. Slowly, she unfolds her arms and unrolls her fingers, until her forearms are exposed, tainted with the suggestion of death. Her defiant body is vulnerable yet stable, revealing pain and questions. Segal wraps herself in her own arms and widens her stance into a slow, sinking collapse. The wrapping here replicates laying *tefillin*, or an absent *tallis* (prayer shawl), and also presents comfort or pain.

Zall begins still, facing downstage in a narrow stance. She pulls her fists tightly into her chest, as if in a frozen moment of beating the breast. As the cantor's voice soars with the first words of the Mourner's Kaddish, Zall's focus floats to the space above her head as she lowers her opening palms in a moment of offering. Her hands gently yield as if to a fair weight before she quickly snatches them behind her back. She raises her open left hand as she appeals to the space above her head. The haunting aural contrast of the full-bodied voice to the stark, interspersed violin and piano chords reflects the movement's counter-tension.

Kruger also begins in a narrow stance. She instead looks down into her upturned palms as if, Weber notes, "reading from the Book."[71] Kruger raises her hands to rest, one on the other, on the nape of her neck. She holds this position as the music begins and then releases her hands, bringing her focus to the space forward and above her head. This moment of cursory interaction with a higher power echoes Zall's initial address of this space with her focus. Kruger folds her torso forward as she steps into a wide, low stance. She touches each hand to the sides of her head and then increasingly circles her arms in front of her body until her torso explodes into a cry.

Two of the most poignant moments in all versions of the dance involve crossed body positions. These stable moments contain strength and weakness, nurturing and supplication. In one of these moments, Segal kneels on her left knee with her weight planted on her right foot. Cradling her face in her own hands, she looks up, pleading from her low

position on the ground. They look like someone else's hands, a child's face in a grand-
mother's loving palm. Segal is at once alive and dead, grieving and grieved. After two
halting steps, Zall seizes her left shoulder with her right hand; her head bows into the
angle of her elbow before she threads her left arm through this small space, grasps the
crown of her skull, and folds her torso forward. Where there was supplication and questioning before, there is now grief. Still in this crossed position, Zall slips her right foot out
into a wide stance and heavily shifts her weight from one leg to the other. Each knee
softens into the weight shift, and provides stability within this grieving moment. After an
increasing whirlwind of arms and a silent full-bodied yell, Kruger's head disappears under
her hands, one grasping the top of her hand and the other clasping her scapula. She
remains in this folded position and heavily rotates her torso, alternating between quick
and sustained twists. Kruger releases her arms and her focus skyward and takes three
wide, weighted steps forward, pausing with one foot in front of the other. Crossed positions also involve the dancers, sometimes violently, wringing their own bodies with a
weight that pulls them down. The ensuing struggle shows a will to overcome grief with
strength amidst suffering.

Segal's and Zall's solos both have punctuations of light movement, followed by kneeling tormented moments. A wide lunge leads Segal into a brief turn, with the only moment
of lightness or hope in the solo as her arms fly out to the sides. After a second lunge, she
turns and beats her breast three times. A third lunge ends with Segal reaching her palm
up (a request?) before spiraling down to a cross-legged kneel, with her torso pushed over
and her palms wide on the floor. She pulls herself up, falls into another direction, and
propels herself up once again with her right hand thrust to the right side of her head,
retaining an asymmetrical, twisted shape, with her gaze open to the ceiling. Segal's repetition of threes, like the *Kaddish* prayer, develops a refraining anchored structure from
which an audience may gather strength. In one of her kneeling moments, Zall spirals
down to her knees and twists backward; her arms extend, palm surfaces exposed, from
her hinging torso. Gently bounding back and forth in the hinge's elasticity, Zall opens her
torso in a spiraling cry before once again grasping her forehead and bending forward.
With subtle twists initiated from deep within her torso, Zall searches the corners of the
room, finding hope, addressing God. This is a moment of lightness, both in terms of spirit
and of weight.

These two kneeling moments in Segal's and Zall's solos complicate the Jewishness in
this dance. Kneeling is not a ritualized movement associated with Jewish prayer; it is
instead central to Catholic worship.[72] Sokolow's kneeling may come from Catholic contexts in Mexican art and culture, where walking on one's knees shows piety and religiosity, especially while visiting shrines or before the Virgin of Guadalupe.[73] Sokolow was
also drawn to this performance of penitence as she witnessed Mexican parishioners
ascending cathedral steps on their knees.[74] Since she premiered this dance in Mexico,
perhaps Sokolow used kneeling to translate the idea of piety to her first audience. Felix
Fibich was reportedly horrified when Sokolow and also Sophie Maslow kneeled in their

Jewish work because kneeling is forbidden in Jewish prayer; kneeling is, however, a modern dance convention.[75] Sokolow's kneework in May's and Zall's versions reflects a secular modernity in modern dance styles. Zall believes that, at least for her version, the kneeling comes from Graham technique.[76]

In a more religious and less secular vein, Kruger and Zall both proceed through motifs of threes to emotional moments. With one foot in front of the other, Kruger shakes her hands three times and clasps her head before dipping into a series of small turns with her upper torso folded forward, keeping her hands clasped tightly together. After a series of tight, narrow turns, Kruger reaches out and pulls her arms in, as if, the glossary notes, to stop herself from crying. Zall takes three petite, halting steps backward, succinctly striking her chest with each one. She runs forward and opens her arms high to the side, looking out and up. Her mature, thin frame and gnarled knuckles summon the forces of the universe. Retreating from this expansion with a whisper of an upper torso contraction, Zall moves sideways and, still entreating to the power in the space above her, gently waves her arms spherically around her head. In live performance, Zall commands the space; her presence is stunningly, powerfully chilling. At once, there is urgency and eternity. She is a widow at the Wall; she bears the weight of the world. Her clear relationship with God yields a debate between two wrathful beings. We, the audience, the witnesses, disappear. Zall is not performing; this moment is between her and her God.

The energy in Kruger's solo, like Zall's, increases fervently, and the movement also incorporates gestures from Jewish ritual. Kruger fixes her focus forward and somewhat downward before circling her hands toward her eyes while bouncing gently. A glossary note states this moment is "based on the Friday night preparation for the Sabbath.... Anna remembered her mother in this religious motion and uses it here."[77] In Jewish ritual, women gather around Shabbat candles, circle their palms toward their eyes a few times, and then hold their hands over their eyes as they recite the blessing over the candles.[78] In Jewish practice, women traditionally perform this ritual without men. During her coaching of Kruger in *Kaddish*, Sokolow insisted that the movements based on Jewish ritual, such as this one, were performed with specific attention to gestural detail. This was in contrast to the majority of movement in the solo, for which the effort about internal struggle was more important than positions in space.[79]

The endings of these *Kaddish* versions diverge in their movement choices. For Zall, where there was grief, there is now light. Three final sharp strikes of her chest—left, right, left—accompany three staccato, exasperated steps backward with her focus directly above her head, addressing a higher power after conversing with it for the duration of the piece, as the cantor wails through the end of the prayer with long, open-throated notes. Kruger, after folding herself into the floor where she lies curled up, brings herself to standing with increasing strength through an invisible backwards turn and a swift punch with her hands. Slowly raising her focus and her upturned palms, she steps haltingly backward until the lights fade. Segal's clenched fists thump against her sternum with the regularity of a heartbeat, recalling the Jewish ritual of tearing one's collar when in mourning. Her

fists embody both ends of the life cycle as they at once represent a heartbeat and the tearing ritual of death. Her face is sad yet defiant, looking out; she is no longer pleading, but
facing the grief. At the same time in her solo, Eryn Trudell again climbs her hands up and
against the invisible stone of the imagined Western Wall.

In the different endings of this dance, Segal faces grief; Zall is defiant and accusatory in
a moment that also holds light and peace; Kruger is reverent; and Trudell finds comfort in
the Western Wall. These endings remain open even as these women deepen their performances or teach their dances to other soloists. According to Samantha Geracht, who performs *Kaddish* with the Sokolow Theatre/Dance Ensemble, this prayer of a dance ultimately ends in triumph.[80] She emphasizes what she calls the extreme movements of "up"
throughout the piece, and that the woman in the solo "is going to make it."[81] This triumph
in the face of tragedy foreshadows how American Jews taught the Holocaust to children in the 1950s, by representing Jews as heroes instead of as victims.[82] Although the
myriad versions of *Kaddish* share elements of grief, accusation, physical and emotional
weight, a sense of loss, interspersed points of light, reverence, countertension, spiraling
through space, and small moments of comfort and stability, the differing endings reinforce
Jews' common heritage and the allowance of every Jew to have his or her own reaction to
the Holocaust. These soloists, who range from adolescence to middle age, represent generations of Jewish women. *Kaddish* is not just about one woman; it is about each woman.
The dance, a woman's ritual, shows a people defiant in the face of annihilation, even against
an imperfect or obstinate god, and it proclaims that those lost are not forgotten.

CONCLUSION

In *Kaddish*, Sokolow expanded her representational power as a Jewish woman when she
transgressed tradition by stepping into a man's space with *tefillin* and with the Kaddish.
Both the dance's gendered Jewish aspects and its pliability as an open work lend it the
power to retain performative relevance to Jewish and non-Jewish audiences at different
points in time. Sokolow continued to rewrite modernism and narrative by assimilating
her Jewishness through the concert dance idiom. *Kaddish* reflected modern dance tradition and modernism within dance through its abstracted shapes, social comment,
universal stance, and performance conventions. Contemporary reconstructions of the
solo reinforce its physical tension and emotional power. They show the continued life of
Kaddish by connecting aspects of Sokolow's 1940s solo to contemporary performance.

ACKNOWLEDGMENTS

Research for this chapter was made possible with the following support: The Ohio State
University Department of Women's Studies and the Coca-Cola Critical Difference for
Women Research on Women, Gender, and Gender Equity Grant; the P.E.O. International

Scholar Award; and The Ohio State University Melton Center for Jewish Studies Samuel M. Melton Fellowship.

FILM AND LABANOTATION SCORE

100 Years of Sokolow. DVD. Bridgewater State College, 2010. Sokolow Dance Foundation.
Anna Sokolow: Choreographer. VHS. Produced and directed by Lucille Rhodes and Margaret Murphy. 1980; Pennington, NJ: Dance Horizons Video, 1991.
Goodman, Karen. *Come Let Us Dance (Lomir Geyn Tantsn): Two Yiddish Dances, Heritage, Style & Steps*. VHS. Burbank, CA: Karen Goodman, 2002.
Jewish Women in Dance. Unpublished videocassette. Presented by the International Committee for the Dance Library in Israel. 1990. Dance Library of Israel, Tel Aviv.
The Joyce Mollov Memorial Lecture and Performance. VHS. Presented by the Continuing Education Program and Center for Jewish Studies at Queens College, Queens College Theater, Flushing, New York. November 4, 1990. The Jerome Robbins Dance Division of the New York Public Library for the Performing Arts.
Mexico on Video. DVD. México, D.F.: Mexican Records, 2007.
Sokolow, Anna. *Kaddish*. Notated by Lynne Weber, 1974. New York: Dance Notation Bureau, 1980. Notation graphics by Mira Kim, 2007.
——. *Kaddish*. Produced by Michael D. Mandell. Performed by Deborah Zall. Forest Hills Space, Forest Hills, New York, 1990. The Jerome Robbins Dance Division of the New York Public Library for the Performing Arts.
——. *Kaddish*. Performed by Hadassah Segal. Unpublished videocassette, 2000. Collection of The Ohio State University Department of Dance.
——. *Kaddish*. Performed by Deborah Zall. *Three Dances: Deborah Zall*. DVD. Produced by Deborah Zall and Niramon Ross, 2007. Gift of Deborah Zall.

REPOSITORIES

92nd Street Y Educational Department Records
Boston Public Library Microtext Department
Dance Library of Israel, Tel Aviv
Dorot Jewish Division, New York Public Library
The Jerome Robbins Dance Division of the New York Public Library for the Performing Arts
The Ohio State University Department of Dance
The Ohio State University Libraries
Sokolow Dance Foundation

NOTES

1. Ze'eva Cohen (dancer, choreographer) in discussion with the author, February 14, 2010.
2. Kaddish is a type of daily prayer, as there is a Reader's Kaddish, a Half Kaddish, and a Mourner's Kaddish.
3. Rabbi Shimon D. Eider, *Student Edition of Halachos of Tefillin* (Lakewood, NJ: Halacha, 1985), 3, 87, 89, 99, 103, 127.

4. Today, women may lay *tefillin*, yet those in Orthodox and Conservative denominations are still discouraged or prohibited from doing so.

5. See Eider, 3, 87, 89, 99, 103, 127.

6. Naomi Jackson, *Converging Movements: Modern Dance and Jewish Culture at the 92nd Street Y* (Hanover and London: Wesleyan University Press/University Press of New England, 2000), 16.

7. For a discussion of Pauline Koner's, Belle Didjah's, and Hadassah's performances in this vein, see Rebecca Rossen, "Hasidic Drag: Jewishness and Transvestism in the Modern Dances of Pauline Koner and Hadassah," *Feminist Studies* 37, no. 2 (2011), 334–64. See also Harley Erdman, *Staging the Jew: The Performance of an American Ethnicity, 1860–1920* (New Brunswick and London: Rutgers University Press, 1997), 40–60, 133. Erdman examines how Jewishness was performed and received on commercial American stages, both by Jews for non-Jews and vice versa, and thus how representations of Jewishness in the United States were constructed from these representations.

8. Cohen, discussion, February 14, 2010.

9. Jim May, post-performance discussion, *Anna Sokolow 100th Birthday Tribute*, presented by Sokolow Theatre/Dance Ensemble, February 14, 2010, 92nd Street YM/YWHA, New York City.

10. Critic Margaret Lloyd noted the "wailing tones of voice" at Sokolow's Boston premiere. Margaret Lloyd, "Dance Recital Presented in Jordan Hall," *Christian Science Monitor* (Boston), May 6, 1946, 4, Boston Public Library Microtext Department (hereafter BPL Microtext). Chanting in Jewish observance is a specific way of singing the melody of prayers, based on a codified system of troches and pronunciation.

11. Anna Sokolow, quoted in *Jewish Women in Dance*, VHS, president of the International Committee for the Dance Library in Israel (1990). Dance Library of Israel, Tel Aviv (hereafter DLI).

12. Ibid.

13. Doris Hering, "Anna Sokolow, YM & YWHA, February 1, 1948," *Dance Magazine*, March 1948, 41.

14. I gleaned this observation through embodying the movement by reading the Labanotation score of this dance. Through this embodiment, knowing Sokolow's work with the Stanislavsky Method, I applied my own experiences of instability, and as an American Jew, my knowledge of the Holocaust, to inform the structure of the movement from the notation.

15. Ze'eva Cohen in phone discussion with the author, September 14, 2010.

16. Gay Morris, *A Game for Dancers: Performing Modernism in the Postwar Years, 1945–1960* (Middletown, CT: Wesleyan University Press, 2006), 94; and Anadel Lynton (Mexican-based dancer, choreographer, dance scholar), in discussion with the author, June 20, 2009, Stanford, CA.

17. Sarah Rubidge, "Identity and the Open Work" in *Preservation Politics: Dance Revived, Reconstructed, Remade*, ed. Stephanie Jordan (London: Dance Books, 2000), 213, note 1. Although Rubidge specifically discusses the open work in postmodern dance of the 1970s in general and in the work of Yvonne Rainer in particular, the idea of the open work relates to *Kaddish* reconstructions owing to the many versions and the lack of a concrete "original."

18. There is also the danger, in analyzing a film of a dance, of considering that filmed version "the dance" instead of recognizing that it is one version of "the dance." Peggy Phelan points out

that often we—students, historians, video audiences—get used to a specific filmed version of a performance, and that particular document becomes the art, instead of understanding that the performance was the art and the film is a documentation of it. See Peggy Phelan, *Unmarked: The Politics of Performance* (London and New York: Routledge, 1993), 31.

19. For discussions concerning the interrelations of discourses of gender and Jewishness, see Ann Pellegrini, *Performance Anxieties: Staging Psychoanalysis, Staging Race* (New York and London: Routledge, 1997); Miriam Peskowitz and Laura Levitt, eds., *Judaism Since Gender* (New York and London: Routledge, 1997); and Daniel Boyarin, Daniel Itzkovitz, and Ann Pellegrini, eds., *Queer Theory and the Jewish Question* (New York: Columbia University Press, 2003). Additionally, clear gender divides between men and women remain in Orthodox denominations of Judaism in the early 21st century.

20. The "second generation" included the largely secular children of Eastern European immigrants, who settled mostly in New York City during the immigration wave of 1881–1914. See Deborah Dash Moore, *At Home in America: Second Generation New York Jews* (New York: Columbia University Press, 1981), 4–5; and Beth Wenger, *New York Jews and the Great Depression: Uncertain Promise* (New Haven and London: Yale University Press, 1996), 7. Wenger expands this definition to include the general time period of the 1920s through the postwar era, extending the term to include the idea of "a cultural generation."

21. Women were the cultural guardians of Judaism, charged with keeping a Jewish home and raising Jewish children, but in Orthodox and Conservative Judaism they were prevented from praying alongside men in synagogue. In Reform congregations, Jewish women gained power through their charitable work with sisterhood organizations, but they were still wholly restricted from men's prayer space. In secular American society, leftover prejudices from late-19th- and early-20th-century racialist discourses effeminized Jewish men. In a sense, Jewish women were thus doubly alienated, as their devaluation as Other replaced Jewish men as feminized Others. See Larry Warren, *Anna Sokolow: The Rebellious Spirit* (Princeton, NJ: Princeton Book, 1991), 2; Paula Hyman, *Gender and Assimilation in Modern Jewish History: The Roles and Representation of Women* (Seattle and London: University of Washington Press, 1995); Pamela Nadell and Jonathan Sarna, eds., *Women and American Judaism: Historical Perspectives* (Hanover and London: Brandeis University Press/University Press of New England, 2001); and Alice Kessler-Harris, "Organizing the Unorganizable: Three Jewish Women and Their Union," in *American Jewish Women's History: A Reader*, ed. Pamela Nadell (New York and London: New York University Press, 2003), 102–3 and 111. See also Ann Pellegrini, *Performance Anxieties;* and Daniel Boyarin, Daniel Itzkovitz, and Ann Pellegrini, eds., *Queer Theory and the Jewish Question*, for discussion of the feminization of Jewish men and what space is left for Jewish women when Jewish men were considered feminine.

22. See Karen Brodkin, *How Jews Became White Folks and What That Says About Race in America* (New Brunswick and London: Rutgers University Press, 1998), 107, for gender equality ideals of the Bund, the General Jewish Labor Union of Russia and Poland, and the political leadership of women associated with *Yiddishkeit*. See also Alice Kessler-Harris, "Organizing the Unorganizable;" Paula E. Hyman, "Immigrant Women and Consumer Protest: The New York City Kosher Meat Boycott of 1902" in *American Jewish Women's History: A Reader*; and Wenger, 114–27. Additionally, Sokolow's mother was an active Socialist and one of the many Jewish women active in the ILGWU. See Warren, 4–6.

23. Judith Butler, *Bodies That Matter: On the Discursive Limits of "Sex"* (New York and London: Routledge, 1993), 187, 241.

24. In one photograph that appears in Warren's *Anna Sokolow: The Rebellious Spirit,* plate page 6, dated 1945, Sokolow is caught in motion, her long wavy hair haloed around her head as the result of a turn, and she wears *tefillin* around her left arm. This image also appears in the *Dance Magazine* anniversary book edited by Doris Hering, 25 *Years of American Dance* (New York: Rudolf Orthwine, 1954), where it is unlabeled (see 112). Two other images of *Kaddish,* photographed by Marthe Krueger and held in the Sokolow Dance Foundation, which have been the most prominent in recent scholarly print, feature the *tefillin* on Sokolow's left arm, and her long, loose, wavy hair. In one, Sokolow leans with her torso folded over her right side, with her left, *tefillin*-bound arm dangling in the air; in the other, Sokolow sits on her right hip, with her *tefillin*-covered left hand holding her hair back from her face. In 1946, Sokolow sent the latter photograph to Bessie Schönberg, with a note on the back inviting her to the May 12 New York performance. Anna Sokolow to Bessie Schönberg, n.d., Box 11, Folder 17, Bessie Schönberg Papers, the Jerome Robbins Dance Division of the New York Public Library for the Performing Arts (hereafter JRDD, NYPL). Though neither of these Krueger photographs is dated except by the date of the *Kaddish* premiere (1945), Sokolow's dated note to Schönberg places that photograph as existing prior to May 12, 1946. In two later photographs of *Kaddish* in the Sokolow Dance Foundation, also by Krueger, Sokolow wears the *Kaddish* costume but without the *tefillin.* Her hair is shorter in these pictures—shoulder-length—and half of it is pulled back. Similarly to the first two Krueger images with *tefillin,* these photographs are also dated simply with the 1945 date of the *Kaddish* premiere. However, one of the images, of Sokolow reaching forward while on her right hip, accompanies Doris Hering's review of Sokolow's February 1, 1948 performance of *Kaddish* at the 92nd Street Y (and the original copy in the Sokolow Dance Foundation has the specifications for magazine publication written on the back), whereas the other, of Sokolow covering her eyes with her hands as she looks skyward, is on a flyer advertising the February 1, 1948, performance at the 92nd Street Y. Doris Hering, "Anna Sokolow YM & YWHA February 1, 1948," *Dance Magazine,* March 1948, 41–42; and flyer, *Dance Theatre presents Anna Sokolow in a program of New Dances Sunday Afternoon February 1st at* 3:30, 92Y. It appears that Sokolow removed the *tefillin* from *Kaddish* between her American premiere of the dance and her next performance of it two years later, for reasons still unknown. I discuss these images further in the following sections.

25. Riv-Ellen Prell, *Fighting to Become Americans: Assimilation and the Trouble Between Jewish Women and Jewish Men* (Boston: Beacon Press, 1999), 8, 13. Prell argues that stereotyped images of Jews portray this. See also Barbara Welter, "The Cult of True Womanhood: 1820–1860," *American Quarterly* 18, no. 2 (1966), 151–74.

26. This Jewishness specifically relates to Jewish identity in the United States for Jews of European descent. Jews from the Mediterranean, Middle East, and Africa have different traditions and ways of using their bodies because of their assimilation into those cultures.

27. Rebecca Rossen, "Dancing Jewish: Jewish Identity in American Modern and Postmodern Dance," (Ph.D. dissertation, Northwestern University, 2006), 34.

28. Judith Brin Ingber, "Felix Fibich, Dancer and Choreographer: Excerpts from Oral History for the New York Library for the Performing Arts, Dance Division, 1997," *Jewish Folklore and Ethnology Review* 20, no. 1–2 (2000), 81.

29. Felix Fibich, quoted in *The Joyce Mollov Memorial Lecture and Performance,* VHS. Presented by the Continuing Education Program and Center for Jewish Studies at Queens College, Queens College Theater, Flushing, New York, November 4, 1990, JRDD, NYPL. It should also

be noted that since many Jewish women were in Martha Graham's company in the 1930s, there was most likely a reciprocal relationship between their Jewish embodiment of Graham's movement ideas and her resultant development of technique.

30. Lynn Matluck Brooks applies language of Laban's theory of space harmony in order to discuss style, intent, and choreography, and Ann Daly introduces LMA as a tool for meaning making. See Lynn Matluck Brooks, "Harmony in Space: A Perspective on the Work of Rudolf Laban," *Journal of Aesthetic Education* 27, no. 2 (1993), 40; and Ann Daly, "Movement Analysis: Piecing Together the Puzzle," *TDR* 32, no. 4 (1988), 40–52. In relying on the dialogical relationship between the different versions of *Kaddish* and the discourses of Jewishness and gender that they reflect, I also reference Naomi Jackson's use of an intertextual lens to interpret dance. See Naomi Jackson, "Dance and Intertextuality: Theoretical Reflections" in *Dancing Bodies, Living Histories: New Writings about Dance and Culture*, eds. Lisa Doolittle and Anne Flynn (Alberta: Banff Centre Press, 2000), 218–31.

31. See Irmgard Bartenieff and Dori Lewis, *Body Movement: Coping with the Environment* (New York: Gordon and Breach, 1997); Peggy Hackney, *Making Connections: Total Body Integration Through Bartenieff Fundamentals* (New York: Routledge, 2002); Vera Maletic, *Body—Space—Expression: The Development of Rudolf Laban's Movement and Dance Concepts* (Berlin and New York: Mouton de Gruyter, 1987); and Rudolf Laban, *The Language of Movement: A Guidebook to Choreutics*, edited by Lisa Ullman (Boston: Plays, 1974).

32. The historical anti-Semitism and sympathy with Nazi ideology associated with Rudolf Laban complicates this inquiry. Laban's theoretical framework is an appropriate tool for examining Sokolow's work because she worked contemporaneously to when many of Laban's ideas were applied in movement. Discrimination was embedded in dance in the early 20th century, in Europe and in the United States, but it was not acknowledged in scholarship until the late 20th century. Although choreographers such as Martha Graham and Doris Humphrey specifically brought Jewish and African American dancers into their companies, not without incident, the Laban systems of movement analysis and notation became embedded in American movement systems and values after Laban's post-German-exile work in England during World War II. Its absorption into American modern dance is part of the larger universal whiteness of the form. See Susan Manning, *Modern Dance, Negro Dance: Race in Motion* (Minneapolis and London: University of Minnesota Press, 2004); Julia Foulkes, "Angels 'Rewolt!': Jewish Women in Modern Dance in the 1930s," *American Jewish History* 88, no. 2 (2000), 233–52; Lillian Karina and Marion Kant, *Hitler's Dancers: German Modern Dance and the Third Reich*, translated by Jonathan Steinberg (New York and Oxford: Berghahn Books, 2003); and Evelyn Doerr, *Rudolf Laban: The Dancer of the Crystal* (Lanham, MD: Scarecrow Press, 2008).

33. See Sarah A. Buck, "The Meaning of the Women's Vote in Mexico, 1917–1953," in *The Women's Revolution in Mexico, 1910–1953*, eds. Stephanie Mitchell and Patience Schell (Lanham, MD: Rowman & Littlefield, 2007), 73–98; Jocelyn Olcott, *Revolutionary Women in Postrevolutionary Mexico* (Durham, NC, and London: Duke University Press, 2005); and Jocelyn Olcott, Mary Kay Vaughan, and Gabriela Cano, eds., *Sex in Revolution: Gender, Politics, and Power in Modern Mexico* (Durham, NC, and London: Duke University Press, 2006).

34. José Herrera Petere, "¡Aleluya! en México," *El Nacional*, August 24, 1945, reprinted in "What the Mexican Press Says," *Tribuna Israelita*, September 15, 1945, 22–23, Dorot Jewish Division, New York Public Library (hereafter Dorot, NYPL).

35. On May 12, the day of Sokolow's New York *Kaddish* premiere, the "Arts" section of the *Jewish Daily Forward*, which is an arts and life section, featured photographs of Polish Jews who survived the Holocaust. See "The condition of the surviving Jews in Poland is reflected in this picture," *Jewish Daily Forward*, May 12, 1946, Section 3, 1. Similar coverage appeared through at least June 2, 1946.

36. See Hannah Kosstrin, "Dance in Another Dimension: The Photographic Work of Lois Greenfield" (master's thesis, Ohio State University, 2003) for a discussion of the documentary qualities of dance photographs when they are used for publicity purposes or for documenting the movements or essence of a dance. Dance photographs through the 20th century were often staged for what made an effective still image, sometimes departing from what the movement looked like in performance. This must be taken into account when discussing and describing dances from photographs.

37. Reprinted in Warren, plate page 6, and dated 1945, with the photographer unknown. A note accompanies the image, saying that it is from the "Anna Sokolow Collection," which was Sokolow's personal collection. Also reprinted, though unlabeled, in Hering, 25 *Years of American Dance*, 112.

38. Printed in Giora Manor, "Creation of Peace about Anna Sokolow in the National Homeland, 1912–2000," *Dance Today: The Dance Magazine of Israel* 2 (2000), 21. The caption reads, " 'Kaddish' by Anna Sokolow."

39. See footnote 24 for my dating system for these images.

40. Herrera Petere, "¡Aleluya! en México," 22–23, Dorot, NYPL; David Zellmer, "Anna Sokolow: YM & YWHA May 12, 1946," *Dance Observer*, June–July 1946, 75–76; Walter Terry, "Four Solo Recitals Here Called Indicative Future of Dance," *New York Herald Tribune*, May 19, 1946, Dance Scrapbook, JRDD, NYPL; Doris Hering, "Two Concerts," *Dance Magazine*, June 1946, 23–24, 26; and Albertina Vitak, "Anna Sokolow, May 12 at the YM & YWHA Dance Theatre, N.Y.," *Dance News*, June–August 1946, 6. Jules Wolffers focuses on the formalist aspects of Sokolow's performance in Boston's *Jewish Advocate* of Sokolow's May 4, 1946, performance there, and simply notes that the Jewish dances on the program were "intelligently worked out." Jules Wolffers, "Anna Sokolow in Dance Recital," *Jewish Advocate* (Boston), May 9, 1946, 22, BPL Microtext.

41. Steve Siegel (92nd Street Y archivist) in email communication with author, January 21, 2010.

42. Deborah Zall (dancer, teacher) in discussion with the author, October 17, 2009, New York City.

43. According to Naomi Jackson, Sophie Maslow received criticism from local rabbis for her piece *The Village I Knew* (1951) in which, during different scenes of traditional Jewish rituals, "dancers kneel[ed] on the floor for the blessing of the Sabbath candles," and the movements of kneeling and rolling on the floor "showed the women's legs, which was considered indecent." 92nd Street Y Education Director William Kolodney invited the rabbis specifically to see Maslow's dance. See Jackson, "Jewishness and Modern Dance in Sophie Maslow's *The Village I Knew*" in *Dancing Texts: Intertextuality in Interpretation*," ed. Janet Adshead-Lansdale (London: Dance Books, 1999), 91–92.

44. See Warren, 104; and Perelman, "Choreographing Identity: Modern Dance and American Jewish Life, 1924–1954," (Ph.D. dissertation, New York University, 2008), 273.

45. Anna Sokolow, quoted in Beth McHenry, "Anna Sokolow: Trip to Mexico," *Daily Worker*, September 20, 1943, 7, Ohio State University Libraries (hereafter OSUL).

46. Elie Wiesel on *The Jewish People: A Story of Survival*, PBS, June 2008.

47. Thank you to Matt Goldish for this insight.

48. Riv-Ellen Prell argues that in mid-20th-century sociological studies, Jewish women's and men's experiences were assumed to be the same, even though the studies undervalued women's contributions to Jewish life, and as a result women's experience was written out of Jewishness. See Riv-Ellen Prell, "American Jewish Culture Through a Gender-Tinted Lens," in *Judaism Since Gender*, eds. Miriam Peskowitz and Laura Levitt (New York and London: Routledge, 1997), 79.

49. See V. Platon, "Thoughts on a Dance in Progress," *Jewish Life* 4, no. 1 (1949), 36.

50. Nathaniel Buchwald, "The Jewish Dance in America," *Jewish Life* 3, no. 4 (1948), 15.

51. This kind of spectatorship relates to "cross-viewing," what Susan Manning pinpoints as the moment when "some spectators may catch glimpses of subjectivities from social locations that differ from their own." Manning, *Modern Dance, Negro Dance*, xvi. Here, the non-Jewish audience members cross-viewed the *tefillin*.

52. See Karen Goodman, *Come Let Us Dance (Lomir Geyn Tantsn): Two Yiddish Dances, Heritage, Style & Steps*, VHS (Burbank, CA, 2002).

53. In this discussion, and the one that follows in the next sections, my use of the word *weight* denotes it as a movement quality, and I draw from Laban Movement Analysis (LMA) for this meaning. The LMA system comprises four main areas: Body, Effort, Space, and Shape. Within the study of Effort, there are four Motion factors: weight, time, space, and flow. Each Effort has two polar qualities, one considered fighting and one considered yielding. Weight is strong or light; time is quick or sustained; space is direct or indirect; and flow is bound or free. These efforts are grouped into states, which are composed of two efforts, and drives, which are composed of three efforts. States and drives are named descriptively and metaphorically based on what the resulting movement from the effort combinations look like. The passion drive is made up of weight, time, and flow, with little attention to space. See Bartenieff and Lewis, *Body Movement*; Hackney, *Making Connections;* Maletic, *Body—Space—Expression;* and Laban, *The Language of Movement*.

54. For discussions relating to the mid-century U.S. discourse of "ethnic" dance, see Yutian Wong, "Artistic Utopias: Michio Ito and the Trope of the International" in *Worlding Dance*, ed. Susan Leigh Foster (2009; New York: Palgrave Macmillan, 2011), 144–62; Rebekah Kowal, "'The World Dances through Manhattan:' Parsing the Postwar Resurgence of 'Ethnologic' Dance" (paper presented at "Topographies: Sites, Bodies, Technologies," annual meeting of Society of Dance History Scholars with Dance Critics Association, Stanford University, Stanford, CA, June 20, 2009); and Kowal, Rebecca Rossen, Paul Scolieri, and Susan Manning, "Ethnic Dance and American Modern Dance in the U.S." (panel presented at "Dance Dramaturgy: Catalyst, Perspective and Memory," annual meeting of Society of Dance History Scholars, York University and University of Toronto, Toronto, Canada, June 24, 2011).

55. Martha Coleman, "Anna Sokolow: YW & YMHA February 1, 1948," *Dance Observer*, March 1948, 32; and Doris Hering, "Anna Sokolow, YM & YWHA, February 1, 1948," *Dance Magazine*, March 1948, 41.

56. Morris, *A Game for Dancers*, 97.

57. Deborah Jowitt, "Staring into Darkness," *Village Voice*, December 16, 1986, 117.

58. Anna Sokolow, quoted in *Anna Sokolow: Choreographer*, VHS, produced and directed by Lucille Rhodes and Margaret Murphy (1980; Pennington, NJ: Dance Horizons Video, 1991).

59. Laban, *The Language of Movement*, 14. Thank you to Melanie Bales for helping me define this.

60. Rabbi Yossi Marcus, "Why Are Many Things in Judaism Done Three Times?" http://www.askmoses.com/article/228,503/Why-are-many-things-in-Judaism-done-three-times.html (accessed June 3, 2008).

61. Morris, *A Game for Dancers*, 93–97. Morris works from Deborah Zall's 1990 performance of *Kaddish*.

62. *The Joyce Mollov Memorial Lecture and Performance*, VHS. Presented by the Continuing Education Program and Center for Jewish Studies at Queens College, Queens College Theater, Flushing, New York, November 4, 1990, JRDD, NYPL; Anna Sokolow, *Kaddish*, unpublished videocassette, performed by Hadassah Segal (Ohio State University, 2000). Collection of the Ohio State University Department of Dance. During the process of learning all the repertory for her M.F.A. concert, Segal also worked with dancers Risa Steinberg, Ze'eva Cohen, and Sharona Rubenstein; *Jewish Women in Dance*, DLI; and 100 *Years of Sokolow*, unpublished DVD, performed by Bridgewater State College Department of Theatre and Dance students (2009), Sokolow Dance Foundation (hereafter SDF). I have viewed this last version, but do not specifically reference it in this discussion. I also do not discuss Ze'eva Cohen's or Linda Diamond's versions of *Kaddish* here.

63. *Three Dances: Deborah Zall*, DVD, performed by Deborah Zall, produced by Deborah Zall and Niramon Ross (2007). Gift of Deborah Zall; Anna Sokolow, *Kaddish*, VHS, performed by Deborah Zall, produced by Michael Mandell (New York: Forest Hills Space, 1990). JRDD, NYPL; and Anna Sokolow, *Kaddish*, performed by Deborah Zall, *Anna Sokolow* 100*th Birthday Tribute*, presented by Sokolow Theatre/Dance Ensemble, February 14, 2010, 92nd Street YM/YWHA, New York City.

64. The original score was handwritten for the Dance Notation Bureau, and the revised score was translated into Labanwriter graphics by Mira Kim in 2006. The score contains a glossary with notes from Weber about the background of the dance, motivation for moments of the dance as dictated by Sokolow, definitions of clusters of symbols that the notator generated for an accurate symbolic representation of the movements as she saw them, and notes about the dancer's timing.

65. Sokolow often used the Stanislavsky Method for motivation. Stanislavsky's Method of Physical Action, or the Method, relates to the outward physical manifestations of inner emotions on the basis of the performer's experiences. See Valentina Litvinoff, *The Use of Stanislavsky Within Modern Dance* (New York: American Dance Guild, 1972), 9; and Ellen Graff, *Stepping Left: Dance and Politics in New York City, 1928–1942* (Durham, NC, and London: Duke University Press, 1997), 70–72; and Warren, 116.

66. This is relevant because not all Labanotation scores include effort symbols.

67. Thank you to Mara Penrose for this observation.

68. Zall, discussion.

69. Weber does not know the reason for the costume and was not able to discuss the choice with Sokolow at the time of the notation rehearsals. Lynne Weber (notator), in telephone conversation with the author, January 25, 2010. It is possible that Hadassah Badock Kruger did not want to wear *tefillin*.

70. This is my interpretation. May told me that Sokolow did not tell her what different parts of the dance meant because she wanted the dancers to find their own motivation. Lorry May (dancer, Sokolow Dance Foundation director) in discussion with the author, November 23, 2009, Attleboro, Massachusetts.

71. Sokolow, notated by Weber, xi. It is unclear if "the Book" refers to a prayer book or to the Torah.

72. Thank you to Judith Brin Ingber for bringing this to my attention.

73. Thank you to Donna Guy and Stephanie Smith for this insight. See also *Mexico on Video*, DVD (México, D.F.: Mexican Records, 2007).

74. John Giffin (dancer, choreographer) in discussion with the author, April 20, 2010.

75. Judith Brin Ingber (dancer, dance scholar) in discussion with the author, June 20, 2009.

76. Zall, discussion.

77. Sokolow, notated by Weber, xiii.

78. I use the Hebrew word *Shabbat* interchangeably with the English equivalent *Sabbath*.

79. Weber, phone conversation.

80. Geracht understudied Lorry May in *Kaddish* when she first joined Sokolow's Players' Project. Geracht also learned Zall's version from Zall, and Dian Dong's version from Jim May.

81. Samantha Geracht (dancer) in conversation with the author, October 26, 2009, New York City.

82. See Rona Sheramy, "Resistance and War: The Holocaust in American Jewish Education, 1945–1960," *American Jewish History* 91, no. 2 (2003), 287–313.

II

Developing the American Ballet Dancer

THE PEDAGOGICAL LINEAGE OF ROCHELLE ZIDE-BOOTH

Jessica Zeller

WITHOUT A CENTRALIZED national institution for ballet, the typical American ballet dancer's training has been far more eclectic than that of dancers raised in conservatories or national academies such as the Paris Opera Ballet School or the Vaganova Ballet Academy. Rochelle Zide-Booth is an example of one mid-twentieth-century professional American ballet dancer with a heterogeneous training background. She turned to teaching more than forty years ago, and her pedagogy can be described as uniquely American: it acknowledges and cultivates individuality, eclecticism, and vibrant physicality, and it encourages an analytical approach. At the core of her work are those qualities and characteristics that have come to be accepted as the American ballet style: bold, direct, rhythmic movement that has few stylistic idiosyncrasies or embellishments; clear directions and spatial intentions with a keen sense of focus; and an energetic, spirited, intellectual approach to dancing.

Numerous twentieth-century dance writers, critics, and scholars have tried to define the American qualities of American ballet. As early as 1913, writer Willa Cather quoted Anna Pavlova, who described American dancers as "quick and confident."[1] The impresario, philosopher of dance, and foremost advocate for American ballet Lincoln Kirstein stated in 1937 that the "American style springs or should spring from our own training and environment, which was not in an Imperial School or a Parisian imitation of it. Ours is a style bred also from basket-ball courts, track and swimming meets and junior-proms.... It is frank, open, fresh and friendly. It can be funny without seeming arch, and serious without seeming pained."[2] Critic Edwin Denby referred to American ballet as displaying "a lovely freshness in classic dancing."[3] In his 1949 book *Ballet: The Emergence of an American Art,* George Amberg described his sense of the American style: "it is not meticulously accurate in the traditional virtuoso fashion, but it is full of bodily self-confidence and youthful stamina."[4] Zide-Booth's pedagogy reflects most of these qualities, which emerged from her multifaceted experiences as an American ballet dancer in the United States during this formative period for American ballet. In addition, her work embodies several prominent American ballet traditions that were central to her individual development as a dancer: the legacies of the ebullient Ballet Russe de Monte Carlo and the youthful, tenacious company of Robert Joffrey; the vaudeville lineage of her teacher Harriet Hoctor; and a potpourri of influences from a number of European and Russian teachers with whom she studied throughout her career.[5]

Like many American dancers of the mid-twentieth century, Zide-Booth's training was a bricolage: she studied with numerous teachers from different national schools and perspectives, whose approaches were often contradictory. At the same time as she was challenged by the inconsistencies of her instructors' various demands, she had to navigate the technique with an unconventional physique for ballet: at five feet tall, she did not fit the then-emerging aesthetic of the wiry, long-limbed Balanchine dancer. Using her individual body to guide her experimentation with the technique, Zide-Booth began the arduous process of reconciling her teachers' discrepant approaches and, along the way, developed her own methodology for teaching ballet. Her pedagogy is, in this way, an extension of her work as a dancer. It is American by virtue of its inherent plurality and its unbridled individualism. It is the fusion of her teachers' often contrasting methods as mediated through her physical facility. It does not adhere to an established syllabus but rather includes elements of several approaches that have been filtered through her unique capacities as a dancer. In contrast to the Balanchine technique—the only American approach to have been supported by an institution, codified, and passed down—Zide-Booth's American pedagogy is entirely dependent upon her body, her intellect, and her eye. From this perspective, her work is comparable in its influence to that of the most notable modern dancers, who have long been acknowledged for their unique approaches to movement based on their individual bodily capacities. American ballet teachers such as Zide-Booth, who, unlike their Euro-Russian counterparts, have been given the formidable task of assembling sound methods from a variety of materials, have likewise used their unique bodies as vehicles for discovery. Because ballet has often been viewed as an immutable form that does not absorb or reflect the mark of the individual, however, these teachers' innovative contributions to ballet technique have been largely overlooked.

Zide-Booth's development and dissemination of a cohesive, unified approach from a miscellany of sources is a pedagogical accomplishment that places her among the most influential of American ballet teachers. The versatility of her methodology has allowed her to teach in a variety of locales, including professional companies, conservatories, universities, and private studios.[6] Having sent numerous students into regional ballet companies, Zide-Booth is an exemplar of the predominant system of training in America, wherein most regional dancers are trained outside the ballet academy and are the products of such eclecticism, which they themselves are encouraged to resolve through their individual physiques.[7] Although Zide-Booth has not altered the course of classical training, she has in this way contributed to a more pervasive dialogue that examines the meaning of being American in a Euro-Russian form. Through her diverse and individualized methodology, Zide-Booth trains dancers—American or not—to identify and embody those characteristics that distinguish American ballet and American dancers on the international stage.

BIOGRAPHICAL SKETCH

Rochelle Zide began to study ballet in 1941 at the age of three in Boston, with the Ziegfeld ballerina Harriet Hoctor (1903–1977).[8] Hoctor studied ballet from the age of twelve at the Louis H. Chalif Russian Normal School of Dance and with Ivan Tarasov of Diaghilev's Ballets Russes.[9] In 1920, she debuted on Broadway with the Ziegfeld Follies, and in 1928, amid a string of vaudeville engagements and Broadway productions, she was deemed one of the foremost American prima ballerinas of her time.[10] Hoctor appeared in the film *Shall We Dance?* with Fred Astaire in 1935, and continued her career as part of a touring company with which she performed and staged revues until 1945. As a teacher, Hoctor wanted to enable her students to discover their own artistic sensibilities, a notion—likely derived from her vaudeville days—that has since become fundamental to Zide-Booth's pedagogical philosophies.

A few years into her training, Zide-Booth's mother determined that Hoctor's teaching was too unorthodox: it combined principles of the *danse d'école* with more unconventional elements that Hoctor had absorbed from her years of performing in revues. Zide-Booth's mother sent her, instead, to the Cecchetti teacher Alicia Langford, who she believed would provide more structure for a budding young dancer. When Zide-Booth no longer found enjoyment in the syllabus-derived training, her mother stopped her classes altogether, although the break was short-lived. They found a once-weekly class with a former Ballet Russe dancer who recognized the then-eight-year-old Zide-Booth's talent and recommended that she find a teacher who would be able to take her on as a serious student. Zide-Booth began several years of study with Boston Ballet founder E. Virginia Williams, who took her students to New York for a few weeks each year to study with a number of teachers. She also frequently hired guest teachers from prominent New York schools, including some from the School of American Ballet. At age fourteen, after feeling that Williams had routinely overlooked her, Zide-Booth made the decision to return to Hoctor. Hoctor's perspective—that dancing should be a source of enjoyment and creativity for students—was what Zide-Booth had been missing. At the same time, she had also determined that more structured classes were important for the development of her technique, so she found other instructors who could complement Hoctor's classes: Tatiana Stepanova, formerly of the Ballet Russe; Margaret Saul, a Cecchetti teacher who contributed to Cyril Beaumont's book *A Third Primer of Classical Ballet (Cecchetti Method)*;

and Mae Block, a Boston-based teacher who had danced professionally in New York.[11] Zide-Booth continued to go to New York during her school vacations, taking classes with the faculties at the Ballet Russe School, Ballet Arts, and the School of American Ballet.

In 1954, when Zide-Booth was sixteen, Serge Denham asked her to join the newly re-established Ballet Russe de Monte Carlo[12]; he had observed her in Frederic Franklin's ballet class at the Ballet Russe School and other instructors in New York had encouraged him to consider her for the company. By her fourth year with the Ballet Russe she had reached the rank of soloist and was touring the United States for months at a time without the benefit of daily classes. When she returned to New York, she frequented Valentina Pereyaslavec's classes at the Ballet Theatre School, until one day she spied the Danish *danseur noble* Erik Bruhn walking into a class. She recalled thinking, "whatever class he's taking, I'm taking. This is the greatest dancer I've ever seen."[13] Robert Joffrey (1928–1988)[14] was teaching, and his anatomically based approach was a revelation to Zide-Booth, who had natural but still unrefined talent (Figure 11.1).

FIGURE 11.1 Zide-Booth as Peep-Bo in the Ballet Russe de Monte Carlo production of Antonia Cobos's "The Mikado," circa 1957. Photo courtesy of Rochelle Zide-Booth.

Joffrey was born in Seattle, Washington, and studied ballet from the age of nine with Ivan Novikoff, who signed him up to perform with the Ballet Russe de Monte Carlo as an extra when they came into town on tours. He went on to study with Mary Ann Wells, an American teacher who "indirectly furnished [him] with the complete program for structuring the Joffrey Ballet."[15] Through Wells, Joffrey began to conceive of American ballet as a unique entity. In 1953, Joffrey and his collaborator and friend Gerald Arpino co-founded the American Ballet Center, now the Joffrey Ballet School. The Robert Joffrey Theater Ballet had its premiere the following year, and through a few permutations of name and headquarters it became the Joffrey Ballet, which relocated to Chicago in 1995.[16] Throughout his career as a teacher, choreographer, and director, Joffrey championed the training of American dancers and helped to develop a singularly American approach to ballet. He made a number of choreographic contributions, including the psychedelic ballet *Astarte* and his satirical nod to the Romantic ballet, *Pas de Déesses*; he commissioned works that blended the ballet and American modern dance aesthetic, such as Twyla Tharp's pivotal *Deuce Coupe*; and he was dedicated to the reconstruction of lost or historically significant ballets, including Nijinsky's *Le Sacre du Printemps*, Léonide Massine's *Parade*, and Kurt Jooss' *The Green Table*.

Zide-Booth became a regular student in Joffrey's classes in 1957, and he invited her to join his company, though she was still under contract with Denham. While she was studying with Joffrey and waiting out her time at the Ballet Russe, Zide-Booth began to study with Elisabeth Anderson-Ivantzova (1890–1973), a Russian émigré teacher from the Bolshoi.[17] Anderson-Ivantzova had risen to "first rank" at the Bolshoi, earning acclaim for her interpretations of Aurora in *The Sleeping Beauty* and Odette/Odile in *Swan Lake*.[18] In 1923, she immigrated to the United States, where she choreographed the American debut production of Igor Stravinsky's *Les Noces* and won over the critics, including the *New York Times*' John Martin, who wrote that "she is...another excellent reason for the establishment of a ballet in New York."[19] She opened the Anderson-Ivantzova School of Dance in 1937 in her studio apartment on West 56th Street in New York City,[20] where she taught "an almost perfectly preserved version of turn-of-the-century Bolshoi ballet."[21] Anderson-Ivantzova's pedagogical work was, in certain respects, the antithesis of Joffrey's; Zide-Booth would later come to reconcile these contradictions in her own dancing and teaching.

In September 1958, Zide-Booth began rehearsals with Joffrey's company and signed a contract with the ballet of the New York City Opera, for whom Joffrey was the choreographer.[22] The following year, Joffrey brought renowned pedagogue Vera Volkova (1904–1975) from Denmark to teach at his American Ballet Center. Widely considered one of ballet's great pedagogues, Volkova studied under Nicholas Legat, Galina Ulanova's mother Maria Romanova, and with Agrippina Vaganova, who came to define Russian ballet technique for the twentieth century. Volkova's performing career spanned Russia, the Far East, and Europe, where she also studied with the renowned teacher Olga Preobrajenska. On retiring from the stage in 1943 and opening a school in London, Volkova became the regular teacher of British ballerinas Margot Fonteyn, Moira Shearer, and Beryl Gray, among others. Having become the leading expert on the Vaganova technique in the West, she taught at the La Scala school in Milan before accepting the invitation to become artistic advisor to the Royal Danish Ballet in 1951.[23] Dancers flocked from all over the country to study with Volkova at Joffrey's school,[24] and she made a lasting impression on Zide-Booth.

In 1962, on the first day of the Joffrey company rehearsals at Watch Hill (Rebecca Harkness's estate), Zide-Booth suffered a detached retina. She was devastated. The company embarked on a tour to Russia and Afghanistan, and Joffrey decided that she would not accompany them. Only afterward did he explain to her that he was concerned about the questionable medical care that would have been available if she had had any complications with her injury. At the time, though, she was so hurt by his decision that she left the company.

On her recovery, she returned to the New York City Opera Ballet, where Joffrey was no longer resident choreographer, and she became prima ballerina. Shortly thereafter, Joffrey—interrupting Zide-Booth with an unheard of telephone call during a class with Pereyaslavec—asked her to rejoin his company as ballet mistress. The intensity of Zide-Booth's schedule, rehearsing ballets, and teaching for Joffrey during the day and performing with the opera in the evenings caused her to tear her Achilles tendon. She described the end of her career with the same kind of matter-of-fact tone that she uses when she teaches: "And that was it. I never danced again"[25] (Figure 11.2).

Zide-Booth has since held a host of directorial and academic positions internationally, and she is certified through the Dance Notation Bureau to reconstruct dances from Labanotation scores. In 1973 she was named artistic director of the Netherlands Dance Theatre, and she has served as the director of the ballet program at the Jacob's Pillow Dance Festival, director of the New Zealand School of Dance, director of the dance program at Adelphi University, and associate professor in the Butler University Department of Dance. Zide-Booth has been on faculty at the Alvin Ailey American Dance Center and the Boston Ballet DanceLab. As a Fulbright lecturer, she was the first American to teach classical ballet at the Prague Conservatory of Dance and the Ballet of the National Theatre in the Czech Republic. In addition to her work in the United States, she has done various international residencies in such locations as Israel, South Korea, the Philippines, Austria, Germany, Hungary, Norway, Switzerland, Belgium, the Netherlands, France, and Italy.[26] She has since retired from full-time teaching, though she still teaches master classes, stages ballets, and offers teaching seminars worldwide.

ROCHELLE ZIDE-BOOTH'S METHODOLOGY AND PEDAGOGICAL LINEAGE

Zide-Booth's esteem for the traditions of the ballet class is evident from the moment she enters the studio. Although her pedagogy does not follow the conventions of an established syllabus, she believes in many of ballet's time-honored notions of decorum, as

FIGURE 11.2 Zide-Booth in the title role of Thomas Andrew's "Clarissa" with the Joffrey, taken at the Jacob's Pillow Dance Festival, circa 1960. Photo courtesy of Rochelle Zide-Booth.

did Joffrey before her. Joffrey's "reverence for the classroom,"[27] as well as his understanding of the ballet class as an important part of the dancer's work that deserves scrupulous care and attention,[28] have become cornerstones of Zide-Booth's teaching.

One of the areas in which she goes against tradition is in her candid, often friendly approach to communicating with students, both in and out of class. Usually a few minutes early, she often checks in with those who are already in the studio and takes note of students' injuries while making her way to the front of the room. Although she can be jovial at times, she has a particular understanding of the teacher-student relationship. She does not require that her students address her by a specific title, as Anderson-Ivantzova, or "Madame Anderson," did, but Zide-Booth believes that instructors should be given the utmost respect. Asserting the teacher's role in the studio, she has been known to admonish her class for displaying anything other than deference, which she sometimes does tongue-in-cheek: "You have to do what the person in front—who is *God*, by the way—asks you to do!"[29] Zide-Booth has finely honed her voice to express various shades of disapproval, and she does not hesitate to exercise those tones if her students do not appear to share her work ethic. Notably, her exclamations of approval are genuine and reassuring. Former student Erica Lynette Edwards, a dancer with the Joffrey Ballet, recalled her encouraging remarks: "when you tried your hardest, even though it was nowhere close to perfect, [the effort] was acknowledged."[30]

The intensity of her presence and her direct approach make her a revered figure in the ballet studio. Zide-Booth makes it evident that she is there to work, and she expects the same commitment from her students. By nature Zide-Booth is straightforward and optimistic—both particularly American traits—and she brings a sense of pragmatism into her classes. She offered some common sense to a studio full of teenagers, saying, "Where you are now is where you are *now*. It's not where you're *going* to be."[31] In the same class, she also outlined her high expectations: "If you can do it well, if it's easy, it must be done beautifully. If it's hard, it must be done to the best of your ability."[32] By acknowledging that there are steep challenges to be faced, Zide-Booth deals with the practicalities of being a ballet dancer. She pushes her students to look realistically at their obstacles and shortcomings, and she helps them address these issues with optimism and energy in order to find sensible solutions.

Ballet is often taught through sheer imitation, a pedagogical approach that has spawned the myth that dancers are trained not to think critically. In contrast, part of Zide-Booth's American pedagogy involves the theoretical nature of ballet: she teaches her students how to take class, as well as how to be self-reliant, intellectually curious, thinking dancers who are deeply cognizant of their actions. She compels complete focus and physical investment from her students, and by targeting her comments to the thought process that takes place before and during the performance of an exercise she encourages a deliberate approach to movement for which she holds students accountable. If Zide-Booth corrects an individual student, she expects to see the application of that correction on the spot. She watches for the application of the idea throughout the rest of the class and often for days afterward, and she expects to see that concept carried into other related movements. This is an area of her work where she is particularly forward-thinking, emphasizing individual responsibility and providing students with tools for analysis and critical thinking in a field where they are so often expected to simply imitate and replicate. She frequently asks students about how or why they executed a step in a certain way, and her questions are never rhetorical. Her encouragement of student verbalization in the studio is not in accordance with ballet's longstanding traditions—where students are expected to quietly endure whatever criticisms the teacher gives. Requiring students to be conscious of their efforts, and asking them to discuss those efforts with the instructor, is another aspect of her approach that deviates from ballet's traditional authoritarian structure. Her method develops the kind of self-reflexivity and insight in students that enables them to solve their own problems in the technique, and in this way she continues to prepare dancers for professional careers in ballet.

Zide-Booth's desire to teach students how to intellectually monitor their own technique was a concept she learned from Joffrey. As Dayton Ballet Artistic Director Dermot Burke recalls, "[Joffrey] worked in such a way that you believed you could do anything."[33] Zide-Booth remembers being stunned by a similar sense in his classes: "The whole idea that you could actually *decide* that you could be good, that you could actually decide that you were going to do things correctly all the time, that it didn't have to do with what kind of a dinner you had last night, that there was a way of making it happen all the time—*that* I got from him."[34] This idea—which is related to Joffrey's anatomically based teaching—became an integral part of the groundwork on which Zide-Booth has based her methodology. Zide-Booth, too, uses anatomical knowledge to inform her teaching of ballet technique. Her broad references to the musculo-skeletal system are intended to help students learn how to work with their individual bodies, fully using their own physical capacities to accomplish the technique deliberately and consistently.

A major theme of Zide-Booth's pedagogy is her effort to develop American ballet dancers, who have significant qualitative differences from dancers trained in the syllabus-driven systems common throughout Europe and Russia. The American style, according to Zide-Booth, is open, physical, musical, and it employs the full breadth of the movement. "Americans are very direct—be American," was her comment to a class regarding the line of energy and focus over the front arm in first *arabesque*.[35] During an advanced class, she taught an *adagio* in which students ran from the upstage corner along the diagonal before stepping forward into a *piqué arabesque* and lowering the heel of the supporting leg. Many students slowed down, taking a long preparation prior to the *piqué* in an effort to carefully find their balance, and Zide-Booth responded with, "That's very British, but we're not English! Be American!"[36] She went on to fully explain her intent, which was for the balance to emerge from the running so that the preparation was almost non-existent; the *arabesque* should come as a surprise to the audience. Likewise, following a balance on *relevé* at the *barre*, she said to an intermediate class, "How much better was your balance because you held on to the barre for a long time? Holding on to the barre for a long time just makes you nervous."[37] From her tone, one got the sense that she was disappointed in the students, who from her perspective did not learn anything by holding on to the *barre* at length. They failed to understand why they had gone off their plumb lines and thus had missed lessons that might have been useful to them in the future. Her approach, which emphasizes spontaneity and encourages learning through risk taking, finds its resonance in the writings of various American ballet critics across the twentieth century.

There is a distinction in Zide-Booth's philosophy between style and mannerism, which is central to her understanding of American ballet's versatility. She aims to train dancers in what she calls a "pure style," where deliberate stylistic choices inform the movement, rather than unconscious habits that are embedded in the technique. Zide-Booth takes great pride in her diverse training background, which, in her view, has made the American dancer adaptable: "we [Americans] are still the most versatile dancers in the world. *Because* we don't have a system, that's why. Because we learn all systems, in a sense…you don't have to strip away a lot of stuff to get to what you want."[38] This aspect of Zide-Booth's approach distinguishes her from European models as well as Balanchine's style of American ballet, which, for example, requires a specifically crafted hand position that helps to identify the style.[39] Zide-Booth might contend that such positions of the hand are mannered, or that they are not necessarily applicable to other styles of ballet. Her understanding of American ballet is based on openness, physicality, musicality, and breadth of movement, and she tries to reduce areas of the technique in which dancers appear to have a characteristic look. Instead, she trains her dancers to be what she considers stylistically objective, so that they can accommodate an array of choreographic demands.

A typically American pluralist approach is paramount in Zide-Booth's philosophy, and it leads her to champion what she calls the "less than perfect body."[40] Her former student Amy Womer Wrobleski recalled that Zide-Booth "corrected and helped everyone in class, not just the students with the amazing technique or bodies."[41] Zide-Booth abides by the idea that if a pedagogical theory works on a dancer who does not possess the ideal physical structure for ballet, it will be more generally applicable to other body types. She explained: "So if I've got Baryshnikov in class, I am *not* going to base my training on him."[42] Rather, she advises students to turn their attention to dancers who are not as naturally gifted. She suggests, for instance, that students can learn more about turning by watching dancers who have to use the full extent of the technique to accomplish good *pirouettes*, even though it may be more enjoyable to watch dancers for whom turning comes easily. This area of Zide-Booth's pedagogy can be traced back to Joffrey. In the government-backed ballet training programs like those in Europe and Russia, dancers are chosen on the basis of their ideal bodily proportions and possibilities for future success in ballet, while America's democratized approach to ballet training has not adopted such a stringent selection process. In this light, Joffrey found that a potential strength of American ballet was in the raw materials: those highly ambitious dancers who might not have had the innate physical pre-requisites to be selected to study in the conservatory traditions of other countries, but whose less conventional qualities of athleticism, youthful vitality, and wholesome appearance he thought were equally valuable. He was able to address their diverse and non-standardized training with a methodology that emphasized strength, efficiency, and a radiant quality of movement.[43] Especially in the early years of his company and still to some degree today, Joffrey dancers have an array of body types and stylistic strong points. Joffrey biographer Sasha Anawalt writes, "His dancers emphasized energy and spirit over form; their physiques, proportions, and lines were not usually in keeping with textbook ideals. 'Dancers with perfect bodies don't have to work as hard,' he said."[44] These values have become central to Zide-Booth's pedagogy; they have informed her own dancing, her understanding of American ballet, and what it means to be an American ballet dancer.

The male dancers in Zide-Booth's classes are particularly subject to her scrutiny. She often asks the men to dance first in the center or during traveling exercises, in direct contrast to ballet's chivalrous tradition, in which the women always dance first. Joffrey also broke with the conventions of the ballet class in this way; the men in his classes regularly performed the exercises before the women to boost their self-esteem and encourage good working habits.[45] Zide-Booth has continued with this part of Joffrey's approach. Her close attention to the men in her classes appears to be an effort to keep them focused, accountable for their work, and humble about their craft. In addition, she believes that men in ballet should not receive preferential treatment, as they often do in pre-professional programs where they are fewer in number, and thus often cast in multiple roles despite their oftentimes lesser technical ability. Notably, while teaching at Butler University, Zide-Booth gave Bournonville's notated "Wednesday Class" to her men's class every week.[46] Part of her American approach involves using what she feels are the most beneficial components of other techniques, and she likely found the emphasis on *allegro* in the Bournonville technique useful for teaching male dancers.

Zide-Booth is a firm believer in what she calls the "do it first and clean it up later" method, in which the coordination of a step is addressed before technical exactitude.[47] This is likely derived from Hoctor's approach, and it applies especially to children. Zide-Booth reminisced about Hoctor's teaching: "There was magic in that studio. I'm serious. We don't remember her teaching us anything. There was an atmosphere in the studio of…discovery. She encouraged you to discover *how* to do things."[48] As a result, Zide-Booth feels that the youngest dancers should not be given intensive instruction in ballet placement and has noted: "By the time they get to the intermediate level, they could care less about dancing. It's been squeezed out of them that they have to be perfect. They haven't enjoyed dancing since they had their little scarves, and did their little dances."[49] Hoctor, in a 1936 interview, felt similarly about the kind of technical rigor to expect from children: "If they have to practice—practice all the time—the chances are they may come to hate it."[50] In Zide-Booth's teaching, this applies to older dancers as well. Wrobleski recalled:

One day after I had a frustrating class and was stretching in the hallway, Rochelle walked out of the studio and saw me. She asked me why I was holding back in class, particularly in the grand allegro combinations. I told her I was trying not to flail about, that I was trying to execute everything just right. Rochelle told me to not worry about it, that sometimes you have to flail and let go and just dance![51]

Zide-Booth's students often have difficulty completing her exercises with absolute technical clarity on the first attempt. Her approach, however, foregrounds the use of appropriate coordination and energy with the material, at which point a deeper comprehension of the mechanics can be acquired. In this way, she allows students to experience the thrill of trying something for the first time with a sense of physical abandon. This aspect of Zide-Booth's pedagogy, which calls for a bold, fearless sense of attack, promotes Hoctor's emphasis on the enjoyment of dancing while also reflecting some particularly American ballet characteristics.

Musically, Zide-Booth uses various meters and tempi throughout her classes. She encourages students to phrase exercises as they see fit within the parameters she establishes with her delivery of the material, and she reminds them to use forethought in their musicality. Like Anderson-Ivantzova, who was dismayed at the inability of her students to distinguish among a waltz, a mazurka, and a polonaise,[52] Zide-Booth often delineates the differences between these commonly used three-four time signatures. The disappearance of traditional Slavic character dance—which frequently includes mazurkas, for example—in the flurry of American eclecticism may be at the root of both Anderson-Ivantzova's frustration and Zide-Booth's subsequent inclusion of this material in her classes. Although character dance training is an essential component of the more comprehensive Russian and European syllabi, it is often a casualty of the generally less systematic training in the United States. Zide-Booth's effort, in this regard, works to systematize her eclectic American approach by including some elements of the Euro-Russian tradition that are often disregarded in the States.

Probably as a result of her own eclectic American training, Zide-Booth sees ballet as both art and entertainment, and she does not see the need for it to always be "angst and abstraction."[53] She expects to see regular improvement in students' technique, and like Joffrey she promotes a thoughtful atmosphere where students are called on to be mindful of their efforts. Yet, like Hoctor, Zide-Booth also sees personal artistic growth and freedom of movement as imperative to the prevention of student burnout. She whispered to a class, "The secret is that we're dancing for ourselves. The reality is that we're dancing for the audience who buys our tickets and that's why we have jobs!"[54] Zide-Booth's class structure reflects this seemingly irreconcilable dual emphasis: her relatively short *barre* is intended to hone the technique, where the longer center portion of the class, in addition to employing concepts from the *barre* work, is focused largely on developing artistry, expression, and freedom of movement. Zide-Booth has thus crafted the structural elements of her class by blending the divergent concepts of her teachers, which establishes her class design as another American aspect of her work.

Zide-Booth's *barre* is designed to develop "pure technique."[55] She does not look for artistry during the *barre* work, although she does attend to musicality.[56] She describes the movement, articulating the action of the feet and legs slowly and clearly with her hands and arms, occasionally demonstrating an exercise or two in her dance sneakers. Walking around the studio during the *barre* exercises, she emphasizes the qualities of the steps: during a *battement frappé* exercise, for instance, she held her hands up to her ears as if listening, and said, "Let me hear the brush; I don't hear it."[57] Often, when verbal comments do not elicit the response Zide-Booth is after, she becomes a hands-on teacher; she has been known to pull forward on students' inside arms at the *barre*, for example, to help with balance, or to offer physical resistance with her hands to assist with the initiation and coordination of various steps. Her *barre* is made up of a basic order of exercises that shifts only slightly from class to class, but the content and structure of each exercise is variable, since Zide-Booth does not plan her classes in advance. Her extemporaneous arrangement of class material is decidedly different from the syllabus-driven techniques; this likely derives from her diverse American training, which emphasized intellect, unself-consciousness, and spontaneity. Her exercises are based on her interpretation of what the class needs at that time, and thus she relies entirely on her "eye." She explains, "from the first couple of combinations, by the time we've gotten to *rond de jambe à terre*, I can see what's going wrong that day in the class, and I build the whole class around the correction that we need that day."[58]

On coming into the center, she often reminds her students, "These are not exercises anymore; this part's called dancing."[59] The order of Zide-Booth's center work is a mirror of Joffrey's: his classes moved from a small *terre à terre* into somewhat larger *pirouette* exercises and a traveling *enchaînement* before reaching the *adagio, petit allegro,* and *grand allegro.*[60] She often fully and fluidly demonstrates the upper body and arms for each exercise, while walking or indicating the steps with her legs. After standing to deliver the combinations, which she rarely gives more than once, Zide-Booth returns to her seat to observe the students; she sits on the front edge of her chair with absolutely upright posture. She narrates during most of the exercises, describing corrections in short phrases: "standing side forward." Zide-Booth manages to balance her commentary in such a way that it is regular but not intrusive, and the sense of dancing to the musical accompaniment remains strong. Rather, she times her words carefully so that an adjustment can be made before the step is completed.

In his teaching, Joffrey was known for his use of a centralized alignment, where the dancer's weight is distributed evenly through the midline of each leg, and centered between the ball of the foot and the heel. When shifting from two standing legs to one, this central alignment requires only a minimal shift of weight.[61] On the contrary, Anderson-Ivantzova's former student Marion Horosko describes Anderson-Ivantzova's placement as "seeming to lean dancers far toward the barre, freeing the working leg. Yet the hip [was] by no means 'out'."[62] This organization of the body atop the ball of the foot requires a larger shift when moving from two standing legs to one, since the center of weight moves past the center of the foot to the ball. Zide-Booth, echoing Anderson-Ivantzova's approach, often suggests that dancers align their heads over the balls of their standing feet to help achieve balance on one leg. She recalled her experience in Anderson-Ivantzova's class: "I was literally doing a cambré over the barre and saying, 'But nobody can balance like this,' and meanwhile, while I'm talking to her, I'm balancing!"[63] Initially, her success with Anderson-Ivantzova's concept of alignment was distressing for Zide-Booth, who felt a strong sense of allegiance to Joffrey; her published diary entry from 1957 includes the admission "I'm very confused, dear diary. She says one thing and Joffrey says another."[64] Despite her attempt to absorb and integrate Joffrey's central alignment into her own dancing, a lengthy period of trial-and-error led Zide-Booth to select Anderson-Ivantzova's method for her own training, with the alignment of the spine—and thus the weight— over the ball of the foot. Since Zide-Booth is committed to teaching only what she can validate as successful, she has chosen to set aside Joffrey's method of placement in her teaching. Anderson-Ivantzova's theory of alignment has become a central tenet of Zide-Booth's teaching methodology, although she does not deny that Joffrey's approach works for certain types of bodies.[65] The antithetical methods of these two instructors presented

Zide-Booth with the foremost challenge in American eclectic training: the merging of contrasting pedagogies into a coherent approach that works for the individual dancer. Zide-Booth has noted her indebtedness to Joffrey for what he taught her, both as a dancer and a teacher, and she has discussed the pangs of guilt she felt when she had to turn away from Joffrey's theory of alignment.[66] It was a difficult choice for her, but her physical success with Anderson-Ivantzova's philosophy made it easier. Her personal history, in this instance, became the basis for her subsequent pedagogy.

In spite of her rejection of Joffrey's approach to alignment, Zide-Booth espouses several other core aspects of his teaching in her own pedagogy. A 1976 film of Joffrey teaching a workshop class at the Ruth Page Foundation School of Dance in Chicago reveals his emphasis on the downward action of the body as a means to rise. For example, in a *tombé* to *à la seconde* he says, "The leg goes up because you *plié*."[67] When closing the gesture leg from *battement tendu* to fifth position, he stresses the same downward action, only with stability with the result instead of extension: "And reach down."[68] This oppositional work along the vertical axis has become an important element of Zide-Booth's pedagogy as well; she often refers to the feeling of working through or even underneath the floor with the gesture leg, but she also attends to the supporting leg's energy downward through the floor as an anchor to send the body upward. She often notes that the standing leg will eventually become the new gesture leg, and she encourages students to give intellectual priority to the actions of the supporting leg: "Put your brain in your standing leg."[69] In the case of a press or a spring up to *relevé*, Zide-Booth's theory is to engage the heels downward just before the *relevé* to gather momentum for the rising action. In a similar use of rebound, she is adamant that the heels press down into the floor at the bottom of the *plié* in *allegro* steps to allow the dancer to access their full elevation and a sense of *ballon*.

Épaulement—or shouldering—and the use of the back in American ballet have typically been taught haphazardly, in bits and pieces. Contrary to the thorough Euro-Russian methodologies for teaching *épaulement* and *port de bras*, which include a comprehensive series of exercises that address the movements of the back, shoulders, and head, there is no such system in American ballet pedagogy that promotes the development of this defining characteristic of classical ballet. In this light, Joffrey's emphasis on the use of the back and shoulders in opposition to the legs can be considered an American approach to *épaulement*: it gives *épaulement*, which is oftentimes viewed as purely aesthetic, a pragmatic, stabilizing function. In the workshop film, a student executes a *pirouette en dehors* to the left side and finishes in a fourth position *croisé*. Joffrey says, "Reach left to me," referring to the gesture side of the back spiraling away from the gesture leg, which is placed *derrière*. In a related episode, Joffrey's remark to a student in *sous-sus* facing *croisé* in the center is, "come forward," while pointing to her upstage shoulder, which alludes to the standing side moving forward in opposition to the front leg.[70] "Your head hardly moves, it's your torso that changes," is the correction he gives regarding a *temps lié en arrière* from *croisé derrière* to *croisé devant*.[71] He emphasizes the forward spiral of the new standing shoulder as the leg position changes, which endows the *épaulement* with an important role in the security of the dancer's stance. Having integrated Joffrey's theory into her own pedagogy, Zide-Booth frequently refers to this contralateral use of the back. She consistently discusses moving the *barre* arm forward, the supporting side of the back forward, or the standing shoulder forward; she often approaches students struggling to balance in *retiré* at the *barre*, takes their hand from the *barre*, and pulls them forward, moving the shoulder girdle of the standing side forward into squared, balanced positions. At the end of a *grand rond de jambe en dedans*, she instructs her students to bring their standing hips and shoulders forward to counter the arrival of the gesture leg in the *devant* position. In this way, she is a proponent of Joffrey's use of *épaulement*, and his related concept that the standing side of the back spiraling forward in opposition to the gesture leg in the *devant*, *à la seconde*, and *retiré* positions provides greater stability. Her attention to bringing the supporting side forward is in lieu of pulling the hip of the gesture leg back in the *devant* line, which allows the dancer to maintain Zide-Booth's preferred alignment over the ball of the foot.

Zide-Booth's fusion of Joffrey's *épaulement* with Anderson-Ivantzova's alignment over the ball of the foot is where she most typifies an American approach to pedagogy. Though these two ideas originated with teachers from divergent backgrounds and with distinct methodological approaches, Zide-Booth managed to fuse them through the medium of her individual body. Her merging of these theories, not only in her own physicality as a dancer but also as a coherent method of instruction, is where her contribution to American pedagogy is the most pronounced.

Pirouettes hold a special place in technique for Zide-Booth, which is evident when she teaches. Her work with *pirouettes* is indicative of her broader philosophies and her overall approach to teaching ballet technique, and it is one that only Zide-Booth could have made. During her training and subsequent career, she was a natural turner—her individual physique and coordination made *pirouettes* relatively easy for her—and thus she has a particular fondness for this element of ballet. She seems to perceive turning as an area in the technique wherein students can experience the excitement of ballet, and thus she pushes them to experiment and have fun with their discoveries. Zide-Booth has fond memories of Hoctor's instructions to turn as many *pirouettes* as her age,[72] and she often challenges her students to do the same, despite the occasional gasp of disbelief from a sixteen-year-old student. She has extrapolated this idea—where she asks for a greater number of revolutions in order to improve the energy given to a lesser quantity—to *allegro* work as well. She is notorious among her students for asking for *entrechats huit* or triple *tours en l'air*. Although Zide-Booth is earnest about her high demands, she does not expect perfect execution of these largely disused steps. Rather, she contends that asking for an extreme drives students to work with the energy and attack that defines American ballet, a concept that she has gleaned from her training with Hoctor. She reassured her students after one such exercise: "See, now that you have to push more for the *pirouette*, you push more for the rest of it."[73] This contentious aspect of Zide-Booth's methodology has, on occasion, caused both her colleagues and her students to question her motives. However, she argues that asking for more, a triple *tour en l'air* for example, improves the energy and quality of what the student has already been working on, so the double *tour en l'air* is much improved after the grand attempt.

Zide-Booth integrates *pirouettes* or a preparation for turns into many areas of her class, both at the *barre* and *au milieu*. She refuses to give corrections to natural turners that may alter their coordination, and she frequently points this out to them. Eyeing a student who had an inherent bodily understanding of the timing and rhythm of *pirouettes*, she strongly advised, "Never let anybody mess with your pirouettes."[74] Zide-Booth's brief period of study with Volkova prompted her feeling that those students who have a propensity for turning should maintain their instinctive coordination.[75] During a portion of Volkova's residency at Joffrey's American Ballet Center, Zide-Booth was unable to execute *pirouettes* as well as she typically could. After bringing her difficulty to Volkova's attention, Zide-Booth learned that in her endeavor to apply all of Volkova's corrections for *pirouettes*, she was distorting her own coordination. Volkova's lesson to her was that natural *pirouette* coordination should be considered of primary importance, a concept which is still at the core of Zide-Booth's teaching.

Volkova placed great importance on coordination and timing throughout the class, and not only with *pirouettes*. In his tribute to Fonteyn, former Sadler's Wells dancer Gilbert Vernon wrote: "In class I had trouble with the timing of a certain exercise. Vera Volkova suggested that I stand behind Margot at the *barre* and feel it with her."[76] Zide-Booth has a similar approach: she begins by focusing the individual proclivities of each dancer, and drawing them out to their fullest extent. Such individualism is a demonstrably American trait, and it is fundamental to her understanding of American training. However, in the event that a student is unable to find success in certain areas of the technique, Zide-Booth encourages the kind of imitative approach that Volkova used: "The thing is to work with the person's *own* coordination, and not mess with that, and if they don't have it, to put them behind somebody who *does*."[77] She often places students lacking *ballon*, or buoyancy, in their jumping behind those who jump easily and directs them to try to absorb the timing during the exercise. She attributes this to her own bodily understanding of the *allegro* rhythm: "I found a boy who was with the Joffrey for about a month who had this *fabulous* jump...and I just stood behind him in class. Every time he went down I went down; every time he went up I went up, and at the end of a month I was a jumper."[78] Her mixture of a more traditional, imitative approach with her primary focus on the individual dancer is indicative of Zide-Booth's willingness to try any means necessary to ensure success for her students. If one approach fails, she quickly and without hesitation moves on to another, using the same kind of trial-and-error that was central to her own training. Notably, this method of training works outside the boundaries of traditional, syllabus-based instruction.

On occasion, Zide-Booth's American lineage manifests itself in her choreography. While dancing in vaudeville, films, and revues, Hoctor garnered significant acclaim for her deep backbend *en pointe*, which she maintained as she *bourréed* around the stage. An excerpt from Walter Ware's 1936 *Ballet Is Magic: A Triple Monograph*—with chapters dedicated to Hoctor, the Danish dancer Paul Haakon, and Ballet Theatre dancer Patricia Bowman—provides an unmistakable visual image of this step, which brought Hoctor such renown:

Like a wayward sapling on a wind-swept plain, she seems to weave upward and downward impelled by some unknown force until suddenly, with a great crescendo from the orchestra, she sweeps into a low backbend, exquisite in its elliptical perfection. In this same position she *bourrées* backward, never faltering for an instant, across the entire width of the stage. (Miss Hoctor is able to see as clearly in this position as though she were standing upright.)[79]

In the 1999 production of Butler University's *The Nutcracker*, Zide-Booth incorporated Hoctor's backbend into the dance for two soloist Angels during the Act II overture. At the time, those cast in the roles thought it impossible, and the sense among many of the other students was one of relief that they had not been selected to dance those parts. Ultimately, the two dancers were able to perform the step successfully, which most likely came about through a combined effort of their fearlessness and technical creativity, in tandem with Zide-Booth's encouragement and her conviction in her American ballet ancestry.

When coaching dancers and when restaging works, Zide-Booth always begins the rehearsal process with a discussion of the character if there is one, or the type of role for non-narrative ballets such as *Les Sylphides*.[80] One of Zide-Booth's enduring qualities is her absolute belief in and love for the ballet repertoire, including the storylines and characters that so often enter the realm of the fantastic. Her American approach, however, brings a sense of realism to the most elusive of roles. Although *Les Sylphides* is an entirely plotless work, Zide-Booth approached it from the same perspective. She pressed me to consider, "Where do the Sylphides live?" "Where do they make their home?" and "What is the surface that you're walking on?"[81] She also distinguished the sylph who dances the Prelude from the sylphs dancing the Waltz and Mazurka, noting that she is more earthbound, whereas the others are jumpers and more at home in the air. Another distinguishing feature of this sylph, according to Zide-Booth, is that she "hears music that nobody else hears."[82] This motivates the "listening" poses in the first section, and most of the directional changes throughout the variation. She was specific about how this motivation worked, tying the fanciful characterization to the realities of the variation's physicality: "You're hearing it [music] *here*, and it's traveling all the way to those fingers, and you're hearing it over *there*."[83] By bringing her commonsensical approach to the whimsical theme of the ballet, Zide-Booth asks for an American interpretation of the traditional work.

CONCLUSION

In spite of its seemingly unbroken tradition, the *danse d'école* can be seen to have absorbed the individual marks of many a powerful teacher. In the narratives of dance history, however, it is the great modern dancers whose idiosyncratic movement vocabularies are typically considered the most significant individual contributions to the field. More often than not, the dance techniques and styles they developed were derived from their distinct bodies and proclivities, and thus their personal inscriptions on the field are evident. The ballet world has failed to see its teachers' contributions to the classical technique in the same light, and therefore the capacity of individual ballet teachers to leave their personal impressions on the centuries-old technique has been largely overlooked. Even though there is widespread knowledge of historically significant dancers and their distinctive qualities, there is a dearth of literature that details noteworthy pedagogical nuances introduced by singular teachers. As a result, classical ballet is often erroneously viewed as a monolithic genre that does not allow room or scope for the development of individual bodies or personal pedagogies. This close analysis of Rochelle Zide-Booth's work, however, demonstrates that teachers' unique bodies and experiences are the primary vehicles through which they put their personal stamp on the technique as well as the tools that promote ballet's evolution over time.

Zide-Booth's personal, bodily understanding of ballet, which she learned from her various teachers in the context of mid-twentieth-century America, permeates her approach to teaching; she used her physical knowledge to solve those paradoxes in her training that are common in the eclecticism of American ballet. Consequently, Zide-Booth's method both reflects and organizes her heterogeneous American training into a cohesive, broad-based pedagogy that is the essence of both American individualism and American pluralism—an achievement that establishes her as a notable proponent of American ballet outside of the Balanchine lineage. Her classes, though notably pragmatic in both design and execution, evoke an unmistakable sense of history: they are where lessons from her past find their echoes, and where teachers from her past are paid homage. Zide-Booth's incorporation of this personal history into her teaching has enabled her to create a unique philosophy and methodology for teaching future generations in the American art of ballet.

NOTES

1. Willa Cather, "Training for the Ballet: Making American Dancers," *McClure's Magazine* (October 1913): 87.
2. Lincoln Kirstein, *Ballet, Bias, and Belief* (New York: Dance Horizons, 1983): 200–201.
3. Edwin Denby, "The American Ballet," *Kenyon Review* 10, no. 4 (autumn 1948): 638.
4. George Amberg, *Ballet: The Emergence of an American Art* (New York: New American Library; New York: Duell, Sloan & Pearce, 1949): 124.

5. I studied with Zide-Booth as an undergraduate student at Butler University from 1997 to 2000. In 2007, I observed and participated in her classes and seminars, I interviewed her, and I had coaching sessions with her while she was in residency at the Canton Ballet in Ohio.

6. Her students have gone on to dance with the Joffrey Ballet, Richmond Ballet, Dayton Ballet, Charleston Ballet Theatre, Eugene Ballet, the Limón Dance Company, Corpus Christi Ballet, and Peoria Ballet, among others. Many of her students have stayed close to the dance field in other capacities; they have gone on to earn various dance degrees and certifications, manage and teach at local studios and companies, work in higher education, and perform in professional theatre and on Broadway.

7. It is important to note that the teaching faculties in many ballet academies in America often have diverse approaches to teaching technique. Despite the common assumption that ballet academies are cohesive in their methods, American students are often presented with the challenge of reconciling divergent methodologies, even inside many of these professional institutions.

8. There are conflicting reports as to the date of Hoctor's birth. According to her obituaries in *Dance Magazine* and the *New York Times* in August 1977, she was seventy-four years old at her death, but the Library of Congress gives 1905 as her date of birth, which would make her seventy-two. See "Harriet Hoctor Collection," *Guide to Special Collections in the Music Division of the Library of Congress*, 2007; "Obituaries: Harriet Hoctor," *Dance Magazine* (August 1977): 18; and Peter B. Flint, "Harriet Hoctor, 74, Ballet Dancer, Dies," *New York Times*, June 11, 1977.

9. Hoctor also trained with Anton Dolin and Nicholas Legat, though it appears that this study may have been brief, as these notable teachers are not mentioned in more than a few of Hoctor's biographical sketches. See "Harriet Hoctor Collection," *Guide to Special Collections in the Music Division of the Library of Congress*, 2007, iv; "Obituaries: Harriet Hoctor," *Dance Magazine* (August 1977): 18; and Peter B. Flint, "Harriet Hoctor, 74, Ballet Dancer, Dies," *New York Times*, June 11, 1977.

10. "Harriet Hoctor Collection," *Guide to Special Collections in the Music Division of the Library of Congress*, 2007, accessed February 25, 2008, http://hdl.loc.gov/loc.music/eadmus. mu2007.wp.0002, 5.

11. There is conflicting information as to whether Block danced for the New York City Ballet or Ballet Theatre (now American Ballet Theatre). She took Zide-Booth to classes at the School of American Ballet, which would indicate her involvement with New York City Ballet, but her name does not appear on the publicized roster of dancers from 1948 forward. Marjorie Dougherty (formerly Margot Williams), a contemporary of Zide-Booth's and one of Block's students, has asserted that Block danced for Ballet Theatre (Dougherty, telephone interview, June 19, 2009). She cites Block's small stature of four feet eleven inches as a primary indication of this affiliation, since the Ballet Theatre dancers were, at that time, much shorter than those in Balanchine's New York City Ballet.

12. She danced professionally under the name Rochelle Zide.

13. Zide-Booth, interview with author, March 2007, Canton, OH.

14. According to Sasha Anawalt's exhaustively researched book, *The Joffrey Ballet: Robert Joffrey and the Making of an American Dance Company*, there is a discrepancy between Joffrey's stated date of birth, 1930, and the date on his birth records. I have chosen to list the date in accordance with her research, which is "most *probably*" 1928 (New York: Scribner, 1996: 17).

15. Sasha Anawalt, *The Joffrey Ballet: Robert Joffrey and the Making of an American Dance Company* (New York: Scribner, 1996): 45.

16. It is notable that although the Joffrey Ballet School is still located in New York and dedicated to furthering Joffrey and Arpino's educational principles, it is unaffiliated with the Joffrey company. The company has recently opened its own training academy in Chicago.

17. Anawalt, *The Joffrey Ballet*, 116.

18. Lawrence Sullivan, "Anderson-Ivantzova, Elizabeth," *International Encyclopedia of Dance*, ed. Selma Jeanne Cohen, 6 vols. (New York: Oxford University Press, 2004): 85; Marian Horosko, "In the Shadow of Russian Tradition: Elizabeta Anderson-Ivantzova," *Dance Magazine* (January 1971): 37.

19. John Martin, "The Dance: A Triumph of Opera Miming," *New York Times*, May 5, 1929, 11, quoted in Lawrence Sullivan, "Les Noces: The American Premiere," *Dance Research Journal* 14, no. 1–2 (1981–1982): 12.

20. "Elisabeth Anderson-Ivantzova," *Dance News* (December 1973): 6.

21. "Obituaries: Mme. Elizaveta Anderson-Ivantzova," *Dance Magazine* (December 1973): 8.

22. Rochelle Zide-Booth, "Dancing for Joffrey," *Dance Chronicle* 12, no. 1 (1989): 59.

23. John Gruen, *Erik Bruhn: Danseur Noble* (New York: Viking Press, 1979): 55.

24. Doris Hering, "America Meets Vera Volkova," *Dance Magazine* (September 1959): 37.

25. Rochelle Zide-Booth, in discussion with the author, March 2007, Canton Ballet, Canton, OH. During the years I worked with Zide-Booth, she informally recounted to me how she found out that she would not be able to dance anymore. After the surgery to repair her torn tendon, the doctor came into her hospital room and walked directly over to the window. She asked him why he was standing across the room, and he replied that he could not tell a dancer that she would never dance again without covering the windows, in the event that she might feel the need to jump.

26. "Rochelle Zide-Booth," *Boston Ballet*, 2006, accessed February 16, 2008, http://www.bostonballet.org/school/summerprograms/SDP07_Faculty/zidebooth.html (link no longer active).

27. Dermot Burke, quoted in Kate Mattingly, "The Joffrey Ballet School at Fifty," *Dance Magazine* (July 2004): 51.

28. Joseph Carman, "In the Joffrey Tradition," *Dance Magazine* (July 2005): 37.

29. Rochelle Zide-Booth, Intermediate and Advanced Ballet Classes, March 2007, Canton Ballet, Canton, OH.

30. Erica Lynette Edwards, e-mail message to the author, August 1, 2011.

31. Zide-Booth, classes.

32. Ibid.

33. Burke, quoted in Mattingly, "The Joffrey Ballet School at Fifty," 50.

34. Zide-Booth, interview.

35. Zide-Booth, classes.

36. Ibid.

37. Ibid.

38. Zide-Booth, interview.

39. Suki Schorer, *Suki Schorer on Balanchine Technique* (New York: Knopf, 1999): 145–46.

40. Zide-Booth, interview.

41. Amy Womer Wrobleski, e-mail message to the author, August 4, 2011.

42. Zide-Booth, interview.

43. David Leddick, "A School with a View," *Dance Magazine* (August 1960): 48.

44. Sasha Anawalt, "Joffrey, Robert," *American National Biography* (American Council of Learned Societies, Oxford University Press, 2000), accessed July 15, 2007, available with an Ohio State University password at http://www.anb.org.proxy.lib.ohio-state.edu/articles/18/18-00631. html.

45. Leddick, 50.

46. Aaron Selissen, e-mail message to the author, August 4, 2011.

47. Zide-Booth, interview.

48. Ibid.

49. Ibid.

50. John A. Crow and Harriet Hoctor, "The Greatest Thrill," *American Dancer* (April 1936): 8.

51. Wrobleski.

52. Marion Horosko, "Mme. Anderson-Ivantzova: A Little Bolshoi on 56 St.," *Dance Magazine* (June 1965): 56.

53. Rochelle Zide-Booth, teaching seminar, March 2007, Canton Ballet, Canton, OH.

54. Zide-Booth, classes.

55. Zide-Booth, interview.

56. Ibid.

57. Zide-Booth, classes.

58. Zide-Booth, interview.

59. Zide-Booth, classes.

60. Robert Joffrey, "Robert Joffrey Ballet Workshop," DVD, videotaped at the Ruth Page Foundation School of Dance (Chicago, 1976).

61. According to Zide-Booth, this alignment is similar to the alignment developed by the well-known New York instructor from the same period Maggie Black, and it is also similar to the placement used in the Merce Cunningham technique (Zide-Booth, interview).

62. Horosko, "Little Bolshoi," 56.

63. Zide-Booth, interview.

64. Zide-Booth, "Dancing," 51.

65. Zide-Booth, interview.

66. Ibid.

67. Joffrey.

68. Ibid.

69. Zide-Booth, classes.

70. Joffrey.

71. Ibid.

72. While studying with Hoctor at age five, Zide-Booth maintains that she was executing quintuple *pirouettes*.

73. Zide-Booth, classes.

74. Ibid.

75. Zide-Booth, interview.

76. Gilbert Vernon, "Margot Fonteyn: A Personal Tribute," *Dance Chronicle* 14, no. 2–3 (1991): 227.

77. Zide-Booth, interview.

78. Ibid.

79. Walter Ware, *Ballet Is Magic: A Triple Monograph* (New York: IHRA, 1936): 7.

80. My first experience with Zide-Booth's coaching was at Butler University in 1999, where she taught me the title role for the first act of *Giselle*. I worked with her later that year as the Sugar Plum Fairy in the opening of Act II in *The Nutcracker*, and most recently in 2007 for the "Prelude" variation from *Les Sylphides*.

81. Rochelle Zide-Booth, rehearsal, March 2007, Canton Ballet, Canton, OH.

82. Ibid.

83. Ibid.

PART THREE
In the Shape of Written Records

UNLIKE OTHER ART forms that endure as artifacts, dance is both fixed and unstable at the same time. It exists in the form of scores and notated symbols as well as in the visions of choreographers and the muscle memories of dancers. The chapters in Part Three explore the process of translating a visual text, or score, into kinesthesia, and of translating dance into another symbolic language. Thus one line of inquiry looks at how movement can be unlocked from symbols, while a parallel line examines how specific recording systems serve to encapsulate the kinesthetic properties of a dance form in its unique historical moment. All five chapters in this part of the book employ both lines of examination in considering the particular subjects at hand.

Any notational construct is limited by both its application (memory aid, preservation, descriptive tool) and the cultural and individual values of its creators and users; the recognition of this fact presents both challenges and opportunities for the researcher. The viewpoints of the authors in the following chapters reveal understanding of both the special value and the limitations of graphic representations of movement. This includes the inherent mistrust many performing artists bring to written documents being placed alongside embodied experience. In this regard, the expertise of the authors within Part Three as dancers themselves is particularly enriching. Among the opportunities offered by such representations are the ability to consider a dance within alternate frames, and to learn about times and places removed from the here and now; scores open up dance languages of the past and provide materials for analytic and interpretive modes of inquiry through translational processes.

Further, the idea of representing the body or the dance in spatial terms forms a persistent pattern through Western dance history, and it is reflected not only in this part but elsewhere throughout the book as well. Catherine Turocy's chapter on teaching Baroque dance in Part Two concerns itself with how spatial models have formed the basis for dance as early as the Renaissance. Other chapters in that part on choreography employ Laban Movement Analysis with its Platonic solids models (octahedron, icosahedron) to underpin notions about how choreographic use of space both clarifies craft and unlocks meaning. From da Vinci's Vitruvian Man standing inside the circle and the square, to Laban's conception of the dancer inside a dynamic kinesphere, we find a thread of interest in how movement both creates and is determined by its spatial environment. As a performing art that also progresses through time, dance shares much with music, with its highly developed notational system. Two chapters below expand our view of several dances by examining the music-dance interaction through close score reading.

In "Recording the Imperial Ballet: Anatomy and Ballet in Stepanov's Notation," Sheila Marion focuses on the creation of a young Russian whose scores played a pivotal role in the development of the ballet tradition in Europe during a volatile period in history. Marion examines the capacity of the Stepanov notation to record the 19th-century ballets, while she also analyzes the system's grounding in the practical exigencies of ballet of that era and in the experiences and demands of classical dancers and their *régisseurs*. She points out as well how the notation revealed the "geometric beauty" of Petipa's work and was particular in its attention to anatomical description.

Rebecca Schwartz-Bishir's chapter brings *musique dansante* into the purview of dance historiography, explains how it works, and shows how it can inform us about the dancing of the past. Generally dismissed as light, tuneful, but ultimately insubstantial accompaniments to (mostly) forgotten ballets, this hoary musical tradition bears re-examination, argues the author in "Musical Expression in the Bournonville-Løvenskjold *La Sylphide* Variation." The music of specialist ballet composers deserves further study, as these artists were highly successful in their ability to write music that imitates, reflects and supports the kinesthetic properties of the *danse d'école*. Bishir's "musico-choreographic" examination of the first Sylph variation, *La Sylphide*, offers a detailed exposition of structure and phrasing, along with specific terms such as melody, meter and articulation.

As does Marion in her Stepanov chapter, Victoria Watts moves from her inward, dance-specific perspective to make larger claims about several notation systems emerging from the needs and ethos of their unique times and particular cultures. Dance notation presents an object of inquiry through which to explore the inherent corporeality of vision while at the same time allowing the reader to follow the author's firsthand experience in reading and writing scores. In "Archives of Embodiment: Visual Culture and the Practice of Score Reading," Watts intends her "thick description" of that process as an invitation to the reader to enjoy a more embodied examination than previous texts have provided. She begins with a comparative analysis of two Labanotated scores of George Balanchine's

Serenade, overlaying her questions about embodiment and the historical evolution of notation systems with theories drawn from Visual Culture Studies.

"Reading Music, Gesture, and Dualism in Mark Morris' *Dido and Aeneas*" considers Morris' piece in its parallel layers of content and structure across music, text and movement. Rachael Riggs-Leyva uncovers the unifying aspects that lie within a work that joins Virgil's text, Henry Purcell's score of the 17th century, and 20th-century American modern dance. Symbolic gestures and other repeated, recognizable figures are traced across time and genre and are found to be corresponding on several levels within the dance; Riggs-Leyva pays special attention to how these correspondences help underpin the colorful characterizations within Morris' dramatic work.

Candace Feck's experiences as a teacher of university courses that require writing about dance prompted her as a researcher to investigate what lay beneath those responses. In "What's in a Dance? The Complexity of Information in Writings About Dance," Feck takes the opportunity "to render visible the information that dwells within the dance experience by looking at the threads of information woven together" in the papers of nine students writing about a repertory dance concert. Through the analytic framework Feck creates to enlarge and illuminate these texts, the reader is invited to peer into the process of constructing knowledge on several levels, and to consider the breadth and depth of dance as an art form.

12

Recording the Imperial Ballet

ANATOMY AND BALLET IN STEPANOV'S NOTATION

Sheila Marion with Karen Eliot

UNLOCKING DOORS TO BALLET'S IMPERIAL PAST

The Stepanov notation system, devised just prior to the turn of the twentieth century by Vladimir Ivanovich Stepanov, emerged at a pivotal moment in dance's history. It was introduced during the culmination of Marius Petipa's reign over the Imperial Russian Ballet; Serge Diaghilev and his Ballets Russes would soon launch forays into Western Europe, where they would re-introduce ballet as "a magnet for artists of genius and meeting ground for a sophisticated, international elite."[1] Although out of use and fairly obscure today, the notation is probably best known for its role in helping to bring the magnificence of the nineteenth-century Imperial ballet repertory from St. Petersburg to audiences in the West.

Stepanov's notation was one of the few early systems to have been used extensively for recording and staging dances. It was the first fully developed system to modify musical notes and use them as a basis for movement signs to indicate timing, and to directly connect the dance steps with a musical score.[2] It was also the first dance notation system to be developed out of an anatomical analysis of human movement.[3] Its importance to scholars today resides in its potential as a resource for dance historians interested in reconstructing the nineteenth-century repertory and deducing period style. Further, an analysis of the system prompts questions for the dance notator about whether any system is truly capable of both documenting dances and translating the body's movement with anatomical accuracy. A flawed documentation system, Stepanov notation nevertheless has the potential to unlock doors to ballet's imperial past.

STEPANOV AND THE IMPERIAL RUSSIAN BALLET

Stepanov was a twenty-six-year-old artist of the Imperial Theaters of St. Petersburg at the time his system was published in 1892. Just two years before, Imperial balletmaster Marius Petipa and composer Piotr Ilyitch Tchaikovsky had premiered their ballet *The Sleeping Beauty*. The ballet, which has come to be regarded as a masterwork, exemplified the "golden age" of the Imperial Russian Ballet. Petipa's long reign over the Maryinsky Ballet would soon end, but his "stewardship of the company had an incalculable effect on Russian ballet," explains historian Lynn Garafola:

> He presided over the shift from romanticism to what is usually termed ballet "classicism," laid the foundation of the modern Russian school by marrying the new Italian bravura technique to its more lyrical French counterpart and helped transform an art dominated by foreigners and identified with the West into a Russian national expression. Petipa choreographed scores of ballets and innumerable dances, codifying their structure while expanding the lexicon of their movements, and created several generations of distinguished dancers.[4]

However, as Tim Scholl notes, "if the 1890 *Sleeping Beauty* marked the creative apogee of nineteenth-century Russian ballet, the system that brought that ballet to the stage was fast approaching obsolescence by the turn of the century." More progressive-minded dance makers and aficionados already referred to Petipa's work as the "old" ballet.[5] Stepanov's system was introduced at this juncture—between Petipa's greatest triumphs and the passing of the torch to a younger generation of choreographers, including the reform-minded Michel Fokine.

Stepanov became a member of the corps de ballet of the Maryinsky Theater on his graduation from the theater school in 1885. He had been performing with the company for four years when he obtained permission to attend classes at the University of St. Petersburg. During his two years of study there in anatomy and anthropology, he devised his system of movement notation. It was demonstrated to the ballet company officials in 1891. An affidavit of its usefulness was signed by, among others, Petipa and his assistant Lev Ivanov[6]—though Petipa was later to question using notation for revivals, writing that "skeletons...have no place in the choreographic art," and that a talented ballet master "will not come to lose his time and effort copying what was done by others long before."[7]

The demonstration won Stepanov a small stipend to continue his studies in Paris with neurologist Jean Martin Charcot, and it was there that the system was published. On his return to St. Petersburg, Stepanov gave another demonstration of his system. This was more extensive and practical than the first. It involved students writing sequences in the notation that were then read and performed by other students, and a revival of a ballet from notation for an examination performance. As a result of this successful demonstration, the system was adopted into the curriculum of the theater school and Stepanov appointed as its instructor.[8]

Two years later Stepanov was sent to Moscow to teach his system at the Bolshoi Theater School. While there he became ill, probably with tuberculosis contracted during his stay in Paris.[9] He died in early 1896, at the age of thirty. Meanwhile, his friend Alexander Gorsky, who was later to become highly respected in Russia as an innovative choreographer, assumed Stepanov's teaching of the system in St. Petersburg. Gorsky, says Natalia Roslavleva, "considered it his moral duty to continue in Stepanov's steps" and made refinements and published a table of signs geared more to teaching the notation than was Stepanov's book, which had been organized in terms of anatomical possibilities of the body. Gorsky also compiled and published exercises and choreographic examples for study.[10]

In 1898 Gorsky staged Petipa's *Sleeping Beauty* for Moscow's Bolshoi ballet, ostensibly from the dance score, although there is some question about whether or not he actually relied on the notation.[11] Around this time he also composed his own ballet *Clorinda*, using notation instead of setting it directly on dancers. The piece was then staged for a student examination performance in which the performers read their parts from the dance score.[12] Soon after these performances and the publication of his classroom studies, Gorsky was transferred to Moscow to become ballet master of the Bolshoi. Nikolai Grigorevich Sergeyev, who had been his assistant, replaced him at the Maryinsky in teaching the notation.

It was there, for the first time, that a major ballet company attempted to have a large part of its repertory notated.[13] Most of the dance scores were notated during Sergeyev's tenure as notation teacher and régisseur. They were probably recorded by his assistants Alexander Chekrygin and Victor Rakhmanov, though, rather than by Sergeyev himself.[14] When Sergeyev left Russia during the 1917 revolution, he took with him the scores of twenty-four ballets and the dances from twenty-four operas. Subsequently, using scores and probably his memory, he revived classics such as *Swan Lake, Giselle, Coppélia, Sleeping Beauty* and *The Nutcracker* for companies in England and Western Europe from the 1920s until his death in 1951.[15]

Other choreographers who used the notation to record their works were Vaslav Nijinsky and Léonide Massine.[16] Both had learned the notation while students in the Russian theater school. In 1976, Massine published his ideas on choreography with an explanation of his slightly modified version of Stepanov dance notation and his own choreographic studies recorded in the system.[17] Nijinsky, while under house arrest in Budapest during World War I, notated his ballet *Afternoon of a Faun* in his own notation system, which also derived from Stepanov.

A number of factors are thought to have contributed to the demise of Stepanov notation after its initial period of official acceptance and relatively intense use. The system has been criticized for its inability to notate the details of the arm and torso movements, which were beginning to be emphasized in Fokine's choreography.[18] The practice in writing the Maryinsky scores was to record predominantly footwork,[19] but this is not surprising given that dancers in the classical tradition were trained in the conventional arm and body movements for the corresponding "steps." But, an examination of the system shows that it is capable of recording movements of the arms and body as well as the legs. Had he lived, Stepanov might have continued to develop the notation and adapt it in order to record more easily the newer choreographic style. Gorsky made some changes and refinements for his Table of Signs, but he grew critical of the system and did not use it to notate his later ballets.

Another factor contributing to the disuse of the system, suggested by scholar Roland John Wiley, may have been colleagues' hatred for Sergeyev, a bureaucratic martinet known for his political intrigues and capricious dealings with artists.[20] Petipa may have resented the notation when he found his ballets reproduced, for additional pay, by Sergeyev.[21] And as Sergeyev was closely associated with the notation for many years, but apparently lacked facility with it,[22] contempt toward him may have carried over to the notation itself. When Sergeyev left Russia in 1918, he took all the notated scores with him. They were not accessible to scholars or other ballet masters until more than fifty years later, when in 1969, Mona Inglesby sold them to the Harvard Theater Collection.[23]

EXAMINING THE NOTATION: RECORDING CLASSICISM

The most striking and visually accessible features of Stepanov notation are the musical notes and the elaborate plans for the dance's movement through the stage space. The music notes, which are adapted to convey movement information, require deciphering, but the stage plans do not (Figure 12.1).

The designs in the stage space of both individual movement and groupings can be notated, and the large groups with symmetrical patterning and mirroring actions, common to the nineteenth-century ballet, are also well recorded. The notation system reflects the choreography for which it was designed, recording to great effect the "spectacle, symmetry and repetition" of Petipa's dances.[24] (Figure 12.2) Spectacle was achieved by mass, as Petipa's casts were large in comparison to today's staging of the ballets from this era (Figure 12.3). Wiley notes, for instance, that the "Shades" scene of La Bayadere was performed with forty-eight dancers, and that there were sixty dancers in the "Snowflake" section of The Nutcracker.[25]

Sometimes the dancers themselves became the background. Dance critic André Levinson, writing in 1918, described the effect:

The *danseuses* are usually arranged in rows forming a right angle. The geometric structure increases the unity and impressiveness of the mass movement. In her variations the soloist contrasts with this unified background. Another frequent device is arranging the corps de ballet in two rows along the sides of the stage such that they accompany the ballerina or a group of soloists with even, uniform body positions. The path of their dance outlines geometric figures and precisely straight lines.[26]

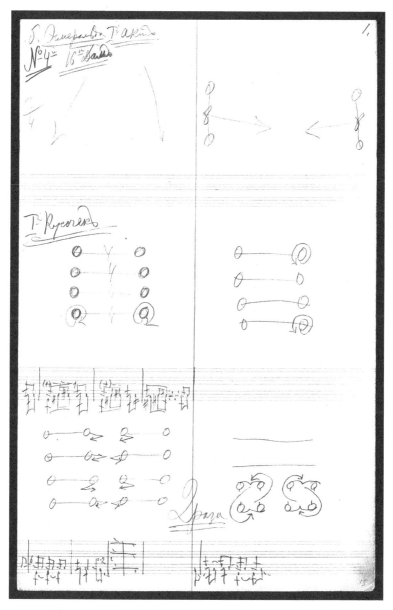

FIGURE 12.1 Nikolai Sergeev dance notations and music scores for ballets, bMS Thr 245 (117), sequence 16, Cesare Pugni, *Esmeralda*. Houghton Library, Harvard University, Cambridge, MA.

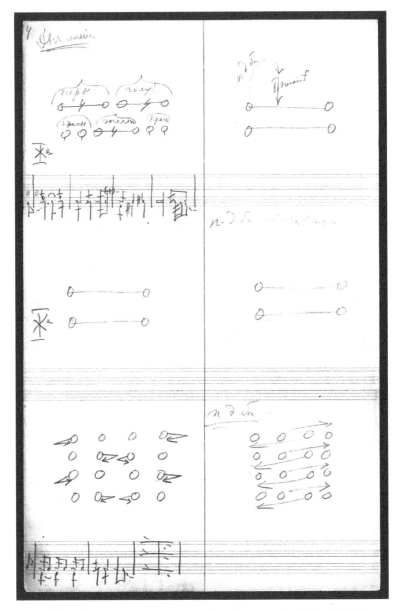

FIGURE 12.2 Nikolai Sergeev dance notations and music scores for ballets, bMS Thr 245 (117), sequence 19, Cesare Pugni, *Esmeralda*. Houghton Library, Harvard University, Cambridge, MA.

The corps de ballet often danced in unison, and the choreography emphasized geometric figures and symmetrical formations. The ballet ensemble in its "most perfect form (as preserved for us by Marius Petipa)," according to Levinson, is based on "the aesthetic principle of 'unity within diversity'" represented by "harmonious movements of a group of dancers—movements which are not only identical in form . . . but which also coincide in time."[27] To Deborah Jowitt, Petipa's ensemble "became an impersonal force—garlands and frames

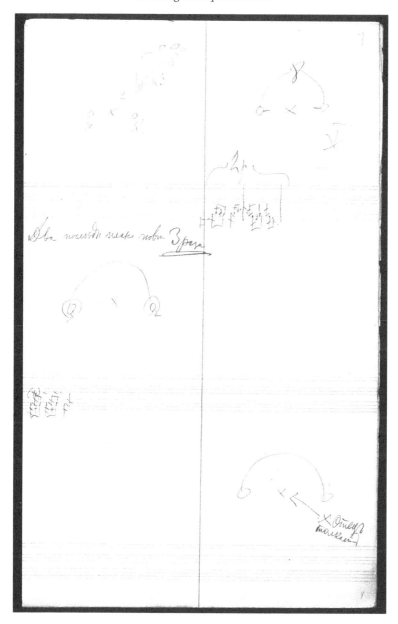

FIGURE 12.3 Nikolai Sergeev dance notations and music scores for ballets, bMS Thr 245 (117), sequence 14, Cesare Pugni, *The Little Humpbacked Horse*. Houghton Library, Harvard University, Cambridge, MA.

and lakes of women...."[28] The "geometric beauty [which] astounded Petipa's contemporaries," according to Russian writer Oleg Petrov, "could elicit a sense of pleasure in the theater and make the audience forget everything that fell short of such beauty." Geometry represented beauty in an idealized world, "in which morality takes on aesthetic form and good and evil become the beautiful and the ugly." Petrov notes that "geometry in Petipa's dances can be found where 'eternal themes' are concentrated."²⁹ The visuality of the stage plans seen in the notation, the clarity of the connections between the movement and the stage plans and the elaborate methods for showing repeated material reflect a concern for staging and patterning that was almost as great as the interest in the dancers' steps.

Stepanov's stage plans show in overhead view the patterns and paths of the dancers in the stage space. Dotted lines and arrows mark where the dancers travel. Pin-like pointers give their orientations and locations onstage at the beginning of each new plan. The pointers show gender: black for a man, white for a woman.³⁰

Plans are read from the dancer's rather than the director's point of view, with the audience side of the boxed plan toward the top of the page.³¹ This perspective suggests the position of a régisseur onstage with the dancers, setting and rehearsing the formations and paths, rather than of a choreographer or director in the theater's house checking their effect

To identify dancers, numbers are placed alongside the notation staffs as well as on the plans (Figures 12.4.1, 12.4.2). Letters above the staffs, sometimes connected by a dotted horizontal line, correlate the dance measures with the location and traveling shown on the plans. Capital letters identify the start of a new plan (lettering begins again with each new page and is not consecutive throughout a sequence). Lowercase letters mark multiple path segments on an individual plan.³² The various connections between the dancers' staffs and the stage plans are simple but clear. Even without training in Stepanov's system, knowledge of music notation could allow one to follow a ballet's score and see its changing choreographic patterns in the stage space, its rhythms and the correlation of both with the music.

Stepanov's notation also shows its roots in Petipa's classicism in the employment of a variety of signs for repeated movement. Repeats of exercises and side-to-side reversal are typical in the ballet classroom, but the number of devices to show repetition indicate that it had substantial choreographic use as well. Petipa frequently called attention to a

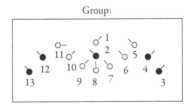

FIGURE 12.4.1 Numbers identify dancers.

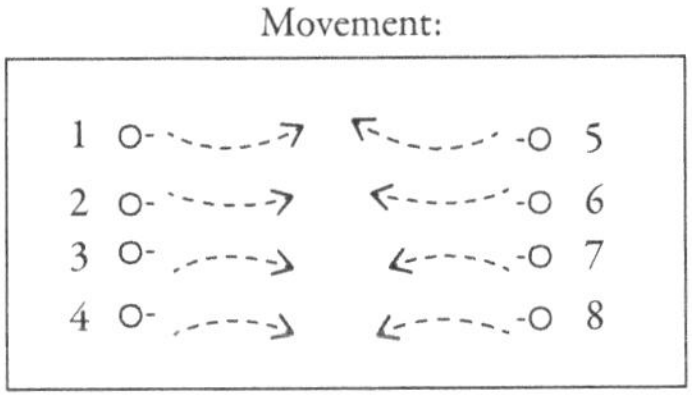

FIGURE 12.4.2 Lines indicate traveling.

particular action by repeating a step or short phrase several times before varying it. An example of extended repeats occurs in the "Shades" scene of Petipa's *La Bayadère*. The corps de ballet, dressed in white tutus, enters single file. Each dancer performs an arabesque, followed by a backbend, and then takes several steps to make room for the next dancer. With each dancer's entrance the phrase is performed again as the line of dancers snakes downstage. Jowitt describes the effect: "the entire act is an opium dream of the bereaved and anguished Solor.... The dance of the *bayadères* has a narcotized slowness and evenness; it suggests a blurring of the hero's vision: seeking one woman in the spirit world, he finds her endlessly multiplied."[33]

Repeated material is identified in the notation by a diagonal line or lines flanked by two dots or four, depending on the length of the lines and the length of the material to be repeated. (Gorsky shows a double line for repeats in his explanatory text and examples but uses single lines in all the choreographic examples.)[34] The lines slant up to the right for an exact repetition, or down to the right for a repeat on the other side.

A number can be placed above a sign to show how many times a brief action should be executed.[35] Or, as shown in Gorsky's choreographic examples, a longer sequence of several measures can be bracketed at the top of the staff with a word note such as "3 times" or "2 times."[36] When dancers' numbers are placed in a box next to the staff, it means thatthey should perform the movement on the other leg, and to the other side (Figures 12.5.1, 12.5.2).[37]

In addition to repeats of several types, Stepanov shows examples of movement in both fully analyzed and simplified versions, suggesting that the abbreviated version could be used once the step was understood.[38] Also, particular movement features that are present throughout a dance can be written as "clefs" at the beginning of a score. Stepanov and Gorsky show a "classical dance clef," in which signs for second degree rotation of the legs

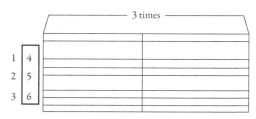

FIGURE 12.5.1 Repeat seven times. Dancers 1–3 as written; dancers 4–6 other side. Movement is repeated three times during two measures.

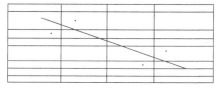

FIGURE 12.5.2 Examples of repeats. Repeat to the opposite side. Repeat two measures to the same side. Repeat four measures to the opposite side.

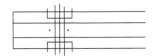

FIGURE 12.6   Classical dance clef showing outward rotation of the legs.

are placed at the beginning of the staff for the legs. This suggests that other "clefs" could be used to identify the central components of a style (Figure 12.6).[39]

The devices for showing repeated material and correlating dance movements, stage patterns and music were not part of Stepanov's original exegesis. Though they seem to have been given a great deal of attention and to be very clearly worked out, these devices are not shown in Stepanov's text and are only briefly mentioned in Gorsky's. The latter's excerpts from choreographic scores, however, show how they work. The devices probably were developed during the process of recording the Maryinsky ballets in order to show the choreographic patterns.

EXAMINING THE NOTATION: MUSIC, ANATOMY AND BALLETIC CONVENTIONS

Although little has been written about Stepanov's design of the system or his intentions for its use,[40] inferences can be drawn from his choices for the framework of the notation and the circumstances surrounding the development of the system. The notation reflects three major influences. One is the connection of music and dance, which is shown by his choice of musical notes as carriers for movement information. Another is his interest in anatomy, as reflected in his description of joint actions. The third is the balletic context, which modifies the notation's anatomical description of movement.

Of these three influences, the use of musical notes is the most visually striking. The modified musical notes not only indicate timing but also show aspects of movement by their shapes, placement on the movement staff and additional marks on their stems. The use of modified musical notes to convey movement information demonstrates the strong movement-music link in Petipa's choreography, a relationship that assumed even greater prominence in his work with Tchaikovsky.

Tchaikovsky's *The Sleeping Beauty*, like earlier ballet music, was composed to Petipa's dictates; nevertheless, the new ballet score was more musically complex than previous dance accompaniment had been, and it posed novel challenges to the performers. Roland John Wiley describes the dancers' "internal resistance" to the music as they began to work with it during the rehearsal process: "each variation went beyond the usual formulas to which the ear was accustomed," writes Wiley, citing composer Ricardo Drigo as his source.[41] Possibly because the music was more complex than the specialist music of the past, Stepanov decided that adapting musical notes for movement signs would clarify the music and dance relationship in the dance notation. The principal aspect of music

FIGURE 12.7 The round note shows jumping or gestures in the air; the oblong note indicates contact with the ground. The downward stem is for the right leg and arm, the upward stem is for the left. The conjoined note shows fifth position of the feet, right leg in front.

notation used is rhythm. In their introductions to the system, both Stepanov and Gorsky show this aspect of the music-movement relationship, citing, as an example, Thoinot Arbeau's sixteenth-century method of writing step names alongside the musical notes to convey rhythm. Stepanov furthers the relationship by using musical notes themselves to convey movement information.

Simplicity seems to have been another of Stepanov's goals. In his introduction, he described his attempt to create a kind of "alphabet," and stated that the point of departure for his system was the analysis of the human body in simple elementary movements, using signs that were themselves extremely simple.[42] The musical notes are indeed a highly economical way to render movement. The shape of the note, oblong or round, determines whether a body part is in contact with the ground or in the air. Extending the note's stem up or down indicates either left or right side. Putting the stem on the right or left of the note, in a position of the feet for example, indicates whether a leg is in front or behind (Figure 12.7).

Placement of the note on the lines or spaces on the staff shows the body part and the type and degrees of movement of its proximal joint. Signs for modifications or additional movements are attached to the note stem. The notes show the relative duration of the movement in the same way that they are designed to show musical rhythms. The note head is open for half notes, filled in for quarter notes, etc. Whole notes are not used because the note's stem is an important indicator. Like a musical score, the notation is read from left to right with direction of reading representing the flow of time. Division of the body into units for recording is accomplished in two ways. One is by means of the staff and movement signs or "notes"[43] for recording "principal" movements (actions of the shoulder and hip joints). The other is by additional signs placed on or alongside the notes for "secondary" movements.

There are some subtle differences between movement and musical timing. Musical notes tend to be discrete and separate tones, accomplished directly and then maintained for a particular amount of time. In movement, though, the amount of time required to move a limb through space might vary. Held "notes" represent held positions. For slow, continuous movement, notes are tied together with a line similar to a musical phrasing bow, or transitions through intermediate positions are written out.[44]

FIGURE 12.8 The Stepanov notation staff, with clefs. The clef's dots show normal positions for the trunk, arms and legs.

In his chapter on anatomy, Stepanov divides the skeleton into three main parts, the head, trunk and limbs; but he locates both head and trunk on one staff.[45] Arms and legs each have a staff, stacked vertically with space between them. The top part, consisting of two lines, is for the head and trunk. The middle group of three lines is for the arms, and the bottom section of four lines is for the legs. A "clef" placed at the beginning of each staff identifies the body part and shows the normal, or starting, position. The clefs and the number of staff lines identify the body part so units can be recorded individually, out of context of the whole, for example when an exercise concentrates on footwork and the arms and torso are not important, or when usage could be assumed to be conventional (Figure 12.8).

Positions—what Stepanov calls the principal movements—are considered to be flexion, abduction and (hyper)extension at the hip and shoulder joints, resulting in the directions forward, side and back for the limbs and torso. These are shown by arranging notes on the lines and spaces of the staffs in tiers to represent positions around the body at angles of 45° and 90° or more, with notes farther away from the starting position (marked by the clef) designating the more extreme range.

Placement for the principal movements varies for each of the three staffs. Notes fan out symmetrically from a center space for actions of the legs. For arm movements (with one exception), notes progress upward, and for motion of the torso notes proceed downward (Figure 12.9.1).

Although the system is not pictorially based, there is visual significance to the placement of the notes on each staff. For the torso, the lower notes represent the increase in range, as the dancer bends. Arm movements (with the exception of 45° backwards, which is marked below the space for normal) continue to rise through forward and side as the notes rise. Directions for the legs are easiest to visualize by turning the page of notation on its side. Then notes on lines or spaces are seen as symmetrical for each leg in the three principal movements; right and left note stems are to the right and left of the body, and stem placement for the forward or backward relationship is in front of or in behind the note.

Stepanov's "principal movements" represent large motions of the torso and limbs as a whole, and only in the major directions of forward, side and back. Because of the anatomical differences between the joints, the same note arrangement does not work for all. For example, movement for the torso occurs to both sides, but Stepanov shows only abduction, movement away to one side, for the arms and legs. Reaching across the body

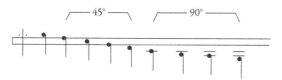

FIGURE 12.9.1 Principal movement of the torso (bending at the hips): forward, right side, back, left side.

is not truly a sideward movement, but its omission makes note correspondence for torso, arms and legs impossible. Similarly, the range of movement Stepanov gives for the arms and legs differs. Movement of the arm is restricted to 45° behind but can be recorded up to 180° forward and side, while the leg is given a range of 90° in each direction. (Figures 12.9.2, 12.9.3, 12.9.4)

The complementary signs for secondary movements are relatively few, reflecting modifications of the principle movements and other basic joint actions, including flexion and extension, abduction and adduction, rotation and circumduction (Figure 12.10).

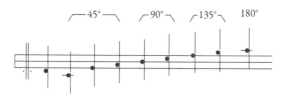

FIGURE 12.9.2 Principal movements of both arms: extension (back), then flexion (forward) and abduction (side).

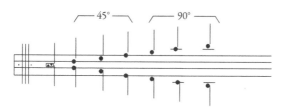

FIGURE 12.9.3 Principal movements of both legs: flexion (forward), abduction (side), extension (back).

FIGURE 12.9.4 The torso bent forward 45°. The right arm lifted forward 45°. The right leg lifted forward 45°.

FIGURE 12.10 Signs from left: secondary flexion and extension; abduction and adduction; rotation right, left, first and second degree; circumduction clockwise, counterclockwise.

Adding the signs to the note stems allows actions to be combined or modify one another. The note stems can carry quite a bit of information, including rotation and movement of the knee, elbow or upper body. This is in addition to the information conveyed by the note itself: right or left limb, relationship of limbs in front or behind, contact—or not—with the floor, and the angle of the principal movement (Figure 12.11).

For positions that fall between the usual 45° angles, signs can be added to increase or decrease the angle of each type of action.[46] If these signs enhance or diminish a principal movement, they are placed above any secondary movement signs; otherwise they are placed directly below the sign they modify.

Although the movement notation is designed to be written along with the music, in practice the two elements are usually recorded separately, and only a few pivotal segments of the music are identified in the dance score. Music notation, when it is included, is placed at the top of the page. Where the musical notation is included, staffs for the dancers are placed directly underneath the music staffs and bar lines are drawn through all the staffs. Double bar lines mark the beginning and ending of a section. Depending on the number of dancers, a brace of staffs may take a full page, or several may appear on a single page. Note values, measure numbers and time signatures are the same in the dance notation as in the musical notation, and musical expressions such as adagio, allegro, moderato and presto give the general tempo. For more specific timing a metronome marking can be added.

Although the stage plans and adapted music notes reflect the choreographic concerns and ballet technique of Stepanov's era, the notation's framework is based on an anatomical description of movement. Surprisingly, Stepanov's was not only the first dance notation system to focus on anatomy as the basis for movement description but it was also the only major system to do so. Though other movement notations are based on the visual design of the body, Stepanov's was the first to describe movements of the whole body by a method other than figure drawing.

The eighteenth-century Beauchamps-Feuillet notation, for example, concentrated on the dancer's footwork and pathways through the performance area. In the nineteenth century, probably in response to the more expressive Romantic ballet, several systems based on modified stick figures opened up possibilities for showing movements of the upper body. Stepanov was familiar with Arthur Saint-Léon's notation[47]; he was also aware of Friedrich Albert Zorn's notation, which was published in Germany two years before he embarked on

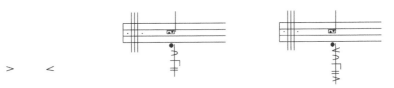

FIGURE 12.11 Signs for augment, diminish. Right hip flexed 90°, abducted (leg forward right) and outwardly rotated, knee bent 90°. The same with leg height decreased and knee bend increased.

his quest. Both systems were based on modified stick figure drawings. There are some hints in Stepanov's writing that he aspired to develop a system that would be more anatomically based than his predecessors' stick figures; he hoped to find a universal solution to the problem of recording human movement. Basing his notation on a scientific study of the body, particularly its skeletal structure, must have seemed to accomplish just that.

CONTEXTUALIZING THE NOTATION: A CULTURE OF SCIENCE AND A NOSTALGIA FOR THE PAST

Basing movement description on anatomy would seem to be one of the simplest and most logical means of recording human movement: there are only so many possibilities for actions in the joints. If one could designate the type and range of each joint action, one could theoretically describe all human movement. Stepanov's system, though, illustrates the difficulties of applying anatomical description to dance. An anatomically based notation system might serve to help dancers understand the functions of particular joints, but this did not interest Stepanov; he regarded notation as a tool for preserving works, for sketching dances prior to their staging and for developing choreographic theory.[48]

Perhaps because his focus was on recording choreography rather than examining technique, Stepanov did not follow strict anatomical analysis. His system contains movement descriptions that do not conform to standard joint ranges, even allowing for the extended range of a ballet dancer. And often his analysis does not express what is required to accomplish a particular movement. It seems unlikely, though, that his knowledge was deficient. He had studied anatomy for several years, and the field was highly developed. It is more likely that his descriptive framework was at odds with the style of movement he was recording. Anatomical description focuses on changes in the angles of joints, while ballet emphasizes the classically defined linearity of body design. Stepanov compromised the anatomical description to allow the notation to more efficiently record the ballet vocabulary. As a result, the system is an uneasy blend of anatomical and spatial description. Such compromise provokes speculation about why Stepanov chose an anatomically based system in the first place. It may be he hoped to give the notation the cachet of science at a time when science and technology were dramatically affecting people's daily lives.

Beginning in the 1890s, Russia experienced a "surge towards industrialization," as the Russian finance minister, Sergei Witte, acted to counter the country's backwardness, inaugurating "new industry and rail lines—including the Trans-Siberian Railroad stretching to the Pacific," and investors moved into eastern reaches of Asia.[49] Excitement about technology and scientific innovation co-existed with a deep conservatism and nostalgic regard for the past. A repressive political atmosphere followed upon the assassination of Russian Tsar Alexander II in 1881; many artists and idealists, according to James Billington, were left with unfulfilled hopes for reform and "fled from the broad arena of history to private worlds of lyric lament."[50] In the ballet, this conservatism was exemplified by *The*

Sleeping Beauty, which was created during "a period of classical revival in Russian culture." Tim Scholl explains that *The Sleeping Beauty* was an ideal vehicle to introduce the "'classical' origins of theatrical dancing to the Petersburg public," much the way that "many Russian artists would begin to revive classical themes in their work."[51] In the creation of his notation system, Stepanov no doubt responded to the conservatism of the era, as much as he did to a general confidence in the possibilities of science to create positive change.[52]

APPLYING THE SYSTEM

The special use of anatomical terms, critical to Stepanov's notation as well as to my comparison of anatomical measures, can be easily referenced by a simple exercise. First, bring your hand up to touch your shoulder and note the elbow *flexion*. Now if you straighten your arm, that action is *extension*. But if you can make your elbow bend backward as some people can, that is *hyperextension* (hyperextension occurs easily at the wrist).

If you move your arm to the side, away from your body, that is *abduction*, while *adduction* is the opposite movement, just as extension is the opposite of flexion. *Rotation* is a twisting action, and *circumduction*, making a circle with the arm, requires a combination of actions. In addition to these six categories of anatomical description, the system accounts for the range of movement, i.e., the degree of flexion, extension, abduction, adduction, etc. For each movement there are thus two qualifiers, the type of action and the degree.

Stepanov's notation is based on positions with movement implied by transitions through the positions. Gorsky writes that

> strictly speaking, we do not notate the movements of the human body; we notate precisely only the poses, that is, the extreme points of each given movement. Taking into account that movements are produced from point to point in a straight line, we in our notating must show exactly every deviation from this straight line; then we must turn our attention to what kind of character the transition from one point to the next has.[53]

The focus on positions corresponds to and probably derives from a similar emphasis in ballet, where the body is sustained in classical poses, or where a clearly defined position may serve as a transitional movement to another position. Anatomical description, however, allows either position or action, and this is where the first major discrepancy occurs between anatomical description and Stepanov's notation.[54] For example, Stepanov uses the terms *flexion* and *extension* differently than would a strict anatomical description. To show a change from a very flexed position to one that is less so, he records the new position as a degree of flexion. However, in anatomical terms, this would be called extension (because it is the act of extending rather than bending the joint). Stepanov, though, uses "extension" only for positions of the arms and legs behind the body, or when a joint is bent backward (hyperextension in anatomical terms).[55]

Stepanov reduces the principal movements of the limbs and torso to the directions forward (flexion), sideways (abduction), and backward (extension).[56] The directions probably reflect the standard repetition of ballet exercises *en croix*, in which an action begins forward and then is repeated to the side and to the back. He establishes a scale of 45° intervals to measure the amount of movement (Figure 12.12).

To accommodate what he refers to as "the choreographic art," Stepanov enlarges the conventional anatomical measures. For flexion, abduction and (hyper)extension of the hips, Stepanov says that the maximum angles, according to anatomical measure, are 76°, 45° and 10° respectively. However, because the angle can be enlarged by an accompanying inclination of the pelvis when only one foot is on the ground, he gives a range of 90° in each direction.[57] Something of the period style can be gleaned from this 90° maximum height for the legs. Today's ballet dancers extend their legs much higher and still maintain the illusion of little displacement elsewhere. Stepanov does say that forward flexion can achieve an angle of 115°, but he qualifies this by stating that the knee must be bent.

For the principal angles of the shoulder (movements of the arms), Stepanov lists anatomical measures as 64° forward, 65° sideways, and 21° backward.[58] Because the range can be extended through involvement of the scapula, he allows a maximum of 180° forward and sideways in the notation. Backward movement, (hyper)extension for the arms, is limited to 45°. Any greater shoulder range involves movements of other joints. The limitation seems unnecessarily restrictive, given the fact that Stepanov overlooks compensating actions and allows a greater range for the arms and legs in other directions. A reason for the notation's limitation in this instance may be that, with the exception of backbends, the space behind the upper body is not much used in classical ballet. However, the limitation may have contributed to complaints that the system could not adequately record the newer style of Fokine and others.

All other movements Stepanov considers secondary. They include modifications of the principle directions, rotation and circumduction of the hip and shoulder, and move-

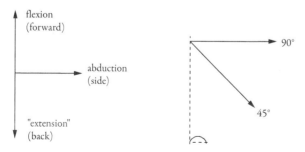

FIGURE 12.12 Principle movements of the hip (viewed from above and from the side).

ments of all the other joints.[59] Anything in between the principal movements of forward, side and back is described as secondary abduction or adduction. For example, if the arm is forward (shoulder flexed), abduction will open it toward the side, while (hyper)adduction will move it across the body[60] (Figure 12.13).

In anatomical terms, abduction and adduction differentiate movement away from or toward the body midline respectively. Gorsky shows a full range of intermediate directions[61] but keeps abduction and adduction as constant references as he moves around the body from front to side to back.[62] What is adduction from a forward position becomes abduction from a backward position (Figure 12.14).

Outward and inward rotation of the limbs and right and left rotation of the spinal column are shown by signs placed on the note stems. Intervals for the amount of rotation seem to vary by body part. For the head and probably for the arms, the first interval of rotation is 45°[63] (Figure 12.15).

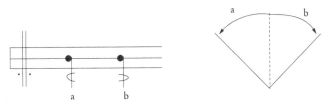

FIGURE 12.13 For the right arm, flexion (forward) with secondary adduction (a) and abduction (b).

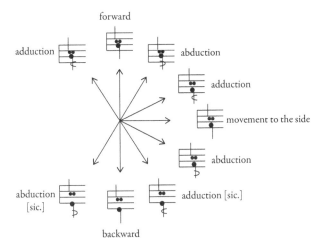

FIGURE 12.14 Principle movements (right leg) with secondary abduction and adduction.

FIGURE 12.15 Outward rotation of the arms. Inward rotation of the arms.

For the legs, the first interval of rotation is 30°—which seems to be measured from a starting point already 30° outwardly rotated.[64] Stepanov states that the "choreographic art" recognizes 45° rotation as its normal position, which is his second interval of rotation.[65] Starting from an outward rotation of 30°, this would be a total of 75°, or 15° less than what is now thought of as an ideal ballet "turnout." Like the notation's 90° maximum elevation for the legs, the maximum amount of leg rotation shows the lesser extremes of range in the ballet of Stepanov's era.

In Stepanov's notation, body configuration is derived from an accumulation of angles, starting from one of the central joints and working outward to the periphery. For example, placement of a hand will depend on where the upper arm is located, how much the elbow is bent, and the amount of rotation in the lower arm. It is surprising, therefore, that as one of the critical qualifiers, the angles of rotation seem somewhat ambiguous in the notation.[66]

Movements of the upper body include flexion of the spinal column: forward, right or left sides and backward, like the principal movements, as well as rotation (Figure 12.16)

Only one interval for bending is given, which in Stepanov's drawings appears to be 30°.[67] For intermediate positions, two signs are combined, such as forward and side, for a position between the two.

Knee and elbow joints allow movement in two opposing directions only. Knee and elbow flexion are marked by one, two or three small lines across the notes to indicate angles of 45°, 90° and 135°[68] (Figure 12.17).

Signs for movements of the head (cervical vertebrae), wrist, ankle and foot go on small lines in front of the note stems. Stepanov mentions combining signs to show intermediate angles for the head, and presumably this device is also possible for the wrist and ankle (Figure 12.18).

FIGURE 12.16 Bending at the waist: forward, back, right, left, and combined signs for forward-right, back-left.

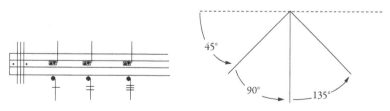

FIGURE 12.17 Degrees of bending the knee.

FIGURE 12.18 Head inclination forward, back, right, left; rotation right, left.

Because they have no time value by themselves, these signs probably would not be written without the notes for principal movements (Figure 12.19).

For movements of the head, and for flexion and (hyper)extension of the wrist, the interval is 45°.[69] The angle also appears to be 45° for wrist rotation in Stepanov's drawing.[70] For other wrist actions, and for movements of the ankle and foot, Stepanov departs from his usual 45° intervals and, as for leg rotations, particularizes the angles of movement.[71]

For the wrist, Stepanov reverses the usual anatomical descriptions of abduction and adduction. He labels movement toward the thumb side of the hand as adduction and toward the little finger side of the hand as abduction.[72] This is because his neutral position is opposite to the anatomical position for defining movement.[73]

For movement of the ankle, particularly plantar flexion (the action that results in the "pointed toes" of ballet) Stepanov's maximum angles for the ankles—like the 90° arabesque, and the 75° "turnout" of a leg—suggest a less extreme range of movement than today. He assigns 40° for the first angle of plantar flexion.[74] His second degree of planter flexion is 60° or 70° for the "pointed" ballet foot.[75] Gorsky's 90° maximum plantar flexion is probably closer to today's ideal[76]

Neither Stepanov nor Gorsky discusses angles for abduction, adduction or rotation of the ankle. Probably, since ranges are small, they correspond to the anatomical measures given by Stepanov.[77]

Stepanov also reverses the definitions of ankle flexion and extension. For Stepanov, "flexion" means plantar flexion and "extension" means dorsal flexion: "Les mouvements du pied sont; la flexion (flexio plantaris), l'extension (flexio dorsalis)."[78] This is the opposite of standard anatomical description.[79]

These discrepancies between Stepanov's notation and anatomical description may also reflect movement assumptions derived from ballet. For example, ballet stresses plantar flexion, to bring the foot in line with the ankle, whereas dorsal flexion is seldom used except in character dance. Similarly, Stepanov's neutral position for the arms corresponds to their placement in the low, *bras bas* position. For recording ballet, it would seem more natural to derive the movement from there rather than the typical palms-forward anatomical position.

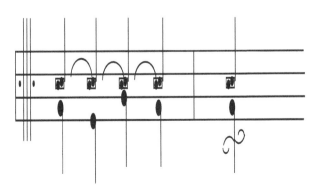

FIGURE 12.19 Measure 1: right leg, rond de jambe en dehors (side, back, forward, side). Measure 2: the same, abbreviated.

Stepanov attempts to base description on anatomical capabilities, yet in his efforts to create an economical system he employed only a few signs that can be manipulated into a great many combinations.[80] As a result, there is a disparity in the notation between individualized angles that reflect particular joint actions and standardized angles that are consistently applied to a number of body parts. As long as signs and rules are understood contextually, their meaning is clear. But Stepanov's system is not contextually consistent. Most of the angles for notated intervals do not relate to joint capabilities or to the anatomical measures Stepanov describes. Instead, they are absolute, often extending beyond the anatomic measures and bearing no mathematical relationship to them.

Stepanov's inconsistencies strike a balance between describing movements anatomically and making generalities that can apply to more than one body part. The joints governing the movements of the extremities—wrist, ankle and foot, cervical vertebrae—have fewer similarities than the shoulder and hip joints, or the knee and elbow. So it may make sense for movements of the principal and secondary joints to have standardized angles in common, and for angles of tertiary joints (wrist and ankle) to be more individualized and anatomically based.[81] Also, it is not as critical that the angles for the extremities be fixed exactly since the placement of other body parts does not depend on them. But movements of the extremities are often the most expressive, and subtle differences can affect style. (Figure 12.20)

Dictates of the technique and style of ballet of the period led Stepanov to concentrate on the large angles created by movements at the center of the body. These are Stepanov's "principal movements," and they show the main lines of most ballet positions. The notation shows the broad outlines of the dance and the large defining features of style in the somewhat restrained, geometrical proportions.(Figure 12.21) Details and nuance are not added. This implies that a knowledge of the style is assumed, and that expressive details are left to the performer. The greater standardization of angles in

FIGURE 12.20 Contact (from left) with ball of foot, tips of toes, heel (stepanov). The same (Gorsky).

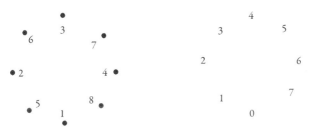

FIGURE 12.21 Numbering for orientation in turns, with 1 (Stepanov) or 0 (Gorsky) facing toward the front or audience, and 2 toward stage right.

Gorsky's *Table of Signs* seems to show the direction in which the notation was headed. Whether this was Stepanov's intention or represents changes made by Gorsky is unknown. What is clear is that Stepanov had not yet come to terms with the issue of standardization versus particularization of description, or perhaps had not even seen it as an inconsistency.

Because it is based on joint angles, Stepanov's analysis focuses attention on the point of attachment of a limb or its parts, rather than the extremity. There may be some spatial connotations in the choice of forward, side and backward directions for the principal movements and the actions of the upper body, but there is no attention to movements of the periphery as they produce paths in space or show the overall body shape. As a result, it is difficult to visualize the position of the body from the notation. To understand an action, it is necessary to calculate all the angles for the parts of the limbs and torso. Compounding the lack of visual clues is the division of the body onto three staffs, which further breaks up the body image. Also, the shapes and placement of the signs themselves give little indication of their meaning.

Curved signs like open figure eights denote circumduction. This combination of actions produces right or left circling, such as a *rond de jambe*[82]

Another set of signs either modifies the contact of the foot with the ground or shows the shape of the hand. Two or three small lines next to a note for the leg show whether the tip of the toe, ball of the foot or heel is touching the ground.[83] The contact may or may not be weight bearing, depending on the direction of the leg.[84]

For the hand, the same two or three small lines placed next to notes for arm movements show half or complete flexion of the fingers.[85] Though there seems to be little similarity between finger flexion and foot contact, the use of the same signs for both probably has to do with degrees of flexion (greater plantar flexion is required for contact with the toes than with the ball of the foot).[86]

The balletic context of the notation's development is clearly reflected in the omission of any means to detail hand movements beyond partial or complete flexion of the fingers. Unlike Asian dance, where positions of the fingers are crucial to the style and meaning of a dance, ballet hands are usually downplayed. They extend the line of the arm, as "pointed toes" complete the line of the leg.[87]

The shoulders can be shown moving forward, backward or upward by adding "notes" (Stepanov) or "Xs" (Gorsky) to the signs for principal arm movements.[88] These signs for shoulder movement are placed on the lines or spaces above or below a note for an arm position

The focus of the notation is on individual joint action, and whole body movements such as turning, jumping and traveling must be inferred from other indications. Turning is implied by changes in "positions of the body," that is, the orientation to the stage or room space[89]

To show that a turn has occurred, a number representing the new facing is placed between the arm and leg staffs. The direction of the turn is toward the closest side. Stepanov and Gorsky differ in their numbering system and in their methods for showing a full turn or multiple turns.[90]

Slow turns are indicated by a series of numbers connected by dotted lines. For whole turns, Stepanov marks the starting orientation and gives a number in brackets to determine the turn's direction. For example, "1(5)" means start facing downstage and turn clockwise, making one full turn. For multiple turns, he adds a small number in superscript to show the number of turns, for example "1(5)^2." Gorsky uses a plus sign for clockwise and a minus sign for counterclockwise instead of the number in brackets[91] (Figure 12.22).

Direction for traveling is determined by the direction of the leg movement preceding a step. The notes for both the non-contacting and contacting positions are tied together by a dotted line; the time values of the notes must be adjusted accordingly[92] (Figure 12.23).

Because principal movements for the legs are defined in 45° intervals, steps always seem to be preceded by a lift of the leg. Possibly the step modifies the height of the leg lift just as a contact of part of the foot modifies an otherwise 45° angle. But some ballet combinations require a 45° preparation for a step. Whether the lift is present or not would probably be determined by context, including the timing and the type of movement. Gorsky's examples from his ballet *Clorinda* simply note, "They run," or, "He runs after her."[93] This suggests that there was a standard, understood way to run, as there is today in ballet technique.

The round form of the notes for the legs indicates either jumping or gestures in the air. If both legs are simultaneously without contact with the ground, the body is assumed to

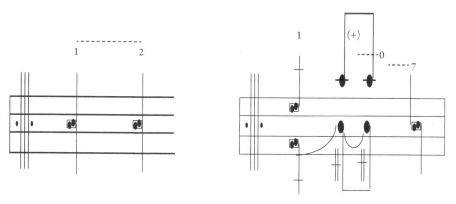

FIGURE 12.22 Example of a slow turn, 45°. Pirouette à la seconde (one and three-quarter turns).

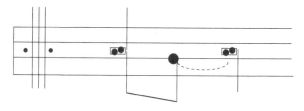

FIGURE 12.23 A step forward.

be elevated.[94] *Plié* preparations and landings for jumps are usually omitted unless the step is analyzed in detail or unless the particular position preceding or following the aerial step is important (Figure 12.24.1 and 12.24.2).

Traveling jumps are shown the same way as steps, that is, by a new contact/support occurring in the spot underneath the lifted leg—though in one example of *pas glissés*, where both legs are active and the movement is analyzed in detail, Stepanov shows a transitional contact/support for one leg while it is to the side[95] (Figure 12.25.1 and 12.25.2).

Perhaps the most undeveloped description in the system is the means for showing weight bearing on parts of the body other than the hands and feet.[96] Gorsky includes an excerpt from Petipa's *Sleeping Beauty* in which two women are "resting" on their partners' knees. One man is on his right knee with his left leg forward for his partner to sit on, and the other couple mirrors them[97] (Figure 12.26).

The woman's position gives no indication of how her weight is supported. She twists toward her partner with her head and body inclined to the side away from him, her arms are crossed in front of her body and her legs are extended forward with toes touching the floor.[98] Only her bodily configuration suggests that she has to be supported by something

FIGURE 12.24.1 Assemblé, plié preparation (right leg).

FIGURE 12.24.2 Pas balloné, plié on landing (left leg).

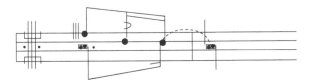

FIGURE 12.25.1 Brisé Télémaque Battu.

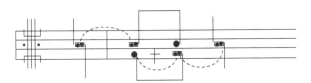

FIGURE 12.25.2 Pas Glissé.

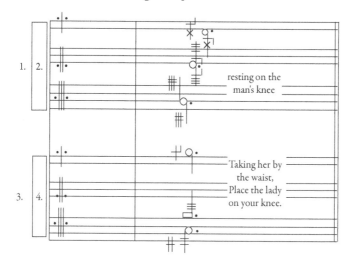

FIGURE 12.26 Adagio excerpt from *The Sleeping Beauty*.

not too far above floor level. Without the word notes, it would be difficult to decipher their relationship, especially as there are no signs showing contact between the partners. Other types of supporting, such as lying down, could probably be recorded by noting the position and marking contact where possible. The oblong or rectangular note shape usually means contact with the whole foot or hand. However, the shape is defined generally as contact with the ground and is not specific as to body part.

Since partner work is common in ballet, it seems surprising that neither Stepanov nor Gorsky give examples of a method to record dancers' contact. Staffs for dancers moving at the same time are connected in a vertical brace similar to parts for musicians in an orchestral score. Floor plans show dancers' relative positions on the stage, and numbers show their orientation vis-à-vis each other and the audience. Simultaneity of actions can be determined by calculating time values of the musical notes, even if two or more dancers' movements are in different rhythms. In Gorsky's partnering examples, word notes such as "by the hand" or "Hold the lady by the waist" accompany the notation.[99] This leaves open the question of how the hands are used and where contact is made; it also implies that hand contact was understood, and that the choreography adhered to conventions.

It appears that the specific application to choreography, particularly dancers' interactions, came later in the system's development and was not easily integrated into the system's design. Stepanov was a dancer, not a choreographer. His thinking about movement shows attention to the individual dancer and what he or she must do, from a bodily standpoint—particularly the steps and positions she or he must learn. His thinking does not show attention to the overall patterning of the dancers' actions and their effect from the audience's point of view.

Stepanov's elegant and economical system was inherently impractical. The compromises he made in his anatomical analysis in order to notate ballet show the difficulties of basing choreographic documentation on a method that inherently lacks reference to the overall design of the body. For instance, the arabesque, a principal motif in Petipa's works,[100] demonstrates Stepanov's compromises between anatomical analysis and his attempt to convey design and to record a well-known movement simply and economically. In Stepanov's notation, an arabesque is analyzed as (hyper)extension of the hip, resulting in a movement of the leg to a 45° or 90° angle behind the body. This is what the dancer strives for and what the viewer sees, but it isn't what happens anatomically. In fact, the hip has very little range, if any, in hyperextension and the action is actually accomplished through movement of the spine. Sally Fitt explains: "The hyperextension that occurs in arabesque is actually made possible by action in the lumbar spine with an accompanying forward tilt of the pelvis."[101] In order to analyze an arabesque anatomically, the notation would have to show extension (a straightening of the hip, not a backward movement), accompanied by flexion at the hip of the standing leg to allow the pelvis to tilt forward, and hyperextension in the lumbar vertebrae. In reading the notation, however, it would be difficult to deduce that the combination of such indicators adds up to an arabesque, which is simply marked by a backward raised leg.

Stepanov's anatomical analysis was in part undermined by his system's emphasis on simplicity. What makes simplicity possible is his standardization of joint angles in 45° increments with finer gradations achieved through combining signs. This method breaks down with joints that have a more limited range. In those cases, the angles seem to be based on individual joint range rather than standardized directions and intervals. If this approach were applied to all the joints, it would probably result in better anatomical description, but it would be much more complicated to learn and apply.

In the end, the least problematic aspect of the notation is that which received the least mention by Stepanov and Gorsky: the various methods for correlating dance phrases with movement patterns in the stage area. Measuring the complexities and multiple possibilities of the human body against the selectivity that makes recognizable a particular movement style, and balancing attention to individual joints against the perception of body shapes or spatial paths, suggests that an anatomically based analysis may not be viable for recording dance.

CONCLUSION

Born at a particular moment in ballet's history—during the transition from the "old" ballet of Marius Petipa to the choreographic innovations of artists including Michel Fokine and Alexander Gorsky—the Stepanov notation system eventually faded into disuse. In some sense, it was a victim of historical circumstance as its creator, Vladimir Stepanov, died before he could test its weaknesses and fully develop its significant potential, and because it later became associated with the much maligned *régisseur* Nicolai Sergeyev. Still, for all its strengths and flaws, the system warrants examination as a record of nineteenth-century classical ballet and for the larger questions it raises about the possibilities of notation systems to record the body in motion. Elegant and economical in its own way, it was targeted for use by a group of readers and notators who were familiar with the conventions of classical ballet. In his efforts to align music with dance and represent elements of human anatomy, Stepanov shined a light on the period's assumptions about ballet and the culture from which the notation emerged.

In yet another irony of history, the system would once again emerge into prominence with the "re-discovery" of the scores at Harvard University and their use in major projects such as the 1999 Maryinsky (Kirov) reconstruction of the original 1890 version of *The Sleeping Beauty*.[102] The renewed interest in these scores, legacies of the unpopular Sergeyev, brought new attention to the possibilities of recording, staging and preserving balletic classicism.

NOTES

1. Lynn Garafola, "Introduction, The Legacy of Diaghilev's Ballets Russes" in *The Ballets Russes and its World*, eds. Lynn Garafola and Nancy Van Norman Baer (New Haven: Yale University Press, 1999), 2.

2. Ann Hutchinson Guest, *Choreo-Graphics* (New York: Gordon and Breach, 1989), 69; Ann Hutchinson Guest, *Dance Notation* (New York: Dance Horizons, 1984), 73.

3. Guest, *Dance Notation*, 73.

4. Lynn Garafola, "Russian Ballet in the Age of Petipa," in *Cambridge Companion to Ballet*, ed. Marion Kant (New York: Cambridge University Press, 2007), 151.

5. Tim Scholl, *The Sleeping Beauty, a Legend in Progress* (New Haven: Yale University Press, 2004), 64.

6. Lev Ivanov choreographed *The Nutcracker* and sections of ballets (including the second and final acts of *Swan Lake*) often attributed to Marius Petipa.

7. Roland John Wiley, "Translator's Preface" in *Two Essays on Stepanov Dance Notation by Alexander Gorsky*, translated by Roland John Wiley (New York: Congress on Research in Dance, 1978), xii–xiii.

8. Ibid., xiii–xv.

9. Ibid., x.

10. Natalia Roslavleva writes that Gorsky's own choreography bridged this transition from the "old" to newer, reform-minded work. In his choreography, he broke "with all accepted clichés of ballet," adopting Stanislavsky's Art Theater principles. Natalia Roslavleva, *Era of the Russian Ballet* (London: Victor Gollancz, 1966), 157.

11. Wiley, "Translator's Preface," xiv. According to Roslavleva, Gorsky had previously notated *The Sleeping Beauty* on his own initiative after his request for funding and assistants to record the ballet was turned down. Roslavleva, 157.

12. Wiley, "Translator's Preface," xv.

13. Roland John Wiley, "Dances from Russia: An Introduction to the Sergeyev Collection," *Harvard Library Bulletin* 24, no. 1 (January 1976): 94. My spelling of names follows Wiley, "Translator's Preface," ix.

14. Wiley dates the bulk of the scores from 1892 to 1913, "Dances from Russia": 107–8.

15. See Karen Eliot's "Dancing the Canon in Wartime," Chapter 1 in this volume.

16. Nijinsky and Massine followed Fokine as choreographers for Diaghilev's Ballets Russes. Massine later became known for his character ballets and his more abstract symphonic ballets. For descriptions of their ballets, see Lynn Garafola, *Diaghilev's Ballets Russes* (New York: Oxford University Press, 1989); Vincente García-Márquez, *The Ballets Russes: Colonel de Basil's Ballets Russes de Monte Carlo, 1932–1952* (New York: Knopf, 1990); and Jack Anderson, *The One and Only. The Ballet Russe de Monte Carlo* (London: Dance Books, 1981).

17. Léonide Massine, *Massine on Choreography* (London: Faber and Faber, 1976).

18. Wiley, "Translator's Preface," xv, xvi. Attitudes vary today among contemporary notators regarding the desirability of writing out all details versus producing a score that is simple to read and aids memory in staging a work.

19. Wiley, "Dances from Russia," 107.

20. Wiley, "Translator's Preface," xvi. For a description of Sergeyev's role in the 1905 artist's strike, see Roslavleva, 172–73.

21. Wiley, "Translator's Preface," xii; "Dances from Russia," 96.

22. Wiley, "Dances from Russia," 97–98.

23. In an interview published in *The Telegraph* on August 3, 2000, Mona Inglesby describes how she came to purchase the notations from Sergeyev's friend, who, she said, was "not a dance lover." In the 1960s, Inglesby offered the notations to the Royal Ballet and the Kirov Ballet companies. Both directors rejected them, prompting her to sell them to the Harvard Theater Collection for £6,000 in 1969.

24. Deborah Jowitt, *Time and the Dancing Image* (New York: William Morrow, 1988), 244.

25. Wiley, lecture on the Russian Ballet before Diaghilev, Arizona State University, February 26, 1986, private notes.

26. André Levinson, "The New Ballet Versus the Old" in *Ballet Old and New (1918)*, translated by Susan Cook Summer (New York: Dance Horizons, 1982), 68–69.

27. Levinson, 68.

28. Jowitt, 244.

29. Oleg Petrov, "Russian Ballet and Its Place in Russian Artistic Culture of the Second Half of the Nineteenth Century," *Dance Chronicle* 15, no. 1 (1992): 46–47.

30. Stage plans in Labanotation show a striking resemblance to Stepanov's, though there is no documented connection between the two.

31. Stepanov and Gorsky do not discuss perspective for the stage plans. I base my judgment on the placement of a set in *Clorinda* and the relationship of the *corps de ballet* to the couples in the excerpt from *Swan Lake*. Gorsky, 62, 69.

32. Gorsky, 66.

33. Jowitt, 246–47.

34. Gorsky, 16, 20, 42–57, 63–70.

35. Gorsky, 48, 54–55.

36. Gorsky, 56–58, 64, 67.

37. Gorsky, 20, 69–70.

38. V[ladimir] I[vanovich] Stepanov, *Alphabet des Mouvements du Corps Humain* (Paris: M. Zouckermann, 1892), 62; Stepanov, *Alphabet of Movements of the Human Body*, translated by Raymond Lister (Cambridge, UK: Golden Head Press, 1958), 37.

39. Stepanov, 49; Lister, 32; Gorsky, *Two Essays on Stepanov Dance Notation*, 36. Gorsky says this sign also indicates that when the legs are in the air, the instep and toes are extended (plantar flexion), though there are no signs to show either the ankle or toe actions.

40. See Wiley, "Translator's Preface" and "Dances from Russia" for sources.

41. See Roland John Wiley, *Tchaikovsky's Ballets: Swan Lake, Sleeping Beauty, Nutcracker* (Oxford: Clarendon Press, 1985), 161.

42. Stepanov, vi, vii; Lister (trans.), 9, 10.

43. Stepanov, 12–13; Lister (trans.), 16–17. I follow Stepanov's use of the term *notes* for movement signs: "Les notes qui servent à indiquer les mouvements...."

44. Stepanov, 48–49; Lister (trans.), 32; also Ann Hutchinson, "Stepanov System of Dance Notation, Notes given by Léonide Massine to Ann Hutchinson, Stockholm, April 27, 1958," (ms., Ohio State University Library Special Collections, DNB file no. 8).

45. Stepanov, 3; Lister (trans.), 11.

46. Stepanov, 44; Lister (trans.), 28–29; Gorsky 13–14.

47. Stepanov, iv; Lister (trans.), 9.

48. Stepanov, v–vi; Lister (trans.), 9.

49. Richard Stites, "The Russian Empire and the Soviet Union, 1900–1945," in *The Oxford History of the Twentieth Century*, eds. Michael Howard and Wm. Roger Louis (New York: Oxford University Press, 1998), 117.

50. James H. Billington, *The Icon and the Axe* (New York: Knopf, 1970) 436, 438.

51. Tim Scholl, *From Petipa to Balanchine: Classical Revival and the Modernization of Ballet* (New York: Routledge, 2002), 26–27.

52. For a further discussion of the political conservatism of ballet in Petipa's era in relation to realism in other Russian arts and its implication for reform, see Petrov, "Russian Ballet and its Place in Russian Culture," 40–51.

53. Gorsky, 21.

54. I compare his anatomical descriptions and measures of joint actions with those of kinesiologists Sally Fitt and Katharine Wells: Sally Sevey Fitt, *Dance Kinesiology* (New York: Schirmer Books, 1988); Katharine F. Wells, *Kinesiology*, 5th ed. (Philadelphia: Saunders, 1971).

55. The neutral state is shown by the absence of the signs for flexion or extension.

56. He describes them through both directional and anatomical terminology: "Les mouvements principaux se font dans les directions suivantes: en avant (flexion), de coté (abduction) et en arrière (extension)." Stepanov, 12.

57. Stepanov, 18–20. Outward rotation of the elevated leg, which is a part of ballet style and facilitates the lift, is recorded separately. Compensating movements of the lumbar spine or the opposite hip joint are not recorded.

58. Fitt points out the difficulty of applying anatomical terminology to the shoulder joint beyond the horizontal line for the arm. To account for a full 360° range of motion, she uses the terms hyperflexion and hyperextension for movements in the sagittal plane behind the body and hyperadduction or hyperabduction for actions in the frontal plane crossing the body. Fitt, 84–86.

59. Stepanov, 15; Lister (trans.), 17.

60. Stepanov illustrates these combinations only with forward movement but uses them in his choreographic examples with side movement as well. Stepanov, 30, 21, 64; Lister (trans.), 19, 22, 39.

61. The 30° interval Gorsky describes is a change from the original notation. Stepanov designated the angle of secondary ab/adduction at 45°, creating one position between each of the

principal directions, whereas Gorsky's method allows two intermediate positions. Gorsky, 6–7, 20; Stepanov, 21; Lister (trans.), 20.

62. Gorsky defines secondary abduction with (hyper)extension as "when we lift the leg back and abduct it almost 30° further back (right leg to the left, left to the right)"—in other words, using abduction for crossing the body midline in back, the opposite of what it is in front. Gorsky, 20.

63. Stepanov does not mention the interval of rotation for the arms, but it appears to be 45° in his drawings (arm rotation is measured with the elbows bent to distinguish twist in the shoulder from that of the lower arm). Stepanov, 31–32, 41; Lister (trans), 22, 26.

64. Stepanov writes that due to anatomical construction, each foot is outwardly rotated approximately 30° (Stepanov, 21; Lister, trans., 20). This seems to be the position from which he measures subsequent rotation. The first "degree" of inward rotation, 30°, would bring the legs to what dancers today refer to as "parallel," with toes pointed forward. The first "degree" of outward rotation would bring the legs to 60° from parallel.

65. Stepanov, 22; Lister (trans.), 20, Massine, 40–41.

66. Except in a few instances, Stepanov doesn't discuss amounts of his two "degrees" of rotation for different parts of the body, whereas Gorsky refers only to first degree or second degrees, also without stating amounts. Gorsky, 15, 34.

67. Neither Stepanov nor Gorsky specifies the amount. Stepanov's drawings show approximately 30°, but Gorsky lists the angles along with knee and elbow flexion, which leads me to think his intervals are 45° for all. Stepanov, 40; Lister (trans.), 27; Gorsky, 30.

68. Anatomical extension, the return from flexion, is shown in the same way as principal movements: by the next flexed position or the neutral state. Stepanov discusses rotation of the bent knee in his chapter on anatomy but doesn't notate it (Stepanov, 9, 23; Lister, trans., 15, 20–21). Also, though some people can hyperextend their elbows, he doesn't include this action in his notation.

69. Stepanov, 42–43, 33. Gorsky shows both 45° and 90° for flexion (the palm surface of the hand closing toward the lower arm). Gorsky, 14.

70. Neither Stepanov nor Gorsky specifies intervals for wrist rotation. Stepanov, 34; Lister (trans.), 24; Gorsky 6–7, 14.

71. Neither Stepanov nor Gorsky specifically states the angles for abduction or adduction of the wrist, though Stepanov's drawings appear to show 30° for each. Since Stepanov states that the anatomical measures are 27° and 35° respectively, 30° would be a reasonable compromise. Gorsky's angle is 30°. Gorsky lists wrist and ankle ab/adduction with secondary ab/adduction of the hip and shoulder, which makes me think his angles are the same, 30° for all. Gorsky, 14.

72. Wells gives the following definitions for abduction and adduction of the wrist: "Radial flexion (abduction)…a sideward movement in the frontal plane, whereby the hand moves away from the body and the thumb side of the hand approaches the radial side of the forearm"; "Ulnar flexion (adduction)…a sideward movement in the frontal plane, whereby the hand moves toward the body and the little finger side of the hand approaches the ulnar side of the forearm." Wells, 229–30.

73. In the notation's neutral position for the arms, "wrists [are] turned so that we see both the back side of the wrist and the thumbs at the same time." (Gorsky, 8). In the anatomic position, palms face forward (Wells, Kinesiology, 8). Stepanov shows a different angle in his drawing for wrist rotation (Stepanov, 34).

74. Stepanov's first angle of plantar flexion corresponds to his anatomic measure, but in his drawing this angle appears to be smaller than the angle for dorsal flexion. His drawing of the angle

for dorsal flexion seems to be about 30°, close to his anatomical measure of 27°. Stepanov, 24; Lister (trans.), 21.

75. Stepanov, 24; Lister (trans.), 21.

76. Gorsky shows angles of 45° for dorsal flexion and 45° and 90° for planter flexion. These angles are probably measured from the position of the ankle in a normal standing position, in which the sole of the foot is at approximately a right angle to the leg. Gorsky, 14.

77. Stepanov's anatomical measures are 16° adduction, 6° abduction, 10° inwards rotation, and 20° outwards rotation.

78. Stepanov, 24; Lister (trans.), 21.

79. Wells's definitions: "Dorsal Flexion (flexion). A forward-upward movement…so that the dorsal surface [top] of the foot approaches the anterior surface of the leg"; "Plantar Flexion (extension). A forward-downward movement…so that the dorsal surface of the foot moves away from the anterior surface of the leg." Wells, 295.

80. Stepanov simplifies body movement rather than detailing it. For example, his classification of joint capabilities includes just three categories: those that permit movement in all directions, those that allow movement in two opposing directions and all others. (The notation system mainly addresses the first two.) Stepanov, 6; Lister (trans.), 13.

81. For categorization of principal, secondary and tertiary joints, see chart, Gorsky, 20.

82. Stepanov only briefly mentions the signs, but Gorsky gives quite a few examples, including rond de jambe and grand rond de jambe of the legs, and circling at the shoulder, elbow, wrist, ankle, "waist" and cervical vertebrae. Stepanov, 44; Lister (trans.), 28; Gorsky, 16–17.

83. The signs' designs, but not their meaning, differ slightly according to Stepanov or Gorsky.

84. The signs are only placed next to round notes, as the oblong or rectangular note shape shows contact with the full foot or hand. (Stepanov uses an oblong shape and Gorsky uses a rectangular shape to show contact.)

85. Stepanov, 25, 35; Lister (trans.), 21, 25.

86. Gorsky, 14, 38, 67, 68.

87. Although the toes must work in conjunction with the ankle to achieve the pointed look for the foot, there also is no means for writing flexion or extension for the metatarsals.

88. "Xs" are also used to show secondary (hyper)extension, but since elbow hyperextension is not recorded in the system, and wrist (hyper)extension is marked on a separate, single line, there is no possibility for confusion.

89. Stepanov, 50; Lister (trans.), 32.

90. Gorsky's method shows the increments of a turn more clearly. Stepanov's method, however, permits intermediate orientations by numbering the spaces between the walls and corners with another consecutive set of numbers.

91. Stepanov, 50–51; Lister (trans.), 33; Gorsky, 19.

92. Stepanov, 49; Lister (trans.), 32; Gorsky, 18. This somewhat indirect method for recording steps probably has to do with the system's contextual approach to determining whether or not a contact with the floor is weight-bearing. One foot can fully support the body if the leg is straight down, but not if it is forward, side or back.

93. Gorsky, 58–59.

94. Stepanov, 13; Lister (trans.), 16.

95. Stepanov, 63.

96. Neither Stepanov nor Gorsky discusses other types of contact or support.

97. As described in the notation: the man's body is upright and his left leg is forward 90°, knee bent 90°, with contact of the whole foot. (The rectangular note shows contact that may or may not be weight-bearing.) His right leg is straight, knee bent 90°, with the ball of his foot touching the floor. Gorsky, 70.

98. As described in the notation: the woman's body is inclined left, rotated right and arched back at the waist. Her neck is arched back and her head turned left. Her arms are forward 45°, rotated inward, with elbows bent 135°. Her legs are forward 45°, and her toes are touching the floor. Gorsky, 70.

99. Gorsky, 69.

100. Petrov, 50.

101. Fitt, 56 (Fitt's emphasis). Wells finds hyperextension of the hip "extremely limited." "Except in dancers and acrobats," she states, "it is possible only when the femur is rotated outward and is probably completely absent in many individuals." Wells, 254.

102. See Scholl, *The Sleeping Beauty*.

13

Musical Expression in the Bournonville-Løvenskjold *La Sylphide* Variation

Rebecca Schwartz-Bishir

FOR ALL THAT is known about nineteenth-century ballet, much of what happened in the actual *dancing* remains speculative. Dancing is ephemeral: it vanishes as soon as it is performed. Sculptures, drawings, and photos capture only an instant. Critical accounts and memoirs can suggest moments of performance, but they rarely include a detailed description of actual movement. The teaching of dance is largely an oral tradition, and what is passed down from generation to generation frequently suffers some alteration and distortion in reproduction. Notation created at the time of first performance is rare and sketchy; frequently missing but needed is a living expert to explain and demonstrate exactly what the notation means.[1] The scholar is left with a lot of pieces of the historical puzzle, but a largely incomplete picture. There is, however, an essential source that can illuminate much about the nature of the dancing itself.

Dance reaches out to the scholar from inside nineteenth-century ballet scores. These sources, although frequently overlooked, allow researchers to consider the relationship of music and dance and to deepen their understanding of ballet variations. Modern musical notation has been standardized for more than four hundred years and, as such, offers the historian a codified text that can be widely interpreted and understood by many people. Although such scholars as Marian Smith, Mary Beth Clarke, and Ann Dhu McLucas have explored music for pantomime, little work has been done on the relationship of nineteenth-century music for dancing the *danse d'école*, the codified school of movements that distinguishes ballet dancing and its aesthetic from all other dance.[2] *Musique dansante*, which is music that suggests the

341

bodily motion of nineteenth- and twentieth-century ballet dancing, has much to tell us about the history of the classical ballet variation.[3]

This chapter offers insight into the dance of the nineteenth-century ballet variation from the perspective of what its music can reveal.[4] After bringing *musique dansante* into the purview of dance historiography and explaining how it expresses dance, this chapter will feature a close musico-choreographic analysis of the Sylph's first variation from August Bournonville's 1836 version of *La Sylphide* (Figure 13.1). Analysis will be based on composer Herman Severin Løvenskjold's holograph score[5] (Figure 13.2) and on two filmed performances of the work, the earliest known film record of this variation from 1903 and another from 1988.[6] By showing in this variation how music and dance are connected, and how their content, form, and ideas interact with each other, it will become clear how music can be a useful historical record for dancing.

MUSIQUE DANSANTE IN HISTORY

The term *musique dansante* came into use by Russian balletomanes in nineteenth-century St. Petersburg.[7] These ardent and influential lovers of the art were concerned with ballet music as well as with ballet dancing. By the 1860s they had coined the term. Balletomanes who wrote on ballet and its music applied *"musique dansante"* (sometimes also expressed

FIGURE 13.1 August Bournonville. By permission of The Royal Library, Copenhagen.

FIGURE 13.2 Herman Serverin Løvenskjold. By permission of The Theater Museum in Court Theatre at Christiansborg Palace, Copenhagen.

in the Russian language as *dansantnost'*) without formal definition, but their meanings connected to the notion of how they understood the relationship of ballet music and movements of the *danse d'école*. Critics in France, such as Théophile Gautier, also used the word "dansante" to refer to music that had the quality of ballet dancing; however, ballet music was, in general, an issue of lesser importance for them. The Russian balletomanes had a knack for knowing when music suited dancing, and when it did not. Thus, they recognized that *musique dansante* is specialized music, a sub-genre of ballet music essential to the very concept and history of dancing the *danse d'école*.

Specialist ballet composers wrote music for ballets, including *musique dansante*.[8] They were expected to write lots of music very fast, and to be willing and able to adjust their music immediately while in rehearsal. Creating good music for dancing the *danse d'école* required a person with an affinity for academic dance and the ability to write physically redolent music. Indeed, composers such as Adolphe Adam, who wrote *Giselle*; Cesare Pugni, who wrote *Pas de Quatre*; and Ludwig Minkus, who wrote *La Bayadère,* had a special talent for translating the sensual and visual qualities of ballet dancing into music.[9] These same composers, and others, were also essential to figuring out the conventions of *musique dansante*. Although the conventions of ballet music may seem ordinary because they are ubiquitous, they presented a compositional problem that could not be solved by just anyone.

The prevalence of these conventions and qualities in nineteenth- and twentieth-century ballet music is a testament to their importance to the art.[10] The music of specialist ballet composers has much to reveal about the connection of music and the *danse d'école*.

The collaboration between choreographers and specialist ballet composers was highly influential on the music written for ballet dancing. In the nineteenth century the choreographer had the ultimate power in the collaboration because he had the most direct experience with what succeeded in dance spectacles. Many works were conceived and directed by these men as well; thus they had a unifying vision of their ballets and the ultimate say. Choreographers did not routinely compose music for ballets, but they did exert influence over what the composer wrote for dances. In order to produce music suitable for their dance plan, choreographers sometimes gave specialist ballet composers the exact requirements of a dance piece, including the dance genre, the tempo, the number of measures, and even a melody or rhythm. For example, Charles Louis Didelot, choreographer of the Russian ballet in St. Petersburg during the first third of the nineteenth century, is remembered for his active guidance of ballet composers.[11]

The famous Danish choreographer August Bournonville took collaboration with composers a step further in the creation of his dances and treated them like partners, not just subordinates. Writing of original music composed for his ballets, he said:

When I have completed my libretto, I set it aside for a while. Then, if I read through it again with the same interest and every picture stands clear before me, I consider it ready for composition. I turn to the music composer, who receives a separate outline for each scene that makes up a musical number; he then comes to an agreement with me as to rhythm and character. Usually, by means of gestures and *pas,* I manage to give him a rough idea of what is to be performed; I improvise a melody to it; sometimes this melody contains a useful theme, which may be picked up, shaped, and modulated.

Now the composer works until an entire piece is finished. I get to hear it…it is completely different from my original conception; I need to become familiar with it, but it is lovely and good music. The length and character are determined. My own working out of the ballet now assumes a new form. From the music, I get ideas for details of which the composer himself has not even the faintest notion. I become thoroughly acquainted with his composition, find an episode in every measure, and then, after the piece has been rehearsed, it appears as if both the composers [the composer and the choreographer] had agreed on every note and as if they had been of one mind.[12]

In the last third of the nineteenth century, Marius Petipa approached his work with Pyotr Ilyich Tchaikovsky in a way similar to Didelot and Bournonville and their specialist composers, giving Tchaikovsky a list that guided the composition of *Sleeping Beauty*.[13] The collaborative model established in the nineteenth century continued to influence the creation of *musique dansante* in the twentieth century.[14] *Musique dansante* and the customs surrounding it were essential to the very *process* of creating a classical variation.

THE CONVENTIONS AND PROPERTIES OF *MUSIQUE DANSANTE*

Musique dansante has conventions that help music and dance go together and properties that imitate or reflect the kinesthetic qualities in the ballet dancing of the nineteenth and twentieth centuries. *Musique dansante* is frequently the result of a composer's conscious reaction to a choreographer's dance plan and the dancers' requirements for performing that choreography, or it is his response to the prospects of composing for ballet.[15] It is influenced by and imitates the style, types of steps, and types of gestures of a given dance.

Unlike mimetic music, which describes specific gestures that symbolize specific meanings, such as "I love you," "you will die," or "we will dance for you," in *musique dansante* families of sounds are analogous to families of academic movements. Musical context limits the possibility of analogous movement combinations and how they are performed. For example, the sounds that suggest big leaps are different from those that suit slow extensions. Although a choreographer always makes the final decision about the dancing, at least some kinship between musical suggestion and choreography unifies music and dance.

Musique dansante's conventions create norms and expectations for choreographers, dancers, and audiences in several ways. The music is easy to follow because it is melody-dominated, highly tuneful, and built in regular phrases. As a rule, it has clear downbeats and a regular pulse with a limited number of repeated rhythmic motifs, which help music and dance unite. To help coordinate music and dance, percussion or brass instruments often punctuate beats or musical goals. The custom of adjusting music to suit a performer's or chorographer's needs is easily recognized in the forms of *musique dansante*, which are simple and easily modified. Each section of the form suggests distinct movement motifs. Simple harmonic progressions that center on the tonic, I, and its most closely related key, the dominant, V, not only reinforce location and progression in the music but also define one section of the form from another.[16] Homophonic textures, with a melody in the forefront and an accompaniment in the background, also make this music easy to follow. Variations are short, lasting from twenty to sixty measures so as not to overtax performers, and are often gender-specific. Dynamic levels not only indicate the caliber of dancing expected for a particular number but also may reflect the sex of the dancers who would perform a given variation or *pas*. In the case of the Sylph's first variation from *La Sylphide,* strings and woodwinds playing mostly *piano* help to highlight the feminine qualities of the ballerina, her role, and dancing *en pointe*.

The distinguishing properties of specialist ballet music are the traits of melody, rhythm, and articulation. Other elements of music, such as harmony, texture, timbre, and dynamics, support melody, rhythm, and articulation and will be discussed in the analysis as they make their impact.[17]

Melody connects directly to the bodily motion of dancing and the sensory experience of it. On the simplest level, it tells when to start and stop moving, and most of the time choreographic beginnings and endings coincide with musical beginnings and endings. The lengths of phrases in *musique dansante* are congruent to the lengths of phrases in its corresponding choreography: combinations of movements typically last two to four bars, and they often parallel the antecedent and consequent content of this music. Melodic goals appearing at the ends of phrases and sections are called cadences; they are the places to and from which motion goes in both music and dance. Two kinds of melodic motion, conjunct and disjunct, relate to a dancer's connection to the floor. In instances of predominantly conjunct motion, which occurs in a melody built in adjacent pitches, choreography is frequently *terre à terre*. In instances of mostly disjunct motion, which occurs in a melody constructed by skipping over adjacent pitches to non-adjacent ones, choreography is frequently *en l'air*. By contrast, melodic contour in *musique dansante* connects to both the size of movements and their direction. Contour does not call for Mickey Mousing but invites commonness of expression in music and dance. Most important about melody is that its lines connect to the lines of the *danse d'école* through the lines of the body. Through melody, one gets a sense of the motion of dancing in a particular piece.

The three categories of rhythm—rhythmic pattern, meter, and tempo—order and express dance in time. Rhythmic patterns limit families of movements that may fit the music. They serve as a guide to the dance motions that a choreographer may relate to them in the context of a particular variation. Meter provides the basic means of synchronizing music and dance, the pulse. Inherent in music-dance synchronization is the connection of the beat to the exchange of weight from one foot to the other. In addition, the number of beats per measure and how they are grouped or divided in a meter provide impetus for dance motion. Tempo is the most flexible aspect of rhythm; it affects music's suitability for a given motion or set of steps. Slight gradations in tempo have a significant impact on the look and feel of dancing.

Articulation in *musique dansante* links the way one plays music with the way one dances movements. Articulation can reflect the physicality of dance movements as well as project a potential approach to choreographing and performing steps. Music that is written *legato*, for example, not only has pitches joined in a connected line but also expresses smooth and flowing motion from one movement or pose to another. *Staccato* articulation indicates detachment in music and dance, and often quickness. *Pizzicato*, or the plucking of a stringed instrument, can express quick, pricking movements *en pointe* as well as a soft bouncing or buoyant character in the dancing. Both music and dance articulation depend on the body to make their expressive concepts reality.

THE MUSICO-CHOREOGRAPHIC EXAMPLE

The Sylph's first variation occurs at the beginning of Act 1.[18] While the Sylph dances around the room, James sleeps in his chair until the end of the variation, when she awakens him with a kiss.

The dance analysis in this chapter is based on two film recordings of performances by the Danish Royal Ballet ballerinas Ellen Price de Plane (1878–1968, henceforth referred to as Ellen Price) and Lis Jeppesen.[19] According to Knud Arne Jürgensen, the Sylph's choreography was passed down directly to Ellen Price from her aunt, Juliette Price, who danced the role from 1849 to 1859.[20] Peter Elfelt made a silent film of Ellen Price performing the variation in 1903.[21] An essential record in and of itself, the Elfelt film is as close in historical terms to an actual nineteenth-century performance of this variation as one can get. Lis Jeppesen's performance provides a record of the variation that is clear, in color, and with orchestral accompaniment. *La Sylphide* has remained in the Danish Royal Ballet's repertory since 1836; however, certain "modernizations," such as higher extensions and more sustained pointe work, have been incorporated into Jeppesen's performance. The musical analysis is of Løvenskjold's holograph orchestral score that was used by Bournonville in his 1836 production of the ballet.[22]

Figure 13.3 is a table of musical symbols and their function in the examples and is intended to help with reading the score.

MUSICAL EXPRESSION OF DANCING IN THE SYLPH'S FIRST VARIATION OF *LA SYLPHIDE*

A descending F major scale (the dominant of the coming key of B-flat major) over the course of two measures leads to the first downbeat of the variation. (See Musical Example Introduction and Section A, Flutes and Violin 1.) The fast descending scale fits running; however, it could also suit very gradual movements or a pause if required by either the stage constraints or the ballerina. This music allows the dancer to run to her place on stage beside the chair or to pose momentarily before dancing. In the 1988 film, Jeppesen runs from across the room around James's chair and steps directly into an *arabesque*. In the 1903 film, Price performs a slow *arabesque promenade* in place, probably because the choreography is constrained by the camera frame. Although running and a slow promenade involve distinctly different movements, the steadiness of these motions links them both to the evenness of the scale. As the performances show, these measures can go with either danced introduction.

In the first section of the variation, A (measures 1–8), Bournonville's choreography defines the Sylph's distinctive dance persona, a weightless inhabitant of the air. The three jumping movements of this section—*sauté cabriole arabesque, double ronde de jambe,* and *sauté arabesque*—convey the ethereality and liveliness of a winged creature. The lightness and buoyancy of this choreography are hallmarks of Bournonville's style.

Measures 1–4 of section A begin with the implication of detached, *en l'air* dancing as indicated by the staccato dots over the melody's eighth notes.[23] (See Violin I for the melody in this section.) This articulation conveys general lightness to the dance while the accompaniment's repeated chords imply continuous suspension, in this case *ballon*. In measure 1 of the string parts (contrabass, violoncello, viola, violin II, and violin I), the b on the downbeat acts as a propelling force that launches the ballerina upward in her *sauté*

Table of Symbols:

Symbol	Name	Function
A,B,C,D	Formal section markers (appearing at the top of the music scores in boxes)	Identify a section of the form and distinguish it from other sections of the form. Provide an easily found marker for rehearsal and performance purposes. Indicate such musical concepts as statement, contrast, development, recapitulation, or · restatement, all of which affect the choreographic structure.
I	Tonic chord	An analysis symbol used in music to identify a chord based on the keynote of the piece, the first and most important pitch in the scale of the key. In B-flat major, the key of the *Sylph's* first variation, a tonic chord is based on the pitch of B-flat. See Section A, measure 1, beneath the staff.
V	Dominant chord	An analysis symbol used in music to identify a chord based on the fifth pitch of the scale, the second most important pitch in the scale and the one that leads the earback to the tonic chord. In the key of B-flat major, the dominant chord is based on F. See Section A, measure 7, beneath the staff.
p	Piano	A dynamic mark meaning soft. See the beginning of the Introduction. *Piano* is often associated with smaller movements.
f	Forte	A dynamic mark meaning loud. *Forte* is often associated with larger movements. Variations of this directive are found in the score. They include *mf* in measure 17 for *mezzo forte* (meaning medium loud), and *ff* in measure 33 for *fortissimo* (meaning very loud).

FIGURE 13.3 Continues.

	Fermata	A small curved semi-circle with a dot in it placed above or below a notehead or rest. See Section C, measure 24. This symbol indicates the protraction of a note or rest's value beyond its normal length. This extra time may be used by the dancer to balance, pose, flirt, or catch her breath.
	Slur	A curved line that arcs over or under a group of notes. Slurs join notes together into a musical idea. For examples, see Section B, the Motif in Violin 1, the arpeggio in Violin 2, and the Sigh in measures 12 and 16. Slurs may be used to indicate legato articulation in music and flowing, connected movements with smooth transitions in the dance. The ends of slurs, especially at the ends of phrases, frequently present places to take a breath in the melody.
•	Staccato dot	A small dot placed either directly above or below a notehead. See section A, Violin 1 measures 1,2,3,4,5, and 6. A mark of articulation indicating the note should be played detached from the notes around it. Staccato dots typically suggest a quick, precise movement that may be performed with a sharp attack or a bounce.
>	Accent	A small arrowhead placed either directly above or below a notehead. See Section C, measure 18 (oboe) and measure 20 (flute). A mark of articulation indicating the notes should be played sharply and with emphasis. Accents typically indicate movements that are stressed.

NOTE: Staccato is a different indication from pizzicato, or the plucked note on a stringed instrument. Pizzicato articulation is also detached from the notes around it and indicated by a dot placed directly above or below a note head, but its dots always appear in the context of the word "pizzicato" or the abbreviation "pizz." in the score.

cabriole arabesque en arrière. The distance between the first two notes—the low b and the high d that begins the melody—corroborates the Sylph's elevation from the floor. Articulation and accompaniment also throw into relief the melody's gradual line of descent, which is suggestive of a combination of movements carried out over the length of two measures. In this case the ballerina continues upstage and repeats the *sauté cabriole arabesque* in measure 2. The phrasing of the melody in this section, which elides the ending of one phrase with the beginning of the next, reflects Bournonville's way of making a landing also a takeoff. The figuration in sixteenth notes at the ends of bars 2 and 4 terminates each phrase and increases the music's motion.[24]

Bournonville's choreography brings diversity to the near repeat of the first two measures' music with the double *sauté ronde de jambe* and the *sauté arabesque* that correspond to measures 3 and 4. The *sauté ronde de jambe,* a characteristic Bournonville step, incorporates elevation in place instead of a jump within a line of traveling movements.[25] The *sauté arabesque* completes the dance phrase and punctuates the musical phrase without copying the fast figuration of the music. The fact that the *cabriole* and *ronde de jambe* differ but both fit the music brings to light the fact that *musique dansante* does not express *specific* movements but rather limits the *motion* of families of movements that could

FIGURE 13.4 Musical Example: Løvenskjold, *La Sylphide*, Sylph's First Variation, Introduction and Section A.

correspond to it. The music is context for the choreography but is also defined by the choreography's content.

The verbatim repetition of the choreography in measures 5 through 8 eliminates the need to discuss it, but the corresponding music has changes that broaden its implications for dance motion. The antecedent phrase in measures 5 and 6 is similar to that in measures 1 and 2; the obvious differences between these measures are a change in harmony (which anticipates the transition to the coming section's new motifs and new physicality) and the descent and ascent of the figuration pattern at the end of measure 6. Measures 7 and 8, however, make new suggestions to the dance by introducing a fluttering motif in the melody and an extended trill in the accompanying flute. A musical metaphor suggestive of the beating of the Sylph's wings, the fluttering motif is created by the rapid, wavelike motion of the sixteenth notes, the speed of the pattern, which contributes to a sense of lightness, and the legato articulation, which suggests continuous motion. Repetition of the same chord of the dominant harmony over the course of measures 7 and 8 directs attention to the melody's motion and articulation. The music's energy serves to drive it and the dance toward their mutual goal, the downbeat at measure 9, and it conveys the Sylph's general excitement of being near the man she loves. Although Bournonville did not take advantage of the fluttering motif, its presence in the music helps characterize the Sylph.

FIGURE 13.5 Ellen Price de Plane as the Sylphide. By permission of The Theatre Museum in Court Theatre at Christiansborg Palace, Copenhagen.

In the second section of the variation, B (measures 9–16), Bournonville's choreography introduces filigree footwork typical of a woman's variation while it continues to emphasize the Sylph's airy qualities. (Figure 13.5) The ballerina alternates lacing *pas de bourrées* in patterns that show off the precision, speed, and delicacy of her footwork with *sauté ballonnés* that continue to emphasize her lightness. A *grand jeté* concludes each phrase.

Measures 9 through 16 permit at least two kinds of movement groups, and Bournonville's choreography brings out both types of motions inherent in Løvenskjold's music. The B section's music contrasts that of the A section with its new melodico- rhythmic motifs and the slurs over them, which suggest smoothness of motion suited to fast *terre à terre* footwork. (The melody is once again in the Violin I part.[26]) The composer introduces a series of thirds ascending and descending in groups of three; a musical sigh concludes the phrases that end at measures 12 and 16. (See Musical Example B.) The rhythmic motif taken on its own—sixteenth note, thirty-second note, thirty-second rest—which emphasizes each sub-beat, suits dancing small, quick steps. In measures 9 and 10, when the melody repeatedly ascends, the corresponding choreography's three-step *pas de bourrée dessus* and *dessous* patterns, which take one step on each sub-beat, coordinates with this rhythmic motif. The choreography is linked to the melody because each time a new group of the intervallic pattern of three begins, a new *pas de bourrée* sequence starts. If the rhythmic pattern is considered as part of the larger melodic phrase and linked with

FIGURE 13.6 Musical Example: Sylph's First Variation, Section B.

FIGURE 13.7 Musical Example: Sylph's First Variation, Section C.

the two main beats of the measure, however, it is suited to the other movement motif Bournonville choreographed, a *sauté ballonné* on each beat. While the *pas de bour-rées* emphasize the sense of six in the bar, common to a moderate 6/8 meter, the *ballonnés* emphasize the sense of a meter of (or divisible by) two. One can see how the choreography might be counted to reflect the two possibilities of the meter by reading the numbers between the Violin I and Violin II staves of measures 13–16. The alternation of the accompaniment's harmonies in this section, between B-flat major (measures 9–10, 13–14) and E-flat major (measures 11–12, 15–16), with the change in melodic contour from ascending to descending supports the division of the dance motifs into filigree footwork and small jumps, *terre à terre* and *en l'air* dancing, respectively. The sigh, which is distinguished by its dotted eighth note (in measure 12) and its fast downward motion in sixteenth notes (measures 12 and 16), constitutes a mini-goal at the end of each consequent phrase. Bournonville paired a *grand jeté* with each sigh, reflecting its high suspension and arcing descent, and bringing the inherent physicality of this musical figure to life.

By writing three groups of the ascending (and later the descending motifs) over the two-bar phrase, Løvenskjold observed the dance custom of showing a step or group of movements three times. (See measures 9–12.) Whether Bournonville asked for this phrasing is unknown, but his choreography, which repeats both the *pas de bourrée* pattern and the *sauté ballonné* movement three times each, reflects the presence of this convention in the music.

In the third section of the variation, C (measures 17–24), Bournonville choreographs changes in the direction and momentum of the dance. In the first two phrases, the Sylph runs upstage on the diagonal and jumps in an *arabesque cabriole* in which she rotates toward the audience; this is immediately followed by a *glissade petit jeté* to the downstage side. In the last two phrases, she walks *en pointe* and then poses. The jumps link the choreography to the airborne qualities of the previous sections, whereas the walks calm the dancing, slow it down, and lead it to a pose. While posing, the ballerina can catch her breath, display her balance, and flirt with members of the audience. In the Price performance, the position is an *arabesque penché* on a flat foot; in the Jeppesen performance the position is an extension *à la seconde en pointe*. The pause at the end of section C is a significant event in the variation that divides the dancing of its beginning and middle from its finale.

In measures 17–20, the music modulates to a new key, d minor (symbolized on the score by i), and introduces fresh color by writing the melody for a solo oboe, flute, and clarinet.[27] (See Musical Example C.) The pizzicato articulation in the accompaniment makes the music's texture sparse and reduces its dynamic level, which brings to mind lightness in the dance. The section's new melody is made up of a musical turn and descending arpeggios that can be paired with quick, jumping motions and changes in *épaulement*. Along with changes in harmony and articulation, the melody highlights a signature of Bournonville's style, unexpected changes in dance motion and direction. For example, in measures 18 and 20 the combination of the dominant harmonies and the accents on the melody's non-harmonic tones create musico-physical stress; resolution of

FIGURE 13.8 Musical Example: Sylph's First Variation, Section D.

that stress on the upbeats of these measures is signaled by the accent in the melody and the return to the key of this section, d minor. Bournonville's choreographic response to the visceral sensations of stress and release is a sudden ninety-degree shift from the upstage run and jump to sideways movements (the *glissade petit jeté*).

Legato articulation in the clarinet and the pizzicato accompaniment in the strings combine in measures 21–24 to suggest smooth movements performed *en pointe*. Each beat has a change of harmony that with the melody implies the exchange of weight. The appoggiaturas[28] in bar 21 and on beat 2 of bar 22, which are composed of a longer note value (the quarter note) followed by a shorter note value (the sixteenth note immediately following it), suggest brief balances followed by a downward motion indicative of controlled lowering between steps in a series. Bournonville's walks *en pointe* of one *piqué* per beat complement the music in these measures, reflecting the calmer and more intimate nature of this music. The grace note that decorates the neighbor figure on the downbeat of measure 22 anticipates the practice of ornamenting steps that is likely in this section; it could be accomplished through the use of *batterie*, the adding of a decorative beat of the foot as it passes the other leg. It is possible that the musical ornament was a reflection of Bournonville's choreography; in both films, Price and Jeppesen walk with beats. The syncopation that occurs in measures 23 and 24, which places a rest on each beat of the melody rather than a pitch (except for the last note of the phrase), still implies the exchange of weight associated with every beat but with new timing. The syntax of the syncopation

motif is significant: it adds interest to the music's rhythm and diversifies the flow of movements. As the films show, the syncopation's displacement of the melodic groups delays
each of the Sylph's steps behind the beat, changing the ballerina's momentum and helping
her motion come to a stop. The addition of a *ritardando* in measure 24 slows the music
and the dancing further. Extending the pause at the phrase goal is a fermata that allows
the ballerina to control the length of the pose.

Section D jolts the ballerina into motion again, and leads her to her first encounter
with an awakened James. In a circle around the still sleeping James she dances a pattern of
sauté arabesques followed by *chassés en avant;* she then leaps across the stage in *saut de
basque* jumps. Before the variation concludes, the Sylph pauses a moment, gestures of her
love for James, and then runs over to his chair and in an *arabesque penchée* kisses him on
the head, waking him up.[29]

Measures 25 through 32 return to B-flat major and a thicker texture, and they feature
fast figuration in the new melody, which suggests a flurry of steps and more active movements than in the closing measures of section C. Measures 25 through 28 of the melody,
which has returned to the Violin I part, alternate their goals, from lower (the accented f
in measures 25 and 27) to higher (the accented d in measures 26 and 28). (See Musical
Example D.) The rapid and repeated notes in the string parts of the accompaniment contribute to the sense of speed in the melody: there is increased activity in all parts. Bournonville's choreography alternates the ballerina's motion from one side of her body to the
other on each beat. His simple combination of jumps and traveling steps coordinates
with the underlying sense of increased motion while it asserts its independence by dancing
through each measure's melodic accent in a continuous flow of movement.

Measures 29 through 32 signal the variation's end. In these last four measures the
spinning quality of the melody's repeated turn figure is indicative of the fast *pirouettes,
pique* turns, or *chaînés* turns that frequently end a woman's variation. Løvenskjold's music,
however, also renders the main beats buoyant and supportive of movements with *ballon,*
such as a leap or jump. Bournonville ingeniously incorporates both of these possibilities
in his use of *saut de basques* in the first two bars at 29 and 30. These jumps that both turn
and travel while hovering over the ground are *tour de force* movements appropriate for
ending a variation and capturing the excitement and energy in this music. Rather than
having the Sylph dance a series of turns, Bournonville reflects convention with a creative
substitute. In the last two bars, amidst the flurry of notes in the music, the Sylph briefly
pauses to mime that she is taken with James and then runs over to give him a kiss. The
ending of her variation's music is elided to her first encounter with a conscious James (on
the downbeat of measure 33).[30]

CONCLUSION

An essential piece of the historical puzzle, ballet scores shape the written record of
dancing. Respective of each variation, *musique dansante's* conventions and properties

give us a detailed, moment-by-moment account of a dance's motion. In so doing, this music suggests both the form of the dancing as well as its content. By providing a written context for the style and the kinds of steps that fit a particular variation, *musique dansante* informs historians about the very nature of the dancing done to the music.

The case study in this chapter is but one example of the value of musico-choreographic analysis in answering the question "Where is the dance?" in the nineteenth century. As in so many other ballets, the dancing is in the musical expression of the variation.

NOTES

1. In the twentieth and twenty-first centuries, Ann Hutchinson Guest has made significant contributions to the research and understanding of dance notation systems and has notated dances. See her *Choreo-graphics: A Comparison of Dance Notation Systems from the Fifteenth Century to the Present* (New York, Gordon and Breach, 1989); and *Labanotation: The System of Analyzing and Recording Movement* (New York: Routledge, 2005). Rudolf and Joan Benesh have also contributed a system called Benesh Dance Notation that is used to preserve and reconstruct dances. See their book *Reading Dance: The Birth of Choreology* (London: Souvenir Press, 1977). The overwhelming majority of choreography, however, was not notated and is unfortunately lost.

2. In addition to pantomime music and music for the *danse d'école*, ballet has other musical categories that can inform our knowledge of dancing in the past, including national music (for folk dance) and music for character dancing (for such categories of characters as commoners, workers, nobles, animals, toys, and witches or sorcerers.). National, character, and pantomime music are beyond the scope of this essay and will not be discussed in this chapter.

3. For a detailed discussion of the topic in the nineteenth and twentieth centuries, see Rebecca Schwartz-Bishir, "*Musique Dansante* and the Art of Ballet" (Ph.D. dissertation, University of Michigan, 2008).

4. In her book on twentieth-century ballet, Stephanie Jordan examines the relationship of music and movement using detailed musico-choreographic analysis. Her pioneering work has opened the door to a new genre of study. See *Moving Music, Dialogues with Music in Twentieth-Century Ballet* (London: Dance Books, 2000). See also chapter 2 of *Stravinsky Dances: Re-visions Across a Century* (Alton, Hampshire: Dance Books, 2007) for her discussion of *musique dansante* in Stravinsky's works.

5. This score was used in all productions of Bournonville's *La Sylphide* in Copenhagen during his lifetime. Changes were made to Act I, Scene 1 in the measures following the first variation for a performance of the work in 1862 at Stockholm's Royal Theater in Sweden and interpolated in later re-stagings in Copenhagen, but the score shows that the Sylph's first variation was *not* cut or expanded from the 1836 version. See Knud Arne Jürgensen, *The Bournonville Tradition: The First Fifty Years, 1829–1879*, vol. II: An Annotated Bibliography (London: Dance Books, 1997), 35, 273. I am grateful to Dr. Jürgensen for his assistance in acquiring a digitized copy of the score.

6. Herman Severin Løvenskjold (July 30, 1815, Holdensjärnbruk, Norway, December 5, 1870, Copenhagen, Denmark). He was born to a wealthy family who ran an ironworks and planned a military career for him. After the family moved to Denmark and the composers Frederich Kuhlau

and Christoph Weyse noticed his talent, he was allowed to pursue music. In his twenties, he studied in Vienna with composer Ignaz Ritter von Seyfried. Løvenskjold's first ballet *Sylphiden*, completed when he was twenty, was a huge success and became the work for which he is known. Other ballets for which he wrote music include *Sara* (1839) and *The New Penelope* (1847). In addition to ballets, Løvenskjold wrote overtures, including *Festouverture*, which was composed for the coronation of Christian VIII, piano chamber music, and an opera, *Turandot* (1854). He was appointed court organist at the church at Christiansborg Palace in 1851.

7. Among the St. Petersburg Balletomanes were the writers Sergei Khudekov, Sergei Plesh-cheyev, and Konstantin Skal'kovsky. These men worked for the newspapers that most often and most generously covered dance performances, including the *Petersburg Gazette* (*Peterburgskaya gazeta*) and *The New Time* (*Novoye vremya*). See Roland John Wiley, "Three Historians of the Imperial Russian Ballet," *Dance Research Journal* 13, 1 (Autumn 1980): 3–16. Interestingly, many of the St. Petersburg writers on ballet and music chose not to identify themselves or to sign their reviews only with an initial or two, such as S—kov for Sergei Khudekov or I— for Mikhail Ivanov. Of course, there were also many other people in the crowd of dance admirers who left no writings for historians to ponder but who likely cared about this aspect of ballet. For a general discussion of balletomanes, see Anatole Chujoy, "Russian Balletomania," *Dance Index* 7, 3 (March 1948): 45–58; and "In The Kingdom of Terpsichore," *Dance Index* 7, 3 (March 1948): 58–71; *A Century of Russian Ballet: Documents and Accounts, 1810–1910,* selected and transcribed by Roland John Wiley (Oxford: Clarendon Press, 1990), 250–75; and Roland John Wiley, *Tchaikovsky's Ballets: Swan Lake, Sleeping Beauty, Nutcracker* (Oxford: Clarendon Press, 1985; reprinted in paperback 1997), 10–17.

8. For an overview of the job and music of specialist composers in the Russian Imperial Ballet system, see Wiley, *Tchaikovsky's Ballets,* 2–8. For a list of specialist ballet composers at the Paris Opéra and their famous compositions, see Ivor Guest, *The Romantic Ballet in Paris* (London: Dance Books, 1980), 10–13. Also see Marian Smith, *Ballet and Opera in the Age of Giselle* (Princeton: Princeton University Press, 2000), 15 for general characteristics of ballet music; and 18 for a brief summary of the duties of ballet music composers at the Paris Opéra during the 1830s and 1840s.

9. Adam wrote fourteen complete ballets, Minkus wrote approximately twenty, and Pugni wrote or added to about three hundred.

10. In the nineteenth and the twentieth centuries, the conventions were the outlines on which dances were built. The customs were influential even when they were rejected in order to produce something distinctly different, such as in Merce Cunningham and John Cage's chance creations. Thus, the effect of specialist ballet composers and their music reaches beyond ballet to modern dance.

11. Adam Glushkovsky, Didelot's student and successor in Moscow, remembers Didelot providing composers with musical plans that included tempo, length, and orchestration for each section of a ballet. On occasion, Didelot sang motifs that he wanted composers to use. Relying on the public's memory of the texts, Didelot also suggested that composers incorporate tunes (known as *airs parlants*) from recently performed operas or popular songs. When an *air parlant* was combined with a scene of similar content in the ballet, the text of the tune helped audiences comprehend the mime scene. See "Recollections of the Great Choreographer Ch. L. Didelot, and Some Deliberations Concerning the Art of Dance" by Adam P. Glushkovsky in *A Century of Russian Ballet,* 23–25. For more on the *air parlant,* see Smith, *Ballet and Opera in the Age of*

Giselle, 101–10. Use of the *air parlant* was widespread in the first half of the nineteenth century and not exclusive to Didelot and his collaborators.

12. August Bournonville, *My Theatre Life,* translated from the Danish by Patricia N. McAndrew (Middleton, CT: Wesleyan University Press, 1979), 30–31. According to Knud Arne Jürgensen, Bournonville's "collaborative process" was established early in his career. See *The Bournonville Tradition: The First Fifty Years, 1829–1879,* vol. 1: A Documentary Study (London: Dance Books, 1997), 81.

13. For the list, see Selma Jeanne Cohen, ed., "Marius Petipa (1818–1910): The Sleeping Beauty," translated by Joan Lawson in *Dance as a Theatre Art: Source Readings in Dance History from 1581 to the Present,* 2nd ed. (Hightstown, NJ: Dance Horizons/Princeton Book, 1992), 95–102.

14. For example, the Stravinsky-Balanchine ballet *Agon* was created using the nineteenth-century model. For more on *musique dansante* in the twentieth century, see Schwartz-Bishir, "*Musique Dansante* and the Art of Ballet," chapters 4 and 5.

15. Other instances in which *musique dansante* may occur are beyond the scope of this chapter. See throughout Schwartz-Bishir, "*Musique Dansante* and the Art of Ballet," for their discussion.

16. The tonic is the home key of a piece, and it is the pitch that names the first note of its scale. All music gravitates to the tonic in a piece of tonal music.

17. For an in-depth introduction to the properties, see Schwartz-Bishir, "*Musique Dansante* and the Art of Ballet," 30–80.

18. *La Sylphide* is a two-act ballet celebrated as the first complete Romantic-era ballet. It premiered in Paris on March 12, 1832, and starred Marie Taglioni, who performed choreography by her father, Filippo Taglioni, to music by Jean Schneitzhoeffer. After seeing the ballet in Paris in 1834, August Bournonville created his own version of *La Sylphide.* It premiered in Copenhagen on November 28, 1836, and starred Lucille Grahn, who danced new chorography by Bournonville to music by Hermann Severin Løvenskjold. Both ballets were based on the libretto by Adolphe Nourrit. A conscious imitation of Taglioni's version, Bournonville's ballet featured new dances for his performers. Although Taglioni and Bournonville's ballets share the same story line, the holograph scores render their versions different works because the same choreography could not fit the music of both ballets. Special thanks to Marian Smith for sharing her holograph of the Sylph's first variation from the 1832 Schneitzhoeffer score. For a copy of the libretto, see "August Bournonville (1805–1879): *La Sylphide.* A Romantic Ballet in Two Acts," translated from the Danish by Patricia N. McAndrew, ed. by Selma Jeanne Cohen in *Dance as a Theatre Art: Source Readings in Dance History From 1581 to the Present,* 77–85.

19. The recording of Ellen Price may be found on YouTube at http://www.youtube.com/watch ?v=l7xkcloI6zA&feature=related. Lis Jeppesen's performance may be viewed on *La Sylphide: Choreography by August Bournonville Performed by the Royal Danish Ballet,* executive producer Robin Scott, 62 minutes, Kultur, 1988, DVD. Film recordings have been chosen for the dance analysis because they eliminate the problems of dealing with dance notation. In addition, they present a unique opportunity for discussion in that they exist, they are accessible, and they show the choreography of this variation as part of an ongoing repertoire.

20. *The Bournonville Ballets: A Photographic Record* 1844–1933, compiled and annotated by Knud Arne Jürgensen (London: Dance Books, 1987), page 20. Whether this variation was altered from its original version in 1836 has not been determined. For more photos of the 1903 production and a few other productions, see *The Bournonville Ballets,* 20–33. In 1979 Elvi Henriksen

added to the film a recording of the variation's music performed on a piano. See endnote 2, Erik Aschengreen, "Bournonville Style and Tradition," *Dance Research: The Journal of the Society for Dance Research* 4, 1 (Spring 1986): 61.

21. The court photographer Peter Elfelt (1866–1931) was the first Danish filmmaker. He dominated the first decade of Danish film production and made more than two hundred films in his career. He made films of the dancers Hans Beck, Valborg Borchsenius, Richard Jensen, Wania Tartakoff, Gustav Uhlendorf, and the aforementioned Ellen Price, which are available for viewing at the New York Public Library (The *Royal Ballet* 1902–1906, Motion Picture). For more on Peter Elfelt, see Ron Mottram, *The Danish Cinema Before Dreyer* (Metuchen, NJ: Scarecrow Press, 1988), 4, 11–12, 14, 22, 34, 42, 109, and 163; and Stephen Herbert and Luke McKernan, eds., *Who's Who of Victorian Cinema* (London: British Film Institute, 1996), 49. See *Danmarks Radio Praesenterer Elfelt Film,* compiled by Ole Brage (Copenhagen: Danmarks Radio, 1975) for the catalogue of his motion pictures. The black-and-white film of Price performing the Sylph's first variation was made in 1903 and is 53 seconds long.

22. The score before you is a clean edition of Løvenskjold's 1836 score of the Sylph's first variation. There are marks on the manuscript not in Løvenskjold's hand that have been omitted from the transcription and in the following discussion unless pertinent. The few notes and sections of text that are bracketed like this [] in the score have been added in my role as transcriber and editor of the music. Each bracketed addition will be addressed separately. Measures have been numbered here for ease of presentation and are not the actual numbers of their location in the complete ballet score. A *répétiteur* (rehearsal score for two violins) was also consulted. Its provenance is undetermined—it is unsigned and undated—but it appears to be the one dated [1836] in Jürgensen's *The Bournonville Tradition,* Vol. II, 37. Handwriting in pencil between a few of the variation's staves is too faint to be deciphered, but all musical marks are clear. The répétiteur corroborates the holograph in the content and key areas of the sections of the form; however, sections B, C, and D are repeated, making the form of the *répétiteur* A, B, C, D, B, C, D. Each section is eight measures in length. Lines in pencil strike out the first D and the repeat of B and C, which, if followed, make the form and the length of the répétiteur the same as that of the holograph score (A,B,C,D; thirty-two measures long). (The repeated sections of the music and their cross-outs, of course, reflect the convention of allowing for the form to be modified to suit the stamina of the dancer performing the role.) In a section that is similar to A and that precedes it, some of the melody is outlined rather than a verbatim reproduction of the holograph score. This pre-A section has been crossed out with pencil. Thus, the *répétiteur* has the potential to be a variation of sixty-four measures rather than thirty-two, but the cross-outs in it suggest that it too was held to the length of thirty-two measures. My thanks to Dr. Jürgensen for his assistance in acquiring a digitized copy of this *répétiteur.*

23. Brackets surround the tempo *Allegro non tanto*—fast, but not too fast—because this directive is written on the score in a hand other than Løvenskjold's. The tempo is included here because it is consistent in all performances consulted.

24. Figuration is a lot of notes, often arpeggiated or written as a scale, that fill out a chordal structure. Figuration adds motion to music and increases its decorative qualities.

25. In her entry on August Bournonville, Patricia McAndrew lists the following movements as characteristic of his style: "attitude *effacée; grand jeté en avant en attitude; grand jeté en attitude en tournant; attitude effacée sautée; ronds de jambe en l'air sautés;* myriad *batterie* steps such as *brisés, entrechats, sissones,* and *assemblés;* and *pirouettes*—many done from second position, *en attitude* or

sur le cou-de-pied—with characteristic *port de bras*" Selma Jeanne Cohen, ed., *International Encyclopedia of Dance,* vol. 1 (New York: Oxford University Press, 1998), 513.

26. Brackets have been added in the French horn parts and the triangle from measures 11 to 16 because these pitches are absent on the holograph. The addition of these notes is made here because they would be consistent with typical orchestration in a ballet variation and because all of the orchestral performances consulted include these parts.

27. The bracket around the *mezzo forte* (medium loud) indication in measure 17 is a matter of editorial discretion. *Mezzo forte* is a logical dynamic level following the crescendo of the preceding measures. The *mezzo piano* (medium soft) indication that immediately follows reflects the drop in dynamic level with the sparse texture and solo instrument.

28. An appoggiatura is a melodico-rhythmic figure that has a stressed note followed by an unstressed note. Appoggiaturas typically occur at points of harmonic tension and need resolution. The appoggiatura frequently implies movement from a balance, lift, or pose to a new step, a landing, a new pose, or a transition.

29. The conclusion of the Price performance gets cut off in the film, so the analysis of the very end of the variation is based solely on the Jeppesen performance. There is a second Elfelt film of Ellen Price from 1906 performing the Sylph's first variation; however, that performance is longer and has altered music and choreography. Sections A, B, and C are virtually the same as in the 1903 performance; section D has new music and choreography. See YouTube video http://www.youtube.com/watch?v=ob86BOYez8A for the 1906 performance. It is not used in this analysis because it is not as early as the 1903 film and because of the differences in the choreography, which do not render it a parallel comparison to the Jeppesen performance.

30. In the holograph beginning at measure 33, there is music written for percussion, brass, and woodwind instruments in addition to the strings. These other parts have been omitted from the musical example here because they are not germane to this discussion.

14

Archives of Embodiment

VISUAL CULTURE AND THE PRACTICE OF SCORE READING

Victoria Watts

Victoria Watts

AN OPENING GESTURE

STAND IN PARALLEL, feet together, weight over the balls of your feet, and feel yourself pulling up from the floor to the crown of your head. Long spine, long neck, relaxed shoulders, arms held loosely by your side. Now, gesture your right arm to the right front diagonal corner, so that your right hand is about head height. Bend back at the wrist so that your hand is vertical and your palm faces outward. This is the basis of your starting position. In all likelihood you already recognize this as the iconic opening position from George Balanchine's *Serenade*. This is also the starting position notated in the two extracts of Labanotation given in Figures 14.1 and 14.2.[1] You can see that the symbols in each figure, though not identical, are very similar. If you have a rudimentary reading knowledge of Labanotation you will also have noticed that the description of head facing differs between the scores. In the first, you are directed to orient your face up toward the right diagonal, whereas in the second you are instructed to orient your face toward your right hand.

Now, in terms of spatial displacement from an untwisted, upright state, these two descriptions lead to an identical performance. However, if both are read with precision, there is a difference in the focus of the eyes that might not be easily perceived from a distance but that will subtly alter the dancers' performance. Both scores supplement this graphical description of the opening position with a word note that tells the reader "Looking out but shielding the eyes from the sun" or "The hand is shading the eyes from the light." The choice of words meshes with the movement descriptions: the score that

363

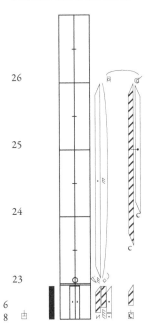

FIGURE 14.1 Arm gesture, *Serenade*. Transcribed into Labanwriter by the author from Ann Hutchinson Guest and Harry Haythorne's Labanotation score (1964).

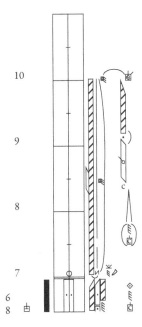

FIGURE 14.2 Arm gesture, *Serenade*. Transcribed into Labanwriter by the author from Virginia Doris's Labanotation score (1983–1988).

mentions "looking out" describes the dancers looking to the high corner, in effect looking past their hands. The other directs the dancers' focus to the act of shading the eyes from the light. It is worth trying this for yourself. In your starting position, either look at the hand or look beyond toward an imaginary sun. I suggest coming back to neutral between the two versions. Indubitably, there is a difference in sensation. For me, it resides in a sense of greater expansiveness when I look beyond my hand, imagining my gaze reaching out to the sky. When I bring my focus in to rest upon the back of my right hand, avoiding the imaginary glare, my energy feels subtly contained, limited to my immediate kine-sphere.

INTRODUCTION

In this paper I draw the reader's attention to dance notation both as a class of visual objects and as a physical analytical practice that has been neglected or misapprehended by critical scholars and philosophers writing about dance. My purpose in doing so is two-fold. First, I intend my thick description of the process of reading and writing notation to act as a corrective to the wholly disembodied accounts of dance notation that occur in the very few philosophical texts that address the topic.[2] Second, I intend my outline of a Visual Culture Studies approach to dance notation to situate the insights of notation practitioners within a broader disciplinary frame and to suggest possible avenues for more in-depth analysis. In all this, my overriding concern is to demonstrate the impor-tance of a somatic understanding of dance notation. For this reason, I urge readers to either dance or use their kinaesthetic imaginations to conjure the feeling of dancing the score extracts I have included. Readers who cannot fathom the notation might try fol-lowing my verbal descriptions. I have tried to make the material come alive for notators and non-notators alike. It is this practical understanding, in tandem with the insights gleaned from Visual Culture Studies, that leads me to claim an analysis of dance notation systems and their scores can provide insight into changes in embodied subjectivity. In parallel to Susan Leigh Foster's recent genealogical account of kinesthesia,[3] I regard dance notation systems and their scores as an archive of historical material on embodiment.[4]

VISUAL CULTURE STUDIES: A WAY OF LOOKING AT DANCE NOTATION

Visual Culture Studies is an interdisciplinary field that draws on the traditions of art his-tory, cultural studies, sociology, philosophy, film and media studies, and feminist thought.[5] Scholars in this field attend to a heterogeneous set of objects and practices, and their points of view about the role of the visual in contemporary Western culture are diverse. However, I identify three key areas of inquiry that, even though not exactly unit-ing the field, connect otherwise quite disparate scholarly enquiries. These strands unite the topic area in that they each interdependently reflect on the pre-eminent notion of vision as a field of power: the critique of visuality itself and the act of looking; the relationship between the social and the visual; and the synaesthesia of seeing. Any aspect of visual culture demands that attention be paid to all three categories since they are fully imbricated one in the other. At the heart of Visual Culture Studies, then, there is an understanding that practices of seeing are culturally determined, that consequently the visual is always symbolic rather than natural, and that the embodiment of the percipient and the thing perceived are crucial in forming an understanding of our intersubjective visual world.

If this understanding of the field is focused on dance notation as a highly corporeal visual practice, a number of contentions present themselves. At the most general level, dance notation systems form part of broader "scopic regimes" in which particular ways of seeing shape how the visual world is constructed. I take this term from Martin Jay's seminal work in Visual Culture Studies, "Scopic Regimes of Modernity." He suggests that, although the modern era has traditionally been characterized by Cartesian perspectivalism, there are various regimes of vision and visuality at play throughout this time. Scopic regimes are thus best understood as forming a contested terrain rather than "a harmoniously integrated complex of visual theories and practices" (4). Comparably, in *Choreographing Empathy* Foster argues for the existence of "corporeal epistemes that participate in the production of knowledge and the structuring of power" (13). The connection between vision and motility is well documented. It takes no great leap of imagination to see how dance notations instantiate and articulate scopic regimes and corporeal epistemes in the graphic traces of their various visual-kinaesthetic practices.

With regard to methods of transcribing dances within particular scopic regimes, the ornate cursiveness of the Feuillet system would seem entirely consonant with the Baroque era in which it was devised. First published in 1700 by Raoul-Auger Feuillet, this system is now referred to as the Beauchamps-Feuillet system since it came to light that much of Feuillet's work was plagiarized from that of Pierre Beauchamps.[6] The illustration here (Figure 14.3) shows the combination of formal order and decorative flourish that also characterizes Baroque architecture and design. The score shows symmetry along the vertical axis and a balance between the top and bottom of the visual image redolent perhaps of the façade of a Baroque church. The curved lines that ornament the structure of the notation echo the curves of leaves, shells, and abstract swirls that adorn furniture, mirrors, wallpapers, and tableware from the era.

Likewise, early Laban Kinetograms (Figure 14.4) call up associations with examples of early European modernism influenced strongly by the Bauhaus school of design.[7] At the same time, I also see echoes of Art Deco leaded windows with thin, angular, geometric panels. The precise linearity of the page layout seems to refute any inference that this may have been drawn by hand. It looks mechanized, automated, and standardized and thereby appears to me to be self-consciously Modern.

This link between the visual characteristics of a notation and dominant features in design, architecture, or fashion of the era in which it was devised might seem banal.

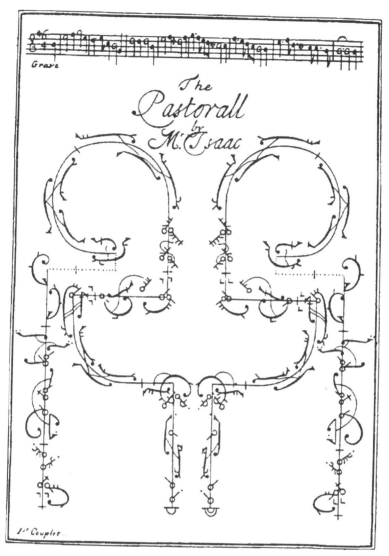

FIGURE 14.3 A page from *Chorégraphie; ou, l'art de décrire la danse*, published by Raoul-Auger Feuillet in 1700.

However, it underscores that dance notations are historically located cultural practices that visually instantiate a complex of particular values. To regard them out of context, perhaps as flawed attempts on the route to notational perfection, is always reductive. The only major account of the history of dance notation in the West takes just such a view. Ann Hutchinson Guest's work in *Choreo-Graphics* is impressive for the extent of primary source material it brings together. Guest's breadth of understanding of notation systems allows her to draw comparisons that less experienced and less knowledgeable scholars could not. However, her comparisons are focused on which system is "best," predicated on the assumption that she can make objective evaluation in spite of the fact that different

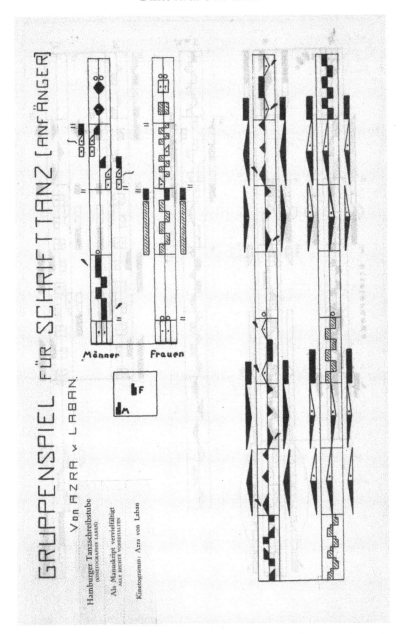

FIGURE 14.4 Example of an early kinetogram written by Azra von Laban, exact date unknown.

systems have avowedly different aims. Her analysis is not concerned with what any system might tell us about the way its users thought, saw, moved.

If vision itself is not a purely natural phenomenon but is also subject to cultural and historical variation then systems of movement observation cannot be objective accounts of what is *there*, dancing in front of the notator, because what is seen to be *there* is altered according to the social and historical context in which it is seen. Thus, on a less abstract level, dance notation practices must always involve the imposition of a conceptual framework that guides perception. This framework might in some instances be so strong that certain features of a dance could be rendered invisible while others come to dominate the perceptual field. Nonetheless, the notation alone cannot divulge whether its omissions reflect a set of "givens" so ingrained that they appeared corporeally "natural" or whether those same omissions denote a perceptual system in which certain variations in performance just did not register. A more in-depth study of any system in context is needed in order to draw conclusions about the significance of the various perceptual frameworks used.

The Beauchamps-Feuillet system (Figure 14.3) combines a representation of the dancers' pathways with a detailed analysis of the dance's steps. This system establishes a framework for analysis of the dance movement primarily in terms of transference of weight and location in the performing space.[8] For each step, marked with a black dot on one or other side of the staff followed by a line that traces the pathway of the step, annotations are given for whether the weight is rising or sinking and whether the step slides, jumps, or turns. The emphasis on manner of performance of steps anchors a conceptual framework in which some facets of the dance are elaborated with a high degree of sophistication—transfer of weight, leg gesture, body location,[9] and relationship—whereas others, such as carriage of the torso and head; most arm gestures[10]; and elements of expression to include dynamics, phrasing, and facial expression, are implicit and not subject to analysis, or are beyond the scope of vision the system offers to its readers. Consequently, body shape recedes from view while body location and manner of locomotion occupy the foreground.

Eugene Loring's Kinesiography, invented in 1954 in collaboration with D. J. Canna pictures neither body shape nor body location but appears to conceive the dance in terms of discrete instructions to a body made up of isolated parts. From the left along the grid-like staff are columns for left and right hip, three zones of the left leg, three zones of the right leg, the torso, left and right shoulder, head and neck, three zones of the left arm, and then three zones of the right arm. The organization of the columns acknowledges the symmetry of parts, placing left and right in relation to each other, but it does not represent the symmetry of the body as a whole unit. The way the columns have been assigned to zones of the body represents a point of view about the hierarchical organization of the dancer's body and prioritizes skeletal structure over bodily surfaces. The details of hand movement, the richness of facial gesture, and complex articulations of the torso recede from view here: the picture of the dancing body is dominated by gross

FIGURE 14.5 Arm Gesture, *Serenade*. Handwritten in BMN by the author.

motor movement of constituent parts. Loring generated his system for use with dances in the ballet genre. Since so much detail can be taken as read, literally, in the standard vocabulary of classical ballet, it is understandable that he saw no need to specify facets of the form that were either not subject to change or else were always determined by context.

Within any system of communication, there are elements that communicate meaning and others that do not. In his structural analysis of language, Ferdinand de Saussure notes that it is only the differences between signs conveying meaning that need to be marked. For example the phonic difference between *bath* and *path* is crucial whereas the difference between *bäth* and *bath* (a difference in pronunciation that is common between accents from the north and south of England) is unremarkable because it conveys no change of meaning in the word. Likewise, within ballet it may not be crucial precisely how the dancer forms her hand—although schools have their preferences—because this facet of the performance is not considered an element of the dance that is subject to any change that would alter the meaning. Of course, Balanchine cared deeply about the shaping of the hand, and the score by Virginia Doris includes a meticulous analysis of this and of the general carriage of the arms in its glossary. The point here is that the shaping of the hands is not generally a significant feature of ballet, outside of mime, whereas the shaping of the hands is highly significant within some other dance genres. It would be unthinkable to record *bharata natyam* and neglect to describe the various *mudras*. Likewise, gestures with the eyes and face are more significant in this form of dance than within ballet. As Jonathan Culler explains, "signs are not simply given to perception: to perceive the signifier at all is to confer on some patterns and not on others the status of meaningful expressions."[11]

When I look at Loring's system with my layperson's eye, I struggle to find an understanding of the body that resonates with my own. I cross-reference this example with explanations of how the system works, but it does not come alive to me in the way that my equally novice reading of Beauchamps-Feuillet permits. The grid itself puts me in mind of computer punch cards. Perhaps if I were a robot, a mechanized dancer awaiting instructional data, I would be able to feed these matrices of information in through a slot in my side and my processors would decode and send an electrical impulse to jolt each mechanical joint into action. This system seems wholly appropriate for an understanding of the body as a biomechanical feat of engineering and is congruent with a sense of optimism about technology and computing that infuses much graphic design of the 1950s.

Loring's approach to dance notation does not cohere with my understanding of the dancing body. Doubtless, there are a host of reasons some notation systems achieve wider adoption and influence than others, many of which have little to do with the general efficacy of the visual scheme and the appropriateness of the analytical framework for the era in which it is created. However, it is fair to say that not all the notation systems that have been proposed in the past five hundred years have been equally fit for purpose. Loring's system may well be a case in point. His associates adopted his system for a limited time, but it spread no further. A good fit between the framework a notation imposes and the "corporeal episteme" in which it is located could constitute a reason for widespread acceptance, and a bad fit might equally speed the demise of notation's use.

In Western culture vision has been prioritized because it was thought to be less "base" than the other senses, but many visual culture scholars have insisted that the discipline must begin by "postulating the imbrication of vision with the other senses."[12] In relation to the synaesthesia that inheres in vision, and our other sense perceptions, the inescapable corporeality of the dance score makes it a perfect medium through which to consider how observation is always necessarily somatic.[13]

The notator relies on the intimate relationship between vision and motility in the writing process as well as in the reading process. For example, in writing the opening gesture from *Serenade* in Benesh Movement Notation (Figure 14.5), I begin by observing the movement and making a quick annotation of the basics of the starting posture, the relationship of hands and feet within the visual frame used in the system.[14] The first body shape illustrates that there is a direct correspondence between the way I see the arm gesture—above head height, away from the centerline of the body and forward of the horizontal plane—and the manner in which it is marked on the stave. To borrow a term from semiotics, this plotting of the hand as a single frame of the notation creates a simple icon.[15] Even for this apparently simple transference to paper of what might seem to be purely visual data—the arm *appears* to be at head height, so I write it on the stave where it *looks* as if it is at head height—I have an empathetic, embodied response to what I see. I am not certain that I would pick up on the key visual features of the opening position quite so quickly if I were not already somewhat familiar in my own body with elements of the movement and its style.[16]

I might have chosen to simply write what I see for the flexion and facing of the wrist direction, but I prefer to play with the movement in my own body to double-check the degree of flexion. Somehow it is just easier and clearer to *feel* the small distinctions of fine motor movement than it is to see them. When it comes to the turn of the head, I have no option but to recreate the body shape myself. I need to feel how much turn and how much tilt combine to make the head position. I try breaking it down to check that the components I have identified "add up" to give the appropriate inclination. I have performed this movement enough by now not to need to check in a mirror to see if what I am doing looks correct, although with less familiar material I certainly would use a mirror.

I observe that the arc of the arm gesture as the hand moves toward the temple happens over more than one count of the music. Several frames later in the score, I draw the path it takes, writing it at the point in time at which that action completes, and I tie it to the opening position with a legato line above the stave in order to indicate when the movement starts. Although the spatial path of the gesture is rendered visually, its timing is not.[17] And my perception of the duration of the action has an aural component. I listen carefully to the rhythm of the movements as they play against the melody of Tchaik-ovsky's *Serenade for Strings*. It takes more than one frame of writing to describe this action, and since more than one part of the body is moving during this time span I must again double-check my own performance against my observation to determine what to write. In this instance, separate indications are needed to show that the head does not begin to turn straight away, and that it passes through an upright and untwisted state.

I have a choice about whether to analyze the detail of the wrist at the initiation of the gesture visually or dynamically. My choice depends in part upon the nuances of the performance and in part on my own preferences as a notator. In the version here, I have opted for a simple analysis. However, if my aim were to provide a more nuanced descrip-tion of this one action, I would write the movement in several ways, wait a while, and then attempt to re-perform my own writing. I would choose the version that seemed to get me closest to both the look and feel of the action. Here, I have written that the hand bends forward slightly at the wrist, in an accented manner, at the beginning of the arm gesture.

Dance notation scores have the capacity to do much more than document any particular choreographic work. Indeed, they can never do just that. Instead, each score contains a record of the movement under observation and also a trace of how the notator thought about and understood what she observed. That much should be evident from the very brief explanation of my recording the opening gesture of *Serenade*. Dance notation systems and their scores are, in essence, a form of "seeing made visible,"[18] and for as much as the notated score is a visual record of the synaesthetic process of seeing at a particular moment in time, it also leaves a tangible trace of an historically and culturally determined mode of embodiment. My example from *Serenade* at the beginning of this chapter (Figures 14.1 and 14.2) illustrates how each score discloses the way a notator sees the dance within the framework of the notation system employed. However, the "pic-ture" of the dance conveyed by the score is not just visual. If you try the simple examples at the opening of the chapter you will find that it is also necessarily kinaesthetic.

In this section, I have suggested that dance notation systems not only document bodies in motion but also form a visible trace of how movement is seen. I have provided a hand-ful of illustrations to indicate how dance notation systems and their scores are embedded within scopic regimes and corporeal epistemes. Each system graphically represents a conceptual framework that reveals and obscures different facets of the dance. I have sug-gested that dance scores are necessarily synaesthetic, and I have provided very brief descriptions to illustrate this point in terms of both reading and writing a notation score. These ways of seeing operate at multiple, interrelated levels: the individual notator, the institutional framework of the system, and the cultural context in which the recording is made.

In claiming that the knowledge a score analysis generates is necessarily corporeal, I posit that a visual culture approach to dance notation must also engage a body of work that critiques mind-body dualism, refutes the theory-practice dichotomy, and counters logocentric epistemologies.[19] In the next section, I draw on the insights of notation professionals to show that practice has served as both an alternative and a complementary route to access the insights I have detailed above. This notation practice is grounded in the engagement of an embodied mind and unsettles the foundations of a conception of knowledge based on the sole authority of language.

DANCE NOTATION: GENERATING KNOWLEDGE THROUGH PRACTICE

There is a tenacious belief that insight is gained primarily through theoretical reflection and should subsequently be applied to an understanding of practice. A review of conference presentations, articles, and books by notators brings to light understandings about perception and embodiment that run parallel to those generated within Visual Culture Studies. Practice, it would seem, can generate the kind of understanding that is normally considered the province of theory. It is not a matter of reversing the binary, but of acknowledging that there are many valid routes to knowledge and that the distinctions between them are not nearly so marked as the history of Western thought might lead a reader to believe.[20]

The remarks presented here, made by notators, allude to a notion that the dance score serves as a repository of information, simultaneously corporeal and textual, on changing ways of seeing and changing ways of moving. These perceptions are nearly all buried in conference proceedings of the International Council of Kinetography Laban (ICKL) or in the short reports from notators contained in *The Choreologist*.[21] As such these insights have not been disseminated to a wider community of dance and visual culture scholars. With rare exception, they are made in passing as part of papers that have some other agenda, and consequently there is little sustained argument or documented empirical evidence to support them. This may be because to each notator these remarks reflect a self-evident "truth" discovered through sustained practice. There has yet to be an intellectual dialogue in print that does justice to the conversations notators engage in between themselves on these matters. A useful first step might be to simply ascertain who said what, in print, when.

As early as 1979, Judy Van Zile commented on the importance of using notation as a source of information on the nature of dance.[22] In 1983, still a good decade before Visual Culture Studies established itself within the academy, Nadia Chilkovsky Nahumck pondered, in connection with her reflections on Laban's "scientific thinking," whether changes in lifestyle produce changes in body-space relationships, and whether there was an interpenetration or overlay of movement styles from one generation to the next.[23] A year later, Suzanne Youngerman wrote: "Notation scores embody perceptions of movements. Furthermore, they can provide data, in an unusually revealing form, for research on a variety of topics, including the exploration of the concept of style, of the ways in which movement can be conceptualized, and of the bases for aesthetic evaluations."[24]

Sheila Marion's 1991 comparative analysis of two scores of Eugene Loring's *Billy The Kid* is the first work to systematically explore what changing perceptions of embodiment and what changing perceptions of the dance might be found in the altered visual and theoretical frameworks employed. It is a nuanced analysis in which Marion is careful to point out that just as a dance evolves over time, so does a notation system, such that it can be hard to separate out the effects of the notation system itself on perception of the movement.[25] In reading Liz Cunliffe's reflections on her work with the Notation Study Group, formed in London in the mid-1980s for dialogue between BMN and Labanotators, it is apparent to me that she too is noticing the problem of teasing out the connections between perception of movement, analysis in the terms of the system employed, and the notator's own personal movement preferences. She writes:

Although we appear to have no problems recording the timing of the same movement pieces, it has become clear during practice dictations that studies are subconsciously constructed which fall most readily into the timing structure of the "familiar" system. While this tends to lead us into thinking that our perception of time is affected by the structure of the system we use, we have not attempted to prove whether or not this is, in fact, the case.[26]

Also at ICKL in 1991, Vera Maletic comments that "variants in the perception of qualities...are determined by period, culture, and individual characteristics."[27] Moreover, it seems that notators themselves are aware that their perception of movement can change as their careers progress. Faith Worth was the first permanent notator employed by Britain's Royal Ballet, taking up her post in 1960. Reflecting on her career there, she suggests: "Each new ballet seems to develop in the choreologist an awareness of something new, something one had not noticed before. This is characteristic of the heightened analytical awareness developed by working with the Benesh Notation."[28]

The partiality shown toward the Benesh system here is a consequence of the "turf war" between the systems that was taking place at this time. I suggest that the prolonged engagement with detailed, systematic observation and description of dances makes notators into *connoisseuses* (and *connoisseurs*) of movement, able to discriminate more finely in their perceptions of the mechanics and intent of choreography than a regular observer.

In 1995, Dominique Dupuy, co-founder of the French Federation of Notation Systems, boldly claimed in his opening address to the conference that it is essential to see notation as a bridge between dance and the history of though.[29] At the same conference, Rhonda Ryman and John Beatty commented that the notator's choice of symbols reflects her or his perception of the movement, and that consequently "notation allows us to see how the writer thinks about movement."[30] In her presentation of the conclusions of her doctoral dissertation, Sheila Marion makes it clear that the notation score does not just show how the individual writer thinks about movement, but that any notation system is itself replete with concepts and values deriving from the movement context in which it originated or was primarily developed.[31] What the writer sees and thinks is already somewhat formed by the premise or premises of the system she or he uses.[32] Finally, Lucy Venable cites an anonymous respondent to the Dance Notation Bureau Labanotation Survey Report of 2001: "Notating allows me to simultaneously digest movement on both a kinetic and intellectual level. It provides the engine for the process of synthesis of body, mind and soul."[33]

With rare exception, these insights are presented as self-evident truths gleaned from practice; they are not, for the most part, set forth as conclusions drawn from meticulous, purposeful inquiry. They represent a body of knowledge that accrues to experts in movement observation and documentation as a result both of their ongoing attempts to capture the infinite nuances of living, breathing movement within necessarily finite notational systems and of their work fleshing out these same two-dimensional symbols when it is time to resurrect the performance from the page. Only Marion makes a really strong, sustained argument, with detailed exemplary material, to support a contention that dance scores, and the systems they are written in, do more than unproblematically transcribe movements into symbols.

In no way am I criticizing the notation community here. Rather, I am pointing out, as has been done before, that professional practice can bring to light many of the same insights as theoretical reasoning. In this section, I have shown that my inferences about analyses of dance notation formed under the aegis of Visual Culture Studies have their counterparts in the experiential knowledge that accrues to notation practitioners. I take this as confirmation of the validity of my claim that an analysis of dance notation systems and their scores can provide insight into changes in embodied subjectivity.

AN ARCHIVE OF VISION AND EMBODIMENT

Using notation scores as an archival resource for research on embodied subjectivity demands that the scholar put her own body at the center of her research practice. A comparison of scores at the level of the differences in individual symbols used might be interesting, up to a point. For example, the shift in Labanotation from analysis of torso movements in terms of chest tilts to descriptions of very similar actions in terms of folding[34] after the formal acceptance of those signs in 1977[35] might in itself reveal something about how notators conceived what they saw. Certainly, I can identify this difference whenever it occurs in my *Serenade* scores and then turn to my notation texts for a theoretical description of how these movement concepts differ. I can then conjecture a more fluid use of the torso when I read *folds* because the concept of folding considers the degrees of articulation of the spine as a whole. I get a sense of curving and curling. When I read a comparable displacement of the upper body described as a chest tilt, generally I have the idea of a more rigid and segmented use of the torso. I need to think of my spine in sections, isolating whatever might be thought of as the fixed and free ends and maintaining the integrity of that chunk of my upper back as I move away from the vertical. However, the real advantage of using a dance score to find out about the way people saw movement and thought about movement at the time it was written is that the score gives the scholar an opportunity to experience something of that way of moving for herself. It demands an understanding of the symbols in context as a dance. The difference between a tilt and a fold might be quite minimal in some cases, or it might alter the style of the piece entirely in others. It may depend on the tempo, on the actions that precede and follow, and on what else is happening in the body simultaneously. The significance of each individual symbol becomes fully apparent only in the dancing.

Notators know from experience that the dance gradually coheres as a whole in the moving body, and that predictably the whole is much richer and more complex than the symbols used to describe it. I believe this may be because the meaning resides *between* the notation symbols as much as it does *in* them.[36] Or rather, the symbols become meaningful only when the complexity of their relationships is given bodily form. In reading the opening phrase from *Serenade*, as written in Figure 14.1, I can articulate verbally that the lower right arm will take three measures to move to the side ending with the back of my hand touching the top right of my temple, but in practice I have to make sense of that with my body. When I move my lower right arm toward the horizontal, away from its former position reaching up to the front diagonal corner, I end with the back of my wrist closer to my nose. My arms are short and my neck is long. So, some adjustment is needed. If you try it, it may be different for you. What can I do to make *my* body make sense of the score? In this instance it is easily resolved with a little less flexion in my elbow and some minor adjustments to the position of my upper arm. When I see that my head should tilt and turn to the left, I find that it becomes a little easier to make the contact between hand and temple while keeping my lower arm horizontal, but only if I also adjust the degree of turn of my head. With a fraction less than a quarter-turn, it works for me. If I turn it the full quarter, as instructed in the score, it does not. With regard to the head gesture, I note that the tilt starts after the arm gesture, and then the turn begins slightly after that. It does not take much practice to co-ordinate the timing, but it does not happen automatically either. And still, this very simple gesture is not complete. Both the accent as the arm begins to move, and the vertical alignment of the hand that gives way to a sense that the wrist leads the movement of the lower arm, must be understood, bodily, as part of the whole. As I practice adding in one detail, some of the others get lost, until the moment when the notation makes somatic sense to me. At that point I can think of the action as a whole rather than having to contemplate the interrelation of its component parts. This is one of those moments where language seems to effect a distortion. When I "think of" the action as a whole as opposed to troubling myself with an analysis of its component parts, I really mean I can dance it. I do it. I understand the meaning of that tiny portion of the score. My "thinking" the movement is demonstrated in action and shows thereby that I know what I read.

This is quite different from simple recognition of the symbolic meaning of each of the signs used in the score. In a corporeal reading, each symbol or cluster of symbols affects the bodily sense of the others. And the specificity of small clusters of symbols needs to be balanced against the intention of the movement as a whole in terms of individual dance phrases and in terms of the way those phrases are shaped to make a dance. That is what I want to convey when I say the meaning of the notation lies *among* or *between* the symbols, and in their relation to each other, as much as or more than it resides in individual symbol instructions.

It might be argued that this somatic knowledge of the dance lacks objectivity.[37] The experience of the symbols cohering in performance and the interpretation the scholar lends to this in terms of notions of embodiment might be misconstrued as unacceptably solipsistic. Certainly, how I need to adjust the details of arm, neck, and head movement in order to achieve the gesture described above is peculiar to my body. Another dancer may not need to adjust at all, or may need to make entirely different adjustments. However, given that the meaning of the movement described arises *between* the symbols, the adjustments we each make in embodying these discrete signs should lead us to the same dance insofar as any two performances can ever be considered the same. Moreover, because notation systems rest on explicitly shared understandings about the look, feel, and intention of the movement in their purview, the notator's synaesthetic perception as reader and writer is always inextricably enmeshed in an intersubjective conceptual framework. The very visual way in which that conceptual framework is represented and articulated means it is always amenable to external scrutiny. This was made clear when I worked on the first section of *Serenade* with a small group of notation-literate dancers at The Ohio State University.

At first I worked alone in the studio, preparing the phrases of the dance to teach to my dancers and co-researchers, Sarah Barber, Alex Bowden, Julie Fox, and Mara Penrose. Then in rehearsals they waited, watched, and followed my demonstrations. They asked for clarifications and pushed me to return to the scores to check and double-check my understanding of the finest nuances of the movement. Through their endeavors, I saw more clearly what the notation articulates, and what it leaves out as being either already understood or else unimportant. At times we looked at short passages of the score together, discussing possible interpretations. They helped to confirm and extend my own kinaesthetic response to the Labanotation scores. It was surprising and exciting to discover just how different these two versions of *Serenade* are. The earlier version felt more "squared off," a little more angular, perhaps more austere. For my part, I felt as if I was dancing in "black and white" through the opening allegro phrases: I strove for a no-nonsense, modernist precision in order to fulfill what I infer as Guest's intent in those symbols. My dancers described the later version as lusher: there seemed to be more softness and pliability through the torso and richer flourishes with the arms.

The significance of each difference in analysis and each alteration of the choreography is slight by itself. Little by little, though, these differences accrue: a change in the path of the arm here, a turn of the head there, a *fondu* where before there was a straight leg. No single example in the score can really serve as a synecdoche in this analysis without seeming to overreach itself. Nonetheless, I am including two tiny score fragments (Figures 14.6 and 14.7) to indicate the kinds of features of the dance that shaped our interpretation. The two measures in these figures show a gallop backward with a large circling of the arms.[38] In each case the dancer is instructed to pause for a moment with one leg *degagé devant*, arms extended outward, before shifting the weight into a quick *assemblé soutenu* turn. After this, not shown, the dancers flock across the stage in preparation for the memorable sequence of *posés piqués* backward with alternating, almost "swimming," third *arabesque port de bras*.

In the earlier score (Figure 14.6), the head is described facing directly up to the ceiling at the end of the gallop while the arms reach out diagonally behind the body. This is marked with an accent, giving a sense of impactive phrasing on the arm circles. The position, though held only for a moment, feels more extreme than the later version (Figure 14.7) in which the arms are carried to a horizontal second position, palms down, and the head twists to the side. The arch in the back is described as just a slight fold backward in this later score. It is barely more than a lift through the chest. Combined with the description of a big step backward *en fondu* into extension of the supporting leg, it gives a sense of coming "up" out of the gallop. By contrast, the earlier score moves the chest 45° off vertical, and this extension into the backspace of the kinesphere makes the position seem rather more forceful and dynamic.[39] The sense is one of dynamic counter-tension through the body along the sagittal axis.

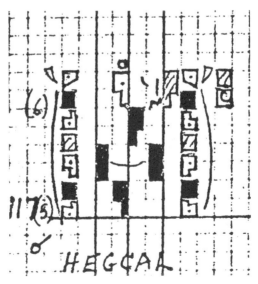

FIGURE 14.6 Galop detail, *Serenade*, from the Labanotation score by Harry Haythorne and Ann Hutchinson Guest (1964).

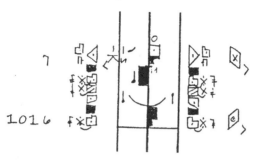

FIGURE 14.7 Galop detail, *Serenade*, from the Labanotation score by Virginia Doris (1983–1988).

The earlier score (Figure 14.6) shows the arms making a very direct path into fifth *en haut* for the execution of the turn. From an extended position, the dancer must pull everything back into tight vertical alignment above her standing leg. She turns "underneath herself" rather than stepping out through space. There are no flourishes of arms or legs, but rather a straightforward and efficiently fast turn that will lead off into a run. There is much more going on in the movement recorded in the later score (Figure 14.7). Rather than pulling up to a tight fifth for the turn, the dancer steps forward *en fondu* and takes the working leg out through a low second before pulling into fifth for the turn. At the same time, the arms make a more elaborate *port de bras*, sweeping down through *bras bas* and up through first on the way to fifth. And whereas in the first version the arms come swiftly to fifth and stay there as the turn is executed, in the later score although the sweep down is swift the arms arrive in fifth at the completion of the turn. I urge readers to try these two sequences for themselves by reading the notation. My verbal description is an impoverished substitute for the exactitude of the notation scores and the plenitude of experience involved in dancing the differences.

Across the notation of this first movement of *Serenade*, higher leg extensions, full turns in lieu of simple changes of directions, and the addition of *batterie* to some of the soloist's *petit allegro* indicate that the technical challenges of the dance increased in the later version. Then again, for the first solo entrance, my dancers and I found the *allegro* phrase in the 1964 version (Figure 14.8) far more challenging to perform. The dancer must stay in the air for longer and transition swiftly on landing through *petit developpé* to *piqué attitude*. The momentum is arrested before the sequence repeats.

In the later score (Figure 14.9), this phrase has a more fluid preparation into the *grand jeté*, and the dancer is never required to stay elevated for longer than one count.[40] The flow of travel is continuous and relaxed. This brief entrance has the brio of exuberant *grand allegro* in both versions. The "ta-da!" moments of display when the dancer is balanced momentarily in *attitude* in the first version feel more formal, aware of and acknowledging an audience. The second version feels more "natural" (if such a thing can ever be said of ballet), more easygoing and generally freer.

The BMN version of this same phrase (Figure 14.10), notated by Faith Worth in 1964 and shown here on the staffs marked "Svetlana," is not a final master. Nonetheless it is

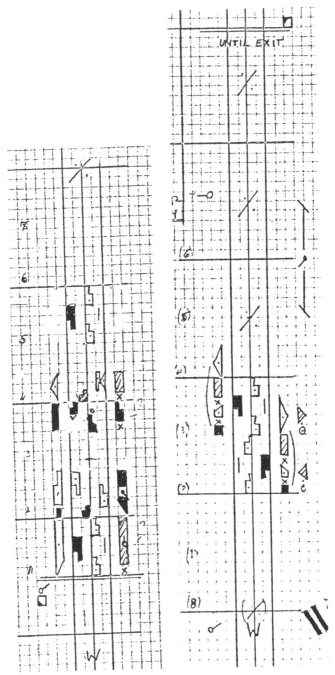

FIGURE 14.8 First solo entrance, *Serenade*, from the Labanotation score by Harry Haythorne and Ann Hutchinson Guest (1964).

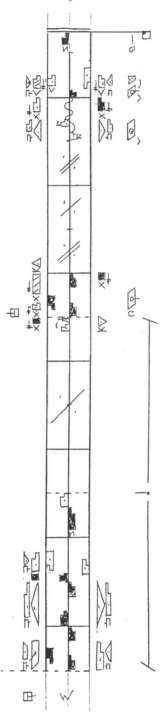

FIGURE 14.9 First solo entrance, *Serenade,* from the Labanotation score by Virginia Doris (1983–1988).

FIGURE 14.10 First solo entrance, *Serenade*, from the BMN score by Faith Worth (1964).

clear enough to show that this solo entrance is given comparable form by two notators using different systems.[41] I can be confident that the difference between the two Labanotation scores is indeed a change in choreography and performance rather than an error in recording. Worth uses dancers' phrases of a group of eight followed by a group of six counts rather than musical measures to mark out the timing. This timing maps closely, though not exactly, against the dancers' counts written in parentheses alongside the staff in Figure 14.8.

There are slight differences in analysis in the BMN version. For example, in this score the exit from the *attitude,* after the *grand jeté,* folds through a *retiré en fondu* and quickly into a little hop as the working leg extends *devant* in preparation for the next *temps levé.* In Guest's Labanotation score (Figure 14.8) the dancer simply steps forward. With no specific analysis for this action, the dancer will perform it in the most straightforward way. Ordinarily if the leg is written extended behind and is then supposed to step forward, the absence of analysis would lead a reader to conclude that the leg should move directly and efficiently en route to the step. In context here, the working leg is likely to move through *retiré* rather than simply lowering before stepping forward. The performance of that transition is not necessarily a choreographic choice as much as a technical one. The Labanotation score tells the dancer to just "get there" for the repeat. The BMN score suggests how that "get there" might be accomplished. A reader who is able to decode the symbols but cannot reconstitute them as performance might overplay this difference bet-ween the scores and hence make more of the transition in Figure 14.10 than is really required, or else struggle to achieve the "get there" in time if following Figure 14.8.

There is also a different specificity in the analysis of the timing of the *port de bras* in the BMN score. Because the score shows the position reached at the top of the jump, the arms and leg reach *arabesque* simultaneously. By contrast, the first action recorded in Figure 14.8 shows that the arms take the whole count to reach the *arabesque* line while the leg gets there beforehand. It is physically possible to do the *temps levé* in *arabesque* this way, but it seems unlikely to me. I think it seems awkward, unballetic somehow, to try to do it sequentially, and I imagine that most dancers reading Guest's score would reach the *arabesque* while in the air without thinking too much about the way the timing of the arms is written. The tempo, the dynamics of the movement, and the conventions of ballet all suggest as much. The analysis in Labanotation of the same action is shown in Figure 14.9 reflecting this more usual understanding of the coordination of arms and legs.

CONCLUSION

My contention, that changes in the theory and practice of dance notation reflect changes in embodied subjectivity, will remain speculative until a much wider-ranging synchronic and diachronic analysis of notation systems can be undertaken. However, in this chapter I have demonstrated that dance notations and their scores are an unrivaled resource for understanding movement and choreography for dance scholars and researchers who are interested in questions of embodiment. Dance notation systems permit the scholar to see the "seeing" of times passed and to grapple with incorporating different ways of moving into her or his somatic understanding of dance history. They do this in a way that is personal or in some way intimate but that is also easily shared and hence debated. Calls for forms of scholarly enquiry that integrate the soma persist, but it remains common to encounter writing that treats the body as a text to be deciphered, effacing the embodied subjectivity of the scholar. I have shown that a disembodied objectivity becomes unten-able when using a score.

The understanding of movement as it is instantiated in each score arises from a detailed reading of the specific instructions inhering in each symbol, but an analysis of these symbols alone cannot generate the holistic knowledge my dancers and I sensed in the movement. As I remarked earlier, any meaning of the notation lies *between* or *among* the symbols as much as or more than it resides in individual symbol instruc-tions and the principles of movement and of observation that organize them. Further, this meaning remains inchoate unless the reader figures out how to *dance* what is writ-ten. The pioneering semiotician Charles Saunders Peirce suggested that for all sys-tems of signification meaning is "the proper significate effect of a sign"[42]; in other words, signs show their meaning through usage. Dance notations are a kind of technology of vision: they are systems of signification that communicate ideas about vision and embodiment specifically as they pertain to dance. They show their meaning through being danced.

NOTES

1. Figure 14.1 is copied from Ann Hutchinson Guest's Labanotation score of 1964, based on an earlier incomplete draft by Harry Haythorne. Guest completed the score following observations of rehearsals when Una Kai staged the work for Great Britain's Royal Ballet for the 1964 season. Figure 14.2 is transcribed from Virginia Doris, written between 1983 and 1988, from the production taught by Suki Schorer to students at the School of American Ballet.

2. I am thinking specifically of Nelson Goodman, Joseph Margolis, and Graham McFee. It suffices to say that each of the writers mobilizes an idea about notation to service their respective arguments about the nature of dance. In each instance there is a considerable gap between the dance notation as they describe it in the abstract and the practical workings of any system that has withstood sustained professional use. Goodman, *Languages of Art* (Indianapolis: Hackett, 1976); Margolis, "The Autographic Nature of Dance," *Illuminating Dance*, ed. Maxine Sheets-Johnstone (Toronto: Associated University Presses, 1984); McFee, *Understanding Dance* (London: Routledge, 1992).

3. In *Choreographing Empathy,* Susan Leigh Foster aims to track how "physicality and with it a specific experience of the kinesthetic have changed radically" (75). She includes a discussion of Feuillet notation, but understandably, given the broad historical scope of her study, she does not consider a broad range of notation systems nor the kinesthetic practices each might engage. Foster, *Choreographing Empathy* (Abingdon, Oxon, UK: Routledge, 2011).

4. The idea that modes of moving, in even the most everyday ways, change through time was first most persuasively set forth by the French sociologist Marcel Mauss. In his influential essay "Techniques of the Body," he pointed out that how people sit, sleep, walk, work with tools, and so forth is culturally and historically specific. He described with some humor how preposterous the method of swimming that was taught to him as a boy now appears. Comparably, George Balanchine, giving free range to his thoughts on the art of ballet in a short piece titled "Mr. B. Talks About Ballet," wrote that "one hundred years from now there won't be ballet as we're doing it today. Just like one hundred years ago, you'd laugh if you saw Carlotta Grisi or Taglioni dance today" (206). Mauss, "Techniques of the Body," *Economy and Society*, 2.1 (1973); Balanchine, "Mr. B Talks About Ballet," *George Balanchine,* ed. Robert Gottlieb (New York: Atlas Books, 2004).

5. There are a couple of excellent books that provide an overview of Visual Culture Studies. Margaret Dikovitskaya surveys the debates surrounding the constitution of Visual Culture Studies as a discipline and presents an argument for a methodology of Visual Culture that lies somewhere between art history and cultural studies. She also concerns herself with the institutional make-up of programs for Visual Culture and their pedagogical perspectives. The book concludes with transcripts of interviews with nearly all of the influential scholars in the field. James Elkins provides both an overview of Visual Studies as it stands and a polemic about its future. He surveys the antecedents of the field, interrogates the canonical texts used and the methodologies employed, and makes suggestions as to how the field might become more innovative theoretically and ideologically. Dikovitskaya, *Visual Culture: The Study of the Visual After the Cultural Turn*

(Cambridge, MA: MIT Press, 2006); Elkins, *Visual Studies: A Skeptical Introduction* (New York: Routledge, 2003).

6. For more on the history of the Feuillet system, see Jean-Noel Laurenti, "Feuillet's Thinking," *Traces of Dance* (Paris: Édition Dis Voir, 1994); Ken Pierce, "Dance Notation Systems in Late 17th-Century France," *Early Music* 26.2 (1998).

7. Vera Maletic notes that Laban was very much a product of his time when she provides an overview of his career and the development of his ideas in her book *Body-Space-Expression*. She draws a number of connections between his work and trends in German culture during the early twentieth century (32–36) and explicitly references the Bauhaus when talking about Laban's articulation of a new sense of space. Maletic, *Body-Space-Expression* (New York: Mouton de Gruyter, 1987).

8. Jean-Noel Laurenti discusses the high degree of analysis built into the system, suggesting that the steps are broken into small units and then combined in such a way that this one notational lexicon can record dance steps from various dance traditions across Europe. In such a way, he argues, the Feuillet system began to codify and homogenize the court dances of Europe in a universalizing way and in a way that is very much in line with the Age of Reason and the burgeoning of the Enlightenment. Laurenti, "Feuillet's Thinking."

9. Early dance historian Belinda Quirey objected to the confusion a term such as "position" can cause in describing dances, especially in light of what she saw as a distinctly modern pre-occupation with shaping the body at the expense of attention to spatial patterns. She suggested instead body location and body shape, and I follow her example here. Quirey, "Dance and Movement Notations," *Journal of the English Folk Dance and Song Society* 8.2 (1957).

10. Some scores in Beauchamps-Feuillet do give indications for arm gestures. But beyond the routine statement of whether dancers are holding hands or not, this is not a common feature of the system.

11. Culler, *Ferdinand de Saussure* (New York: Cornell University, 1986), 127–128. Clearly, and in spite of the fact that academic fashions have turned away from structuralism in recent years, there is much to be gained from applying a Saussurean analysis to dance notation systems. Jonathan Culler's book on Saussure is exemplary for both explaining and assessing the impact of Saussure's work. For a more general review of semiotics, Roland Barthes' text still presents an excellent starting point. Finally, Winfried Nöth's handbook is a useful reference text. Barthes, *Elements of Semiology* (New York: Hill and Wang, 1985); Nöth, *Handbook of Semiotics* (Bloomington: Indiana University Press, 1990).

12. W. J. T. Mitchell "Interdisciplinarity and Visual Culture." *Art Bulletin* LXXVII, no.4 (1995), 543. For more on the history of the hierarchy of the senses, see Anthony Synnott, "Puzzling over the Senses: From Plato to Marx," *The Varieties of Sensory Experience: A Sourcebook in the Anthropology of the Senses* (Toronto: University of Toronto Press, 1991); Suzannah Biernoff, "Carnal Relations: Embodied Sight in Merleau-Ponty, Roger Bacon and St. Francis," *Journal of Visual Culture* 4.1 (2005).

13. Phenomenologist Merleau-Ponty is widely cited in Visual Culture scholarship. I recommend his meditation on Cézanne's painting as a lucid demonstration of how crucial the integration of the visible world and the world of motor projects are in his thinking. Merleau-Ponty, "Eye and Mind," *The Merleau-Ponty Aesthetics Reader* (Evanston, IL: Northwestern University Press, 1993).

14. In brief, Benesh Movement Notation is written on a five-line stave, slightly larger in scale than that used for music. The lines of the stave represent the top of the head, the lines of the

shoulders, the waist, the knees, and finally the floor. For a simple explanation of the basics of the system, see Rudolf Benesh, *An Introduction to Nenesh Dance Notation* (London: Adam and Charles Black, 1956); Julia McGuiness-Scott, *Movement Study and Benesh Movement Notation* (London: Oxford University Press, 1983). For a more in-depth explanation in the context of classical ballet, see Monica Parker, *Benesh Movement Notation: Elementary Solo Syllabus—Ballet Application* (London: Benesh Institute, 1996).

15. Thomas Sebeok's book *Signs: An Introduction to Semiotics* includes a very clear taxonomy of sign types. Sebeok, *Signs* (Toronto: University of Toronto Press, 2001).

16. John Martin invoked this same kind of kinesthetic empathy in his theory of metakinesis to explain how audiences might find dance meaningful. Subsequently, neuroscientists have discovered that "mirror neurons" fire in the brain whenever people see movement. When I watch someone else jump, turn, or stretch, those same areas of my brain respond as they would if I were moving myself, albeit to a more limited extent. However, there is some dissent as to how significant the existence of mirror neurons really is in terms of making judgments about the nature of mind and its relationship to the body. For more on "mirror neurons" and the insights cognitive science brings to an understanding of the relationship between mind and body, see Shaun Gallagher, *How the Body Shapes the Mind* (Oxford: Clarendon Press, 2005); Raymond W. Jr. Gibbs, *Embodiment and Cognitive Science* (Cambridge, MA: Cambridge University Press, 2006).

17. This is in direct contrast to Labanotation, in which rhythm and the relative timing of gestures is highly visual.

18. I take this turn of phrase from W. J. T. Mitchell, one of the earliest champions of Visual Culture Studies. This is another excellent introduction to and overview of the Visual Culture Studies project. As a dance scholar, I find his willingness to acknowledge the materiality of embodiment as a constitutive aspect of culture to be particularly helpful. Mitchell, "Showing Seeing: A Critique of Visual Culture," *The Visual Culture Reader* (New York: Routledge, 2002).

19. In addition to heavyweights of the canon, such as Derrida, Merleau-Ponty, and Kristeva, see, for example, Thomas J. Csordas, "Embodiment and Cultural Phenomenology," *Perspectives on Embodiment* (New York: Routledge, 1999); Eugene T. Gendlin, "The Wider Role of Bodily Sense in Thought and Language," *Giving the Body Its Due* (Albany: State University of New York Press, 1992); Mark Johnson, *The Meaning of the Body* (Chicago: University of Chicago Press, 2007); George Lakoff and Mark Johnson, *Metaphors We Live By* (Chicago: University of Chicago Press, 2003); Paul Stoller, *Sensuous Scholarship* (Philadelphia: University of Pennsylvania Press, 1997).

20. I find that dance notation is a rich field for exploring the dissolution of binary thinking. See my article "Dancing the Score: Dance Notation and *Différance*" for an exploration of Derrida's critique of logocentrism as it might apply to dance notation. Watts, "Dancing the Score," *Dance Research* 28.1 (2010).

21. *The Choreologist* started out as a student journal for dancers training at the Benesh Institute (then known as the Institute of Choreology) and became the journal/newsletter whereby the institute and its professional members kept in touch and shared information.

22. Judy Van Zile, "Exploring Notation as a Research Tool: Implications of Selected Projects on Asian and Pacific Dance," *Proceedings of the 11ᵗʰ Biennial Conference of the International Conference of Kinetography Laban* (1979), 32.

23. Nadia Chilkovsky Nahumck, "Space–Consequent Movement," *Proceedings of the 13ᵗʰ Biennial Conference of the International Conference of Kinetography Laban* (1983), 134.

24. Suzanne Youngerman, "Movement Notation Systems as Conceptual Frameworks: The Laban System," *Illuminating Dance: Philosophical Explorations*, ed. Maxine Sheets-Johnstone (Toronto: Associated University Presses, 1984), 101.

25. The first of the scores of *Billy the Kid* under analysis was notated in 1942, the second in 1983 with further revisions in 1988–89. Sheila Marion uses her analysis to explore developments in the system of Labanotation, showing how the same movement was written differently over an interval of approximately forty-five years. She notes that some patterns emerged that may have broader implications. For example, "[i]nclusion in the score of elements supplementing the notation speak to a more inclusive approach to documentation, while dissimilarities in movement description create a different feel to certain aspects of the dance" (107). Marion, "A Comparison of Two Scores of *Billy the Kid*," *Proceedings of the 17th Biennial Conference of the International Conference of Kinetography Laban* (1991).

26. Liz Cunliffe, "The Study Group—A Personal Reflection," *The Choreologist* 31, Winter (1985), 9.

27. Vera Maletic, "Qualitative Annotations of Labanotation Scores," *Proceedings of the 17th Biennial Conference of the International Conference of Kinetography Laban* (1991), 73.

28. Faith Worth, "My Work as a Choreologist with the Royal Ballet," *The Dancing Times*, June 1967, 469.

29. Dominique Dupuy, "Believing in Notation," *Proceedings of the 19th Biennial Conference of the International Conference of Kinetography Laban* (1995). This comment resonates with Joan Benesh's claim, made in her tribute to her husband just after his death, that BMN made possible "the preservation of creative thought." *The Choreologist* 6 (1975).

30. Rhonda Ryman and John Beatty, "Basic Issues in the Laban Notation of Ballet Vocabulary: Code Versus Analysis," *Proceedings of the 19th Biennial Conference of the International Conference of Kinetography Laban* (1995), 63.

31. Sheila Marion, "Towards a New Paradigm for Exploring Dance Notation," *Proceedings of the 20th Biennial Conference of the International Conference of Kinetography Laban* (1997), 139.

32. Ilene Fox makes a similar claim, albeit purely anecdotally, in a conference paper that is predominantly concerned with the question of what counts as "movement." Having remarked upon the importance of avoiding cultural or genre bias within the system, she then states: "A style of early German modern dance was clearly based on relationship to space. When notating a reconstruction of Oskar Schlemmer's *Bauhaus Dances* and a work choreographed by Hanya Holm (who came out of that German tradition), I felt that their work had been choreographed to be notated by our system" (9). I would suggest then that genre bias clearly exists in some form in Labanotation and in all other systems when it appears as though some styles of choreography are much more readily suited to its description than others. Fox, "What Is Movement?" *Proceedings of the 19th Biennial Conference of the International Conference of Kinetography Laban* (1995).

33. Lucy Venable, "The Dance Notation Bureau Labanotation Survey Report," *Proceedings of the 17th Biennial Conference of the International Conference of Kinetography Laban* (2001), 118.

34. For a brief explanation of folding for the torso, see Guest, *Labanotation* (London: Routledge, 2005) 287–88.

35. See the conference proceedings for a detailed record of new theory adopted and decisions regarding ongoing attempts to synthesize practices in Labanotation and Kinetography Laban. *Proceedings of 10th Biennial Conference of the International Council of Kinetography Laban* (1977).

36. Here again, there is a correspondence with Saussure's analysis of language. It is in the differences between individual sounds, individual words, that meaning is formed. See Saussure, "From 'Course in General Linguistics,'" *Critical Theory since* 1965 (Tallahassee: Florida State University Press, 1986).

37. I point readers again to the work of scholars such as Mark Johnson and George Lakoff, who show that the "objectivity" in question here is always mythic and promotes a dichotomizing between objectivity and subjectivity that runs in tandem with other discredited modes of binary thinking. I am taking seriously the contention that cognition is embodied and that we, as subjects, are not radically "other" to the environment we live in but rather are, as Merleau-Ponty suggests, wholly enworlded. Thus, there is no "object world" as such out there. As Lakoff and Johnson write: "The real world is not an objectivist universe, especially those aspects of the real world having to do with human beings: human experience, human institutions, human language, the human conceptual system" (218). I follow their lead, then, in adopting what they term an "experientialist perspective" (230). Lakoff and Johnson, *Metaphors We Live By*.

38. I am aware that these two examples show the gallop backward on different legs. Although this motif is performed in canon along different facings on both the left and right legs, the gallop prior to the turn is performed on the right leg by all dancers in the later production and on the left by all in the earlier version.

39. In Labanotation scores written prior to 1969, the absence of a pre-sign in the third column indicated a tilt of the chest. In Kinetography scores of the same era, this third column was used for a different kind of analysis of the upper body that had its origins in the style of dance employed in the mass movement choirs with which Albrecht Knust was so well acquainted. I am relatively certain that the meaning intended here is a chest tilt because of the context of the movement and the provenance of the score. For an explanation of the analysis of upper body movement used by kinetographers, see Guest, *Labanotation* 442–45.

40. It is widely known that Balanchine changed his choreography to accommodate weaknesses and showcase the strengths of his favored ballerinas. For example, speaking about *Apollo*, Alexandra Danilova remarked: "Today, it's a different ballet. For one thing, the steps for Terpsichore's variation are different. What I danced was lighter, smaller, and quicker. I did fifth, arabesque, fifth, arabesque—nobody does that anymore. And then I did sissonnes—my version was jumpier than the one they dance today. Balanchine changed it when Suzanne Farrell learned the part because she couldn't jump so well—she's taller than I am, and she couldn't move as fast.... The adagio I did was the same as every Terpsichore's, but lately I notice that dancers tend to emphasize the angular aspects and accelerate everything in between, which I didn't do" (1004). Danilova, "Apollo," *Reading* Dance (New York: Pantheon, 2008). Moreover, Balanchine re-choreographed *Serenade* repeatedly, so in order to infer significance from the differences between the scores, I will need to do more extensive contextual and historical research.

41. As mentioned in note 1, both Faith Worth's BMN score and Ann Hutchinson Guest's Labanotation score were recorded from rehearsals of Britain's Royal Ballet production in 1964.

42. Cited in Nöth, *Handbook of Semiotics*, 101.

Dido, Queen of Carthage, has fallen in love with the Trojan Prince Aeneas. Meanwhile, the Sorceress, with her coven of witches, plots their downfall.[1]

15

Reading Music, Gesture, and Narrative in Mark Morris' *Dido and Aeneas*

Rachael Riggs-Leyva

THIS TEXT OPENS Mark Morris' videotaped staging of *Dido and Aeneas*, directed by Barbara Willis Sweete, and set to 17th-century English composer Henry Purcell's opera of the same name (c. 1689).[2] Morris' staging generally follows the narrative produced by Purcell and librettist Nahum Tate, translating music and language into movement. In Morris' *Dido*, the dancers play the stage characters, voiced by off-camera singers. The prologue text, and the staging of the Overture, act as exposition to the dramatic narrative and serve to key the audience in to the choreographic world Morris has established, where music, libretto, and choreography fuse in communicative cohesion.

Text, music, and action invite the audience into the musical, gestural world of Morris' dance adaptation of Purcell's opera. The opening of the Overture collages a series of several shots moving from extreme close-up to an extreme wide shot, creating spatial-dramatic tension and anticipation. Aeneas and Dido's separate groups pass through the frame of each shot, their collective weight evenly rocking with the solemn pulse of the music. The dancers approach the stage space in a grave procession that they will repeat when they exit the stage space at the close of the opera. Everyone pauses. This moment of stillness holds great tension through the device of an extreme wide shot: the dancers perch in anticipation, ready to cross the threshold, their bodies dwarfed by the larger-than-life title text "Dido and Aeneas" that fills the gulf between them.

On a staccato chord, everyone quickly turns away from the center, releasing the palpable pressure between Aeneas and the group that now disperses into a completely new energy. The strings quicken, playing running eighth notes; the group of courtiers skitters forward, each one holding his or her sarong with one hand while the other hand daintily points to the side. The posture and abruptness of the skitter do not completely upend the grave weight and melodrama of the dancers' unceasing entrance, but suggest a wry sense of humor to come; the stage is set for irony and tragedy.

A multi-layered choreographic text such as Morris' *Dido and Aeneas* communicates meaning across visual, aural, verbal, and non-verbal mediums. New perspectives on reading and literacy, as described by David Barton, broaden definitions of literacy to that of taking meaning from many sorts of texts: "Literacy is based upon a system of symbols…used for communication, and as such exists in relation to other systems of information exchange. It is a way of representing the world to ourselves."[3] Reading is a meaning making; an interpretive enterprise, and symbolic systems are abundantly pictorial, gestural, notational, or even social, making reading across systems an activity that is salient to analyzing Morris' *Dido and Aeneas*. Morris' version is skillfully crafted, weaving musical score and libretto into complex relationships with the choreography, ripe for reading and interpreting. Although Morris' venture is story telling, his means of communicating the narrative rely on various symbolic systems—musical score, libretto, and choreography—joining physical, visual, aural, and written forms.

Parallels between symbolic systems aid in interpreting the music/libretto-dance relationship essential to Morris' version of *Dido and Aeneas*. Morris' choreographic conventions embody values similar to 17th-century music in his expression of emotion and words through systematized, conventionalized compositional devices. During the 16th and 17th centuries, European composers developed a canon of musical figures, meant to translate various rhetorical practices and devices for musical purposes: "In the same way that an orator was to ornament and heighten his [sic] speech through rhetorical figures to lend it greater persuasive effect, so too could the composer portray and arouse the affections through comparable musical figures."[4] These devices would have been widely understood by musicians and musically educated audiences and were thus effective in portraying various affections, abstract ideas, and even specific words or passages in the vocal text. Morris does not adapt actual devices or figures from the 17th century, but he creates his own lexicon that operates in a similar fashion. Morris employs symbolic gestures to represent specific words, characters, and concepts within the text of the libretto. Through their repetition, they become memorable, infused with meaning, instructing one how to read the choreography. Using these mimetic actions within the choreography, the dancers' bodies express dialogue between characters, evocatively visualizing the libretto through movement.

In addition to examining a visualization of the libretto, this essay analyzes the choreographic translation of the musical score. Morris is famous for his treatment of the dance-music connection. Joan Acocella, his biographer, describes how he chooses music: "Is the music danceable? Is its structure clear?…Almost always, the idea for the dance is born from the music."[5] Because of the order—music leads, dance follows—the music becomes the guide to the form and content of Morris' work. One framework for analysis I will use is from the Eurhythmics system, developed by the early-20th-century Swiss musician and movement theorist Emile Jaques-Dalcroze for training the physical expression of musical elements. In the Eurhythmics system, movement and music are parallel mediums, and one can be used to understand the other. Morris' choreography visually translates various elements of Purcell's musical score into movement, a method known as music visualization. Dalcroze's framework provides a starting place for drawing connections between what is heard and seen.[6] Dance scholar and musicologist Stephanie Jordan further develops the theoretical construct of musical visualization in choreography to include not just the parallel relationships proposed by Dalcroze but also counterpoint and oppositional relationships.[7] When so much of the choreography creates a parallel relationship with the music, moments of contrapuntal relationship become especially important and meaningful to the dramatic narrative as contrasts.

Finally, Morris' *Dido and Aeneas* evokes the principle of dualism. With the advent of the 17th-century philosopher Descartes' mind-body split, dualist constructs spread into the arts and sciences. For Baroque music, dualism emerged in the contrast between freedom for extravagant expression and disciplined compositional order[8]: between free-rhythms as in *recitative* or *cadenza* and metered time, between loud and soft dynamic contrasts, or between major and minor keys, consonant and dissonant harmonies, for example. In Purcell's and Tate's score and libretto, dualism is most noticeably marked by the presence of the "good" Dido with her court, and the "evil" plotting Sorceress and her coven of witches.

Dualism appears in Morris' work as contrasts, juxtapositions of opposites and extremes, sometimes within the same character or dancer. Morris' choreographic sensibility amplifies the "good-evil" contrast, mixing the tragic and the sardonic. The exaggerated characterization and bawdy movement vocabulary of the witches contrast the chaste and restrained actions of Dido and the courtiers. Yet the relationship is more complicated than a simple "good" versus "evil" narrative. Interlaced with musical visualization and symbolic gestures, Morris' dualism leaves room for reading parallels between the two characters. These parallels and juxtapositions are intensified because they are contained within one body—Morris' body—and suggest a worldview in which beauty and the grotesque, order and chaos, irony and tragedy, exist only in the context of the other.

THE PLOT SYNOPSIS

Purcell's opera, and by extension Morris' re-telling, primarily follows the plot of the narrative between Aeneas, the future founder of Rome, and Dido, the tragic queen of Carthage, from Virgil's *Aeneid*. At the start of the opera and Morris' adaptation, Aeneas, the only remaining survivor of the downfall of Troy, has already shipwrecked on the shores of Carthage. Purcell's original score, as performed by the girls' school in Chelsea (1689), is considered lost to history; the score consulted for this chapter is from *The*

Works of Henry Purcell, edited by William H. Cummings.[9] A Prologue for the opera exists without a music score, and Morris' production omits it completely, replacing it with a shorter exposition text and staging for the Overture, described previously. In the opening of Act I in Dido's court, Belinda, Dido's handmaiden, danced by Ruth Davidson, tries unsuccessfully to cheer Dido into pursuing the relationship with Aeneas; Dido expresses her inner torment and trepidation. Aeneas joins the queen, prompting the court to dance and rejoice. He proposes marriage; she accepts.

Purcell's opera invents the Sorceress and her coven of witches, who were not included in Virgil's narrative of Dido and Aeneas. In Act II scene 1, the Cave, the Sorceress beckons her "wayward sisters" (mm. 17–18) to create a plot against Dido. The foundation of this rivalry is never clear from Tate's libretto, but it may have arisen because the dramatic action necessitates a villain to create opposition against beauty, love, and prosperity found in Dido and her court. The two characters never directly interact or even share a scene. The Sorceress and her coven plan to send a storm to end the court's hunting party, forcing them back to the palace; in the confusion, they will trick Aeneas by appearing as fate to call him away to continue his voyage toward Rome.

In scene 2, the Grove and Hunting Party in Morris' version, we witness a passionless consummation of Dido and Aeneas' love.[10] Afterward, the hunting party attends to a lively story of Diana, sung by the Second Woman, danced by Rachel Murray. As plotted by the witches, a storm erupts, and all hasten to town. A witch disguised as Mercury appears to Aeneas to call him back to his destiny to found Rome, twisting the traditional narrative of the myth. Rather than actually being called to continue his quest by the gods, Aeneas is deceived into accepting his fate. A song and dance by Aeneas' sailors follows as they prepare to leave Carthage, in the opening of Act III. The witches reappear, delighting in the execution of their plot; they further predict Dido's downfall and suicide. In Purcell's opera, a dance follows, while for Morris it is a melee and orgy between the Sorceress and her coven. In the final scene in the palace, Dido mourns her forsaken state, having been abandoned by Aeneas after their brief affair. When Aeneas briefly reappears to plead his case, she sends him away once and for all. The story ends with Dido's final lament and suicide.

LIBRETTO VISUALIZATION AND SYMBOLIC GESTURES

Just as Morris' *Dido and Aeneas* is a visualization of the music, it is also a translation of the libretto. Because the dancers act the sung roles, they communicate their lines through gesture and movement, extending the concept of music visualization to include the libretto. Morris' use of repeated gestures does not simply follow repetition in the libretto; it instructs the viewer how to read the dance. Repetition connects the present performance of a gesture to a previous performance of the same gesture, and the nature of that performance can further signal continuity or change. As with musical development, symphonic devices cross-reference material over time.[11] Repetition creates familiarity and can drive progression, or stress circularity, within the narrative.

Morris' use of symbolic gesture is not unlike certain 17th-century musical principles where ideas and emotions were thought to be represented in music through a "systematic, regulated vocabulary."[12] For example, a minor key was used for sad music, a bouncing rhythm could represent running or playing, or rising notes could represent joy or heavenly subjects. This was the case for both instrumental and vocal music, and meanings within the text were expressed through conventionalized musical devices, many adapted from classical rhetorical practices. According to Bartel, a composer "sought to analyze and define his [sic] linguistic source and then construct a parallel linguistic structure.... The text was to be depicted and explained, reflected on and taught. This process included a search for analogies between text and music."[13] More simply, this practice is known as word painting.

As a 17th-century composer, Purcell uses word painting throughout the opera.[14] The libretto of the final chorus, "With drooping wings," sings about drooping wings of cupids (mm. 1–10) and scattering roses on Dido's tomb (mm. 11–14). The drooping wings are represented in the music melodically with melodic passages lilting down the scale; one can hear the wings drooping. The scattering roses are shown rhythmically and melodically by eighth-notes running up and down the scale. The tragedy of Dido's death is further iterated by the frequent use of chromatic accidentals and non-harmonic tones.[15] Likewise in Morris' choreography, the drooping wings are danced with drooping torsos and swinging, wing-like arms, matching the lilting rhythm of the text.

Libretto visualization in the choreography consists primarily of symbolic and mimetic gestures, which represent and illustrate specific words or ideas within the sung libretto. When Morris created his *Dido and Aeneas* in the late 20th century, there was no highly codified, systematic vocabulary of symbolic gestures in common currency in concert dance.[16] In lieu of an established set of conventional gestures, he created his own vocabulary of gestures for the opera. Repetition and re-enactment of events and actions link the current moment to previous moments, and it is through repetition and re-enactment that these events and actions gain symbolic and referential meaning. Paul Connerton, in *How Societies Remember*, describes the rhetoric of re-enactment as "causing to reappear that which has disappeared...the permanent making present of [a] temporal situation."[17] In Morris's staging/work/version many words and ideas have specific gestures attached, which are repeated whenever that word is sung:

- "Fate" is typically displayed as both arms twisted outward and stretched to the sides, with the fingers grotesquely splayed apart, as if to show fate's cruel, controlling nature.
- References to "thought," "remember," and other synonyms move with the palm of the hand lightly touching the forehead.

- References to "desire," "heart," or heavy "pressed" emotions are danced with the hands sliding down the front of the torso, fingers pointing downward toward open and bent legs.
- "Forsook," in reference to Dido's encounter and abandonment by Aeneas, is performed with the backs of the hands hitting the inner thighs.
- "Dido," "beauty," "fair," and other synonyms employ a hand circling the face.
- "Aeneas" and references to him such as "Trojan guest" or "hero," as well as "triumph" and "conquer," use a sideward bow with arms curved upward or a muscleman biceps flexing pose.
- For "flames," the fingers flutter.

That gestures and movement motifs recur with specific words, concepts, and phrases implies that the movement is meaningful and referential. Recognizing which gestures match words or ideas becomes a game, to find as many links as possible. The list here is not exhaustive of all the word-gesture pairings.

When these gestures are combined in sequence, they inscribe visual monologue and dialogue in the dancers' bodies. Rather than translate every word of the libretto, the word painting catches the most salient words in each line. Recalling Belinda's opening *aria* "Shake the clouds" from the top of Act I, dancer Ruth Davidson's gestures demonstrate soprano Ann Monoyios' sung lines. Davidson shakes her hands as Monoyios sings "Shake the clouds from off your brow" and embraces Morris while gesturing to his brow (mm. 3–5^2). For "fate your wishes does allow," Davidson grandly performs the fate gesture and then curtsies and holds her palms open to Morris; on "Empire growing, Pleasures flowing," Davidson's arm and focus sweeps around the stage as if to reference the vastness of Carthage, and then she hops from foot to foot while rippling her hands, evoking the flowing pleasures. Monoyios sings "Fortune smiles and so should you," and Davidson's hands draw upward toward her face, straining the very corners of her mouth upward before sitting next to Morris with an open palm, inviting her to smile. With the final chorus in Act III, scene 2, "With drooping wings," the libretto implores "keep here your watch and never part." The dancers emphatically point their fingers in place on "here," then bow their heads and hover with their arms as cupids watching from above. They repeat a carving "never" gesture, and part their arms as though pinching a long string. These examples show how the gestures illustrate the words literally through mime-like actions, and symbolically through abstract gestures repeated over time.

The narrative of Morris' *Dido and Aeneas* owes as much to Purcell's musical score and Tate's libretto scores as it does to Morris' own choreographic and directorial tastes. The basic story arc and character development reside within the scores, but from those scores Morris forms his own telling of the story. His repeated use of symbolic and mimetic gestures allow him to add foreshadowing and thematic subtext to the choreography. For example, imagery from the final *recitative* and *aria* are foreshadowed in the choreography at the beginning of the opera. In the *recitative* of her final aria before her suicide, Dido sings, "Thy hand, Belinda; darkness shades me, On thy bosom let me rest." Dido stretches her hand toward Belinda, who wraps her arms around Dido's chest and brow. These same images are seen in two places in Act I: the embrace during "Shake the clouds," and the reaching for Belinda's hand during "Ah! Belinda." As Dido's handmaiden, it is Belinda's job to soothe and comfort her, which she jovially tries to do in "Shake the clouds." The embrace is sudden, quickly rebounding into the next action, and Dido receives it stiffly. When repeated in the final aria, Dido deliberately and slowly pulls Belinda toward her into the embrace, explicitly seeking comfort. In Act I, Dido sings, "Ah! Belinda I am pressed with torment, not to be confessed" and performs the "pressed" gesture on her own body. This same gesture is repeated in her final *aria*, when she sings, "May my wrongs create no trouble in thy breast." Here, Dido transposes the gesture onto Belinda's body, visually expressing her own forsaken torment to Belinda while vocally proclaiming her wish for the opposite.

When the Sorceress and witches plot how they will destroy Dido, their choreography previews the action to come. In Act II, scene 1, the two henchmen witches, danced by Tina Fehlandt and William Wagner, describe how the storm they conjure will drive Dido et al. back to court. Both dancers spring and push their arms like shovels, each herding a group of cowering witches across the stage. The court repeats this same action in scene 2, when the storm approaches, singing "Haste, haste to town." Rather than herding, however, the courtiers use this movement motif to position themselves into two straight lines, creating a safe path for Dido to traverse.

Fate is perhaps the strongest recurring gesture of the opera. As a theme and plot device, fate plays an important role in the opera as written by Purcell and Tate. Fate brought Aeneas to Carthage, fate causes Dido's demise, and fate calls Aeneas to return to his journey. Morris magnifies the presence of fate through subtle layering of the fate gesture throughout the opera. Even when the libretto is not specifically mentioning fate, the gesture insidiously appears. On Aeneas' first entry in Act I, he stands on the balustrade with his back to the court and both arms holding the fate gesture high. Even before one begins to associate the gesture and the word through the libretto, it is visually present; Aeneas is meant to be in Carthage. In the short "Cupid" chorus after Aeneas declares his fate is with Dido, Belinda and the Second Woman form an arch with their arms in the fate gesture, under which the courtiers process and sharply poke at Aeneas with their fingers. They literally pass through fate to prick Aeneas with Cupid's arrows. In Act III, Dido slaps Aeneas in the face, sending him abroad forever. She turns to face the empty stage, the fate hand pressed close to her chest as she resolutely walks away from Aeneas' exit; fate forced Dido's hand to her ruin, and it was not her choice to send Aeneas on his way. To conclude her final *aria*, "When I am laid," Dido and the court travel upstage, as in a funeral procession. All arms hold the fate gesture overhead, a last reminder that Dido's end was decided before the story even began.

MUSIC VISUALIZATION

Choreographic translation of musical elements into movement, typical of Morris' work and known as music visualization,[18] involves creating a direct and visible representation to any aspect of the music: rhythm, pitch or melodic line, instrumental grouping or soloing, tonality, dynamics, or poly- or homophonic structure,[19] for example. At a given moment, the movement can represent one or more musical aspects and is able to change to a different aspect. In the Eurhythmics system of musical training, musical concepts are physicalized in the body. Dalcroze's theory outlines three areas of musical-movement elements he finds present both in music and in moving plastic, his term for dance movement: dynamics (energy and force), agogics (time division), and space. Dalcroze's dynamics for music refer to the force or weight of a sound, such as loud, soft, crescendo, decrescendo; time refers to metric (mathematic) and pathetic (flexible, felt) duration, and speed, acceleration and deceleration, rhythm, or pause; and space is understood in terms of planes, axes, and distance, both generally and personally 273–276. Dalcroze's elements are similar but not identical to 20th-century movement theorist Rudolf Laban's analytical categories of Weight, Time and Space. As general categories of analysis, some flexibility in the use of each is necessary to read a music-movement relationship.[20]

Additional categories of cross-over include structural and compositional elements. The table in Figure 15.1 is based on Dalcroze's own categorization, but revised to include some Laban Movement Analysis to suit the needs of this essay. Because musical concepts are physicalized in the body, moving plastique creates visual representation of the music. Dalcroze writes that

we have a right to demand from dancers that elements of musical phrasing, shading, time, and dynamics should be observed by them as scrupulously as practicable. To dance in time is not everything. The essential is to penetrate the musical thought to its depths, while following the melodic lines and the rhythmic pattern, not necessarily "to the letter"—which would be pedantic—but in such a way that the visual sensations of the spectator may not be out of harmony with those of his [sic] auditive apparatus.[21]

Dalcroze's views on the emotive and natural purposes and relationship between music and dance are particular to the late 19th and early 20th century. It is at times one-sided, favoring harmonic and cohesive relationships, whereas in dance it would serve to portray musical content through the body in a one-to-one relationship. Mark Morris' choreography often fits the cohesive, parallel music-dance union. Acocella describes how Morris' choreographic process includes a long period of analytic work with the music score that is always accompanied by an emotional idea. "The emotion/movement idea," she writes, "is generated in his mind by the musical structure."[22] In *Dido and Aeneas*, one can see the music in the dancing, with visual and auditory content reinforcing one another. Rhythmic

Music	Dance
pitch	level, position in space
dynamics	dynamics, Weight, size
timbre (texture)	diversity in bodies and/or movement vocabulary, texture
duration	duration
time, speed	Time
rhythm	rhythm
rests	pauses
melody	continuous succession of isolated movements or phrase/sequence
counterpoint	opposition of movements, or more than one gesture/movement occurring simultaneously
chords	arresting of several associated gestures at once (or gestures in groups)
phrasing	phrasing
structure/form	structure/form
orchestration	casting/number of bodies or part(s) of the body, or the arrangement of the part to the whole

FIGURE 15.1 Music-Dance analytical categories.

form, phrasing, orchestration, and structure are the most common types of music visualization used by Morris.

Stephanie Jordan describes this kind of parallel relationship which "creates a kind of meaning, drawing attention to itself as special, as music and dance seem to clarify each other."[23] Emotive or affective content can be enhanced through a cohesive, or parallel relationship. In her final *aria* in Act III, "When I am laid in Earth," Dido sings her last lament: "When I am laid in Earth, may my wrongs create no trouble in thy breast. Remember me, but Ah! Forget my fate." The bass line of this *aria* is musically famous for its repetitive, oppressive nature, with its pitches lilting downward chromatically by half-steps. This five-measure phrase repeats nine times as the foundation for the *aria*. During the introduction to the *aria* (mm. 1–5) and at its end (mm. 39–47), the dance chorus slowly processes upstage toward Dido, decreasing the space around her, enhancing the feeling that she is being trapped. On the second procession, each dancer holds one hand high in the air, displaying the fate gesture, as though pushing Dido to her inevitable end. The slow, uneven rhythm in the bass is visible in the dancers' collective centers of gravity, which rock forward and backward, their weight stepping on each note in their slow procession upstage[24] (see Figure 15.2).

In Morris' staging of the opera, reading the music visualization creates a meaningful connection between the visual and aural. Canon and other compositional structures become more prominent and easier to understand. The sung chorus "Banish sorrow" (mm. 16–28) during Belinda's Act I *aria* "Shake the cloud from off your brow" begins in unison/homophony (mm. 16–20), breaks into a four-part counterpoint/polyphony (mm. 20–25), and then returns to unison/homophony (mm. 26–28). The dancing chorus is arranged in four columns to show the four vocal parts in order—soprano, alto, tenor, and bass—exhibiting Dalcroze's orchestration category. Like the vocal chorus, the dancers begin in unison and then break into visual counterpoint, with each group simultaneously performing a different action. The sung text, "Banish sorrow, banish care, Grief should ne'er approach the fair," bounces between the four vocal lines: soprano and tenor share "Banish, banish sorrow," before splitting into momentary soprano-alto and tenor-bass pairings; they split into four such that "Grief" is sung separately by each (see Figure 15.3). The dancing and gestures highlight the rhythm of the vocal phrases, and the counterpoint between the vocal lines visibly bounces from one column of dancers to the next.

Orchestration also applies to instrumental parts of the music. For the entirety of Belinda's Act I sung solo "Pursue Thy Conquest Love," the bass accompaniment follows the vocal line in canon. Davidson dances to Belinda's line, while Rachel Murray, who plays the Second Woman and is active throughout the rest of the scene, dances to the bass line. As a result, the two dancers swirl around each other, increasing the intensity and flurry of arms, as well as encouragement for Dido to pursue Aeneas (see Figure 15.4). During several moments of *recitative* in the Palace, the courtiers accompany the action of the scene with their presence and minimal movement. Rhythm and pulse in *recitative*, musical dialogue or monologue meant to mimic natural speech, are more free than metered. Instrumental accompaniment is typically minimal; often chords are sparsely timed to fall on emphasized words or strong beats within the measure, or to decorate pauses in the vocal lines. The court in Act III, scene 2, acts as the accompaniment in a similar fashion; they do not match the instrumental accompaniment note for note. Rather, they act as the music visualization category of chords—the arresting of associated poses or groups of gestures. As Dido rushes around the stage, decrying earth and heaven and fate for her ill state (mm. 1–14), the chorus sits on the upstage balustrade in a line; they point one arm at a time toward the center of the line, with palms upward and wrists flexed backward, an

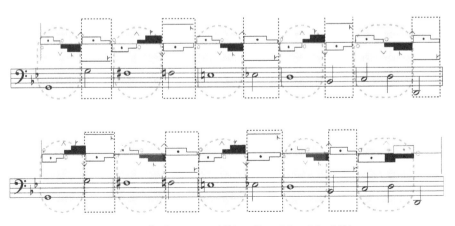

FIGURE 15.2 "When I am Laid" bass line with weight shifting.

echo of the "Heaven" gesture Dido repeats many times. When Aeneas tells Dido, "How, royal fair, shall I impart the god's decree, and tell you we must part?" (mm. 20–23) the chorus members thrust their elbows forward and faces toward the sky (m. 22^1); they curl their upper bodies forward as in shame or sorrow (m. 23$^{3-4}$). Dido responds, "To your promis'd empire fly, and let forsaken Dido die" (mm. 32–34), the chorus members swiftly twist their bodies toward the wings as if watching Aeneas fly away (m. 33^1), and then they turn away and arch their bodies upward, echoing Dido's position on "die" (m. 34$^{1-3}$).

Orchestration can be shared between body parts, as in the Second Woman's *aria* "Oft She Visits," in Act II scene 2, and the Grove and Hunting Party. The solo uses orchestration for bass and voice, divided between the Murray's feet and upper body. The layering is complex, showcasing polyrhythms between Murray's upper and lower halves, as well as between Murray's gestures and singer Shari Saunders' rhythmic and vocal phrasing; Acocella describes it as a kind of Dalcroze exercise.[25] Off and on throughout the solo, Murray's feet pound the ground in time with the running eighth notes of the bass. In the first sung phrase, "Oft she visits this lone mountain," Murray's hands tap the air twice on the strong beats of measure 5, flip and carve from high to low along with the rhythm and pitches of "this lone mountain"; her arms dig, lift, lower, and stretch to the phrasing of "Oft she bathes her in this fountain," in measures 7–8. Murray points emphatically, matching, "Here [rest], Here" (m. 92, 4); she then makes a dipping gesture that becomes a bow and arrow, before exploding her arms outward into the fate gesture, following the phrasing of "Acteon met his fate"[26] (mm. 13–14; see Figure 15.5).

Murray shares her solo in "Oft she visits" with the chorus ensemble, alternating phrases while Saunders always sings solo. Within the gestures matched carefully to the lyrics and vocal rhythms, Murray's and Saunders' dynamics mirror and complement each other: Saunders' voice presses when Murray rebounds and then explodes the consonants and clips "fate"; Murray circles her upper body with smooth phrasing, riding across Saunders' dotted rhythms; both punch voice or action on the staccato "hounds"; and to emphasize "mortal wounds," Murray slightly varies her timing to Saunders' timing and uses impactive dynamics that highlight the stabbing of the mortal wounds and contrast Saunders' more even and unaccented dynamics. Even though orchestration of dance solo-group to vocal solo, and several of the dynamic and rhythmic choices, do not correspond to a one-to-one relationship, they are still complementary, working together on a different basis.

Melodic contour and dynamics are paralleled in the movement for Dido's final *aria*, "When I am laid in earth," Act III, scene 2, following Aeneas' exit. As soprano Jennifer Lane sings "When I am laid in Earth, may my wrongs create no trouble in my breast," Morris as Dido circles around Belinda, his arm rising to his side as the sung pitches rise, and increasing his speed to a run with the *crescendo* in the music (mm. 6–11^3). Morris matches the growing dynamic sense of the vocal phrase through his speed rather than note for note or pitch for pitch. Lane sings "No trouble," in a falling melody with a long-short-short-long rhythm, beginning in a vocally high pitch and ending in a low pitch (mm. 11^3–13^1); Morris spins by leading with his arm, then swipes high overhead, and carves downward through the space next to Belinda, using the same rhythm as the singer. Space and size in movement also follow dynamic contrast. Lane sings "Remember me, remember but ah! forget my fate, remember me but ah! forget my fate" on a strong *mezzo forte* dynamic (mm. 17^{3+}–28^2); with each imploring "Remember me," Morris pulls apart his arms wide apart and arches backward. When Lane repeats the phrase with a *piano* dynamic (mm. 28^{3+}–34^2), Morris repeats the gesture using less space, bent lower to the ground, and moving more delicately. Both previous repeats appeal and beckon to the court. The final "Remember me" (mm. 34^{3+}–35^3) repeats with the loudest volume, and in a drastic change of space, Morris's arms stretch the farthest upward—the camera positioned in a dramatic bird's-eye view pointing down onto Morris—suggests, perhaps, an appeal to something beyond the court.[27]

Not all relationships between music and movement need be cohesive, as envisioned by Dalcroze. Non-harmonic, contradictory, or ironic relationships would have been unac-

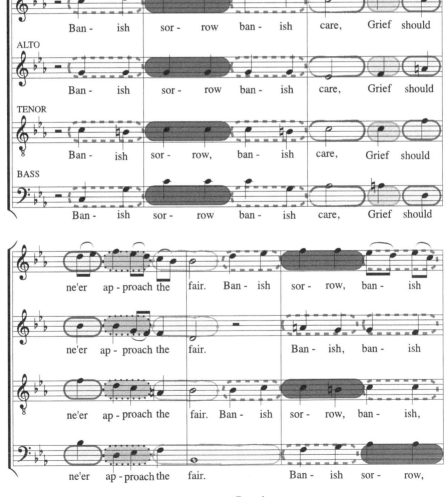

FIGURE 15.3 Continues.

FIGURE 15.3 "Banish Sorrow" Unison and Counterpoint.

ceptable in Dalcroze's time, but especially since the rupture created by the postmodern dance movement in the 1960s such relationships are prolific. Choreographically, general patterns emerge when a match is most effective; at other times, matching the libretto takes precedence over matching the music, and at still other times service to movement phrasing or narrative trump both. Thus Morris inscribes his own artistic sense into the telling of the story. Jordan refines the idea of music visualization to include what she terms parallelism and counterpoint because "all dance bears some kind of relationship to music, however much it does or does not attend to the detailed internal mechanisms of the score"[28]; a parallel relationship is akin to Dalcroze's harmonic matching of sonic and visual elements, while in a counterpoint relationship any number of oppositional or non-relationships between sound and visual material occur.

FIGURE 15.4 "Pursue Thy Conquest Love" Voice/Belinda and Cello/Second Woman canon.

Parallelism is most prominent in *Dido and Aeneas*, and even counterpoint relationships are more cohesive than opposing. When Dido and Aeneas consummate their love in the Grove during *Ritornelle* in Act II, scene 2, the closest discernible relationship to the music is between the phrasing of the action and larger phrases of music. The music is constantly in motion, each of the strings overlapping lines of eighth notes, so that the long, unison chord at the end of each phrase draws attention as the focal point. At the start of this interlude, Dido and Aeneas are in a stiff embrace, Aeneas gazing in the distance. Dido slowly unwraps herself and melts to the floor, pulling Aeneas with her, in one continuous action; though this is timed relative to the larger phrase structure of the music, the dancers' simple, sustained action contrasts the music's complex, four-part motor. It is fitting, however, and slightly humorous, that they climax on a phrase-ending chord.

The Witches' Chorus and Dance of Act III, scene 1, is the most fractured music-dance relationship of the entire work. In this dance, the Sorceress leads her coven in a mock hoe-down celebrating Dido's destruction. The chorus sings "Destruction's our delight, Delight our greatest sorrow; Elissa dies tonight, And Carthage flames tomorrow!" (mm. 1^{4+}–9^2). During the hoe-down, the witches clap and stomp, rub their eyes in a gesture of mock crying, and pretend to die—each dancer melodramatically improvising a unique end—all to the beat of the music. Two couples perform a mock pantomime of two lovers kissing and one killing the other. Although most of the witches lie on the floor pretending to be dead, the Sorceress mockingly mimes masturbation. At her climax, the coven engages in a melee, embracing, taunting, pushing, throwing each other.

FIGURE 15.5 "Oft She Visits" Voice and Bass Visualization.

According to former Mark Morris Dance Group member Susan Hadley, this was one of the only times during her tenure with the company that Morris allowed the dancers to improvise.[29] The improvisational character of this scene drastically ruptures the structural cohesion between music and movement, as no single aspect of the dance explicitly follows the music score. The witches' improvised chaos is the most dramatic disjunction between music and dance in the entire opera. Reserving chaotic improvisation for the witches is significant because it reinforces the dualism between the Sorceress/witches and Dido/courtiers: the witches engage in wild debauchery and ignore the music, while the courtiers would never abandon their bodily restraint, nor the musical structure.

DUALISM AND NARRATIVE

Baroque music espouses a principle of dualism, which Morris extends into his choreography and staging. As mentioned, dualism in Baroque music often plays out in dynamic contrast, switching between major and minor harmonic bases, free rhythm and metered time, and extravagant expression and restrained compositional structure. Dualism in this respect does not refer solely to Descartes' mind-body split, but more broadly to a juxtaposition of opposites. This sort of dualism is a theme found in much of Morris' other works: "[Morris has] a kind of double-sidedness that is absolutely fundamental to his vision, an ability to see and express two opposing aspects of an experience simultaneously. Often these two aspects are the solemn and the ridiculous."[30] In Morris' staging, dualism as the juxtaposition of opposites serves the dramatic storytelling. Divergent physical characterizations and movement choices of Dido/court and Sorceress/coven visibly mark these characters as opposites: good-evil, beautiful-grotesque, ordered-chaotic, tragic-satirizing. Through these characterizations, the seriousness of Dido's tragedy and the sardonic mocking of that tragedy by the Sorceress re-mix the opera into a strange combination of classical music and form, with satiric and grotesque humor.

Morris' postures for the two characters differ greatly, furthering their characterization through their contrasting movement. Dido's and the court's movement stylization appear as pseudo-classical lines, curves and formations. Their poses mimic ancient classical vases or friezes, with the control and decorum one might expect to see accompanying Purcell's Baroque music. Dido's actions primarily emphasize the vertical dimension and her elongated limbs in clear spatial positions, result in a narrow range of dynamic contrasts. I would not generally describe Morris' movement style as Light, but Dido moves with more Lightness than the Sorceress because of the vertical emphasis.[31] As discussed previously, Dido and the court primarily operate in parallel relationships to the music score; they embody structure, restraint, and order.

The Sorceress' movement emphasizes body and dynamic range over space and form. The Sorceress's and the coven's movement stylization is grotesque: the witches crawl, slither, writhe, and spasm, creating a substantial visual disassociation with Purcell's refined, classical music. Dido sits upright and uses minimal shoulder or hip isolations, portraying the decorum of a queen. The Sorceress, however, lounges, catwalks, flips her hair like the sassy "queen." In Act II, scene 1, the Sorceress's movement is full of contrasts by comparison: between Strong and limp actions, and Sustained and Sudden[32] timing. Lying upside-down over a bench, she crawls on her knuckles to one end, rolls over letting her arms fly and flop to the ground, and drags herself from one end to the other with one arm. This movement sequence alternates slow, tense movements with sharp, vibratory, and loose actions. After the Sorceress knuckle-crawls and flops over, she flutters her hands and feet, drags her body across the bench, flips her hair over her shoulder, squats and beckons her coven with wringing hands, slithers up out of her squat, and then suddenly springs into a stiff seated position, punching one leg to the side and her opposite arm firmly slicing the air. In Morris' adaptation, the singing ensemble at times uses a thin, nasal quality for the witches, particularly noticeable in the Act I "Ho! Ho! Ho!" choruses. The coven rushes on and off stage between the Sorceress' *recitative* with the First and Second Witches, in ironic counterpoint to the stately processions of the courtiers. Singing the laughter "Ho!" the witches spasm and vibrate, the voices of the ensemble becoming increasingly distorted and obnoxious. If Dido embodies restraint and structure, the Sorceress embodies disorder and extravagant expression.

Morris uses this dualism to contrast the tragic with the satiric, with the witches subverting the tragedy. Dalcroze's timbre category refers to the unique physical and visual texture of an individual body, as timbre in a musical instrument refers to the unique aural texture of that instrument. Although Dido and the Sorceress have opposing movement profiles, both arise from Morris' body. Nevertheless, the two characters' distinct physical timbres allow audiences to read the reiterated gestures with different meanings. As Dido performs the "thought/remember" gesture, Morris' hand gently approaches his forehead; as the Sorceress, he bangs his hand to his head as if to sarcastically say, "duh!" Performing the "forsook" gesture, Dido's hands slap her knees while standing in a deep second position, and the allusion to her deflowering is restrained yet easily read. This same gesture performed by the Sorceress and her henchmen is nothing short of a "crotch taunt"—their pelvises thrust forward, the sides of their hands slap their thighs closer inward toward their hips. The "forsook" gesture highlights the sexuality of each, with special emphasis on the wild, brazen attitude of the Sorceress and witches.

The witches' scenes operate similarly to satyr plays in ancient Greek theater that fused tragedy with comedy featuring Dionysian debaucheries. The witches further satirize Dido's tragedy in the Act III, scene 1, Chorus and Dance. This final scene for the witches brings the climax to their mockery of Dido's movement, tryst with Aeneas, and suicide. The witches mockingly pantomime the movements of Dido and the courtiers in the Overture and Act I. In this parody, they move abruptly, hit their postures with more gusto and flair, and grimace in campy smiles and inflated looks of longing.[33] The "female"[34] witch presents her lovely face (a reference to Dido) and then skitters to the "male" witch, who sticks out his chest in a manly fashion (a reference to Aeneas); they kiss, and he slits her throat. This lovers' kiss-and-kill pantomime makes fun of Dido's tragedy—giving herself to Aeneas, only to be forsaken and then commit suicide. Dido's suicide is further mocked in the Chorus immediately proceeding the kiss-and-kill pantomime. Each witch exaggeratedly feigns suicide in a manner reminiscent of an old cartoon: enlarged self-stabbing and throat slitting, over-played bodily spasms, mock choking on poison, a finger gun to the head. In the actual moments of Dido's end, Morris treats the moments of tragedy as tragedy, but through the witches he thumbs his 20th-century nose at the construct of a tragic figure, at suicide-over-love-turned-sour.

The Dido-Sorceress dualism is more complex than a counterpoint between the good and the bad, the beautiful and the ugly. Morris' decision to cast himself as both protagonist and antagonist injects the work with narrative possibility.[35] Dual casting can suggest continuity and circularity, the way repeated musical and movement motifs do. In light of Morris' choreographic use of music visualization, symbolic gesture, and dualism, the connection between Dido and the Sorceress is meaningful. The Sorceress' first appearance in the Cave at the top of Act II is striking: draped prone over a bench, arms twisted and dangling to the sides with hands resting on the ground, hair hanging wildly toward the floor. From this position, she slithers and slinks. In her death scene, Dido stands, head down, as if contemplating what is to come. Without warning, she sinks to kneel and gracefully drops onto the bench, landing in the same position maintained by the Sorceress in her introduction.

Morris' Dido and the Sorceress act as two connected opposites, suggesting the possibility for conflicting natures to reside in one body. In an interview, Morris comments on dualism in his work: "It's [dualism is] always contextual, always. It can't not be. It's life. You can't just have prettiness.... Why is that beautiful and this is not? Beauty doesn't exist separately. It exists in the world of everything else and it is also subjective."[36] Tragedy cannot exist without comedy, nor beauty without the grotesque, nor order without chaos; to know one is to know the other.

In the opera's final moments, Dido is deceased, and the courtiers slowly advance upstage to exit, recalling the somber procession and mood of the Overture. Dido lies slain, draped prone over the bench with twisted arms dangling to the side—the pose she shares with the Sorceress. Only Belinda remains, sitting on the edge of the bench, her head curled toward her lap in mourning. We never know who the Sorceress is, where she comes from, or what drives her motives against Dido. Some scholars have considered this a major flaw of the opera, but with Morris' re-telling we don't need to know. Through the dualism and connection between Dido and Sorceress, Morris holds a mirror up to a classic tragedy for an uncanny ending. He smirks and pokes fun at the tragedy through the Sorceress while honoring it through his sincere performance of Dido. A circularity lies between Dido's ending and our introduction to the Sorceress—in which we see her inverted, limp to the ground, debased. In Dido's fall, we are reminded of her antagonist; we see beauty and order transformed into the grotesque and chaotic.

NOTES

1. Prologue, *Dido and Aeneas*, Mark Morris, directed by Barbara Willis Sweete, DVD, Rhombus Media, 1995.

2. I am using the 1995 videotaped version of Morris' choreography for my analysis. Although Virgil's original story and the videography add to the layers of this version of Morris' work, my

project is not to critique them. Rather this chapter is primarily about the interplay between Purcell's score and Morris' choreography, and the video is my source for this analysis.

3. David Barton, *Literacy: An Introduction to the Ecology of Written Language* (Malden, MA: Blackwell, 2007), 34.

4. Dietrich Bartel, *Musica Poetica: Musical-Rhetorical Figures in German Baroque Music* (Lincoln: University of Nebraska Press, 1997), 82.

5. Joan Acocella, *Mark Morris* (New York: Farrar Straus Giroux, 1993), 168–69.

6. I have not found evidence of Morris directly or formally studying Dalcroze Eurhythmics. Acocella alludes to *L'Allegro* being inspired by "Duncan and Humphrey and the Dalcroze dancers" and juxtaposes photographs of Dalcroze dancers in a similar pose to the dancers in *L'Allegro* (249–50). Nevertheless, it is my argument that Dalcroze's music-movement analytical framework can be a pertinent tool for analyzing Morris' music-movement relationships.

7. Stephanie Jordan, *Moving Music: Dialogues with Music in Twentieth-Century Ballet* (London: Dance Books, 2000).

8. Donald Grout, *A History of Western Music*, 3rd ed. (New York: Norton, 1980), 299.

9. The William H. Cummings edition of the score was published by Novello, Ewer, and Co. in 1889 as Volume III of *The Works of Henry Purcell*. The focus of this chapter is on Mark Morris' adaptation of Purcell's opera into a dance theater work, rather than on Purcell's opera itself. This score was chosen over other scores because it includes full orchestrations and libretto and, as far as I can discern, seems to follow the score used by Morris. Additionally, all figures of music excerpts in this chapter are transcribed from this score.

10. Purcell's score and Tate's libretto lack an explicit statement or demonstration of consummation. Morris places the consummation during the Act II scene 2 *Ritornelle*, for which Tate and Purcell give no dramatic action. Instead, the libretto shows Aeneas, Dido, and court entering at the end of the *Ritornelle* for the hunting party scene (138–39). In Virgil's version, the consummation occurs in a cave as Dido and Aeneas take shelter from the storm during the hunting party.

11. Jordan, 89.

12. Grout, 299.

13. Bartel, 63.

14. The purpose of this section is not to engage in an in-depth analysis of musical rhetoric and word painting in Purcell's score. The practice is mentioned and a brief example given as a link into Morris' libretto visualization. An in-depth analysis of musical rhetoric and word painting in Purcell's score is left for another writer.

15. Chromatic accidentals and non-harmonic tones are musical devices that momentarily deviate from the given tonal center or key signature. They are used to create harmonic tension, anticipation toward harmonic resolve, and can be used to elicit unstable states of being, emotions, or drama. Accidentals are the "sharp" (#) and "flat" (♭) symbol indications in the music score used to denote a half-step tonal deviation upward or downward, respectively. When a series of notes moves along the scale by half-steps, it is considered chromatic. Non-harmonic tones are dissonant tones used to create harmonic tension that begs for resolving.

16. Ballet has a history of including elements of pantomime, and in the late 19th and early 20th centuries, Delsarte developed a series of symbolic actions and gestures. However, at the time of Morris' *Dido*, Delsarte had long fallen out of practice, ballet pantomime was primarily limited to story-based ballets, and no other symbolic or mimetic vocabularies were widely used enough to be easily recognized by concert dance audiences.

17. Paul Connerton, *How Societies Remember* (1989; reprinted Cambridge: Cambridge University Press, 1995), 69–70.

18. The specific choreographic style of certain Ruth St. Denis and Doris Humphrey works have become associated with the phrase "music visualization," in which a strict one-dancer, one-instrument relationship is maintained. However, I am using the phrase "music visualization" more broadly as the visible representation of musical elements.

19. Polyphony and homophony describe the relationship of multiple voices or parts. Monophony is the simplest, with a single voice or part. Homophony may have several voices or parts, but they move with rhythmic unison. Polyphony has multiple independent voices or parts and is also known as counterpoint.

20. In the Laban framework Weight specifically deals with force in relation to gravity as Strength or Lightness; Time is an attitude of Suddenness or Sustainment; and Space is both an attitude of Directness/Indirectness as well as a larger category that includes spatial pathways, orientation, shape, reach, and size; and a fourth parameter is Flow, where movement progresses freely or is impeded. For this chapter, I will primarily draw on the Dalcroze theoretical system, but will strive to be clear when I use words from by both systems. When I am referring specifically to Laban Efforts, the words will be capitalized, as is usual practice, and also to provide a visual difference within this text from Dalcroze or musicological terms. In addition, Italian musical terminology will be italicized.

21. Emil Jacques-Dalcroze, *Rhythm, Music and Education*, translated by Harold F. Rubinstein (New York: Arno Press, 1976), 297.

22. Acocella, 171.

23. Jordan, 75.

24. All music excerpts in this chapter are transcribed from the 1889 score edited by Cummings. I have chosen to use Labanotation/Motif Description, including dynamics and phrasing indications developed by Vera Maletic in the examples because it is the dance notation system with which I am most familiar. The Labanotation score is horizontal instead of vertical to match the music notation score, so the symbols are flipped onto their sides. Both will be read left to right. In Figure 15.2, the blue and green coloring show the relationship in phrasing between the long notes of the cello and the rocking of the feet.

25. Acocella discusses the relationship of Dalcroze Eurhythmics to American modern dance of the early 20th century in Morris' biography. Describing some Dalcroze exercises, she writes, "The Dalcroze system was designed to inculcate musical sensitivity by having students translate musical rhythm into bodily movements, often one rhythm in the arms, one in the legs. (The Second Woman's dance in *Dido* is thus a sort of Dalcroze exercise)" (177). Thus, the way Morris separates the differing rhythms of the strings and the vocal line between parts in a single body is similar to the way certain Dalcroze exercises split rhythms between students' body parts.

26. Again, the Labanotation/Motif symbols are turned on their side to move along the music score, and both read left to right. The upper body movement is shown above the music, and the heel drops are shown below the music for the sake of proximity to their matching music staffs.

27. The camera angle is mentioned here because of the role it plays in creating the drama for this moment. Most of the dance was shot from an angle that mimics the view one might have sitting in the audience of a proscenium theater. The overhead angle or bird's eye view is used sparingly in this video. Using this camera angle at the climax of Dido's lament heightens the emotion of the moment by changing the viewer's perspective.

28. Jordan, 73.

29. Susan Hadley, personal interview with author, May 8, 2008.

30. Acocella, 65.

31. In Laban theory, Lightness is associated with the "up" of the vertical dimension.

32. Strong, Sudden, and Sustained here refer to the Laban Movement Analysis Effort qualities, which are conventionally written with capital letters to distinguish from more colloquial uses of those words.

33. Dido maintains a composed expression except when she allows a demure smile or a faint furrow of her brow to disturb her features. By contrast, the Sorceress's face is alive with exaggerated facial expressions: smug amusement, satiric delight, eye-rolling annoyance, and parodied pleasure.

34. More than one witch couple performs the pantomime, alternating the gender of the dancer with the gender of the pantomime role. With the first couple, the female dancer pantomimes the woman, and the male dancer pantomimes the man. With the second couple, the roles are switched, with the male dancer pantomiming the woman's role, and the female dancer pantomiming the man's role.

35. In an interview about a 2008 revival of *Dido*, Morris commented on the decision to retain the practice of dual-casting Dido/Sorceress. "It makes more sense. When they [Amber Darragh and Bradon McDonald] split the roles, I wasn't sure if either of them could pull it off. But they more than proved they were each capable of doing the whole piece. It's better for continuity—it's over in a second. I like that whirling activity of one person getting worn out by the end of it." This chapter does not focus on gender constructions, but I would like to point out that both a man and a woman alternate performing both roles in this revival. To me, this reinforces the importance of the theatrical device of dual casting for Morris' narrative over the gender of the performer. Lloyd Schwartz, "Maestro!: Interview: Mark Morris picks up the Baton," *Boston Phoenix*, May 19, 2008: n.p. Web. December 21, 2010.

36. Quoted in Janet Lynn Roseman, *Dance Masters: Interviews with Legends of Dance* (New York: Routledge, 2001), 70.

Writing is not typing; it's thinking on paper. [1]
—MARCIA B. SIEGEL

16

What's in a Dance?

THE COMPLEXITY OF INFORMATION IN

WRITINGS ABOUT DANCE

Candace Feck

DANCE IN ITS many forms, whether its purpose be theatrical, social, ritual or religious, can be accessed by its viewers in diverse ways. It may be fascinating, satisfying or repugnant to watch for any number of reasons, depending on a wide variety of factors, such as its particular content, its viewing context and the predisposition and aesthetic preferences of its viewers. It can be engaged at face value, providing an exhilarating or curious

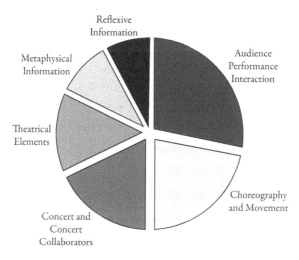

FIGURE 16.1 Threads of Information.

or unsettling viewing experience, scrutinized closely and analytically, read for its social, cultural and political implications or simply ignored. But in the moment-to-moment fluctuations that transpire over the brief lifetime of a given performance, dance rarely yields up the entirety of its information in readily digestible form. The purpose of this chapter is to ferret out "what's in a dance" by examining the complexity of this information, to render visible the information that dwells within the dance experience by looking at the threads of information woven together by a group of student viewers who were asked to respond to dance by writing a paper (Figure 16.1).

THE POWER OF WRITING

In lecture halls and dorm rooms, in library cubicles, newspaper offices and behind internet blog sites, laments are raised about the challenges of witnessing a fleeting and nonverbal art form and wresting from it the elements of verbal expression. Once likened to the act of placing a tattoo on a soap bubble,[2] the task of writing about performance requires close attention to the unfolding event, a process of reflective engagement afterward and finally, the daunting business of choosing and organizing words that will convey an accurate and persuasive account of the experience to a reader, once-removed.

In most academic contexts where dance is studied, students are regularly expected to attend performances and produce written responses about their experiences. Having taught such courses for many years, I have been a frequent witness to the power of writing assignments to open pathways to knowledge acquisition that remain clogged through standard lecture, reading and performance-viewing approaches alone. When such assignments are required in a course, students participate in the performance event with an increased level of engagement, and they produce written reactions that are more satisfying and complex than the brief verbal responses typically offered in classroom discussions. The necessity of fulfilling a prescribed allotment of words or pages with observations and reflections about performance, and the task of organizing these observations into a logical and compelling text, can prompt an integration of course concepts that might otherwise remain unassimilated. Moreover, as students discover personal routes for linking dance with their own lived experience and accumulated knowledge, their writing often demonstrates what Koroscik, Perkins and others refer to as knowledge transfer,[3] that highly desired cognitive goal in which fresh connections are forged between previously acquired knowledge and new learning experiences.

The abbreviated tale of a former student who was a member of a large general education course devoted to the study of contemporary dance history illustrates this phenomenon. Having been assigned to view and respond to a challenging performance by DV8 Physical Theatre that quarter, Michael approached me the morning following the performance to set up a meeting, and as I correctly surmised from the tone of his request, his intention was to argue that he had not understood the performance and couldn't possibly write about it. Thinking it wise to "give it a try" before pursuing our meeting, Michael appeared at my office door several days later with a long sheaf of paper in hand, seeking feedback. After discussing his excellent draft and encouraging him to continue, I commended him on his work. Gesturing with obvious satisfaction and surprise to the paper with his free hand, he blurted, "When I sat down to write, this stuff just came out!"

UNPACKING THE WRITING

Variations on Michael's experience have steadily come to my attention through many years of teaching, prompting me to investigate both student and professional writings about dance in an effort to identify their constitutive properties. What transpires in that undefined space between witnessing a performance event and writing about it? What materials do writers invoke in constructing their responses to dance, and what might their texts in turn suggest about the nature of the art form?

In a 2002 study of nine student papers,[4] I devised an analytical framework to explore these questions, and to identify some of the elements called on by writers in making sense of a dance performance. The subject of the analysis was a paper assigned in response to an MFA concert at The Ohio State University, an evening of repertory dance that featured the works of six individual choreographers,[5] offering a variety of movement styles and choreographic approaches for the writers to consider. The six dances on the program were *Ciona* (1973) by Pilobolus, *Plum Tarts* (1997) by Allison Tipton, *Passing* (1992) by Susan Hadley, *Partial* (1997) by Angie Hauser, *Carpe Diem* (1988) by Susan Van Pelt, and *Circle Walker* (1985) by Alan Boeding. In addition, these works were interspersed with short video excerpts that introduced the choreographers to the audience and revealed selected rehearsal footage. Students were required to compose papers of approximately a thousand words, reporting on the event and addressing themselves to a fictional audience of interested readers.

The construction of writings about dance offers a rich field of investigation for dance research; by peering deeply into these texts, much can be discovered about how they are composed and how dance opens itself up for reflection and discussion. A wealth of information that may not be visible to the passing observer becomes legible; in language on the page, the ephemeral takes on a form of tangibility. Because this method of analysis turns to the dance itself as source, it is congruent with the conceptual aims of this book, which professes to consider dance from the inside out. In a sense, this approach sits outside the issue of whether, as Franco and Nordera have recently conceptualized it,[6] one is concerned with the study of dance from an aesthetic or a cultural studies point of view. Rather, an analysis of dance writings might be useful from either perspective as a method of extracting and identifying those elements that form the constituents of a dance performance through the eyes of its viewers.

THE COMPLEX ACT OF WRITING

Writing about dance necessitates an *active* process of toggling between the lived experience of the writer and the phenomenon of viewing and writing. Calling on hearing and observation, opinion, memory and personal information, domain knowledge, association and self-awareness, the writer weaves an intricate and distinct tapestry of information. Contemporary theatrical dance, the kind of dancing that was the subject of these papers, requires the ability to track a three-dimensional moving body or bodies that interact with space and time in ways that are unique and specific to a given work. In conventional performance settings for this type of dance, the moving bodies are enhanced by a variety of theatrical elements, including costumes and make-up, and performances are typically presented in venues supported by technologies of lighting and sound, among others. A viewer is met with a spectrum of sensory information in watching dance: costumes have shape, texture and color and often connote specific thematic, historical or character elements. Lighting serves to focus the viewer's gaze, mold the moving shapes, establish mood, or in the case of one dance in this study play a narrative role in the piece. The performance environment may also contain elements of set design, and in some cases, exemplified by another of the dances in the study, the set may become an integral partner with the dancer. Furthermore, with the exception of the costumes and make-up, these production elements are as transient as the movement itself: lighting plots change according to the designer's cues, music evolves in a temporal frame that it shares with the movement and the permutations and interactions among these elements vary exponentially.

The moving bodies of dance, its *raison d'être*, add considerable complexity to an already dense field of information for the viewer. How many dancers are there? Are they men or women? How do gender, age, race, body type or any of a long list of social markers figure in a consideration of this work? In group dances, exemplified by the majority of works considered in these writings, how do the performers relate to one another, to the audience, and to the other elements of the performance? Directions, levels, patterns and shape present compositional elements to track, as do the means for dividing time, whether rhythmically steady or unpredictable, syncopated or smooth. The manner of performing a given action may be focused and swift, sequential or simultaneous, silky or jagged; a given performance of movement might suggest restriction or freedom, lightness or buoyancy or strength. Dance may tell a story or emphasize formal properties of the art form. A given dance or section of a work may invoke a feeling, a place or a time. It may celebrate a piece of music or commemorate a memory. It may be silly, serious, sarcastic or sinister. The rules of contemporary theatrical dance are fluid, inherently innovative and, therefore, frequently changing. The possibilities are innumerable, and the possible interactions among all these elements both incalculable and evolving.

Enter the writer. In a live performance, there is only one chance to see each performance; it will never be repeated in exactly the same way again. The viewer must remain vigilant, attending to each dance to learn from it what is important; as well, the viewer is obliged to track all its components as they unfold, committing to memory what cannot be stored any other way. This viewer *cum* writer arrives at the performance with his or her own set of preconceptions, concerns, physicality—in short, lived experience. Observation and hearing are often cited as sensory channels for the dance experience, but tactile and kinesthetic responses are also part of the viewer's equipment; associations, information from the program and publicity are also among the sources available to the writer.

PREVIOUS SCHOLARSHIP

Various guides for writing visual art criticism exist, but there is to date only one recent text that deals specifically with dance criticism.[7] Writing about dance, however, entails challenges that distinguish it from critical writing about its more stationary artistic relatives. Dance critics must track a moving subject without the luxury of a stable material event for repeated reference after the performance has been completed. In the absence of the performed event at the time of writing, writers are obliged to weave their accounts after the fact by drawing upon a variety of information.

Among the established literature detailing particular methods for writing both visual art and dance criticism are an array of handbooks on writing art criticism, articles and dissertations about dance critics and criticism, as well as an extensive pool of critical writings about art and dance themselves. The existing analytic work, however, tends to be almost entirely prescriptive, contextualizing and advancing specific strategies for guiding the writing experience. Although these important guides are very useful, including works by Larry Lavender and Wendy Oliver, among others, this study was designed as a descriptive approach.

An important exception to previous work is Sally Banes' 1994 article "On Your Fingertips: Writing Dance Criticism," which provides an excellent descriptive survey[8] that examines critical operations in professional dance criticism. In the design of my analysis, however, I elected to focus on student writings and, building on Banes' work, sought to press beyond an examination of the standard critical operations of description, interpretation, evaluation and contextualization.

METHOD OF ANALYSIS

To address these objectives, content analysis offered a means of scrutinizing and categorizing core elements of the writings. An analytical method that allows the researcher to excavate texts for their contents, content analysis enables the analyst to "go beyond the data as physical phenomena, and to make inferences about their meaning as symbolic representations."[9] Each utterance of each paper was thus subjected to a series of research questions, yielding responses that were collected and categorized by means of coding sheets. In short, content analysis offered a way to "unpack" the selected texts, lay bare the writings to a degree not possible by means of a superficial reading, see what they might offer up for future course development in critical writing and consider what kinds of issues they might bring to light as a varied group of individual papers composed in response to a common topic.

Because the study examined a small group of papers about a single concert, the results were not intended to be generalizable; another group of writings written by a different group of writers about another concert, for example, would certainly produce varied results. The value of the information harvested in the study and featured here lies not in its specific applicability but rather in what it illuminates about the complexity of both the writing endeavor and the art form of dance.

DESIGN OF THE STUDY

The design of the analysis emerged from a grounded process of inquiry,[10] with categories arising from questions unique to the specific agenda of the study. Though I focus in this discussion on only one of the primary categories of the analysis, the Type of Information used by the writers, analytical typologies were also structured to investigate what kind of understandings about dance the student writings would reveal, how similarities and differences among writers' understandings could be conceptualized, from what sources of information the students derived their information and what critical operations were used to articulate them.

HARVESTING THE DATA

Through a process of experimentation, a coding sheet of seven columns emerged that guided the collection and organization of data from the papers. On the basis of an analysis of sentences, which were in turn divided into smaller segments, each iteration of each paper was accounted for in the study design. Figure 16.2 presents a truncated template of these coding sheets, displaying a skeletal version of the structure for the first two paragraphs of the analysis for one writer.[11]

Writer #	Paper title	# of words
	Sentence/Segment	**Type of Information**
Paragraph #	Introduction	100
1		
2		
3.1		
Paragraph #	*Ciona*	77
1		
2		
2.1		

FIGURE 16.2 Abbreviated coding sheet for one writer; Type of Information column is indicated in boldface.

	Sentence/segment	Type of Information
1.1	*Plum Tarts,*	concert basics
1.2	to the contrary,	reference to concert structure: part/whole relationship
1.3	featured a cast of distinctive characters,	movement/meaning relationship
1.4	each trying to assert her presence within the group.	performer/ensemble relationship

FIGURE 16.3 Coding Sheet excerpt for one writer, showing one sentence, with Type of Information.

TYPE OF INFORMATION

In order to generate the data for the Type of Information category, each sentence segment was subjected to these questions: "In general, what type of information has the student used in writing this segment? What sort of thing does it deal with?" Figure 16.3 presents a single sentence written by one of the writers, followed by the Type of Information column from the coding sheet.

The intention of this category was to locate and identify generally what kind of information students use when they write about dance. As the first category to follow the actual unit of text written by the student, this column was intended to paint the type of information employed by the writer in broad strokes. Of all the coding categories, the Type of Information column produced the most extensive list of possible responses, consisting of ninety-one general types of information, represented alphabetically in Figure 16.4.

SUBDIVIDING THE CATEGORY

As the extensive range of possibilities that made up this category proved unwieldy for further analysis, the data was divided into five major groups of components, conceptualized in Figure 16.5 and briefly defined here:

- *Audience/Performance Interaction*: those segments of writing broadly conceptualized as referring to the relationship between the audience and the performance
- *Intrinsic Information*: those segments that referenced the empirical information of the concert itself
- *Extrinsic Information*, those segments that dealt with information outside of the empirical elements of the concert experience
- *Meta-Information*: those segments of writing that dealt with the relationship between performance and the extended public, beyond the confines of the audience attending the concert on a particular evening
- *Reflexive Information*, those excerpts that brought acknowledgment of the writer directly into the written material

Types of Information

art/culture relationship	director/work relationship	performer/set relationship
audience composition	directorial role	performer/work relationship
audience/art relationship	history: dance	performers' physical attributes
audience/concert relationship	history: music/dance	production elements
audience/dance relationship	history: work	program order
audience/director relationship	(isolated word/phrase)	program order/audience relationship
audience/music relationship	lighting	publicity
audience/performer relationship	lighting/meaning relationship	publicity/audience relationship
audience/set relationship	lighting/mov't relationship	set
audience/work relationship	lighting/performer relationship	set/meaning relationship
cast selection	lighting/shape relationship	sound
choreographer bio	lighting/space relationship	sound/meaning relationship
choreographer/performer relationship	movement/costume/music/ meaning relationship	statement: choreographer
choreographer/work relationship	movement/lighting/meaning relationship	statement: director
choreographic comparison	movement/meaning relationship	title/meaning relationship
choreographic process	movement/music relationship	title/set relationship
choreographic structure	movement/music/meaning relationship	video
choreographic style	movement/set relationship	video/audience relationship
comparison of concertworks	movement/set/meaning relationship	video/concert relationship
concert basics	movement/sound relationship	video/work relationship
concert collaborators	movement/space relationship	viewer/concert relationship
concert comparison	movement by category	viewer/dance relationship
concert concept	music	viewer/video relationship
concert content	music/meaning relationship	viewer/work relationship
concert documentation	nature of art form	work/meaning relationship
concert structure	nature of performance	work/visual art relationship
concert type	performer bio	writer identification
costume	performer's skills	writing agenda
costume/meaning relationship	performer/concert relationship	
dance/culture relationship	performer/ensemble relationship	
director bio		
director/concert relationship		
director/dance relationship		

FIGURE 16.4 Alphabetical list of entries compiled from student writings for Type of Information.

Though the last two categories had only slight representation in the student papers, the other categories were substantial, and several of them required further sub-division. In order to illustrate the complexity of information brought to bear in these papers, each category will be discussed in turn and illustrated with selected examples.

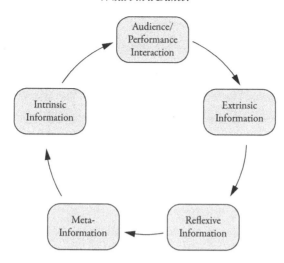

FIGURE 16.5 Five Types of Information.

AUDIENCE/PERFORMANCE INTERACTION (API)

When a viewer attends a dance, what ensues is an ongoing, interactive process in which she or he responds to the unfolding event. Any sentence or segment that referred to this recursive process, either directly or indirectly, was determined to be fundamentally concerned with the relationship between the spectator and the performance, and was broadly designated as Audience/Performance Interaction (API). Variations within this category were accounted for by designating sub-divisions of General, Particular or Meta Audience/Performance Interaction. For example, the excerpt "The applause from the audience was warm-hearted and very enthusiastic" was designated as General API, since it refers to the audience as a singular entity. The designation of Particular API was reserved for information that was concerned specifically with the relationship between the individual viewer—normally, the writer—and the performance, rather than with a generalized notion of the audience as a group, as in the "viewer/concert" relationship, exemplified by the segment "Jim Cappelletti's concert did a rare thing for me." Finally, the category of Meta-API refers to excerpts that reference the relationship between the performance and the extended public, beyond the confines of those viewers attending the concert on a particular evening. An example of this category can be seen in the "dance/culture" category, as in "I don't know if the real world can support a truly populist modern repertory dance company."

As the designation of General comprised the majority of the API category, it was further divided into Sections I and II, represented in Figure 16.6. The first section consists of writing segments that *explicitly* referred to the existence of the audience as an element of the concert experience, as in the category "audience/concert" relationship: "The diversity

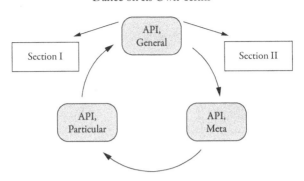

FIGURE 16.6 Audience/Performance Interaction (API), subdivided.

of this collection was a successful formula for pleasing this audience."[12] Segments of writing that incorporated references to publicity for the concert were also viewed as components of this audience/performance interaction, as in the "audience/publicity" relationship, exemplified by "Due to a thorough advertising campaign, the concert was presented to sold out audiences."

The writers' efforts to make meaning of the concert were conceptualized in the study as a discrete function of the spectator's interaction with the performance and therefore were partitioned to form Section II of General API. Exemplars include the "movement/meaning" relationship category, illustrated by such segments as "the dancers' movements were at times contrastingly free and energetic, suggesting youth, and memories of days gone by," or the category of "title/meaning" relationship, as in this excerpt about the piece *Plum Tarts*: "Short, sweet, not more than the title suggests, the plum tarts are five young girls."

The broad category of Audience/Performance Interaction thus ranges from segments in which students tapped information concerning the composition of the audience, or speculations about the relationship between the audience and art in general or dance in particular. It includes segments that describe how the audience responded to the concert and to the director of the concert, as well as references to the impact of music on the viewers. Excerpts that characterize the possible impact of both the video footage and the set on the audience are represented in this category, as are discussions of the opportunity the concert afforded the audience to view specific works. The category also includes characterizations of the audience response to specific performers, as well as remarks that theorize about the impact of the program order on audience members. Information about publicity or the likelihood that the publicity campaign for the concert attracted the large numbers that attended the concert is also represented in this category.

In their writing, students also ascribed meaning to the dances of the concert, positing connections between a variety of elements of the concert and the meaning of individual dances, and because this activity of making meaning was conceptualized as a function of

Audience/Performance Interaction

GENERAL:
audience composition
audience/art relationship
audience/concert relationship
audience/dance relationship
audience/director relationship
audience/music relationship
audience/performer relationship
audience/set relationship
audience/work relationship
lighting/meaning relationship
movement/costume/music/ meaning relationship
movement/lighting/meaning relationship
movement/meaning relationship
movement/music/meaning relationship
movement/set/meaning relationship
music/meaning relationship
set/meaning relationship
sound/meaning relationship
program order/audience relationship
publicity
publicity/audience relationship
title/meaning relationship
video/audience relationship
work/meaning relationship
PARTICULAR:
viewer/concert relationship
viewer/dance relationship
viewer/video relationship
viewer/work relationship
META:
dance/culture relationship
art/culture relationship

FIGURE 16.7 Three Types of API Information, listed alphabetically, by subdivision.

the spectator's interaction with the performance, it was placed within the API Type of Information. In making meaning of the concert experience, writers drew on various kinds of information, including lighting, costume, music, movement, set and sound, and they often drew on various combinations of these elements. Some writers also incorporated the titles of works in these discussions, and in many cases authors cited specific works as they wrote about meaning within the concert. Figure 16.7 presents the entire Audience/ Performance Interaction category.

INTRINSIC INFORMATION

Borrowing from aspects of critical writing delineated in art educator Terry Barrett's works on art criticism,[13] I adopted the notion of identifying information as either intrinsic or extrinsic to the work under consideration. Thus, the second broad category of information is that which encompassed any statement in the students' papers that dealt with Intrinsic Information, the immediate and material elements of the concert experience. Within this category, three significant sub-divisions emerged in the student writings: Movement and Choreography, Theatrical Elements, and Concert and Concert Collaborators (Figure 16.8).

Intrinsic Information

Movement and Choreography

| choreographic structure |
| choreographic style |
| movement: by category |
| movement/space relationship |
| performer/ensemble relationship |
| performer/work relationship |
| performer's skills |

Theatrical Elements

| costume |
| lighting |
| lighting/movement relationship |
| lighting/performer relationship |
| lighting/shape relationship |
| lighting/space relationship |
| movement/music relationship |
| movement/set relationship |
| movement/sound relationship |
| music |
| production elements |
| set |
| set/performer relationship |
| title/set relationship |
| video |
| video/work relationship |
| video/concert relationship |

Concert and Concert Collaborators

| **Concert:** |
| concert basics |
| concert concept |
| concert documentation |
| concert content |
| concert structure |
| concert type |
| program order |
| **Concert Collaborators:** |
| cast selection |
| choreographer biographical information |
| choreographer/performer relationship |
| choreographer/work relationship |
| concert collaborators |
| director biographical information |
| director/concert relationship |
| director/dance relationship |
| director/work relationship |
| directorial role |
| performer biographical information |
| performer/concert relationship |
| performers' physical attributes |
| statement: choreographer |
| statement: director |

FIGURE 16.8 Intrinsic Information.

INTRINSIC INFORMATION: MOVEMENT AND CHOREOGRAPHY

The Movement and Choreography category, included in Figure 16.8, groups those statements concerned with the raw materials of dance, the movement of the body[14] and its organization into the dance works that make up the concert experience. Writing segments included discussions of choreographic structure, as in the excerpt "The repetition and manipulation of this recognizable phrase was enough to provide a satisfying sense of clarity," and descriptions of the movement of individual dances of the concert, such as this exemplar of the movement from the dance *Carpe Diem*: "Dancers stream from the wings with even, sliding leaps, arms raised and heads upturned." They incorporated information about the movement/space relationship, as in "the only obstacle to a completely successful piece was the apparent lack of space needed to execute specific paths"; further, they drew on the relationship between the performer and the ensemble in group works, as exemplified in "The six performers appeared to be a tightly bonded company." They also brought into their writing information about the relationship between performers and the specific works that made up the concert, such as "These dancers brought a sense of maturity and professionalism to a well choreographed, post-modern piece," including references to the skills required by the performers in executing the choreography, as in "I was impressed by Cappelletti's sense of balance."

INTRINSIC INFORMATION: THEATRICAL ELEMENTS

The next sub-category of Intrinsic Information, also represented in Figure 16.8, consists of that type of information concerned with the production elements of the concert, such as lighting, costume, sound, music and set, as in "Gradually, the dancer manipulates the sculpture, its motion responding to physical movement," as well as the video footage, which was an integral element in this concert. The lighting/movement relationship, for example, is brought into play in the excerpt "at one point, she slowly makes her way towards the light," for example, while the lighting/shape relationship is incorporated in the segment that claims "the saturated merlot hues softened, leaving us with the black silhouettes of five female bodies."

Students brought into their writing information about all of these individual theatrical elements, as well as various relationships between them. In referencing the role of these production elements, writers also incorporated information about the relationship between these elements and the performers, the performance space and information about movement and shape, among others. They also drew on the titles of works in their particular relationship to these elements, as in the excerpt "the large circular sculpture after which the dance is named" in discussing *Circle Walker*.

INTRINSIC INFORMATION: CONCERT AND CONCERT COLLABORATORS

The final subdivision of the Intrinsic Information category of information, represented in Figure 16.8, is that which deals with student statements using information about the concert itself and those who participated in producing it. The category was further subdivided into two units, coding segments about the concert and the concert personnel separately.

INTRINSIC INFORMATION: CONCERT

In the first group of information, culling segments that dealt with the concert itself, students included basic journalistic information (the who, what, where and when of the concert); discussed its conceptual foundation, as in "the concept of accessibility was evident in Cappelletti's choice to place a premium not only on the product, but also on the process"; and referenced specific contents of the concert, as in "the choreography presented was certainly varied, in line with the artistic director's intentions." Writers also brought into their papers information about the fact that the concert was to be documented for later presentation on local television, as in this excerpt: "Cappelletti's efforts also included an arrangement to have the concert videotaped by WOSU for future airing." Other segments included information about the structure of the concert, as in "the evening concludes with a duet by Cappelletti" as well as the fact that as a repertory concert, it was a concert of a particular type, as in this reference to "Cappelletti's graduate project, an elaborate repertory concert." The category also included information about the program order of the concert: "a very wise choice as a program closer for several reasons."

INTRINSIC INFORMATION: CONCERT COLLABORATORS

The second group within the Concert and Concert Collaborators category consisted of information about the concert personnel. In these segments of writing, students discussed cast selection for the concert, such as "He culled performers from the ranks of graduate and undergraduate students in the Department of Dance," and referenced biographical information about the performers, choreographers and directors, including direct statements made by individuals in these roles, such as "Cappelletti states in the first segment of the video that he wanted a concert that had 'something for everyone.'" They incorporated information about the relationship between the performers and choreographers, and between the choreographers and their works, as in "Hauser has worked well within the trio structure, playing with unison, duets and solos." The writings often featured remarks about the very fact of collaboration, bringing into the papers information about the cooperation among various people that was necessary to achieve the concert.

choreographic comparison
concert comparison
history: dance
history: music/dance
history: work
work/visual art relationship

FIGURE 16.9 Extrinsic Information.

Other segments featured information about the role of the concert director, such as "Jim Cappelletti served as creative liaison between his company of dancers...and an array of choreographers," to his relationship to dance in general, as well as his relationship to the concert and its specific works. Writers also incorporated information about the relationship between specific performers and the concert, and information that described the physical attributes of selected performers.

EXTRINSIC INFORMATION

Again calling on aspects of critical writing referenced by Barrett, the category of extrinsic information inventories any type of information that was derived from outside of the immediate performance event, as represented in Figure 16.9. Although it was not a large category, given this group's relatively modest level of domain expertise, it is nonetheless a significant one, as it gives the writer a means of inserting relevant personal knowledge into the discussion of the concert works. Students constructed their responses using information that compared this concert to other concerts, and works within this concert to other works, such as in this "choreographic comparison" category excerpt: "This work offers a Cirque Du Soleil-like interface for its viewers." Inserted information that contextualizes the concert or the work with reference to dance or music history, such as "Modern dance in the US has been primarily a movement driven by the idiosyncratic vision of choreographers," falls in this category, as does information that contextualizes specific works with regard to their previous histories of performance, such as in this segment about *Partial*: "Hauser, Cappelletti and Jacobs are the original dancers of this work, which has appeared at the American College Dance Festival and on other Ohio State University programs." Writers also called on information that placed the concert works into play with other works of art, as in this excerpt about *Circle Walker*: "The pair is introduced to the audience in a DaVinci-like image."

METAPHYSICAL INFORMATION

Yet another category of information was identified in the students' inclusions of what was conceptualized in the study as "metaphysical" information. This term was used here in

nature of art form
nature of performance

FIGURE 16.10 Metaphysical Information.

the sense of what is theoretical or philosophical, relating to principles underlying the subject of dance in particular or art in general. Although this category comprises only a small fraction of the types of information used in these papers, it does occur in several instances and was thus coded and identified in the analysis, as indicated in Figure 16.10. Segments of writing that referenced the nature of dance or the nature of performance, such as "Possibly, Cappelletti underestimates how much of the meaning of the dance is inherent not only in the dance itself," which gestures to the nature of the art form, were included in this category.

REFLEXIVE INFORMATION

The last category of information is the kind of writing that brings the writer directly into the discussion. As in the previous category, this component of the writing was small, but it fulfilled a function in the writing that could not be conflated with any other. Here, the writer departs, however briefly, from writing about the concert: in a sense, she steps out of the discussion of the concert to introduce herself or to comment on the writing as it is evolving (Figure 16.11), as in an example of writer identification, "I realize immediately, this dance will never again be repeated as I see it now," or this example of information about the writing agenda: "Writing this paper takes me back to the moment when I got chills during the concert."

SUMMARY AND CONCLUSIONS: A WEB OF INFORMATION

The analysis discussed here has attempted to make visible some of the variegated threads that writers stitch together to make sense of a dance performance. In the act of pulling apart these threads, I am reminded of Brenda Dixon Gottschild's summoning of a dreadlock as a metaphor for the task of teasing apart the intertwined Africanist aesthetic in American performance[15]: it is at once an impossible endeavor, and simultaneously one that is worth undertaking for the sake of discovery and visibility. In the end, a dance is always greater than the sum of its threads. The study was undertaken to bring into relief the complexity of both the writing project and the art form.

writer identification
writing agenda

FIGURE 16.11 Reflexive Information.

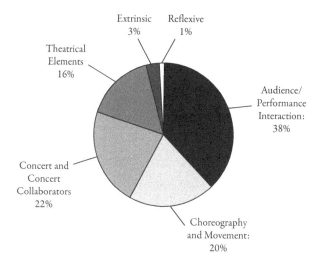

FIGURE 16.12 Type of Information Composite for Writer #12.

In the collection, analysis and illustration of particular examples within these writings, a rich and complex snapshot emerges of the kinds of information embedded within the experience of viewing a dance. The data that emerged reveal texts that were composed from a complex web of information and drawn from a variety of multi-sensory sources, which gestures to the richness of the dance experience. In writing about a single evening of dance, featuring one work each by six choreographers, and framed within the context of a concert that consisted of approximately forty-nine minutes of dancing plus twenty-eight minutes of video footage, nine writers brought more than ninety types of information into their written responses to this event. As conceptualized and evidenced in the coding process, these types of information ranged from various facets of the audience/performer relationship to discussions of the movement, concert, concert personnel, theatrical elements and information extrinsic to the event. Figure 16.12 provides a composite image, illustrating the range of categories of information enlisted by of one of the writers in the study.

While a dance is ticking by, its viewers are collecting and storing a range of sensory, conceptual and associative information. They are absorbing information about interactions between the performance and the audience, including a range that incorporates their own subject positions as individual viewers, addresses the larger community of viewers assembled to witness the event and includes speculations about the hypothetical "audience" beyond the confines of the particular observed event. They are gathering information intrinsic to this particular concert, including a range of detailed information about the choreography and movement, about the concert itself and the many personnel involved in producing it and about the various theatrical elements that have played their own complex roles in the overall production. To varying degrees, the writers also consider information extrinsic to the event, such as related historical and cultural knowledge,

P4	Sentence/Segment	Type of Info
1.1	'Passing,' choreographed by Susan Hadley	concert basics
1.2	depicts two women's struggle with the death of their friend.	movement/meaning relationship
2.1	They begin moving quickly	movement: time
2.2	from the floor to the air,	movement: space
2.3	taking turns supporting and throwing each other.	movement: contact
3.1	These repetitive movements	choreographic structure: repetition
3.2	stay in one corner of the stage,	movement: space
3.3	a metaphor for the mundanity of daily life.	movement/meaning relationship

FIGURE 16.13 Sample of Integration in Types of Information.

and some also include what I have chosen to call metaphysical information, information that is philosophical in substance, such as musings about the nature of the art form.

Afterward, in order to produce an act of writing, this range of information—stored almost entirely in the form of memories of the event—is sorted out, organized and presented not as individual types of information but through an integrative process. In this process, the web of many strands of information gets translated, through the ordering practice of writing, into intelligible prose. This webbing effect is already visible at a micro level, as writers typically incorporate a variety of types of information within a single sentence, indicating that a connection has been made between discrete parts. Even a cursory glance at one of the coding sheets provides evidence of these inter-connections, as exemplified in an excerpt from the analysis of one writer's paper as illustrated in Figure 16.13, information that encompasses "concert basics," the movement/meaning relationship, elements of movement including time, space and contact, and choreographic structure—already interwoven in a matter of three short sentences.

It is, in part, through this integration of multiple strands of information that the phenomenon researchers on cognition refer to as the coalescence of all learning, knowledge transfer, occurs. When students go beyond the accumulation of information to synthesize and apply what they know, and to extend it into other areas of knowledge, they forge new connections. Among the findings to emerge in this analysis of student writings, there is evidence that writing about dance provides this kind of activity, the ability to relate learning from one strand of information to learning in another. By excavating from the student writings their constituent threads of information, drawn from multiple sources, a kind of blueprint of knowledge transfer becomes visible.

The analysis of student writings that emerged from the study not only yielded implications for the teaching of dance criticism but also provides insights about the complexity of the art form. It is in the complex and multi-sensory nature of dance that the catalyst for rich learning experiences exists for its witnesses. By generating a list of types of information, and giving evidence to their integration within the student papers, the study holds up a mirror to the rich human activity that is dance. Elsewhere, I have argued that the opportunity to reflect on dance and produce an act of writing creates a kind of sensory loop, through which the writer re-enters the dance experience to harvest the information it contained.[16] Here, in a sense, is the inverse of that project; the writings themselves become the source for peering into the abundant field of information that is a dance. This harvest reveals dance as a container, one that is brimful of various kinds of information. A given viewer will bring to bear his or her own lived experience, associations, domain knowledge, and cultural sensibility to interact with a given dance performance because the art form itself is so richly evocative, so full of information and so open to multiple points of entry.

NOTES

1. Transposing a criticism once leveled at Jack Kerouac by Truman Capote, "That's not writing, it's typing!" Marcia B. Siegel has frequently made this statement in lectures and writing workshops at The Ohio State University and elsewhere.

2. In Roger Copeland and Marshall Cohen, eds. *What Is Dance? Readings in Theory and Criticism* (New York: Oxford University Press, 1983). 424, quoting theatre critic John Mason Brown.

3. This important pedagogical concept is concerned with the connectedness of knowledge and the ability to transfer knowledge from one learning situation to another, and is referenced in the works of many educational theorists: Judith Smith Koroscik et al., for example, discuss knowledge transfer in their "The Function of Domain Specific Knowledge in Understanding Works of Art," in *Inheriting the Theory: New Voices and Multiple Perspectives on DBAE* (Los Angeles: J. Paul Getty Trust, 1990), 14; and Perkins and Salomon have made it the subject of their article "Teaching for Transfer" in *Educational Leadership* 46 (1), 1988: 22–32.

4. Feck, M. Candace. "Understandings About Dance: An Analysis of Student Writings with Pedagogical Implications." Ph.D. dissertation, The Ohio State University, 2002.

5. The concert, entitled "The *Consigliere* Collection," was completed in partial fulfillment of the MFA in Dance by Jim Cappelletti and was offered at The Ohio State University in October, 1998.

6. The premise laid out in the preface to Susanne Franco and Marina Nordera's book *Dance Discourses: Keywords in Dance Research* (Oxford and New York: Routledge, 2007) is to address the perceived divide between dance scholars who have considered dance from aesthetic, historic, and philological perspectives, and those who have embraced a multi-disciplinary, cultural studies perspective.

7. This volume is recent indeed, having been published contemporaneously with the writing of the present chapter: *Writing About Dance*, ed. Wendy R. Oliver. Champaign, IL: Human Kinetics, 2010.

8. In Sally Banes, *Writing Dancing in the Age of Postmodernism* (Hanover, NH, 1994), 24–43.

9. Krippendorff, Klaus. *Content Analysis: An Introduction to its methodology.* (Thousand Oaks, CA: Sage Publications, 1980), 21.

10. See Corbin and Strauss, who, among others, advocate for grounded theory as a research method in which theory emerges inductively from the data, rather than as a preliminary hypothesis generating data.

11. The top three rows of the coding sheets contain general labeling and categorizing information. The first row presents the identification number assigned to each writer, the title of

the paper, and the number of words used in its composition. The second row identifies the labeling categories that apply to the rest of the analysis, including columns in which each sentence or segment of the paper is presented in its original order, as well as the identifying information for the remaining analytical categories; for the sake of simplicity, in this truncated version of the coding sheet, only the Type of Information column is highlighted. The third row identifies those columns that are used to record each paragraph number, the subject of that paragraph, and the number of words in the paragraph. The bulk of the analysis follows these identifying rows of the coding sheets. Sentence and segments for each paper, represented by numerical designations, occur in the exact sequence in which they were written, interrupted only by a variation of the third row, which identifies by name and number each new paragraph.

12. All exemplars used in this chapter are taken directly from the study.

13. Works by Barrett that use this distinction include his *Criticizing Art: Understanding the Contemporary*, 2nd ed. (New York: McGraw Hill, 2001) and his *Criticizing Photographs: An Introduction to Understanding Images*, 2nd ed. (New York: McGraw Hill, 2005).

14. Movement of the body, as the central medium of the dance experience, occupies a predictably substantial portion of the student writings. I adopted a two-part system to examine this information, listing it both as a type of intrinsic information (movement) as shown here, and later separating the movement components into conceptual groups (by category) in a subsequent section of the analysis. In proceeding through the coding sheets, I also wanted to differentiate the kinds of movement components that the students chose to articulate. Although my analysis of movement is informed by the systems and language of Rudolf Laban, I also resisted the practice—both in labeling the student papers and in my discussion of them—of relying on a lexicon that is too specific to be generally understood. Movement categorization, then, was considered in two stages of analysis. At the first level, the category called "movement" was placed in the Type of Information cell of the coding sheets, allowing movement references to be distinguished from other types of information in the student papers. Following a colon, an additional label distinguishes between thirty-four basic types of movement, providing a layer of analysis that contributed to the characterization of individual dances, discussed elsewhere in the larger study.

15. Brenda Dixon Gottschild. *Digging the Africanist Presence in American Performance: Dance and Other Contexts* (Westport, CT: Greenwood Press, 1996).

16. See M. Candace Feck. "Writing Down the Senses: Honing Sensory Perception Through Writing About Dance." Dancing in the Millennium International Joint Dance Conference Proceedings, July 2000, Washington, DC, 168–74.

CONTRIBUTOR BIOGRAPHIES

MELANIE BALES is a professor in the Department of Dance at The Ohio State University where she teaches courses in dance technique, dance history, and Laban studies and is active as a choreographer. A former professional dancer of both ballet and modern dance, she has also performed solos from the repertories of artists including Daniel Nagrin, Catherine Turocy, Tere O'Connor, and Iréne Hultman. She received her B.A. in German from Carleton College and an MFA in dance from University of Illinois Urbana-Champaign, and was certified as a Movement Analyst through the Laban/Bartenieff Institute of Movement Studies. Her book, *The Body Eclectic: Evolving Practices in Dance Training*, co-authored with Rebecca Nettl-Fiol, dealt with approaches and attitudes toward technique training since the Judson era.

HARMONY BENCH is assistant professor of dance at The Ohio State University, where she teaches in the areas of dance, media, and performance studies. She completed her Ph.D. in culture and performance at UCLA and holds additional degrees in performance studies, women's studies, and ballet. Her current research focuses on mobile media, social media, and videogames as sites for choreographic inquiry and analysis, and their collective impact on movement, gesture, and cultural belonging. Bench's writing can be found in *Dance Research Journal*, *The International Journal of Performance Arts and Digital Media*, *Participations*, and *The International Journal of Screendance*. She is currently working on a book that addresses dance onscreen and the politics of mediality.

BETSY COOPER teaches at the University of Washington, where she serves as Director of the Dance Program and Interim Divisional Dean of Arts. She has published articles about the WPA Federal Dance Project in *Theatre Research International*, *Dance Research Journal* and *The International Dictionary of Modern Dance*. She is on the editorial review board of the *Journal for Dance Education*, where she has contributed articles on engaged learning and writing practices. Cooper remains active creatively as a choreographer and principal dancer with Seattle Dance Project. She holds an MFA in dance from the University of Washington and a B.A. in archeological studies from Yale University. Cooper is a recipient of a 2004 Distinguished Teaching Award from the University of Washington.

ANN DILS directs the Women's and Gender Studies Program at the University of North Carolina, Greensboro, where she is a professor of dance. Her recent writing appears in the journal *Screendance*, as part of the Dance Heritage Coalition's 100 American Dance Treasures digital project, and in the edited collection *Revisiting* Impulse: *A Contemporary Look at Writings on Dance 1950–1970*. She received the Dixie Durr Award for Outstanding Service to Dance Research from the Congress on Research in Dance (CORD) in 2010 and is a former editor of *Dance Research Journal* and a past president of CORD. She co-directs Accelerated Motion: Towards a New Dance Literacy, a National Endowment for the Arts–funded digital collection of materials about dance.

KAREN ELIOT danced in the Merce Cunningham Dance Company. She is now a professor in the Department of Dance at The Ohio State University. Her book *Dancing Lives: Five Female Dancers from the Ballet d'Action to Merce Cunningham* was published in 2007. Her current research is on the British ballet during the Second World War and has been supported by an OSU Arts and Humanities Seed Grant, College of the Arts Research Grants, and a Coca-Cola Critical Difference for Women Grant. In 2010 she was awarded the Howard D. Rothschild Fellowship in Dance at Harvard's Houghton Library for research on choreographer Mona Inglesby and the International Ballet. She serves on the advisory board of *Dance Chronicle*. Her articles appear in *Dance Chronicle, Dance Gazette, The American Society for Eighteenth-Century Studies Book Reviews Online*, and *Dance Research Journal*.

M. CANDACE FECK teaches courses in contemporary dance and theatre history, theory, and criticism at The Ohio State University. She holds a B.A. in cultural anthropology from Webster College in St. Louis, an M.A. in dance and a Ph.D. in art education from The Ohio State University. Her essays, criticism, and pedagogical research have been published on the CD-ROMs *Victoria Uris: Choreographer and Videographer*, for which she received an award from the National Dance Association in 2000; and *Prey: An Innovation in Dance Documentation* by Valarie Mockabee Williams; *Dance Research Journal, The Teaching Artist Journal*, the proceedings of CORD and SDHS, in Terry Barrett's *Interpreting Art: Responding to Visual Culture*, and on the website *Accelerated Motion: Towards a New Dance Literacy in America*. She is currently at work on a book about choreographer Elizabeth Streb.

DEBORAH FRIEDES GALILI received her B.A. in dance history from Brown University and her MFA in dance from The Ohio State University. She began researching Israeli contemporary dance on a Fulbright grant in 2007–08. Besides founding danceinisrael.com, she has covered Israel's dance scene for publications including *Dance Magazine* and *The Jerusalem Post*. Galili teaches dance history for Dance Jerusalem, a study-abroad program initiated by the Jerusalem Academy of Music and Dance and Hebrew University's Rothberg International School. From 2011 to 2012, she studied to become a teacher of Gaga, Ohad Naharin's movement language, in the training program's inaugural class. She is the author of *Contemporary Dance in Israel*.

CARRIE GAISER CASEY is a lecturer at St. Mary's College of California in the LEAP (Liberal Education for Arts Professionals) program. She is a guest lecturer for the San Francisco Ballet and also serves on the board of the Museum of Performance and Design. She completed her Ph.D. in performance studies at the University of California, Berkeley, in 2009 with a dissertation on women in early-twentieth-century American ballet. Prior to her academic career, she danced professionally with the Fort Worth Dallas Ballet and was a full scholarship student at the Kirov Academy in Washington, DC. Current publications include articles in *Theatre Journal* and *Dance Chronicle*.

HANNAH KOSSTRIN is visiting assistant professor of dance and humanities at Reed College, where she teaches courses in dance studies, Labanotation, contemporary technique, and introductory humanities. Situated at the intersection of dance, Jewish, and gender studies, she researches Jewishness and gender in Anna Sokolow's choreography from the 1930s to the 1960s. She has recently directed a project supported by the National Endowment for the Humanities Office of Digital Humanities to make a mobile dance notation app. Her publications appear in *Art Criticism* and *The International Journal of Screendance*. Kosstrin holds a Ph.D. in dance studies from The Ohio State University with a minor in women's history.

SHEILA MARION is retired from the Department of Dance at The Ohio State University. She served as the director of the Dance Notation Bureau for Education and Research at OSU from 1995 to 2011. Prior to OSU, she taught at Arizona State University. Marion received her Ph.D. in performance studies from New York University. She has master's and bachelor's degrees in dance from UCLA.

GERALDINE MORRIS is a former Royal Ballet dancer and now senior lecturer at Roehampton University London. Together with Stephanie Jordan, she produced a DVD: *Ashton to Stravinsky: A Study of Four Ballets*. She has also published substantial articles in *Dance Research*, *Research in Dance Education* and *Dance Chronicle* and her book *Frederick Ashton's Ballets: Style, Performance, Choreography* was published in 2012. As a dancer she worked with Ninette de Valois, Frederick Ashton, Bronislava Nijinska and Kenneth MacMillan among others, and alongside the work of Ashton, she is particularly interested in exploring how philosophic thinking can be applied to dance.

RACHAEL RIGGS LEYVA is a dance director, notator, scholar, and teacher. She earned her MFA in dance directing from The Ohio State University and is working toward her Ph.D. in dance and literacy studies. Her Labanotation score of a duet from Trisha Brown's *M.O.*, the first dance notation score of Brown's choreography, explored the documentation movement intention and release technique. As an archive fellow with the Dance Heritage Coalition, Riggs Leyva worked with the Bebe Miller Company archive housed at the Jerome Lawrence and Robert E. Lee Theatre Research Institute and experimented in an "archivist in the studio" role during the company's 2011 residency at the Krannert Center for the Performing Arts.

REBECCA SCHWARTZ-BISHIR is a specialist in the relationship of music and movement in nineteenth- and twentieth-century ballet with a Ph.D. in historical musicology from the University of Michigan. In addition to her research and her ballet and tango dancing, she is a freelance editor and an academic writing, dissertation, and tenure coach. Among her publications are the entry on dance critic Sarah Kaufman and fifteen other biographies in the *Grove Dictionary of American Music*, Second Edition; "Aleksandr Nevskiy: Prokofiev's Successful Compromise with Socialist Realism," in *Composing for the Screen in Germany and the USSR*; and the Academicladder.com newsletters "A Christmas Carol for Academics: Lost Your Way? 9 Steps for Finding Your Light" and "Stay out of the Comparison Gutter."

CATHERINE TUROCY is a leading choreographer/reconstructor and stage director of eighteenth-century opera-ballet. She has been decorated by the French Republic as a Chevalier in the Order of Arts and Letters and has received numerous awards for her work, including the Bessie Award. As a founding member of the Society for Dance History Scholars, Turocy lectures on historical performance practices; her papers have been published by the society and many translated into French, German, Japanese, and Korean. An accomplished performer in her own right, she has been given a chapter in Janet Roseman's book *Dance Masters: Interviews with Legends of Dance*. She began her historical studies at The Ohio State University with Shirley Wynne.

VICTORIA WATTS works as head of Global Education Partnerships and Qualifications at the Royal Academy of Dance, where she also leads the Master of Teaching (Dance) and takes responsibility for the development and supervision of practice-based graduate research in dance teaching. She holds a Ph.D. in cultural studies from George Mason University, an MFA in dance (with a concentration in multimedia technology) from The Ohio State University, and a B.A. (Hons.) in dance in society from the University of Surrey, along with advanced certifications in Benesh Movement Notation and Labanotation. She is a former recipient of the Selma Jeanne Cohen Award from the Society of Dance History Scholars and of a dissertation proposal development fellowship in the area of visual culture from the Social Science Research Council funded by the Andrew W. Mellon Foundation. She is currently serving as chair of the British Fulbright Scholars Association in the UK.

JESSICA ZELLER is an assistant professor of dance at Texas Christian University. She holds a Ph.D. in dance studies and an MFA in dance from The Ohio State University, where she completed her doctoral dissertation, "Shapes of American Ballet: Classical Traditions, Teachers, and Training in New York City, 1909–1934," in 2012. As a dancer, she studied with Maggie Black, Rochelle Zide-Booth, and Jan Hanniford Goetz; her article on Black's teaching and pedagogical lineage appeared in *Dance Chronicle* in 2009. Zeller's research examines the development and genealogy of nineteenth- and twentieth-century ballet pedagogy, and it explores the integration of progressive pedagogical approaches into modern-day ballet classes.

Printed in the USA/Agawam, MA
October 18, 2016

641760.015